BARDIZAG
AND ITS PEOPLE

by

Krikor Mkhalian

Translated and annotated by

Ara Stepan Melkonian

Gomidas Institute
London

 FUNDAÇÃO
CALOUSTE
GULBENKIAN

The publication of this book was made possible with the support of the Calouste Gulbenkian Foundation.

© Translation copyright 2014 Ara Stepan Melkonian

ISBN 978-1-909382-14-5

For more information and updates about this work please visit our website (details below)

Gomidas Institute
42 Blythe Rd.
London W14 0HA
United Kingdom
www.gomidas.org
info@gomidas.org

*To my beautiful birthplace, Bardizag, and the memory
of my dear and unforgettable forefathers*

Krikor Mkhalian, 1938

and

*To all the descendants of Zobi Melkon of Bardizag
and his compatriots, who live and have died
in every corner of the world, having survived the
genocide of the Armenian people in 1915*

Ara Stepan Melkonian, 2014

ՊԱՐՏԻԶԱԿՆ
ՈԻ ՊԱՐՏԻԶԱԿՑԻՆ

ՊԱՏՐԱՍՏԵՑ
ԳՐԻԳՈՐ Յ. ՄԻՍԱԼԵԱՆ

1938
ՏՊ. ՍԱՀԱԿ-ՄԵՍՐՈՊ
Գահիրէ

Bardizag and its People
Original title page

CONTENTS

Translator's note	xiii
Biography: Krikor Mkhalian	xxv
Map: Bay of Izmid, Bardizag and surrounding villages	xxviii
Map: Bardizag	xxix

Preface	1
Onnig Mkhalian's note	4
Introduction	5

PART 1 – FROM THE BEGINNING

Chapter 1 - The foundation of Bardizag and the origin of the migration

1 – Bardizag's location and position	11
2 – The origin of the migration and the first families	13
3 – Bardizag's boundaries according to the Imperial firman [decree]	15
4 – The origin of the Armenian population of Izmid (Nicomedia)	16
5 – Traces of a Turkish population in Bardizag	17
6 – The life and occupation of Bardizag's first settlers	18

Chapter 2 - The early days – the first priests and notables

7 – The building of Bardizag's first church	21
8 – Bardizag's first priests (kahanas)	21
9 – The building of Bardizag's second church	25
10 – The priests who served in the second church	26
11 – Village government, Armenian ishkhans [notables] and Turkish aghas	27
12 – The collection of young men for naval service	30

Chapter 3 - The Agha Krikor Great Hadji Khacher Bab era

13 – Great Hadji Khatcher Bab and the beginning of his rule	32
14 – The procuring of the *cham* fuel trade for the Ottoman Mint	33
15 – The newly-ordained kahanas [married priests] who served in the second Church	34
16 – Great Hadji Khacher's opponents	37
17 – Sericulture and the silk harvest in Bardizag	39
18 – The pilgrimage site of St Minas (Sokhmiar-Soghouk Pounar)	40
19 – Sourp Dirouhi [Holy Lady or Holy Mother of God]	42

20 – Great Hadji Khacher Bab's public works	43
21 – Hadji Khacher's family circumstances	44
22 – Bandits capture priests from Bardizag	45
23 – Hovhannes Kahana of the Great Derder family is exiled	47
24 – The supply of charcoal to the Ottoman Mint passes into the hands of the people of Bardizag	50
25 – The port of Seymen's trade movement	52
26 – Attempts at hermit-like living	53
27 – The building of the third church	54
28 – The great death	56
29 – A prodigal's sad death	56
30 – Apraham Kahana's ordination	57
31 – Great Hadji Khatcher's death	57
32 – The *derebeys* in Bardizag	58

Chapter 4 - The Apraham Kahana Khacherian era 1809 – 1825

33 – Apraham Kahana and Hovhannes Kahana of the Great Derders family	60
34 – Apraham Kahana's position and authority	62
35 – A border dispute between the villagers of Bardizag and Dongel	64
36 – The billeting of army detachments in the villages	65
37 – Preparation of building materials for the church	66
38 – Prelate Archbishop Boghos Karakoch's church reforms	66
39 – The newly ordained kahanas who served in the third church	68
40 – New attempts at hermit-like living. The founding of the Manoushag pilgrimage site	69
41 – The construction of the old houses in Bardizag, their parts and furnishings etc	75
42 – Village weddings in olden times	79
43 – The foundation of the community school, the first teachers	82

Chapter 5 - The Garabed Agha Mgerian era 1825 – 1850

44 – Apraham Kahana's fall and exile	83
45 – Garabed Mgerian	85
46 – The newly-elected notables' relationship with Apraham Kahana	86
47 – Apraham Kahana's revenge on his opponents	86
48 – Mgerian introduces horseshoe-making skills and trade in horseshoes into Bardizag	88
49 – The visit of Giragos, the exiled Catholicos of the Great House of Cilicia, to Bardizag	89
50 – One or two anecdotes about the *shoushdag* vartabed Mesrob of Bardizag	90

Contents

51 – Apraham Kahana's second exile	91
52 – The building of the fourth and last church	92
53 – Apraham Kahana's return from his place of exile	94
54 – The *ghonakh* [government building] and the Turkish aghas	95
55 – Artin Amira Ghazaz's intervention in Bardizag's community affairs	98
56 – Accusations and slander against Mgerian	99
57 – The deaths of Nerses Kahana Kardeshian and Krikor Agha Kahana Krikorian	101
58 – A government census in Bardizag	102
59 – The construction of a separate school building (1833)	102
60 – A personal educational initiative	104
61 – Apraham Kahana's death and the fate of his supporters	105
62 – New arrangements for the supply of charcoal to the mint	107
63 – The plan to build a paved road between the port (Seymen) and the village. Opposition to this plan	108
64 – A Bardizag martyr (May 1st 1838)	110
65 – Mgerian, wheat and cereals merchant, builds his own warehouse in Seymen	113
66 – The financial auditor Garabed Vartabed (nicknamed Yanghendji) in Bardizag	116
67 – The death of the venerable Sarkis Kahana: an outline of his character	118
68 – A new census taken and government records compiled of agricultural produce and property	118
69 – Mgerian purchases new land and makes it into a farm. He also buys up all the houses surrounding his and makes the area his own	119
70 – A new door is created in the church wall in the market, at the corner of the building owned by Mgerian	121
71 – Mgerian has a large horseshoe workshop belonging to him built opposite the cemetery	122
72 – Mgerian sells his property sited next to the church wall to the village community	123
73 – The ordination of two sargavaks [deacons] as well as a kahana from outside Bardizag	124
74 – New agitation in the village concerning community accounts	125
75 – A visit by Armenian amiras to Bardizag	126
76 – Mgerian's final years of personal and public works	127
77 – The church's water problem	131
78 – The origin of Saroukhanian's and Ayvazian's emnity towards Mgerian	131
79 – An attempt to conscript Christians into the army	132
80 – The re-use of a site within the port by building a community bakery and coffee house on it	134
81 – Deacon Megerditch Mardigian (Miapanian)	135

82 – The *bazar khayeghs* [caiques, boats] belonging to the
 Bardizag community — 136
83 – The teacher Mourad of Peria — 138
84 – Garabed Kahana Der-Krikorian sent to Armash monastery to repent — 139
85 – The ordinations of Sahag Kahana and Nerses Kahana — 139
86 – The death of the venerable Sahag Kahana Bedig Sarkisian — 141
87 – The purchase of church fittings and carpets — 141
88 – Exiles from Bardizag in foreign lands — 142
89 – Hadji Artin Agha Der-Antreasian, the Hadji Artins' and
 Der-Antreasians' ancestor — 146
90 – Archbishop Stepannos Maghakian, prelate and locum tenens
 of the monastery of Armash and Izmid (1855) — 152

PART 2, 1850 – 1919

Chapter 6 - Present times – transition period 1850 – 1919

91 – The development of Bardizag's economic life — 155
92 – The Mgerians after Garabed Agha Mgerian's death. Sarkis
 Effendi Mgerian — 158
93 – The bandit chief Lefter — 159
94 – The formation of a Catholic community and its life in Bardizag — 161
95 – Hovsep Vartabed Ayvazian's return to the mother church in 1876 — 165
96 – The entry and spread of Protestantism in Bardizag — 166
97 – The foundation of the Saroukhanian and Mgerian silk spinning factories — 173
98 – The Mgerians in this new situation — 175
99 – The ordination of kahanas on March 6th 1866 — 176
100 – Community authority — 178
101 – The foundation of an American girls' school — 182
102 – Mr Parsons' martyrdom — 184
103 – The immigration of the mountaineer Cherkez [Circassians]
 into Turkey — 185
104 – Educational work in Bardizag during Sarkis Effendi Mgerian's time.
 Kevork Effendi Shirinian as inspector of the community schools and
 director of the *ousoumnaran* — 186
105 – A bandit group that robbed a government courier in Bardizag — 190
106 – Clashes between the young men of Bardizag and the Circassians — 194
107 – The immigration of the *Giurdjis* [Muslim Georgians] to Turkey
 and the settlement of a group of them on the heights around Bardizag — 195
108 – Thieves made a forced entry into Hagop Agha Djergants' house one
 night and burgled it — 198

Contents

109	Educational work in Bardizag after Shirinian's departure	200
110	Mr and Mrs Armen Lousinian in Bardizag's community schools	204
111	A new and final census in Bardizag	208
112	Records of ownership and government taxation	209
113	Horse thieves and Bodour Gabe	212
114	Mr Pierce succeeds Mr Parsons as a missionary, and the foundation of the American Boys' School	215

Chapter 7 - Present times – the Tourian era 1880 - 1914

115	Government representation	220
116	The building of the road from Bardizag to Seymen	224
117	Tset Khacher's son Levon's unexpected act of bravery	226
118	The rebirth of silkworm breeding and the silk trade in Bardizag: the Pasteur method	228
119	An ordinary bandit named Nouri Bey achieves a very wealthy and influential position among the notables of the province of Izmid	230
120	Yeghishe Vartabed Tourian in Bardizag as preacher and community schools' inspector (1880)	231
	1. The construction of the new school building	232
	2. The fundamental organisation of educational work	234
	3. A new generation of teachers	235
	4. Cultivation of spiritual life. Tourian the preacher	237
	5. Lecture hall and theatre	239
	6. Tourian's family, social and personal life	243
121	New ordination of kahanas in Bardizag	248
122	Stepannos Vartabed Hovgimian, prelate of the Izmid diocese: biographical outline, work and character	249
123	The ordination of a young man from Bardizag as a celibate monk	252
124	The repair of St James church and the building of the church of the Holy King	253
125	Khachig Agha Avedian becomes a silk spinning factory owner	254
126	Helvadjian builds his own silk spinning factory in Bardizag. Helvadjian's water problem	256
127	The enclosing of the old cemetery with a wall	258
128	The first revolutionary act in Bardizag	260
129	Mr Chambers, the third American missionary in Bardizag	264
130	Garabed Effendi Helvadjian, the son of the family, is abducted by bandits and taken to the mountains. The fate of the Helvadjians' silk spinning factory	272
131	Ordination of Mgerdich Vartabed Aghavnouni	275

Chapter 8 - Present times – The next phase

132 – Educational work in Bardizag after Tourian's departure	277
133 – The ordination of a vartabed: Mr A Mazlemian dedicates himself to celibate priesthood	284
134 – Days of terror in Bardizag	285
135 – The Yildiz bomb: new and terrible fear in Bardizag	286
136 – Fire calamities	287
137 – Nshan Agha Sinanian and his farm	289
138 – Laz-Armenian bandits	292
139 – The construction of the community bath house	297
140 – The Ottoman Bank incident in Constantinople and its repercussions on life in Bardizag	298
141 – The final ordinations in Bardizag	300
142 – Antranig Garabedian becomes director of the community schools	303
143 – The links between Armash seminary and Bardizag	304

Chapter 9 – 1908 – 1915

144 – The re-establishment of the Turkish constitution (July 1908): days of freedom	307
145 – Various organisations in Bardizag	311
1. Protection of Village Cultivable Land	311
2. The organisation of the Armenian General Benevolent Union (AGBU) Bardizag branch	314
3. The establishment of the People's Bank of Bardizag	314
4. The Steamship Company	315
5. The Diurger [Builders'] Association	317
6. The Dashnaktsagan (ARF) retail co-operative	319
7. The Public Garden Association	319
146 – New plans being considered	321
147 – Theatrical and artistic life in Bardizag	322
148 – The founding of a kindergarten and the purchase of its own building	324
149 – The conflict between the community authorities and the local committee of the ARF	325

Chapter 10 – Deportation and short-lived post-war life

150 – Incidents that were precedents in Armeno-Turkish relations	330
151 – Collection of weapons and deportation	335
152 – Bardizag during the years when it was empty of its population	344
153 – After the Armistice	349

Chapter 11 – A composite picture of Bardizag's public life

154– Explanation ... 356
    1. Bardizag's position, geography and topographical description ... 357
    2. Climate and health ... 362
    3. Economic life ... 370
    4. Family life ... 387
    5. Social life – leisure ... 404
    6. Public life ... 411
    7. Religious and spiritual life ... 415
    8. Educational work ... 420
    9. Popular superstitions and beliefs ... 429

APPENDIX

Photographs ... 437-460
Documents, illustrations and tables ... 461-472
Sources ... 473

TRANSLATOR'S NOTE

My original aim in translating this work was to provide the descendants of Armenians from Bardizag with a tool to help them understand their past as, due to the circumstances that led them to settle in the places they live now, many of them may not speak, read or write Armenian, cannot find anything in English (or any other language for that matter) about the village and are hungry for information about their families, their families' past and the origin, history and demise of the place itself.

Since beginning it, however, I have come to see things with a wider perspective, and think that my work might be useful for those (both Armenian and non-Armenian alike) who want to know what a large Armenian village was like, as Krikor Mkhalian's monumental work is detailed and all-embracing.

Bardizag was not a typical Armenian village in distant Anatolia, nor was it a metropolis; but it was the epitome of a relatively prosperous conglomeration of people with a link to the main city of the Ottoman Empire, Constantinople,* who mostly shared a common ancestry, outlook, customs, Armenian dialect,† education and ideals. Influential and educated Constantinople Armenians trumpeted it as an example of the best kind of Armenian village during the final decades of its Armenian existence.

But for those of us who are descended from families that originated in the village, know something of its history and are able read Armenian, Krikor Mkhalian's book *Bardizagn ou bardizagtsin*,‡ which first appeared just over 76 years ago, is something of a tantalising myth. Many people have heard of it; it was known to have been published by the Sahag-Mesrob Press in Cairo, Egypt in 1938 and is much sought-after; various Armenian authors have made use of it, but copies were – and are – almost impossible to find in the diaspora. It took me 40 years to find and actually read a copy – the one kept in the Nubarian Library in Paris. I know of only four other copies in Europe, although there must be others. Who knows how many copies were printed, sold or discarded? It is no wonder that accurate information about Bardizag before 1923 is therefore very scarce...

---

* The name Constantinople is used throughout this work, as the author is referring to the time before it officially became Istanbul.
† The people of Bardizag didn't use Turkish in the village, speaking their version of the Sepastia (Sivas) Armenian dialect; in fact their knowledge of Turkish was poor, generally speaking.
‡ The title, in reality, should be translated as *Bardizag and the (Bardizag) villager*, but I have preferred to take a broader, simpler approach. I trust the reader will forgive the liberty I have taken with it.

My translation and annotation of this book are part payment of the debt I feel I owe my particular heritage. I began paying it in 2005, when I realised that in actual fact there were only a handful of books in Armenian about Bardizag, and none at all that I had heard of in English or any European language.

The author, Krikor Mkhalian, was a well-educated community activist and talented teacher in Bardizag. He and his family were deported with the rest of the village's population in 1915. They survived and he continued his teaching career in Aleppo, Cairo and Jerusalem. He died suddenly in Cairo on the 5th of April 1937, having suffered poor health for the last few years of his life.[*] He was much respected for his abilities and erudition, and many people who were his students, colleagues or who knew him well held him in great esteem.

It fell to his nephew Onnig Mkhalian to complete the efforts to publish the work as his uncle,[†] by a cruel twist of fate, passed away just when the book had gone to press, never actually seeing the results of his long, arduous efforts.

I must say that although its publication was much acclaimed in the countries where Armenians from Bardizag found refuge – such as Egypt and Greece – some personalities from the village and their adherents considered Mkhalian's work to be, shall we say, not to their taste. This of course was because they were perhaps not written about with the fulsome praise or approbation they would have liked...

As I have worked through the original Armenian text, my respect for the author has grown by leaps and bounds; he has recorded, without fear or favour, in as much detail as he could muster, all he knew about the village and many aspects of life there.[‡] To me, as a translator, it is a tour de force that has lain unrecognised for too many years, with the author's magnificent achievement remaining hidden for far too long.

Mkhalian, ever the teacher and educator, takes care to explain things in great detail, using a rich, long form of western Armenian that is without any literary pretensions. This is a boon to the reader on several levels – first, the facts and details he recalls are not available elsewhere; secondly, his language is of a standard that we can hope to consciously emulate, but which to him was natural; and again, his patience and the extent of his memory, set down on paper, lead us to appreciate the substance of his work even more. Although the author's writing is mostly dispassionate in tone, I have to say that his nature ensures that he can become lyrical, satirical, critical or personal about various subjects, events and people. This is especially true of the descriptions of his career in education and his contacts with the theatre and the arts.[**]

---

* See his biography below.
† Krikor Mkhalian was his father's brother.
‡ He does, however, show some (restrained) bias against people or organisations that he considered to have done less than their best for the community, or did not fit in with his particular views.
** I have changed his third person singular prose, in which he describes events relating to himself, into first person, thus 'the writer of these lines knew' becomes 'I knew'.

Translator's Note

I am surprised at the extent to which he was involved in community enterprises. Although he says very little about his activities (and that in third person, as I've noted), he was the originator or instigator of some of the worthwhile community projects that lasted until the deportation of 1915.*

One cannot over-emphasise the fact that Mkhalian's work is *the* source book for anyone who wants to know about Bardizag. Some of the few authors who have penned works about the village – and who, incidentally, would have known him personally - have used it without even having the grace to acknowledge their debt to him. Without the use they made of it, their works would be poorer indeed.

It should be said that Mkhalian himself stated that he didn't set out to write a history, laconically writing:

> I had no intention of sketching out a history of the village, considering it to be absolutely beyond my capabilities, especially as Bardizag's history was outside my field of study and preferences.†

He actually prepared this book on the basis of his experience of living in Bardizag from his birth until middle age, aided by various written sources,‡ his recollections and the encouragement of famous individuals from the village itself who later achieved high ecclesiastical office. He wrote with hindsight, ending the work in his final days in Cairo, Egypt, knowing he would never see his birthplace again – something that makes his writing all the more poignant.

I have the impression that various sections were written at different times, as his prose style varies from one section to another; I think that individual chapters and sections might have been the basis for articles he might well have written, although I have no proof of this. My conviction that he wrote the book over a long period is bolstered by his statement concerning the time and effort he made over research he carried out to ascertain certain things, as well as the correspondence he used to check his knowledge.

There are, however, some startling omissions in his work. Here are two examples. He never mentions, even in an oblique way, the one and only *Armenian* miudir of the group of villages *(nahie)* centred on Bardizag – Hagop Der-Hagopian, the Constantinople journalist who held that office in Bardizag from 1908 until 1914 - although Mkhalian must have been in direct contact with him at least on a weekly

---

* See Section 145.
† See Preface.
‡ He had access to Kasabian's work, for example - Minas Kasabian (Farhad), *Hayere Nikomedio Kavarin Mech* [The Armenians in the Province of Nicomedia], Azadamard Press, Bardizag 1913.

basis due to his community commitments. One is left to wonder why.* The second is about the group of approximately 250 people from the village who went into the mountains rather than be deported in 1915.†

His work shatters the myth of the idyllic agrarian Armenian village that is popularly imagined to be nestling in the hills, with the sheep on the mountainside, and a relatively thriving population, albeit subject to Turkish or Kurdish raids etc. It shows the reality: a place where Armenians lived as Armenians and agriculture took second place to industry; where the notables and priests were in the ascendant with the villagers very much the underdogs, although prone to mass rebellion; and where the ever-present yoke of arbitrary Turkish rule (sic) had to be reckoned with. But it also shows how a relatively small group of people built a village which survived many economic problems,‡ how it grew and produced great and famous sons and retained its individuality. In fact it became one of the favourite places, by the end of the 19th century, where Armenians from Constantinople, including famous personalities, came for holidays, to be in and enjoy the Armenian milieu, climate and beautiful natural surroundings.

The book also sheds light on the morals and patriarchal form of village life in Bardizag; the author demonstrates the various influences that pervaded village society and the battles between the different factions that occurred at various times. It also highlights the role played by the priesthood, notables, industry, agriculture and education in the lives of the villagers and the development of the village itself right up until 1915.

The author lingers on the schools and teachers he had known. He talks about the Shirinian era and recalls Yeghishe Vartabed Tourian (later Patriarch of Jerusalem) and the community boys' school. He recounts his tenure there with all the problems he suffered. He deals in detail with Dr R Chambers and the American High School where he was a teacher... All these people and situations made a great impression on him and provided the grounding for his subsequent – and very fruitful - career.

Another aspect that he dealt with is the villagers' relations with the Muslim immigrants from the Caucasus (Georgians, Circassians and Laz) and *Hamshens*

---

* When cross-referencing this work with Hagop Der-Hagopian, *Bardizage Khadoudig* [Dappled Bardizag], published in Paris in 1960, I could not help noticing that, although Der-Hagopian mentions this book and even uses paragraphs from it without attribution, he makes no mention of Mkhalian's work on the village council – of which he (Der-Hagopian) was chairman. He does, however, say that Mkhalian was a conservative, (pro-Hnchak) and anti-Dashnak. I can only assume that this might be part of the reason that there seems to be a mutual antipathy between them, each expressing it by his silence towards the other and their respective works!

† See Hagop Der-Hagopian, *Bardizage Khadoudig*, Paris 1960, pp. 53-54 and Section 151 below.

‡ Bardizag's economy was never put on a firm footing, being dependant on the vagaries of climate and the general economic and political situation.

Translator's Note

[Laz Armenians] from Trabzon, and their effect on the commerce and life of Bardizag. The government-assisted immigration of *Guirdjis* [Muslim Georgians] and Laz[*] changed the demographic composition of the local area,[†] which was, until their arrival, almost completely devoid of a settled population except fot the Armenians, who themselves were immigrants from various parts of the Ottoman Empire.[‡]

The reader will note that the major part of the work concerns the period from about 1825 until the villagers' deportation in 1915. It also has a section on the return of survivors of the genocide in 1918 until the final abandonment of the village in 1923. Mkhalian apologises for this, but tells us that the scarcity of records – even in Bardizag before 1915 – meant that much information about the village's early times had already been lost before that date.

The events of 1915 etc. are related in detail.[**] Mkhalian was one of the people who personally suffered the beatings and harassment meted out by the Turkish authorities in the months before the deportation. The demise of the village, beginning in 1914 with the conscription of over 1,000 young men between the ages of 18 and 45 into the Ottoman army,[††] followed by the deportation of the remaining population of approximately 8,000 people in 1915, makes harrowing reading.

The return of some of the refugees to the village, beginning in 1918, and their efforts to rebuild their shattered community and lives that lasted until 1923 can be seen, once more with hindsight, to be doomed. But what does shine through is the dogged Armenian spirit that imbued the community – they were all Armenians and wanted to live as such - and they did everything in their power to do so...

The final chapter (Chapter 11) of this translation is a summary of Bardizag life. The author has divided it up into sections and sub-sections – and rightly so - for it embraces all aspects of village life. I feel that it is perhaps the best *handbook* on the village that could have been written. In view of its length and subject matter, I have created sub-sections within it for birth, marriage and death.

I should like to commend this work to all those who are interested in the village. It is erudite yet down to earth; it is full of history yet is dryly humorous. It is – yes – long, but a joy to read in its individual sections. Briefly, it is very satisfying,

---

[*] The Laz Armenians, however, received no assistance whatsoever.
[†] This was a Turkish government policy, and extended to all areas inhabited by non-Turks.
[‡] The Armenians of Bardizag, for example, originated in Sepastia (Sivas), while those of Bolu were from Karabagh (Artsakh). Both communities spoke their original dialects right up until 1915!
[**] See Chapter 10.
[††] The actual number is not known; we do know that 500 went as conscripts to Karamoursal on 9th August 1914, and *at least* another 500 went three days later. Hagop Der-Hagopian, *Bardizage Khadoudig*, p. 35.

providing much information concerning our lost community and even about many individual families and their origins etc.

*****

Mkhalian's sources are interesting. He made great use of the notebook that was found in the library of the Armenian Apostolic Patriarchate of Jerusalem. This document was penned in Armenian by Garabed Kahana Mkhalian – one of his relatives from a previous generation. This churchman was known in Bardizag by the nickname of *Gentani Domar* [living ledger or archive] for his knowledge and superb memory. Other important points in the narrative in Mkhalian's book we know (from his own words) also originated with this long-serving cleric. Mkhalian also had access to the Bardizag church's library or archive before 1915 and often quotes documents that were held there.

Despite his care to use written sources, he also relates many instances of arguments and strife, often in considerable detail and sometimes with dry humour, giving an extra flavour to his narrative. He however adds a note of caution about his work; in one place, talking about the records that were lost in 1915, he says: 'In my present circumstances I can only rely on facts held in my fleeting and uncertain memory.' He is far too modest!

The work is unusual in its structure; although it generally follows a pattern based on time, it is divided into parts, chapters, sections and in a few cases, sub-sections, based on subjects that are separate items in their own right. Not only this. Mkhalian also includes much important and fascinating family and personal detail in these sections by just adding them, often in parentheses, in the text or as footnotes or illustrations.*

I have had to amend certain part, chapter and section numbers. Part 1 was not numbered or titled; a chapter number (5) has been repeated; this has also happened to section numbers, for example (89) and (141). Mkhalian has not always been consistent in his structuring of the sections. Some are very short, while others are of chapter length. I have made all these follow the general structure of the work and have added titles to chapter headings as necessary, re-working the contents pages to reflect the changes made. Part, chapter and section titles remain the same where used by the author, except in the case of the one single-section chapter – Chapter 10, Section 149 – I have deleted the chapter heading and appended the section to the end of the previous chapter. I have also split Section 152 into two parts: its first retains the title, and second I have numbered 153 and given it the title of 'After the Armistice', using the author's title that appeared in italics on page 645 of the original work.

I have retained the footnotes to the text the author himself inserted as they were in the original. They are shown by the notation (Author's note).

---

* In fact, with a little effort, whole family trees may be compiled from the information provided in this work.

Translator's Note

I should perhaps comment on the number of annotations I have made. Mkhalian writes in a bald style, omitting various events, names and details which may be gleaned with confidence from other sources. I have added many items that throw extra light on the text, so that the current generation of readers, who perhaps cannot read Armenian, may have a better understanding of the subject. I make no apology for this.

I have retained the ecclesiastical titles used in the text that may be unfamiliar to the reader. They are placed within the name of the individual concerned, as they would be in Armenian. These are:

Kahana – married priest
Avak kahana – senior married priest
Avakerets – leading married priest (prelate's deputy in the village)
Vartabed – celibate archimandrite
Dzayrakiun vartabed – celibate archpriest

I have used the following definitions for certain recurring words and terms:

Parish for *tagh*
Notable for *ishkhan*
Parish council for *taghagan khorhourt*
Village council for *taghabedagan khorhourt*
Village authority for *azkayin ishkhanoutiun* in the *village* context
Community rather than national for *azkayin* in the *village* context
Silkworm house for *sheramadoun*
Silk spinning factory for *manaran*

I have also used a simple transliteration system without diacritical marks that is suitable for western Armenian; thus Bardizag *exactly* reflects the Armenian name, rather that the system that seems to have recently come into vogue, based wholly on eastern Armenian and thus totally unsuited to western Armenian, that makes it 'Partizak' which looks incorrect to the native English speaker, jars on the ear and is at odds with the gentle accent of the original – local – dialect.

The reader will note that various Armenian words and phrases are retained in the text; my translations of them into English are shown in square brackets.

I found that the transcription of personal and other names from Bardizag Armenian into their English equivalent was a problem, as the author used an old style that might lead to confusion today. I have therefore rearranged them to be consistent with current usage, allowing for the titles, descriptions and other soubriquets that were used in the village in the past.

Mkhalian's occasional use of Turkish in the text should be noted. He used words and sentences from that language in places where he wished to add emphasis, or give flavour to the short conversations he recorded. This was acceptable in the 1930s when people from the village and their descendants still understood Turkish, but the present generation doesn't necessarily have the knowledge their grandfathers had. All such usage has been rendered into English, hopefully without affecting the tenor of the work.

I should like to add a short note concerning the contents pages of the original (Cairo, 1938) publication (pages 977-983). It does not accurately reflect the part, chapter, section, or sub-section titles and lacks their numbers, just providing a sketchy version of the titles themselves and page numbers. There is no list of illustrations or documents and maps either. My impression is that it was put together in a hurry, to try and make the book complete after the author's sudden death.

One concern, generally, is the lack of available illustrations of the village and its inhabitants before 1915. I should like to point out that the narrowness of the village streets and the closely-built houses did not lend themselves to being recorded in photographs. There are only a limited number in existence, all of which have been reproduced numerous times, with the resulting degradation of their quality. It has proved possible, however, to use a considerable number of the 68 illustrations, 3 maps and 2 documents that appeared in Mkhalian's work thanks to modern technology. Some, although of considerable interest, are so poorly printed that their further reproduction is impossible. I have also used some that have appeared in various editions of Garo Kevorkian's *Amenoun Darekirke* [Everybody's Yearbook].

Finally, all errors and omissions in this translation are solely my responsibility.

* * * * *

A note on numbers and units of measurement to be found in this work:

There are no accurate figures for the number of people living in Bardizag at any given date;[*] I have seen numbers as low as 8,000[†] and as high as 12,000 quoted for 1915.[‡]

The number of houses quoted varies between 1,200 and 2,000 for the same date.[**]

---

[*] Boghos Vartabed Natanian quotes a population of 6,000 for 1870. Boghos Vartabed Natanian, *Arachin deghegakroutiun vidjagis Nicomedio* [First report on the diocese of Nicomedia], Djezvedjian Press, Constantinople 1871, p. 19.
[†] Kasabian, in the census table he presents, quotes the number of people in the village as 4156 males and 4100 females totalling 8256 people. See Appendix, Table 2 below.
[‡] A more realistic figure, although the source is not quoted, is 9,024. See Raymond Kevorkian, *The Armenian genocide, a complete history*, I B Tauris, New York, 2011, p. 551.
[**] Boghos Vartabed Natanian quotes 1100 for 1870. Boghos Vartabed Natanian, Arachin deghegakroutiun vidjagis Nicomedio, p. 19.

Translator's Note

A further question is of the number of people absent[*] from the village for various reasons, such as business, employment as servants or wet-nurses in Constantinople or elsewhere. Figures range from 600 to 950.

It will be seen that distances are quoted as being '…hours distant'. This is based on the distance that an average man could walk in the time quoted.

The monetary system in the Ottoman Empire was:

40 paras = 1 kurush

100 kurush = 1 lira.

An arshin is about 28 inches (180mm).

* * * * *

I have not translated Part 3: 'Bardizag Armenian', as I think that to appreciate it one must already know western Armenian well. It is made up of the following:

'Observations concerning the Armenian spoken in Bardizag' (not given a section number; pp. 814-822).

'Bardizag dictionary' (not given a section number; pp. 823-878).

Section 155: 'Forms of expression, explanations, sayings' (pp. 879-913).

'Grammar' (not given a section number; pp. 914-944).

'Pieces of poetry'[†] (not given a section number; pp. 945-973).

* * * * *

I had long since sent the manuscript of this translation for final editing when, on 15 October 2013, I received a copy of Minas Kasabian's book *The Armenians in the Province of Nicomedia*, published by the Azadamard Press, in Bardizag in 1913 (in Armenian) from Mr G Aghjayan in the USA, for which I am profoundly grateful.

This book is of fundamental importance for those who wish to make use of a scientific publication about the Armenians of the area around Nicomedia/Izmid/Kocaeli, as it is packed with many statistics concerning the whole province in the last phase of our people's existence there.

I determined to review my translation with a view to including as much of the information provided by Kasabian as possible, as his work compliments Mkhalian's to a very great degree, although his political views (pro-Dashnak) are diametrically opposed to Mkhalian's. I think, however, that they tolerated and respected one an-

---

[*] Kasabian, in his book compiled during 1912, quotes the number of houses as 1460. Minas Kasabian (Farhad), *Hayere Nikomedio Kavarin Mech*, p. 31.

[†] The title *panahiusoutian badarigner* is used here.

other as colleagues in the High School and perhaps were on cordial terms.* Mkhalian did, however use Kasabian's book for various facts such as population figures.

My instinct was totally justified, as his painstaking work has provided a great deal of information on Bardizag until 1911/1912. In fact his work – in terms of Bardizag alone – goes far beyond Mkhalian's book.

I know that my work has now been significantly enriched by these additions and hope readers will have an even better appreciation of Bardizag and its people. It has proved, however, very difficult not to include *every scrap* of information about even obscure things concerning Bardizag as I have had to keep in mind that *this is a translation of Mkhalian's work with annotations – not a history.*

* * * * *

I should like to acknowledge my debt to the following: the pictures, maps and documents in this translation have come mainly from Mkhalian's book itself, as well as from a few other sources such as rare early 20th century publications, from friends whose property they are and from the Internet. I should like to make a blanket acknowledgement to all for them, and express my thanks.

I should also like to take this opportunity to thank several people who have encouraged me, in one way or another, to undertake the translation of this large, important work. First, my good friend Ara Sarafian, director of the Gomidas Institute, London, Great Britain, who has unfailingly given me the greatest encouragement to continue to translate, from Armenian into English, works that are of importance. Next, my cousin Janna Davidian Lusk, who has given me so much encouragement and introduced me to many relatives I did not know. Thirdly, Krikor Mukhalian (the author's grandson) of Los Angeles, USA, who helped me discover relatives originally from Bardizag I previously knew nothing about. He also kindly supplied various documents and photographs that belonged to his grandfather for this publication. His whole family provided me wonderful hospitality and encouragement when I was in Los Angeles. I also thank my good friend Andranik Michaelian, who had the arduous task of editing my work.

I would also like to express my greatest appreciation and thanks to my wife Anne Melkonian, who has always been a constant source of encouragement and support in my efforts to impart some of what I know through translations, articles and lectures.

Finally, I should also like to add a heartfelt note of thanks to the Calouste Gulbenkian Foundation of Lisbon, Portugal, for their very generous grant that enabled me to complete the translation of this work.

---

* Kasabian makes many references to the ARF in his work; for example he quotes the organisation as being the mediator in disputes between strikers and management in the silk-spinning factories. See Minas Kasabian (Farhad), *Hayere Nikomedio Kavarin Mech*, p. 196.

Translator's Note

* * * * *

The 99th anniversary of the deportation of the population of the Bardizag villagers by the Turkish authorities will son be with us. Approximately 8,000 people were forced to take to the road to exile, deportation and, for a great number, death. But the spirit of those martyred people lives on and their descendants, spread around the world, cherish it and their memory.

I hope that, for non-Armenian readers, this will prove of interest and – I pray – lead to a better understanding, in a small way, of what and who Armenians are and have been in the recent past.

Finally, this is for my immediate family, relatives and the descendants of the people of Bardizag generally and for future generations – a significant part of your Armenian heritage is here...

Ara Stepan Melkonian
Plymouth, Great Britain
2014

BIOGRAPHY: KRIKOR MKHALIAN

The son of a well-known village family, Krikor Mkhalian was born in Bardizag on 12 June 1866. He was educated in the Bardizag community boys' school and graduated in 1884, during the Tourian years.* He then took up a post as a teacher in the same school from that year until 1890.

During that time he was also part of a group (all former Tourian students) that was instrumental in creating the Bardizag village theatre, having collected funds for its construction and furnishing.† He and his friends produced plays for the villagers too.

He studied sericulture at the same time as he was teaching and received a first class certificate as a silkworm breeder from the Turkish government Sericulture School in Boursa in 1889.‡

He then taught in the Chengiler School in Boursa (1891-1893), then in the theological seminary of the monastery of Armash (1893-1895). Following this, he taught in the school in Ovadjekh during the school year 1895-1896.

He was fortunate to escape the massacre of Armenians in Constantinople that took place after the Ottoman Bank incident in 1896. He had gone there on business, and managed to board a ship to return to Bardizag on the day after the massacre started.**

He accepted a post in the American High School in Bardizag and taught there from the start of the school year of 1896 until 1915.

His competence as a teacher was recognised by the award of a certificate from the Armenian Apostolic Patriarchate in Constantinople in 1911.††

Apart from being a teacher, he also held administrative posts on the *taghabedagan khorhourt* [village council] in Bardizag from 1908 onwards, including the temporary one that lasted until 1915. He was a community schools *hokapartsou* [trustee] from 1908 onwards.

When the prelate of Nicomedia was forced, in 1908, to activate the diocesan assemblies he had not called in years, Mkhalian was seconded to it as one of the four lay members representing Bardizag until 1915.‡‡

---

* Later Armenian Apostolic Patriarch Yeghishe Tourian of Jerusalem.
† See Section 120 of this work for details.
‡ See the facsimile of his sericulture certificate in the Appendix, Document 4.
** See Section 140.
†† See the facsimile of his teaching competence certificate in the Appendix, Document 5.
‡‡ See Section 145.

He was one of the leading lights in several community enterprises after 1908, such as Bardizag's People's Bank and the Steamship Company.[*]

He co-edited, with Hagop Alodjian, the YMCA newspaper *Paros*, which was printed in Constantinople from February 1910 until August 1911, a total of 17 issues. It consisted of literary, moral and news sections.[†] It was also distributed in Bardizag and was the only journal of its kind in the entire Ottoman Empire.[‡]

Another of his activities was the formation of the first Armenian General Benevolent Union (AGBU) branch in Bardizag, of which he, with Dr Hovsep Der-Stepanian, was chairman. He was also known as a leading conservative and anti-Dashnak[**] thanks to his erudition and debating skills.[††]

He was one of the two people[‡‡] who were given a permit by the miudir of Bardizag to go to Constantinople just before the deportation in August 1915. This was to solicit extra donations totalling 100 to 150 liras from wealthy people from Bardizag for the Ottoman military aid organisations named *Tekalife Harbiye* and *Hilale Adjmer*, in the hope that the village population, having already collected 200 liras and promising to pay for and maintain a 100-bed hospital would, with this extra sum, be allowed to remain in the village. Before he and his companion had collected all of it, they were recalled to the village by their relatives, as the deportation was beginning.[***]

He and his entire immediate family were deported in August 1915 with the rest of the Bardizag Armenian village community. The members of his family that survived[†††] finally found shelter in Kilis from 1916 to 1918, where they lived a very gruelling life.

The whole family moved to Aleppo after the Armistice in November 1918, where he was appointed a teacher in the newly-established Anglo-Armenian School in 1919.

From there he and his family went to Cairo, Egypt at the invitation of the Armenian General Benevolent Union (AGBU), becoming the director of the well-known Kaloustian School from 1919 to 1922. Later, at the end of 1922, he and his

---

[*] See Sections 144, 145 and 149 of this work for his activities in the village after 1908. It should be said that, in his modesty, he has somewhat belittled his work and influence in Bardizag.

[†] Hagop Der-Hagopian, *Bardizage Khadoudig*, p. 225.

[‡] Minas Kasabian (Farhad), *Hayere Nikomedio Kavarin Mech*, p. 269.

[**] The famous 'Shahrigian incident' is an illustration of this, but he made certain that his students weren't affected by it. See Garo Kevorkian, *Amenoun Darekirke* (Everybody's Yearbook), Beirut 1956, pp. 211-212.

[††] Hagop Der-Hagopian, *Bardizage Khadoudig*, p. 219. See also Section 144.

[‡‡] Mkhalian doesn't provide the other person's name.

[***] See Section 151.

[†††] He recalls that his family consisted of five houses, totalling 31 people. After the catastrophes of the war, the number who survived was 21. See Section 153.

Biography

family moved once more, helping to set up and becoming the educational director of the two AGBU orphanages in Jerusalem during that year and 1923. He taught in the Jerusalem seminary from 1924 until the time of his death, lecturing in Armenian language, mathematics, French and bookkeeping.*

He suffered poor health in the last few years of his life and died suddenly, aged 71, on 5 April 1937 in Cairo, Egypt, where he had gone to settle various details of the printing of this work, and is buried there.

May he rest in peace.

His known published works are:

Paros, the YMCA newspaper he edited in concert with Hagop Alodjian, printed in Constantinople from February 1910 to August 1911 (17 issues). (In Armenian)

Joghovourti zavagi me hishadagnere (The memoirs of the son of a community) (originally serialised in the newspaper *Baikar* of Boston, Mass., USA), and subsequently published as a separate book by Baikar, Boston, in 1924. (In Armenian)

Bardizagn ou bardizagtsin (Bardizag and its people), his great achievement, was finally published after his death by the Sahag-Mesrob Press, Cairo, in 1938, thanks to his nephew Onnig Mkhalian's efforts.† (In Armenian)

---

* An abbreviated biographical outline appears in Bishop Mgerdich Aghavnouni, *Members of the [monastic] brotherhood and visitors to Armenian Jerusalem*, published by the St James' Press, Jerusalem 1929, pp. 528-529.

† See Onnig Mkhalian's note at the beginning of this work.

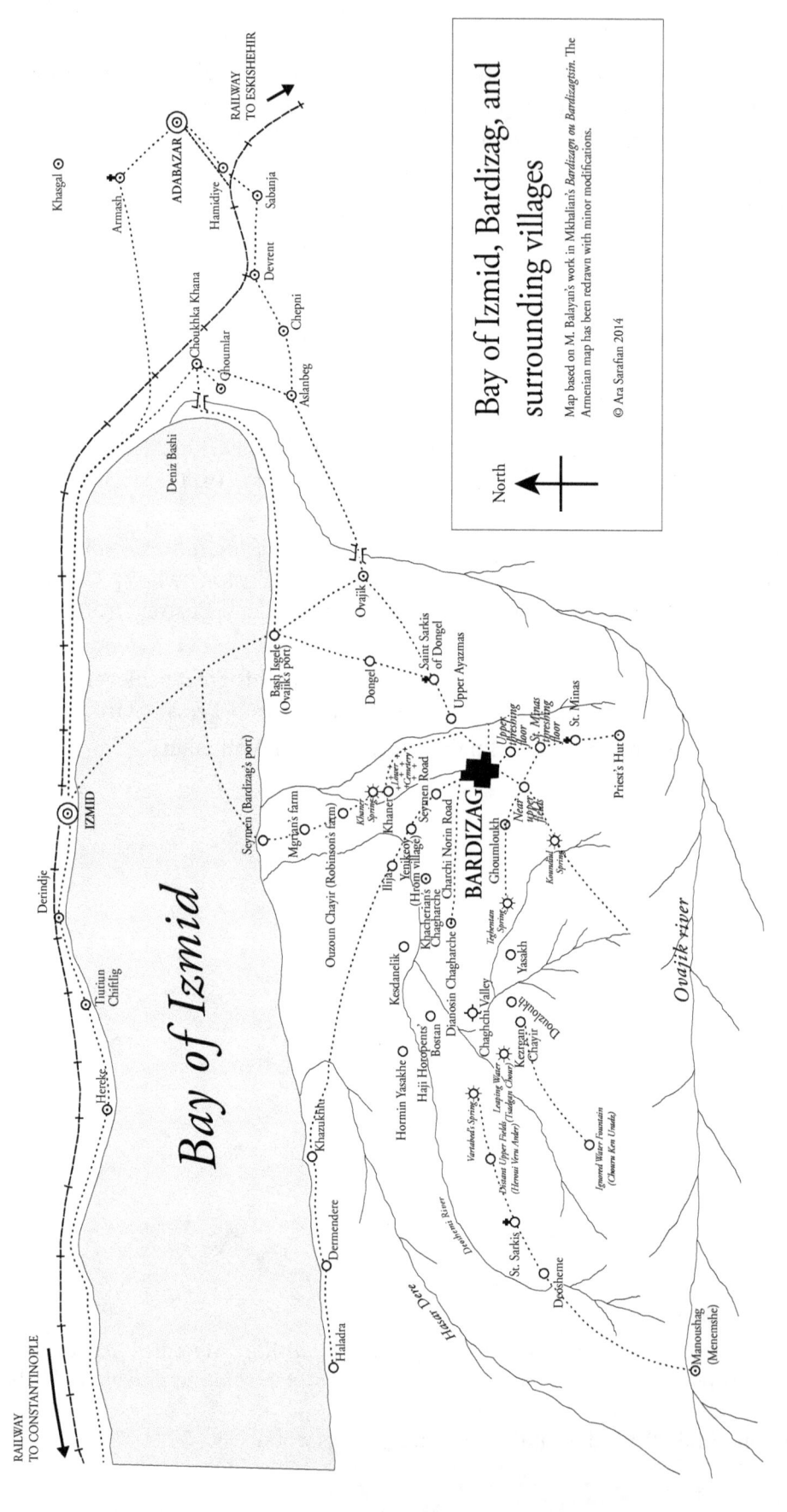

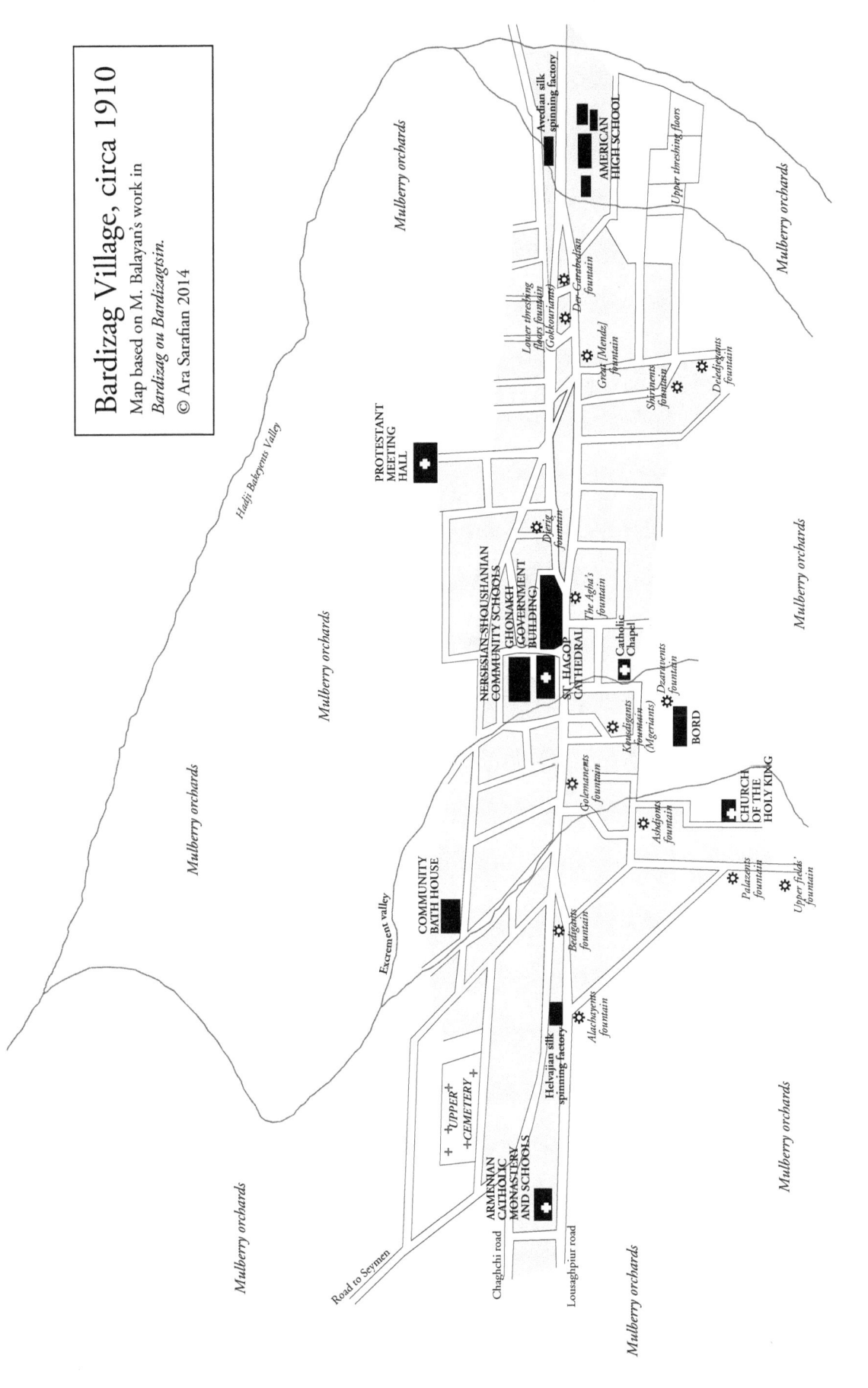

BARDIZAG

AND ITS PEOPLE

Preface

I prepared the first five chapters of this work from the contents of a notebook edited by the well-known Bardizag kahana Garabed Kahana Mkhalian. I was able to find it among his sons' possessions, through the efforts of the famous teacher Minas Dzalian, now deceased. He had, at my request, been good enough to obtain it and send it to the library of the Armenian Apostolic Monastery of the Two Jameses in Jerusalem, where it is now kept.

Garabed Kahana Mkhalian wrote it diligently and in great haste, with trembling hands, untidy script, and untrustworthy and poor composition, in his advanced years. He did so with the object of leaving a legacy for future generations of people from Bardizag. He was concerned to immortalise the memory of his unforgettable birthplace. He was the only person left from the generation that had lived in the village that had the ability and experience to tell its authentic story, more or less, from its foundation until 1912 and relate it to future generations.

Indeed, Garabed Kahana Mkhalian was regarded as Nicomedia (Izmid) province's living and speaking historian. Blessed with faultless memory and just right-mindedness, he had evinced great interest in the history of the Armenians of Bithynia. He especially built up his knowledge of the historic events and personalities of Bardizag, from the beginning to our times, by listening to clever old people's stories, reading colophons, official papers, tombstones and inscriptions. At the same time, he used his intelligence, to bring out of the dim shadows many things and personalities from bygone times.

He was regarded as the province's greatest historical authority with his ability to throw light on past events and the dark areas of our origins.*

When the monk Yeghishe Vartabed Tourian was the director of the schools in Bardizag – as he would relate the story – he suggested that Garabed Kahana write about the village's past, including the notes he had collected, assuring him that he, Tourian, would try to put them in order and have them published.

This fired Garabed Kahana's enthusiasm and he began to write the history of Bardizag based on his research and interests. He was able to untidily fill four notebooks, none of which were edited very much. The first two contained Bardizag's history from the beginning until the time of his advanced years. The third contained details of the origins of more than 1,500 families, tracing them to 28 original families that must have been, in his estimation, the first refugees to move there. Finally, the fourth notebook contained his (Mkhalian's) family tree. They all

---

* Indeed, his nickname in the village was 'Living Archive' *('Gentani Domar')*.

contained much of interest concerning the life of Bardizag. One or two of these notebooks were quite large but, unfortunately, only one remains in our hands today. It is one of the first two, containing the history of the village from 1625 until 1850, a period that stopped about a decade before his ordination.[*]

Garabed Kahana, in a preface to this notebook, with the greatest modesty, explained that he had no pretensions of writing a regular and accurate history, and didn't want what he had set down to be published in the poor form in which he had written it. He called (or rather begged) for some of the respected teachers who were his contemporaries in the village to take what he'd written, edit and tidy it, correct the language, put it into order and then, if possible, place it in a suitable form in the public domain.

As for me, I had no intention of sketching out a history of the village, considering it to be absolutely beyond my capabilities, especially as Bardizag's history was outside my field of study and interest. But when Patriarch Yeghishe Tourian[†] was dying and everyone had gone to hear his last words I, with others, approached his bed, where Catholicos Papken of the Great House of Cilicia introduced me to him in his final dying state, for him to give me his last wishes. The dying man did not forget to bring Garabed Kahana's notebook to my attention, asking me to look at it and bring it to a presentable state.

That sacred commission, placed on me by the great patriarch, appealed to my feelings. It was to write the history of this much-loved village, especially as, like all Armenian villages, it belonged to the past and was worthy of having its historical record presented to others. Further, Patriarch Torkom Koushagian,[‡] Archbishop Mgrdich Aghavnouni and I all thought that when the surviving members of our generation died out, it would be impossible to record the village's history properly in the future. This was because, among all the others, I was the one person who had spent many years in Bardizag, as a teacher in both the community schools and the American High School during its heyday, and as a public activist who had worked there during the community's final years. I felt it incumbent on me to complete Garabed Kahana Mkhalian's legacy up to the time of the village's final destruction.

The genesis of this work was the result of this commission. I have attempted to complete the history penned by Garabed Kahana and to append a small study of Bardizag's Armenian dialect to it.[**]

I too, in my turn, confess here that this is not a regular chronologically ordered, wide and serious study. Instead, I have the satisfaction of giving a memoir of the

---

[*] He was ordained in 1866. See Section 99.
[†] Armenian Patriarch of Jerusalem from 1921-1929.
[‡] Armenian Patriarch of Jerusalem from 1929-1939.
[**] Part 3 of the original work. (See Translator's Note, above).

Preface

history of Bardizag in general terms, on the principle that the poor effort I have made is better than nothing at all.

My involvement in this work was to utilise my personal memories, as well as information and recollections from several of my friends and acquaintances from Bardizag, who, at my urging, were good enough to send me what they had concerning Bardizag's history and final events. I am indebted to all of them.

When my plan to write Bardizag's history became public knowledge, it was received with the greatest enthusiasm from all sides, from people from the village and those who loved it. This gave me the greatest encouragement to dedicate myself to the task, with the strength to work to fill a public need.

I am delighted to have been able to complete this work and present it to my dear compatriots, who I believe will read it with pleasure, finding in it old memories and reliving the wonderful life that unfortunately has been lost forever.

K. Mkhalian
Cairo, 18 March 1937

Onnig Mkhalian's Note

The compiler of this history – Krikor Mkhalian – my late lamented uncle,[*] as is well known, passed away suddenly on 5 April 1937 in Cairo, Egypt. This was after a life full of good works, when only a few sections of this book had been printed. He was thus deprived of the comfort of seeing the complete production of his hard work.

His sad and sudden death had the effect of handing me a sacred trust: to complete the publication of the entire work, overcoming every difficulty. I am delighted that I was able to do so, completing the part concerning the Bardizag dialect with the help of my friend and compatriot, the Kalousdian Community School teacher Mr. Ghazaros Nahabedian. Thus I too bring my warmest filial feelings both to the dear departed and the memory of unforgettable Bardizag.

O. Mkhalian
Cairo, 20 June 1938

---

[*] Father's brother.

Introduction

The Imperial *firman* [decree] concerning the founding of Bardizag is dated 1625.* That decree, without doubt, must have been granted years after the village's creation. By then the first settlers had established themselves there, built their houses, formed families, prepared fields and planted gardens in that previously uncultivated area.†

There was a valley, on the south side of Bardizag, at about a quarter to half an hour's distance, which was known as Chiftlig Valley.‡ Farming had never been carried out on that side of the village, going back one to two hundred years from my time, but the name shows that a *chiftlig* [plantation or farm], belonging to Turkish aghas or pashas, on which Armenian or Muslim slaves had worked, existed there previously.

We can have some idea of the reasons** that forced Armenians and other Christians living in the interior provinces of the Ottoman Empire to abandon their centuries-old homes and come and settle in these places by recalling the Empire's internal conditions.††

Sultan Mohammed III ascended the throne in 1595.‡‡ The great Djelali rebellions*** exploded during the years of his reign††† in Asia Minor and throughout the inner provinces of the Empire, terrorising the ordinary people and

---

* This was during the reign of Sultan Mourad IV (1623-1640).

† Kasabian states that the *second* westward migration of Armenians (the first took place after the collapse of the Kingdom of Lesser Armenia (Cilicia) starting in 1374) started in 1513 and lasted until 1670. See Minas Kasabian (Farhad), *Hayere Nikomedio Kavarin Mech* [The Armenians in the Province of Nicomedia], Azadamard Press, Bardizag 1913, p. 11.

‡ Chiftlig means plantation.

** One of the major factors in the westward drift of the Armenians was the famines that took place in 1577 and 1607. See Minas Kasabian (Farhad), *Hayere Nikomedio Kavarin Mech*, p. 15.

†† Another reason for the migrations was the forced Islamisation of Christians en masse in the Ottoman Empire that lasted from 1551 until 1640. See Minas Kasabian (Farhad), *Hayere Nikomedio Kavarin Mech*, p. 16.

‡‡ This was, in fact, Sultan Mehmed III Adli, who reigned from 1595 to 1603.

*** The Djelali rebels were the armed forces and their commanders that were sent against the Persians. They rebelled against Ottoman authority and became masters of vast areas of eastern Turkey. Minas Kasabian (Farhad), *Hayere Nikomedio Kavarin Mech*, p. 14.

subjecting them to pillage and destruction, resulting in the country's population, especially the Christian and Armenian elements, to abandon their homes and find peace and safety around Constantinople and Roumeli.

The foundation of Bardizag in the province of Bithynia in the hills on the southern side of the Bay of Izmid at the beginning of the 17th century was one minor result of this general catastrophe.

In those days persecuted Armenians from the interior created a number of villages around the bay, close to or somewhat distant from the seashore. Four Armenian villages, Bardizag [Bahchedjoukh, later Bahchedjik], Dongel, Ovadjekh and Arslanbeg fell within our borders, on a west to east axis. Apart from these, Armash, Khasgal, Ferizli and Tamlekh were set up northeast of Izmid, on the slopes of the Sakaria river valley in Khodjeli province. Sabandja, Geyve, Ortakiugh, Ghendjelar and Kourtbelen were further to the east, on the hills and plains along the same valley. They had been built by Armenians and were either completely or at least partially inhabited by them. The Armenian villages of Merdigeoz and Yalak Dere were located in the mountains to the west, towards the bay above the port of Karamoursal.* The Armenian villages of Shakhshakh, Kartsi and Kheledjekeoy, on the slopes of the mountains of Yalova, were also on the same axis, towards Constantinople. There were other Armenian settlements located higher than the latter villages, on the parallel mountain slopes at the northern and southern ends of Lake Niceae. These were Chengiler, Ortakiugh, Bazarou Medz Nor Kiugh, Keremet, and, opposite, Seoleoz, Giurle, Gharsakh and, near the Marmara, Benli.

This chain of newly-established Armenian villages extended further and was enriched by others, scattered in the mountainous plain between the cities of Biledjig and Broussa (Boursa), right up to the border of the province of Engiuriu. There were more than 40 of them.

We could still see many other Armenian-inhabited villages around Rodosto and Bandirma,† the majority of which were founded during the time of that dreadful internal disorder in the immediate area around Constantinople, on both the European and Asian shores of the Marmara.‡

---

††† In fact the first Djalali rebellion, led by Djelal, a Shiite preacher from Tokat, began in 1519. It then broke out again from 1526 to 1528, during the reign of Suleiman I the Magnificent, flaring up again in 1595-1610, 1654-1655 and 1658-1659.

* There were 10 Armenian families living in Karamoursal until 1883, which had been organised by a certain Serovpe Vartabed into a proper community, with a chapel, school and a dwelling for a married priest. They were forced to leave when there was an influx of Muslim settlers. Minas (Farhad)Kasabian, *Hayere Nikomedio Kavarin Mech*, p. 79.

† It should be borne in mind that he was writing in the 1930s.

‡ See *The Chronology of the Vartabed Krikor of Taranagh*, published by the Jerusalem Patriarchate. (Author's note)

Introduction

Once Murad Pasha had been able to stamp out the Djelali rebellion and destroy the rebels in 1609 (during the reign of Sultan Ahmed),* the country returned to tranquillity. A *firman* was then published instructing all refugees from the interior to return to their original homes. This government order naturally created new terrors for the newly-established Armenian communities that had created their new life and work in the places they had now settled.

These Armenians were therefore subject to great disillusionment in view of this unexpected order and tried by direct and indirect means to remain where they were. It is probable that, to escape attention, they left and found refuge among other distant new communities, while some of them were forcibly returned to their places of origin.

It is very probable that, as Krikor Vartabed of Taranagh tells us, the first Armenian villages were founded near the European and Asian shores of the Constantinople waters. But when the above-mentioned Imperial *firman* was promulgated and the people were forced to leave their newly-established villages and return to the interior provinces, an important group of them seem to have returned, in separate groups, to Asia Minor as if to comply with the order, and then scattered over the mountains south of the Bay of Izmid. There they founded new villages and were careful to stay away from the shoreline, thus remaining out of sight. It could be that Bardizag was founded in this way, as were the surrounding villages, off the routes of their return journeys.†

---

* Sultan Ahmed I, Dec 1603 –Nov 1617.

† The author of the first part of my story, Garabed Kahana Mkhalian, recalls Arakel of Tabriz's *History* in his notebook, having seen it in Krikor Kahana Somoundjian's (Hatsouni) home. The rebellion described by Taranagh was included in this *History*, which came to the same conclusion about the foundation of the newly-created villages. (Author's note)

PART I

FROM THE BEGINNING

Chapter 1

The Foundation of Bardizag and the Origins of the Migration

1 – Bardizag's location and position

Our forefathers, in their escape from the seashore around Constantinople, appear to have greatly hesitated about where their new settlement should be. It is highly probable that, in order to remain out of sight and in accordance with the enthusiasm given by age-old Armenian custom, they wanted to settle in a place near the eastern end of Lake Nicaea.

That region was an area mostly occupied by Turks from the past until present times, with only Nicaea having relics from the days of Christianity and the Crusades, and whose population included a Greek minority.

Our people came to that region and chose, for their settlement, a mountain called Eoren, near the present-day Turkish village of Tejir, which had been a certain Nouh Bey's *vakef*.* Naturally, they cleared the area of trees and woods and created cultivable fields about 4-5 hours journey from the Bay of Izmid. The people of Bardizag called that place *antereres* [the other face] in my day.†

Our ancestors were unable to feed themselves while the soil was still not ready for cultivation, so they sent their young men to work on the neighbouring farms owned by Turkish aghas. All the remaining people, old or young, spent their time preparing the soil of their new homeland for cultivation.

Large farms were to be found at that time on the edges of the plains on the southern side of the Bay of Izmid. These were located near the ports of Ghazekhli and Deyirmendere, which stretched almost to Bardizag. This was where, in our times, we had a tract of land called Chiftilig Valley. The newly-arrived young refugee men went to these farms as *yanashma* workers [hired hands], to work on the fields owned by the Turkish aghas.‡

---

* *Vakef*: pious endowment.
† Kasabian relates the legend that the first settlers comprised seven families that were later joined by 13 more. Minas Kasabian (Farhad), *Hayere Nikomedio Kavarin Mech*, p. 31.
‡ These farms were, according to Kasabian, owned by a certain Khalil Pasha who, according to legend, was of Armenian origin, becoming a Muslim when he was captured and inducted into the Janissary corps. He seems to have been a grandee during the time of Sultan Ahmed. Kasabian also states that at the time of his writing (1910-1912) land deeds were recorded as being *Khalil Pasha vakefe* [Khalil Pasha's religious endowment or foundation]. Minas Kasabian (Farhad), *Hayere Nikomedio Kavarin Mech*, p. 32.

It became obvious that the Turkish aghas were very pleased with these new arrivals' cheap and hard work as well as with their expertise in cultivating the soil. They approved of them and tried to find a way of retaining them for their lands. The Turkish aghas, when the new arrivals' parents occasionally came to visit them, found the opportunity to speak to them and persuade them to come down from those distant mountains where they wouldn't be able to find work and protection. They suggested that they settle in a place near the farms, where they would be closer to the provincial centre, Izmid, where an Armenian community already existed. Our ancestors agreed with the Turkish aghas' suggestion and left their pioneering work, descending from Mount Eoren. Carefully avoiding the lowlands filled with thorn bushes, they chose to settle on the thickly forested foothills of the mountain looking towards Izmid. That place was named St. Minas' Hill by our ancestors. They found a flat piece of land on the side of the mountain that stretched west to east just below St. Minas Hill. There they founded the village called Baghchedjoukh. It was well supplied with fresh, clean water, and had healthy air, in every way suitable for settlement. The site was covered with trees called *ghezel aghadji*.

Our ancestors' chosen place became centre of the extended village of our times. The supply of water increased in winter on both sides of a small valley that they called Charsouvi or Jamoun Tsor [Church Valley] due to the flow of rainwater from the surrounding hills. They once more cleared a rectangular area of the forest, stretching on all four sides to the borders of the areas taken up by the Djangaloz, Mikayelian, Khashman and Amouents houses, having the church and school as their centre. The church, school, prelacy and *ghonakh* [government building] were all built in this space and the houses belonging to the Delihadjis (of the Ghochoum clan), Ghareveleg Azarians, Alemshahs, Abadjis, etc. were constructed around them. Our ancestors built the walls and roofs of these first huts with the timber from the trees cut down in the forest. The huts had beaten earth floors. The hearths were in the centre, and the smoke escaped through a hole in the roof or through the door, just like in houses built by primitive man.

With its position, the newly-established village took in a beautiful and wide panorama. St. Minas Hill was on the southern side, its summit crowned with centuries-old copses of trees. The gentle downward slope to the shore of the bay was set before it in a northerly direction, where a sizeable field was prepared, later to be the villagers' agricultural centre called Khaner. Beyond this, the semicircular strip of blue water stretched from west to east. The age-old capital of Bithynia was opposite, its back to a line of low hills and with villages framing it on both sides within a cordon of tall trees which, rising, closed off the horizon towards Constantinople.

The village, in this position, would eventually spread solely east and west, as there was a steep upward slope behind it to the south and a downward slope to the north. In my day it would present the appearance of a great saddle, with its horns rising above the sides of St. Minas Hill, forming the short and narrow lines of the upper threshing floors and upper fields.

2 – The origin of the migration and the first families

Where had the migrants to Bardizag come from? There is no answer to this question with an historical basis.* The thought among us, however, that they came from the province of Sepastia [Sivas] has become an established fact, based on the close similarity of the Armenian dialect spoken in the village with that of the areas around Sepastia, in terms of words, grammar and pronunciation, as well as village customs and character.†

Hovhannes Kahana Mgerian tells us that, on one occasion, when he was making a pastoral visit to a number of refugees sheltering in Constantinople, he heard a mother singing a lullaby to her baby. There was such a similarity of her language, lilt and accent of the song with that of Bardizag that for a moment he had the idea that he was with a woman from the village. He asked her where she was from. She replied 'I'm from Sepastia.'

It is also a well known fact that there was a village in the province of Sepastia called Baghtchejoukh,‡ and it was a very widely held view that our forefathers came from that village and named their new homeland after their original one, wanting to link their old life with their new one.

There is an old tale concerning the name 'Bardizag' which is at odds with the above conclusion. It tells that Sultan Murad IV, on his way with a large army to capture Baghdad from the Persians, passed through the province of Nicomedia and rested there for one night. In the morning he looked out of the window at the hills opposite and saw the village that had been recently founded by our forefathers and asked his attendants 'What is this view? It seems like a *baghchedjoukh* [small garden].' He also saw the nearby village of Ovadjouk and supposedly said 'It looks like a *youvadjoukh* [small nest].' This legend says that the two villages were thus named by the words

---

* Kasabian, quoting Hovhannes Avak Kahana Mgerian's book *Mahartsank yev hishadagarank* [Tombstones and Memorials], published in Constantinople in 1877, p. 227, says that the immigrants arrived in two groups. The first was composed of seven families that were later followed by 19 more. He has based the latter figure on Roupen Zartarian's article in *Azadamard* in 1911. Minas Kasabian (Farhad), *Hayere Nikomedio Kavarin Mech*, p. 31.

† Kasabian states that the people of Bardizag were not only from Sivas, but also from Agn. See table in Minas Kasabian (Farhad), *Hayere Nikomedio Kavarin Mech*, pp. 102-103. We also know that several families from Zeitun also immigrated to the village in the early 19th century such as the Moskofians, who retained their links with their cousins in Zeitun until 1915, although they adopted all the village customs and speech.

‡ This village, with its 65 houses and its church of St. Kevork, still existed in 1915. Teotig, *Koghkota hai hokevoraganoutian yev ir hodin aghedali 1915 dariin* [The Golgotha of the Armenian clergy and its flock in the calamitous year of 1915], edited by Ara Kalaydjian, St. Vartan Press, New York, 1985, p. 115.

spoken by the Sultan.* Garabed Kahana Mkhalian, the author of these historical notes, is of the opinion that it is entirely possible that the legend is correct.

For me, these tales are the stuff of legend, as it's not possible to believe that people would found a village and wait for a Sultan to arrive by accident and name it.

There is a greater degree of probability in the idea that the villages were already named and that the Sultan, with those depictions, gave a witty explanation for their names and, as a sort of proof, I can present the name Ovadjekh, which rather than looking like a small nest can be linked to the description of a small field as it is situated on the edge of a small promontory, which the villagers called, for many years, Yazi.

It seems to me that this explanation is the more probable, especially as it was customary for the people to create a legend concerning any one place, based on its name, as they've done for the nearby village of Dongal, or Dongel, saying that the name springs from the Turkish saying 'Don gel' [depart and return], trying to show its remoteness and poverty.

It's a natural thing for people to link the past with the present, as our people have done. Families were used to keeping old names alive in new generations and keeping priests' names for those newly ordained. This is also the case for villages and places of pilgrimage.†

We have a legend that among the first immigrants was a large family named the Deli Hadjis. The story about them is that they, with all their relatives, had arrived at the site of the village and founded it. Garabed Kahana Mkhalian, in his youth, had known an old woman named Perteg Neneh [grandmother] who, if she had remained alive in 1909, would have been 160–170 years old. This old woman used to say that she had married one of the members of the family named Vahan Deli Hadji and that her father-in-law would say that he was one of the original immigrants.

There were two Deli Hadjis brothers, one of whose houses was to the west of the Jamoun Tsor [Church Valley] with the other on the side of the valley itself. According to Garabed Kahana Mkhalian‡ the Khotchoums, who in our time had a

---

* This is also recorded by Kasabian. See Minas Kasabian (Farhad), *Hayere Nikomedio Kavarin Mech*, p. 33.

† Kasabian tells us that *Bardizag* is the translation of *Baghchdjoukh* and, before settling on its final Armenian form, was *Baghchdjik (Bahçeçik)* and is recorded as such in official documents. See Minas Kasabian (Farhad), *Hayere Nikomedio Kavarin Mech*, p. 33. See the land sale document No 1 in the Appendix, Document 6, below.

‡ In my opinion this name was retained in the current name 'Deledjeg', the name of a family related to the Ghouchoums and which had a house near them. They later sold it and had a new house in another part of the village. The Deledjegs still existed in my day. Their house and fountain still existed at the foot of St. Minas' hill. The word Deledjeg is formed from the corruption of the surname Deli Hadji, with the 'l' and 'h' letters lost and becoming 'Deledjeg, with the 'k' becoming 'g'. (Author's note)

house at that very spot, were descendants of the Deli Hadjis, this latter name having been lost in the village.

The Ghaladjis of our time also belonged to the Deli Hadji family. They were an old Bardizag clan, because the above-mentioned Perteg Neneh was the mother of the great Hadji Krikor and Little Ghaladji Garabed, the names Vahan, Krikor and Garabed being retained in the Ghaladji family even until my day. It would appear that this family, descended from the Deli Hadjis, took this surname because of their tin plating trade. The people of the village, when the second church was to be built, approached the Ghaladji family to give up part of their property for the expansion of the church. They, like their Deledjeg relatives, left their house and went to the east of the village and built a new one there.

There were two Ghaladji houses in that area in my time, a little distant from each other, both being notable families of the village. Garabed Kahana tells us that Perteg Neneh was a very shrewd and clever woman. She had a *charkh** and carried on the old trade of preparing warp threads, the skill probably brought from the original village in Sepastia.

There is every possibility of checking this information, but at the least it shows that others apart from the Deli Hadjis were among the original families, a proof of which was Perteg Neneh's marriage into the Deli Hadji family.

3 – Bardizag's boundaries according to the Imperial *firman* [decree]

Bardizag's imperial decree was promulgated during the reign of Sultan Mourad IV in the Turkish era 1040, which coincides with 1625 A.D. It was later lost, but the village notables of the time, 80 or 90 years ago,† succeeded in obtaining a new copy. It was kept in the church's library until 1915, the year of the deportation.

The boundaries of Bardizag were fixed, according to the contents of this decree, as follows:

The village boundary, following the line of the coast, went from Batakh Dere or Chatal Dzov to Ghara Ghalderem, a distance of one hour on horseback. It then turned south from the former's boundary on the landward side, rising up the slope to Bardizag's western side, to the place called Sakar Bghche or Deosheme. It went from there to Doghan Dere (Nebi Dere). From that point it turned east, reaching the place called At Yailase, opposite Gharpoz Pounar (St Minas). It continued on to a point near Ghara Dere Bashe, in other words near the source of the Chamerli Boghaz River. It included Bal Ghayan and Bazirgian's Chayir, and then extended to the border of Dongel village. It then ran to the head of Patsperan [Open Mouth] Valley *(Yoriukler Yailase)* and descended along that valley towards the seashore to Tash Keopru and Lebi Deria.

---

* Charkh is Turkish for wheel. It was a sort of spinning wheel.
† The book was published in 1938, so the author probably means during the 1850s.

I should add that in connection with this decree determining Bardizag's borders, there have never been empty or deserted places within the defined area. As I said before, there were farms and fields there worked by Turkish *marabas* [destitute workers]. The places quoted in the decree are ancient ones that existed long before Bardizag was founded.

Secondly, the decree also includes the nearby Greek-inhabited village of Yenikeoy or, as the people of Bardizag called it, Hormin Kiugh [Roman Village], that was always regarded as part of Bardizag by government departments. Its tithe was paid to the *multezims* (tax collectors) in Bardizag. The two villages were separated thirty or forty years ago[*] and a border was determined between them from Chakhchi Valley to a stretch of water called Engezli Boghaz, although the people of Bardizag owned considerable land (gardens, fields etc) beyond the latter.

Government records assigned the village area as Meri Meran Khalil Pasha's *vakef* [pious endowment]. There was an extensive farming area near the seashore called 'The Pasha's Chiftelig'. Khalil Pasha had assigned this *vakef*'s annual earnings to a mosque near the sea at Uskudar, and the foundation officials would come to Bardizag each year to collect it, at a cost of one and a half to three *kurush* per head of population. In the old days the villagers paid this tax with wheat, barley, oats etc.

A Turk from Agn, who spoke Armenian like a native, arrived in Bardizag from Constantinople in the Turkish year 1291 to check on the area of land belonging to the village. Garabed Kahana Mkhalian saw the above-mentioned land tax recorded in that man's books and that the yearly tax on barley was specifically set at 30 *kiles*.

The *vakef* [foundation] including the neighbouring villages of Dongel and Ovadjek was assigned to an important man named Roum Pasha.

4 – The origin of the Armenian population of Izmid (Nicomedia)

The Armenian immigration to the Byzantine Empire, especially to Constantinople and other important cities among which was Nicomedia (Izmid), began very early. Whether the immigrants retained their national identity in those ancient times is very doubtful. An important part of these Armenians lost their language and church and were assimilated into the Greek population. However we cannot regard this as absolute. There were communities in various places in the country that were able to retain their national characteristics and identity, despite persecution and Greek fanaticism.

People have said that there was an Armenian community in Izmid from the date the Turks conquered the Byzantine Empire.[†] A pasha by the name of Pertev began building the Yeni Djami mosque in the town in the Turkish year 989 (1574 AD). This was domed and built of stone and cement, and became one of the ancient and

---

[*] Approximately 1890-1900.

[†] 1453.

notable edifices of Izmid. Pertev pasha brought Armenian workers and master craftsmen in to build it.[*] Its construction took a long time, so the pasha, to keep the workers at their building, recommended that they bring their families to the city. The Armenian workers obeyed the pasha's recommendation and brought their families and goods from the provinces. They settled them in a place assigned by the pasha on the deserted heights that, from that time onwards, was called *Karabash mahalesi* and known as a Christian quarter. He also gave them a piece of land called *Djin Bayir* where they used to bury their dead.

These Armenians left their quarter after a time, selling their houses to Turks, and moved lower, to a square area known as *Ghadi Bayir*. They also bought some land for themselves near the coast as a new cemetery and began burying their dead in it. They visited the old cemetery at least once a year to bless their dead buried there.[†]

The community of Izmid was thought to have been formed in this way, and its existence encouraged new refugees to found their villages on the slopes of the surrounding hills.

5 – Traces of a Turkish population in Bardizag

Until my day the area below Bardizag's upper cemetery was known as Korel. We Armenians called Turkish tombs by that name. In our times that area consisted of Tavit Kahana's tannery, the Kiutners' silk spinning factory and mulberry orchards, and the Dzallans' orchards, and stretched as far as Hadji Minas Teoleol's newly-built silkworm house. Bardizag and the villages around it were inhabited solely by Armenians, so the name Korel must have been kept because Turks had also previously lived there – according to the tradition described below.

Turks established themselves among us, just like the people of Bardizag, to secure employment on the surrounding farms where there was always work to be had and the opportunity for making a living.[‡] Obviously they must have arrived and settled there after the Bardizag Armenians as, if they had been there previously, they would have prevented the 'infidels' from settling near them. The Turks would not have permitted the Armenians to settle in the higher, more wholesome and better watered places, as there wasn't a spring or water to be had in the area where they

---

[*] Kasabian says that '…everyone, be they Turks, Armenians or Greeks, all agree that the founders of the Izmit Armenian community were stonemasons and builders from Palu.' Minas Kasabian (Farhad), *Hayere Nikomedio Kavarin Mech*, p. 28.

[†] They later built the church of the Holy Mother of God in the city. Minas Kasabian (Farhad), *Hayere Nikomedio Kavarin Mech*, p. 25.

[‡] Kasabian states that they too (between 8 and 10 families) were refugees from the Djelali rebellions, but does not indicate when they arrived. Minas Kasabian (Farhad), *Hayere Nikomedio Kavarin Mech*, p. 31.

lived. Naturally the Armenians wouldn't have liked the Turks to live near them, and would have wanted to find a way of removing them from their village.

The Armenians found an opportunity to realise their desire. A Turkish judge came to Bardizag at some point about a legacy. The village notables provided hospitality, treated him with deference and became friendly with him. They then suggested that he find a way of sending the Turks away beyond the village boundaries, making the idea more palatable of course by using a bribe.

The judge then visited the Turks, called in their elders, talked to them and, striking their most sensitive nerve, asked, 'What business do you have among these infidels? You haven't got a place to pray in and your wives and daughters have no shame, going about with their faces uncovered, like infidels. You have greatly sinned. The Prophet will punish you, condemning you all to hell.'

The elders became confused and replied, 'Oh sir, what are you saying, and what can we do to be good in the Prophet's eyes?'

The judge added, 'What are you doing here, in this dry and barren place? Go down near the sea shore. There is good land and plenty of water there. I'll talk to the infidels; they'll buy your land.'

The Turks agreed, sold their land to the people of Bardizag and departed for the sea shore, settling in a Turkish village called Ghoumlar.

The people of Bardizag have only retained a memory of them - the name Korel - as the name of that former burial ground.

6 – The life and occupation of Bardizag's first settlers

Naturally, farming was the settlers' first occupation. They cleared the forest around their dwellings, converted it into fields and planted grain. In my day, the areas occupied by mulberry orchards were all former fields, and the grain produced was brought to the village threshing floors. Eventually only the threshing floors remained - as playgrounds for the children – Upper Threshing Floor, St. Minas' Threshing Floor, Khashman's Threshing Floor, Amou's Threshing floor, the Bordj Oghlou's Threshing Floor and others.

In my day the fields near the village were called the Upper Fields and, naturally, those below it the Lower Fields, located around the lower threshing floors and the upper cemetery. These fields were later converted into mulberry and fruit orchards. The stony land to the east of the village was called Kirazlekh and that around the lower cemetery Dantsin Broun [Pear Marsh].

The villagers also maintained small gardens adjacent to their houses where pear, apple, quince, fig and cherry trees were cultivated, providing fruit for their owners. There were also vines cultivated against walls and over arbours that provided grapes. There was an ancient vine near our house that covered the Momdjonts' barn and was still growing in my day. Years later, vineyards were planted on the sunny slopes around the village in the area above the Upper Fields, on St. Minas' Hill and Kirazlekh, of which very little remained when I was young. The gardens attached to the houses were, of course, also used by the villagers to grow green vegetables in the shade of the trees and in the sun: onions, garlic, cabbage, beans, several marrow plants, cauliflowers, tomatoes, aubergines (egg plants) and legumes.

The villagers reserved a considerable area of land for vegetable cultivation a little distance below the village, on the edges of Hadji Bakeyents Valley, Kak [Excrement] Valley and near the so-called *Khoshmish* [Stinking Water]. The name *Khiyare Boghaz* [Cucumber Valley], on the side of Hadji Bakeyents was still remembered in my day, where they grew cucumbers, marrows, sugar melons, watermelons, legumes etc. Lentils and chick peas were similarly grown on the dry, upper slopes.

The people also kept domestic animals and henhouses in the yards: a few goats or sheep, one or two cows and oxen for cultivation purposes, nags for transporting goods and especially horses. Beehives were set against the walls. Fallow and open areas for grazing domestic animals were left around Kirazlekh, on the slopes of St. Minas' Hill, as well as below the Lower Threshing Floors and Zepperin Chayir.

Agriculture and domestic animal breeding thus formed the new settlers' main occupations. Skilled trades hadn't begun among them, apart from those which concerned their ordinary work, such as the making and repair of ploughs, carts, preparation of firewood, charcoal and timber and planks for building houses. Skilled blacksmiths were probably available to make horseshoes, as were saddle makers and people who produced footwear.

The villagers' nourishment mainly consisted of bread and soups, bulghour [cracked wheat], flour and legumes prepared by boiling; milk, dairy products and eggs were added to this, as was the meat from chickens, goats, lambs and calves occasionally. Hunting must have been common in those days, with birds, rabbits, deer and boars being the main targets, the latter two mainly during the winter. Famous hunters such as Seghos, Palabeyukh and others were remembered from the old days.

Autumn presented the villagers with the opportunity to supplement cultivated crops with the harvest of wild plants - wild grapes, pears, apples, medlars, cornel berries and chestnuts – all of which were plentiful in the nearby forests.

Our ancestors lived a full and busy life. The women and girls were especially busy as they not only helped in the fields but also prepared the winter food stores and essentials: vinegar, preserves, syrups, items for soups and fine flour. They would use the home's grinder, singing as they worked; they worked thick cloth, washed wool and hair, and used them to make beds, pillows, coverlets and socks.

The villagers only rested on Sundays and festival days, when everybody rushed to the church for prayer and Mass, while not forgetting their prayers at home every morning and evening.

There were no coffee houses or drinking places in the village in those days.

The marriage season began during the winter and wedding celebrations and dancing took place during those months. The faces of all those in the home would also brighten with the appearance of new-born children – each newly born child was a tangible God-given blessing - filling the house almost to busting point and increasing the population.

The people would create opportunities for social gatherings through everyday friendly relationships, contacts and visits with in-laws and neighbours, the birth of infants, weddings and by the sadness of death. They would eat, make merry, dance, sing, and organise games in the home or outdoors on happy occasions.

Much chatter took place during the long winter nights in the house. People would meet in summer and talk in the open spaces and in front of the houses. They would do the same on the threshing floors and in the shade of the gardens, near the cold fountains and on the banks of the streams and rivers. These chats would be interspersed with serious conversations about their work and occupations; time would slide by with joy and longing that guaranteed their work and noble, devout lives.

The notables and the priest would come together and make decisions when important public works were to be carried out, having the village's good and safety as their main concern. Village and home disputes would be settled through mutual compromises and the spirit of forgiveness. The elderly were respected and the children were looked after with affection.

This, in a few lines, was the newly-settled Armenian refugees life, just as it was when, in my youth, we saw Armenian or Muslim refugees build their new villages nearby.

Chapter 2

The Early Days – The First Priests and Notables

7 – The building of Bardizag's first church

Bardizag's history stretches back just over 300 years from 1900. As we've seen, the Imperial decree was granted in 1625 and, if we accept, which is most probable, that the village had been founded about 10 to 20 years before the decree was issued, then the Armenian exile took place at the beginning of 1600 – 300 years ago.*

It was only after the villager, at the beginning, had prepared the soil, built his first hut and completed all that had to be done, that he thought about the need to have his own place of prayer and worship, especially as it would appear that the new village didn't have a priest to conduct morning and evening prayers or Masses, which was probably the main reason for the delay in building a church.

As the Armenian community of nearby Izmid had been established and organised long before Bardizag was founded,† the Bardizag villagers would go there as a body for baptisms, weddings and funerals. It was perfectly natural, after they had completed the preliminary work to establish themselves securely, that they persuaded one of Izmid's kahanas to be their resident spiritual leader, and he took up residence in the village.

The presence of a kahana made the building of a church a necessity, and it was not difficult for our refugee forefathers to build a small chapel.

We know that they built the first church under these circumstances; a small wooden building resembling their huts, with woven lath walls and roof, and an earth floor. It was a sort of little chapel with a small altar and very simply furnished. This first church, as we'll see later, was destroyed by fire and a larger and more solid one was built in its place.

8 – Bardizag's first priests (kahanas)‡

A *Mashtots*** printed in Amsterdam used to be kept in the church's library that had the name of a certain 'Srabion Kahana' and the date 1140 of the Armenian era

---

* But see the author's preface.
† The bishopric of Nicomedia was not, however, organised for another hundred years; the first prelate of the Nicomedia diocese was Bishop Margos, who served from 1687 until 1698. Minas Kasabian (Farhad), *Hayere Nikomedio Kavarin Mech*, p. 111.
‡ The priests who served in Bardizag were always married (known in Armenian as kahana). Unless otherwise stated, 'priest' will mean a cleric of this rank.
** A special prayer book.

[1691 A.D.] written on the endpaper. Because the Imperial decree was dated 1075 of the Armenian era [1626 A.D], that inscription showed that that priest served in the church in Bardizag some 65 years after it was promulgated. Srabion Kahana, in the same inscription, adds that he was ordained a kahana by Baron [Bishop] Margos.* It seems to show that this 'Srabion Kahana' was probably the first priest to be ordained in Bardizag itself. Again, the following could be seen at the bottom of an old bill: *Srabion veledou Antreas* [Srabion, son of Antreas]. It is probable that this Antreas, Srabion's father, was himself a priest. As proof, it is possible to present the following. Agha Krikor Great Hadji Khacher, called *Djed Ishkhan*, had his son Mikayel ordained a priest many years later, as we'll see in subsequent pages,† and the name given to him on ordination was Antreas Kahana.‡ There was a good tradition in Armenian families, according to which the names of ancestors were retained by the new generations.** The same tradition was utilised in the Armenian Apostolic Church for later priests, so on that basis it is possible to say that in the old days there was an Antreas Kahana, whose name was perpetuated by naming the newly ordained Hadji Khacher's son the same. If this supposition can be accepted, then Srabion Kahana's father was also a married priest, especially as in those olden days the priesthood passed from father to son as if it were a legacy. Thus the first Antreas Kahana, Srabion Kahana's father, was Bardizag's first priest, brought in from outside.

Another historic circumstance may be brought forward to justify the truth of our supposition concerning the existence of the first Antreas Kahana. This is that at the time of the second Antreas Kahana's ordination the most senior priest was Srabion Kahana's grandson, Hovhannes Kahana, one of Hadji Khacher Agha's fanatical opponents. It appears that Hadji Khacher Agha, having his son ordained and called by the name that had become an exclusive one retained by the priest's family, wanted to transfer it to another – his own.

In 1866 Garabed Kahana Mkhalian and Hovhannes Kahana Mgerian became interested in Bardizag's early history and, to clarify the origins and descent of the old Bardizag families, searched for old documents. They visited Kel Krikor's house for the same reason, as it was thought that he had old documents: encyclicals, letters etc. They entered his tumbledown house, an old one full of past attributes and features, asking the inhabitants, 'Have you any old papers?' They replied, 'We did, fathers,

---

* In those days it was usual for bishops to be titled 'baron' (equivalent to 'lord'), just like the Patriarch of Jerusalem was called Baronder. Bishop Margos is regarded, according to one tradition, as the founder of the Monastery of Armash. (Author's note)

† See Section 15.

‡ Anyone who becomes a priest of the Armenian Apostolic Church is rechristened at ordination, being given a new name as a symbol of rebirth.

** This tradition still exists.

The Early Days – The First Priests and Notables

but one day we needed to examine them, so we called Vandar Baba as someone who understood these things. He looked at what we had and threw most of them into the fire as useless.' The priests were very sad over this important loss. It was true that Vandar was a human Mashtots, knowing all the church's ceremonies, festivals prayers and readings by heart, but he was a person who understood nothing of history and had destroyed a batch of papers that may have somewhat clarified Bardizag's early history. But two documents – two bills – survived in that house, one written in Armenian, the second in Turkish.[*] The latter was a debt statement. One of the family's forefathers, the notable called Tateos, had contracted a loan of 250 *kurush*, in other words the value of a golden bracelet of 64 *mskhals*[†] from a Jewish moneylender in Izmid that he paid off at the right time and so retrieved the statement. That was the gist of the contents of that document.

The other was an important official paper with the following content:

> The reason for this document is as follows.
> In the Armenian era 1159 [1710 A.D].
>
> We, the undersigned Garabed Vartabed[‡] and Khodja Khachadour, in accordance with the Imperial decree [firman], have visited the Armenian villages and came to Baghchedjouk [Bardizag] where we removed the priest Srabion Kahana from his position and transferred his parishes to Tateos, Melkon, Tavit and Hagop. These are Bison, Khashman, Shahbaz and Yailakhan, 29-30 houses in all. They will collect the tithes of these parishes that belong to either the prelacy or the patriarchate until next year and, when the collector arrives, give them to him.[**]

By 1909 this document was 200 years old and brought out several historic facts concerning Bardizag's history. First, Srabion Kahana's removal from office; secondly, the names of the four notables of the village and, at the same time, demonstrated the prelacy's and patriarchate's authority over the public concerns in the villages, and details of the revenue assigned to the prelacy and patriarchate.

Why was Srabion Kahana removed? A tradition relates that his wife died young and he had become a widower, due to which accusations – true or false – were levelled against him. A scandal developed and, when the patriarchate's representatives, Garabed Varatabed and Khodja Khachadour visited the village, the priest's case was put before them. It was examined and they removed him from office

---

* Ottoman (Arabic) script.
† This word is not understood.
‡ Vartabed: archimandrite, one of the ranks of the celibate priesthood.
** This important document had been retained with certain others by Hovhannes Kahana Mgerian, but were all destroyed by fire in 1870. (Author's note)

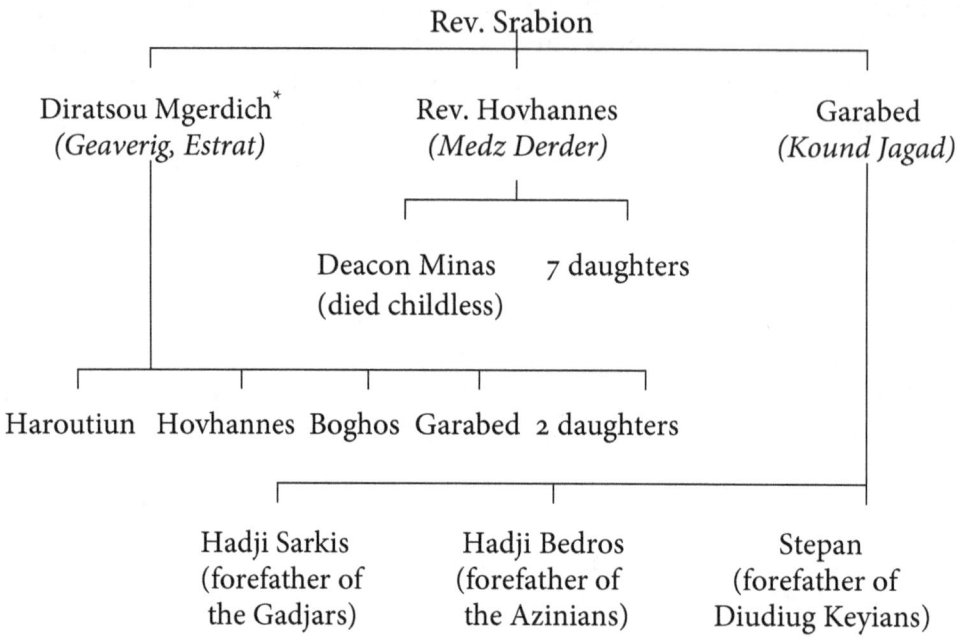

Estrat Diratsou Mgerdich's two daughters became wives of a Khashman and a Zobi Melkon. (Author's note)

People also recalled that, in Srabion Kahana's time, there was a Kevork Kahana whose signature was seen on various bills of debt. He too was probably born in Bardizag. This Kevork Kahana's existence can be proved by a historical fact that much later, Krikor Kahana, of the farming Khashman family, had his son-in-law ordained priest and the name Kevork Kahana was given to him in accordance with tradition.

Srabion Kahana was released from his sentence and resumed his ministry a year or two later. He had his son ordained with the name of Haroutiun Kahana during his lifetime. Kevork Kahana and Haroutiun Kahana were probably ordained together, as the village's population had significantly increased.

Apart from Krikor Kahana Khashman, another Krikor Kahana is remembered, a contemporary of Srabion Kahana, who lived before Kevork Kahana. It is probable that when Srabion Kahana was removed from office, the first Krikor Kahana was either ordained or brought in from outside so as not to leave the church without a priest. The descendants of the first Krikor Kahana or his children in Bardizag were the Beroushes, the Balams, Demirdji Kousdigs and Mgerian families. This priest's own house was also Beroush Hekim Hovhannes' house.

Krikor Kahana was a strict, good and devout cleric. He was never absent from church and often spent the night praying and reading the scriptures in it. Apparently neighbours would, out of curiosity, go and listen to his night-time services, thinking that they heard angels' voices. For that reason they considered

The Early Days – The First Priests and Notables

him to be holy and greatly revered him. When he died, his tombstone – which until the end could be seen in the upper cemetery – became a place of pilgrimage; the villagers would bring sick people to his tomb, place them on it, and bathe them there as an act of washing away their sins for them to recover from their pain.

The old people used to tell these stories in my youth.

Srabion Kahana's family has given rise to many well-known Bardizag families, and we give their family tree here (See table above).

Based on the details given in the preceding pages, the first priests were:

Antreas Kahana (brought in from outside)
Srabion Kahana
Krikor Kahana
Kevork Kahana

All these priests served in Bardizag's first church.*.

9 – The building of Bardizag's second church

The villagers built the first wooden church around 1625. It stood until 1724, for approximately 100 years, when it accidentally burnt down. † The villagers therefore got together and began to construct a new one in the same year. Because the population, in 100 years, had grown considerably, possibly to as many as 120 families, it was necessary to build it much larger and with materials that would, to a certain extent, be resistant to fire.

Bardizag's soil was mostly clay, so the villagers cut block-shaped pieces and, having dried them in the sun, used them as building bricks. The church was built as

---

* When, in the Armenian era 1159 [1710 A.D.], Garabed Vartabed and Khodja Khachadour came to Bardizag, the latter suggested to the notable Tateos that he purchase a 'Medz Haismavourk' [Great Book of Days] printed in Constantinople at that time (during the reign of Sultan Ahmed) for the church in Bardizag. Tateos agreed and contributed 60 *kurush*; Khodja Khachador added another 20 *kurush* and, with that sum, a copy was bought that was kept in the church's library even in my days. It carried Khodja Khachadour Kurd Oghlu's signature. Tateos also added his ancestors' names under the descriptions of the martyrdoms of the saints. (Author's note)

† Rev. Garabed Mkhalian found that the 100 year life of the first church was too long, bearing in mind that the first one was built to serve from 20 to 25 families, and therefore couldn't cope with the requirements of the rapidly increasing population. So he thought that the first church didn't burn down, but the second did.

He thought that it was more likely that after a time, about 40-50 years later, the first church was demolished because it couldn't cater for the needs of the people and a second, larger, wooden church was built in its place that was burnt down. Despite this, in accordance with the accepted view, he states that the first church was the one destroyed by fire. (Author's note)

a collective enterprise, with thick clay walls reinforced by wooden *hatels** on the inside to ensure their strength. The roof was probably covered with tiles.

Clay-built houses from the old days still stood in Bardizag in my time, with their thick and wide walls, firmly established, with the same *hatels* on the inside and without windows. The roofs were made of timber and tiled, and had small skylights.

This clay-built church lasted until 1800, when the further increase in population made the building of a new church necessary.

10 – The kahanas who served in the second church

We see new priests appear during this time; the first, Boghos Kahana, was the ancestor of the Garakian or Bordj oughlu family as they were also known. Boghos Kahana's forefathers had been the godfathers to the well-known Khacherian family that holds an important place in Bardizag's history. It was said that these two families had left their former homes and become refugees, settling in Bardizag together.

Srabion Kahana's son, Haroutiun Kahana, also grew old in this second church.

A Vosgi Kahana or Vosgan Kahana is also remembered alongside Boghos Kahana, whose descendants formed the Partsigian house (Voski or Voskan Kahana's grandson's name Hampartsoum having been shortened to Partsig); similarly this priest's descendants were the Chelengers (their forefather's name was Mardiros); the Depe Delens (whose forefather was someone called Hagop) and the Voskians, who kept the priest's name.

Vosgan Kahana was named in a Turkish document belonging to the Giullo family† concerning the sale of a house's *arsa*,‡ where one of its borders is determined as 'The dead Vosgan *papaz*'s [priest's] house'. Vosgan Kahana's house was that of the Chelengers, located near the church, and behind which was Giullo Chakhr's house. This latter house later became the beadle Khachadour Pandig's (Pandigian) house, (he was the father of Great Sahag Kahana) as the Pandigs' sister, Giullo Chakhr's wife, had died childless.

A certain Garabed Kahana with the nickname of Bougha [Bull] is also remembered with Boghos Kahana and Vosgan Kahana. Bougha Garabed Kahana is linked to the family known as Hadji Stepans that later branched out to become the Hovhannesians, Ghennobdjonts and Semerdji families.

---

* This word is unknown to me. It probably means beam or post.
† The Giullos weren't from Bardizag, but had come from the Armenian village of Geol Pazar and settled in Bardizag. These new people were the first to introduce the *mazman* trade [making string from animal hair] into the village. (Author's note)
‡ This word is unknown. Probably (from the text) a piece of land of a certain size or use.

Garabed Kahana's nickname Bougha (Bull) suggests many things to me. It would seem that he was a very powerful, confrontational and unsatisfied person. He carried on a vendetta against Srabion Kahana (Great Derder) for years and defeated him. He took over all the land covering the old cemetery that subsequently belonged, in my day, to the Djangaloz, Djerga and Matos families, his heirs having sold it off after a time. Of those pieces of land, only a part remained the property of someone named Hagopig Hovnanian, who was the Hadji Stepans' grandson. Bougha Garabed Kahana also owned land within the borders of the lower threshing floors, starting from them and extending as far as Hadji Bakerents Valley. This too was sold by his heirs, apart from one part that remained the property of Garabed Kahana's grandson, also named Garabed.

Vosgan Kahana, whom we mentioned a little earlier, had a very sad life; like Srabion Kahana, he was left a widower and had nervous crises. He died in a very sad state.

These then were the kahanas who served in the second church. Although there were other priests ordained in this church, we will recall them in the section concerning the third church.*

11 – Village government, Armenian *ishkhans* (notables) and Turkish *aghas*

Bardizag's population rose to about 300 families from the beginning until the start of the 1800s; Garabed Agha Mgerian and people of his generation who were important in my day have assured me that this figure is correct.

In my day, a generation later, 350 *esems* [families] were recorded in government registers. Naturally such a community would have had its public bodies – both community and governmental - that would run the community's public affairs. We lack historical information as far as village government was concerned, especially about the earliest period. The only thing that is obvious is that the avakerets [married archpriest]† or kahana was the main community activist‡ in a Christian village in the old days. The priest was the de facto village head, as he was almost the only person who could read and write and was the people's shepherd. This was the case from Bardizag's foundation and for many years afterwards. He would naturally be visited by people coming to the village, with the ishkhans [notables] or representatives of its great families around him.

Visiting government officials would be entertained in the priest's house in those days. There is a Turkish proverb that says: 'the priest's house is my house'; this was

---

* See Section 39.
† The title *avakerets* is the highest that a kahana can reach. He is the first among equals, and frequently acted as the representative of the diocesan bishop.
‡ I use the word activist for the Armenian *kordzich*.

the truth in the early days of the villages, and it is well known that the kahana or married archpriest ruled Bardizag until Great Hadji Khacher's time.

The official document I referred to in previous pages* states that in the first priest's – Srabion Kahana's – days the village ishkhans or notables were individuals named Tatos, Melkon, Tavit and Hagop or Garabed.

Tatos' descendants, based on the colophons in the above-mentioned Book of Days, were the Kel Krikors, Ignatioses, Boghosians, Mourad Krikors, Giulesers and the Bedig Der-Sarkises.

Melkon is linked to the Melkonians or Zobis, Bakradzes, Aslans, Chelemboshes, and Tekerdjis.

Tavit, it would appear, was either Agha Krikor's father or nephew, whom the notable Agha Krikors or Great Hadji Khacher's family are descended from, as we shall see anon.†

The families descended from Hagop or Garabed remain unknown.

These four men and the representatives of their houses were the village's important people, going back 200 years from my time.

There have always been Turkish aghas in Bardizag who had certain rights. From very early on there were the *chiftilig* [farm] owners or their representatives whose land was worked by the farmers from Bardizag and to whom, or to special tax collectors from Constantinople, they paid the *vakef* tax.

Later, Turkish aghas took over, known as *multezim* (tax gatherers), who were the owners of *ghatars* (carts) ships and capital *(sermie)*, and who employed the villagers to make charcoal. This trade was very important and brought in great profits for the people of the village and its economy, bringing great changes and leaving the villagers' original trade of farming as a secondary activity. These aghas' signatures may be found on very old promissory notes called *seneds*.

These later Turkish aghas were mostly from Haladara. This was a Turkish village located on the south side of the Bay of Izmid, on a mountain between Deyirmendere and Karamoursal. They had rented the monopoly of the collection of the *vakef* tax from the government – which towards the end became the 'tenth' tithe,‡ from which they gained the *multezim* title. In my time the tithe collectors were known as *multezims*.

The aghas, with their official positions as government representatives, had the right to intervene in the village's public affairs. They were usually accompanied by a *yaghedji* [book keeper or secretary] who held the ledgers and a *zobi* [policeman]. They would arrest malefactors and question them, often using beatings, then try and punish them either by imprisonment or by extracting monetary fines from them.

---

* See Section 8.
† See Section 13.
‡ In Armenian *dasnortagan pajin* or *ashar*.

Armenians could also be found in their service who acted as their servants and to whom the title of *agha* was customarily given.

The Turkish aghas, as we said, had introduced a new trade into Bardizag, that of making charcoal, carried on in the thick forests around the village; there was a great variety of trees – oak, ash, linden, hornbeam, chestnut and others, whose wood was suitable for the trade. There were no coniferous trees - cedar, pine or fir - in these forests, whose altitude above sea level wasn't very great. Those kinds of forests were located a great distance away, in the interior, on the heights of Ghendjelar and Ghourtbelen in the county of Geyve.

The people of Bardizag were unfamiliar with the charcoal-burning trade for a long time. The Turkish aghas used charcoal burners from Roumeli from very early times. The men from Bardizag learnt the trade from them, soon denying work to people from outside the village's borders.

The aghas would agree terms for the production of charcoal with the burners, on the basis of *zenbils* or *chouvals* [large sacks] full of charcoal, to which the name *ayar* was given, and would send them into the mountains to prepare it. The charcoal would be brought down from the mountains in horse-drawn carts to Bardizag's port of Seymen, from where it would be transported on the agha's ships to be sold on the Constantinople market.

Carpenters* and *barmakhdjis* worked as timber preparers alongside the work of charcoal burning. The Turkish word 'barmakh', meaning the size of a finger, was used to describe these tradesmen, because timber was prepared using the finger as the standard measure and the baulks produced were assessed using it.

I said that these trades linked to the forests brought about a revolution in the economy of the village. This was because the villagers were gradually forced to go below the village to areas suitable for farming near the seashore when the population grew and the need for more cultivable soil became necessary. The land around the village had been mostly made into orchards and vineyards, whose fruit was more important and brought bigger profits. As a result of this, an agricultural centre appeared in the fields below the village which were called Khaner. Only cereal crops were cultivated in these lower areas because they were considered to be fertile, ready-prepared fields, while the upper slopes were covered in forests.

Malaria, weakness, anaemia, stomach problems and early aging began to cause havoc among the farmers who worked within the borders of Khaner, thanks to the accumulation of stagnant water and the ground becoming marshy. This created genetic problems and destroyed whole families. When, thanks to the Turkish aghas, charcoal burning and timber preparation began in the mountains on the heights that had clean, healthy and safe water, also bringing greater profits, the villagers mostly left arable farming and began working there. Thus the people of Bardizag

---

* The word used here is *paidahad* which could be taken to mean 'timber preparers'.

developed a generation of robust, healthy and strong mountaineers. The people of the village gradually became craftsmen and gardeners. This economic movement slowly gained impetus and the villagers forsook the lower, unhealthy ground. Thus the villagers became more prosperous, strong and healthy, and the cultivation of cereals and agriculture was discontinued permanently.

12 – The collection of young men for naval service

The government, during the days of the *aghas* - the date unknown - used to collect young men to work on board its ships. They used to be given the name *chouloumpa*. They were expected to wash the sailors' clothes and clean the ships. The aghas, when the command came from Constantinople, would seize six young men from Bardizag and forcibly send them to the city. Young men are also known to have volunteered. These young men, as future government servants, would become arrogant and create trouble in the village before their departure, wandering the streets armed with pistols, killing people's chickens, stealing sheep from outside the houses, eating and drinking to excess and shouting and screaming. Everyone in the village was frightened of them. They would get leave every two years, given so they could return to their birthplaces. When they returned, they would go to the upper threshing floors with their friends, dance and shout scandalous epithets.

The following was related about these young men: a young man from Bardizag named Doghrou Ese (Yesayi) was hired as a farm labourer by the Turkish aghas. He was later involved in an accident and, being frightened of the consequences, ran away to *Giavour Izmir* ['Infidel' Izmir, Smyrna] that, in those days, was a sort of criminal centre. The guilty, those in debt and criminals usually went there to cover their tracks. Ese became the servant to the tenant of a coffee house there. Being a bold and fearless young man, he was much liked, earning the customers' esteem with his readiness to please, nimbleness and quick service and, as a result, the number of customers increased.

This was at the time when the Janissaries still existed.[*] Someone named Arab terrorised Izmir at that time, being known as a dangerous, aggressive person. Turks, Greeks and Armenians were all afraid of him, while the local government respected him. Ese heard his name every day, said with fear and emotion, in the coffee house. Doghrou Ese finally became annoyed and asked the customers, 'What sort of people are you? Has an Arab terrorised a big place like Izmir? I'm astonished. Ever since I got here all I've heard is "Arab, Arab".'

He was reprimanded by the coffee house tenant, who told him to be careful. Someone told Arab what the young man had said. Arab entered the coffee house one morning; everyone was terrified. He asked 'Who is it who is apparently against me?' Ese understood that the man was referring to him and rushed forward, shouting 'It's

---

[*] The janissary corps was disbanded by force in 1826.

The Early Days – The First Priests and Notables

me' to his face. When Arab got to his feet to teach the 'child' a lesson, Ese pulled his gun from the sash around his waist and shot him in the stomach, making him fall to the ground. The customers rushed out of the coffee house in terror and Ese disappeared during this disturbance.*

Elderly people of the time used to tell this story, having heard it from the Turkish aghas. Brave and intrepid young men like that were much loved in those days. The village elders used to respect them, because such men could provide great service during times of danger in those barbaric days.

Apart from what has been related in the last two chapters, we have very little reliable information about Bardizag's early years, which remain obscure from the foundation of the village (about 1600) until 1750. I will therefore move forward to the second era, closing this dark and impenetrable page in the history of the village. We will soon find a considerable number of things to relate concerning life in Bardizag.

---

* *Doghrou Ese* seems to have been descended from 'Shidag Minas' and 'Shidag Haroutiun's Hovhannes' *(Gharale)* and lived at the beginning of the 1800s. The first left no descendants and the second had a son and daughter. (Author's note)

Chapter 3

The Agha Krikor Great Hadji Khacher Bab Era
1750 – 1809

13 – Great Hadji Khatcher Bab and the beginning of his rule

Great Hadji Khacher Bab was born in the first quarter of the 18th century and was the head of the community ruling body from the time of his youth until his death in 1809. He was one of the few people of his time who could read and write and has left us a brief notebook concerning Bardizag's ruling families and their activities, where he writes:

> In the old days the notables were from the Alemshah or Azarian families. Hadji Tatos, son of Azaria, Tatos' son Rapayel and so on from father to son in succession.

The powerful Azarian family's house was immediately opposite the *ghonakh* [government building], right next to the agha's fountain – that large area where, in my time, the shops belonging to the Khacherians, Hadji Artin, Kousdig Merger, the Alemshahs and Semerdji Rapayel were located. The houses belonging to the Avedians, Semerdjians and Melekons,* as well as the Amouents' *magharan* [flour sifting works] were also located in the same place. It was a large neighbourhood, surrounded on three sides by public streets, through which the Church Valley passed, before it reached the church itself. It was the most important part of the first settled area in Bardizag.

The Azarian family also owned a watermill and extensive land outside the village. Even in my day the names 'Chaghchi Valley's Edge', the 'Azarian Hollow' (Valley) and 'Azaria's Forest' were well known.

This family's representatives ruled Bardizag's community affairs until the beginning of the 18th century, but it appears that after a time discontent and hatred against them developed among the villagers, culminating in the abolition of this form of compulsory hereditary rule.

The village peasants, with this movement, achieved their freedom and selected several men to be ishkhans [notables] and to whom they passed the village's governance from among themselves. Almost none of them, however, could read or write, so they added the young Hadji Khacher to their number as someone who was educated and well read.

In Hadji Khacher Bab's above-mentioned notebook, he refers to his election and says: 'The notables took this sinner to be one of their elected members.'

---

* This might be a misprint, the name possibly being 'Melkons.'

Great Hadji Khacher had an older brother, Nalband Hadji Varteres (Hadji Bak) who worked with his younger brother in village affairs.

When Great Hadji Khacher gradually began to build his authority and position and became the most influential person in the village, antagonism developed between him and Srabion Kahana's grandson Hovhannes Kahana of the Great Derder family, the influential avakerets [archpriest] of the time. Led by him and the leaders of the old regime, this antagonism is known to have been an attempt to weaken Great Hadji Khacher's position.

14 – The procuring of *cham* fuel for the Ottoman Mint

The Ottoman Mint was located in Constantinople, in the place known as Sara Broun Top Kapu, and charcoal produced from coniferous trees, known in Turkish as *cham keomiur*, was required for its operation.

Turks provided the majority of the Mint's workers and officials, as it always had been in all the other Turkish government establishments. But there had been Christian, especially Armenian, work masters who were very experienced in producing gold and silver wares from the earliest times. Almost all the well-known goldsmiths in Constantinople were Armenians, some of whom had positions in the Ottoman Mint. Individuals appeared from their ranks that, over a period of time, achieved great authority and were entrusted with the management and responsibility for the entire Ottoman Mint. Some of these were the Diuzians, Krikor Chelebi, Sarkis Chelebi Diuzian and their successor, Artin Amira Kazaz.[*]

We saw, in the previous chapter, how the charcoal burning trade began and developed in Bardizag in the time of the Turkish Haldaran aghas.[†] They were then approached by the Mint authorities as experienced dealers and took over providing fuel for it.

Bardizag's forests, however, were bereft of coniferous trees, forcing the aghas to get the raw timber from the heights of Khendjelar and Ghourtbelen,[‡] burn it into charcoal there and bring it down by mule, over a long and difficult journey, to Bardizag's port, Seymen.

The Turkish aghas used charcoal burners from Bardizag who worked for them in those distant places to do this. It was then transported from the port to the Mint.

---

[*] Artin Amira Kazaz (1771-1834) was Sultan Mahmoud II's banker. He was a self-made man. He never neglected Armenian interests, and was a great benefactor to the Amenian community. Bardizag was just one of his beneficiaries. See Pascal Carmont, *The amiras, lords of Ottoman Armenia*, Taderon Press, London, 2012, pp. 115-117.
[†] See Section 11.
[‡] Mkhalian sometimes names Ghourtbelen as Khourt Belen. I have used the first spelling throughout.

The notables of Bardizag seeing, after a time, the great profits to be made from this trade, and utilising the reality of the Armenian presence in the management of the Mint, succeeded in completely taking over the trade, becoming *sermayedjis,* cart and ship owners and making the trade into a monopoly for a long time.

This interesting initiative was widened to include neighbouring Armenian villages – Ovadjek and Arslan Beg – thus the provision of charcoal to the Mint became, to all appearances, an Armenian trade and occupied numbers of Armenians for many years.

I will have the opportunity to refer to this trade that was the reason for the appearance of rich and notable men in Bardizag and the surrounding villages in future pages.*

15 – The newly-ordained kahanas [married priests] who served in the second church

Hovhannes Kahana of the 'Great Derder' family was the most prominent among these and lived until 1820. He was, for a time, in his old age, the only priest in Bardizag, as the older priests had died and the new ones hadn't yet been ordained.

Great Hadji Khacher Bab and the newly-elected notables, seeing this, met and decided to assure the presence of a new priest to spare the strength of old Hovhannes Kahana and perhaps in some way curb his pretensions. It would appear that they couldn't find a suitable candidate for the priesthood in the village, so Vartan Kahana of Ghendjelar was invited to be the resident priest for Bardizag's church. Vartan Kahana agreed to the suggestion made by the notables and moved with his family to Bardizag. The notables assigned a piece of land for his house in the village, on the site that in my day was that of the one belonging to Hadji Mgrdich Khacherian (the grandson of Great Hadji Khacher), and built a very good house for Vartan Kahana on it.

Vartan Kahana began his ministry in concert with Hohvannes Kahana Great Derder. Vartan Kahana's eldest son was ordained a short time later, taking the name Pilibbos Kahana and began to minister to the villagers with the other two priests.

Vartan Kahana's descendants, in my day, formed the Basmadji family. Vartan Kahana became related through marriage with Great Hadji Khacher's family; a Khacherian daughter being married to his eldest son - a very significant factor in understanding the nature of the relationship between Great Hadji Khacher and Hovhannes Kahana. It would seem that Great Hadji Khacher wanted to ensure that a priest would be on his side – to spite Hovhannes Kahana.

* The provision of charcoal to the Mint began in 1750-1760 and lasted until approximately 1838, a period of about 80 years. (Author's note)

Vartan Kahana, alongside his ministry work, introduced a new trade to Bardizag – that of *basmadji*, a method of dying pictures or patterns on cloth in various colours. The articles produced were much esteemed in those days, especially in the Turkish aghas' houses. When Vartan Kahana settled in Bardizag, he and his children continued the trade for some time. It needed running water, so he bought and utilised the water on the road to Kirazlekh owned by a woman named Tavani Neneh, and where he planted a grove of mulberry trees. Hadji Hagop, Garabed Kahana Mkhalian's father, bought this grove, years later, from Vartan Kahana's descendants. In my day it was located in front of the American High School.

Vartan Kahana's trade was continued until my day by Pilibbos Kahana Der-Vartanian's son-in-law Mardig Bedros Andon's grandson Basmadji Minas.

Krikor Kahana, the grandfather of the Demirdji Diannos family, was ordained after Pilibbos Kahana. This priest and his wife were killed in an unfortunate accident. They went to Jerusalem on a pilgrimage and on their return journey were drowned when the ship they were in was wrecked. Krikor Kahana was a member of the farming Khashman family (the Diannos family were khashmans); one of his brothers was the ancestor of the Khashman Bedros family and of the farmer Garo. Krikor Kahana Khashman's son-in-law was also ordained after Krikor's death, taking the name Kevork Kahana.

Another priest is also recorded alongside these – Sarkis Kahana Bedigian, a descendant of the notable Tatos's son Giuleser.

All of these priests, Pilibbos Kahana Der-Vartanian, Krikor Kahana Khashman, Kevork Kahana and Sarkis Kahana Bedigian were all ordained in Bardizag's second church.

Antreas Kahana Agha Krikorian, the eldest son of Great Hadji Khacher Bab, was a contemporary with the others but was ordained before Sarkis Kahana. He however didn't live very long, dying in 1863, the year of the 'Great Death', when Great Derder Hovhannes Kahana was still living.

Great Hadji Khacher Bab, to neutralise his main enemy Hovhannes Kahana, appears to have used some diplomacy to secure the ordination of his first son, Antreas Kahana, by first inviting Vartan Kahana to Bardizag. He then, after some time, had Vartan Kahana's son, Pilibbos Kahana and others ordained, until he considered the time ripe for the ordination of a member of his family as a priest with the aim of strengthening his authority. Unfortunately his ordained son died and he lost hope. But Great Hadji Khacher Bab continued this policy, the result of which was that, much later, he had his second son Krikor ordained as Apraham Kahana. He also had Nalband Varteres' son (his nephew) ordained as Krikor Kahana, when his enemy was very old. I will return to these historic events in due course.*

---

* See Section 16.

With his death, Hadji Khacher's son Antreas Kahana left two orphans – Kelesh Hagop and Hadji Artin. Their grandfather took them under his wing and brought them up, making each independent. Antreas Kahana's house became Kelesh Hagop's family home, located opposite Djanig Agha Khacherian's, on the other side of the road, which eventually became Kelesh Hagop's two sons' property. Hadji Artin built himself a house a little to the west.

Before closing this section, I should like to present the stories told by the old people about Sarkis Kahana Bedigian. This priest had a stroke when he was old, but lived for a long time in that ill state. He moved about leaning on a staff, and always went to church although he was unable to carry out his ministry. Later his parish was ministered to by his son, Sahag Kahana, the first of those priests in Bardizag who were ordained during their father's lifetime, after those mentioned above.

Sarkis Kahana was a brave and fearless priest. He was never reticent in front of the Turkish aghas, officials or gendarmes. One day his grandson, Sahag Kahana's son Hadji Boghos, was arrested and imprisoned by the Turkish agha of the day as the result of an accusation at the *ghonakh* [government building]. Sarkis Kahana, trembling, leaning on his staff, went to the building and asked for the agha when he entered the courtyard. The agha appeared at the top of the stairs and asked Rev. Sarkis, 'What do you want, *ekhtiar* [venerable] priest?'

'Let my son go; have some respect for my beard,' he replied.

'Go, reverend priest, I'll release your son,' the agha answered.

And in truth, Hadji Boghos was released without being beaten like his friends were.

On another occasion, when the body of the martyr was brought to Bardizag and hung from a tree at the end of the street,[*] and while everyone, terrified, hid wherever they could, Sarkis Kahana hauled himself to the tree and, seeing the martyr hanging there, surrounded by ten wolf-like policemen, looked at the body with pity. The dead man's face was covered with a cloth, and Sarkis Kahana said, 'Oh, holy God, until now we read about martyrs in the Book of Days, and now we have seen it with our own eyes.' Then he returned home.

Sarkis Kahana's son, Mardiros, whom we referred to above, was ordained in 1820, with Nerses Kanana Gardeshian.[†]

Sahag Kahana's wife died in childbirth sometime later and left one son, Hadji Boghos. The kahana, in this wretched state, became the subject of a woman's slander and, not being able to control his feelings would, every time he passed the woman's house, sigh and say 'May God take revenge.'

The Der-Sahagian many-branched, rich family was descended from Sahag Kahana, the son of Sarkis Kahana Bedigian and was called, from then on, by his name.

---

[*] See Section 64.
[†] This could be a misprint. The name might be Kardeshian or Kardashian.

16 – Great Hadji Khacher's opponents

We saw in previous sections* that Great Hadji Agha Khacher gradually became the most influential person in Bardizag, enjoying indisputable authority and respect, who became friends with contemporary diocesan church leaders, Izmid's notables and the village's Turkish aghas.

It was only natural that a person becoming a public figure of that stature would have enemies, the chief of which was Hovhannes Kahana of the *Medz Derderants* [Great Derder] family, whom we referred to above. Hadji Khacher's grandchildren would say that his enemies went so far in their hatred and enmity as to plot his assassination.

The Turkish aghas of Bardizag lived, at one time, with their families in the neighbouring Greek village,† part of the border of which adjoined that of Bardizag's government-determined one. Hadji Khacher's opponents learnt, one day, that he would be going there to visit the Turkish aghas, so they bribed several unknown Turks to ambush and kill him on his journey.

Our villagers, it would appear, maintained their primitive harshness and violent habits in those days. The Turks who had been bribed went to lie in wait on the route he normally took, hiding in the Azarians' forest. Hadji Khacher, by a lucky stroke, decided to go a different way that day and, instead of going to the Greek village by the usual route, took the one to Ayazma, where he had bought a new field in a place called Indjiridag, wanting to see it on his way.

After waiting without success for a long time, the Turks left their hiding place and went to the Greek village. They saw Hadji Khacher there and were astonished. They saw the finger of God in this and, repenting, confessed the assassination plan and said to him, 'You, agha, are a good man. God preserved your life and prevented us from committing the crime of killing you, an innocent person, for which give thanks to Him.'

For this reason, that field owned by the Khacherians was known as the 'Blood Field'.

The Great Derder clan's and its adherents' opposition to both Hadji Khacher and, after him, to his son Apraham Kahana, lasted for many long years and as usual divided the village into opposing camps, between those for the influential clan and those who were envious of it.

People said that during the *miusellim* (voivoda) period the Great Derder clan, also known by the name of Estrat, enjoyed the great respect and honour of a notable Turk by the name of Hadji Pasha and his people. For this reason Estrat Hovhannes Kahana wrote letters to various places, slandering Great Hadji Khacher. One of

---

* Sections 13 and 15.
† This was Yenikeoy, known to Bardizag Armenians as *Hormin Kiugh or Hrom Kiugh* [Roman Village].

those letters had been preserved, until the end, in the church's library, and in which the following slanders could be read:

> ...that Hadji Khacher collected the villagers' silks in his house and, instead of selling them at high prices to merchants unknown to him, profiteering by actually selling them at lower prices to those whom he knew, embezzling the poor people's rights.
>
> Additionally, he seized the villagers' or village lands by underhand means, having them registered to himself in the village's Turkish aghas' registers.

We don't know on what basis these accusations were made or what value they had, but we do know that the appropriation of land was a common and well-known thing in those days. This ploy was used so that not only Hadji Khacher Agha, but all of the notables of his time, thus added to their existing land holdings. There was unused government-owned or *vakef* land around the village or at some distance away, and all those who, thanks to their position and influence, could make friends with the Turkish aghas, had those lands registered to them. This was, of course, not a reprehensible act by them, but a method of utilising their position and the opportunity with a view to the future.

Hadji Khacher Bab, for example, had an extensive forest near Deep Valley registered in his name in this way. Similarly, his descendants had a mulberry tree wood near the Upper Threshing Floors located behind the Arab family's threshing floor known, when I was young, to be the area from the rear of the Baghjis' house right up to Bilidj Krikor's house. He also made some derelict land into a mulberry plantation between the Osmans' house and gardens; his descendants profited from them even in my day.

The Mikayelians, similarly, had an extensive area of derelict land registered in their name, which extended from the Lower Threshing Floors' fountain alongside the Kirazlekh road and spreading eastwards as far as the Lower Threshing Floors road. Bedig Sahag Kahana's brothers did the same, as did all the influential and wealthy families in the village. Rev. Hovhannes Mgerian began to cultivate some land near the Upper Fields and had it registered in his name even in my day. The Mgerians would also say that Dants's Broun was their property, but they had no official, legal document to prove it.

All the notables had good relations with the *chorbadji, rais* and *keyia* Turkish aghas in those days. As an example, let me quote the family named Ghara Keyia, that existed even before before Hadji Khacher's time and whose descendants still lived in the village in my day. This family had registered all the land near the fountain on the Upper Threshing Floors, starting from the edge of the Kokorents houses, along the edge of the land belonging to Hadji Khacher and as far as the Upper Threshing Floors, to themselves.

There were pieces of unclaimed land, about half an hour to one hour distance from the village, where anyone would go, prepare the ground and, after profiting from it for a number of years, find the means to have it officially registered to themselves by government officials. This took place even when I was a boy. This is what happened in the case of Enor Keyia's *ashman* on the slopes of Upper Ayazma. Many other *ashmans* that this or that villager had appropriated and developed for farming and later officially turned into his own property in accordance with the law also existed.

Hadji Khacher Bab's opponents would relate the following, with the object of besmirching him. A person called Sermayedji Hadji Agha Zakar had made a name and position for himself, and whose descendants were the Selis, Kafadars, Hairabedians and Zakarians. This man had two great *ghatars* [large carts] and sent vast quantities of charcoal down to Bardizag's port, where it would be stored. He was also the owner, like the rest, of extensive lands starting from the village as far as the port, about which the villagers used to say 'Hadji Zakar would travel from the village to the port on his own land'. This was probably an exaggeration, but bearing in mind that his descendants had great holdings of land in my day in that area, the saying was perhaps justified.

Hadji Khacher Bab was apparently jealous of Hadji Zakar's position and wealth and had his two *ghaterdji* [carter] sons killed by Turks in the mountains. This doesn't seem probable to me, especially as a little after the incident the two houses became related by marriage, with Hadji Khacher's grandson's daughter (Antreas Kahana's daughter) becoming Zakar Agha's son's (Kafadar Asadour's) wife.

There is a version of this story that is probably nearer the truth. In those days the need for charcoal was very great on the Constantinople market, and Turkish sailors would fight with knives to buy charcoal in Seymen. Hadji Zakar, who was the greatest merchant in that trade, usually only sold his stock of charcoal to a particular Turkish ship-owner whom he trusted. For this reason the other ship-owners held a grudge against him and had his two sons killed in the mountains.

17 – Sericulture and the silk harvest in Bardizag

I mentioned the production of silk in Bardizag in a previous section.[*] This shows that sericulture was already one of the village's important occupations. We also saw that many people worked to secure land around the village and planted groves of mulberry trees on it. Mulberry leaves, of course, are the silkworm's sole sustenance. It would appear that sericulture had begun in the village at the beginning of the 18th century as a profitable initiative. It was greatly suited to the climate and the people's way of living and as work that brought a huge return for the utilisation of a small area of land.

We also know that Bardizag's expanding population didn't have enough farmland. The villagers therefore had the intelligence and foresight to assign small areas of land that were suitable for cultivation to specialist crops such as vineyards, mulberry trees and fruit growing. These brought in large profits in proportion to the

---

[*] See Section 5, where it is mentioned in passing.

area of land used, at the same time keeping the people free from malaria that flourished in the plains.

Although I have no historic basis for saying so, I think that the first settlers were ignorant of sericulture, as it didn't exist in their former homeland in the interior of Anatolia. On the other hand it is well known that from the days that the Turks first conquered the country, and even earlier, sericulture had begun in Bithynia (Nicomedia and Boursa) and Syria. So when the Armenian refugees from Bardizag in Sivas settled in their new home, they absorbed the experience that was all about them concerning the trade. It is also possible to conjecture that the trade was practiced in the Turkish farms that for a time employed the new settlers.

Sericulture, with all these considerations, was the women's, girls' and young boys' home occupation. It did not involve grown men, especially when it was carried out on a small scale, as it must have been in the beginning. At the same time silkworm breeding took place in the spring months of April and May when, after the work of ploughing and sowing having been completed, there was still time until threshing. Thus with the aim of utilising their free time women, girls and boys pursued the production of silkworms and silk, an article that was as much valued as gold was in those days.

We will return in future pages to this important village trade that became, in time, the greatest source of profit in the village economy.[*]

18 – The pilgrimage site of St. Minas (Sokhmiar-Soghouk Pounar)

St Minas was a pilgrimage site located on the top of the hill above Bardizag, where there were wind-blown trees, a grassy area and a cold stream.

That stream was there from the earliest days and the villagers believed that it cured fevers, like the Greek *Ayazmos*. Bardizag's people began to visit that miraculous spring, swear oaths, light candles on the stones around it, make one or two signs of the cross and pray, wash their hands and faces and drink the water as if it were a heavenly medicine.

The village priests and notables invited the then diocesan bishop, probably Bishop Avedik[†] – who served long before the tenure of Bishop Bartoghomeos[‡] –

---

* See Section 118.

† Actually Archbishop Avedik. He was diocesan prelate (based in Armash Monastery) from 1766 until his death in 1780. He sent an encyclical to Bardizag in 1766. It is not known where he was buried. Minas Kasabian (Farhad), *Hayere Nikomedio Kavarin Mech*, p. 112.

‡ Bishop Bartoghomeos Gaboudig. He was prelate (based in Armash Monastery) from 1784 until his death in 1809. He was buried near the north wall of the Armenian Apostolic church in Izmid. He rebuilt Armash Monastery. Minas Kasabian (Farhad), *Hayere Nikomedio Kavarin Mech*, p. 115.

when he was in the village during the summer on a diocesan visit, to that particular spring to honour him with cold water and shish kebabs.

The Bishop saw that village women had come there, lighting candles on the stones and praying, with tears in their eyes and with great fervour. He was very surprised and said, 'What is this? You've created Ayazmos here; we're not Romans (Greeks). All this is superstition – I forbid it.' But seeing that it would not be easy to forget an old custom, he recommended that a small chapel be built there and an icon of St. Minas be put inside it, calling it 'Finder of lost things, St. Minas.'

We know that the name St. Minas had already been given to that place by the people of the village. From then on it was formally known as St. Minas and was an official pilgrimage site. The bishop said that from then on candles should be lit in the chapel, in front of the icon of the saint.

The villagers built a small chapel above the spring on a flat area in accordance with the bishop's recommendation and it was rebuilt four times from its foundation until the end of our time there.[*] Its pilgrimage day was determined as being during the summer, in August, on the feast day of the Holy Mother of God, when the priests and a great crowd of villagers ascended the height, where prayers, worship, vespers and a service were held. *Madagh* [sacrificial animals] were butchered, cooked and the blessed food distributed among all those present. In my day the great madagh cauldrons were kept in the church[†] and the hearths for the fires to cook it on were still located on the summit of St. Minas.

The Armenian and Greek people, when they found the remains of holy places or relics within the area of their villages, such as expensive smoothed stones, foundations or walls, stones with carvings of crosses on them and so on, considered them to be sacred places, which they hurried to make into pilgrimage sites. They gave these places names, gave them days of pilgrimage and, on one day a year, would go to them with religious fervour, sacrifice animals – cockerels, chickens, sheep and so forth – and try to find remedies for their spiritual ills by reviving the ancient sites of the Christian religion.

The people found several holy or pilgrimage places in this way around Bardizag: *St. Minas, Vartabedin Sourpe* [The Priests Saint],[‡] *Manoushag, Hormin Sourpe* [Romans' Saint] (in the vineyards), as well as St. Sarkis, which was also known as Gharibough Hagopigants Sourpe, located about an hour's distance from the village, on a hill. One villager had the temerity to make lime from several of its fallen stones

---

* It stood for over 150 years. The ruins were demolished in the 1960s and the site excavated, the local people looking for 'Armenian gold'. The site is now a restaurant.

† The author does not say which church, but it seems that he meant the one in the village.

‡ This might mean 'The Priests Holy Place' and refer to one of the places that Bishop Hovannes of the Goudjoukian family venerated. See Section 40.

– considered to be a sacrilege by the rest of the village. There was a place of pilgrimage further away in the mountains called Oulou Geol, called St. Yeghia, which was said to have been a large and important monastery in Byzantine times. There were still, in my day, some remains left of it – walls made of polished white marble, the lead-covered cupola of the monastery church, with a mosaic floor, the two doorposts made of great smooth stones, cross stones and carvings. People from nearby villages had taken the majority of the stones and used them as building materials. One of the stones had even been brought to Bardizag, where it was used as the threshold of the main door to the Megrian's silk spinning factory.

The festival day for this monastery was the Sunday of the Exaltation of the Holy Cross,[*] when Christians would go there to make vows. Turks too would visit it for the same reason, calling it *Top Aghan Manastere*, a name derived from a grove of trees that grew there.

19 – *Sourp Dirouhi* [Holy Lady or Holy Mother of God]

I should also like to recall, amongst these places, a pilgrimage site called *Sourp Dirouhi* [Holy Lady or Holy Mother of God], within Bardizag, that has not been noted by Garabed Kahana Mkhalian in his historical work, either being forgotten or recorded in his second notebook which I was unable to find.

In my day this place was an area of unused ground in the western part of the village, about five minutes from the church, on the western side of Bardizag's well-known valley, near the Dayetsi (Daiyan) house. There were trees and a spring that later must have become the one called *Ashdjonts Aghpiur* [Ashdjonts Fountain]. This was when it was still outside the borders of the newly-established village. Our ancestors wanted to re-establish a familiar pilgrimage site there, near their settlement, trying to maintain sacred memories of their past. They constructed a chapel there in the early days like that of St. Minas, where they could gather on a specific day of the year, probably on the day of the Assumption of the Holy Mother of God,[†] before St. Minas had taken its final form, as I described in Section 18.

This chapel was, of course, entrusted to the care of a neighbouring devout family, the Daiyans, where devout people under spiritual stress – mothers and women – would go at any time, bearing gifts of incense and candles for the Holy Mother of God (Holy Lady or *Sourp Dirouhi*), seeking relief and spiritual comfort for their ills.

After St. Minas was recognised as an official pilgrimage site, over the course of time, with the gradual expansion of the village, it probably lost its importance, with fewer and fewer people going there. The popular saying 'the distant saint is powerful' had become reality in this case, the result of which was that it was left deserted, the chapel fell down and the trees died. The people had no wish to

---

[*] This was in September.
[†] In mid-August.

reconstruct it as they had a distant saint endowed with pomp, as well as natural and Godly beauty. In my day the place where *Sourp Dirouhi* had stood was an open place, used as a playground by the local children.

The *Sourp Takavor* [Holy King] church and pilgrimage site, established at time of the anchorites within the village area, suffered the same fate, as we shall see later.[*]

20 – Great Hadji Khacher Bab's public works

Hadji Khacher Bab's rule was useful for the village with public works being carried out. He had the Chaghchi Valley road paved, with the participation of the villagers, even before he had become the owner of a mill. He also had the streets in various sections[†] of the village paved and public fountains constructed. It was in his time that the cold and pure water from St. Minas was brought to the village, split into two and a fountain for each flow set up at the borders of two sections of the village. They were called *Medz Aghpiur* [Great Fountain] and *Agha Krikorents Aghpiur* [Agha Krikor's Family Fountain]. (The latter was known, in my day, as Garabed Kahana's or Kondayents fountain.)

Agha Krikor's two houses, one belonging to Great Hadji Khacher and the other to his brother Nalband Varteres, as well as their neighbours, would get their water from a spring near Gelder Ghodja Keole Stepan's house before the water from St. Minas was brought to the village. (This stream was also called Chayir Keoliun's spring.) It provided between 5 and 6 *okhas* of water a minute, and its source was located a little higher up, below the Gannons' (or more correctly) Khachan Papaz Djele's house. This flow of water, due to the growth of that part of the village, eventually proved to be insufficient. As a result, Agha Krikor's two sons, Great Hadji Khacher and Nalband Varteres, having thought about it and in agreement with the people of that section of the village, began work with the object of bringing water to it from St. Minas.

Under the leadership of the two aghas the people of the section dug trenches, starting at St. Minas, as far as just below the Gannon's house, near the old spring, in which they installed a line of linked earthenware conduits. They split the flow of water into two at this point, making one part flow past the front of the Gannons' house as a public fountain for the people of the section. This was equipped with an iron tap and a large stone trough in front of it, almost always full of water, allowing the animals belonging to the people who lived there and others to drink. The second flow was directed, through new channels in the street, down the slope, as far as the front of the Mikayelian's (Kondayents) house, where Nalband Hadji Varteres'

---

[*] See Section 124.
[†] I have used the word section to mean a part of the village; later, when Bardizag was divided into six official sections, each became a parish in its own right and is described as such.

house was located. Hadji Khacher's house was built higher up, near the Gannons' house.

The two brothers had something of a disagreement when they were distributing the water. This was because Nalband Hadji Varteres wanted to divide it into two equal parts. His brother Great Hadji Khacher, however, wanted the greater proportion of the water to flow to the upper fountain, where the section was much larger. Finally clear-sightedness prevailed, and the two brothers agreed to split the water: three fifths to the upper fountain and two fifths to the lower, to Nalband Hadji Khacher's section. Great Hadji Khacher had a modest inscription put on the Great Fountain: '*Sebeb yeghoghats orhnoutiun**

They demolished the old fountain, which didn't provide clean water, after constructing the new ones, but the people of that part of the village continued utilising the water below the Gelders' house to 'pull mandjelekh' for a time.†

These works demonstrate that Hadji Khacher Bab was a modest, practical man who was dedicated to the public good. At the same time he was a very devout and church-loving person, never missing a morning or evening service.

21 – Hadji Khacher's family circumstances

The generations that descended from Hadji Khacher's and his brother, Nalband Varteres' families form many well-known families in Bardizag today (see the family tree below).‡ Great Hadji Khacher Bab, however, had many family difficulties and tragedies. He became a widower twice. His first wife was from the clan of the notable Tatos, the sister of Sarkis Kahana Bedigants, who died young and childless. His second wife was from Arslanbeg, who gave birth to sons and daughters: Mikayel (Antreas Kahana); Krikor (Apraham Kahana); a daughter Soultan who married Shelem Bolo; Mariam the wife of Garabed Konda; Kayiane, wife of Govdji Gharevleg Arakel; and Hripsime, the wife of Boghos, Vartan Kahana of Ghendjerlar's son.

People tell an interesting anecdote about Great Hadji Khacher Bab's wife from Arslanbeg. One day, when he was still a young man, Hadji Khacher visited his friends in Arslanbeg. A local woman saw this stranger from a window when he was walking along the street. She asked about him, admiring his great height, his looks and said, in truth, 'He's a real man, he looks good.'

Time passed. Hadji Khacher's first wife died and he decided to go to Arslanbeg, wishing to choose a suitable wife for himself. The previously mentioned woman's husband had

---

* 'May this be the reason for blessings to all'. (This is an approximate translation as the inscription was in classical Armenian.)

† This is the old method of unwinding silk from cocoons by submerging them in boiling water and then winding it onto a wheel by hand.

‡ The family tree shown is only an outline; this text supplements it.

died and so she was a widow. Hadji Khacher's friends told him about her, suggesting that she would be a suitable candidate for a wife. Hadji Khacher approved, and married her. Thus by a strange twist of fate, she married the man she loved.

Unfortunately his second wife died too, having given birth to many children. Great Hadji Khacher married for a third time, to a widow also from outside Bardizag, from whom he had a son, Hovhannes and a daughter, Dirouhi.

Great Hadji Khacher, alongside all his other qualities, had a peasant's simplicity of mind and was open-hearted, something that was characteristic of all the great people of that time, who had no qualms about expressing their feelings in the most basic and coarse way.

22 – Bandits capture priests from Bardizag

In the old days, it was the rule that kahanas read the night Psalms while it was still dark and before the church bell sounded. Pairs of officiating priests would carry out the readings in turn, probably in the church's anteroom, as was the custom.

When the two kahanas were reading the Psalms in church one day, they suddenly found themselves faced with four armed Turkish bandits who ordered them to accompany them. The poor priests were extremely frightened, but had to agree to go with them. The bandits took them, via the road through the Upper Fields to the rear of St. Minas Hill, then to a place on the other side of the Ovadjek River. Having tied the kahanas to a large rock, the bandits went to the road in the hope of stopping a passer-by. They finally met some Turks from Anteres, who were taking goods to Bardizag via this route. The bandits told the travellers to inform the notables of the village that they had captured the kahanas, taken them into the mountains, and now demanded a 4,000 *kurush* ransom for them, a very large sum in those days. They added that if the ransom was not forthcoming, they would kill the priests.

Hadji Khacher Bab, the village notables and priests held a meeting and were able to procure the sum demanded, which was sent to the bandits. The bandits, having received the money, released the priests.

Until my day, people pointed out a large rock in the mountains which had been given the name 'The rock the priests were tied to.'

After some time, one of the bandits, who was from Khodjeli's Tash Keopru village, told the story to an acquaintance from Bardizag who was there as a travelling merchant. He said, 'A few of us were in the Baghchedjouk [Bardizag] area then and suddenly, during the night, we heard the sound of the wooden bell in the bell tower of the church. One of our comrades, who had been a bandit for a long time, persuaded us to go there. We entered the church and, driving the kahanas ahead of us, took them to the mountains.' This act by the Turks not only betrays their customary appetite for robbery and looting but also their fanatical hatred for Christians.

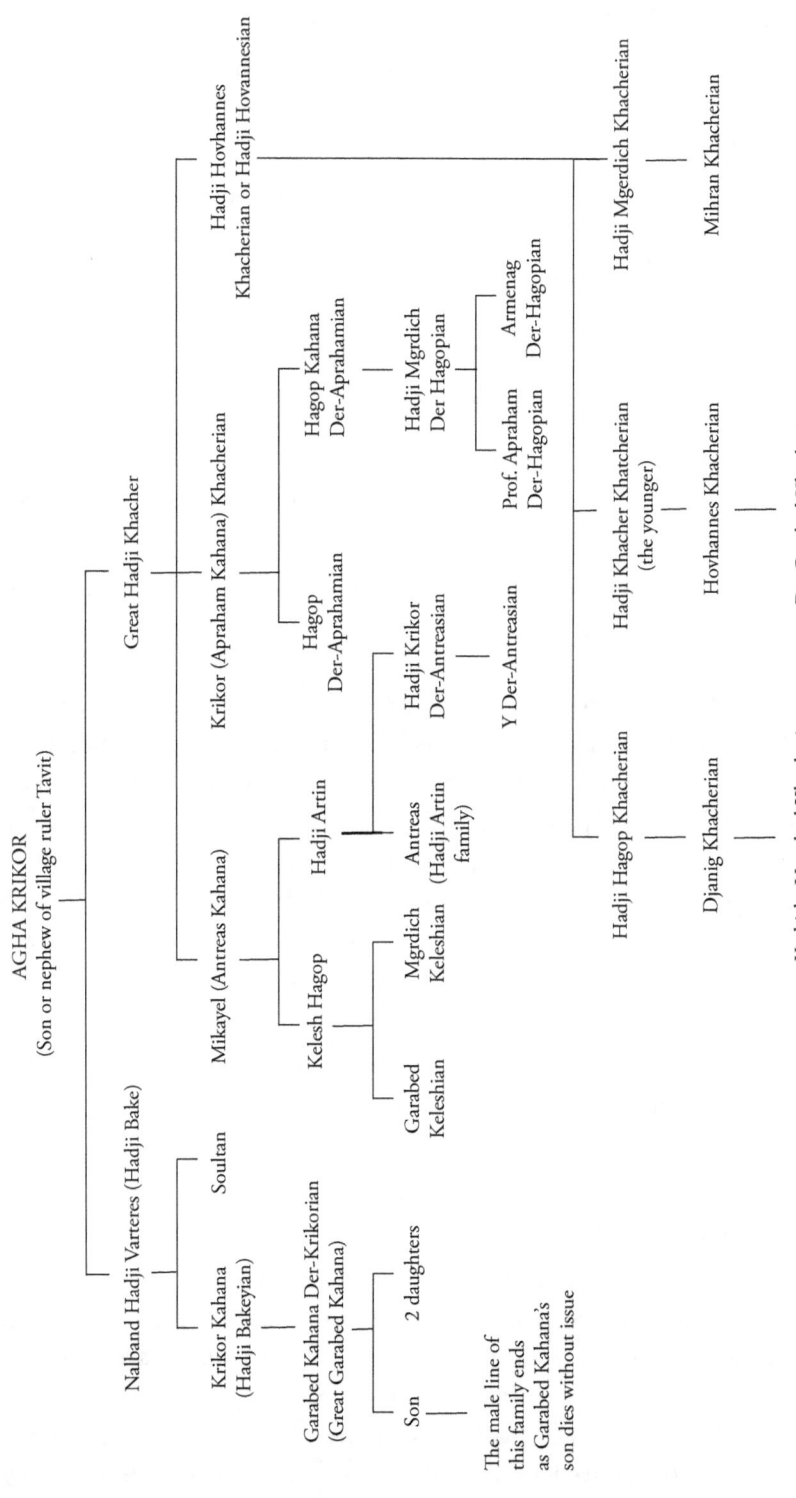

NOTE: The family tree above shows only the main generations, simply to show the names of those who had important positions in their lives or in the village. Great Garabed Kahana's line continued through his two daughters, one of whom, Dirouhi, used the name Der-Garabedian. Patriarch Torkom Koushagian's mother was from this family. He therefore was Great Garabed Kahana's great-grandson.
Nalband Hadji Varteres' daughter, Soultan, married into the Bournazian family, being the wife of Bournaz Hovannes, the ancestor of the well-known Megerian family.

Churches were also looted in those old and dark days. Robbers made nocturnal visits to the Greek church near us in Yenikeoy and the one in Kara Depe near Arslanbeg.

The thieves who had robbed the Yenikeoy church came to Bardizag on the same night with their loot. There they opened one of the blacksmith's shops, lit the forge and melted down the looted church silver. They must have had Christian helpers, because it is difficult to explain how Turkish thieves, without any qualms of conscience, could have come to a large Christian village like Bardizag and spend hours there, never mind the fact that it was night time and especially that they had the skill to melt silver.

23 – Hovhannes Kahana of the Great Derder family is exiled

The hatred that existed between Hovhannes Kahana of the Great Derder family and Great Hadji Khacher from the early days became more pronounced over time and was to have scandalous repercussions.

Hovhannes Kahana was the leading priest[*] during the days of Hadji Khacher's rule, and was the representative of the oldest priestly family and the oldest person among the priests, at the same time being an able and knowledgeable person.

He had a wonderful voice and knew all the *sharagans* [canticles], having sung them in the services during the time of his grandfather and father who were both priests. He also wrote with a good and neat hand, and had developed great skill and ability in composition. He edited all the official documents sent to the diocesan bishop, the Patriarchate and the amiras.[†] The titles of his official letters to the patriarchs were especially rich and filled with long, bombastic explanations and adjectives, affected phrases and grandiloquent sentences.

These skills were dangerous for Hovhannes Kahana. Due to his great hatred towards Hadji Khacher, he continually sent letters of protest about him to the head of the diocese and to the patriarchate in Constantinople, making accusations against him and later about his son Apraham Kahana. In one of his letters that still exist, written in Ottoman Turkish,[‡] we read the following story:

> A Turkish official brought, on behalf of the governor of Izmid of the day, a written order to Baghchedjouk [Bardizag] one day in which he demanded the sum of 4,000 *kurush*. (It was not made clear in the letter why the governor made this demand). Hadji Khacher, the notables and the kahanas convened a meeting to discuss the governor's demand and invited Hovhannes Kahana to attend too. Hovhannes Kahana didn't want

---

[*] *Avakerets* – the most senior rank among kahanas.
[†] *Amiras* – rich Armenian merchants and industrialists of Constantinople, who had great political influence in various quarters.
[‡] This document is now lost. It was written in Ottoman (Arabic) script.

to participate in the meeting. Threats were made to bring him to it by force, so he was obliged to attend, despite his unwillingness.

The order was read in the meeting, after which Hovhannes Kahana said 'I have no opinion', withdrew from the meeting and tried to leave. The Turkish official intervened and forced him to sit down. Under these circumstances the meeting couldn't come to a decision about the governor's demand. At this, the Turkish official took Hadji Khacher, Hovhannes Kahana and the village notables to Izmid with him to see the governor.

The consultations about the demand continued there, with conflicting views appearing. Finally the governor, annoyed at this continual delay, grew angry and, turning to Hovhannes Kahana, said, 'Oh *papaz* [priest], so is it you who has stirred up things in the village and opposed my rule.'

'Oh sir' replied Hovhannes Kahana, 'I am a priest, it is not my job to create trouble...'

The governor, in answer to this, pointed Hadji Khacher out, saying, 'This person gave me the news.'

The priest protested and said, 'He is insulting me, sir.'

This is one of Hovhannes Kahana's - Hadji Khacher's adversary's - stories, the aim of which was to show that Hadji Khacher was the author of his subsequent exile and to belittle him. In any case, without denying Hadji Khacher's involvement in these events, it becomes apparent from the story that by escaping from the meeting and not agreeing to the governor's demand, he wanted to secure another opportunity to level accusations against Hadji Khacher. This was while the latter and the other notables, put in a difficult position, didn't dare refuse the governor's demand. In these circumstances, it remained for Hovhannes Kahana, as a right-minded person, to either join the others or reject the governor's demand, accepting all the consequences.

The story continues:

> An order arrived to exile Hovhannes Kahana a few days after these events. It cited him as a trouble-maker and a person who refused to accept government commands. This was backed up by Hadji Khacher's side, including the diocesan bishop, Bartoghimeos, the patriarchate and the government.
>
> Hovhannes Kahana was therefore arrested by Bardizag's Turkish aghas and remained under guard that night. He was then moved, on the following morning, to Deyirmendere by road, as the first stage of his journey to Constantinople and from there to his place of exile. He was imprisoned in a stable there with his legs in chains. He was able, however, to open the stable door while still shackled and escape towards the mountains. (It is probable that the aghas' servant assisted his escape.)
>
> Wandering about in the mountains, he reached a Greek-inhabited village called Foulanekh that evening, located near to the Armenian villages of Yalakdere and Merdigeoz. He was careful not to enter the latter

two, as the inhabitants would be forced to send news of his whereabouts to the Armenian diocesan authorities in Izmid. The Greek Christians of Foulanekh village took pity on Hovhannes Kahana and, at his request, moved him to the isolated port of Dil Iskele, between Karamoursal and Yalova. He went by boat from there to Constantinople, like an ordinary traveller.

When he arrived in Constantinople, he approached sympathetic amiras, one of whom was Ghazar Agha of Ghapan and was able to secure his release from the exile order through his intervention. He wrote a letter to Hadji Takvor Agha (who was either his friend or relative) in Izmid, as well as to his sons-in law in Bardizag - Kelesh Atanas (the patriarch of the Cheopdjis, Chepels and the Banbern families), Eleg (real name Boghos Mardigian), Peto-Stepan (patriarch of the Peto family), Semerdji Hadji Hovhannes (patriarch of the Semerdjians) and Balaban Arakeli Hovhannes (patriarch of the Arakelians – the Hadji Horops). Hadji Horop (Hripsime) was Hovhannes Kahana's daughter, Arakel Hovhannes' wife.

He gave them the news of his release, thanks to the approaches made to highly-placed Armenian amiras in Constantinople on his behalf.

This took place in 1797-1798, and is verified by a copy of the exile order kept in the monastery of Armash[*] that was brought to Bardizag by Torkom Vartabed Koushagian as an important document concerning Bardizag's history. The prelacy of Izmid and the abbacy of the monastery of Armash were united at that time.

Hovhannes Kahana remained in Constantinople for some time, giving time for tempers to cool, and then returned to Bardizag. But he, before anything else, was not a quiet person; he once more fanned the flames of the ancient enmity between the two parties: 'Old stone, old bath house.'[†]

I close this sad page in Bardizag's history that has been repeated on other occasions, as we shall see.

Hovhannes Kahana, despite his restless nature, had his merits. He was studious and an able priest. He made great efforts to educate himself, a hundred years before our times, in those days of ignorance and darkness. He collected books on medicine and sermons and aspired to learn Turkish and Greek – grammars for those languages were found in his papers – that were subsequently kept in the church's

---

[*] The monastery of Armash, which later became a famous place of pilgrimage known as Charkhapan Sourp Asdvadzadzin [Evil-slaying Holy Mother of God], was founded in 1611 by Bishop Tateos, an emissary from Echmiadzin, when he was conducting a visitation to the Nicomedia prelacy. Minas Kasabian (Farhad), *Hayere Nikomedio Kavarin Mech*, p. 55.

[†] An old Turkish proverb, translated by the author.

library. Among them was an important document, his spiritual father's* encyclical concerning his parishes.

24 – The supply of charcoal to the Ottoman Mint passes into the hands of the people of Bardizag

I have previously told how the supply of charcoal to the Ottoman Mint was in the hands of the Sermayedji Turkish aghas in Bardizag.† When the Diuzians were appointed managers of the Mint by the sultan, they heard that the charcoal was being prepared by Armenian charcoal burners from Bardizag. The village notables were called in and agreement was reached about its supply.

The notables of Bardizag returned and organised the work. The charcoal was prepared by men from Bardizag in the Ghourtbelen Mountains, just as before. Mule trains were organised for the transport of the prepared fuel from there to Seymen. Each well-to-do villager bought one or two mules for the community's trains, which were used to bring the prepared charcoal from the mountains once or twice a week. Two officials were appointed in Seymen– an accountant and a supervisor – whose duty it was to calculate the weight of the charcoal and cost of transport. These arrangements were made in the first instance in Hadji Khacher's time, as a Bardizag co-operative operation and owned by the village.

There was then the question concerning the charcoal's movement by sea from the port to Constantinople. Turkish boats were utilised at first but, during Apraham Kahana's rule and upon his suggestion, the people of Bardizag obtained their own cargo boat, a large, swift vessel captained by Armenians that went from Seymen to Constantinople loaded with charcoal twice a week. Seli Hagop, his brother Seli Khachadour, the Reizes and other Armenian captains may be recalled. Thus Bardizag people took over the preparation and transportation of the charcoal completely. This organisation worked for many long years, and the notables and people of the neighbouring Armenian villages of Ovadjek and Arslanbeg also took part.

When the charcoal, packed in bags or baskets was brought from the mouintains to Seymen, the accountant, who at one time was Zakar Kevorki Hagop, got his *cheteleh* (a short wooden rod) which at that time was a form of tally‡ and would join it to the one carried by the muleteer. He would then make a mark with the point of a knife on his for each load, returning the muleteer's own to him. The number of marks on each had to match, the muleteer's tally stick acting as a check on the accuracy of the calculation of the total number of loads.

---

* This term is generally used for the bishop or archbishop who ordains a celibate priest or kahana.
† See Section 14.
‡ The word used here is *hashvedoumar*. This literally means 'account book'.

The supervisor, who at one time was Djerga Hadji Sarkis Baba, the grandfather of Sarkis Agha Djergayian of my day, watched over the work of storing the charcoal in the warehouses and loading it on the boat.

Payment by the Mint's officials per load at the agreed rate was made to the notables of the village every month and the charcoal burners would then be paid according to the quantity of charcoal each had produced. The revenue obtained was used by the notables to pay the cost of mule transport, the officials' salary, boat repairs etc.

It seems that the actual profit made went to the church and the community school.

There have been occasions when an official specially sent from the Mint would come to Seymen to oversee the general running of the business. Naturally their salaries were paid directly to them by the Mint, but their living expenses – food and board – were paid by the business. Abdullah and Emin Effendis as well as others may be recalled among them.

During Sultan Mahmoud's reign the mint extended its operations to include the making of new coins *(metaliks)* and gold ornaments* *(mahmoudieh)*,† resulting in a vast increase in the amount of charcoal provided by the organisation owned by the people of Bardizag, reaping rich profits. This coincided with a considerable part of Apraham Kahana's and, after him, with Garabed Agha Mgerian's rule.

Much later, one of the notables of Ovadjek, Zakar Agha, took over the whole business of providing charcoal, the work having been taken away from Bardizag during the Mgerian period. As a result the sending of officials from the Mint to Bardizag ceased.

I don't know the reason for the change, but it is probable that one of the main reasons was that by moving the business to Ovadjek, there were savings made in the cost of charcoal and transport, as its port, Bash Iskele, was closer to the charcoal producing mountains. Perhaps, there were also suspicions of profiteering through the collusion of the officials and the Bardizag organisation.

Zakar Agha became very rich as a result of the change, and gained an important position, his becoming the only great house in Ovadjek. He had the charcoal transported to Ovadjek's port, Bash Iskele, which in my day was the port serving Ovadjek and Dongel, half an hour to the west of Seymen, right opposite Izmid.

It is probable that the Bardizag charcoal burners continued to produce charcoal, as the more experienced masters in the trade.

Many years later, however, the work of producing charcoal ceased completely in our region, with the Mint installing new, European machinery and replacing charcoal with mined coal, the use of which had already started in Europe at that time.

---

*   The word used here is *zartoski*.
†   This could mean commemorative gold coins.

25 – The port of Seymen's trade movement

As I've mentioned previously, the port of Seymen had been in existence even before the beginning of the 18th century as an important centre for the movement of charcoal, firewood and timber to the Constantinople market, since the time of the Turkish aghas. Much later we can see that the people of Bardizag also became occupied with this export trade, among the early protagonists who can be recalled being Sermayedji Great Hadji Zakar Agha, whose enterprises continued for many years after him, through his sons, Hairabed and the others. After them new undertakings began by people from the village, such as the Amous (the Kiutners), the Zobis (the Melkonians) and, with them, the Aparigs (the Mkhalians), who in my day had warehouses or storage areas in Seymen.

There was an old story told in relation to this trade about Hadji Zakar Hairabedian's two sons' deaths on their return journey from Izmid to Seymen. Their boat, caught by the ferocity of the wind and waves, capsized, and the travellers – Hairabed's two sons and Gatsan Yesayi, father of Gatsan Hovhannes – drowned. After that, Hairabed's wife, affected by the loss of her sons, never ate fish again, thinking she was eating her sons' flesh.

Seymen, in my day, was the centre of a vigorous export trade.

Turkish ship owners usually bought the fuel and firewood ready for export and were sold on the Constantinople market. Greek ship owners, on the other hand, bought the timber (*varol* – baril) also known as *samanli* and took it to the Arshibeghakos Islands, where it was used to make containers for wine, oghi[*] and olive oil. These Greek ship owners, when they were buying timber, used the opportunity to import, through Seymen, the local produce of the islands – raisins, dried figs, wine, oghi, olive oil, olives, soap and earthenware vessels (tubs, pitchers, urns and *gelibolous*) the latter being a kind of large, convenient vessel used to transport water.

We will see, in subsequent pages, that both trade through Seymen increased, such as the export of silk from cocoons, horseshoes and nails and baskets and the import of things such as European wheat, flour and engineering products, through which Seymen became one of the notable ports in the Bay of Izmid, even for shipment of goods to distant countries.

26 – Attempts at hermit-like living

Great catastrophes, such as wars, epidemics, famine and other natural disasters are often the reason that particular psychological states or appearances are generated in a people's consciousness. These have consequences leading to the scorning of life and its false promises and withdrawal from the world and adopting concerns about

---

[*] *Arak* or *raki*.

heaven or the world beyond the grave. Some people would dedicate themselves to a life of contemplation, to aspire to be in permanent communion with their God, especially in the times when God's religion had an overwhelming place in the souls of simple and virginal souls. Exactly this kind of spiritual state was created among some people of Bardizag at the end of the 18th and the beginning of the 19th centuries, when hermits or anchorites made their appearance.

These people wished to withdraw from worldly occupations, distance themselves from places where others lived, to wander the mountains, dedicate themselves to hermit-like living, pray, fast and be nourished by grass and salad-like food.

A certain kind of individual also appeared among them who had gone to Armenia – to Gdouts Monastery on Lake Van. Most of them were men – brothers, uncles, cousins etc. – from the Mkhdji family, also called Sapenk (of the Sap family – *sap* meaning idiotic, crazy or mad in Bardizag dialect) who had immigrated to Bardizag and settled in Ghourtbelen about 200 years before.

They lived there for some years like hermits and formed a hermit brotherhood, called the 'Seven Bligs' (*beoliugs*). They then petitioned the abbot of the monastery to ordain them as celibate members of the church – deacons, monks and vartabeds. Among them may be recalled a bishop named Hovhannes, vartabeds named Garabed, Mardiros and Arakel, a deacon named Stepannos or Panos as well as others.

They were joined, after a time, by Mger Bab, the ancestor of the Mgerian (Bournaz) family, Garabed Agha Mgerian's grandfather. This Hadji Bab, from early in his time there, served this community as a lay brother. It is said that Brother Meger Bournaz constructed a water vessel in Gdouts Monastery with his own hands that was customarily known, until the end, by his name. Bishop Hovhannes never ever returned to Bardizag, but Garabed Vartabed and Mardiros Vartabed did for a time, then returned to Gdouts. Deacon Stepannos' son Arakel Vartabed also came back to the village and lived for a long time in his sister's (she was Benbel Garabed's wife) house, never returning to Gdouts, dying in Bardizag between 1830 and 1840. The old people in Bardizag who knew him said that this vartabed, after ordination, was sent on a mission to Nor Nakhichevan* to collect funds for Gdouts Monastery, but instead of returning there, came to Bardizag instead. It would appear that he never presented any accounts and kept the money he collected.

According to people from the village these clerics who returned from Gdouts had no education, but were good, honourable, devout individuals. They occasionally attempted to preach in Bardizag, but the sermons they gave were poor in terms of language, meaning and inspiration. For example, they used a sort of parable to emphasise the importance of charity – 'Aunt Soghig put caps on the heads of poor children' – and other silly stories.

---

* Novo Nakhichevansk near Rostov-on-Don, Russia, where there is still a large community of Armenians.

Deacon Stepannos also returned to Bardizag and was the *jamgoch* [church beadle] for a time. He had learnt to read a little, so the village priests gave him permission, once a year, to read the Gospel (that he'd probably learnt by heart) during Mass during the seven days of Theophany. When this deacon finally moved his family to Bardizag, clerics from Gdouts Monastery who came to Bardizag would stay in his house, as if they were in a monastery. After some time the deacon built a small building near his house, where the returning clerics, with certain devout villagers, could say prayers and sing the evening service. This building was known as Sourp Takavor [Holy King] and became a sort of pilgrimage site.*

It later became the custom to take sick people there, from both Bardizag and outside, saying that they would receive a cure there from their ills, thus making the Holy King building famous as a miracle-working pilgrimage site. Its fame spread and the number of visits by sick people, pilgrimages by the devout and *madagh* [sacrifices] increased with time.

Many years later, the deacon returned to Gdouts Monastery and wrote a letter from there to his two sons – the beadle Mardiros and Arakel Vartabed - to look after the Holy King pilgrimage site, to hang lanterns and burn candles there and to conduct evening services, giving it the form of a second Gdouts. His sons loyally continued to do so, even after Arakel Vartabed's death. They were assisted in their duties by the devout Koukoug Krikor Aghpar (also known as Peylivan) and the deacon Garabed, known as Eski, who was the son of Hovhannes Daiyan.

While Deacon Stepannos was still in Bardizag, the Turkish Agha or his servant, I can't determine which, went to the Holy King building one day, called him and said, 'Open this church and let's take a look at it.' The deacon opened the door and the Turk entered. He examined every part of it and, when he wanted to ascend the steps to the altar with his tobacco pipe in his hand, Deacon Stepannos intervened, saying, 'My lord, don't go there, it is a sin…' The Turk replied, 'It is a sin for you, but it is no sin for me…' With that the Turk, in that irreverent manner, ascended the steps to the altar.

27 – The building of the third church

The second church was found, after a time, to be too small as a result of the increase in the village's population, especially as the people retained all their love, enthusiasm and zeal for it. Everyone without exception was used to hurrying to the church both morning and evening, even before the *Haismavourk* [Book of Days] and *Zartik* [Arise] were read, squashing one another and pushing and shoving to find a place in the church. The notables and priests of the village, seeing this, decided to demolish the now too-small church and build a bigger one, to solve the problem.

As we saw in the case of the hermits' Holy King church, there was no real difficulty in building churches in those days, especially in villages; there was no need

---

* An unfinished chapel of this name was later built in the village. See Section 124.

to await an imperial *firman* [permit] to build one. It was enough to present a petition to the local governor and obtain his permission. People thought that it would be easy to explain the need to the *miuselim* and obtain the desired permit from him. The *miuselim* was therefore given a *gift* of 10,000 *kurush*; permission was given to demolish the old church and to build a new one according to the style and size the people of Bardizag wanted, on the condition that the whole work was completed in one month. They couldn't afford to complain about this.

Hadji Khacher Bab and his brother Nalband Hadji Varteres, with the village elders and priests, led the villagers to complete the accumulation of materials needed to build the church. They sent woodcutters to the mountains to prepare lumber and timber, the *baltadjis* to bring down centuries-old trees and carters to bring all of it to the village. The construction of the church was started at the same time to make best use of the time allowed.

The village notables supervised the building work, some in the village and others in the mountains; the latter to encourage the *baltadjis* when they struck tree trunks with powerful blows and felled them, singing this devout, simple song:

> Tree, don't cry, tree, don't scream, there is good news for you;
> We are going to build God's House, shameless one!

The entire village - old and young, boys and girls – all worked hard, without regard for night or day and built the church in exactly one month. Of course a building built so quickly and in such a short time couldn't last very long; it stood for only about 30 years.

This church lasted until 1830, having been built in 1800.[*] As we shall see, the fourth and final church was built, the solid, wonderful church of St. James of our days.[†]

The diocesan bishop, probably Bartoghomeos,[‡] had a Greek master brought from outside when construction was completed who made three cross holders of metal and gilded in bronze. Terzi Hadji Stepan, the father of Terzi Hadji Srab, whom I knew, paid the whole cost of gilding them. The church was dedicated and services began. Terzi Hadji Stepan was from Izmid, had settled in Bardizag, and was the son or grandson of a kahana. A manuscript *jamakirk* [breviary] and a *badaraki khorhrtadedr* [service book] were to be found in his house.

---

[*] According to the diary kept by Krikor Kahana, this church was built '...In the year 1799 the building of the church began on January 17th and was completed in one month. Its dedication took place on the Saturday of the *Poun Paregentan* (the beginning of Lent, in the second half of February). Hagop Der-Hagopian, *Bardizage khadoudig* [Dappled Bardizag], Paris 1960, p. 23.

[†] See Section 52.

[‡] It was Bishop Bartoghomeos Gaboudig, who served as prelate from 1784-1809. Minas Kasabian (Farhad), *Hayere Nikomedio Kavarin Mech*, p. 114.

Hovhannes Kahana (the *avak kahana* or leading priest), Krikor Kahana Agha Krikorian, the son of Nalband Hadji Varteres, Great Hadji Khacher's son Antreas Kahana and Pilibbos Kahana (from Ghendjerlar) were the priests who continued their ministry in this third church and who, between them, satisfied the spiritual needs of the community.

A fund was set up specifically for the priests called 'The Perpetual Fund', on the occasion of the building of this church, to provide for their old age and illnesses, with the whole community contributing, starting with Great Hadji Khacher, his brother Nalband Hadji Varteres and Terzi Hadji Stepan from Izmid.

28 – The great death

The epidemic called the 'great death' occurred (it was probably cholera) in 1803, shortly after the construction of the third church. This illness was unknown in the regions around Bardizag at that time. It took hold in the region very swiftly and Bardizag was also contaminated.

Those sick with the illness suffered dreadful diarrhoea and died in just a few days. Many died in Bardizag that year. Antreas Kahana was also affected and died. The epidemic lost its impetus after his death. There was a saying among us that was used in such dire circumstances: 'a priest should die so that this catastrophe ends.'

29 – A prodigal's sad death

Djezel Hadji Garabed, son-in-law of the Azarians, had two sons, Ghazaros and Hovhannes. Ghazaros married first and had two children. Despite this, he led a life in the village that was full of scandal; he carried a *Shishli*[*] cane and wore a scarf round his neck, things that were regarded as scandalous in those days. He boldly wandered the streets without shame. There were other more serious crimes he was seen as guilty of... At all this, the villagers, scandalised and losing patience, petitioned the village notables to rid them of that *noxious weed*.[†] They prepared an accusation against him and gave it to the government. Ghazaros was arrested and sent to Constantinople, was tried there for his crimes and beheaded in the Balek Bazaar.

The Djezelians, after that, and especially the beheaded man's grandson, the Djezel Ghazar of my day, accused Great Hadji Bab of being the instigator of Ghazaros' trial and execution. This happened sometime between 1803 and 1807.

30 – Apraham's Kahana's ordination

Great Hadji Khacher felt great sorrow at the unexpected death of his son Antreas Kahana and, as a form of spiritual comfort, wanted his second son Krikor to be

---

[*] Word unknown.
[†] Author's italics.

ordained as a kahana. It is also probable that he also thought that this would weaken the position of his enemy, Hovhannes Kahana.

He therefore suggested to the notables and priests that his son should be ordained. Without doubt, in those days of his most powerful rule, it wasn't difficult to find a way to succeed in his request, but it was obvious that he wanted to be courteous to those around him and to receive their assent, knowing that they wouldn't refuse.

Hovhannes Kahana was naturally opposed to the suggestion, but finding himself alone in being against Hadji Khacher, was forced to agree to it.

The diocesan bishop, Bartoghomeos, was invited to Bardizag to carry out the ordination, which he did, naming Hadji Khacher's son Apraham Kahana. Apraham Kahana was to be one of the most famous characters in Bardizag's history, and the greatest authority for a long time in the following years. He had already worked alongside his father before his ordination, becoming his right-hand man, and had gained great experience in the economics of public works and relations with the government.

31 – Great Hadji Khatcher's death

The patriarch Great Hadji Khatcher had the presentiment that his death was near just after Apraham Kahana's ordination. He therefore went on foot to church one day (although due to his lack of strength he usually remained at home), made confession and took communion. He begged forgiveness and peace of everyone he met on his way home.

He reached home, got into bed and, a few days later died peacefully. His funeral was conducted with great solemnity and pomp, with the whole village attending. This was in 1809. During my time his tombstone, which his sons and grandsons had placed on his grave with an inscription in poetry on it, in which the deceased was named as a 'Djed Ishkhan',[*] was still to be seen in the Old Cemetery.[†]

32 – The *derebeys* in Bardizag

Anarchists called *derebeys* who lived like bandits were to be found all over the country in those times. They existed in our part of the country; one near Adabazar was called Arab Osman, another in Ghodjaeli was called Abbas Ali, and there were others too.

One of these men, called Chaker Beoliuk Bashi, came to Bardizag one day and told the *chorbadji* (steward) of the time to prepare a place for him to stay for the night. In those days it was the custom to provide a bed and meal for a passing soldier

---

[*] 'Prince of the race'.
[†] The old cemetery was in the centre of the village.

or policemen, especially if he was visiting the village. The same hospitality was provided for this man and his band, according to his wishes; he was given Srab Nerses' house on the edge of the village, the walls of which were built of fired bricks. The inhabitants left it for that night and Chaker Beoliuk Bashi and his men took it over.

Night came, and the newly-arrived men began to knock holes in the walls like defence bastions, apparently for self-defence purposes. They were given bread, water and fire; they spent the night in the house and began preparations to depart in the morning. Several young men from the village got together well before dawn however, armed themselves and decided stop the band en route, probably with the *chorbadji's* knowledge, and kill the whole derebey group.

It would appear that the derebeys had told the *chorbadji* that they'd be taking the route to the Greek village of Yenikeoy (known to the people of Bardizag as 'Horom Kiugh'). The young men from the village went and settled themselves in a hiding place in the Azarians' forest on that route before dawn.

Beoliug Bashi and his men set out, without any inkling of the trap planned for them. When they reached the point where the young men from the village were hidden, a rifle was accidentally fired from nearby; Beoliug Bashi's group, becoming suspicious, thinking there was danger, therefore changed their route and, emerging from the forest, tried to take one towards Seymen. The young men from Bardizag seeing this, and not wanting to lose their prey, started firing at the derebeys. One of attackers, from the Kachol family, rushed out of his hiding place, approached the retreating men, aimed and fired at them.

The derebeys returned fire; one of their bullets hit the thoughtless young man and killed him on the spot. The derebeys suffered three wounded in the exchange of fire. The band carried the wounded and, retreating up the slopes, took the mountain road, going towards Manoushag. The young men from the village brought their dead comrade's body back to the village and buried it. This was a completely stupid and thoughtless action on the part of the young men from the village.

Chaker Beoliug Bashi realised that the attackers were from Bardizag, so he decided to take his revenge on anyone from the village he met. It was a Saturday and, on their way through the mountains, the band met three charcoal burners and lumber workers who were returning from the mountains to the village. They were Alig Baboug, Badel Manoug's son and Mangasar of the Baboukh family. The derebeys stopped them and asked where they were from. The innocent reply was that they were from Bardizag, as they knew nothing of the incident that had taken place. At this, Chaker Beoliug Bashi, pointing to his injured comrades, told them, 'People from your village wounded these innocent men, so you'll have to carry them.' They put one of the wounded on each of the backs of the poor workmen and forced them to go with them until they reached a village. The derebeys saw that the Armenians were so tired after a time that they couldn't walk another step. They stopped them and said, 'We'll let you go free, but we'll mark each of you with a sign as a lesson for your fellow-villagers.'

Chaker Beoliug Bashi assigned each of the villagers to one of his men and, telling them to go into the depths of the forest, ordered then to cut off the villagers' ears and noses and release them. Mangasar was freed without injury. The Turkish bandit felt sorry for him and told him to run away as fast as his legs could carry him, shouting 'Amman...!' Alig Baboug and the Badelents boy weren't so lucky; the punishment was carried out and they were freed, bleeding heavily.

The derebeys continued their journey and, when they saw other people from Bardizag on the way, guessed that they would have trouble, so took care to avoid meeting them, escaping through the mountains until they found safety.

Mangasar, who was uninjured, fell into bed sick from terror, and died. The Badelents boy died from his wounds becoming infected. It was only Alig Baboug who remained alive; after the incident he was called 'Cut nose Baboug.'

Chapter 4

The Apraham Kahana Khacherian Era 1809 – 1825

33 – Apraham Kahana and Hovhannes Kahana of the Great Derders family

After Great Hadji Khacher's death, his authority and rule transferred to his son, Apraham Kahana, who had put great effort and individuality into his activities. Apraham Kahana knew the Turkish aghas who had always been his family's friends and sympathisers. He was also known by the diocesan prelate and his circle and had great experience in village public affairs. Being the son of one of the village notables, he had grown up to be fearless and a bold speaker, and thus became, for many long years after his father's death, Bardizag's *atoragal* [seat-holder]* and the Turkish aghas' advisor and co-worker.

Hovhannes Kahana held the clerical leadership, as before, as the leading priest and church blesser, but Apraham Kahana made all the announcements in church as the representative of the village authority.

The diocesan prelate, Bishop Bartoghomeos, also died after Hadji Khacher's death. He was buried in the courtyard of the Armenian Apostolic Church in Izmid. He was succeeded by Bishop Boghos Karakoch of Gesaria (Kayseri) as the prelate of the united sees of Broussa (Boursa) and Izmid.†

When the newly elected prelate visited his see of Izmid for the first time, Apraham Kahana and a few of the notables of Bardizag visited him and welcomed him in the village's name. The prelate was impressed by him as a clever and able priest and visited Bardizag a few days later. Apraham Kahana entertained him in his own his house as the village notable. He also took the opportunity to get to know the prelate's assistant, a monk named Stepan Vartabed Aghavni (who had been ordained by him) and became good friends with him. It was this monk who later became the well known Bishop Stepannos Aghavni Zakarian, prelate of the Izmid diocese.‡

During Apraham Kahana's era, long-standing enmities surfaced once more: on the one hand Apraham Kahana and his cohorts and on the other hand Hovhannes Kahana – now very old – of the Great Derder family and his friends.

---

* I don't know what this title meant in practice.
† He was elected to the prelacy in 1810 and served until 1825. He was buried in Armash Monastery. Minas Kasabian (Farhad), *Hayere Nikomedio Kavarin Mech*, p. 115 and 117.
‡ The diocese was also known as the diocese of Nicomedia.

Hovhannes Kahana, not accepting the position that Apraham Kahana had achieved, wrote secret letters of protest to the Patriarchate in his usual way, making accusations against Apraham Kahana and the Turkish agha Osman, showing them as obstructing affairs in the village.

In one of his letters of protest, Hovhannes Kahana expressed himself in the following manner about his opponent:

> These two pharaohs, these two demons (Apraham Kahana and Osman Agha) are trying to destroy Bardizag, creating trouble for the poor and incapable.

In another, written in Turkish using Armenian script, he wrote:

> They are destroying Miri Mian Halil Pasha's *vakef*. (He was referring to Bardizag.) They are oppressing the poor people. We have suffered a great deal at the hands of these tyrants. Now we are in no mood to put up with it any longer.

Hovhannes Kahana not only wrote protest letters and sent them post-haste to Constantinople, he also did everything in his power in the village to obstruct any of his enemy's enterprises. He obstructed, for example, the idea put to the villagers that they should own their own boat to transport charcoal, but he wasn't able to prevent its enthusiastic adoption and implementation.[*]

These two able and influential priests, under these circumstances, always remained at loggerheads, and made great efforts to discredit each other and create quarrels and scandal – things which occasionally even happened inside the church.

Hovhannes Kahana was used, when entering the church, to take off his shoes and, holding them in his hand, advance in that unseemly manner through the congregation and take them to the antechamber. It would seem that he was frightened that they would be stolen if he left them in the *kavit* [narthex].

One day he entered the church late, carrying his dirty *yemeni* shoes. The choir was standing in the nave singing a canticle of blessing[†] and the priests, wearing copes, were at their head under Apraham Kahana's supervision. When Apraham Kahana saw Hovhannes Kahana in that scandalous state, he became angry, took several steps forward and, taking the elderly priest by the collar, ordered him to go back to the narthex and leave his shoes there. Hovhannes Kahana, startled by this, lost his balance and fell to the ground. The congregation became very agitated, but no one had the courage to open his mouth against Apraham Kahana. Without doubt, Hovhannes Kahana's conduct wasn't justified, but neither was Apraham Kahana's, at that moment, in church. It was scandalous and reprehensible. As a result, things became worse between the two parties.

---

* See Section 24.
† Orhnoutian sharagan.

Hovhannes Kahana asked the prelate of the diocese, at one point during a cordial conversation, if he would ordain his only son, Deacon Minas, as a kahana. The prelate agreed to make arrangements do so on an appropriate occasion. Hovhannes Kahana repeated his request by letter as the ordination was delayed, basically saying that he was very advanced in years and therefore he had no strength in his legs, adding that he needed an assistant in his dotage. I don't know why, but the prelate never replied to the letter; the suspicion being that Apraham Kahana and the other priests, hating him, had changed the prelate's mind. Angry about this situation, Hovhannes Kahana now began to write letters of protest about the prelate to the Patriarchate, in such terms as:

> A false hermit and silver-lover, the prelate is a person who destroys families. When he is against someone, he works, without a pang of conscience, to destroy his house. He is a very bad person. He has closed four churches in Adabazar...

In the same letter, as proof of his accusations, with a total absence of tact and proportion, he stated that he had heard all this from the locum tenens of the diocese, Stepannos Vartabed Aghavni.

As for the fable of the closing of the churches, the story gained currency from the following. A number of kahanas in Adabazar had created church-like places - under their houses, in yards or in shops – and, collecting their parishioners, held proper masses, evening and morning prayers in them, also collecting money from those present. This was against church law, so Bishop Boghos Karakoch closed them down, strictly forbidding them. Even today those kinds of places seem not to be legitimate and might be considered to be unseemly. Hovhannes Kahana's foolhardy conduct and this new protest was added to his previous activities and were the reason for the increased influence and strength of his opponents, fuelled by his own suspicious and continually restless nature. We'll read, in subsequent pages, of the results of his actions.

34 – Apraham Kahana's position and authority

Apraham Kahana's first concern was for the dilapidated and ruinous condition of the church, because at that time, although it was only 24 years old, it was in danger of collapse.[*] The walls had cracked and the roof, now damaged, let in the rain. He therefore decided in his own mind to demolish it and build a new one with his own hands, 'to immortalise my name.'

Apraham Kahana, as we already know, was the man of the moment, the village elder, *the* village leader. He was Osman Agha's friend and advisor and all the accounts concerning the business of supplying charcoal to the Imperial Ottoman

---

[*] This must have been in 1824.

Mint were in his hands. Deacon Garabed Der-Krikorian, who was his paternal uncle's grandson, was the willing, obedient servant of the all-powerful priest, hoping to retain his patronage to make him a kahana, something he really wanted.

Apraham Kahana was annoyed at Deacon Garabed and his father (Krikor Kahana) for some reason, but this coldness between them didn't last long and Deacon Garabed got his wish. Apraham Kahana had him ordained in 1825 at the beginning of Bishop Stepannos Aghavni's* prelature. He was renamed Garabed Kahana. The newly-ordained priest was, at the same time, appointed the church's *avantabah* [sacrist or trustee] by Apraham Kahana.

Although I have told this story ahead of its chronological time, I shall continue this history in my usual way.

Apraham Kahana not only commanded respect through his authority and rule, but was also a rich businessman. He operated a bakery and grocery shop in the village marketplace run by his sons. The villagers, to please this powerful man, would buy almost everything from them.

The people gradually became discontented with his many deals and his contemptuous and bold ways in the village. For example, people said that during the zenith of his rule, he took over, without any recompense, a piece of fallow common land near the lower threshing floor where the villagers were used to resting and grazing their cattle. Sometime later, one of his sons, Hadji Garabed, who lived in Cairo, Egypt, gave it to one of his relatives. They also said that Apraham Kahana's conduct was not in keeping with his position. He was an aggressive man and, what was worse, he was not averse, when angry, to using language that was not fit for a priest to utter. Many such things have been recorded in the diary kept by Garabed Kahana's father Krikor Kahana,† in which, if there seem to be exaggerations, the probability is that the information he provided cannot be totally wrong. It would appear that Apraham Kahana lacked his father's – Great Hadji Khacher's – noble circumspection.

Krikor Kahana also recounts of him that when the church bell pealed for the morning service, everyone would rush to the church and wait for Apraham Kahana to arrive for it to begin. He was usually a little late. Apraham Kahana was used to entering the church through the door to the St. Stepannos chapel. When the priests and congregation heard that door open and saw him appear in the church, they all got to their feet with great respect and the service would then start.

Slavery has always been the reason for rebellion in all societies. Occasionally Apraham Kahana would turn to the congregation and give a homily or make an announcement, but he never spoke tactfully. He wanted to rule by fear and often

---

* Bishop Stepannos Aghavni Zakarian served as diocesan prelate from 1825-1853. Minas Kasabian (Farhad), *Hayere Nikomedio Kavarin Mech*, p.119.

† See Hagop Der-Hagopian, *Bardizage khadoudig*, pp. 22-28.

said, 'I'm a snake, I'm a snake, and I bite.' In response, Hadji Hovhannes Dzallan, who was from Hovhannes Kahana's family, quietly said, from where he sat, so that only those closest to him could hear, 'I'm *tiriak, tiriak* [anti-venom, anti-venom].'

It is obvious that his rule and position had gone to his head and he gradually accrued powerful enemies who were far more dangerous than Hovhannes Kahana.

Many were also scandalised by his ordination as a kahana. It was often seen that after the morning Mass, instead of retaining the awe inspired by the church and the service, he would go to the *ghonakh* [government building] to visit the Turkish agha as soon as he left the church, where he said what he liked, without taking his position as a priest - and extremely critical public opinion - into account. He often didn't know how to forgive, something that would have been in keeping with his position. If he got angry at someone, he would hand him over to the Turkish agha to be imprisoned and beaten, apparently to teach him a lesson. Unfortunately this, of course, had the opposite effect, making the objects of his wrath rebellious. All these scenarios led to his loss of position in the affections and hearts of the villagers.

Despite these failings, he was a worthy, vigorous and authorititive leader, a notable rather than a servant of God. When he was called to either the prelacy or government office in Izmid, he would remove his priest's hat, replacing it with a fine scarf; he would also wear a silk coat, a garment that would enhance his personal presence.

35 – A border dispute between the villagers of Bardizag and Dongel

A dispute arose over the boundary between the villages of Bardizag and the neighbouring village of Dongel,* with incursions by villagers into each others' territory. One day a large crowd of villagers from Dongel ascended the mountain as far as St. Minas. They erected a flagpole, complete with flag, and declared that the boundary of their village reached that point.

The notables of the two villages, seeing this, got together and began negotiations, hoping to resolve the matter amicably on the basis of the *firmans* [permits] issued to the villages. This was unsuccessful, the resolution of the dispute therefore falling to the government. Special officials were sent by the government to listen to evidence locally, to examine the case and present a report. The Bardizag villagers produced their *firman,* in which the border with Dongel was determined as from the summer dry point called Chinar Dere down to the place towards the sea called the Bostan of the Open Mouth.

---

* Dongel villagers seem to have shared their village at one time with Turks. Minas Kasabian (Farhad), *Hayere Nikomedio Kavarin Mech,* p. 33.

The people of Dongel didn't have a *firman* or didn't want to produce one, but insisted, without proof, on what they thought were their rights, and made noisy attempts to gain them. It was therefore necessary to find witnesses.

The people of Bardizag provided two Turkish witnesses, men between 60 and 70 years of age, knowledgeable of details concerning those areas, including the boundaries previously agreed and implemented in the days of their youth. They bore testimony that what the people of Bardizag said was true, and as proof, showed the government inspectors a line on the ground, saying that it was created using charcoal dust, put there to fix the border between the villages by government inspectors in the past. The ground was dug up at that point in front of the people from Dongel and they did, indeed, find the remains of the line of black charcoal dust.

The government inspectors, on the basis of this testimony and proof, prepared their report and the government, in its turn, gave its decision in favour of the villagers of Bardizag.

I should like, in this connection, to record here an arrangement that was later made about the forests that belonged to the village. The forests had being cleared for a considerable distance around the villages. The charcoal trade, wood cutting and carpentry had used most of the trees, and there was a danger of wiping out the forest resources altogether.

Each village, therefore, with a view to the future, wanted to put the rich forest resources under their care and protection by limiting the amount of woodcutting that took place. To do this, it became the custom to select a considerable expanse of forest and to forbid, for a specific time, any woodcutting in it, giving the trees time to grow. The parts of the forests put under this restraint were called *yasakh* (forbidden belt). Thus Bardizag had its *yasakh*, as did Dongel and Horom Village (Yenikeoy). Paid foresters were appointed who made sure the ban was adhered to. This was a very good arrangement made by the villagers, but timber was stolen and excessive cutting was carried out by ignorant people and by those who needed to, short-sightedly, take enough for their daily needs, despite the ban.

In my time no forests remained around the village. The villagers and new immigrants had used and destroyed them; it was only possible to gather brushwood and bunches of twigs from what was left. Virgin forests were hours away and firewood, charcoal and prepared timber were similarly very expensive by the end.

36 – The billeting of army detachments in the villages

The regular army, known as *nizam* or *nizamie*, would rest in any village along its route, either going to war or returning from one. This happened to Bardizag too.

It was considered to be the villagers' duty, under such circumstances, to empty several houses on the edge of the village and allocate them for the soldiers' temporary use. They also had to provide all the fodder for the troops' horses and pack animals, while any other expenses were paid by the government. Apraham Kahana was used, when this happened, to take off his clerical coat and wear a form of robe called a *balekeser* and to oversee the distribution of fodder so as to prevent any scandal or undisciplined acts by the soldiers. When he saw a soldier annoying a villager, he would intervene and even had the boldness to beat one of them, with the officers' agreement of course, after securing permission.

Ghapan Oghlu's *sipahis* (cavalry) stayed in Bardizag for 40 days in 1832. They utilised the lower threshing floors as their cavalry exercise area and would carry out military exercises there during specific hours every day. The villagers only provided them with temporary quarters and firewood.

37 – Preparation of building materials for the church

I have referred to Apraham Kahana's wish to build the new church with his own hands in previous pages.[*] To this end he began to have bricks and stone stockpiled and lime prepared. But during that period (the 1820s) the freedom of Greece was ensured with the intervention of the European powers[†] and, because of the political climate, the government of Sultan Mahmoud didn't look at Christian minorities in the empire with favour. Permission to build schools and churches was therefore denied for a time. It was at this juncture that the Armenian Patriarch of Constantinople, Archbishop Garabed, sent an encyclical to all his people in which he declared that the Greeks and the *voivodas* of Oulah Boughdani (Romania) had revolted against the Ottoman government and advised the people to adopt a careful and cautious stance, not to cultivate relations with foreigners, and not invite them into their homes.

Even in my day a copy of this encyclical was kept in the Khacherians' (Hadji Apraham's) house, but they destroyed it with others papers during the 1896 persecution.

It was impossible to obtain a permit to build a church under these conditions and the materials collected by Apraham Kahana were lost or destroyed over the years thanks to lack of care and attention.

38 – Prelate Archbishop Boghos Karakoch's church reforms

Archbishop Boghos Karakoch was an alert and robust shepherd of his flock, and a zealous and demanding churchman.[‡] The Izmit prelacy and the work of shepherding his flock were both subject to great changes during his tenure. Before his time, prelates would make diocesan visits perhaps once a year to their scattered flock, not with the

---

* See Section 34.

† Greece achieved its independence in 1826.

‡ He became diocesan prelate in 1810 and served as such until 1825. Minas Kasabian (Farhad), *Hayere Nikomedio Kavarin Mech*, p. 115.

thought of giving satisfaction to its spiritual needs, but with the wish to collect their profits. These accrued from the fruit harvest, the souls of the dead, the fees for weddings and engagements and so forth. On these occasions they would recite memorised and appropriate sermons and, having secured what they wanted, move on.

Archbishop Boghos didn't act like that. With his frequent visits, he also displayed concern and care to make important church reforms. He made his first visit to Bardizag in August 1813, remaining in the village until the feast day of St. James of Nisibis.[*] He regularly preached, examined the progress of community affairs and the clergy, organised a choir, and began baptism and death registers (December 15, 1813). He gave the following form to the register of baptisms: to record, in a special book, the name of the baptised infant and the names and surnames of the father and godfather. He strictly ordered the priests to record every baptism without fail, threatening to punish the miscreants if this was not carried out properly.

Naturally that register didn't have the expected order and accuracy in the early days; the priests would record the baptisms in notebooks of their own making, and even on scraps of paper. Some priests only recorded baptisms in their parish, without any system or order, so there were cases when records were not kept or were even lost.

In 1825, when Garabed Kahana Der-Krikorian was ordained a kahana by the diocesan prelate Bishop Stepannos Aghavni, he created a special book made of large, clean sheets of paper called 'Osmanli', bound in a stout leather cover. He wrote a good preface in classical Armenian on the first page and began to make entries regularly. He collected all the previously poorly made and kept notebooks and records, and entered them, in order, in the book he had created. He used the Armenian era dating system[†] until the date of his ordination. After that he continued to religiously compile the records during the whole of the time he was a priest adding, to the basic information, the month and day of baptism and the name of the officiating priest, thus giving the records a whole new appearance.

Krikor Kahana Somoundjian continued this work after Garabed Kahana's death, was followed by Mesrob Kahana Simonian and finally by Nerses Kahana Balabanian.

A certain indifferent attitude appeared among the priests with regard to the records after a time. It would appear that each assumed that the other would keep the necessary records and they began to make one of the assistant teachers of the day create them: first Deacon Nazaret Geloyian, then Deacon Krikor Mkhalian[‡] and finally Hovhannes Mkhalian (later Garabed Kahana Mkhalian).

---

[*] This is celebrated in December.
[†] The Armenian is 551 years behind the current system used throughout the world. Thus the Armenian era of 1225 equates to 1826 (1225 + 551 = 1826).
[‡] The author's paternal uncle.

The records were then kept by the *avak kahana* [leading priest] Hovhannes Kahana Megrian for a whole year (1865). At that point the register created by Garabed Kahana became full, and a new one was started, maintained by Garabed Kahana Mkhalian beginning in January 1866.

39 – The newly ordained kahanas who served in the third church

We saw, in previous pages, that when the building of the third church was completed,* there were only four priests left from those previously ordained. They were Hovhannes Kahana, Pilibbos Kahana, Apraham Kahana and Sarkis Kahana. Of those four, Hovhannes Kahana and Sarkis Kahana were very old, leaving only two young priests who were still vigorous: Apraham Kahana and Pilibbos Kahana. Seeing this, two candidates were chosen at Apraham Kahana's suggestion and according to his wishes, one being his cousin† and the other the son of Demirdji Takvor. The latter was a simple skilled worker who, pulling threads, made saddles and looked after horses.

Archbishop Boghos Karakoch was invited to Bardizag to perform the ordination of these two candidates. He interviewed them*u*‡ Minas and the other, Krikor Kahana's son, *Diratsou* Garabed. It would appear that this time Hovhannes Kahana's state and his advanced age moved both; one was the son of a notable, well dressed and neat, the other a simple villager in short drawers, unclad legs and bare feet. The prelate was amazed and said, 'Who is this with bare legs that is going to be a priest?'** But he endorsed their election and ordained them both. He called the first Krikor Kahana, and the second Kevork Kahana. This took place in 1815. The two new priests began their ministry after their 40-day retreat.††

Hovhannes Kahana, seeing that his request for his son to be ordained was without result and that others were ordained instead, became enraged and began to write complaints about the two newly ordained priests to various places. He finally lost all proportion when Sarkis Kahana's son Mardiros and one of the Kardeshians (whose baptismal name I've not been able to ascertain) were ordained as deacons and were thus future candidates for the priesthood. They were to perform deacon's duties in church for five years. Before the term was up, however, Sarkis Kahana and Hovhannes Kahana were no longer capable of performing their ministries. The two were therefore ordained priests by Bishop Stepannos Aghavni, who had been

---

* See Section 27.
† His father's brother's son.
‡ *Diratsou* was a title meaning 'lord to be' and used for deacons, but it was also used, in those days, as an honorific title.
** Archbishop Karakoch said this in Turkish as he was from Kayseri.
†† Monks and priests of the Armenian Apostolic Church go into seclusion for forty days immediately after ordination.

ordered to do so by the prelate. This was in 1820. Mardiros became Sahag Kahana, and Deacon Kardeshian became Nerses Kahana. Two new deacons were also ordained at this time, for a period of four years. Hovhannes Kahana's son *Diratsou* Minas and the other, Krikor Kahana's son, *Diratsou* Garabed. It would appear that this time Hovhannes Kahana's state and his advanced age moved the pity of his enemies and the past was forgotten.

Hovhannes Kahana died shortly after this ordination, his life having been like a stormy sea. But he didn't die wanting; he saw his son ordained deacon and it is probable that he was laid to finally rest, as Bishop Aghavni wrote in one of his diary entries, in Armash.

But Deacon Minas Der-Hovhannesian only served as a deacon for two years. He suddenly left his office and resigned from his candidacy as a future priest. The following reasons were given for his actions: it was said that he would occasionally become dumb due to a physical abnormality when he was reading aloud and his friend, Deacon Garabed, would laugh at him. Apparently annoyed and unnerved, he decided to resign from his deaconship. This seems to me to be a childish way to come to a decision. People also said that he apparently became cold towards the position of a priest thanks to the things that happened to his father and the enmity and persecution that existed. He already knew that when he was ordained a deacon. This too doesn't seem like a valid reason for such a decision. It is probable that his mood changed as his family and his father were in an uneasy situation in which he was involved. The reality was that the many years of ministry in the Great Derder family ended with Deacon Minas' resignation.

I related the facts about Deacon Garabed's ordination which took place in 1825 in previous pages,[*] during the final years of Apraham Kahana's rule.

40 – New attempts at hermit-like living. The founding of the Manoushag pilgrimage site

People said that it was about this time one of the Mavi Goudjouk clan, the son of Varteres Goudjouk, by trade a *ghatardji* [carter] and a good, devout person, had visions every day. He was invited to lead a hermit's life. Listening to those heavenly voices, he left his trade and village and followed in the footsteps of the first hermits, going to the Monastery of Gdouts.[†] He was ordained a monk there, being given the

---

[*] See Section 34.
[†] Situated on Lake Van. See also Section 26.

name Hovhannes Vartabed, later being consecrated with the dignity of *koryebisgobos* [suffragan bishop]. Twenty years later he returned to Bardizag.*

The mountain known as Ghodja Beroun is about three hours away to the west of Bardizag. Bishop Hovhannes established his hermitage there, giving it the name Manoushag [Violet] and continuing his monastic existence. He collected students around him who took up his lifestyle.

At that time no one lived in the place called Manoushag; it was a high place covered with age-old trees and the remains of ancient Christian habitations and churches, cross stones and foundations. There was an ancient fountain which gushed from the earth over a marble lip. Bishop Hovhannes called that fountain Lousaghpiur [Fountain of Light]; it was called *Tash Delen Su* by the Turks.

Based on a biography of Bishop Hovhannes,† that good, pious and uneducated peasant churchman may be presented as one who, affected by the example of the Saps family's hermit-like living, went to Gdouts many years after them. He served as a lay brother there, then he was ordained a *vartabed* [monk] and then a bishop in the monastery of the Catholicos of Aghatmar.‡ He had manuscripts transcribed for him while he was in Aghtamar: sermons, *sharagans* [canticles] and church books. Some of them remained in the Bardizag church library, while the remainder were given away or sold after his death by his brother Hagop, apparently in accordance with instructions in his will.

Bishop Hovhannes came to Bardizag with these books, dressed in a hair shirt like a hermit and wandered, for a time, in the nearby forests. Then he built himself a hut that was known as *Vartabedin Khoutse* [the priests' hut] even until my day, in the forest above St. Minas. He lived there, spending his time singing psalms, praying and fasting. For that reason the height that the hut was built on quickly became a place of veneration in the eyes of devout people, and the place and trees sacred;

---

* Another person from Bardizag is recalled alongside Bishop Hovhannes. He was the monk Sarkis from the Baboukh clan. It would appear that he too was ordained at Gdouts Monastery, and for a time ran the prelacy of the town of Van or was its locum tenens. He later returned to Bardizag where he died in 1829. His tombstone could still be seen in my day in the cemetery. Another person, Bishop Hovhannes' cousin (paternal uncle's son), the monk Garabed, lived for a time in Bardizag and then returned to Gdouts where he died. A third, also from the bishop's clan, was the monk Kevork, who died in Rodosto. (Author's note)

† This biography was written by one of his followers, Deacon Boghos, son of Topal Simon of Ovadjek, who signed the work as 'The meek Deacon Boghos Simonian'. This notebook was found, later, in Ghazig Sarkis' house in Bardizag. (Author's note)

‡ The Catholicosate of Aghtamar was located on the island of the same name in Lake Van. It ended with the death of the last catholicos of that title, Khachadour III Chiroyian (reigned from 1864-1895), although the monastery continued its existence until about April 1915, when the monks on the island were massacred.

mutilation of the trees was considered a great sin. People said that Donba Mardiros dared to cut down one or two of the trees, sometime after the bishop had abandoned the place, and took them to his house. God punished him: becoming ill, he died soon after. Bishop Hovhannes was surrounded by students and followers there and with whom he created a religious brotherhood.

Bishop Hovhannes left his hut after a time and went, with the same aim, to the place where he used to have visions in his youth – the mountain called Ghodja Beroun (Manoushag). He established his new pilgrimage site there, which I referred to at the beginning of this section. He determined the area of a church, foundations were excavated, crosses were buried in them in the name of the twelve Apostles, and a modest building was erected there as a church and hermitage.

It was not long before this new pilgrimage site and the hermit bishop became well known everywhere, and a pilgrimage movement of devout people began. The sick from the surrounding villages were brought there in the hope of healing; some people were cured and its fame spread far and wide as a holy site of miraculous healing.

The bishop determined the site's pilgrimage day as the Sunday after Assumption,* procured an icon of the Virgin Mary and put it in the church and called it 'The Church of the Holy Mother of God'.

The fame of this new pilgrimage site gradually spread further afield – as far as Biledjik and Broussa (Boursa). People would go in great numbers, a few days before the Sunday after Assumption, to 'St Manoushag, the healing St. Manoushag' with devout longing. Minstrels would create songs about it which would then be sung by everyone, and joyful expectations would increase. Animals would be sacrificed at the site and *madagh* [the sacrificial meal for all] prepared. It was a time of joy and festivity. There were six or seven fountains in the vicinity, which became sacred, bearing the names of great church saints, such as St. Garabed, St. Nicholas etc.

The monks of the brotherhood of the Armash *Charkhapan* [Evil-slaying] Monastery of the Holy Mother of God became angry as a result of all this. The stream of pilgrims to the monastery began to go elsewhere. A diocesan general assembly was convened in the Izmid prelacy with the assistance of the notables and kahanas of the diocese, during which it was decided to demolish the new Manoushag pilgrimage site as a sham and false establishment.

A group of delegates was sent to Manoushag for that purpose, accompanied by representatives from Bardizag – both kahanas and notables. The people from Bardizag became angry at the decision made and reproached the representatives from their village. The delegation, however, calmly continued to the site, demolished the pitiful chapel, dug up the foundations, removed the crosses and turned the result of Bishop Hovhannes' years of toil into ruins. The majority of the

---

* Usually about the third Sunday in August.

people of Bardizag, however, remained firm in their devotion and zeal towards the new pilgrimage site and continued to visit it every year with a greater emphasis. That was the expression of the strength of their faith.

The prelacy, seeing this, sent a monk from Broussa (Bursa) named Hagop Vartabed to Bardizag to talk to the people there and persuade them to resign from their fervent stand in favour of Manoushag. Hagop Vartabed's mission was a failure.[*] The people loved their hermit monk who, having descended from the mountain, lived in his brother's house in the village.

There were also opponents of the bishop in Bardizag, who ridiculed him and called him 'false hermit, deceitful, cross-stealer' etc. Deacon Hagop Bodourian was the main opponent, later to become a kahana under the name of Nerses Kahana Balabanian. This man, taking the side of the notables opposed to Manoushag, tried to serve his own ends,[†] which he did, by becoming a kahana.

The people, however, despite all these persecutions and insults, would seem to have been even more against those who perpetrated them, remaining firm in their belief in the Manoushag pilgrimage site. The situation became even worse and took on a serious aspect; the Patriarchate was informed by letter, with Bishop Hovahannes being accused of being the sole reason for the unrest. He was called to Constantinople, where a written promise was extracted from him, over his signature, to resign from his previous conduct and he returned to Bardizag. A patriarchal encyclical was also sent to the village, presenting the bishop's written undertaking and, at the same time, calling him 'the deceitful, false hermit', wanting, in this way, to warn the people of Bardizag not to follow him.

A copy of that encyclical was kept in the church's library. At the same time another copy was sent, in error, to the village of Bardizag in Sepastia (Sivas), due to the two villages having the same name.

The people of the village remained even more firmly fixed in their belief and the Patriarchate's intervention and advice was considered to be of no importance.

Bishop Giragos,[‡] the Armenian Patriarch of Jerusalem of the time was at the Monastery of Armash at this time. He heard about Bishop Hovhannes and what had occurred and, on his way back to Constantinople, went to Bardizag and expressed the wish to see him. Bishop Hovhannes declined. A deacon from Jerusalem

---

[*] Especially when the monk, in his effort to persuade the people, made scandalous and impious announcements (in Turkish) during his sermons from the church's altar saying, for example, 'The Holy Mother of God had such long legs that one foot was on Armash mountain and the other on Memenshe mountain.' As a result of these tactless and disgraceful words, the people of the village, instead of being convinced, became angrier and more firmly fixed in their belief. (Author's note)

[†] The words used here are: 'to dye the cloth he wove'.

[‡] Armenian Patriarch of Jerusalem from 1846-1850.

accompanied Bishop Giragos, and would, years later, become the famous Patriarch, first of Constantinople, then of Jerusalem, named Haroutiun Vehabedian.[*]

Garabed Kahana Der-Krikorian was the head of the faction opposed to Bishop Hovhannes in Bardizag, probably because of his partiality for the Monastery of Armash. I have mentioned, in connection with this, the deacon named Hagop Balabanian (Bodourian). He was a teacher in the Bardizag community school and a lackey of two of the notables of the day – Garabed Agha Mgerian and Garabed Kahana. This individual showed himself to be on the bishop's side for a time. He often visited his house. The bishop innocently believed what the man said and wished, if he accepted to do so, for the visitor to write the history of the Manoushag brotherhood. Bodourian, to become the darling of the anti-bishop faction, told Garabed Kahana what had been said. The bishop heard about the trap that was set for him, took no further interest in the man and dismissed him from his presence.

When it proved impossible to calm the people of Bardizag concerning the Manoushag brotherhood,[†] the familiarity enjoyed by the deacon Hagop was used as the basis of accusations that the bishop was intransigent and rebellious – directly opposing the agreement he had made. People in the Patriarchate, the brotherhood of the Monastery of Armash and his opponents in both Bardizag and the province approached the diocesan prelate to write to the Patriarchate that the bishop wasn't abiding by his agreement and that his presence in Bardizag was a permanent reason for unrest.

At this, the Patriarchate approached the government and obtained an imperial order for exile against the bishop.[‡]

The bishop, who had aged and suffered through the persecution he had been subjected to, took the road to exile by land during the winter of 1839, to Kayseri. After a dreadful journey full of distress and injustice, he reached there in a state of exhaustion and illness. The local Armenian population gave him a very warm welcome and looked after him with all the care they could muster. Unfortunately, wasted by the troubles he had suffered, his age and exhaustion, he didn't live for very long. He died a few days after his arrival and was buried in the courtyard of the church in Kayseri, where his tomb became a place of veneration, like a shrine.

The bishop's exile didn't achieve its aim. The people of Bardizag became even angrier and their devotion to Manoushag was given greater emphasis. Pilgrimages still took place as usual. The pilgrims themselves sang the evening and morning

---

[*] Armenian Patriarch of Constantinople 1885-1888, then of Jerusalem from 1888-1910.

[†] The word used here is *oukhd*. This can mean vow, devotion, pact, alliance, covenant, religious ceremony, congregation or brotherhood (in eccliastical terms), pilgrimage, order, treaty or clergy. I have assumed 'brotherhood'.

[‡] His place of exile was designated as St. Garabed Monastery, Kayseri. Minas Kasabian (Farhad), *Hayere Nikomedio Kavarin Mech*, p. 97.

services, singing 'Lord, have mercy...' Chopdji, Kemelo Garabed and Deacon Mgerdich, who were some of the minstrels of the day, created songs in praise of Manoushag.

Deacon Mgerdich's song was in Armenian, in which he described the trials and tribulations of the bishop's exile. Kemelo Garabed's creation was also in Armenian and was in praise of Manoushag. Each of the stanzas ended with:

Ghoul Garabed sang praise,

And the praise was for the name of St. Manoushag.

When the notables and priests noted that the people still went to Manoushag, they decided to send their own priest there on its feast day, taking heed that it was not seemly for devotions to be made without a priest. From then on, on the seventh day after Assumption (in August), it was the custom for a priest to be sent to Manoushag, to conduct morning and evening worship and to display the relics there.

The picture of the Holy Mother of God was brought from the bishop's brother's house on these occasions and taken to Manoushag. People would set up an altar there, putting the picture at the centre, and sing psalms and 'Lord, have mercy'. If the pilgrims wanted it, the relics were displayed, with vows being made at Lousaghpiur, with candles being lit and prayers offered. On these occasions too, the faithful would put their contributions on the plates set up for the purpose; they provided a considerable sum which would be brought to the village and divided among all the priests. The leading priest Garabed Kahana also took his share, even though he had persecuted the bishop so much at the time.

These events concerning Bishop Hovhannes and Manoushag lasted for over half a century. They lasted from the days of Apraham Kahana's rule until that of Garabed Agha Mgerian and Garabed Kahana Der-Krikorian's assumption of the role of *avakerets* [leading priest]. I thought it best to insert the whole history here.[*] I will be able, in the following sections, to return to the subject of pilgrimages to Manoushag that took place in my day.

---

[*] Manoushag village, which sprang up around the pilgrimage site and chapel, was founded after 1830. It had about 30 houses and was split into 4 sections: (1) *Manoushag's Church section*, (2) the *Chapel section* about a quarter of an hour's walk to the east, (3) the *Soubatoum section* half an hour's walk to the south and (4) *Almasou*, about one hour away. There were five families that settled there first: the Zadigians, Keshishians and Ichmezians from the villages of Tepe and Sosadja about five hours from Ordou. 15 further families arrived the following year: the Avedisians, Dertliyians and Minasians from the same villages and from Chamashe. The first kahana ordained from among them was Krikor Kahana Avedisian, well known as a hunter. Minas Kasabian (Farhad), *Hayere Nikomedio Kavarin Mech*, p. 97.

41 – The construction of the old houses in Bardizag, their parts and furnishings etc.

1. Houses

A house in Bardizag that had been built before 1800 was usually constructed of clay bricks dried in the sun called *kepidj*. It had thick walls right up to roof level. The roof itself was made of lumber and planks, covered with tiles, with eaves that projected well beyond the walls, allowing water to drip to the ground away from the outer sides of the foundations.

The important part of the house was the room containing the oven (*odjakh*) to which the name *nerse* [inside] was given. If this room faced the street, then it would have one large window; if not, then the roof would be pierced in several places and bell-shaped glass covers (called *depe djami*) placed over them, to allow light to enter. These skylights would be obscured by snow in winter and it would then be necessary to light the room with lamps.

A lamp was a vessel made of a block of clay or sheet metal (called a *sadj*) which was filled with linseed or olive oil, with one sharp end (the beak) holding the wick, the lower end of which was in the oil. When it was necessary to light the lamp, the housewife would take a smouldering piece of wood from the fire, blow on it with all her might until it burst into flame, then bring it to the lamp and light the wick. The lamp would be hung over the door of the stove (oven), using a nail hammered into the wall so that the smoke from it would go up the chimney, otherwise it would fill the room and make it impossible to breathe.

When the oven had to be lit, the housewife would rake any smouldering coals left in it under the soot, place them on its floor and add some dried leaves or other kindling on top. Then getting down on her knees, she would blow on the coals, until the kindling caught light. She would then carefully add more kindling and, when it was all well alight, add thicker pieces of wood, piled up. When the fire had really taken hold, she would put long lengths of wood in the stove, with their tops leaning against the back wall and the lower ends in the fire itself. This allowed them to gradually dry and burn from the bottom upwards.

The family would sit in a semicircle around the door to the oven to get warm on cold days. Occasionally a thick, hardwood log would be added to burn slowly, gradually becoming one large burning mass. At the same time a container holding the soup or meal would be cooked in the corner of the oven on a tripod made of iron, with a part of the fire moved under it.

Open areas outside this 'inside' room were called *oda*s, which, unlike the 'inside room' were not protected by walls on every side: one side would be open. The 'inside' room was where the family lived; it was there that they sat, received guests, food was cooked, and the place they slept, especially in cold weather.

The floor of the 'inside' room would be covered with mats or rugs in winter and there would be flat woollen mattress-like seats with hard pillows against the walls to lean on. The parcels containing the beds would be piled up in one corner and would be undone and spread out on the floor next to one another when it was time to sleep. The bed, coverlet and pillow were generally filled with wool. At bedtime, everyone, old or young, would remove their outer clothing and pile it up next to their beds and bury themselves in their bedding in only their white underclothes.

During the beautiful summer weather the family would use one of the outer rooms (one of the *oda*s) to live and sleep in, where it was cool and airy. In those days there were no bugs but there were parasites that appeared in lumber and timber imported from Europe. There were, however, fleas and lice, although the people of Bardizag had early followed the rules of cleanliness, with the majority of houses being free from them. The fleas, however, with their swift and light movements and ability to jump would continue to make those asleep uncomfortable, especially in summer.

Water was plentiful in Bardizag, drawn from a reliable and clean stream or fountain, but its transport from the source to the home was quite heavy and tiring work for the women and girls. It was the custom for everyone, old or young, having completed their daily tasks, to wash their feet in cold water in winter and summer; this was especially true of the little ones, who mostly wandered about in the streets with bare feet, as did older people when they were working. They took a bath in hot water in a wooden tub once a week in the house yard – there was no bath house in those days – often making its floor wet and creating a permanently damp area within the house, as the sun never reached it to dry it out.

House toilet facilities were very poorly arranged. They were either behind or at the side of the house and far from public view, long and narrow passages, with wooden boards for a floor, one of which had circular or triangular holes cut in it, set over a channel, without any piping. One could see the channel through the holes. The holes were the seats on which the family members relieved themselves in a disgraceful, unsuitable manner. It was impossible to keep the toilet seats (the board) clean; urine would wet the edges of the holes and the wood would rot, causing accidents. The whole thing stank. They would often be fouled by excrement and although they were cleaned several times a day, they were dirty, irritating and noisome.

Human waste would pile up for days and months in the narrow streets and in every corner of the village and smelled terribly. The dreadful stench often affected passers-by. The atmosphere in the houses would not always remain fresh, and there was the constant worry that a burst of heavy rain would carry the sewage into the houses themselves. Often the men, during those storms, would wear sacks on their heads, and using spades, assist the streams of rainwater to complete the work of cleansing the village.

2. Clothing

The clothes the people of the village wore in those days and what they were made of were simple and the result of the work the women did. The main clothes were made from linen made from flax. The women would reap it from the flax fields, separate the threads from the stems, weave them using simple hand tools and make cloth using pit looms. A quantity of the cloth produced would be dyed black, while some would be left in its natural state (white). The white cloth was used to make underclothes for both men and women, while the black dyed cloth was used for outer clothing.

The clothes both sexes wore were very similar. Underclothes comprised an undershirt that reached the knees and a pair of drawers. Outer clothing consisted of a blue or black pair of trousers and a shirt called a *zeboun*, the ensemble being completed by a white woollen belt around the middle made by the women and which was only worn by the men. The drawers and trousers were made like wide sacks, from the waist to the feet, with the bottom sewn and the corners open for the legs to go through. The trousers had a drawstring at the top. The clothes would be gathered in the trousers and the whole secured by the trouser drawstring. The only difference between the trousers the men and women wore was that the top of women's trousers were higher and, because they were wide, would form pleats as the drawstring was pulled tight. The men's was shorter, with the waist cut lower and the bottom, extending from the knees to the ankles, gradually grew narrower, tight to the legs. Grown men, however, often wore trousers like those of the women. The shirt *(zeboun)* would extend below the waist, and would open in the centre, being held closed by a tie. A woollen coat *(aba)* would also be worn in winter when it was cold.

Earlier, elderly women could be seen wearing a different outer costume, beginning from the shoulders; a cassock-lik coat *(barecod)* with sleeves, open from top to bottom, that was worn and closed at the waist with a scarf. This *barecod* had slashes in its bottom half, allowing the edges of the white material the shirt was made of to be seen near the feet.

The men wore felt caps or a fez, around which either a piece of material *(chalma)* or a folded veil *(yazma)* would be wound. Before this some men wore turbans. The women had a form of headcovering: the head covered with a veil *(yazma)*. Over this a second veil was worn, long enough to cover both cheeks and the ears, with only the eyes and nose being left uncovered. The women also did their long hair into many plaits, like snakes, sometimes only making one or two.

3. Living

Tables or chairs weren't used when a meal was eaten. A large square tablecloth *(seni bezi)* would be spread out on the floor of the 'inside' room, in front of the door to the oven. The family elder would sit at the right-hand corner of the oven, at one end of the cloth, in the place of honour. The oldest boys would be next to him, then the girls, next to the lady of the house. They would all sit cross-legged in their places, and the women who had married into the family would sit near their mother-in-law (sometimes they would kneel, rather than sit, as a sign of respect), with the children near them or on their laps. The bread would be cut into long strips by either the father or eldest son and would be distributed along the edges of the cloth, which would be pulled over the knees of each person. Then the large, deep bowl made of earthenware or copper containing the soup would then be placed at the centre of the cloth. Everyone would use the spoon previously placed before them to spoon the soup into their mouths with the bread that had been dipped in it, with the greatest appetite. They would occasionally chew a portion of fresh or dried onion to improve the taste. Soup was the main and everyday meal.

The meal would begin and end with the Lord's Prayer, originally recited by the house elder, but later relegated to one of the children of the house. The only implements used at the table were wooden spoons, a bread knife and a cloth (towel) for wiping the hands. Fish, meat and other foods were eaten with the fingers, using the bread as a fork. There was also a pitcher full of water to drink at the table, brought to the lips and drunk from directly, until the individual had drunk his fill.

The soup was generally made with cracked wheat *(bulghour)* and dumplings which were cooked with clarified butter or sheep's tail fat. The lady of the house would cook the soup early in the day and it would be brought to the table when everyone was seated. In the evening too it would be brought in to be eaten with pieces of bread broken into it.

A piece of bread would be chewed on at midday, without sitting down for a meal. It was either dry or accompanied by a piece of salted cheese and some fish and a few olives.

In those days various special dishes for guests or on festival days consisted of spit-roasted meat, broth, chicken, eggs in oil, fresh fish either fried or roasted, and various kinds of pastries that were considered to be foods suitable for fasting days.

When guests were present only the grown men would eat together, the women and children eating after the guests finished their meal. The lady of the house, her daughters-in-law and daughters served the guest table, often under the envious eyes of the children, who would see tasty and steaming dishes brought in.

Oghi - and occasionally wine - was always on the table, reserved for the grown men and being accompanied by various pickles.

There were no curtains at any window; in the winter they were hung with cloths or rugs. The windows, however, had external shutters which were shut against the sun and, in the evening, against the cold wind.

The water from the fountains flowed down to the village through earthenware pipes that kept the water clean and cool as they were buried quite deeply underground. The women, girls and daughters-in-law brought water from the fountains every day in earthenware containers *(gelibolou)* balanced on their hips. Each container held about 12-15 *okhas* of water. This was exhausting, heavy work for them.

42 – Village weddings in olden times

Weddings in the village in those days took place in a very rough and unseemly manner. The well-to-do and rich, to enliven the joyful wedding festivities, would hire musicians to play drums and wind instruments *(zournas)*. During weddings the streets, the bride's house – in fact the whole village – would be the stage for primitive music.

There was also a strange custom in those days. On the Sunday of the wedding, the groom's friends would assemble in his house, take him to a dark corner away from prying eyes, strip him of all his clothes and solemnly, with singing and great excitement, bathe and dress him in his wedding attire that had already been blessed. In my day the bathing had been abolished, with his friends only getting his wedding clothes and dressing him.

The wedding clothes would be blessed in the groom's house on Sunday during the day or in the evening. The opportunity was taken, at this time, to crown the groom's head with a ridiculous, enormous turban.

The groom and his people would go to the bride's house at dawn on the Monday morning to fetch her. The bride would be heavily veiled, then seated on the back of a horse and taken to the church. A crowd of small boys would, at that point, run around the village streets and congratulate any man they saw. They called these boys *lapoustag* or *nabastag* [rabbits].

The groom's turban would be fringed with delicate metalised ribbons, strings of raisins and Egyptian corn. He would carry a sword, as did the godfather. The bride was enmeshed and buried within her dense veil and had a sort of hat on. Garabed Kahana couldn't remember what it was called.

The bride would be taken off the horse when the procession reached the church door and two women, each taking one arm, would lead her inside, as it was impossible for her to see anything under her veil.

The wedding ceremony took place in church, on the Monday morning, without the usual Mass. Then the priest and choir singing *sharagans* [canticles or hymns], leading the bride and groom, would go to the groom's house in procession. When the wedding procession arrived in front of the house, the officiating kahana, taking the bride's, groom's and godmother's hands, would dance a *shourchbar* [circle dance] of three complete circles, singing at the same time the canticle 'King, coming to Your world'. Garabed Kahana Mkhalian, stated, concerning his own wedding:

> That custom still existed when I was married. My groom's dance was led by the senior priest, Garabed Kahana Der-Krikorian.

It was usual to pin the groom's and godfather's shoulders with a sort of decorated handkerchief (called a *chevre*) until the Wednesday after the wedding ceremony, to distinguish them from ordinary people. I think the crown was taken down[*] on the Monday. The circlet (*narod*)[†] would be stuffed into the groom's turban, with a part of it showing below it.

After the crown has been taken down, the groom, godfather and friends would visit the groom's close relatives' homes. Dishes containing various pastries and, in the centre, a boiled chicken would be set before them on tables. They were all gathered up and brought to the groom's house, carried on the groom's friends' heads. The relatives would also send packets of dried foodstuffs – cracked wheat, aubergines, beans, chickpeas, lentils etc. - to the groom's house.

Wine was plentiful at weddings; *cherchoug* (diluted) oghi would also be available, although this was only for old people. Pure, undiluted wine from the villages was drunk by everyone present using gourds or copper vessels, all of which had to be submerged in buckets filled of wine to be filled. Many people would get drunk, make merry, dance and sing songs in Armenian and Turkish, often taking on the laughable appearance of masked people at *Paregentan*.

When dancing began, someone from the group of dancers would go to the head of the group to lead it in a line, determining the movements according to the song being sung and in time to the beat. The (now) leader would declaim the first line of the song, which would be repeated by the dancing group. Gradually the excitement would increase, upward leaps would be made by the dancers, and the song would be sung with greater emphasis, more loudly and joyfully. I can't remember the words of the songs that were sung then, but I do remember one line from one of them – 'Destroy the giant's stone bridge, oh, oh!'

In those days women would wear *diudiuk pacha* (narrow trousers – *shalvars*) and a long coat (*entari*) and hid their heads, cheeks and chins with two pieces of cloth. The bride's headdress was more complicated: her face and cheeks, mouth and chin were covered with a veil (*yashmakh*), over which a veil was added, made of red Bitlis linen which completely closed her mouth, leaving only her eyes and nose exposed. Women would also dance and sing silly songs in Turkish with stanzas like 'I lost my horse and am now tired', often laced with scandalous and immodest expressions.

If a man or woman was seen in a scandalous situation, an Armenian or Turkish song would be made up about them and sung at social gatherings even in my time.

I mentioned the use of musical instruments at weddings, but more seemly and upper class weddings would invite a minstrel with an *indje saz*[‡] to entertain the great and the good of the village and the Turkish aghas in the best - and best furnished - room in the house. They would listen to the minstrel with great attention and

---

[*] This is the literal translation of *bsage var arnel*.
[†] I have used the word 'circlet' here, in lieu of a better definition of *narod*. It could have been a sort of crown, ribbon, headdress etc.
[‡] A stringed instrument a little like a mandolin, but with a very long neck.

admiration, who would play and, at the same time, harmoniously recite *semayis*, *divanis*, *ghazels* and *manis*,* or tell stories about *Ashugh* (Minstrel) Gharib.

Minstrels with *indje sazes* were rare after 1850 and a wandering minstrel would only occasionally appear in Bardizag. He would sing and play songs created by others or by him, while seated in a corner of a coffee house. When he had finished, money would be collected from the men present† and given to him as his reward.

There was also, at weddings, the custom of 'playing' with the bride, something that now seems somewhat abnormal. The bride's neighbours and relatives would arrange to meet outside the bride's house for this purpose. The bride, with a single female friend or relative (or more), would dance in their presence. Those present would, on this occasion, give the bride money and other gifts.

The groom's friends would also go to the bride's house to do the same. There the bride would dance in front of the groom and his friends as well as with the groom, his friends and other engaged couples. Every young man, on these occasions, would give his fiancée 5-10 *kurush*, and half or one *kurush* to each of her friends.

The custom of taking the dowry (*sachou, ojid*) to the bride and groom by friends, relations and neighbours took place during the days following the wedding. On this occasion there would be a specific individual to whom the title *karoz*‡ was given, who held each proffered gift in his hand, showed it to those present, stated the giver's name and adding, 'He hasn't eaten, nor has he drunk, but has given this gift to the bride and groom...' Then he would end by expressing good wishes to the donor.

The custom was different to this in earlier times. The dowry bringers with their gifts would be welcomed at the door of the wedding house by the bride and groom and godfather. The three of them would then take the gifts on their shoulders if the gift was something made of cloth or carry it in their hands and, in that state, would do a small dance, as a mark of respect for the donors.

Most of these customs ended after 1850, but traces of them remained, in an improved form.**

The wedding menu, in those olden days, would have been very interesting for us, in terms of knowing contemporary customs. Among them was the officially much-

---

* Different styles of poetry.
† Women never went to coffee houses.
‡ The word means sermon.
** It should be noted that there was a set of rules drawn up in 1864 by the village council and endorsed by the prelate of the time concerning behaviour and customs at engagements and weddings. It was first published in the Armash Monastery journal *Huis Troashag Haireniats* [Hope, the flag of our homeland] No 5. Minas Kasabian (Farhad), *Hayere Nikomedio Kavarin Mech*, p. 283. The text is given in Hagop Der Hagopian, *Bardizage khadoudig*, pp. 421-423. The translation of these rules appears in the Appendix as Document No. 2.

respected *dolma* (vegetables stuffed with ground meat and rice etc). This was known as 'meat filled dolma'. If it was made using olive oil (and therefore without meat) it was called 'false dolma'. The women neighbours would get together to make the dish days before the wedding, something that was considered to be an honour for each individual. A second important dish was meat and onions, eaten with large salted olives. 'Tub cheese' was later added to this. Each guest at the table would also be given a fresh leek as a spice to excite the appetite.

After a time it became the rule to conduct the wedding ceremony during Mass. The reasoning behind this was that any nervous attack (*spasm*)[*] or fainting the bride might suffer in the future could be regarded as the result of a profanity, because the couple's marriage hadn't been solemnised during Mass. It was therefore considered necessary to marry couples during Mass. People said that, from then on, that kind of illness was never seen again.

43 – The foundation of the community school, the first teachers

Everyone knows that there was no school in Bardizag in the early days, but the old people have said that when the second church was built, a room was constructed adjoining it where the boys[†] were led by a kahana or deacon in learning to read, write and sing church hymns and canticles until the age when they went to work – which was early. This modest form of schooling continued until about 1830. This 'school' served only to prepare people to read or act as choristers in church and prepare future candidates for the priesthood.

A native of Erzerum (Garin), by the name of Mello oghlou (I don't know his real name) came to Bardizag sometime between 1822 and 1825 purely by accident. He had a powerful voice and great experience of singing in church. The village notables approved of him and retained him for a few months to teach the boys how to sing in church. He was the first outsider recognised as a teacher in Bardizag. Unfortunately, however, he was a drunkard and an unreliable character so the village notables were forced to get rid of him after a short time.

After Mello oghlou, a certain teacher from Adabazar, Apraham, who had a good voice and was an expert in church canticles, was invited to Bardizag to take up the same position. He was a drunkard too, as his assistant deacon, who later became Garabed Kahana Der-Krikorian, relates. Despite that failing, Apraham spent three years teaching in the school-room, after which he was removed from his position. Bardizag always had, from the time of that teacher, a community school and hired teachers, be they from the village or outside, whose stories will be read in the following pages.

---

[*] The word *spasm* is used in the text.
[†] The word *dghak* is used here. It can mean 'children' or 'boys'. I have used it in the latter sense, as girls' education started much later.

Chapter 5

The Garabed Agha Mgerian Era 1825 – 1850

44 – Apraham Kahana's fall and exile

Apraham Kahana's absolute rule started at the beginning of the 1800s, but a rebellious movement began among the people against his despotic regime that was becoming intolerable. Two opposing parties thus appeared in Bardizag, each bent on destroying the other.

A government *miubashir* arrived in Bardizag in, I think, about 1827, with an order to exile certain men by making them oarsmen in the galleys, the object of which was to quieten the village. Apraham Kahana's party were delighted, thinking that the order had been made to smite his enemies.

Apraham Kahana, Hadji Artin Der-Antreasian (Apraham Kahana's brother's son) and, from among their opponents, Dervish Hadji Mikayel (father of Tavit Kahana Mikayelian), Dzallan Hadji Hovhannes of the Great Derder family, and similar notables like them from the village were invited to the *ghonakh* [government building]. There the official read the order he had brought with him to the village's Turkish agha and all those who had been invited, in which it stated that the leaders of the two opposing parties were to be exiled – Apraham Kahana, Hadji Artin, Dervish Hadji Mikayel and Dzallan Hadji Hovhannes. When the latter two heard their convictions and sentences of exile, they quietly went into hiding.* Only Apraham Kahana and Hadji Artin were arrested and put under guard. It would appear that they seemed to think that they were untouchable.

There is no doubt that each side had, secretly from each other, applied to have their opponents silenced and brought into line on many occasions, using the government's heavy hand. But the government wanted to punish the leaders of both factions and to preserve the peace in the village, which shows that Apraham Kahana had gradually lost his old authority and influence in government circles. It also showed that his opponents had managed to create new friendships and obtain protection for themselves. This had therefore resulted in the government arriving at the decision to punish both sides, so that peace might be made between them.

Time has altered much in ways of thinking and feelings. We can see that in those days old friends and relatives had stood against one another, becoming bitter at Apraham Kahana's somewhat haughty and cynical ways. It got to the point that his opponents included almost all the priests who, in Great Hadji Khacher's time, had

---

* The phrase used here is 'kept their faces'. I have taken that to mean 'concealed themselves'.

been his minions. Pilibbos Kahana Der-Vartanian, Garabed Kahana Der-Krikorian, Sahag Kahana Bedigian and Nerses Kahana Kardeshian were cases in point – the last three having been ordained at Apraham Kahana's insistence and under his protection. Sarkis Kahana Bedigian (the father of Sahag Kahana) remained neutral, probably due to his advanced age and loyalty to his family links to the Khacherians.

Among Apraham Kahana's opponents was Bournaz Hadji Meger's grandson, the son of Bournaz Hadji Hovhannes, named Deacon Garabed. He had gradually, starting from that time, already begun to gain position and authority in Bardizag and would become one of the leading notables in the future. He would later be called Garabed Agha Mgerian.

The *miubashir*, thanks to the intervention of Dadjig Agha Osman, allowed the arrested men to go to their homes to prepare for their journey into exile.

Apraham Kahana and Hadji Artin were taken to Izmid and were sent from there to either Constantinople or Broussa (Boursa) – I cannot establish which – but after only two months were able to obtain their freedom, returning to Bardizag, where Apraham Kahana regained his former position and authority.

One of Apraham Kahana's main opponents, Pilibbos Kahana, died soon after his return. I heard the description of all these events, in every detail, directly from Gochgoch Hadji Mgerdich, who was Pilibbos Kahana's grandson.

Apraham Kahana's and Hadji Artin's exile was not sufficient to extinguish political passions in Bardizag. On the contrary, they became stronger, because Apraham Kahana's opponents, especially Dzallan Hadji Hovhannes, were frightened of his potential revenge, as the latter had become his most virulent opponent. It was as if he had inherited the anti-Apraham Kahana will of his relative, Great Derderents' Hovhannes Kahana. This party decided to finally – by all means – end Apraham Kahana's by now intolerable rule and to disarm his protector Dadjig Agha Osman of Deyirmendere. They found an advisor in the person of one called Nayib Hassan Effendi of the Turkish village of Sarayli, who was knowledgeable about the law and the way the government operated,[*] and whose word reached the government. This individual was Dzallan Hadji Hovhannes' house guest one night when he visited Bardizag, hence their acquaintance and friendship.

A small incident that occurred between Apraham Kahana and his protector Osman Agha considerably eased the work of the former's opponents against him. One day he had an argument with the agha about a member of his parish, one Korto Melkon Asadour, whom the agha had seized and beaten without his knowledge. A certain coldness developed between the two old friends as a result of this beating, to the delight of Apraham Kahana's opponents.

Osman Agha, utilising the opposition to Apraham Kahana, incited the villagers against him. They massed in front of the government building in great numbers and

---

* This is the best definition I have been able to make of the the word *varchaked*.

shouted, 'We don't want the priest!' in Turkish. In response to this, Rev. Apraham and his people organised a counter-demonstration against the agha, shouting, "We don't want Osman Agha, he is bringing revolution to our village', also in Turkish.

When Apraham Kahana saw, however, that his opponents grew in number from day to day and their boldness against him increased, he became depressed and tried to alter appearances to retain his position and authority in the church and among the people.

His opponents, however, secure in the knowledge of their strength, arranged for a new election of village leaders and managed to sweep the board. Among the newly elected notables was Deacon Garabed Mgerian, Bardizag's new man. This election was the sign of Apraham Kahana's final fall and the destruction of his authority.

45 – Garabed Mgerian

As I said, Garabed Mgerian was Bournaz Hadji Meger's grandson. His grandfather, from whom the clan had taken the name, was a cutler by trade. Deacon Meger was a naturally talented person, learning to read and write when he was a boy. He was noticed in the village as there wasn't another person who knew so much at that time. His father, Hovhannes, to allow him to gain experience in work, took him with him when he went around the Turkish villages where he sold the knives he produced. There Garabed was able to develop relationships with the Turkish notables and, strengthening his knowledge of Turkish, became experienced (according to the standards of the time), being able to use the correct forms of language with the notables.

At one time the *barmakdji* [lumber producer] group, the *ghatar* [carters] and labourer's employers sent him to Constantinople as their representative, to sell their products and to look after their accounts for them. He obtained excellent experience in the trade and had the opportunity to get to know and become friends with Armenians and Turks with positions and wealth there. Mgerian became a master of his work through these opportunities.

These experiences and on-the-job training became useful to him. He respected the village elders and was liked by them. He lived closed to them during his visits to the village, and accompanied them to church. He respected Apraham Kahana as a leading cleric and as a person with great position and authority. He called him *dayi* [uncle] – Mgerian's grandmother was from the Khacherian family – and would kiss his hand with filial respect. In other words he made his name as an experienced and polite young man throughout the village.

Deacon Garabed had a brother Mgerdich, and four sisters: Pepron, married to Teoleol Hadji Khachadour Keoseyan (she was the Teoleolians' grandmother); Mariam, married to Maya Israyeli Garabed; Srpouhi, married to Seli Minas (the grandfather of the Protestant notables of my day); and Soultan, married to Stepan, who was known as Shelem Krikori Anison (Magarian). All of them, brothers and sisters, were respected in Bardizag as clever and noble people.

46 – The newly-elected notables' relationship with Apraham Kahana

The newly-elected village notables appointed *Diratsou* Garabed Mgerian as their *kordzagadar* [agent] in place of Apraham Kahana – in those days *diratsou* was a title of respect, like Mr. or *Effendi* is today.

The majority of the newly-elected members of the assembly belonged to the party opposed to Apraham Kahana. They tried to win him over, however, to ensure peace in the village. They also promoted the merit of their new position. This was because they appreciated his personal qualities and the strength of his clan, all of whose families being well-to-do. They also knew that he had powerful friendships in Constantinople and the diocesan prelate, Bishop Stepannos Aghavni, looked on him with favour. When they were approached by Apraham Kahana, as the *avakerets* [leading priest], to have a new priest ordained to replace the deceased Pilibbos Kanaha, they decided, in line with this peaceful policy and with the greatest tact, that his son Garabed, who served in church, should be the candidate.

Apraham Kahana was satisfied with the meeting's decision and tact and said, 'If it is God's command and you want it too, it remains for me to conform.' In this way, during his lifetime, his son Garabed was ordained priest and was renamed Hagop Kahana. This took place on the feast of St. James, on the 15 December 1828.

47 – Apraham Kahana's revenge on his opponents

Despite the newly-elected notables' tact, Apraham Kahana couldn't forget the plot against him and his sentence to be exiled. He therefore began to secretly work against his opponents, while apparently accepting the situation.

He presented protests against them in the Patriarchate and to the amiras who knew him, and he was able to obtain an order for their exile. The management of the Imperial Ottoman Mint, hearing this, summoned Dzallan Hadji Hovhannes (he was Minas Effendi Dzalian's grandfather), who was Apraham Kahana's main opponent, Djerga Hadji Sarkis (the Mgerians' relation by marriage), Pattouk Minas, *Diratsou* Garabed Mgerian and someone called Pehlivan oghlou from Ovadjek to Constantinople. It would appear that these individuals were accused of fraud in the matter of supplying charcoal to the Mint, which was still in the hands of the villagers of Bardizag at that time.

As soon as Dzallan Hadji Hovhannes heard this, he decamped and ended his flight in Keotahia (Goudina). He was said to be a wily, persuasive person but, as soon as he found himself in a difficult position, would escape. Whatever is said of Dzallan, however, it is certain that there was clan enmity between the two houses from olden times, as we have seen in the details of the Great Derders' Hovhannes Kahana's story.*

The other four individuals were arrested and were taken under guard to Constantinople in a *karat* ship, where they were incarcerated in the Mint's prison.

Artin Amira Ghazaz was the head of the Mint's management at this time. When he had gone to his office one day, he remembered the Armenian prisoners, had them brought to him and asked their names. When he heard their strange names, he made sarcastic asides about each of them, saying, to Djerga Hadji Sarkis, 'Oh, djerr...'; to Pattouk, *'patakiut, patakiut...'*; to Pehlivan oghlou, 'Oh, you are a real *pehlivan* aren't you..?' When it came to Garabed Mgerian's turn, Mgerian said, 'Your servant Garabed Mgerian...' He then began to severely reprimand the four of them: 'What have you been doing? You've been stirring up the village and there are many protests about you.'

'Agha,' Djerga oghlou Hadji Sarkis replied, 'we are not at fault; others carry out the crimes and blame us.'

'I am going to have you released,' the amira told them. 'I will call you again.' Finally turning to Mgerian, he said, 'Come and see me tomorrow.'

Garabed Mgerian went to the Mint the following day to see the amira, who said, 'Tell me what happened.'

Mgerian told him what had happened in the village in order and in detail.

The amira listened to him with great attention and came to the conclusion that the accusations against the four were the result of political hatred. He then said, 'I'll give you a letter for the prelate advising him to call the leaders of the two sides together and reconcile them.'

The amira took to Mgerian as a result of this and told him, just before he and his companions left, 'If, after this, you have a problem, come to me.' Mgerian and the others, carrying the letter, returned to Bardizag.

When Apraham Kahana and his cohorts heard of the four's release and their return to the village, they panicked and spread a new rumour. 'They've duped the amira, they've told lies. We will beat them once more and turn their joy to bitterness.'†

Mgerian, hearing this, mounted a horse and without losing any time, left for the Monastery of Armash that night with a companion, to see the prelate, and to give him the amira's letter. He'd not been able to do this before as the prelate had gone there from Izmid.

Bishop Stepannos Aghavni, the prelate, read the amira's letter and, turning to Mgerian, said, 'You have secured the water at its source, well done!' He immediately

---

* See Section 33.

† The actual words of this last phrase are: 'leave their joy in their stomachs.'

wrote a letter to Apraham Kahana and advised him and his people to remain calm. He added that if they didn't, the situation could become very grave and the responsibility and punishment would be on their heads. He also said that he'd received a letter from Artin Amira Ghazaz about this. He sent Apraham Kahana his letter, enclosing a copy of the amira's.

Apraham Kahana read both letters and became confused. He didn't dare, after that, to oppose things openly, especially against Mgerian. The latter had scored a victory and had achieved an unassailable position. From that day, Mgerian was regarded as being under the amira's protection. He was respected by all in the village and *Diratsou* Garabed now became *Baron* Garabed* and his political adherents took heart, working boldly and openly.

Apraham Kahana gradually accepted his fate; his star had been extinguished. The people and children around him didn't represent any great value. His daughters, although clever and astute, didn't dare give their father advice. Apraham Kahana's once absolute authority within Bardizag passed to Mgerian, who gradually accumulated the rule of the village into his own hands.

It was expected, of course, that the new man would face difficulties, just as there had been against Apraham Kahana, greatness and rule being dangerous supports. Despite that possibility, he enjoyed the villagers' esteem for many years with his activity, astuteness and circumspection. Mgerian conquered so many difficulties that one of his main opponents, Varteres Kondaiyan, who was one of Apraham Kahana's sister's sons said of him, 'Let me tell you something: when God chooses to raise a man up, the whole world can't humble him.'

48 – Mgerian introduces horseshoe-making skills and trade in horseshoes into Bardizag

Horseshoe-making was introduced, spread and developed in the village thanks to Mgerian's enterprise. Its commercial exploitation soon assumed great importance. In Mgerian's day there was small-scale trade in the production of horseshoes in the region, which hardly covered the needs of the local population. Mgerian saw that there were great profits to be made in the trade, and he began to study it. People knew that he had the opportunity to satisfy his interest when he was the *barmakdjis* [lumber producers] representative in Constantinople. He brought a master horseshoe-maker who was from Erzerum (Garin) – the people of Erzerum were considered to be masters of the trade – to Bardizag. That man, commonly known by the name of Ghourou entered, with his son Krikor, into Mgerian's service. Mgerian established a smithy where father and son began to produce horseshoes. The

---

* *Baron* (baron or Mr. in English) had a higher status in those days.

villagers became interested in this new trade and many men subsequently learned how to make them.

Mgerian doubled the size of his horseshoe works, saw that there was great demand for the product in the country and, with iron being cheap, began to make great profits. He enlarged the trade. He set up a large horseshoe manufacturing facility, with five to six forges, employing 20-25 workers, on a piece of unused ground in front of Pandig Mgerdichian's house. He rented a warehouse in Constantinople to stockpile the horseshoes produced by his workshop in the village. He also used it as a depot from which he sold vast quantities to other merchants who, in their turn, sold them in the trading centres of Anatolia and Rumelia. As a result, the fame of his abilities spread far and wide. Through this trade he made a great deal of money and became very wealthy.

Other wealthy people in Bardizag followed Mgerian's example, establishing workshops in various places in the village. I can recall the Dzallans, Djergas, Arakelians (the Hadji Horops), the Kiutners,* Dions, Pashas, Kondas (Minas and Varteres) and the Selis, thus making Bardizag a well-known centre for the production of horseshoes. Ghourou, the master smith from Erzerum finally settled in Bardizag. His son's family became the Diubegs and Hokos.

49 – The visit of Giragos, the exiled Catholicos of the Great House of Cilicia, to Bardizag

When Sultan Mahmoud ascended the Ottoman throne in 1807,† the Turks in Cilicia defamed the local Armenians, accusing them of storing great quantities of weapons, cannon and military materials in the premises of the Catholicosate of Cilicia. The sultan had the catholicos brought to Constantinople for examination.‡

The Catholicos Giragos** came to Constantinople and enquiries proved that the accusation was baseless. He was then allowed to return to his seat. On his way to Sis, however, he was recalled to Constantinople as the accusations had been repeated. The second examination ended with the same result. The sultan was filled with remorse. He saw a miraculous change in the catholicos and felt that he was in the presence of a man of God, a man in whom there was no deceit. He honoured him and ordered him, for the second time, to return to his seat in Sis.

The catholicos began his return journey by land and reached Izmid. The notables and people of Bardizag heard about the catholicos' arrival and sent a delegation there, inviting him to visit the village. He came to Bardizag, led by the delegation.

---

*   The author has used the name Kiuters, which I think is a misprint.
†   This was Sultan Mahmoud II, who actually reigned from 1808 to 1839.
‡   This incident took place in 1810.
**   This was Giragos I the Great, Catholicos of the Great House of Cilicia from 1797-1822.

All the villagers, without exception, met him at the entrance to the village – it was the very first time they had seen the catholicos – and welcomed him with great honour and respect.

The catholicos conducted Mass one Sunday with great solemnity. Then, under a formal canopy, he toured the village with an entourage, while the villagers placed parcels of white cloth on the streets, so that the catholicos could walk on them. This visit by the catholicos to the village was a spiritual pleasure and an opportunity for joy for all the villagers.

He remained in the village for a few days, after which he was, with the greatest respect, seen on his way. Every villager, young and old, man and woman, accompanied him as far as the Lower Threshing Floors. As he was saying goodbye, the catholicos stopped, looked at this great crowd, said a prayer of benediction and blessed it, saying, 'May you increase like the grains of sea sand.' The people of Bardizag, from that day on, held the belief that they were a blessed people and usually regarded the great and rapid increase in their population as the result of the catholicos' blessing.

When Archbishop Nerses Varjabedian was prelate of Izmid, later becoming a bishop in the Catholicosate of Cilicia at Sis, he would talk of the catholicosses of Cilica with great praise and say, 'They were never the illiterate and worthless churchmen that people thought they were.' He especially remembered Catholicos Giragos' words, 'My name begins with the letter G; whichever way you turn it, it keeps its form,' wanting people to understand his inflexible and robust character.

50 – One or two anecdotes about the *shoushdag* vartabed[*] [celibate monk who was formerly a kahana] Mesrob of Bardizag

Mgerdich Ayvazian, who was a widower, was ordained as an archdeacon at the time that Hagop Kahana (Apraham Kahana's son) was ordained. He continued in his position for some time in the church in Bardizag, also becoming the *jamgoch* [beadle]. He then left and went to the Monastery of Armash where he was ordained a *shoushdag* monk with the name of Mesrob Vartabed. He was usually called 'The Ayvazents monk'.

There was a monk called Tateos who was a simpleton in Armash at that time. He related these anecdotes, as if he'd heard them from Mesrob Vartabed about his time in Bardizag.

When Mesrob Vartabed was the beadle before his ordination, he would stealthily climb on to the roof of Apraham Kahana's house and hide there to hear the conversations that took place inside the house. He apparently reported them to

---

[*] *Shoushdag* is a title given to a kahana who, after his wife and children have died, becomes a celibate monk.

Mgerian. It is possible that this story is not true, but as is often the case in the character of a steward, beadle, deacon or some such person, amongst whom right-mindedness and nobility don't hold much sway: 'fallen people have no friends' apparently justifies the popular saying. The mentality of a slave or lackey was usual among those kinds of people.

The same monk apparently related that the church was beginning to collapse, and that Mgerian and his cohorts wanted to demolish and rebuild it. Apraham Kahana with his group was against this plan, because he wasn't the plan's initiator. So the notables and priests of the day who wanted to rebuild the church advised the beadle (Mesrob Vartabed) to bring down some of the plaster of the altar arch one night with a pole, so that it could be demonstrated that the rebuilding of the church had to proceed, and Apraham Kahana's opposition be obviated. Apparently he did so.

This seems probable, because a beadle would have liked to carry out the strangest or most absurd action to please those in power.

51 – Apraham Kahana's second exile

As we've seen, the second church only had a short life of about 30 years[*] and had become ramshackle, with everyone in the village, be they priest, people in authority or the ordinary people, concluding that it should be demolished and a new one built. But the rebuilding was delayed for a time due to political unrest, and now it was delayed further due to internal dissention in the village.[†]

Mgerian, however confident in his strength and his increasing authority, decided to take the initiative to bring the problem of the rebuilding of the church to a successful conclusion through the locum tenens of the diocese,[‡] Boghos Vartabed Taktakian, who was visiting the village. At that time the Turkish agha of the village was Omar, the son of Osman, the previous agha, who had fallen under Mgerian's influence.

Mgerian invited the village elders, influential people and the priests to a meeting. Apraham Kahana was among the latter. In the meeting he raised the subject of the rebuilding of the church. In subsequent sessions he pursued the matter and, during one of these, an unexpected protest by a mass of the villagers caused the subject to be closed without resolution. One day, when Mgerian and the other elders were in the *ghonakh* [government building][**] with the agha, a crowd of people gathered in front of it and began to shout, saying "Meger Oghlu ashaghe ensin, istemeiz, biz fukarayez, kilisa yapadjak halimiz yok, khasere serib biz douameze yapa biliriz."

Boghos Vartabed happened to enter the ghonakh just at that moment, saw the crowd, heard their shouting and ordered one of their number, Tsatgan Hadji Boghos

---

[*] From about 1800 to 1830.
[†] See Section 27.
[‡] Bardizag came under the diocese of Nicomedia, based in Izmid.
[**] It was located in the main street, in the market area.

(one of Apraham Kahana's relatives by marriage and one of his men), to quieten the crowd and make them disperse. Tsatgan Boghos innocently replied that the priest should speak to the crowd, referring to Apraham Kahana, who was attending the meeting with the other priest and the village elders. Boghos Vartabed Taktakian then entered the *ghonakh* and ordered Apraham Kahana to quieten the crowd. So Apraham Kahana went to the window, put his head out and told the crowd to be quiet and for everyone to return to their homes. The crowd did so immediately. Apraham Kahana, who perhaps wanted to demonstrate his authority, was viewed as the instigator of the demonstration by all those present in the meeting.

The locum tenens, Mgerian and his supporters then convened a separate meeting, in which they decided to write a report to the bishop of the diocese, Bishop Stepannos Aghavni, to the effect that 'Apraham Kahana must be exiled so that we may continue our work, for as long as he is in Bardizag, there will never be peace.'

The bishop, on the basis of this report, wrote to the Armenian Patriarchate (in Constantinople) so that an Ottoman government order could be issued to exile Apraham Kahana from Bardizag for a time. The government issued the order, the result of which was that he, his wife, his son Hagop Kahana with his wife and three year-old son Mgerditch, and his other son Hadji Hagop with his wife and young daughter Dirouhi were forced to leave the village to go to Merzifon (Marsovan).

All of Apraham Kahana's relatives and friends got together, and weeping and wailing, said goodbye to the exiles, heaping curses on those responsible for the exile order, especially Sahag Kahana and Garabed Kahana.

The exiles were voluntarily accompanied by some of their relatives. They all reached Marsovan safely, where they received a great welcome – Apraham Kahana had many acquaintances there – and were all honoured with oil and honey.[*] The exiles' relatives returned three weeks later, while the exiles themselves remained in Marsovan for a whole year.

52 – The building of the fourth and last church

After Apraham Kahana's removal, the village authorities called all the skilled tradesmen together, demolished the old, decaying church and stored all the materials worth saving in a safe place for future use.

Thanks to Artin Amira Ghazaz's intervention, the imperial *firman* (permit) for the construction of the church was swiftly obtained. As the dimensions of the church to be built hadn't been specified in the *firman*, the Izmid authorities sent special officials

---

[*] A traditional sign of esteem and welcome.

to determine them on site. The village authorities were able to win the officials' benevolence and the dimensions were agreed according to the villagers' wishes.

Construction was started under the direction of Boghos Vartabed Taktakian, the locum tenens of the diocese.[*] He blessed the foundations, as the bishop of the diocese hadn't been able to carry out the ceremony personally due to illness. The people - men and women, the old and the young - began construction with the greatest devoutness and dedication, working like ants. Every villager, according to his ability, helped to defray the costs of construction, the builders working faithfully and with great dedication.

A certain Deacon Garabed, the village teacher of the time, was appointed as assistant to the locum tenens, and both oversaw this pious construction. The building of the church was completed in nine months, on March 31, 1831, with the surrounding wall being built later.

Invitations to the dedication ceremony were extended to the diocesan bishop, monks from Armash and the parish priests from the surrounding villages after the church had been completed. This was conducted with the greatest solemnity.[†]

The senior parish priest, Garabed Kahana Der-Krikorian, who wrote this account of the building of the church[‡] with all its details, presented the cost as 361,500 *marchils* or 663 purses. Hadji Haroutiun Kutnerian, his son Kevork Kutnerian and grandson Serabion Kutnerian, who never handed over this account register to the village authorities, kept the original accounts. In my time Serabion Kutnerian was asked for the account book so that it could be kept in the church's archives. His reply was 'We haven't got anything like that in our house,' so it was never retrieved.

The first anniversary of the completion of the church, 31 March 1831, fell during Lent. On the anniversary, a solemn, full service was held, with the altar curtain

---

[*] The prelate of Nicomedia of the time was Bishop Stepannos Aghavni (Zakarian), who held the post from 1825-1853. Minas Kasabian (Farhad), *Hayere Nikomedio Kavarin Mech*, p. 119.

[†] The dedication of a new Armenian church involves using Holy Chrism to 'open the church doors', blessing, anointing and dedicating every pillar to a saint and symbolically cleaning and anointing the altar, naming it for the saint the church was dedicated to. In Bardizag this saint was always St. James of Nisibis.

[‡] This account was carefully written down in a notebook, in classical Armenian, which also contained the story of the martyr, as well as a few notes on the foundation of the village.

People said that Rev. Garabed subsequently altered the master of the original account, removing references to the efforts made by Garabed Agha Mgerian and even his name, as a result of the coldness between them that began after the construction of the church. In an attempt to return the account to its previous state, the senior priest Rev. Hovhannes Mgerian added notes in the margins of the manuscript, which was kept in the church's library. (Author's note)

open* and with the *sharagan* [canticle] from the previous evening 'Holy church be joyful' being sung and the 'Eve of Feast' ceremony also being conducted. This continued until 1838, when the custom ceased. Garabed Kahana, in his account, stated 'I haven't found, in church law, any reference to the celebration of the completion of the construction of a church, but it would appear that our people decided for a time that it was fitting to do so.'

53 – Apraham Kahana's return from his place of exile

Archbishop Garabed, the Patriarch of Constantinople, died in 1831 and the prelate of Izmid, Bishop Stepannos Aghavni was elected his successor. He petitioned the government to free Apraham Kahana. This was granted and the local government at Mersifon (Marsovan) was informed.

Apraham Kahana collected his family and began the return journey to his birthplace, Bardizag. He heard, when he reached one of the Armenian villages near Broussa (Boursa), that one of his opponents, the locum tenens Boghos Vartabed Taktakian, was there on a pastoral visit. He pretended that he was unaware of this and didn't visit him, at which Boghos Vartabed became angry and decided to punish him for his tactlessness.

Apraham Kahana sent word to his friends of his arrival when he and his party reached Sabandja. His friends and relatives went on horseback as far as that village in great numbers, returning to Bardizag with him with great solemnity.

The whole village assembled at the entrance to the village at the Lower Threshing Floors – curiosity had some part in this welcome – where the exiles and those arriving with him dismounted. The people, to the accompaniment of drums and pipes, danced in welcome and then joyfully returned to their homes.

Boghos Vartabed arrived in Bardizag several days later and summoned Apraham Kahana. He severely dressed him down for lacking respect and ordered him to stand in the nave of the church, next to one of the pillars for 40 days and repent.

Of course, Apraham Kahana was not going to bow his head before such a cleric, but he obeyed the order. He showed penitence with the object of securing the people's sympathy. He knew that this new punishment, after a year's exile, would have its adverse effect on the people and inflame them against his enemies.

His son Hagop Kahana began his ministry. Apraham Kahana too, after his 40 day repentance, resumed his place in the chancel and his office as leading priest.

Apraham Kahana, who was a person endowed with great individuality, looked around and found that everything had changed. The church had been rebuilt and

---

* The altar curtain is kept closed for the whole of Lent, except for Palm Sunday, and a truncated form of Mass is conducted in front of it.

his enemies were more powerful. Mgerian was now the absolute notable of the village, and the church keepers and seat-holders* were his people. He wasn't able to accept all this and wrote a letter of protest, depending on the new patriarch's old friendship with him, complaining especially about Mgerian. But he forgot that Mgerian now had a powerful defender in Constantinople, Artin Amira Ghazaz, who was the most influential man of the time in governmental and Armenian community circles.

The patriarch enclosed Apraham Kahana's letter in one of his own and sent it to Mgerian. Apraham Kahana heard of this, became frightened of a new calamity and was forced to try and make peace with Mgerian.

He went to the Kousdik house (they were his relatives, as well as being related to Mgerian by marriage), inviting the latter to see him there. Mgerian replied, accepting, and the two great men of Bardizag met face to face there. Apraham Kahana bowed and said, '*Baron* Garabed, I did this - forgive me; we are worldly beings and all of us make mistakes.'

Mgerian replied, with great restraint and deference, 'Lord father, let's forget what's passed, you carry out your priestly duties and let others do what they can for the people. We all make errors; may God forgive all of us.' The two men were reconciled and the matter was closed.

54 – The *ghonakh* (government building) and the Turkish aghas

The *ghonakh* (government building) where the Turkish aghas lived from the old days was located to the east of the church, in the market, in front of the 'aghas fountain' and was owned by the community.† In the old days it was known as *ambar iustiu*. There was a cellar underneath it where, at the beginning, the *vakef* [foundation] tax portion of the community's harvests was stored.

The area the *ghonakh* held extended to a point well behind the church, as far as Jamoun Tsor [Church Valley]. This had been the Ghochoums or, by another name, the Deli Hadjis (the Deledjegs) property from the early days. It is certain that it had been the site of the houses belonging to Ghourt Asadour and his brother Mikayel of that family, and was purchased by the notables of the day to build the *ghonakh*. The two brothers were given, in place of this site, a large, community-owned green area above the village. This was just below the St. Minas threshing floor, where the Deledjegs had their house, surrounded by gardens and with their own fountain, called *Deledjegents aghpiur* even in my day.

The Deledjegs belonged to Apraham Kahana's party. Because the site was purchased when Mgerian was patronising the ruling body, the priest had, apart from persuading them to accept the new site, to give them a sum of money.

---

* The words used here are *yegeghetsban yev atoragalner*.
† In other words it was the property of the village of Bardizag.

It should be explained that there had been a community-owned building already on the site near the two Deledjeg houses even before Mgerian's day. So to build a new, enlarged *ghonakh*, the two houses had to be bought and demolished. The new one was built on the whole site during the time of Mgerian's stewardship. It was demolished in 1890 and the final *ghonakh* was then constructed.

When I was a child the *ghonakh* had the following sections. There was an entrance in the market onto an open-air courtyard about ten paces deep, around which there were a stable, and a store left over from old times. There was a staircase in one corner of the courtyard leading to an apartment on the first floor, located over the stable and the store, consisting of a small room, kitchen and a room specially set up for the Turkish secretary and was his official office and living area. The *ghonakh* had a second apartment, higher up, where there was a large hall and the Turkish agha's office. On one side of the yard was a room belonging to Mkhig Hagop Reyisian (Ghourt oghlou's brother) that had been converted into the *zaptiehs'* [gendarmes'] mess hall.

The Turkish aghas of Deyirmendere, Hadji Pasha, Chelebi Agha, Osman Agah and Omar Agha lived and worked in this *ghonakh* until 1835. I don't know where they conducted official business before the one in the village was built.

The Turkish aghas' families, however, lived in Horom Village (Yenikeoy). This was lower down, three quarters of an hour's distance from Bardizag as I have already stated. The aghas would call upon the people of Bardizag, once or twice a year, to provide all the stores necessary for their house and for their gardens to be cultivated. The people of the village had to carry out all the tasks that were expected of them.

Reyis Garabed, a man with a deep and loud voice, on these occasions would go into the market and the streets and shout, 'People, its time to dig the agha's gardens in Horom Village. Everyone should take his spade and go there tomorrow, but in the end you know best.' At other times chickens, eggs, vegetables and many other things were collected for the agha's house using his same coercive shouts.

There is an anecdote about this Reyis Garabed. One day one of the agha's sheep was waiting to give birth and the shepherd was late. The agha said, 'So the lamb didn't come, eh?'

'No my lord, there is no lamb. Will the shepherd now bring the cudgel?' he replied.

The agha understood the joke and began to laugh loudly.

The aghas had the right to try and punish miscreants, with the knowledge and assent of the local notables – in those days courts didn't exist in the country and the administration of justice was in the hands of the highest official of the region. The agha would order the miscreant's arrest and question him. When the accused's guilt was established, one of two punishments would be decided upon, in accordance with the severity of the crime: beating and imprisonment, or a fine (*djerme*). To beat the guilty person, he would be laid on the ground and his legs would be rendered immovable using a form of tie called a *falakhan*, and two policemen (*zaptiehs*), facing each other, one on either side of the prisoner, and armed with wet canes, would beat his feet with the number of strokes decreed by the agha, in his presence. The prisoner's feet would be washed with salt water and he'd be thrown into prison after this punishment had been carried out. Someone who was guilty of a minor offence would have his feet beaten with a thin cane called a *chergesteh*.

This official method of trial and punishment began during Great Hadji Khacher's day, if not before, and lasted through the whole of Apraham Kahana's rule and the first few years of Mgerian's. The Turkish government re-established this unjust and pitiless punishment during the First World War, when Armenians were declared to be outside the law...*

The aghas would also collect the village's *vakef* taxes in advance and, later, the one-tenth (*ashar*) tax. The aghas were, for this reason, also known as *ashar* tax collectors (*miultezims*). For example, when the silk cocoons were harvested, and the silk was collected using the the old *mandjelekh* method [putting cocoons into boiling water and unwinding the silk by hand onto a spindle] the *reyis* would go to the different parishes on a particular day and let the people know that that day's silk production would be taken as *ashar* tax. It was also the agha's right to arrange matters regarding inheritance (*tereke*, estate).

According to ancient Turkish law, if someone didn't have a male heir, that person's agricultural harvest was *mahliul* (government property) and the deceased person's wife and daughters were not considered to be heirs. As for buildings (*emlak*) – house, shop, bakery or storehouse – the deceased person's wife and daughters were entitled to a certain portion of them. This unjust law was reformed in the Turkish year 1260 (1845), under which, if the agricultural harvest was *vakef*, then females were allowed the same proportion as males, and if the harvest was real (*serf arazi*), the son took a whole portion and the daughter only half; later daughters were given the right to take, from the forests and fields, the same portions, but not from vineyards or gardens.

According to ancient law, *mahliul* (government appropriated) land was permitted to be sold in the name of the government by the aghas at knock-down prices, sometimes almost by force, to anyone who appeared and was able to pay the price. These people were usually wealthy.

Omar Agha of Deyirmendere, during his time, forcibly sold such land to Kechedji Hadji Garabed Baba and Semerdji Hadji Hovhannes. They didn't want to buy it so as not to deny the female heirs their inheritance.

The aghas would also endorse the acts of buying and selling property and issue promissory notes (*sened*s) in the purchaser's name.

---

* About 40 people from the village suffered this punishment during the collection of arms episode in 1915. See Section 151.

Apart from this, they would sell government-owned unused land, forests and uninhabited areas, issuing the purchasers with the above-mentioned promissory note.

When the land that had been forcibly sold by Omar Agha to Kechedji Hadji Garabed Baba was being examined in terms of its cultivation (*yokhlaman*), the latter gave it as a gift to Bardizag's church. Pandig Baba had the idea of registering it under the name of 'Yeghisapet veledi Hovagim' [Elizabeth, mother of Hovagim] which he did. After Hadji Garabed Baba died, his grandchildren, urged on by his son-in-law Kiutner Hadji Artin, were able to reclaim it as their rightful inheritance, arguing that there was no such person known in Bardizag as 'Yeghisapet veledi Hovagim'. Kechedji Hadji Garabed Baba's land thus returned to the previous owner's heirs, who sold it to Greeks and Laz Armenians. This was against the donor's will, therefore denying the community its property.

55 – Artin Amira Ghazaz's intervention in Bardizag's community affairs

I've mentioned, in previous pages, the intervention made by that great community figure in the Apraham Kahana-Garabed Mgerian affair, and his sympathy and protection for Mgerian.[*] I should like to say a few words here about his beneficence and help in the matter of building the church in Bardizag.

It was he who obtained the Imperial permit to build the church in three short days! He also gave the huge sum of 20,000 *kurush* in cash and 1,000 *okas* weight[†] of lead sheets as gifts to aid its construction and to roof the cupolas over the altars. The amira was thus Bardizag's greatest benefactor.

He was not only a generous benefactor and a just person who interceded in Bardizag's community affairs. He also assisted individuals to find solutions to their difficulties through his wish to help and the greatness of his spirit. Among these works, he was extremely helpful, especially in the case of a poor orphan from the village that was able, through his intervention, to gain his inheritance under the following circumstances.

The reader will remember, of course, that a man named Djezel Ghazaros from Bardizag was beheaded in the Balekh Bazar in Constantinople, in Great Hadji Khacher's day.[‡] This man left an orphan named Krikor, whose paternal uncle Djezel Hovhannes took his inheritance, Krikor's father having died while his grandfather was still living. Krikor was therefore regarded as disowned (*dede mehroumi*), and, according to law, stopped being his grandfather's heir, if his grandfather had not made special provision for his son's orphan child during his lifetime. Djezel

---

[*] See Section 53.
[†] Equivalent to approximately 2700 lbs or 1200 kg.
[‡] See Section 29.

Ghazaros had not made any such arrangement for Krikor and the boy, left without an inheritance, lived in poverty.

Krikor, having turned bitter at this injustice, told some people his story when he was in Constantinople; one of them suggested that he approach Artin Amira Ghazaz.

Krikor, holding a petition, waited on the amira's route one day. When he saw the amira, he approached him with much trepidation and fear and proffered the petition. The amira, scowling, asked, 'What is this?'

'It's a petition,' Krikor replied very softly.

'Am I judge?' shouted the amira and, slapping Krikor hard in the face, sent him away, but kept the petition.

Krikor, confused and feeling hopeless, escaped.

After some time, however, the amira searched for the boy. Krikor appeared before him and, at his command, told his story in every detail. Having heard it, the amira wrote a personal letter to the prelate of Izmid, advising him to write to the notables of Bardizag with the suggestion that they rectify the injustice in some way for this poor orphan.

Krikor took the amira's letter, went to the prelate in Izmid, and gave it to him.

The prelate read the letter and enclosed it in one of his own, which suggested that the notables of Bardizag give the boy his rights, adding 'otherwise the end result would not be good.' He gave the envelope to Krikor and sent him to Bardizag.

The village notables summoned the boy's uncle Djezel Hovhannes, told him of the orphan's petition and the contents of the letters, and advised him to give his brother's son a portion of his inheritance. Hovhannes agreed and returned his dead father's portion of the estate to Krikor.

Artin Amira Ghazaz died in 1834, leaving a blessed memory in the annals of the Armenian community. He was a great and good man, giving great lustre to the community as well as being a great benefactor. He was a protector of the weak, and was Sultan Mahmoud's greatly esteemed servant,[*] who gave great service to the government and his nation and to all those, without any national bias, who needed his help and protection, earning everyone's greatest respect and esteem, especially in the Turkish Armenian community.

56 – Accusations and slander against Mgerian

In Section 54 (above) I recalled the *ashar* (the one-tenth tax) that was one of the rights belonging to the Turkish aghas, in his role as a tax gatherer (*miultezim*), especially in relation to silk.

---

[*] The words used here translate as 'he was the light of the eyes of Sultan Mahmoud'.

The aghas, to establish the amount that would be one-tenth of the crop, would appoint a trustworthy person from the village as their middleman for the sale of silk. This individual would receive the buyers at his house. They would give the price of a *tefe* (600 *drams*) of silk and the middleman would arrange for the *reyis* to go to all parts of the village to let the people know that the silk merchants had arrived and the price they were offering. The merchants, who wanted to buy the silk from the villagers, would do so through the middleman, who would calculate the amount in each transaction and the total cost. The actual amount of one-tenth tax each villager had to pay was based on this, and was remitted at the time the silk was sold.

Apraham Kahana had been the middleman and followed by Garabed Kahana's brother of the Bakey family. He was succeeded by Hadji Artin Der-Antreasian, and finally by Garabed Agha Mgerian. It was natural that the middlemen would be the subject of slander and criticism by this or that person as profiteers and embezzlers and thus be discredited. The people were always inclined to accept these accusations without question.

Whether it was an agha or notable – this was the villager's stubborn belief – the person involved would ensure that he profited by his position. Of course there have been people who were not scrupulous and did profit at the expense of the people, but the people themselves were always ready to exaggerate the facts and tar all of them with the same brush.

Thus when Mgerian was the middleman for silk sales, he was accused of committing fraud and embezzling the one-tenth tax. He was taken to Constantinople and imprisoned there as a result, but relevant examinations showed that he was innocent. When he was released, he soon returned to Bardizag and resumed work in his mercantile and engineering enterprises.

Mgerian was also accused of being a fraudster in the matter of building the church, such as the claim that he embezzled a proportion of the materials obtained for its construction and, using them, built an expensive and well-appointed guest apartment (*selamlik*) at the side of his house, with painted and decorated walls and ceilings; a main hall (*tahlidj*) painted with sprays of flowers and expensively furnished; a pond in his front garden with live fish swimming in it and benches round it, shaded by a great vine arbour. The top of the pond wall had pots containing flowering and green plants, shade-providing trees etc.

These then were opulent things in a simple village life which led to so much suspicion against Mgerian. The number of his opponents grew and his friends began to distance themselves from him when they grew less important and when new, more powerful people were present. The amira had died and so he was easy prey.

Tongues were loosened: 'Mgerian has built his own house with materials belonging to the church and the community...' could be heard everywhere.

Mgerian became angry. He called a meeting and demanded that an accounting be carried out. The church building treasurer, Hadji Artin Kiutnerian, had apparently made revelations about it... The meeting was convened, Kiutnerian was summoned to it to determine the truth of the accusations against Mgerian, but he was hardly able to mumble anything. The so-called accounting proved nothing and the accusations were not substantiated.

It was that account book that had gone missing and was searched for years later. The old people in the village told this story.

57 - The deaths of Nerses Kahana Kardeshian and Krikor Kahana Agha Krikorian

Nerses Kahana Kardeshian went to Jerusalem on a pilgrimage with his family when he was old. He became ill and died and was buried in the Holy Redeemer cemetery, where his tombstone may still be seen. It was used to place the dead on from then on.

Simple people said that when this priest was setting out, he went to say goodbye to Apraham Kahana. The latter apparently said, 'May you go and never return,' and that the curse worked.

Nerses Kahana, according to people who knew him well, was a restless, quarrelsome priest. He was in continuous dispute with the Khochers over the borders of a *mal* [a piece of land]. He was articulate and knew Turkish well. He often went to Izmid and would find ways to obtain *fetvas* [judgements] against his opponents.

Apraham Kahana didn't like him, and they were against one another until the end.

Garabed Kahana Der-Krikorian, speaking of this priest, said that he wasn't faithful to his calling and didn't fulfil his duties. He often didn't come to church, making the excuse that he was ill. He spent his time on worldly things such as farming and the yield of his crops at harvest. It was also said that he spent occasional nights in his field wanting to water his maize plants. When his neighbours retired and returned to the village and he was left alone, he would quietly divert the community stream into his field and lie down next to his neighbour's dry irrigation ditch so that when the water was made to change course by someone else when he was asleep, he would be awakened by the noise of the water and once more divert it into his field.

It would appear that he was disillusioned by his position as a priest.

Krikor Kahana, Garabed Kahana's father, died in 1832. He was one of the most powerful of Apraham Kahana's opponents – Nerses Kahana was still alive – and Apraham Kahana led the burial service. In those days it was the custom to turn the dead priest's coffin to the four cardinal points of the compass in the church, as if the canticle *Antastan* [The Homeland] was being sung. When they were doing this at

Krikor Kahana's funeral, Apraham Kahana apparently said, whispering in Hagop Kahana's and the choristers' ears, as if he were talking to Nerses Kahana, '*Bodour*, lift the *djafs*' and '*Bodour*, put the *djafs* down.' '*Bodour*' meant Nerses Kahana, and '*djaf*' was Krikor Kahana. It is surprising that in the old people's customs, respect and gravity was lacking even in the presence of a coffin and the smallness of their souls and feelings would come to the fore, even on the most solemn occasion, when passions should have been stilled.

58 – A government census in Bardizag

Bazar Bashi Ali Effendi, a government official, was despatched from Izmid in the same year (1832) to conduct a census in the villages of Bardizag, Ovadjek, Dongel and Yenikeoy.

Ali Effendi made Bardizag his headquarters and stayed in Hadji Hovhannes Khacherian's newly built house. The latter was Great Hadji Khacher's youngest son.

This census only took account of the male population. Garabed Kahana Der-Krikorian copied the results of this census into a separate book. It showed the villagers' surnames and the order of houses. He also added the 32 village section names in accordance with the division made at the time when charcoal was being supplied to the Imperial Mint. Rev. Garabed's book contained 639 houses or families and was kept in the church's library.

59 – The construction of a separate school building (1833)

Bardizag had no special school building until 1833. The priests, from the early days, would gather their own and the notables' sons and teach them how to read and write and give them exercises to do, either in the church or in their own homes. Later the *mazman* [string-makers'] shops were a kind of school, to which children who wanted to read and write went to take lessons from the master craftsmen who worked in them.

In Apraham Kahana's days, when the teacher Apraham of Adabazar was brought in from outside as a paid teacher, the diocesan prelate advised the village notables to build a small extension next to the church as a special school building. One was therefore constructed that became the first school building in the village.

When, however, Bardizag's last church was being constructed on Mgerian's initiative, it was found necessary to appropriate the site of the school to extend the church itself. The school was therefore demolished and its site incorporated into that of the church, meaning that there was no longer a building for the school. After the completion of the church, one of its anterooms was assigned to the school. This lasted for about a year. After some time the school moved to the church gallery because of concerns about the scholars' health, as they were sitting on the stone floor every day. It should be said that from the beginning until that time, it was felt that only boys needed to be educated – to learn to read and write – while the girls weren't taught at all.

These provisional arrangements having been made, it was found necessary for the school to have its own building.

The building of a new school was therefore taken in hand with Apraham Kahana's, Mgerian's and the notables' participation. A piece of land belonging to the community to the north of the new church and outside its wall was chosen as its site. The church was bordered by walls and streets on all four sides; the school was located on the northern side of the one that ran from west to east outside its northern wall, towards the Chelengs' and Pandigs' houses. This street led from there to the main street, passing the Khashmans' house.

The church wall had a door in it, linking the school directly with the church's exterior *kavit* [narthex]. We knew that another door had been let in to the church wall when the church was built to allow women to enter it. It was located near the Chelengs' house and was kept closed when the church wasn't used, preventing passers-by entering the church through it.

One part of the school itself (containing two classrooms) was built over the street skirting the northern wall using the wall itself as the base for the upper storey, leaving the street going through a tunnel under the first floor of the building.

This new school building was my boyhood one and had the following parts: *dzaghgots* [the first school], which was quite a large hall, located on the ground floor. There was another large hall upstairs reserved for the older boys. A door in the corner, facing the direction of the school entrance, led to another hall used as a lecture room for the more educated boys. There were two classrooms on one side of the stairs in the wing over the street below, the entrance to the first being from the boys' hall, the second having a separate door at the end of the building nearest the church wall. There was a third classroom too, between the lecture hall and the second classroom, with a wall made of glass panels, towards the front of the building, which was arranged over the toilet.

The boys' upper hall, in other words the study room, occupied the eastern wing of the building. It had a high stage constructed against the back wall with a long seat on it, reached by a few steps. This building had been constructed in accordance with Ousta Mgrdich Paragham's plan – the Paraghams were a well-known family of *diurgers* [builders] in Bardizag.

The school was inaugurated with great solemnity after construction had been completed, with the priests, notables and a great number of villagers present. For such solemn occasions a high gallery built over the study hall door was used, reached by a staircase built into the wall itself. This gallery was also used for public prayer meetings and lectures.

The school had its own prayer which began with 'Glory to You, Lord God'. This prayer was intoned on inauguration day by Garabed Kahana Mkhalian's elder brother, Mgerdich Mkhalian, who died at the age of 21, on 5th December 1840.

The school's teacher (when it was located in the church's anteroom) was *Diratsou* Garabed, the son of the sister of the Protestant pastor from the Chamourdji Deroyents family. This was the same teacher who was appointed as the aide to the locum tenens – Boghos Vartabed – during the building of the church.*

In those days the *diratsou* had great renown as a person well versed in the Armenian language who also gave important lessons in grammar to the pupils. An argument broke out between *Diratsou* Garabed and the local teachers over these lessons after some time. It would appear that the local teachers were supported by the people, considering lessons in grammar to be superfluous. There were teachers who knew nothing of the subject, but that didn't harm their teaching. Dzallan Hadji Hovhannes Baba, the church guardian, also incited† the opposing teachers further under the following circumstances. A small room in the narthex below the stairs to the church's gallery had been assigned to *Diratsou* Garabed as his living quarters. The *diratsou* committed the 'sin' of working after dark and using up some of the church's candles each night, which Hadji Hovahnnes regarded as wasteful. Uniting the 'waste' of candles with the grammar lessons being superfluous became a powerful reason to make the *diratsou* resign, to save candles and the boys. He did, and the man they called *vareg* (*Diratsou* Garabed) was sent away.

The teacher appointed to the new school was *Diratsou* Hagop, who was known as Sari Hagop, of the Somoundjents family. He had a good voice and was an expert in singing canticles, and ran the school with an assistant (known as a *khalfa*). It would appear that he only taught things that were important to the boys. The textbooks of the time, from the easiest to the most difficult were the alphabet; spelling; Psalms; breviary; Gospel and Nareg. In those days nearly every boy in school set himself up as a class of his own, receiving his lessons on a one-to-one basis. The teacher would take a group of boys and would make each of them read the lesson from his own textbook.

Garabed Avak Kahana Mkhalian wrote the history of the new school with a preface written in marvellous classical Armenian, in which he inscribed the following: 'Great Solomon, wise in the Lord, said, "Love the light of wisdom"'.

60 – A personal educational initiative

I related, in the previous section,‡ the story of the construction of the first proper school building in Bardizag for the education of the village children. I'm sure,

---

* See Section 52.

† The actual expression used here is 'rubbed oil onto their bread'.

‡ See Section 59.

however, that it's not been forgotten that the only concern of the ordinary person from Bardizag, until that date (1833), was boys' education, girls' education being considered unnecessary – even a scandal.

Eight or nine years later, a native of the village, from the well-known Daiyan family that had shown such partiality towards devout, God-loving hermit life appeared. He had been an enthusiastic follower of the newly-established brotherhood of The Holy Mother of God in Manoushag. This man, by the name of *Diratsou* Stepan, collected all the little girls of the neighbourhood together and dedicated himself to teaching them to read and write in his house. This was the very first time in the whole of the province that it had happened and seemed to be another example of the faith his family held.

The people of Bardizag, however, being alert and intelligent and pursuing education and progress, liked and appreciated that sort of individual initiative, and wanted to adopt it. The village notables, seeing that the newly built school in the village could hardly cope with the great number of boys attending it, bought the neighbouring house owned by Stepan Magarian of the Geolliu family to serve as a girls' school. A significant number of small girls attended it learning to read and write, entrusting them to *Diratsou* Stepan, who was appointed their teacher.

This individual initiative, as a result of the circumstances described above, was the first community school in Bardizag to have classes for both boys and girls, something that continued until my day, in other words for almost a century, while the work of boys' education was older and was an enterprise lasting for two centuries.[*]

61 – Apraham Kahana's death and the fate of his supporters

Rev. Apraham died near Christmas 1834[†] and his burial took place with great solemnity. Garabed Kahana Mkhalian couldn't identify the name of the vartabed who led the funeral service.

---

[*] In my day, a young lady from the same family, Miss Marine Daiyan, with the help of German philanthropists, ran a small girls' orphanage in her own house near St. Dirouhi, where the orphans were given a simple primary education, food and family care. The orphans were gathered from all the places where Armenians had been massacred. The orphanage maintained its existence in Bardizag until the orphans reached maturity and, with the philanthropists' help, were settled and raised their own families. (Author's note)

Kasabian tells us that this orphanage was called 'the German orphanage' and was founded in about 1900. It looked after 16 orphan girls and had one teacher. Minas Kasabian (Farhad), *Hayere Nikomedio Kavarin Mech*, p. 255.

[†] The author refers to the Armenian Apostolic calendar, which places Christmas – or rather Theophany – on January 6th.

After Apraham Kahana's death, his supporters were led by Hadji Artin Der-Antreasian Bab, Apraham Kahana's nephew (his brother's son), who had been his right hand man during his lifetime. He was an important personality in the village. He knew how to read and write quite well; he ran a tailoring shop and many men worked for him in the trade. He had powerful and influential friends among the most important Turks and Armenians outside the village.

Hadji Artin, in Apraham Kahana's time, had not been able to secure a noteworthy position as a director and leader due to the kahana's very strong character. Perhaps he lacked the qualities and competence required for those things. Despite being respected even by his opponents in the village, in his day Apraham Kahana's party continued its slide and wasn't able to recover its old strength and authority. This party was somewhat aristocratic and clannish in its makeup, based upon house and family, from father to son.

Mgerian's party, on the other hand, represented the bourgeous class of people. By their individual efforts they created a name for themselves through hard work. They secured their positions and futures according to the demands of the time and belonged to this class as people born of their own efforts. The following anecdote describes them.

In my day, many years later, people said that a grandson of Hadji Artin Baba might be considered to be a bourgeois, thanks to the successes he achieved in work, but that he had a different spirit. This man got into an argument in the street with an ordinary person for some reason and, to prove his superiority and honourable standing, shouted at the man, 'I'm a hearth, a hearth!'[*] The man replied, 'How many *paras* does your so-called hearth cost? If you put three stones together, they form a hearth.' That man, with his illustrative, witty answer, announced a new principle in the social structure of the time.

On this basis Mgerian was a man of his times. The village notables now resembled him, gradually making his party stronger; the Turkish aghas also felt the value of that new force and grew closer to him.

People said that Eomer Agha, whose father Osman was such a sympathiser and Apraham Kahana's ally, had fallen completely under Mgerian's influence. He had the sensitivity to present Mgerian's young son Artaki with a field as a gift when he was born. People and times had changed and the future belonged to those who knew how to adapt.

62 – New arrangements for the supply of charcoal to the mint

I provided certain details about this trade in the pages above, and described its importance to Bardizag and its progress over years past.[†] I should like to provide some new information about it and close this page of Bardizag's history.

---

[*] The hearth was the most important part of the house.
[†] See Sections 14 and 24.

I already explained how, when the Turkish aghas' intervention ended, specific officials were sent by the Mint to Bardizag to supervise the trade. This new arrangement was made in 1835, during Mgerian's days.

These newly appointed 'aghas' didn't, however, want to live in the *ghonakh* [government building], so to give them satisfaction Mgerian persuaded the husband of one of his *kenagals* [sister-in-law], Ghanbour Ashdji Hadji Toros' Hadji Sefer[*] to assign his newly built house, near the Ayvazents gardens, to the aghas to live in, and he and his family moved to the government building that was otherwise going to remain empty. Hadji Sefer agreed and moved. By obligingly doing this, Mgerian gained the new aghas' sympathy and friendship. He then appointed one of the people under his protection, *Diratsou* Garabed Ayvazian, to work under them as their agent, as a result of which he would know everything that happened.

The board of the Mint, in those days, imposed a new tax the villagers called *binnime*. This was utilised to pay those working in the trade, the costs of the feed for the mules transporting the charcoal, as well as the expenses incurred by the new aghas for their living and food.

A ledger was used to record the expenses incurred by the aghas that was constantly added to by those collecting the tax. One of these collectors, Gadjar Sarkis, was given the nickname *gragi ti* [fire shovel][†] by the people of the village. It was an accurate description of the contents of the ledger.

This new method of payment for charcoal – the tax and limitless expenses that fell on the villagers' shoulders – became the reason for dissatisfaction and complaints. It meant that the trade would lose its value and appeal in the eyes of the villagers and so disrupt its regular flow. It would extinguish the initial enthusiasm felt by the villagers and their abandonment of the trade, the results of which would almost certainly be the transfer of the work to Zakar Agha of Ovadjek and the people of that village. After that, the Turkish officials' position was ended, something I mentioned in one of the sections above.[‡]

I should like, in connection with this, to give a few details about Ghanbour Ashdji Hadji Toros and his family. This man wasn't a native of Bardizag, but someone from the provinces who had served as a cook for many years in Artin Amira Ghazaz's house. When the amira died, he moved, on Mgerian's advice, to Bardizag, where he finally settled down and built himself a new house. He was a widower and had two sons, Hadji Sefer and another, as well as a daughter, Anna.

---

[*] The relationship of the two isn't really made clear here, but Hadji Sefer was Hadji Toros' son (see below).
[†] *Ti* means shovel, oar, rudder or helm.
[‡] See Section 24.

Ashdji Hadji Toros then married a widow of the Bodosian family of the village. He also married his son Hadji Sefer to Mgerian's sister-in-law named Haiyots and gave his daughter Anna in marriage to Kevork, son of Hadji Asadour of the Kiutner family.

63 – The plan to build a paved road between the port (Seymen) and the village. Opposition to this plan

We have already seen in this work how Bardizag's port – Seymen - grew and blossomed, but the way to it, taking about an hour from the edge of the sea to the village, often became almost impassable during the winter due to mud and water, not only for horses and carts, but for people too, as it was a rutted and neglected trackway.

The winter of 1836 was one of the longest and most severe. Snow fell for days on end. Great amounts of snow weighing a very great deal collected on the roofs in the village, some of which collapsed. Early every morning everyone would have to clear them of the snow that had fallen during the night by sweeping it into the streets to prevent any more collapses.

No one dared to go out.

By arrangement, two candidates for the priesthood,[*] *Diratsou* Tavit Hadji Mikayelian[†] and *Diratsou* Hagop Somoundjian, Hadji Sarkis' son, had been sent to Constantinople in the autumn to be ordained and, after their 40-day seclusion, were to return to Bardizag. There wasn't a bishop in residence in the diocese at that time.

The two were ordained there and, having finished their period of seclusion, started the return journey to Bardizag. They reached Seymen, but the route up to the village was almost impassable and thus a dangerous venture. Snow and ice had piled up in drifts, and the storms froze the blood. So the villagers, to ease the new priests' journey, sent quite a number of strong young men down to the port with the idea of making a path through the fields that were smothered in snow.

The state of the road from Seymen, as a result of the severity of the winter, captured Mgerian's attention and, convening a meeting with the village notables, he suggested that the road be paved to make it passable at all times. The meeting agreed. But certain people from the party that opposed Mgerian began, outside, to stir the people up against the plan and tried to thwart its implementation. They said, 'Mgerian wants to ensure a source of profit for himself; if he needs the road, let him have it built.'

One of these people was Hadji Krikor of the Ghaladjis, Apraham Kahana's brother-in-law and both Stepan Ghaladji's and Hadji Khacher's father, who at that

---

[*] They were to be ordained as kahanas.

[†] I believe that the author has given this individual the wrong baptismal name. We know that his *ordination name* was Tavit, so his *baptismal* name must have been different.

time was plying his trade of silvering vessels in Deyirmendere. He heard of Mgerian's plan to build the road and began to say whatever came into his head against Mgerian from there, cursing and swearing at him - Hadji Krikor of the Ghaladjis was known in Bardizag as *kiufiri dobrag* [bag of curses]. Those who heard him came and told Mgerian, who protested to the Turkish agha about him. Hadji Krikor was brought back to the government building in Bardizag from Deyirmendere. The Turkish agha cross-examined him, asked various questions and finally said, 'Don't you want the village road built?'

The answer was: 'Let the person who wants the road built build it.'

At this, the agha imprisoned him and had him beaten without mercy during the night.

Hadji Krikor's beating proved to be salutary. The opponents of the road scheme withdrew and kept their mouths shut 'because of pagan terror', but a mute hatred of Mgerian began among them, and they planned to assassinate him.

Several people from the ranks of those opposed to Mgerian were deputed to carry out the plan. Among them were Dovdji Hagop, Shelem Arabi Hagop, Deledjeg Asadour and Boghos, the son of the elderly priest Sarkis Kahana, all of whom, armed, would wait behind the Baghdasarians' house on Mgerian's route at night, to kill him when he left the government building to go home.

Fortunately, the plot became known before it was put into action, under the following circumstances. Dovdji Hagop's wife got to know of the plot and of her husband's participation in it. She begged and pleaded for them not to carry it out. She wasn't successful, so she went to see her sister who was the teacher *Diratsou* Hagop's step-mother. She told her of the plot and the fact that her husband was a part of it and begged her sister, 'I wasn't able to persuade him out of it; let my brother-in-law see and talk to him, otherwise our hearth fire will be extinguished,' and she wept. *Diratsou* Hagop heard this from the next room and rushed to *Diratsou* Sarkis Ayvazian, a teacher in school like him, and told him what he'd heard. Sarkis, in his turn, told his brother, *Chorbadji* Haroutiun Ayvazian, who was Mgerian's man. The four men were then arrested and taken to the government building. The Turkish agha decided on punishing three of them with a beating, with the fourth, Deledjeg Asadour, who was old, being punished by being shamed publicly, making him sweep the market area from one end to the other with a broom, with his feet squeezed into stocks.

The punishments were carried out. Deledjeg Asadour, a man of some dignity[*], was very affected by his punishment and fainted in the street with the broom in his hand. He was then taken home. Two of the other three were very severely beaten, while Boghos, the son of Sarkis Kahana, who was a much loved and respected cleric, was set free at the priest's request.

---

* The text reads 'a man with a beard.'

This incident added to the problems Ghaladji Hadji Krikor already had, and the opposition to the plan disappeared completely.

The road-building plan was then put into operation, on a collective work *(medji)* basis, with the whole village participating. Whoever had horses, used them. Those who didn't acted as labourers, using their physical abilities. The wealthy contributed by giving donations. Albanian builders were hired as experts in paving, joined by master builders from the village such as Leyloz, Lat Kashogh[*] (Andon oghlou) and so forth. The road was then completed, becoming a blessing for the village.

Thus, although Mgerian had been slandered, cursed, accused and regarded as a tyrant, he nevertheless did great things for the village, being able to have the church and school built, and the road constructed.

After doing these things, he undertook the building of sewage drains in the houses and parishes in the village, probably having to use reproaches[†] to do so.

64 – A Bardizag martyr (May 1st 1838)

The story of the martyr, in prose and poetry in classical Armenian, with repeated editing, was written by Garabed Avak Kahana Der-Krikorian. I am going to present it here in its broad outlines, as an incident in Bardizag's history. Those who want to read it in greater detail should read Garabed Kahana's book.[‡]

The martyr, Hovhannes Pirenian, was the son of Stepan and Takouhi Pirenian (who was Kevork Kahana's sister). This young man entered the service of a Turk named Ghoulakhsez Mehmed of Yordjiun as a farmworker. This Turk was known to the people of Bardizag as *Diratsou Meymed*, as he had learnt Armenian songs and often sang them. One such was 'Spring, spring! The time has come, come my love, be joyful…'[**]

Mehmed was a wealthy man, a charcoal merchant. He had two daughters, one married to a man with the title of *emir*, the second still unmarried. These two sisters, joking and perhaps with some fanaticism suggested, at every opportunity, that Hovhannes became a Muslim. Having become almost part of the family, he would innocently reply, jokingly, 'I will, why not?'

---

[*] Also known as 'Latakash'. The word means 'cloth puller'.
[†] He uses the dialect word 'chekh' here.
[‡] The book is *Vgayapanoutiun Hovhannes Bardizagtsvo yev badmoutiun himnargoutian Bardizagi yev shinoutian yegeghetsvo yev varjarani* [The martyrdom of Hovhannes of Bardizag and the history of the foundation of Bardizag and the construction of the church and school], published by the Armenian Apostolic Patriarchate of Jerusalem in 1933. (In classical Armenian)
[**] '*Karoun, karoun, hasial e jam, yeg, sireli, ourakhatsir.*'

One day it happened that he fasted as a devout believer on the feast day of St. James of Nisibis. (It should be explained that the feast of St. James was embraced with great fervour by the people of the village, as it was their church's feast day.) This coincided with the Muslim month of Ramadan. At this the two sisters and the turbaned emir were overjoyed that Hovhannes was fasting with them and spread word in Yordjiun that he had accepted the true faith. This resulted in preparations being made for the supposed convert's formal conversion, with Muslim religious men being invited for the ritual circumcision and the official conversion act to take place.

There was a Greek baker in that Turkish village at that time who heard of these things. He secretly met Hovhannes and advised him to escape to Bardizag, then to disappear.

Hovhannes, who hadn't even thought of conversion, seeing that the joke had become serious and dangerous, fled from the agha's house by night and went to Bardizag through the mountains.

His flight became known. The turbaned emir, at the head of a fanatical crowd, petitioned the *miusellimin* (governor) of Izmid, with the situation being presented with much exaggeration and false comparisons. The governor wrote to the agha of Bardizag telling him what had happened and ordering him to bring the boy to him so that he could cross-examine him.

Through the intervention of the notables of Bardizag, the Turkish agha replied to the governor's official letter: 'I have examined the problem. All that has been said is lies and calumnies about the young man.' At this the governor got rid of the fanatic mob.

The villagers, however, being careful, hid Hovhannes in the deceased Apraham Kahana's house, in the room which only he entered in his lifetime, thus putting Hovhannes under Hagop Kahana Aprahamian's protection. This encouraged Hovhannes not to be frightened and remain true to his Christian faith.

After some time the stories about Hovhnnes died away and he, after staying in Apraham Kahana's room for 40 days, returned to his father's house and even, after a time, thinking that everything had been forgotten, began to go out and about in the village.

The turbaned emir, however, continued to pursue the issue. His father-in-law, *Diratsou Meymed*, never agreed with this pursuit, but unfortunately wasn't able to forbid fanaticism even in his own house. The turbaned emir, despairing of the Izmid governor's position on the matter, approached one of Sultan Mahmoud's senior courtiers, a person named Kurd Hodja, who had been the sultan's boyhood teacher and was a fantical Muslim. This man, the Sultan's hodja (religious official) sent a severe and threatening letter to the governor of Izmid, demanding that he immediately arrest Hovhannes and send him to Constantinople.

The governor, frightened for his life, prepared an arrest warrant and passed it to a captain who, leading some policemen, went to Bardizag to carry out the order with the help of the local agha, and arrest Hovhannes and those protecting him.

Hovhannes was arrested and taken to Izmid and from there to Constantinople, to Kurd Hodja. Hovhannes was accompanied by Garabed Agha Mgerian, who was accused of harbouring an apostate. Mgerian took Hadji Garabed Dakhdag Baboukh, who had once been Apraham Kahana's personal bodyguard with him, as he had the same role in Mgerian's service, and was fearless in such situations.

Mgerian was able to free himself from the accusations and threats levelled against him through Saraf Misak Amira of Agn and returned to the village with his bodyguard. Meanwhile Hovhannes had been sentenced to death as an apostate and was sent to Izmid for the punishment to be carried out in Bardizag.

In Izmid, attempts were made to persuade Hovhannes to save his life by accepting Islam. He always refused, so was handed over to a squad of ten policemen to be taken to Bardizag and hanged. When the villagers saw their arrival, with Hovhannes in chains as a condemned man, they all scattered and hid, and the market and streets became absolutely deserted. The police looked for priests or notables without success. Finally they found the steward (*kehya*) of the day, Margos Reyis, son of Hadji Sarkis Reyis, and made him walk in front of them. Then they looked for somewhere to hang Hovhannes.

Finally, at the lower end of the market, at the entrance to the Baghdasars' street, they saw a mulberry tree and, passing a rope over one of its branches, hanged Hovhannes, keeping his body hanging for 27 hours (this was on 30 April 1838). Then, satisfied that they had carried out their orders, they gave the body to the village's notables for burial. The martyr was buried in a high place in the upper cemetery. When the police had left, the body was exhumed by night and brought by the notables and priests to the church. His right arm was cut off to be kept as a relic and he was then buried in the church's courtyard, next to the north wall.

After a time this right arm was encased in a silver reliquary at Ghalfa Garbed Amira's expense. The amira had one finger cut off and put in a silver case for himself. This silver-cased right arm relic was kept in the church's vestry, not being taken out until 1909.

A marble tombstone was made at Arakel Bey Dadian's expense (the son of Hovhannes Bey Dadian), eight years later. He had an oil lamp hung above the tomb, paying for the oil himself for many years.

The martyr's tomb in the cemetery, however, immediately after his death, became a place of pilgrimage for devout people who didn't know of his body's transfer to the church. The priests, falling into line with this expression of the people's fervent faith, held services, lit candles and swore oaths there. Many said that light came down from the sky at night and shone on his tomb, where miracles happened. The priests encouraged all these religious feelings, probably respecting the people's pious expressions, especially as all this brought them an income. The kahanas of that time were Kevork, Sahag, Garabed, Hagop, Tavit and Krikor Kahana Somoundjian.

The inscription on the martyr's tombstone, composed by Bishop Stepan Aghavni, reads:

> Come, happy children of men
> To see the ceremony of martyrdom,
> This is Hovhannes Stepannosian,
> A fit young man of the Pirenian family;
> He grew to the age of twenty,
> He suffered torture in prison, in the dungeon,
> Was tried twice because of an infidel
> After professing his faith in the Holy Trinity.
> In Bithynia's city of Nicomedia
> And in the palace in Byzantium's Constantinople
> Then in his village birthplace
> He was hanged by the wicked hands of the Turks.
> This tomb is the reliquary of his bones,
> The heavenly altar rejoices with his soul;
> May the pilgrims who visit this tomb with their pleas
> Have them satisfied, may they please you, Lord Jesus Christ.[*]

65 – Mgerian, wheat and cereals merchant, builds his own warehouse in Seymen

Mgerian, a skilful and able man, aided the development of Bardizag's economy with his enterprises.

We saw, before this, that the villagers gradually moved away from agricultural work and put their efforts into trades and engineering as more profitable occupations and better suited to local conditions.[†] On the other hand the villages' population grew and the requirements for grain for bread increased, as it was the main element in the villagers' diet. The grain was brought in from neighbouring agricultural areas – from Eski Shehir, Bolu, Khodjeli (Izmid) and areas on the other side of the mountains.[‡]

Under these circumstances, Mgerian became interested in the cereals trade and saw that European wheat had begun to appear on the Constantinople market, as did that from Romania and Russia, which were sold at lower prices and competed with

---

[*] This is translated from classical Armenian. It may need some revision. The tomb was located in the church courtyard, near the right-hand ante-room, and was made of marble. Minas Kasabian (Farhad), *Hayere Nikomedio Kavarin Mech*, p. 121.

[†] See Sections 14 and 48.

[‡] I have translated *Anteres* (the other face) like this, as the people of Bardizag referred to places on the other side of the line of hills and mountains behind the village in this way.

local varieties. So he began to deal in European wheat, buying it on the Constantinople market and selling it in Bardizag. This experience showed him that it was necessary to have his own grain store in Seymen.

With this aim in mind, he took over a piece of land next to the sea that, because of the water, was marshy. He had the area filled with soil, drained it, and built a large, capacious warehouse – an empty space enclosed by four walls and a roof – with an office built on part of the roof itself.

It would appear that he had ownership documents for this and other unused land prepared in his name by the Turkish aghas who were his friends. He stored the wheat bought in Constantinople in that warehouse and sold it, little by little, either in the region or the village.

The village had a community-owned warehouse and bakery belonging to it in the port before this, built on land that stretched as far as the sea shore and bought from the Kiurkdji Khanlian family. Mgerian became the owner of ground near this community-owned land and behind it, including a well under a hornbeam tree and, nearby, a place called Korel, where it was known that Turks had been buried in olden times.[*] He joined all this land to his own field that lay towards the village, forming a large property owned by him inside the port area, and on which he had great hopes for future development.

Mgerian's new enterprise and acquisition of the land, followed by his ability to obtain legal title to it, became the subject of slander and envy by his enemies, as someone who profiteered from his position and notability to become a property and land owner. We saw a previous example of this kind of slander, in connection with the construction of the church, and how it had come to nothing.[†] This time it was another attempt, using the building of the church as the basic premise, to make the people he protected– seat-holder Hadji Varteres Hadji Mikayelian and especially *Chorbadji Diratsou* Hovhannes Ayvazian, through whose hands certain purchases made in Constantinople for the church passed - seem suspicious. Among these were a picture of the Crucifixion worth 1,000 *kurush* and some paint. The aim of Mgerian's opponents was to discredit him in his community administration work.

Then whispers began in the village: 'Brother, has it ever been heard that a picture could cost 1,000 *kurush*? It's impossible – 1,000 *kurush*? With that you could build a house!' Another was: 'They bought the packages of paint for half a *kurush* and

---

[*] See Section 5.
[†] See Section 51.

recorded them in the ledger as costing two *kurush*! Can it really happen? They've defrauded the community!'*

These persistent whispers led, between 1830 and 1840, to trouble in the village, but the opposition's observations had no effect: Mgerian always retained his authority and honour. He was powerful and rich.

Over time, however, certain incidents further agitated Mgerian's opponents. For example, when Mgerian was taken to Constantinople, accused of harbouring the martyr and was able to prove his innocence, he remained there for some time with members of his family, probably to stay out of sight and not give his opponents an opportunity to create further problems for him. But when he found that the atmosphere around him had eased, he returned to Bardizag where his sympathisers welcomed him back with great honour, with notables, priests and a great crowd of villagers as well as the church choir meeting him and the members of his family at the entrance to the village, near the upper cemetery. When they saw him arrive, the choir began a song, written by the teacher of the time, Boghos from Armash, in his honour:

> You, the heir of the brave and happy race,
> You came, to the glory of our souls... etc.

They then escorted him to his house in a respectful procession.

His opponents' accusations continued, however, and were concentrated on those he protected. Finally one of his opponents, Hadji Garabed Paboudjonts, a bold and intrepid person, went by land to Constantinople, drawing breath in the Armenian Patriarchate. There he protested about corruption in the building of the church. At this, the Patriarchate decided to send an official communication to the prelacy of Izmid, ordering it to conduct an investigation into the matter. Hadji Garabed, however, dared to say to the patriarch and the amiras, 'Until you appoint an official inspector and send him to the village, your letter will have no result.'

The Patriarchate therefore decided to send a special financial auditor to Bardizag. The person chosen for this task was a monk by the name of Garabed Vartabed, who later, having been consecrated a bishop, became the prelate of Sivas and Kayseri, where much was said of him.

66 – The financial auditor Garabed Vartabed (nicknamed Yanghendji)† in Bardizag

Garabed Vartabed arrived in Bardizag at the beginning of the winter of 1839. He formed a financial auditing body under his chairmanship that held its official

---

* This is the essence of both slanders. It is impossible to replicate the actual dialect speech style in English. See the original in Mkhalian, *Bardizagn ou Bardizagtsin*, Sahag-Mesrob press, Cairo 1938, p. 205.
† Yangendji is Turkish for 'fire person' or 'fire raiser'.

sittings in the church's anteroom. The people who had to submit accounts, seat-holder Dervish Hadji Varteres Mikayelian and the agent *Diratsou* Haroutiun Ayvazian, presented the accounts of the church construction and details of the costs. Abadji Garabed, the well-known creditor and his friends Kel Sarkis Andon oghlou (Latakash),* Topal Hovhannes, Ghazaros Ghochoum, Khachadour Eyolen and others, seeing these never-ending expenses, the presentation of which took days, began to get angry, shouting, 'Brothers, what expenditure is there? There's no end to it! These accounts are like Yerevan's continuous sheep sale.'

The examination of the accounts continued day after day with no sign of ending. Seeing that there was no way of grasping anything from this accounting and understanding the extent of the corruption, Garabed Vartabed began to advise them to forget the past and try to secure peace between the two sides. To this end he said, in the presence of the notables, priests and everyone, 'What's happened has happened; no matter how you deal with it, it will grow until it snaps. Let's leave this accounting and all try to put some order into community work together and not provide any opportunity for discontent after that.' He then suggested that a new election of notables take place. Everyone agreed. Twelve people were elected as notables; a new steward (*chorbadji*) and a collector were also appointed. With this election and appointments, the two sides were somewhat reconciled and accepted the new arrangements.

On the following Sunday evening Garabed Vartabed ascended the steps to the altar to preach and, using the opportunity, to announce the reconciliation and election. When the time came to introduce the new notables to the people, a shout was heard from the women's door to the church, '*Yanghen!* [Fire!].

The people, terrified, rushed out of the church, leaving Garabed Vartabed's announcement unsaid. It was found a little later on, however, that there was no fire, the object of the shout only being to create panic and thus stop the priest's announcement.

Garabed Vartabed came down the steps from the altar, becoming very angry, and went into the vestry. The village priests and notables surrounded him and tried to soothe him. He, however, being extremely annoyed, shouted in Armenian and Turkish and threatened to shut the church and hand the keys over to the Patriarchate. The notables tried to calm him down, but he refused to be assuaged. They were eventually able to coax him into the church's antechamber.

Now it was Stepan Ghaladji's wedding that Sunday. The bride and groom were to be brought to the church for the wedding ceremony as dawn broke on the Monday morning. Garabed Vartabed, still upset and angry at the previous evening's events, refused to allow the church to be opened for the morning service. People came and went, approaches were made to him, and they were finally able to calm him down, promising to find the miscreant, whoever he might be, and punish him.

---

* Also known as 'Lat kashogh'

The church was opened very late, the morning service took place, and Stepan Ghaladji's wedding was solemnised. From that day on Garabed Vartabed's nickname in the village was *Yanghendji Vartabed* (Fire Monk).

He remained in Bardizag until the end of the Easter celebrations. He had a very good voice and pronunciation. On the feast of the Gospel writer John, it was he who read the 'Peace'. When he read the prayers part, he altered the sound of his voice and his style of reading, creating a great impression on everyone, who had never, until then, experienced such a harmonious reading of that passage.

When the service was over, the priests and notables, gathering in the church's antechamber, greatly appreciated Garabed Vartabed's sermon and reading. 70 years have passed since then and it has become the custom to read that passage from John's Gospel just as Garabed Vartabed did, with the priests vying with each other to make the opportunity theirs.

As for the instigator of the panic, it was later found that the guilty person was Hampartsoum Atanasian, Chopdji Atanas' grandson, an immature boy, urged on by the people who wanted to disrupt the announcement.

I should like, using this boy's wrongdoing as the opportunity, to record an important donation by a person from outside the village for the building of the village church. The donor was a person named Nalband Hadji Garabed of Arslanbeg, who having become a widower at about that time, came to Bardizag and remarried the aforementioned Hampartsoum's mother, three of whose grown sons were left in the care of their relatives in Bardizag. He took the fourth, Hampartsoum, and his new wife and returned to Arslanbeg.

Bardizag's notables, taking advantage of the situation, suggested to Nalband Hadji Garabed that he left a memorial in his wife's birthplace. So he had two richly carved panels for the interior *kavit* [narthex] door made from good quality walnut by a talented artisan from Broussa (Boursa) at his own expense.

Two famous kahanas were descended from Nalband Hadji Garabed in Arslanbeg. One was Hovhannes Kahana Nalbandian, his grandson, and Atanas Kahana Nalbandian, his grandson's son.

67- The death of the venerable Sarkis Kahana: an outline of his character

The venerable Sarkis Kahana died in 1839.[*] This priest was from the same neighbourhood as the Mkhalians, being from the adjoining house to theirs.[†] He'd had a stroke years before his his death but, bent over his cane, he used to go to the church. One day, when he was going there, he slipped and fell on 'Amouents' (the

---

[*] This is incorrect. I've seen his tombstone, used as a paving slab set in front of a public fountain in the village, in 1969, on which the date of November 3rd 1838 was inscribed.

[†] The phrase used here is 'of the same party wall'.

Kutners') bridge and was hurt. In spite of this, he continued to attend church. He used to sit on a chair with broken legs in church, continually looking at the other priests, except for Garabed Kanana Der-Krikorian, whom he didn't like.

When he was healthy, he was a learned, intrepid and dutiful priest. He had a book containing details of illnesses* and was interested in learning about medicine. He had books on the subject and many prescriptions written on paper. He was a devout priest. When he left his house to go to church in the mornings, he'd raise his voice in the street and shout 'Hey! All of you! Get up and come to church. Even the dogs are howling and begging for bread from God himself!' It was as if he wanted to start carrying out his Lord's orders, beginning with his family.

If he found a pebble in the road, he'd push it below the nearest wall using his cane. He had another unusual habit. On his way, if he saw a boy near the door to the Great Fountain, he'd gently pat the boy on the back. He played this trick on many people.

This good priest had a very sad life. His wife, who I believe was the neighbouring Momdji's (Momdjian) daughter, died young, leaving two young children. The first later became a kahana by the name of Sahag (the founder of the famous Der-Sahagian family). The younger one, Boghos, was only two years old at the time of his mother's death. Sahag Kahana looked after his old father and his younger brother for many years, looking after his father's parish as well, giving him the earnings from the parish. Sarkis Kahana lived the last years of his life in his younger son Boghos' house.

68 – A new census taken and government record compiled of agricultural produce and property

I wrote about the 1832 census above.† A new census was conducted in 1838-39 and records compiled of property and agricultural produce. The officials sent to Bardizag for this purpose stayed in Berber Alexan's house.

For this census, each citizen had to present himself to the officials, taking with him all his mature sons capable of walking, while the immature ones were recorded according to the declarations made by their fathers. The officials first recorded the father's details (name, surname, age and religion) then, with the same content, the sons. Females were once more excluded.

As far as registering land and assets was concerned, every citizen had to present, written on a piece of paper, a list of what he owned, showing, for each item, its location, category and extent (for land), each calculated by the number of hours a day required to cultivate it. The owner gave the listing to the officials who recorded

---

* The word used here is Armeno-Turkish: *kufenerov*.
† See Section 58.

it in their registers. The village notables appointed two clerks, one being Garabed Kahana Mkhalian's elder brother, Mgrdich and someone else to help those who couldn't read or write. Both of the men stayed in the church's room, where they prepared an ownership list for anyone who came to them. This was then handed to the officials. The government issued each owner with an identity document and ownership *kochouns* on the basis of these registrations, in which the value of the asset and tax payable were inscribed.

69 – Mgerian purchases new land and makes it into a farm. He also buys up all the houses surrounding his and makes the area his own

We saw, in previous pages, how Mgerian bought parcels of land near Seymen.* Now he began to turn it into a vineyard and orchards. He began to enclose all of it with a wall to bring them together and make one entity of them. He also closed the public road that ran through them and re-routed it through the area between his land and the neighbouring field belonging to the Boyadjis.

A mob of villagers, egged on by his opponents, went and demolished the wall. Mgerian prudently didn't interfere with that angry demonstration, but sometime later, when passions had cooled, rebuilt what had been demolished and completed it.

Mgerian was a diplomatic person, his more obvious virtues being generosity and magnanimity. Here is an anecdote that shows that trait in his character.

One day one of the villagers who had taken part in the demolition of the wall had an argument with his neighbour and, finding himself in difficulty, approached the agha (Mgerian), saying, 'Agha, I have a problem, free me from this man.' Mgerian listened carefully to the man's woes and finally replied, 'All right son, don't worry, I'll call him and make him keep quiet. Weren't you one of the people who demolished my wall? Never mind, sometimes people have need of one another,' wanting to take the opportunity to give this man a lesson, but also to sort out his problem.

After creating a farm and vineyard near Seymen he then purchased the houses in the village surrounding his own one by one. This extended his property to the edge of the market and was bounded on all sides by public roads. The houses he bought were Keskgin Stepan's, the Paboudjis', the Beylers', Beloran Movses' (nicknamed 'Yanghen'), Pattoug Ghazaros', the beadle Pandig Khachadour's, the Pirens' and Delo Hagop Krikor's. He did not buy Ghara Demirs', Pattouk Minas', Konda Hadji Minas' and Kachal Kevork's houses or Alacha Badjak Haroutiun's blacksmith's shop. This made a large area in the centre of the village his personal property, bounded by streets on every side, stretching from the market to the Agha's Fountain (Kousdigants' Fountain).

---

* See Section 65.

After making these purchases, he added new upper parts to his house, building a new-style kitchen and dining room and special rooms for the children where they had lessons with their own teacher. He enlarged the front garden, had new trees and flower beds planted, and established his own fountain in the house itself. He had a bakery, coffee house and shops built in the market, thus securing a prominent place in both the village and the province. 'Mger Oghlou's house' was famed far and wide.

These successes created envy and hatred. Envious people, when he was purchasing the houses, advised the owners to sell their properties at the highest possible price, as he would be forced to buy them. 'Let him run out of money,' they said, and prepared to applaud his failure, which they thought wouldn't take long. Mgerian calmly continued to buy up the properties and enlarged the area he owned day by day. When the purchases and building work were completed, Mgerian's friends gradually increased in number, with the important Turks from Izmid – Hadji Emin Bey, Mustafa Bey, Kharaman Zade Bey and others - now becoming his close acquaintances.

During the summer, the best time in Bardizag, he always had more than one visitor in his home every day. Rich tables and entertainments would be arranged at night in his garden, under the stars, with a large lamp being hung from a mulberry tree and a magnificent table set in front of the fountain. Hadji Bedros Mkhig, Mgerian's personal pipe man, would respectfully welcome the guests to the table and act as the waiter.

People used to say of Mgerian that he never ate onions; if he smelled them he would become angry, feel sick and even leave the table. The Turkish notables, who knew of this weakness, often played a trick on him, secretly adding a small piece of onion to his plate while he was otherwise engaged and, seeing his anger, laugh at him. On one such an occasion, when he saw the onion, he rose from the table with such agitation that he almost upset it.

Mgerian was now the one and only great agha in Bardizag. His strength and authority was at its peak. More than 50 families worked in his businesses. Everyone treated him with respect. The village notables sought his friendship and grace. The priests almost never left his house. This especially applied to one of them, Garabed Avakerets, whose paternal aunt Soultan was Mgerian's mother. The whole of Bardizag was in these two men's hands – the church in Garabed Kahana's hands and the public works in Mgerian's.

Garabed Kahana had an older brother named Stepan. This man's work failed and he fell into debt, forcing him to sell an important part of his possessions to pay his debts. On this occasion he sold one of his shops at the end of the church wall nearest to the government building to his brother Garabed Kahana and his cousin Mgerian, who divided it between them. Garabed Kahana's part was nearest the *building* and Mgerian's nearest the wall. Garabed Kahana had a coffee house built on his part, while Mgerian had a bakery and a shop built on his, with a room above it, with an exit [extension] over the market. Garabed Kahana didn't like this exit, so he suggested that Mgerian buy the coffee house. They agreed, thus making Mgerian the sole owner of the whole of Garabed Kahana's brother's former property.

Garabed Kahana, with the profit he thus made, bought part of the house belonging to Gerdjig Tatos (of the Gargedans), and built a coffee house there, known locally as 'Garabed Kahana's barber shop'.

70 – A new door is created in the church wall in the market, at the corner of the building owned by Mgerian

When the wall around the church was built, in the first years of Mgerian's dominance, only two doors were let into it: the main one opposite the Djangaloz's house and another, on the northern side. This was a small door near the Pandigs' and Chelengs' houses. The latter was for use by the women who were attending church from the eastern parts of the village. There was no door, however, at the eastern end of the wall, although there were many houses, with new ones still being built in that area. It was obvious that, in opposition to Apraham Kahana and his supporters – Apraham Kahana and Hagop Kahana were in exile at the time – the notables of the day, under Mgerian's leadership, did not want to create a door there. It was also true that all the old village clans – the Khacherians, Der-Antreasians, Apraham Kahana's, Hagop Kahana's and Garabed Kahana's families, the Der-Sahagians, Mikayelians, the Kiutnerians and so on - that had had such important roles in Bardizag's history had their houses in that part of the village. Garabed Kahana Der-Krikorian, the Der-Sahagians and the Kiutnerians, not wanting to be at odds with Mgerian hadn't intervened, it seems, in this deliberate omission.

After a time, however, Hadji Hovhannes Agha Khacherian, Apraham Kahana's younger brother, thought about the lack of a door there and said, 'Wouldn't it be good to have a door there, so that our mothers, wives and daughters could go to church using a short route? I am ready to have one constructed at my expense on our side.' He applied to the priests with this wish and obtained their agreement. Garabed Kahana also agreed, as he had cooled in his relations with Mgerian over the problem with the shop. Expert masons were called who found no problem in creating a door at the designated place. At this, encouraged by the reception he had received, Hadji Hovhannes, having the wall breached at that point, had a small door constructed right next to Mgerian's shop.

Mgerian, from whom this work was apparently kept secret, heard what had happened and considering it offensive to his honour, got angry and said, 'So! A door is constructed without asking my opinion?' People said that Mgerian protested to the government against Hadji Hovhannes about the change to the building, which had been carried out without permission. This resulted in not only Hadji Hovhannes paying for the door's construction, but also a fine for doing so. But the door was opened nevertheless, with Mgerian later using it to enter and leave his shop, having constructed a door in the shop's wall at that corner.

71 – Mgerian has a large horseshoe workshop belonging to him built opposite the cemetery

Mgerian's horseshoe business, with all his others, still remained his main occupation. We have seen, in previous pages,* that he opened a forge with two hearths in front of the Pandigs' house. He now wanted to enlarge this business and build a new, large facility on his own property.

His sister-in-law's husband, Hadji Toros' Hadji Sefer, had some land opposite the cemetery on which he had set up and ran a tannery. No one knows how Hadji Sefer obtained the land – but he did so by either buying it or by having it registered with the Turkish aghas in his name as unused ground. It is probable that it belonged to Mgerian and assigned to Hadji Sefer for the tannery, which was built significantly below the level of the cemetery. Mgerian began to build his workshop on that piece of ground which, however, was quite small, being only about 150 square *arshins* (about 816 sq feet or 90 sq m) in area; in fact it was too small for Mgerian's plans and needed to be enlarged. It was located between two streets which joined together a little lower down in front of the cemetery, becoming one road. Now this area of land, on one side, fell sharply from the edge of the road into the valley and was covered in wild plants and brambles.

Mgerian decided to have the slope raised and levelled to enlarge it. He therefore planned to have a high, straight wall built as high as the tannery's ground level at the bottom of the slope, and to fill the void inside it with soil. The masons built the wall – a long and high structure - with carters bringing stone and lime. The space between the wall and the slope was filled with soil excavated from around the cemetery on the side where the road led to the port. The final result was a large area, about three times the size of the tannery. No one dared to comment on Mgerian's somewhat cavalier way of doing things; people muttered among themselves, but the boldness required to oppose his plans was lacking. He had used his brains to profit from an empty area, the use of which had not been thought of until that time. It should not be forgotten that he spent money and employed hundreds of people on this project.

After preparing the ground, he had a small, neat house built on the old tannery site and, in front of it, a 20-30 sets of horseshoes' capacity workshop. The buildings on the site took months to construct. Mgerian used many precious, polished and beautiful marble slabs from the ancient monastery of St. Yeghia, located at Oulu Geol, in the construction of his house.

---

* See Section 48.

The forges in the workshop began to glow with heat where there were over 100 workers – master craftsmen, their assistants and apprentices. The workshop produced more than 40 *geyim* (sets of four) horseshoes a day, ready for finishing on the following day. Mgerian's business lasted until 1858, being a great source of wealth for him and providing many villagers with work.

During the construction of this workshop, a terrible accident occurred. One of Leyloz Hadji Krikor's small sons, Alexan, fell from the wall while playing and died.

After some time discontent arose in the workshop, the workers complaining that they were paid in a foreign currency known as *Mango* that Mgerian apparently obtained in Constantinople at a discounted rate from the money-changers in Khaviar Khan. He then paid his workers at the current rate, which wasn't enough to buy what they needed locally. Mgerian replied, 'If others don't accept this coinage at its value, bring it to me, I'll take it. Buy what you need with it from my grocery shop and bakery.' He thus made two profits from his workers: firstly from their work, and then through their purchases from the shops he owned.

To be fair it should be said that at that time this coinage was in circulation and Mgerian was paid in this currency for the horseshoes he sold. There were also Turkish coins in circulation: silver-plated brass pieces called *metalliks* with a face value of 5 or 6 *kurush*; there were halves and quarters of these, as well as those of 20 and 10 *paras*. The following gold coins were also used: the *memdouhie, khairie, mahmoudie, meserli, roubie, charkhli, dabanle* and so on that were later put into general circulation.

72 – Mgerian sells his property sited next to the church wall to the village community

Mgerian decided to sell this property to the community. When Bishop Stepannos Aghavni's locum tenens, Bishop Boghos Taktakian, visited Bardizag on the occasion of the feast day of St. James, he invited the notables of the village to a meeting under his chairmanship – Garabed Kahana Der-Krikorian was absent from the village as he was on a pilgrimage to Jerusalem – and said to those present, 'Brothers, I am going to sell this shop; I'm not interested and I've no time to be involved with it, so I've made my decision. Since the shop is between the community-owned *ghonakh* [government building] and the church, I find it fitting to make the following suggestion. We haven't got a prelature, which is a shame on our village, and the shop is a suitable place for one. Let's meet tomorrow, if it pleases you, and complete the deal.'

Hearing this, the locum tenens said, 'This would be a good thing; the agha's suggestion is *minasib* [fitting]. Don't let anyone else take over that property, I agree.' They were finally convinced and convinced one another. At the following day's meeting they wanted to reduce the price for the purchase. Mgerian demanded 30,000 *kurush*; the bishop intervened, offering 25,000. The people at the meeting agreed on this lower figure and the community became the owner of the property and retained it until my day. Part of the price was paid in advance, the remainder in installments.

With this capital Mgerian managed to buy several new houses in his part of the village and thus moved the boundary of his land towards the edge of the market.

In my day, a second storey was added to this building which, for a time, was used as the prelature. It had a meeting hall and a bedroom. There was also a kitchen and other facilities, and a large entrance way at the head of the staircase, which rose from the western edge of the church wall. Apart from the door in the church wall that has already been mentioned, there was a second one which opened onto the passageway known as the *tolalekh* which extended from the entrance to the left-hand vestry to the narthex.

There were two shops as well as a large coffee house (called the 'Village Coffee house') under the prelature.

73 – The ordination of two *sargavaks* [deacons] as well as a kahana from outside Bardizag

A delegation, accompanying a candidate for the priesthood, arrived in Bardizag from Nor Kiugh [New Village] in Nicaea in 1843. The candidate was a man from Ghendjelar who had married a widow in that village who was Archbishop Khoren Ashekian's paternal aunt. Bishop Stepannos Aghavni, who happened to be in Bardizag at the time, agreed to ordain him.

At Mgerian's suggestion, the notables of Bardizag took advantage of the situation and decided to have two deacons ordained as possible candidates for the priesthood, thus easing the work of the now elderly priests. Mgerian suggested that one should be *Diratsou* Boghos Simonian and the other *Diratsou* Garabed Daiyan (Eskin), the son-in-law of Hadji Boghos Djerga, who was one of his in-laws. When *Diratsou* Garabed declined, Dzallan Hadji Baba suggested his neighbour, Hovhannes Nahabedian (father of Vahan Vartabed[*]), as the second candidate, who accepted. They were ordained deacons at the same time as the person from Nor Kiugh was ordained as a kahana. They were to serve as deacons for four years and at the same time act as teachers in the school. These ordinations took place in the summer. Garabed Avakerets was also present as he hadn't yet departed on his pilgrimage to Jerusalem.

---

[*] The famous Vahan Vartabed of Bardizag (also surnamed Der-Minasian), who wrote several satirical books such as *Apeghatsak*, published in Constantinople in 1894, and who was sent to various places as a representative of the Patriarchate. See also Der-Hagopian, pp. 126-144. Hagop Baronian also wrote a brilliant satirical article about him in his series *Azkayin Chocher* [National notables]. See Hagop Baronian, *Collected Works*, Academy of Sciences, Yerevan 1964, Vol 2, pp. 149-158.

It was later in that same year, on the feast day of St. James, that Bishop Boghos Taktakian was in Bardizag and the property owned by Mgerian was bought by the community, as was described in the previous section.

Taking advantage of Garabed Kahana's absence and to escape his probable opposition, Mgerian suggested to the meeting of the notables and priests that the newly ordained deacons be ordained as priests immediately, claiming the village needed new priests. The priests who were present didn't dare raise any objections and, with the locum tenens' approval having been assured in advance, both deacons were ordained the same year. *Diratsou* Boghos was called Mesrob Kahana Simonian, and *Diratsou* Hovhannes Nahabedian, Minas Kahana Nahabedian.

Both new priests began their ministries after their 40 days of seclusion without having specific parishes, while continuing with their teaching as their way of earning a living. This continued until the elderly priests died and they took over their parishes and left teaching.

People knew that Mgerian, with these swift ordinations, aimed at stabbing Garabed Kahana in the back, as he had cooled towards him, as we shall see more clearly later on in the matter of these new priests obtaining their own parishes.[*]

74 – New agitation in the village concerning community accounts

New agitation began in the village between 1843 and 1846 over government taxes and community expenditure. The people, demanding proper accounting, saw that no one listened to them and lost hope. This was because of the slack attitude shown by the senior community leaders towards those who wielded power. A large number of them therefore went to Izmid to bang on the government's door and protest. These were the same people that had previously made the same demands. However Paboudji Hadji Garabed, the boldest of them, wasn't present as he and a group of friends had gone on a pilgrimage to Holy Echmiadzin. On the way back he left his companions to go to Sis,[†] wishing to be present at the blessing of the Holy Chrism, as he'd not had the opportunity to do so before that date. Unfortunately he became ill there and died soon after he reached Bardizag.

The leader of the protesters in this instance was Seli Minas' son Mgrdich, the father of Minas Agha Seliyian, one of the Protestant notables of my day and who was the late lamented Abadji Paboudji Garabed's brother-in-law.[‡] When the *miuselim* [governor] saw the crowd, he was much surprised and asked (in Turkish), 'What is this commotion? You are acting as if you are in your own state. Who is going to step forward from among you?

---

[*] See Section 85.
[†] The seat, in Turkey, of the Catholicos of the Great House of Cilicia.
[‡] Sister's husband.

At this, Kel Sarkis of the Andonents family (called Lat Kashogh or Latakash) moved to the front and, putting his hand to his chest, replied, 'Effendi, my....'

The governor, probably disappointed at the man's appearance, commanded (in Turkish), 'Take these people to the shipyard and make them work.'

They remained there for a short time, doing forced labour, and were then sent to the Izmid prelacy, so that their concerns could be understood. There they were shown a rough account, which they didn't understand. The people presenting the accountants were Kechedji Hadji Garabed Baba and Semerdji Takvor's Hadji Hovhannes who, although both wealthy and men of probity, weren't people who understood accounts and were unable to provide a clear statement of the transactions they had made.

75 – A visit by Armenian amiras to Bardizag

Boghos Bey Dadian, Khalfa Garabed Amira Balian, Yaghedji Boghos Agha Odian and Haroutiun Agha Chobanian, as members of a government committee, had accepted the task of studying the feasibility of building a cloth factory on the coast of the Bay of Izmid on the bank of the Kilegh (Ovadjoukh) River, at the place called Dermeni. The Armenian amiras had come to the area for this purpose on several occasions and had been entertained in Ghara Melkon's house in Izmid. Mgerian, one of Ghara Melkon's friends, had meetings with the visitors and took the opportunity to invite them to Bardizag, which they accepted.

The whole population of the village turned out at its entrance near the upper cemetery to greet the arrival of the illustrious guests. The amiras, in accordance with an ancient custom, threw bags of small change – ten and twenty *para* coins minted during Sultan Medjid's reign – into the crowd, which were accepted with enthusiasm and high spirits. They were entertained in Mgerian's house and gave gifts to the church, school, priests and teachers. Mgerian was able to capture the sympathy of the Armenian amiras, especially that of Khalfa Garabed Amira Balian.

After some time, an Imperial Cloth Factory was built in accordance with the amiras' report and according to the plan drawn up by the Khalfa Garabed Amira Balian at the above-mentioned location, with Armenians from the neighbouring villages taking advantage of gaining employment as workers and supervisors.

76 – Mgerian's final years of personal and public works

When Mgerian completed the construction of his horseshoe workshop, he had it fitted out and started production. Bishop Stepannos Aghavni visited the newly-constructed workshop, approved of it and congratulated Mgerian, and on that occasion wrote, in his own hand, a memorial that was to be placed over the entrance. It read:

> This iron factory
> Was newly built by the respectable
> Rich, premier notable Garabed
> The lauded heir Mgerian

Mgerian added a Turkish memorial to this and had it all carved on a marble tablet which was fitted into the stonework above the entrance.

Encouraged by Mgerian's example, many others began horseshoe production businesses in the village. The first was a Turk named Mehmed Effendi who lived among us in Aiyazma in my day. A second, called Simonian, an iron trader in Constantinople's Ghourchounlu khan, established a horseshoe workshop in Khaskiugh in Constantinople, which he operated using workers from Bardizag. Finally, the two Djergayian brothers from Bardizag established their own workshops in 1850, followed by the Dzallans, Arakelians, Kiuters[*] and others. The Mgerian house, however, remained the most famous due to the scale of its production, but this trade was about to gradually lose its appeal.

After some time Mgerian decided to build a coal store to cater for the needs of his workshop as well as the separate *mkhi* forges. To secure the area needed for these new buildings, he made an agreement with the village community notables and purchased a piece of land for 400 *kurush* that was part of the cemetery where there had not been any burials, on the edge of the public road, just below the Djangalozes house. At the upper end of that piece of land, near that Djangaloz house, a new door was built to the cemetery and, on the other side of the passage leading to it, Mgerian had an entrance built to his new coal store which, with the new forges, was now located along the length of this passage. It seems that, when these buildings were being erected, bones were found in the lower areas of the ground. He had them collected and reburied inside the cemetery.

The movement of these bones gave rise to a scandal, resulting in the people of the village becoming agitated. Whispers circulated that Mgerian had apparently collected these bones and thrown them into the valley. Although these whispers didn't have any results, they became the reason for the scandal that surrounded the village priests and notables of the day, who had sold that piece of the cemetery to Mgerian with flattering, unforgivable permission.

Mgerian was able to turn his attention to his land and vineyards near Seymen, despite all the efforts he was putting into his various businesses. He bought more land and forests adjacent to that he already owned. He enlarged his farm and planted stands of mulberry and oak trees. He had already built a *sheramadoun* [silkworm house]; he now built two more large ones, as well as a beautiful chalet[†] for his family to live in. He brought his own water from Azariayin Pos [Azaria's

---

[*] This might be a misprint. The name might well be Kiutners.
[†] The author uses the Turkish word *keoshk* here.

Hollow], located near Hrom Village's mill, to his farm and built a fountain like the one in the garden of his house in the village. He carried out changes to the boundaries of his land without reference to anyone. Thus the road to the port, which was once removed from the Semerdjians' land and now went through the forest belonging to the Bordj Oghlous, was returned to its original route in the Semerdjians' field, Mgerian having bought the forest with the aim of joining it to his land. He had many people working and permanent staff on his farm all year round, and kept his own guards there. He began the large-scale production of crops and other produce, especially of fruit and silk worm cocoons.

The extravagant extensions to his farm and workshops required a great amount of capital. To secure it, he exploited not just all his personal wealth, but also borrowed great sums with interest from Khalfa Garabed Amira. The amira encouraged Mgerian to become the greatest landowner possible, believing that the value of the land in Turkey would rise greatly very soon with the probable mass influx of Europeans into that part of the country.

Mgerian also thought of giving his sons the education demanded of the time. After they completed their primary education in the village, he sent them to the monastery of Armash with the wish that they would develop their education. He even, for a time, sent his second son, Sarkis, to the Gymnasium in Uskudar that was, at that time, a centre of the highest educational standards and under the amiras' care.

After preparing his sons in this way, he placed them in his own businesses: the oldest, Hagopig Effendi, in his horseshoe sales office; Sarkis Effendi in his businesses in Bardizag – both the farm and the horseshoe factory. Hovhannes and Artaki were still too young at this time to go to work.

It was natural that, bearing in mind the scale of his businesses, Mgerian would need other people to manage it. One of these was *Diratsou* Hagop Bodourian, who at one time was a teacher in Ghendjelar. This teacher entered Mgerian's service in 1810 and continued working for him until 1845. He had been sent on important missions to Constantinople, Tekirdagh and finally Izmir. While he was there he suddenly left the work he was entrusted with and returned to Bardizag. These developments brought him under suspicion: the accounts were examined and a great deficit was found as a result of his embezzlement. The missing amount was demanded from him. Bodourian, replying 'I've no debt,' refused to pay. The problem was handed over to the Turkish agha of the village, who imprisoned him and kept him under pressure.[*] Despite his will, he was forced to go to great lengths to pay the sum demanded of him.

---

* The word used here is *neghel*: to trouble, vex, plague, pester, annoy, narrow, contract, constrain.

Mgerian also had his brother-in-law working for him, a man called Kherlod Sarkis, who rather than being a man of business was more like a parasite. Every time the accounts were checked, there was a deficit. Mgerian would strongly rebuke him, saying, 'What's this? How many times…?'

The answer, given by Kherlod Sarkis without any embarrassment was, 'Well… write it off to me…'

Mgerian replied, 'Do you have anything else I can write it off to?' and sacked him.

Kherlod hung about in the village without any work and remained hungry. He then went to his sister (Mgerian's wife) who took pity on him and went to her husband, begging and pleading for him to arrange some sort of employment for her brother. Kherlod was sent to Constantinople, not to work, but simply to reside there and draw a salary. This useless individual, instead of being grateful for his brother-in-law's generosity, bore him a grudge and joined Bodourian against him.

The latter, at that time, was in Constantinople, hoping to find work. He was in debt and in a hopeless position. His brother, Magar Reyiz looked after him – Magar Reyiz was a ship's captain and had a good job in those days. Bodourian and Kherlod Sarkis, the two discredited individuals, having found each other, decided to approach Mgerian's friend Khalfa Garabed Amira to protest at the apparent injustice that Bodourian suffered.

They wrote a letter and Bodourian took it to the amira.

The amira read it, felt sorry for Bodourian's state and wrote a personal letter to Mgerian, drawing his attention to the fact that a man who had served for five years in businesses like theirs, even if he had made losses, was worthy of having his debt glossed over, especially as the poor man had children, was unemployed and hungry.

Mgerian was affected by the amira's letter, which was a criticism directed at him; he didn't want to refuse the suggestion made as he had need of that great man. So when Bodourian returned from Constantinople, Mgerian called him to his office and returned the money he had got from him. This individual, instead of being thankful for Mgerian's generosity and keeping his mouth shut, went about with it in his hands, saying to everyone he met, 'Look I got my money back from Mgerian.'

Everyone in the village heard what had happened, it becoming a cause celebre. Encouraged by this, all those who had a problem or had a complaint against Mgerian, real or false, rushed to Constantinople to present it in writing to the amira.

The teacher *Diratsou* Sarkis, son of the beadle Pandig Khachadour did the same after the Bodourian episode. Mgerian had bought a house from his father. In his letter to the amira, *Diratsou* Sarkis complained that Mgerian had bought his father's house very cheaply by pressurising him and that they, the children, had suffered and lost much because of Mgerian's actions.

The amira realised the error of his previous intervention, so he took no notice of it. But it would appear that he told the story on some occasion to Mgerian's son Hagopig Effendi, resulting in the village knowing of this new approach.

The teacher, before he went to Constantinople, had asked the notables of the village to increase his teacher's salary. On his return from the city, a meeting was convened to discuss the matter. *Diratsou* Haroutiun Ayvazian, Chorbadjian's and Mgerian's man, asked why he had gone to Constantinople. The teacher, in all innocence and without embarrassment, told the meeting all about the problem; Mgerian was also present. At this, Ayvazian, beside himself with anger, verbally attacked the teacher and a fierce argument began, with scandalous and despicable words being used. Mgerian intervened and, directing his words at the teacher, said, 'My son, if you had a problem, you could have come to me. Why bother the amira with such a thing? It was wrong of you and demeaning for me.' But to smooth over the situation, he suggested that the teacher's salary be increased and that he kept quiet. People said, regarding this story, that when the teacher's father, the beadle Khachadour, was playing a tune on the wooden and metal bells, Mgerian said, 'Play, you shameful man, play! Your son's a teacher. What more do you want?'

But the situation didn't end there. Mgerian's opponents didn't want to lose the opportunity. Garabed Kahana, whose coldness had deepened against Mgerian, worked with Hadji Artin Der-Antreasian, Djangaloz Kerope, *Diratsou* Hagop and several others, and prepared a document of protest containing 24 accusations, notable among which were: the illegal occupation of land within the port; the purchase of part of the cemetery; the defilement of the remains of the dead; his avoidance of Holy Communion in the previous 12 years and many other similar things. The document was prepared in three copies: one was sent to the Patriarchate, the second to Boghos Bey Dadian, and the third to Khalfa Garabed Amira. They were unsigned: 'We were frightened of signing it.'

At this, Khalfa Garabed Amira called Hagopig Effendi (Mgerian's son) to him, handed him the document and said, 'Go to the village and show this to your father. Let him find out who wrote it and what they want. Don't provide any opportunity for this sort of thing to happen.'

Mgerian called a meeting and had the accusatory document against him put on the agenda. He suggested that the authors come forward and prove their accusations. No one dared to say anything; all of them said, 'We don't know anything about it.' The matter therefore reached no final conclusion.

77 – The church's water problem

There was a small fountain and basin at the corner of the Kousdigs' shop in the market, opposite the church wall. The priests had a consultation with the notables and the decision was reached that the source of the fountain would be deepened to increase its flow, thus enabling them to divert some of the water into the church courtyard.

The Kousdigs agreed, and the work began. The source was opened, the priests performed the ceremony of *khachhankisd* [Repose of the Cross] and the next stage in the deepening of the source of the water began. It was noted that, in actual fact, the amount of water flowing did increase. Mgerian intervened at the last minute, having the excavations stopped, saying that the water he owned had been reduced, as the sources of his and the one that was being diverted were very close to each other.

The people of the village became upset and there were arguments between Mgerian and the notables; the problem grew. On this occasion, one of the priests, to prove the community's rights, said, 'We performed the ceremony of Repose of the Cross; the flow increased. The water is ours.'

'Oh, so you're the prophet Moses, you strike the rock and water gushes out?' Mgerian sarcastically replied, having lost his serious demeanour in his annoyance. The battle took on a more serious air at this scandalous utterance.

The villagers' side was supported by the aghas Stepan Chayian and Haroutiun Saroukhanian – the Armenian directors of the Imperial *Choukhakhane* who lived in Bardizag. This group was joined by Haroutiun Ayvazian, Mgerians former protégée, who now, having left his position as a *chorbaji*, had become friendly with the latter aghas and had gone over to Mgerian's opponents.

The villagers, strengthened by these defenders and despite Mgerian's protests and intervention, diverted a part of the water to the church courtyard, where a fountain and basin were constructed, called *jamoun aghpiur* [the church's fountain]. Some time later, however, the water from the Koustigs' fountain lessened, then ceased. Mgerian, whose star was beginning to wane, had some of the water from his own source diverted into that of the church to allow the fountain to flow, so as not to give his opponents any excuse to inflame the people of the village against him.

78 – The origin of Saroukhanian's and Ayvazian's enmity towards Mgerian

Haroutiun Agha Saroukhanian from Constantinople, as the director of the imperial factory and a person of importance and office, was respected by everyone in Bardizag. He was also, for a long time, Mgerian's friend, tied to him by respect and sympathy.

Saroukhanian had an unmarried sister named Areknaz. His other sister, known as Ilimonia Doudou, was well known in Bardizag. He wanted to have Areknaz marry Mgerian's third son (later Hovhannes Kahana Mgerian) with the wish to strengthen his ties of friendship with Mgerian by this marriage. In one way or other he was able to convey this to his friend Mgerian, who refused the match with great tact and delicacy, saying that his son was still too young. This was the reason for the coldness between the two erstwhile friends.

As for Ayvazian, he was a son-in-law of the Mgerians, and had been his man for many years. He was respected in the village as a knowledgeable and active man. He had an adopted son named Haroutiun who was quite well educated, having learnt Armenian, Turkish, and Greek, and had great experience in accountancy.

Saroukhanian took this boy into his service and appointed him a clerk in the imperial factory. This is how the friendship between Saroukhanian and Ayvazian began, with the latter becoming a member of Saroukhanian's circle of sympathisers; because Ayvazian had cooled towards Mgerian because of the church fountain incident described above, he agreed with Saroukhanian and they took the part of the villagers against Mgerian.

Mgerdich Melikian (Ayvazian) was *Diratsou* Haroutiun Ayvazian's brother who was, for a time, the Patriarchate's Chancery Officer in Constantinople. He then took over the ownership of the daily newspaper *Hairenik* and maintained and edited it for many years. He left an honourable name in Constantinople Armenian intellectual circles as a community activist.

The aforementioned adopted son Haroutiun went to Constantinople after a time, having been promoted, joining the Imperial Zeitoun Broun Factory.

79 – An attempt to conscript Christians into the Ottoman armed forces

An imperial decree published in 1846 put the military conscription of Christians into law. The governor of Izmid, on the basis of this decree, invited the leaders and notables of the Armenian and other Christian communities to see him, and read it to them.[*] He charged the representative of each Christian community to call a meeting, each in its prelacy, and determine the number of those who were to serve in the armed forces from each village and community.

As a result, a meeting was convened in the Armenian Apostolic prelacy of Izmid, and it was determined that Bardizag's share would be six men.

Bardizag's representatives, having heard this decision, returned to the village and began to choose six young men on the basis that the potential recruits were to come from families that had three or more sons, provided that they were more than 20 years of age. They therefore set about identifying them, instructing the *chorbadji* (steward) Takvor Oghlou, accompanied by a single government policeman, to detain and bring them to the government building.

The families that satisfied the criteria were panic-stricken and hid their sons. The steward managed to detain one of the men, Toros, son of Semerdji Sarkis, in the market. Toros didn't want to surrender, and his friends and relatives arrived and were able to help him escape.

The notables decided, in view of this difficulty, to detain six unmarried, defenceless men and hand them over to the government. They arrested one such young man called Djidjig Sahag in the market, where he clung to a cart and refused to go. A crowd collected around the man and the people who wanted to arrest him,

---

[*] The word used here for decree is *Bouyroultoun*.

shouting, 'Brothers, what do you want of this poor man?' Sahag, taking advantage of the disturbance, escaped.

The notables, caught between government pressure and the resistance of the village populace, then decided that those families with sons of conscription age should pay a military service exemption tax and, with the sum accumulated, hire six Armenian soldiers, who in return for the money, would join the army.

One of the greatest of Izmid's Armenian notables, Melkon Agha Dobrashian, was invited to Bardizag to assist in the implementation of this decision. In concert with Mgerian, he and the village notables wanted to carry out the order by every possible means. They convened another meeting, calling for representatives of families with sons of conscription age to attend, and put the decision before them. Some agreed to pay some money, while others, saying they would pay, left and didn't return. Despite this resistance, the notables were able to raise enough money to serve as the military tax.

Naturally all this took considerable time. The government, meanwhile, grew angry and wouldn't wait, and police officials were given orders to arrest any male from Bardizag found in Izmid, without reference to age. With that aim, police squads spread out throughout the town – in the market and the various khans and streets, and were able to arrest the following people from the village: Gabedj (Bodourian), Kel Hagop of the Vartabed family, Agodjig the grandson of Oshin Apkar, Shelem Haroutiun Arabian and Hagop of Giurle, who was married to a woman from the village and had settled there. So there were five men, and the village notables, with the money collected (6,000 *kurush*), hired a young man from Adabazar to make up the number.

These six men were sent to Constantinople as Bardizag's recruits to serve in naval ships. Of these, Gabedj returned to Bardizag within the year, having obtained his freedom through skulduggery. What he did was to urinate in his trousers every night and spread the urine all over himself, making himself stink. His officers rebuked and insulted him on a daily basis, calling him 'dirty rascal', or 'infidel'. Gabedj, however, carried on without worrying, until the officers, sick and fed up with him, discharged him as a person unfit to serve.

Shelem Haroutiun Arabian's parents, paying bribes, were somehow able get him out of the navy before his term of service had ended.

The remaining four continued their military service for the full term and returned to Bardizag alive and well. Their task had been to wash and clean the ships, to do the soldiers' laundry, and to serve in the kitchens and at table: in other words serve without weapons.

Those who returned told how the officers of the ship had given Hagop of Giurle, who had a powerful and sweet voice, the task of shouting *'Padishahm chok yasha!'* [Long live the Sultan] at the top of his voice every time the sultan passed the warships in his twelve-oared barge, as he occasionally did.

The government, before issuing the decree concerning Christians serving in the armed forces, used to collect three levels of military tax from its Christian subjects. The *ala* (highest) – 60 *kurush*; *evsat* (middle) – 30 *kurush*; and *edna* (lowest) – 15 *kurush*. But when it started to recruit Christians into the army and navy, the tax was abolished. Later, however, when this recruitment attempt failed, it re-established the tax, the amount and payment of which was determined by a new census taken in 1848, conducted by a high government official named Kel Pasha.

80 – The re-use of a site within the port by building a community bakery and coffee house on it

Mgerian's in-law Hadji Bedros Djerga was the chief treasurer of the school in 1843. He hardly knew how to write; he would collect the school income, pay the teachers their monthy salaries, pay any expenses, in all about 500 to 600 *kurush*, and have the accounts written up in a notebook by one of the teachers.

Mgerian abolished his position after some years, saying, 'Our in-law has grown old, he can't carry out that function anymore,' and replaced him as treasurer with his cousin* Hadji Hagop Mikayelian.

Diratsou Hovhannes Mkhalian (Garabed Kahana Mkhalian) and *Diratsou* Toligian were the two assistant teachers in those days, with *Diratsou* Sarkis Pandigian being the school teacher.

Diratsou Ayvazian took these teachers one morning to the agha's – Mgerian's – house. The agha, at that moment, was sitting on a chair in front of the fountain in his garden with the mouthpiece to his hookah in his hand, the tube of which was about 12 *arshins* (about 25 feet or 8 metres) long. The *chorbadji* (steward) Takvor Oghlou was seated on another chair and was wearing a rolled turban; he was almost bent double with respect.

Hadji Hagop, the new treasurer, also arrived and sat next to the steward. Mgerian, directing his words to Hadji Hagop, said, 'You're going to be treasurer and these boys,' referring to Mkhalian and Toligian, 'are *khalfas* (assistant teachers) for the school. Pay one 50 and the other 40 *kurush* a month. The salaries of the teachers are already well known. The account has to be obtained from our in-law and the book handed over to you.'

'Thank you, Agha,' Hadji Hagop replied.

Mgerian, turning to the steward, said, 'Is it *minasib* [suitable]?'

'Agha, it is very *minasib*,' Takvor Oghlou replied, with great deference, rising slightly from his seat.

It was during Hadji Hagop Mikayelian's term as school treasurer that the new community-owned bakery and coffee house were built in Seymen. The site itself

---

* Mgerian's mother's brother's son.

belonged, at one time, to Hassan Effendi, who had a store* there, located in front of Mgerian's warehouse and shop on the seashore. They were built on the site after it had been demolished. The coffee house had an upper room that was rented out to the government and used as a customs' office.

Hadji Hagop was responsible for overseeing the construction and use of these new buildings. He employed master craftsmen and labourers and purchased all the necessary materials – lumber, timber, nails etc. When construction was complete, the treasurer's accounts were examined. It was found that he had recorded all the expenses, purchases and wages one below the other, without arranging them – simply writing 'timber this much', 'nails so much', 'wages so much' etc., without invoices, receipts or dates. When the accountants saw the state of the accounts, with everything mixed up, they looked in astonishment at one another and one of them, Dzallan, losing his patience, shouted, 'What is this, brother? Lumber, nails, timber... there is no end to it...'

Hadji Hagop Mikayelian's nickname from that day on became *Kam* (nail) and in my day the family were usually known as the Kamians.

81 – Deacon Megerditch Mardigian (Miapanian)

Deacon Megerditch Mardigian, one of the teachers of the time had been a follower of Bishop Hovhannes† in his youth, as a member of the brotherhood of Manoushag. He had also been ordained a deacon by the abbot of the brotherhood, the same Bishop Hovhannes. The deacon was one of those of the new order about whom songs were written.

He was, from that day on, known as a deacon and served in the church in Bardizag. Some time later he was made a teacher. This deacon was a very good, humble and devout man. He had very good handwriting. His conduct in the school was good enough to serve as an example. He would give the little ones good advice and his influence on his peers was always good and constructive. He died as a deacon, at an early age, in 1845, leaving two orphans, Hovhannes and Hagop Mardigian.

82 – The *bazar khayeghs* [caiques, boats] belonging to the Bardizag community

The journey between Bardizag's port of Seymen and other sea ports, especially Izmid was made by boat from very early on. A *navoghchek* [ticket] cost 10 or 20

---

* The word used here is *maghaza*.
† This bishop is the one who built the the priest's hut *(vartabedin khoutse)* and was an ancestor of the Goudjoukians. He was exiled by the government, after a protest by the monks of Armash to the Patriarchate, and died in Kayseri. See Section 40.

paras. The owners of these boats were usually from Izmid, a coastal people who, from their earliest days, were used to boats. There were Turks, Greeks and especially Armenians among the boatmen. The latter, due to their links with Armenian villages on the opposite shore, were very active and had gained a sort of near monopoly. Thus, right up until my day, the trade with the port for Ovadjekh and Dongel, named Bash Isgele, was in the hands of Armenian sailors from Izmid.

We've already seen that trade blossomed in Bardizag's port due to the transportation of charcoal for the Imperial Mint. In Apraham Kahana's day the people of the village owned a cargo boat for that purpose that plied between Seymen and Constantinople, as they wanted to retain the profit and make the trade their own.* When the charcoal trade was transferred to Zakar Agha of Ovadjekh, the Bardizag notables sold the community-owned boat.

Some of our people saw, however, that trade and transportation between Bardizag and Izmid were increasing on a daily basis. They also had experience of the profits water-borne transport could bring. The Amous, an independent trading family that dealt in charcoal and timber in Mgerian's day, wanted to have their own boat to transport the goods they bought between Seymen and Izmid, especially the barley that was fodder for horses and the flour or wheat for the needs of the workers. At the same time the Izmid sailors continued to transport passengers as usual.

The Bardizag notables, taking their cue from the Amous' initiative, and with the idea of allocating the profits of such trade and passenger transportation to the community schools in the village, reached agreement with the Amou family and bought three large boats or caiques – called *bazar khayeghs* – that were to provide the same services on behalf of the Bardizag community, as the passengers embarking at Seymen were all Armenians from the village.

The Amous' initiative had operated without much notice being taken of it as an independent business. Now that it was becoming a Bardizag community enterprise, the Armenian sailors of Izmid became panic-stricken and the trade became the subject of great arguments and competition between them and the men from the village. This issue became the reason for the embittered relations between the two groups. This occupied the notables of Izmid and Bardizag as well as the local government for a considerable time. It even involved the community and government authorities in Constantinople. Arguments and fighting between the men from Bardizag operating the *bazar khayeghs* and the sailors of Izmid were daily occurrences.

The seaport of Seymen belonged to the Bardizag community; it forbade any Izmid sailor to even approach it. The government stepped in, finding the ban illegal. The people of Bardizag, angry at this, and knowing about their profits and zealous to retain them, declared a strike against these 'foreign' vessels and only transported

---

* See Section 24.

goods and people in their own boats. The Izmid sailors found that they had no customers and were forced to reduce their prices, competing against the Bardizag *bazar khayeghs*. The people of Bardizag, however, paid more and travelled in their own boats, only a few being attracted by the temporary bait of cheaper prices. The Izmid sailors persisted in their hopeless and unsuccessful battle, even transporting passengers free of charge, but their efforts proved self-destructive.

The people of Bardizag endured every difficulty, noting that trade was free and people were free to travel in whatever boats they chose, especially as the *bazar khayeghs* were theirs and what they gave with one hand they recovered with the other.

The Izmid sailors' ire lived on for days, months and years until, under the force of circumstances, they had to finally give up the battle. Thereafter peace was restored on the sea, and the service became a sort of monopoly for the people of Bardizag that lasted until 1910, the days of freedom, when it was transferred to a steamship company that undertook to pay the whole of the community part of the *bazar khayegh* service.* Thus the community budget was freed from the heavy expenses connected with running that business.

This enterprise by the people of Bardizag was a clever and well thought-out arrangement to promote the local community's interests, although without a regular control mechanism; the profits it created were used to improve education in Bardizag, an activity that was one of the most praiseworthy aspects of public life in the village, provided with the greatest assiduousness and sacrifice, and in which the best possible future was seen for its children.

Three sailors sailed each *bazar khayegh*, one of them being the captain, to whom the title *reyiz* [captain] was given. An important number of them were from Izmid, although descended from people from Bardizag, among whom I can recall the following individuals: Khnami, Hovhannes *reyiz*, Garabed (Eolen) *reyiz* and others. The daily income from them was divided into four equal parts: the three sailors received a portion each, with the *reyiz's* portion being slightly more, and the fourth portion belonged to the community. This was used to pay the boats' daily expenses, repairs, fittings, and, if necessary, the cost of a new boat to replace an old one.

Accounts and the overseeing of the service were, for many years, entrusted to the representatives of the Amou family, whose own cargo movements were practically free of charge, something that was winked at, as the Amous were the people who created the original concept.

The amount due to the community was taken by the representative to the school treasurer on a weekly basis. In my day, the fare for one person was two coins (80 *paras*), much cheaper than in the past, of which a quarter (20 *paras*) remained in the community's coffers and from which, as I said, the boats' running expenses were

---

* See Section 145 (3).

paid. That small sum, however, represented the school's most significant income, compared to that provided by the rents of the other community-owned land. Later in my time, the task of overseeing the boats was taken away from the Amous and given to a specially hired official and subjected to a control system, leading to a more satisfactory result, even though the official had to be paid.

83 – The teacher Mourad of Peria

A new, important educational innovation, if not in results, at least in terms of ideology, began in the province of Nicomedia in July 1847. Mourad of Peria, the Armenian language teacher and musicologist, was appointed as general director (a sort of educational inspector) of all the Armenian schools in the province, by the decision of the meeting convened in the prelacy of Izmid of all the representatives of the communities in Nicomedia. His salary and expenses would be paid for by a levy on every school, perhaps according to their budgets.

When Mourad officially visited Bardizag for the first time in accordance with the terms of his office, he met the notables of the village and put before them, for their approval, his educational plans for the village school. It included putting rows of desks in the classrooms, each row being higher than the one before it, so that the students would sit and study while the tutor, in the centre in front of them, could supervise; secondly, giving each student a number to be used in place of his or her name. These arrangements were duly implemented. Then the teachers were reassigned as follows: director, *Diratsou* Garabed Bodourian; teachers, *Diratsou* Kapriel Semerdjian and *Diratsou* Sarkis; music teacher, Deacon Sarkis from Broussa (Boursa); treasurer and accountant, Krikor Kahana Somoundjian (Hatsouni). At the same time an advisory board – a trusteeship of 24 members - was set up.

Unfortunately, these arrangements made by the new general director for the Bardizag community schools didn't provide any significant results. I don't know if, later, any similar arrangements were made by the general director.

84 – Garabed Kahana Der-Krikorian sent to Armash monastery to repent

At about this time[*] the married leading priest Garabed Kahana Der-Krikorian was sent to Armash, apparently to repent, where he remained for two months. I have no idea what sin or wrongdoing was ascribed to him. People only said that in his history of the construction of the church he altered and added things, trying to diminish Mgerian's services in its building and putting, in place of his name, the general word 'notables'. He thus tried to ignore Mgerian's leadership and important role in that work.

Everyone knew that Mgerian had completely lost his trust in Garabed Kahana and Hagop Kahana Der-Aprahamian in his last days. They opposed his plans and he therefore wanted to bring his chief opponent, Garabed Kahana, to order, by taking in

---

[*] The year is not given, but by context it could be taken to be during the 1840s.

85 – The ordinations of Sahag Kahana and Nerses Kahana

Bishop Stepannos Aghavni, the prelate of the Nicomedia diocese, was invited to Bardizag on the occasion of the feast day of St. James of Nisibis on 15 December 1848, and was entertained in Mgerian's house. Mgerian then convened a meeting with the notables, in his house, under the chairmanship of the bishop, the priests not being invited...

During the meeting the village notables decided to have the able Armenian language teacher *Diratsou* Sarkis Pandigian and *Diratsou* Hagop Bodourian, who was quite well educated and had good handwriting, ordained kahanas.

The priests of the village heard of the decision but remained quiet, expecting that their opinion would be sought about this arrangement or, at least, they would simply be told.

At that time there were nine priests in the village, one of whom, Sahag Kahana Bedig Sarkisian, had ceased his ministry because of his advanced years. Several of the remainder were also old, and it would appear that the spiritual welfare of the villagers was not being sufficiently cared for.

On the Saturday following this decision the two candidates, wearing cassocks, were brought to the church by Mesrob Kahana Simonian (who was a staunch Mgerian man) during the morning service. He said nothing, however, to the other priests. When they saw this, three of them, the leading priest Garabed Kahana Der-Krikorian, Hagop Kahana Der-Aprahamian and Kevork Kahana Sarkisian, left the church. The service continued, but several of the notables, led by Hadji Artin Agha Der-Antreasian, tried to persuade the departing priests to return to the church to prevent scandal. The priests hesitated, but when the bishop conferred the rank of sub-deacon [*gisasargavak*] on the two candidates during the 'Fathers' part of the service, they agreed to the notables' suggestion, returned to the church, and were present at the remaining parts of the ordination.

The bishop that day, during Mass, ordained the candidates with the rank of *avak sargavak* [archdeacon] and, on the following day, Sunday, as kahanas. *Diratsou* Sarkis was renamed Sahag Kahana and *Diratsou* Hagop, Nerses Kahana. Hadji Artin Bab, when he heard the name Nerses given to Bodourian, said to those around him, 'The bishop did well to find that name; Nerses Kahana Bodourian will complete what Nerses Kahana Gardeshian left.'

The two new priests, after their 40-day period of seclusion, returned to teaching for a time to ensure their living.

The swift ordination of these priests was, without doubt, a ploy by Mgerian; the decision made by the meeting was simply a diplomatic game played by him, firstly to win over his sometime enemies (about which we have read in previous sections), and secondly, to use them as weapons against Garabed Kahana and Hagop Kahana,* who had started to inflame the people against him.

In reality, the new priests, on Mgerian's advice and under his protection, joined by several of the other priests, soon raised the question of parishes, demanding that the parishes and income be more justly and equitably divided among them without bias. By doing this, their aim was to strike a blow against Garabed and Hagop kahanas, who had appropriated the most lucrative parishes for themselves. The priests making these demands signed a plea, in two copies, one of which was sent to the prelacy of Izmid, the other being presented to the notables' meeting in the village.

This argument over parishes lasted for some time due to the resistance put up by the two previously mentioned priests, who even took it as far as the Patriarchate, distrusting Bishop Stepannos Aghavni's stance concerning them.

Garabed Kahana, in Constantinople, with many others, knew the Protestant pastor Badveli† Chamourdji Deroyents who, in those days, enjoyed a great reputation in the upper echelons of the Patriarchate and the Armenian community. He was able, through the pastor, to obtain a document containing a favourable decision for him, on the basis that a priest's parish belonged to him until his death, after which it was transferred to the diocesan bishop, who was the only person who had the right to give it to a new parish priest as a *Derouni iravounk* [lordly right], each family paying 10 *kurush*, in accordance with the traditional rule.

86 – The death of the venerable Sahag Kahana Bedig Sarkisian

The venerable 67 year-old priest Sahag Kahana Bedig Sarkisian died in 1841, after serving as a priest for 29 years. This priest didn't have much education, but had been a person who knew his duties and was a conscientious priest. He was in church, morning and evening, at his post.

At the same time he was a skilled man who earned money. He had learnt four trades: cutler, felter, mender, and another.‡ He educated his sons, Taniel, Mardiros and Sarkis to a certain level and then ordered them to work. The eldest, Taniel, learned a new trade, painting, that had not existed in Bardizag before. This trade was also learned by Mardiros, who also used it. They worked together for a time and then went their separate ways, both becoming quite wealthy.

After them, the trade of painting was taken up and plied by Hadji Hovhannes Khacherian's sons (he was Apraham Kahana's younger brother), Hadji Khacheres

---

* The actual words used here are: '...to use them as weapons to break Garabed Kahana's and Hagop Kahana's noses...'
† The word means honourable, and was the title given to Protestant pastors. Senior pastors were called *verabadveli,* or 'most honourable'.
‡ The fourth trade is not mentioned in the text.

Agha (the younger), Mgerdich Agha Khacherian and his brother's, Hadji Hagop Khacherian's sons named Apraham Agha and Djanig Agha.

87 – The purchase of church fittings and carpets

Ornaments and fittings as well as carpets were bought for the church during the first eight to ten years after its construction.* First of all six large chandeliers were purchased, the largest being placed in the centre of the *adian* [chancel]; four small ones were put, in pairs, in the apses; and one was to be hung in the choir. The one in the choir, the one in the centre of the court, and one of the pairs in the apses were made of crystal, while the pair in the other apse were made of crystal painted green and red. They were all brought from Constantinople to Bardizag in a dismantled state to prevent breakages, with a drawing or plan of how they were to be assembled and arranged. This was used by the master craftsman Serope Djangaloz, and after assembly, each was hung in its appointed place.

It was decided, in 1846 or 1847, to cover the floor of the church with carpets which would have to be purchased. Ghezel Margos Baba, the church keeper, and beadle Goudjoug Mger's Garabed were sent to Constantinople with the order to buy them. They went and purchased felt floor covering material at 9 *kurush* an *arshin* (about 28 inches or 180mm). This material completely covered the floors of the two apses, beginning at the choir and extending to the narthex wall. But they hardly lasted for ten years: they frayed and wore out, and the pieces cut disappeared from the church. This has always been the fate of community-owned things: people, be they priests, beadles, housekeepers or anyone else would just take them.

Proper furniture and tableware etc. had either been bought or been given as gifts to the prelacy at one time or another. After a time all of them had disappeared. The beadles and other people had taken them all, piece by piece, with no one questioning their disappearance. An important proportion of them had become old and unusable and had been thrown away of course.

The above-mentioned beadle Goudjoug Mger's Garabed, from Manoushag's founder's (Bishop Hovhannes') clan became the son-in-law of archpriest Garabed Kahana Der-Krikorian. He married the priest's youngest daughter, Dirouhi, and moved into the priest's house. He inherited the priest's wealth and most of his income and, changing his name, was henceforth called Hadji Garabed Agha Der-Garabedian. Despite this, the villagers always called him *Jamgoch* [beadle] Hadji Garabed. The priest's other son-in-law was Serope Djangaloz, who only inherited a few crumbs from that house.

---

* The church of St. James was constructed in 1830 and consecrated in 1831. See Section 52.

Beadle Hadji Garabed, after becoming the priest's son-in-law, relinquished his poor post and, as the adopted son of the priest, took over that rich house's economy and work.

88 – Exiles from Bardizag in foreign lands

The Bardizag villager wasn't in the habit of migrating to foreign lands or towns and cities for the sake of work or profit. He has never been daring or adventurous, but there have been some who, because of some fault or by falling into debt, ran away from their birthplace to escape pursuit. The villagers had a saying that had the strength of a proverb: 'The Bardizag villager without doubt will get into a bathtub on Saturday evening.' What they wanted to say was that the villager couldn't stay away from the village for more than a week.

Gozgoz Hampartsoum's three sons, Hagop, Mgerdich and Khachadour (a *badveli* - pastor) harassed by their creditors, escaped to Izmir at the end of the 1840s. The usual remark about this sort of move was: 'even if one of them went for profit or employment, he escaped.'

Deledjeg Stepan and finally Mkhdji Mger and his four sons – Hagop, Garabed, Hovhannes and Stepan all followed them to Izmir too.

The Gozgozian brothers got hold of a case full of cloth during a fire in Izmir. They brought it back to Bardizag, sold the contents, sat back and enjoyed the profits.* They returned to Izmir after a time, where they remained for a very lengthy period. There Gozgoz Hampartsoum's grandsons Mgerdich and Hampartsoum learned how to make *khaitan* and took up the trade. After their father's death, they went to Egypt, then to Massua, on the Red Sea coast, on Ethiopian soil, where they followed the trade of making *serma* string. They amassed a considerable fortune through that trade; their base was a house in Cairo, with one or the other brother remaining in Massua during the year, plying their trade.

They also visited their birthplace during the summer every few years and would remain there for several months at a time, giving gifts and aid to the church and school. Mgerdich, who had married in Egypt and was a widower, remarried, taking Sarkis Effendi Mgerian's daughter, Sirvart, to wife. Hampartsoum, now of marriageable age, chose a young lady from the village as his wife too.

They became bankrupt some years later and lost their once brilliant position. This failure, coupled with their advanced years, became the reason that they couldn't live long after the catastrophe. Mgerdich Effendi left children, while Hampartsoum had none.

Deledjeg Stepan had built a reputation in the village of being a busy man. He had gone to Constantinople for a time and, gaining the trust of a Greek merchant, was

---

* The words used here are '...they sat down and ate.'

involved in the wheat trade. He got into debt, however, and went to Izmir. He took up spinning animal hair to make string* but was not very successful at it.

He returned to Bardizag for a time in his poor state; his brother gave him a house as his portion of their father's estate. He wandered about the village for a time without work or anything to do, then quietly sold the house and, taking his wife and son with him, returned to Izmir. There, his only son was the victim of an accident in a factory; he also didn't last long and died there. His wife, now a widow and living among strangers, returned to Bardizag and, marrying her daughter off early, lived with her until her death.

Mkhdji Baba and his sons rented a shop on the square in Izmir called Ali Pasha Meidan, where they made nails and horseshoes. They made enough money to live on in the town and to send some to their families in Bardizag. They had worked in Mgerian's horseshoe workshop for years and were in debt to him and had escaped to Izmir, not being able to repay it and feed their families.

When Mgerian heard that they were working in Izmir and earning money, he wrote them a letter demanding what they owed him. They didn't reply. Mgerian, realising that there was no hope, found a way for them to pay him, in the following manner.

Mkhdji had a fresh, newly-planted vineyard near Lemberloz. Mgerian summoned Mkhdji's relative, the beadle Mardiros, to see him and persuaded him to appear before the appropriate government official as Mkhdji Mger, to get a *takrir* [certificate] stating that he had sold his land to Mgerian and received full payment for it. Mgerian succeeded in his ploy – with Mardiros being paid a bribe of course – and became the owner of the vineyard.

Mkhdji Mger died in Izmir many years later, as did his son Garabed. His three other sons remained. Of those, Stepan first returned to Bardizag and married; the other two also soon returned. Of the latter, Hagop, who was Mkhdji Mger's first-born son, laid a complaint against Mgerian in the prelacy of Izmid and in Bardizag before the notables' meeting, accusing him of appropriating his father's vineyard.

People said that, after visiting the prelacy several times without any result, he one day finally, and angrily, said to the prelate, 'Your grace, I beg you to give me justice!'

The bishop replied, 'My son, there can only be complete justice before Jesus' court.'

I have no idea how accurate this story is, but I know that Mkhdji Hagop appeared one day before the notables' meeting in Bardizag without any hope of redress. He was ordered to sit down, so he took his *aba* [coat] off, spread it on the floor and sat on it, begging that they sort his problem out. It appears that he appealed to them several times without result. After much discussion, when he became convinced that there was no hope of getting a favourable decision, he suddenly got up and began to

---

* The word used here is *mazmanoutiun*.

recite from the Psalms: 'They made the poor man's words shameful, as the Lord is his hope.' He then left the meeting with swift strides, disappointed.

Mkhdji Mger's vineyard remained, until the end, the Mgerians' property. People told a similar story about it in my day.

We had a neighbour called Doner Ma, a widow with two daughters, who owned her own house opposite ours. This woman married her eldest daughter to a man in the village and then, taking her younger daughter with her, went to Constantinople to go into service with a family. Some time later she was able to marry this daughter to a young man from the provinces who planned to return to his birthplace, taking his wife and her mother with him, freeing him from Constantinople's wearing and tiring life. Doner Ma approved of her son-in-law's plan – she too would escape from strangers' houses – and brought her daughter back to Bardizag to sell her house. She was able to find a buyer and a price for the house was agreed. When she told her elder daughter of the sale, however, she encountered her total opposition and couldn't persuade her in any way to change her mind. She, however, hid her eldest daughter's opposition from the buyer and, with the elder daughter's apparent agreement to the sale, invited the buyer to Izmid, to the relevant official's office, to formalise the sale and obtain the certificate (*takrir*) for it.

Pretending that she had decided not sell the house in the village, she said goodbye to her eldest daughter and quietly left the village, taking the younger one with her, going to Izmid to await the buyer. There she was able to find a girl that looked like her elder daughter and was her age, and in some way persuaded her to pretend she was her daughter and to take part in the signing of the formal sale document.

The buyer arrived, and the document was signed. The buyer knew nothing of the skulduggery, and all the necessary actions were carried out to complete the sale. Doner Ma pocketed the purchase price of the house and, with her younger daughter, went directly to her son-in-law in Constantinople. They all set out a few days later to go to the provinces. We never saw Doner Ma again.

When the buyer, now the legal owner of the house, entered it, Doner Ma's eldest daughter, who was living in the village, understood what had happened. She went to her father's house to eject the unwelcome guest, who was the person that was really tricked.

After that our street became like a battlefield between Doner Ma's daughter and the new owner. She sought any opportunity to enter her father's house and occupy it; the owners tried to stop the attacks on their home. They kept the doors and windows shut at all times. When the woman did succeed in entering it despite all their precautions, she had to be forcibly ejected. At one point the woman was going to make a hole in the house wall during daylight hours to force an entry. There was shouting and screaming in the parish every day, disturbing the other families living there.

Finally, one day, when the owners were absent, this bold woman, who was worthy of being Doner Ma's daughter and who never lost hope, put a ladder to a high window that had been left open and entered the house. She then secured it from the inside. When the owners returned they found the house locked against them by their enemy. Blows, pushing and shoving, words and pleading didn't make any difference. She remained inside, under voluntary siege and her husband supplied her with food through the high window.

The problem, which had been presented to the notables' meeting many times but never achieved a result, was taken to the meeting again by the owner. The notables this time were able to persuade the buyer to negotiate with the woman as she was the one who had really been cheated. Finally a sum that was equivalent to her share of the original sale was agreed that the poor buyer had to pay, so as to be free forever from the problem that threatened to become a chronic one.

One of Apraham Kahana's sons, Garabed Der-Aprahamian, went to Izmir, where he stayed for a number of years and was able to create a remarkable position for himself. From there he went to Cairo, Egypt, where he died. He lived a bachelor existence. He visited his birthplace, Bardizag, and his brothers and relatives several times. He was well-to-do and often assisted his needy brothers or their orphans in Bardizag.

Tavit Kahana Mikayelian's first-born son, Garabed Der-Tavitian, who had joined the Protestants and had undertaken many kinds of work in the village, finally went to Izmir in the 1870s-1880s, where he lived his epic story.

He had taken over some abandoned land to the north of Bardizag in the Upper Fields during the time when Protestants were being persecuted in the village, where he had opened up a cultivable area and had planted stands of mulberry, oak and fruit trees, and built a large silkworm house.

He also had a large, newly-built house in our parish in Bardizag itself but was a person who was difficult to please. The successes he achieved still left him dissatisfied, however. Carried away by the Anglo-Saxon Pilgrim Fathers' enthusiasm, he followed their example and finally went across the sea to Izmir with his entire family to find a new world. He hoped to join Armenian Protestants there who had established themselves early on and had quite a strong community.

He began a viticulture business in Izmir, buying a large vineyard and a fig orchard. Success smiled on him, but a sudden catastrophe ruined his calculations and he became sick of his life there. A powerful earthquake destroyed his small house in the vineyard and one of his sons and his son-in-law were killed under the rubble, while one of his other two sons contracted a severe illness.

Garabed Der-Tavitian's heart became agitated due to these sorrows and crises, so he was forced to gather up his remaining children and return to Bardizag. He returned like a man who had been beaten about the head and lived and worked in the village for a time. However it seemed that bad luck pursued him: first one of his sons died in Bardizag, then, because of the pain of the loss of his son, he died soon afterwards and was buried near his forefathers. His sick wife, his son who was married and a father and his now-widowed daughter finally went to America, where they continued to live until their last days, perhaps unable to find a new place to settle.

His second son-in-law, Garabed Agha of Marash, a manufacturer, purchased his father-in-law's house in Bardizag. He had become a son-in-law in Izmir and became a widower with two sons a little later on. This man established himself in Bardizag and ran a successful carpentry business there, until the storm of the deportations swept everything and the Armenians away.

Garabed Der-Tavitian had a younger brother, Hadji Mikayel, who lived opposite the cemetery in the old family home and occupied himself with an old trade, that of tanner, remaining faithful to the family's traditional trade until the year of the deportations (1915).

89 – Hadji Artin Agha Der-Antreasian, the Hadji Artins' and Der-Antreasians' ancestor

Hadji Artin was Great Hadji Khacher's grandson who had become an orphan on his father's, Antreas Kahana's, death. Hadji Artin had an elder brother, Hagop, who was the ancestor of the Kelesh Hagop family. Great Hadji Khacher raised and settled the two orphans and had a special regard for the younger, Hadji Artin, who had learnt to read and write and became the owner of an important independant enterprise.

After his grandfather's death, Hadji Artin became his uncle's* right-hand man in the governance of village affairs and had an important role in all the events that have been portrayed in relation to Apraham Kahana's rule and adherents.†

Hadji Artin was an honourable and well-to-do tailor in Bardizag who employed many people in his business. He had become the son-in-law of Kevork Kiutner's Haroutiun – the Kiutners were a notable clan in the village.

Apraham Kahana and Hadji Artin, as we saw above, were the two most influential personalities in Bardizag until 1828, when Mgerian first appeared on the scene. The latter succeeded in gathering about him all those who were against their rule – all the unhappy elements that gradually became the majority. Mgerian's new group put an end to Apraham Kahana's and Hadji Artin's power and influence, resulting in the two becoming the new regime's main opponents.

With Apraham Kahana's death, Hadji Artin remained alone as leader of the opposition. But the priest's death was a decisive blow for the opposition that now lacked a personality with his strength and authority. Despite this, Hadji Artin continued to be respected in the village, without having any real authority. He only drew back from Mgerian, whom he really didn't like. For his part, Mgerian tried to win him over, calling him 'Hadji Daiyi' in the same way he called Apraham Kahana 'Derder Daiyi'. Mgerian's grandmother was from the Khacherians' house, as we said earlier.‡

---

* Father's brother.
† See Section 33 and 34 etc.
‡ See Section 45.

Hadji Artin Bab had two sons, Antreas and Krikor, as well as many daughters who were married into well-known families in the village. Antreas had learned and ran his father's trade, while Krikor still didn't have a specific occupation.

Great Hadji Khacher Bab had given a son's portion to this grandson from his many sources of income. He had given his two sons, Apraham Kahana and Hadji Hovhannes, a shop opposite the government building near the agha's fountain. He gave his other shop (that later became a paint shop), located further up the street, to Hadji Artin. His son Antreas plied his trade for a time in that shop, but after Apraham Kahana's death, Hadji Artin rented Hadji Hovhannes' grandfather's shop in the market and turned it into a grocery shop for his son, Hadji Krikor.

Hadji Artin had the habit of sitting in front of that shop, with the idea of getting customers to come to it. He knew that all respected him; but if some of them dared to pass the shop with their bottles for oil in their hands, he would shout, 'Hey you, where are you going? Won't you buy your oil from our shop? Has our oil been mixed with urine?' Many would hide their oil bottles in bags so they wouldn't be seen and thus become the subject of Hadji Artin's rebuke.

After some time Hadji Hovhannes, Hadji Artin's paternal uncle, who was much younger than he was, needed his own shop and told him to vacate it. At this an argument broke out between the two; the sons also joined in, with Hadji Artin shouting, 'This shop is mine!'

'No it isn't,' Hadji Hovhannes replied, 'my father gave it to me!'

Hadji Artin never vacated the shop and became its owner through his shouting and screaming. Hadji Hovhannes was forced to pass the shop, which had been given to Hadji Artin, over to him, where his sons plied their trade of painting in it for a very long time.

He later appropriated the passageway between the agha's fountain and the shop that was used for turning carts, saying, 'This land belongs to my shop' and built a small garden on it. This sort of thing was usual in those days, when appropriation of land legally owned by someone else wasn't considered to be a crime.

Hadji Artin Agha and his sons, so as not to be behind Mgerian, began to copy his enterprises. They had a vineyard and grew oak and mulberry trees like he did. They bought a field from the Kardeshes near Kiraghlekh and grew oak trees on it. The public road passed in front of this field. There was a field that was owned by the Chullers on the other side of the road which had then been bought by the community as a grazing and rest area for cattle. Gradually both the road and the field became mixed with the stand of oak trees.

One day Hadji Artin Agha went and saw the church keeper, Ghezel Margos Baba, and demanded the church's *seneds* [documents]. Choosing the one concerning the Chuller's field, and saying 'I need this one,' he put it in his pocket and left. He also bought Ghaladji Garabed's shop next to his that was near the agha's fountain, which he later exchanged for Koukouts Garabed's barber's shop. The appropriations made by Hadji Artin that I have recalled above and which seemed a little like bold conquests didn't end without trouble. It is true, however, that in those days powerful people gave themselves the right to do things like that, as we've seen in acts carried out by Mgerian and others.

Nerses Kahana Kardesh's son Hadji Hovhannes started a court case against Hadji Artin, accusing him of taking possession of his field, while Hadji Artin Agha had bought it. But Hadji Hovhannes Kardesh replied that they, the legal owners, hadn't sold it, but someone else, saying it was theirs, had sold it to Hadji Artin Agha. The court case was taken to the Izmid government office.

Hadji Hovhannes' son Arakel was a well-known barber in Izmid in those days, and his shop was patronised by the greatest men who came to be shaved. One of these people was Topal Osman Pasha, who liked barber Arakel very much. Hadji Artin, with his son Hadji Krikor went to Izmid when the aforementioned dispute grew and took on a serious appearance, where they succeeded in settling the case through arbitration. They gave Kardesh Hadji Hovhannes a little money to keep him quiet, and confirmed the ownership of the field in Hadji Artin Agha's favour.

The old antagonists, becoming reconciled after a time, became related to each other by engaging one of Hadji Artin's granddaughters (Antreas' daughter) to Kardesh Arakel.

This court case had another beneficial result. Hadji Artin, through it, became acquainted with the important Turks in Izmid: people like Hadji Emin Bey, Mustafa Bey, Hassan Effendi and Siuliman Bey. He also became closer to Saroukhanian Effendi – the director of the Imperial Cloth Factory – who, as we've seen, had been hurt by Mgerian in the case of his sister Areknaz.[*] I haven't been able to ascertain whether Mgerian had anything to do with the court case that seemed to bring Hadji Artin's family and Saroukhanian (Mgerian's opponent) together.

Hadji Artin and his sons now, gaining strength from the powerful friendships they had forged, tried not to be left behind by Mgerian, competing with his business in Seymen. Hassan Effendi, one of their new, powerful friends, created a brilliant business in the port in partnership with Hadji Artin's sons. This Turkish effendi, along with other Turkish personalities, took over the rental of the vast warehouse and stockpiled the harvest – wheat, barley, oats, etc. – which they sold on credit at high prices to the peasants, from whom they could recover what was owed from the following year's harvest. Hadji Artin's sons became the Turkish effendi's factors for Bardizag and secured an enviable position for themselves.

Hassan Effendi, on one occasion, visited Bardizag in connection with this business and was entertained in Hadji Artin's house, which was old and small and totally inappropriate for his wealth and new position. Fired by his emotions against Mgerian, he began construction of a new, large and glorious house, saying 'The camel driver's friend should have a house with a large door.'

---

* See Section 78.

He had already bought several of the houses near his and bought more, thus securing an extensive area on which the new, large, painted house was constructed. It was known as 'Hadji Krikor's house' in my day.

His friendship with Hassan Effendi gradually grew closer. They bought Djezel Hadji Hovhannes' field near the port – Mgerian hadn't succeeded in buying it. They then planted a large grove of mulberry trees and built a silkworm house on it, copying Mgerian. To reach Mgerian's status, all that remained was to own their own warehouse and bakery inside the port.

On the Hadji Artins' advice, Hassan Effendi, who had now become Hassan Pasha, bought Djezel Hadji Hovhannes' warehouse and bakery inside Seymen. They had those old buildings demolished and built a large warehouse on the same site. This was in Hassan Pasha's and their names and extended to the water's edge, closing off the view of the sea from the buildings that belonged to the community from the early days.

Now Hadji Artin's two sons, Antreas and Hadji Krikor, putting their work in the village to one side, would mount their horses and go down to Seymen every morning and return to the village every evening in the same way, being occupied with their new enterprises, the futures of which seemed uncertain. Hadji Artin Bab, who was still mentally active, became unhappy after a time with the progress of the new businesses, boldly shouting in his sons' faces, 'Hey! Your route to the port... I brought you up by selling olives and oil!'

Hadji Artin Agha, thanks to the protection of his powerful Turkish friends, gradually regained authority in Bardizag, enough to cause problems for Mgerian,[*] but he had one fault – he was easily aroused and often couldn't control his tongue, something that was a necessary virtue for someone called upon to control things. He often had arguments with Mgerian in meetings, where he couldn't retain his composure. Let me give you an example of this by relating the following.

Mgerian's cousin[†] Hadji Hagop Mikayelian had become village steward (*chorbadji*) and treasurer at Mgerian's suggestion and under his protection. He had inherited the Bardizag seat[‡] from his father, but was disgraced by Mgerian, who decided to make him resign from his position of seat owner. Hadji Hagop, put in a difficult position and powerless to deal with Mgerian at his own level, approached Hadji Artin for protection.

Mgerian, to achieve his aim, convened a meeting of notables which included respected men in the village with positions. After discussing various village matters, Mgerian made the question of the seat ownership an agenda item, and suggested changing the owner. A close argument began between Hadji Artin and Mgerian: 'He

---

[*] The phrase used here is 'with the strength to put a stumbling block in front of his feet'.
[†] Mother's brother's son.
[‡] The words used here are *Bardizagi atoragaloutiune*, literally 'the ownership of the seat of Bardizag.'

won't resign', 'Yes he will.' Voices rose and the populace rushed to the prelacy wondering what was happening and trying to see what the commotion was all about. Hadji Antreas, Hadji Artin's son, went into the meeting and, seeing that the argument was between Mgerian and his father, angrily shouted at Mgerian, 'Agha, what do you want of my father?'

Mgerian's son, Sarkis Effendi, who had also gone into the meeting, quietly said, referring to his father and Hadji Artin, 'Brother Antreas, lower your voice; you'll see that they'll soon be like brothers again.'

Mgerian couldn't hold a grudge and continued his relationship with Hadji Artin, calling him 'Hadji Aghpar' or 'Hadji Daiyi'.

Hadji Artin, in his final days, did something that badly offended the villagers' pious feelings due to his desire to show his friend Hassan Pasha how great he was.

Hassan Pasha was invited to Hadji Artin's grandson Nigoghos' wedding. Great preparations were made for it. The wedding began and, on the Monday after the wedding ceremony, Hadji Artin sent word to Hagop Kahana Der-Aprahamian – Garabed Kahana was on a pilgrimage to Jerusalem at the time – that the bride and groom be brought home in procession by the priests and choir, led by the priest who celebrated Mass, still in his formal vestments.

The priests, showing weakness and to please Hadji Artin, complied with his wishes, and the celebrant priest, in his vestments, led the procession through the streets to the house, something that had never been done until then. The bride and groom were ceremoniously taken to the room where Hassan Pasha was sitting on a wide and comfortable settee with other important guests. The celebrant priest entered the room and was forced to give a respectful bow to the pasha and complete the remaining wedding home prayers in his presence.

The priests' actions and weakness were scandalous. On certain occasions it was permitted for the priest to wear a cope when performing appropriate rituals such as in houses, at a pilgrimage site or in the open air at a funeral. But for a priest to go through the streets in his Mass vestments, accompanying a wedding procession, where there were not a few drunkards, was a blasphemy against church law. In this Hadji Artin was not at fault. He, in his innocent piety, could have expressed such a wish, but the priests, who knew the established rules and laws, should have refused it as a sin. Hadji Artin Agha, with his faith, would not have wanted to sin in that way.

This incident, naturally, gave birth to popular anger and scandal, and everyone shouted, 'Hey! Look at these priests! They've lost their minds; is it right that the celebrant priest, in his vestments, should lead the bride from street to street, then bow to a Turk in that state? Isn't there anyone in this village, a seat holder, who will write to the diocesan bishop and have these priests' beards shaved?' Feelings ran higher and pervaded the village; there may have been people who incited them even more, just as it always happened in cases like this.

The seat holder, Hadji Hagop Mikayelian, was forced to write a report on the incident to the diocesan bishop's locum tenens, Yeprem Vartabed, in Izmid. The seat holder had it written by *Diratsou* Hovhannes Mkhalian – who was a teacher at that time. The locum tenens wrote a harsh letter, rebuking the priests and threatening to punish all of them. The priests became agitated and looked to everyone for protection.

Nerses Kahana Bodourian informed Hadji Artin that *Diratsou* Mkhalian had written the report. The latter, becoming very angry, rushed to the school and appeared at the door of the hall where Mkhalian was teaching. There, he began to rebuke and berate him, using, in his enraged state, language that was quite unseemly. Despite the fact that he was surprised and crestfallen, the teacher still tried to defend himself, informing Hadji Artin that he was a teacher and had complied with the seat holder's order, to whom Hadji Artin ought to address his remarks.

Hadji Artin, still in an angry state, didn't want to hear any defence and, after shouting and screaming, left the school, with the threat, 'I'll show you!'

At this, at the year's end, *Diratsou* Hagop Mkhalian resigned his post so as not to suffer Hadji Artin's vengeance.

Hadji Artin Bab, years later, in his extreme old age, retired to his bed and died in 1858. Mgerian didn't last much longer, dying only 20 days later.

Many people's livelihood suffered after the deaths of these two men, and when the Crimean War ended in 1855, the entire country suffered an economic shock. Hadji Artin's sons' businesses went bankrupt.

Hassan Pasha, with Melkon Agha and his adopted son Kevork Agha from Izmid, came to Bardizag to liquidate Hadji Artin's businesses. They looked at all the accounts and found that a very large debt had accumulated. To pay it off the Hadji Artins lost everything – the bakery in Seymen, the shop and warehouse and the mulberry trees - all these losses didn't clear the debt. They were forced to sign a debenture. They also owed sums of money to various people.

After some time it was Hassan Pasha's turn; Ahmed Vefik, a well-known senior government official, was sent by the central government to examine his business. Hassan Pasha's sun also set: he lost all his wealth and was disgraced. Taking advantage of this situation, Hadji Artin's son Antreas went to Izmid, put his father's one-time friend in a difficult position, and was able to recover their debenture for 7,000 *kurush*.

90 – Archbishop Stepannos Maghakian,[*] prelate and locum tenens of the monastery of Armash and Izmid (1855)

Bishop Stepannos Aghavni was succeeded as diocesan prelate, locum tenens of the Izmid diocese and of the monastery of Armash in 1855 by Archbishop Stepannos Maghakian. Bardizag went through a number of stormy years during his prelacy. The village Armenian Catholic and Armenian Protestant communities were formed

---

[*] He served from 1855 until 1865. Minas Kasabian (Farhad), *Hayere Nikomedio Kavarin Mech*, p. 122.

during this time. I'll write about them and the arguments and battles that ensued in the following pages.

Archbishop Stepannos Maghakian, a worthy churchman, was, for a time, the locum tenens of the Patriarchate in Constantinople. It was during his reign that the Armenian National Constitution was received and implemented as the basis for the administration of the internal affairs of Armenian communities in the Ottoman Empire.[*]

He then took up his position as locum tenens of the Nicomedia diocese once more; he passed away in Bardizag in 1865 while in office, and was buried in Bardizag's church courtyard, next to the martyr's grave.

After Maghakian's period of office as locum tenens, the Izmid diocese was finally separated from the abbacy of the monastery of Armash which had been, for a long time, united in one person.

Maghakian was succeeded as prelate of the Izmid diocese by Archbishop Nerses Varjabedian in about 1860.[†]

---

[*] The 'Armenian National Constitution', promulgated in 1863.

[†] This is incorrect. Archbishop Nigoghos Aghasian served as locum tenens from 1867 until 1870, when Archbishop Nerses Varjabedian was elected. The latter served as prelate until 1880. Minas Kasabian (Farhad), *Hayere Nikomedio Kavarin Mech*, pp. 123-124.

PART 2

1850 – 1919

Chapter 6

Present Times – Transitional Period
1850 – 1880

91 – The development of Bardizag's economic life

Bardizag, as we've seen in the first part of this work had, in its two-and-a-half century life, developed to a certain economic level, thanks to local conditions and the qualities of its people.

The mainstay of its inhabitants were charcoal burning and timber preparation, horseshoe making, sericulture, fruit farming, and several other trades such as painting, forge trades such as farrier and blacksmith, saddle making, carpentry etc.

Bardizag's oldest trade, tanning, was almost dead as a result of new European technology in my day. Only Hadji Mikayel Der-Tavitian continued it, barely able to make a living for himself.

The cultivation of cereals quickly diminished and had become limited, as it was not possible to compete with European flour imports. There were only a few people left who still hesitated and grew the crops their fathers did in the Khans area – the Khashmans, Garos and one or two others, while the great houses – the Momdjis, Bozigs, Bedigs and others – had long forsaken it.

Painting, although still continued by some families such as the Khacherians and Der-Sahagians, showed all the signs that it would disappear from the market, as it did after 1880.

Mazmanoutiun [string making from animal hair] and weaving trades suffered the same fate.

Horseshoe making still continued, but on a much smaller scale. The Mgerians, the family that first started the trade in Bardizag, would abandon it soon, while others – the Djergas, Arakelians and Dzallans – would continue with it for some time, until machine-produced horseshoes made the trade redundant.

Sericulture, given Bardizag's advantages, would gradually attract many people's attention and lead to silk production for the European market. The example set by Mgerian and Hadji Artin would be followed by all the wealthy families as well as by the village population. For this reason, the number of silkworm houses[*] and mulberry groves would increase, especially around the village, which would soon be surrounded by a green belt.

---

[*] Silkworm house' is the direct translation of the Armenian *sheramadoun*. This was a large building where silkworms would be grown and their cocoons produced.

The four Der-Sahagian brothers built separate silkworm houses in those days, as did the Hadji Bekirs, Gharevlegs, Mikayelians, Der-Garabedians, Torosians, the Kiutnerian brothers, the Dzallans, Ghazarosians, Djergas and, further away, the Kourouns, Garabed Der-Tavitian, the Seliys, Sare Baba, the Gatsans, Gozgozes, Simavons* and many others. At the same time, every house, during the growing season, which lasted for about two months, would be used to grow silkworms.

The old trades of charcoal burning and timber preparation would retain their previous importance and prestige alongside that of sericulture. New names would appear – Nalband Mgerdich and Gosda Asadour Apelian - alongside the old masters in these trades.

Local needs would determine that trades encompassing consumables and finishing would be replaced by several new ones. These were ironworking, shoemaking, European tailoring, the manufacture of *yemeni* shoes, furniture making, and a new, simple trade – that of basket making, the product of which would be used for fruit and vegetable market trading. Carpentry would also increase, and the number of carpenters plying their trade would become considerable.

There would be attempts at using European technologies with the establishment of *manarans* [silk spinning factories]. Bardizag had two of these, set up by the Saroukhanians and the Mgerian brothers.

The government, years before this, had built two factories on the banks of the Kilez River to supply the army's needs for cloth and fezes. Many people from the village, as well as others, gained employment in these factories. Although these new enterprises, using new skills, could offer employment for many people of both sexes, a social problem was created with having girls and women working outside the home.

Due to local population growth and the establishment of new villages by immigrants, large and small trading enterprises would be encouraged, with new opportunities occurring for grocery shops, bakeries, the flour and wheat trade, sale of European manufactured goods and *hiusvadzk* [knitwear], all of which would increase. Bardizag would thus take on the life of a small town.

Villagers would not, despite all these new jobs and opportunities, be able to find sufficient local work for everyone who needed employment, due to Bardizag's own population growth. Many people would have to look outside the village for work, either temporarily or permanently. This drift from the village first started in the direction of nearby Izmid, the provincial centre, where more than one hundred Bardizag families would gradually settle, finding opportunities for work, mostly as carpenters, basketmakers, *khandjis* [resthouse owners], abadjis (weavers), saddlers, ironworkers, officials and finally, hired workers. The Bodourians, Mkhalians,

---

* This might be a misprint. The name might have been Shmavons.

Baldjis, Pattoukians, Batakhanians, Kousdigians, Jamgochians, Bodosians, Azarians, Oghinians, and others in Izmid were noted families originally from Bardizag. Apart from these, many girls from Bardizag married local men and created families there. A Bardizag community would also be formed in Constantinople in a similar way with the Mgerians (the married archpriest Hovhannes Kahana Mgerian and Ardashes Mgerian), the Sinanians, Melkonians (Kembelian), Deledjegians, Pashayians, Torosians, Basmadjians, Boghosians, Geolliuians, Alexanians and many others who have since been forgotten.

This movement also extended to Adabazar, Armash-Khasgal and even abroad – with a branch of the Torosians and the Baboukhians going to Bulgaria. By the comedy of circumstance and fate, while many people from the village felt constrained in their own houses, a number of outsiders settled in Bardizag. They wanted to live the life of ordinary villagers, leaving behind fast and unhealthy lives in towns and cities, or because they saw opportunities for profit in Bardizag. I can recall a certain Hovhannes Agha of Khaskiugh, who spent a lot of money in the Avazoud parish of the village and in Chiftilig Valley to build his house and silk spinning factory and plant mulberry groves. He also built a *keoshk* [chalet] and began cultivating silkworms like a local man. Another person, whose origins and real name are unknown to me, was called Aldermaz by the villagers. He bought land in the Khans and planted mulberry trees and also built a silk spinning factory. He also tried cultivating cotton for a number of years. A third, Krikor Agha Dobrashian, known by the people of the village as Robinson, had lived for many years in the United States and had studied agriculture and animal husbandry there. He arrived during my time to cultivate his brother's land near the Mgerians' farm, apparently by using modern methods. Needless to say, while villagers were successful in earning a living with the labour of their whole families, the people from outside couldn't survive long because they had to pay for all the work done, in cash, sooner or later: the ruins of their properties would be the only things left as witnesses to their unsuccessful efforts.

Others settled among us to engage in trade. The first of these was someone known as Filizer; then there were Nshanig Agha Azarian, Garabed Agha from Marash, an Onnig Agha and others from Constantinople or further afield who began trading in manufactured goods. Many of them, who married girls from the village, and thus became villagers of a sort, were able to survive, supplementing their trade with sericulture conducted in their houses with the assistance of their families. Many of these people were able to set down roots among us and gain reasonable positions in the community.

There was another Onnig Agha from Constantinople, a considerably wealthy person, who began a flour business among us, trying at the same time to cure his poor state of health and nerves in Bardizag's healthy and invigorating climate. He bought a vineyard that was located on a high place right next to the new cemetery and built his chalet there, living in it with his family during the summer. At the same time he ran his business, the management of which he entrusted to an active young man, one Hagopig Hovnanian. Unfortunately Onnig Agha didn't live long and his wife and children closed their business down and left Bardizag.

92 – The Mgerians after Garabed Agha Mgerian's death. Sarkis Effendi Mgerian

Garabed Agha Mgerian died, as we've seen, in 1858. Thanks to his public works he had earned the grateful thanks of the community and was therefore accorded the honour of being buried in the church courtyard, opposite its south apse, near the main door, against the churchyard wall. His sons placed a marble tombstone on his grave and enclosed it with an iron fence.

Shortly after Mgerian's death his first-born son, Hagopig Effendi Mgerian, also died childless, and his wife, a daughter of the Kousdigian family, remarried, becoming the wife of Hadji Taniel Agha Der-Sahagian, who had been a widower since the death of his first wife.

As a result of these tragic circumstances, Sarkis Effendi Mgerian, Mgerian's second son, became the new representative of the Mgerian house. He was quite well educated and had gained great experience in his father's business, having collaborated with him for many years. Sarkis Effendi was an august and presentable personality of great stature who impressed all who saw him. He took the management of all his father's many businesses into his hands and inherited all his influential friendships, authority and charm. Taking after his father, he really was his worthy successor, becoming a noted, authoritative personality in Bardizag's public affairs and, after a time, in the entire province.

It was during his time[*] that the (Ottoman) Armenian community[†] became the owner of its own laws to govern its internal affairs, the National Constitution, accepted and endorsed by the Turkish government. According to the rules of this constitution, Armenian public bodies would take charge of community affairs. These changes meant that the Turkish aghas' former feudal system was now ended and government relations with Armenian communities in the villages took place through an *ekhtiar medjlis* (council of elders). Sometimes the members of the community council also had seats on this council of elders, thus concentrating government and community affairs in the same hands, often for years. The concentration of both kinds of governance often proved to be positive in terms of good order and results.

Sarkis Effendi Mgerian proved to be the overriding personality among us during this new period in Bardizag's public affairs and was able to conduct both

---

[*] 1862.

[†] I have added the word (Ottoman) here, as the author is talking about the Armenians throughout the Ottoman Empire – in other words the Armenian *Millet*.

government and community administration safely. He was the chairman of the first parish council[*] under the Constitution and the chairman of the council of elders.

93 – The bandit chief Lefter

In those days a Greek bandit chief named Lefter made a name for himself at the head of his band of Greeks, Armenians and Turks and terrorised the province of Izmid.[†] This man was from the Greek village located on the heights of Karamoursal and near the Armenian villages of Merdegeoz and Yalak Dere. A young man with a naturally bold, fearless nature, he had served in the police force for years. A person who was used to fighting fiercely and doing brave deeds, he thus earned the appreciation and respect of his superiors for the skill he showed in his post and for his boldness against criminals. He thus became the 'spoilt brat' of government circles before he became a bandit.

He later became bitter at his superiors' changed attitude towards him, which he hadn't expected. They had perhaps wounded his nationalist feelings due to the government's new mentality towards the Greeks resulting from Greece's independence. He suddenly left his job as a policeman and, with a few comrades, went into the mountains. Filled with a natural feeling of revenge over his wounded dignity, he was to carry on a trade that was not unlike that of the police in Turkey until his death.

Lefter operated as a bandit for many years, entrusting his and his band's safety to the inaccessible caves in the mountains, suddenly appearing in the most unexpected way and performing some bold act. He would capture the most important and richest Turkish aghas from the safest towns and villages, pulling them from their beds at dead of night and taking them to the mountains. He would only release them when he had received a large ransom. He left them in perpetual fear and worry, like mice in his claws.

Fear and terror followed the steps of this new king of the mountains. He was full of surprises and acted swiftly, disappearing for a time and then suddenly appearing in a most unexpected place, making every heart tremble with terror.

Every attempt at following and capturing him was in vain. At the same time he was a good, noble man and a friend of the people and the poor. He was the terrible enemy of the tyrannical individuals and those who fleeced the people; everyone held him in esteem and defended him as a restraining angel poised over villains. Only his natural death would allow those in government circles to breathe a sigh of relief.

---

* *Taghagan khorhourt.*
† This was in 1860-1866. His band was made up of 30 individuals. They terrorised the plain of Nicaea and the areas around Armash and Fendekli. Minas Kasabian (Farhad), *Hayere Nikomedio Kavarin Mech*, p. 123.

Two important incidents in his story link him to Bardizag and Armenian life in the surrounding area, which bring to light his boldness and, at the same time, his great nobility.

It was during the silkworm season – April and May – and everyone in Bardizag was busy working, and the great men of the village had temporarily established their homes in their silk spinning factories in the village's deserted outskirts.

Hadji Taniel Agha Der-Sahagian, like everyone else, had moved to his silk spinning factory, outside the village on the Kirazlekh road. With him were his wife Hadji Doudou, his son Zenon and his daughter and some workpeople. Everyone was exhausted from their efforts and had fallen into deep sleep during the short summer night.

Lefter entered the silk spinning factory at this moment, leaving his men outside. He woke the family who, although terrified by the sudden, disturbing appearance of the bandit in their house, tried to remain calm, treating him like a friend. They prepared a meal for him, bringing him wine and trying to enliven the meal with witty conversation. Lefter ate and drank, made jokes and, when it was time to leave, ordered Taniel Agha to accompany him.

Begging, pleading and tears wouldn't move the bandit chief, when Hadji Doudou, in a death crisis, suddenly threw her arms about the bandit's neck, wet his dirty face with her tears, and begged him to release her husband.

The bandit chief immediately relented in view of this female self-sacrificing gesture, soothed her and, with tears in his eyes, said, 'I release your husband,' and withdrew with his men.

The second incident took place in the nearby fields near Ovadjek.

Lefter had, for some time, been following a man called Mirto from that village who, voluntarily working with the government, had joined in an attack on him and his band and had killed one of his dearest friends, Hadji Boghos, with a rifle bullet.

He was finally able to apprehend him one day when he was returning home from the fields. He sat him down next to him and asked him, in the coldest manner, 'Was it you who killed Hadji Boghos?'

'Yes,' Mirto replied, with the same coldness.

'With which hand did you pull the trigger?' asked Lefter.

'This one,' replied Mirto, extending his right arm.

At this, Lefter ordered his men to bring him a branch from a tree. They brought one and laid it down. Lefter ordered Mirto to bare his arm and put it on the branch. Mirto did so. Lefter then ordered one of his men to cut it off with one blow of his knife in front of him. The order was carried out; Mirto's hand was severed from the arm and fell to the ground with blood everywhere. Gritting his teeth, Mirto, with stoical calm, accepted what had happened to him without showing any weakness. Lefter ordered that the stump should be cleaned, the bleeding stopped, treated with medicine, and bandaged up as if they were carrying out a surgical operation.

After all this, Lefter turned to Mirto and said, 'You can go now. Hadji Boghos' soul was satisfied.'

Mirto rose to his feet and began to walk towards the village, but suddenly turned and approached the group, which had not yet departed. Lefter, surprised, asked him, 'Why did you come back?'

'I left my belt under a bush and came to get it,' he replied. It was a rumpled piece of cloth which he took and wrapped around his waist.

Lefter, greatly affected by the man's fearlessness, got to his feet, embraced him, kissed his forehead and said, 'I'm comforted. Hadji Boghos fell from the bullet of a brave man.'

94 – The formation of a Catholic community and its life in Bardizag

The Armenian Catholic Church was recognised as a separate community from the Armenian Apostolic Church by the Turkish government in 1830, after years of battles, mutual persecution and tyrannical acts by the two churches. The Armenian Catholic Church had its sympathisers in Bardizag from very early on. This sympathy gave birth to political passions among certain families with regard to community leadership and the priestly class – with discontent and, to a certain extent, the wish to give children a regular and well-prepared education.

In those days the Armenian Catholic Mkhitarist Order of monks[*] was notable for its incontestable efforts and skill in the literary and educational fields. For the people of Bardizag the need to give children a regular and satisfactory education became an imperative because of political events in the country.

People said that in 1836 Garabed Somoundjian, who was the father of Hatsouni Vartabed of the Mkhitarian order, through some internal village problem, became disenchanted with the village leadership and priests. He gathered a number of like-minded people around him, and petitioned the Armenian Catholic Patriarchate in Constantinople. He then brought an Armenian Catholic kahana to Bardizag, with the purpose of eventually separating from the Armenian Apostolic Church. The Catholic priest became a guest in Garabed Somoundjian's home where, for the first time, the Catholic version of the morning service and Mass took place.

---

[*] Generally known and much respected by Armenians as the Mkhitarian Orders of Venice and of Vienna.

This newly established church continued its existence in this primitive way, without its own church building. Catholic kahanas would occasionally come either from Kaghadia (Engiuriu) or Constantinople to shepherd this newly established small group, among whom the priests Menzilian and Kantarian may be recalled.

They were followed by Hovsep Vartabed Ayvazian as the leader of the Armenian Catholic community of Bardizag, appointed by the Armenian Catholic Patriarchate in Constantinople. Ayvazian remained in the village with that office from 1867-1876.* He bought a house from the Koustigians just above the centre of the market in the village, whose ground floor was turned into a prayer hall known as the 'Catholics' Chapel'. The first floor was assigned to Armenian nuns of the Order of the Immaculate Conception as their living quarters. The priest rented a house owned by Hadji Toros Koustigian as his residence.

Hovsep Vartabed Ayvazian returned to the mother – Armenian Apostolic – church in 1876,† resulting in the abandonment of the newly established Catholic Church for a time. The nuns returned to Constantinople, while the few Catholic families were somewhat confused and divided into two groups. Some returned to the Armenian Apostolic Church with the priest, while the remainder awaited developments.

The leadership of the Armenian Catholic Church in the village was later handed over to the Mkhitarian order. The order sent Nerses Vartabed Djendoyian to Bardizag in 1882 to lead the community (he was later to be appointed Armenian Catholic Bishop of Daron in Moush). This priest worked very hard to reconstruct the disintegrating church and bring the remaining Catholic families back together. He was able to buy a garden near Lousaghpiur in the Avazoud parish of the village belonging to Nshanig Agha Azarian, despite the opposition of the population of the village and began to build a church and monastery on the site, according to the plans drawn up by Kachouni Vartabed, who also supervised its construction.‡

He rid himself of the difficulties the villagers placed before him, when they refused him water, sand and lime for construction purposes, by having an artesian well dug on his land. He then was able to buy another garden near Lousaghpiur, from which the necessary sand and soil to continue construction was extracted. Under these circumstances he was able to complete his plans: a church, a prelacy,

---

* Natanian tells us that there were about 40 houses (about 200 people) who were Catholics in the village in 1870, the faith having been established about 6 years before. They had a church and a school, but were in a poor financial state. Boghos Vartabed Natanian, *Arachin deghegakroutiun vidjagis Nicomedio* [First report on the diocese of Nicomedia], Djezvedjian Press, Constantinople 1871, p. 21.

† See Section 95 below.

‡ This Catholic church was consecrated on 28 April 1891. See Hagop Der-Hagopian, *Bardizage khadoudig*, pp. 171-172.

and a boys' school all housed in a large, strong building constructed of stone with lime mortar.

Djendoyian's successor, Kaftandjian Vartabed, built a nuns' convent and a girls' school next to the first buildings, entrusting them, once more, to the sisters of the Order of the Immaculate Conception. These Armenian Catholic schools, thanks to their services – free education, free schoolbooks and writing materials, as well as other charms – were able to collect quite a number of boys and girls of Armenian Apostolic families, in addition to Armenian Catholic children, as students. But the low standard of the teaching staff and poor basic tuition, as well as Catholic propaganda, weren't able to satisfy the high educational standards required. This was at the time when the community schools were enjoying a brilliant period during Yeghishe Vartabed Tourian's term of office as schools inspector, and the provision of well-run high schools, both for boys and girls by the American Missionary Board.

The impetus given to Armenian Catholic life under these circumstances and the sacrifices made for it had no real effect. The Catholic community remained weak and limited in numbers, without any great influence on the village's educational movement. The one exception was the practical teaching offered to girls by the nuns in sewing and embroidery, which many girls profited from.

It should be kept in mind that the mass disturbances created by the Hasounian and anti-Hasounian battles within the Armenian Catholic community dealt an almost mortal blow to the whole Ottoman Armenian community. In Bardizag, the development and activity of the Armenian Catholic church was like sowing of seeds on a barren and unproductive field.

After Kaftandjian Vartabed, the Armenian Catholic community leaders in Bardizag were successively Serope Vartabed Abdullah, Yetvart Vartabed Sirounian, Teotoros Vartabed Sirounian, then, for a second time, Yetvart Vartabed Sirounian, whose second term of office coincided with the Armenian deportations.[*]

There is, however, an important point to be raised concerning the work carried out in Bardizag by the Mekhitarists. Although the Armenian Catholic school didn't have a noticeable effect on the student population of the village, it did act like a hothouse to prepare pupils for Mekhitarist high schools.[†] A considerable number of boys from Bardizag have followed courses in the Mekhitarist High School in Kade-Kiugh, the educational establishment on St. Lazzaro, Venice and the Mourad-Raphaelian schools, who have reached significant positions.

---

[*] The author is referring to the Armenian genocide of 1915.
[†] There were two Catholic schools in Bardizag in 1909-1910: the boys' school had 110 pupils, while the girls' school had 60. 5 male and 3 female teachers taught in them, and it was thought that their yearly budget was 25,000 *kurush*. Minas Kasabian (Farhad), *Hayere Nikomedio Kavarin Mech*, p. 261.

Students from Bardizag who attended the Mekhitarist School in Venice were Apraham Geloyian (1875); Dikran Pashayian (1875-1880) – later becoming Dadjad Kahana Pashayian; Stepan Melkonian (1854-1855); Arshag Tanielian (1889-1892); Maghakia Gelorian (1897-1898); Aray Jamgochian (1899-1900); Ardashes Kiutian (1901-1902); Haroutiun Aslanian (1908-1910); Torkom Kiutnerian (1924-1928); Hagop Bedrosian (1926-1929) and Garo Djoboyian (1928 – he still continues his studies)*. All these have studied in the Mekhitarist seminaries and were then discharged as unsuitable for ordination as monks.

Students who followed courses in the Mourad-Raphaelian School were: Mihran Der-Krikorian (1883-1886); Mgerdich Gabeyian (1890-1894); Mikayel Alemshah (1890-1894); Ardashes Ghazigian (1895-1896); Krikor Nalbandian (1906-1909); Stepan Daiyan*† (1906-1912); Hovhannes Semerdjian (1909-1910); Moushegh Kechedjian (1910-1912); Bedros Simonian* (1913-1916); Garabed Moutafian (1919); Khachig Alemshah (1919-1922); Kourken Alemshah (1919-1923); Hovhannes Bodourian* (1919-1923); Haroutiun Kehiaian (1919-1924); Bariur Mardigian* (1921-1924); Garbis Alemshah* (1921-1925); Stepan Daiyan (1923-1928); Hrach Kacharents* (1927-1931); Papken Bodosian (1927-1930) and Krikor Bodosian (1931-1934) who was born in Ovadjek.

Young men from Bardizag who joined the Mekhitarist order of monks are detailed below.

> * Hovhannes Vartabed Torosian. He entered the monastery in 1874; took the oath binding him to the Mekhitarists in 1880 and was ordained in 1882. He has been a teacher, director of the Venice seminary, as well as of the Kadekiugh and Venice schools. He has been the editor of *Pazmaveb* and author, secretary to the Mekhitarist order, a member of their executive council and general Abbot of the order itself.
>
> * Yesayi Vartabed Dayetsi. He entered the monastery in 1884; took the oath in 1890 and was ordained in 1892. He has been a teacher, editor of *Pazmaveb*, publisher and the director of the Milan school.
>
> * Vartan Vartabed Hatsouni. He entered the monastery in 1885; took the oath in 1890 and was ordained in 1892. He has been a teacher, director of the Venice seminary (twice), director of the Mourad-Raphaelian schools (twice), general secretary to the Mekhitarist order, a member of their executive council, editor of *Pazmaveb* and an author.
>
> * Arsen Vartabed Ghazigian. He entered the monastery in 1888; took the oath in 1892 and was ordained in 1895. He has been a teacher, translator and author, and has held various administrative posts.

---

*   The author is writing in the 1930s.
† The six names in this list with an asterisk against them were students who also completed university education at the school's expense. (Author's note)

* Mgerdich Vartabed Bodourian. He entered the monastery in 1894; took the oath in 1899 and was ordained in 1902. He has been a teacher, editor of *Pazmaveb*, publicist and publisher.

* Ghevont Vartabed Daiyan. He entered the monastery in 1900; took the oath in 1904 and was ordained in 1906. He has been a teacher, editor of *Pazmaveb*, head of music, an instructor in the Venice seminary and secretary to the Mekhitarist order.

* Agheksantr Vartabed Deolenian. He entered the seminary in 1906; took the oath in 1912 and was ordained in 1916. He has been a teacher. He only remained in the order for a short time.

It can be seen from these lists that a significant number of students from Bardizag received their education and diplomas from the highest Mekhitarist educational establishments and some of them, with the order's help, found the opportunity to attend universities in Europe and thus brought honour not only on themselves, but also on the great Order and their birthplace.

95 – Hovsep Vartabed Ayvazian's return to the mother church in 1876

Although I referred to this incident in a previous section,[*] I feel that it is right to give all its details here, as it was an important event in Bardizag's history. When I was still only a ten year-old boy, a whisper ran through the village: 'The Catholic priest will become an Armenian; he'll be coming to our church tonight with a pointed cowl *(veghar)* on his head.' With the whole village, I too was delighted, and a ray of victory lit up our childish souls.

At that time Protestantism had already been among us for several years. In our childish minds, we could see the centuries-old Armenian Apostolic Church surrounded by enemies. The Armenians' faith was in danger, and that faith was *everything* for all of us. It was Armenia, it was Armenian monasteries and churches, Armenian schools, the Armenian alphabet, Armenian history and the entire content of Armenian community life. We were therefore all happy, as that whisper awoke great hopes in the depths of our souls: the Armenian Apostolic Church would be triumphant!

The evening arrived and we all rushed to the church, imbued with the fervour of a feast day.

The church was lit up. All the chandeliers, lamps and candles had the appearance of being wide eyes waiting for things to happen. The eyes of the entire congregation were on the great door, when suddenly the diocesan bishop's locum tenens, Stepannos Vartabed Hovagimian, with the Catholic priest wearing a cowl, entered the church behind a procession made up of choristers and priests singing the

---

* See Section 94 (above).

canticle 'Be joyful, holy Church.' When we saw the monk under that cowl, we felt that he seemed to have a different aura about him. The procession slowly advanced towards the altar, where psalms and prayers were being read. After a moment or two, the locum tenens, the vartabed, the other priests and the choir took their usual places. The newly-turned monk took his place at the head of the left-hand side. The evening service began. When it was over, Hovsep Vartabed Ayvazian, bearing a priestly staff, was brought to the dais at the centre of the choir, where he began his first sermon as an Armenian (Apostolic) monk. He took his text for the sermon from the Book of Psalms: 'The day gives knowledge, the night shows wisdom.' This sermon, of which I personally understood very little at the time and some of which I can now guess, was a confession of his Armenian faith burning in his Armenian soul, something that had been under a foreign cover that circumstances had now removed, bringing it into the open with genuine truthfulness.

The vartabed remained as a guest in Bardizag for a few days and then went to the Armenian Patriarchate of Constantinople. From that day on he became a worthy Armenian Apostolic churchman, a vartabed, then a bishop, carrying out valuable preaching and diocesan duties in various places.

96 – The entry and spread of Protestantism in Bardizag

The Protestant Church came to the village in the wake of the Catholic Church, as if to rid us of it and to impose its rule on its ruins.

The missionaries of the American Board of Missions first came to the Ottoman Empire in 1825-1830 and began to preach, taking advantage of the reform decree issued by Sultan Medjid* that promised equality for all the races that made up the population of the Empire and proclaimed freedom of conscience at least for its Christians. The American missionaries were devout and enthusiastic Christians. They were the sons of a New World that had swiftly become rich and educated, whose successes and blessings, they believed, were due to Christ's Gospel. The new, comfortable life in a distant America across the ocean undoubtedly gave birth to a religious movement through which they wanted to be free of all restraints to freedom and conscience, without any outside interference between themselves and their God. They knew their God, and they had in their hands His Holy Book, which they regarded as sufficient for themselves. They had now come to this land (Turkey) to teach their experiences and show the new way to others. They had, in their own country, great fervent multitudes that were ready to aid and assist their undertaking which, for them, was God's work.

---

* The author can only be writing about Sultan Abdul Medjid I, who reigned from 1839 to 1861, so the date he is quoting must be incorrect.

The missionaries, in their innocent and sincere devoutness, thought at the beginning that they had come among heathens who did not know of the Law and the Books.* They were driven to look on them with compassion as sinners who, having killed the *spirit* of the Books, had made idols for themselves which they worshipped. They found, among the local Christians - mainly among the Armenians - dissatisfied individuals who, in one way or another, had become disenchanted with their spiritual and temporal leaders. At the same time they found others who were carried away by the prospect of a new dawn of freedom in Turkey and had a yearning for free thought, in whatever way it was presented, after long years of deadly servitude and tyranny. The newcomers, as a result, succeeded in forming small groups of sympathisers who at first met in houses and read, under their supervision and in absolute freedom, the Holy Scriptures in their own spoken language – thus finding satisfaction for their spiritual needs. They prayed in public in their meetings, without having to learn ancient prayers by heart, sang the Psalms in their ordinary language, and created a spiritual and religious movement that in reality was a movement for freedom. It was this that, more than anything else, spoke to the innocent converts whose eyes had just been opened.

The missionaries, with the help of the local people who were their co-religionists, then translated parts of the Holy Bible, religious and moral stories as well as songs, into the local language, printing them as booklets and distributing them, free of charge, among the newly-converted and to others. Through these efforts a Protestant culture began to be built around the missionaries and people became familiar with it. This new movement was restricted for some years to Izmir and Constantinople but gradually spread further with new Protestant educational centres, all based on American lines and methods. When the old churches, inflamed against this new danger, began to persecute those converted to this new movement, the new Protestants, enthusiastically and spiritedly imbued with the new principles they had adopted – we could even say with their fanaticism – doggedly defended their rights to freedom of expression and conscience.

This movement gradually spread through the provinces, especially in Izmid, Bardizag and Adabazar, which were near Constantinople and where, in the same way and using the same methods, similar religious agitation took place.

---

* During an interview by Minas Kasabian with Dr. R. Chambers sometime in 1910-1912, Dr. Chambers provided a statement on the original aims of the Protestant movement in the Ottoman Empire:

> ...The original object of the missionaries in Turkey was to preach the Gospel to all races in the Ottoman Empire. The Armenians were the people that benefitted most from the education and opportunities provided by the missionaries.

For the full text, See Minas Kasabian (Farhad), *Hayere Nikomedio Kavarin Mech*, pp. 130-131.

Writing specifically about the origin of Protestantism in Bardizag, the following anecdote is related, giving the reader the impression that it was a legend rather than actual fact, yet to a great extent it explains the beginning of the Protestant church among us, in parallel with the mentality described in the lines above.

In the course of this history we have often read of the Selihians, who were a large clan descended from a certain Zakar Agha, as were the Zakarians, Hairabedians and Kafadarians. The Selihians were a family noted for a rebellious and independent nature. They would rise to their feet and protest because of supposed or actual injustices and were generally considered to act against the public interest. They had, on many occasions, had arguments in the village because of profiteering and fraud in public accounting.

One anecdote about such events is the following.

The Selhians were the Mikayelians' neighbours, who were an influential and powerful family in Bardizag from the earliest times. The latter demolished their house with the object of building a new one on the site, which was located in the market area of the main street, near the Der-Garabedians' public fountain. During the construction of the new house, the Selihians demanded that, according to the law, the foundations of the new building be moved back, wishing the street to be widened and the area around the fountain enlarged. The village authorities intervened between the two sides and arrived at the following agreement – the new house's foundations should be 10 *arshins** (about 25 feet or 8m) from the fountain and, to ensure this stipulation, they made a measuring pole of that length and kept it in the church store-room.

The Mikayelians, however, relying on powerful friendships, reduced the distance to eight *arshins* (just over 20 feet or 5.5m) and were somehow able to have the measuring pole reduced to that length, having two arshins' length cut off it. The Selihians heard of this trickery and demanded that the official measuring pole be brought out. The pole was brought and checked, but it was only eight *arshins* long. The Selihians didn't forgive this fraud, protested and demanded that the foundations of the house be rebuilt two *arshins* back from their position but, unfortunately, they were faced with a fait accompli and, despite all their efforts, didn't succeed in having their demands met. They ascribed their lack of success to the community leadership and the priests' slackness and partiality. They were scandalised and, with all their relatives and others who thought like them, joined the Protestant movement.

It is not possible, in my opinion, to link the beginning of Protestantism among us to this incident, but it may have been the thing that began the storm that was ready to burst, otherwise we would belittle the significance of the Protestant movement and the spiritual and intellectual value of our people. But it is an

---

* An arshin was 68cm or 28 inches.

indisputable fact that these kinds of incidents and disagreements fanned the flames of the fire that was ready to spring up, as we've seen in the same way with the beginning of the Armenian Catholic Church.

Along with the Selihians, the Protestant movement took the Kafadars (relatives of the Selihians), Gatsans, Magarians, a branch of the Topouzians, Sepetdji Minas, the Simas, Toroums, a branch of the Gevregs, Touma Baba, Tavit Kahana's two sons – Garabed and Hadji Mikayel, the Mgerian father's brother, Djezel Ghazaros, the Avedians, Ghourous, Arabians, Panosians, Gobelians, Pirenians, Youvanians, Kemelos, Diudiug Kehians, Beyzadians, a branch of the Bodourians (in Izmid) as well as many others, whose numbers swelled for a time until the movement itself stopped when I was still young.

The Protestant community was formally recognised by the Turkish government around 1846-1850, about 20 years after the official recognition of the Catholic Church. The Protestant church probably grew in Bardizag after 1850. Mr. Dwight, a travelling missionary, preached in Izmid and Bardizag in the first instance. He had a mission to prepare the way, as we've seen, for the formation of the small kernel of the Protestant Church under the Selihians' leadership. They initially met in Mger Baba Selih's house, which was a little below and to the north of that belonging to the Mikayelians. Mr. Dwight didn't remain long in the area, having founded the Protestant church in Izmid, Bardizag and, probably, in Adabazar.

The American Missionary Board, seeing a great opportunity for its plans for work in that area, sent Mr. Parsons as the resident missionary in the Bithynia plain. He was, sometime later, able to buy the Gharavelegs' silkworm house that was surrounded by mulberry trees in a beautiful position at the eastern edge of the village. He set up his permanent home there, having a small house built for him on the site.

This Protestant movement in Bardizag, at the beginning, was the subject of vigorous, if not violent, hatred and opposition by the rest of the villagers. It was greater and more threatening than that shown when the Catholic Church was formed and there were reasons for it. First, the opposition to the Catholic Church had eased in Constantinople and the official Armenian Apostolic authorities and people had, by now, accepted the fact of its existence. Second, when the Catholic movement first began among us, the Armenian Catholic Church was a completely Armenian church using Armenian (Apostolic) Church ceremonies and the classical Armenian language. It only changed its spiritual leader and differed in a few minor questions that the people didn't really understand. The only real difficulty was that it split from the jurisdiction of the Catholicos in Holy Echmiadzin and came under that of the Pope. When an Armenian entered an Armenian Catholic Church he heard the same prayers, singing and canticles. He saw the same ceremonies and mass. The clergy was Armenian and, in all its ranks, the differences were barely noticeable.

The Protestant Church was completely different and became known in disturbing circumstances. The split or breach between Protestants and Apostolic Armenians being so deep that bridging it seemed impossible. It seemed like blasphemy to the Armenian believer in terms of appearance, ceremony, language and the enormous differences in declaration of faith. The Armenian community in its entirety was armed against this new movement even from the outset, ferociously wanting to get rid of it from its bosom, as an unfeeling and wicked thing. Thanks to this mentality, an enormous battle began between the old and the new, with curses, derision, arguments and fighting, stoning and even murder plots being set up against newly-converted individuals. Life became impossible for the Protestants in the village.

The first Protestants in Bardizag were subjected to heavy and serious persecution by our people at first, and if it hadn't been for their defence by Protestant governments, their church, while taking its first steps, would have been destined to be crushed and destroyed.

The Protestants, sticking to their freedom of conscience, were totally dejected and discouraged. Every link between the two communities – friendship, relationship, work and trade - was severed. The Protestants, for a long time, didn't have the courage to appear in public, even feeling unsafe in their own houses, especially at night, and they were unable to tend their fields. It was an altogether dangerous situation.

The Protestants couldn't sit and do nothing. Life, like their faith, always had its demands, so they decided to find a solution to their situation by creating small Protestant community-like entities for their work and occupations. They chose and transferred their agricultural work to two places – fallow areas – Upper Ayazma and Distant Upper Fields that were outside the village. There they planted mulberry trees and built a silkworm house and found a way, by being close together, of protecting one another, to work there in peace. Following the Pilgrim Fathers' example, they moved to unknown *lands* holding their weapons in one hand and the Bible or their work tools in the other. They lived like this for some time, until passions had somewhat cooled and both sides could tolerate each other as neighbours.

When I was young, violent acts and persecution had ended.[*] Religious arguments then took place in the streets, market and shops, which always attracted

---

[*] Boghos Vartabed Natanian, when he visited Bardizag in 1870, found that there were about 50 houses with 250 people who were Protestants in the village. He stated that they lived in their own quarter, had a meeting hall and school and one preacher. He adds that they have been established in this manner for 20 years, but were in a poor financial state. Boghos Vartabed Natanian, *Arachin deghegakroutiun vidjagis Nicomedio* [First report on the diocese of Nicomedia], Djezvedjian Press, Constantinople 1871, p. 20.

an interested crowd. Sarcasm, jokes and occasional curses aimed at each other were mixed together, but the arguments always ended with witty thoughts but without the use of fists.

Mr Parsons was the first missionary to organise the Bardizag Protestant community. He ensured that it had, firstly, its own place for prayer - the Protestant meeting hall - near the Selih part of the village. This was in the Batakh Baghchai area, to the south of the village centre. The first Protestant families - the Selihs, Kafadarians, Toroum Sare Baba, the Gatsans (Semerdjians), Kourouians, Arabians and others – lived around it. They also had their own cemetery a few steps from their place of prayer. Those areas were probably gifts to the new community from the Selihians or another Protestant family.

The meeting hall was a building with its longest side running north-south, located on a promontory, such that at its southern end the ground was flat around it, and one entered it through the great door there. Inside was a small vestibule with a room on either side, which served as offices for the Protestant leadership and their spiritual leader.[*] A door in the vestibule led into a large, light hall, like a lecture hall, with plain walls, a wooden floor and furnished with tables and chairs. At its northern end was a wide stage or platform that was approximately one *arshin* (28 inches, 68cm) high and about 2-3 *arshins* (maximum 7 feet, 2m) deep which always held a small lectern with a Bible and hymn book in the centre. This hall served as a prayer hall for the Protestant faithful, who assembled there and sat on the chairs, having their Bibles and hymnals on the tables in front of them.

The children sat on benches without tables near the stage; the women and girls on the left side of the hall and the men on the right. Although the separation of the sexes was not the rule, the old custom persisted. The spiritual leader or pastor, who was usually known by the title *badveli* [reverend] occupied the chair at the back of the stage and took the service standing at the lectern. Worship consisted of a short reading from the Bible, a short prayer selected by the *badveli* in accordance with the circumstances, a few hymns[†] followed by the sermon, the most basic and important part of worship, then a blessing, and a short period of silence, during which the individual worshipper said a silent prayer. The service generally lasted for an hour to an hour and a half at the most. The congregation sang in unison and often recited the readings together. The hymns were sung to the accompaniment of a harmonium[‡] placed at the corner of the stage, and usually played by a girl or woman.

Because of the way the building was constructed, it was possible to build a basement hall of about half its area, in the corner of which was a small room. This

---

[*] The word used here is 'shepherd'.
[†] The author uses the word 'songs'.
[‡] The word used here is *yerkehon*.

part of the building was the Protestant school, used to give the children basic education: reading, writing, arithmetic, geography, Bible study and the basics of the English language. After attending this school for five to six years the pupil, boy or girl, went to the American boys' or girls' schools if they wanted to continue their education; if not, then their training began either in the market or at home. The Protestant school was run by a qualified female teacher with the help of an assistant teacher and a housekeeper.*

The *badveli* or pastor was the community's shepherd and preacher, occasionally giving lessons in the school. He was also ex-officio chairman of the Protestant governing body.

The Protestant Church had two distinct classes in terms of voting – that of the communicants who were elected by public testimony for their faith, conduct and honour, and therefore had the right to approach Communion, and the second class, made up of those who weren't communicants. Only church members had the right to vote in executive elections. Every Protestant family contributed, in accordance with its means, to church expenses, and paid fees for their children at school. Naturally, during the first years of the church's formation, popular subscriptions weren't sufficient to defray all the costs of the preacher, school and administration, and the Missionary Board had to cover the deficit through its own resources. The church in Bardizag never managed to become self-financing and always enjoyed the Board's assistance on an annual but declining scale, in accordance with the increasing funds provided by the people.

Protestant weekly services were very simple and few. On Sundays there was a main service, as described above and Bible lessons in the evening, split into classes according to age and gender. During the week there was a short service called the Prayer Meeting, held in the hall, as a public form of worship. There was also a women's prayer meeting held on a specific weekday in various houses in turn, and called the Sisters' Meeting. These were the elements of weekly worship. Naturally every believer read the Bible and prayed regularly, either individually or as part of a family group.

Much later, public evening prayer meetings were held in the meeting hall each day during the last week in December to welcome the approach of the New Year. Talks and sermons were given during these services, not only by the *badveli*, but also by others from the congregation, such as teachers and believers. These took place on set occasions based on a plan drawn up according to particular texts.

---

* By 1909-1910, the Protestants in Bardizag had two schools: the one for boys had 119 pupils and the other, for girls, had 51. The schools were served by 2 male and 1 female teachers and their yearly budget was thought to be 10,000 *kurush*. Minas Kasabian (Farhad), *Hayere Nikomedio Kavarin Mech*, p. 261.

The Protestant church had, during the first few years of Mr. Parsons' missionary work, already developed this organisation in all its parts. Mrs. Parsons, who was a bold and active woman, led the Sisters' Meetings. At the same time she was occupied with practical Christianity, without discrimination, helping those who accepted her aid with the sick, inoculating children against smallpox and providing free medicine and assisting the poor and needy. With all this, she handed out moral and religious pamphlets in people's homes, written in the villagers' simple language.

Similarly, Mr. Parsons, outside his missionary responsibilities, occasionally visited all parts of the province, preaching and distributing whole bibles or extracts from it free of charge in the initial perod. When the Protestant Church organisation became finally fixed and learnt to govern itself, Mr. Parsons planned and achieved more fundamental means of Christian education, which I will have an opportunity to write about later.*

The following people have been pastors in the Protestant church in Bardizag: the *Badvelis* Hovhannes Der-Stepanian, Der-Sahagian, Prof. Djedjizian (before he went to Robert College), *Badvelis* Boughdanian, Abdalian, Tashjian, A Bedigian, P. Iskenderian, S. Manougian and Hovsep Haigazn.

When the church didn't have an official pastor, the faithful ran services themselves. This was done by Sepetdji B. Minas, Gober Baba, Garabed Baroutdjian, Mgerdich Goydourian etc.

97 – The foundation of the Saroukhanian and Mgerian silk spinning factories†

Before silk spinning factories were built, silk thread was removed from the cocoon using the old system called *mandjelekh*. A number of cocoons would be submerged in large pans of boiling water and the silk thread would be wound on to a bobbin at home. The silk, in this state, would be sold to merchants. This method lasted until the middle of the 17th century. Silk machine technology, however, developed in Europe and improved methods were found for the preparation of the raw material and for choosing cocoons, keeping the value of silk high by reducing the cost of choosing them.

Saroukhanian, an Armenian from Constantinople, who had been the director of the government cloth factory for many years, had gained great experience in machine and skilled work. As previously mentioned, he had settled in Bardizag from Constantinople.

---

* See Section 114.
† The author writes about the silk industry in the village with great authority, being a graduate of the sericulture school in Boursa (Bursa). See his certificate in the Appendix, Document 4.

Wishing to have his own independent business, he began work to found a *manaran* [silk spinning factory] in Bardizag. This was a new business in Turkey at that time, with only a few such enterprises located around Broussa (Boursa). Saroukhanian planned to build his own because there was a great crop of cheap cocoons in Bardizag and the surrounding area, plus a low demand for labour, as well as cheap wood or charcoal.

He obtained a large piece of land on the eastern side of the village where the Der-Sahagians' silkworm houses were and constructed a silk spinning factory with machines with the capacity for handling one hundred *tava* [pans]. He also built a *khozak-hane* [a separate store for cocoons], and assured his own water supply for the silk spinning factory, sources being plentiful in Bardizag. He thus completed the factory with all its equipment, had a small house built for his family to live in, and began to operate the silk spinning factory for himself. This was the first in Bardizag and began operations in about 1860. Saroukhanian was successful in this new business. He became known on the Constantinople market and was able to secure great credit with the European middlemen dealing in silk.

The Mgerian brothers – Sarkis, Mgrdich and Artaki – who continued their traditional horseshoe workshop, despairing of its uncertain future and the competition from European machine-made products decided, in their turn, to begin a modern business, encouraged by Saroukhanian's example. They therefore demolished their workshop and, using their own resources and credit, constructed their own silk spinning factory on the workshop site, about the same size as Saroukhanian's, with the same organisation and equipment. Now two factories, one at either end of the village, began to use machines, with spindles turning, operated by male and female workers and their bosses, disrupting the until-then peaceful atmosphere of Bardizag with mechanical whistles and a new work spirit.

The villager was delighted: two huge engineering enterprises had been born in the bosom of his village and great opportunities for work had been created. Woodsmen in the nearby forests provided the silk spinning factories with fuel, horse-drivers transported the fuel and silk, and hundreds of women and girls, who previously had no opportunity to earn money, worked and earned wages. Clerks, cocoon-merchants, porters, woodcutters, cocoon type selectors, cocoon driers – all of these were new professions providing work all year round.

In poor Bardizag, money and riches flowed in extraordinary ways. The demand for cocoons was constant and a source of wealth… It was no longer a case of 'go and return' for work.[*] These two silk spinning factories ushered in a remarkable era in Bardizag's economic life, giving it a completely new direction, and resulting in the expansion of sericulture. Fields were turned into mulberry orchards, the number of

---

* The original saying was *kne egou*.

silkworm houses increased, and the trade in mulberry seeds grew. All this was a stupefying revolution in Bardizag which happened very quickly.

Unfortunately this enthusiasm only lasted between five and ten years, and the enterprises, only just established, stopped for a time, causing the two silk spinning factory owners and the population of the village the greatest disillusionment. The silkworms had been affected by unknown sicknesses and every effort to cure them had been in vain. The crop of cocoons, despite great sacrifices and the greatest care in trying to keep the silkworms healthy, was poor, year after year. The villagers and the silk spinning factory owners, despite all their stubborn sacrifices and continuous effort, fell greatly into debt and went bankrupt, on a scale of a public disaster, comparatively speaking. The silk spinning factories closed their doors for lack of cocoons, the silkworm houses were abandoned, the mulberry tree orchards were uprooted and new, safer crops were cultivated on the same soil. Saroukhanian and Mgerian lost everything – silk spinning factories, buildings, land and gardens and were left with nothing.*

The Saroukhanians, having nothing further to do in Bardizag, finally moved back to Constantinople, tortured simply by the need to have food to eat. Only their widowed sister, Ilimonia Doudou and her family was left to its fate, even though they had taken that poor family into their care. She temporarily acted as the guardian of the silk spinning factory, staying in the family house itself and forced to live on crumbs left from the Saroukhanians' inheritance. She had to rely, to a great extent, on the charity of the villagers.

The Mgerians too, with their arms folded, having lost everything including hope, retreated to their ancestral home that was the only thing remaining in their hands, as if wounded by a shock precipitated by a dramatic fall. They only had a few small vineyards or gardens left in the immediate neighbourhood of the village. To close their enormous debts they sold the complete silk spinning factory, the coffee house in the market, their shop, bakery and *tolalekh*, the land and warehouses in Seymen and the Mgerian farm with all its land. The Mgerian property that still remained in the hands of the community were, either by purchase or by demand arrangements, a bakery, a shop, and a part of the building called *tolalekh*, while their coffee house was retained by *Diratsou* Hadji Garabed Der-Garabedian, satisfying one of his demands. Everything else became the property of European banks.

98 – The Mgerians in this new situation

The three Mgerian brothers – Sarkis, Mgerdich and Artaki, who each had his own family by then, were faced with a very difficult situation resulting from the complete destruction of their economy. The Mgerian house's traditional greatness, the family representatives' personal merits, assisted by a certain degree of education, as well as

---

* The expression used here is 'they sat on ashes'.

powerful and influential friendships were the way to their salvation. Although they had lost everything and had suddenly become poor, they retained their honour and charm in the village and province.

Sarkis Effendi Mgerian later worthily took over the Armenian representative's seat on the provincial council left vacant by the death of Melkon Agha (called Ghara Melkon) of Izmid, uniting in his person the province's Armenian voice with great ability and results, a position he held until his death.

Mgerdich Effendi, as we shall read in the next section, was ordained a kahana in the church in Bardizag, raising his calling and position on himself and leaving a much-loved and respected name in contemporary community history when, after a time, he was accepted into the ranks of the clergy of the Holy Trinity Armenian church in the rich Pera district of Constantinople. Later, as the leading priest *(avakerets)* of the same church, he earned the sympathy and friendship of the wealthy people of the district. He also became, for a time during Nerses Varjabedian's Patriarchate, his locum tenens, a position which was usually entrusted to a celibate churchman, but which he gave value to by his bold activities and authority, endowing the position with noble attributes.

The youngest, Artaki, who was childless, was able to live on the crumbs left from the family's wealth. He was, for some time, appointed the government overseer of the Tiutiun Chiftlig on the Izmid-Constantinople road.

99 - The ordination of kahanas on March 6th 1866

The village council headed by Sarkis Effendi Mgerian, seeing that many of the parish priests could no longer fulfil the needs of their parishioners due to their advanced ages, decided to have three new ones ordained. The candidates decided upon were Deacon Megerditch Mgerian, Hovhannes Mkhalian (who was an assistant teacher at various times in the community schools) and a goodly, spiritual young man (a basket-maker) from the Azarian family who had become a son-in-law to the well-known Kiutnerian clan.

The diocesan archbishop of the day, Archbishop Nerses Varjabedian (later the great Armenian Patriarch of Constantinople)* endorsed the choice of candidates made. He then came to Bardizag and ordained the three men on March 6th 1866. They were renamed as Hovhannes Kahana Mgerian, Garabed Kahana Mkhalian and the Azarian youth Mgerdich Kahana Azarian. Garabed Kahana Der-Krikorian and Hagop Kahana Der-Aprahamian had both passed away before the election had been carried out, leaving Sahag Kahana Pandigian, a great Armenian language scholar, Krikor Kahana Somoundjian and Minas Kahana Nahabedian, none of whom lived very long after the ordination of the new priests. When I was a boy the

---

* He was elected patriarch in 1874. Minas Kasabian (Farhad), *Hayere Nikomedio Kavarin Mech*, p. 124.

priests in the village of Bardizag of the older generation were Tavit Kahana Mikayelian, Mesrob Kahana Simonian and Nerses Kahana Bodourian (Balabanian) and those newly ordained – Hovhannes, Garabed and Mgerditch kahanas.*

After some time Nerses Kahana Bodourian was invited to Manchester, England, to be the community's spiritual leader. Accepting the invitation, he left Bardizag without receiving the approval of the village authorities. Hovhannes Kahana Mgerian became one of the resident priests of the Holy Trinity church in Pera, leaving only four priests for Bardizag who were able to minister to the spiritual needs of the people of the village for a while.

In about 1875 Nerses Kahana Bodourian returned from Manchester in his old age, but wasn't accepted into the ranks of the priests in the village, having previously left the church in which he was ordained without approval. As a form of protest, he wouldn't join the priests when he came to church but would stand, like an ordinary person, among the people, behind the priests. Sarkis Effendi Mgerian, irritated by this unseemly behaviour one day, shouted, in his fierce and booming voice, '*Der Hayr* [Lord Father], it's shameful, join the other priests.' He was thus forced to do so. I think that his unofficial status lasted until his death, when the whole situation resolved itself.

At about this time another priest from Bardizag returned to his birthplace – Simon Kahana, the son-in-law of the Torossians, who had been ordained in the village of Ferizli in the county of Adabazar. He too remained without a position for some time and, not being able to control himself in his depressed state, put a cloth on his head as a Catholic kahana and went over to the Catholic chapel, creating a scandal in the village. Sometime later, however, he repented publicly and returned to the mother church†, where he began to officiate as an officially recognised kahana, having his own parish, at the time when Mesrob Kahana and Tavit Kahana were both very old. When they too were unable to carry out their duties, the entire work of ministering to the people of the village was left solely to Garabed Kahana Mkhalian and Mgerditch Kahana Azarian.

The church in Bardizag had another priest born in the village who didn't have a position for some years after 1880. He was Krikor Kahana Paboudjian, Arshavir Kahana Varteressian's paternal uncle.‡ Krikor Kahana had been ordained in the village of Nor Kiugh [New Village] in Niceae but, after some time, had left that

---

* Boghos Vartabed Natanian tells us that the kahanas officiating in Bardizag in 1870 were Krikor (Somoundjian) (the senior priest), Mgerditch (Azarian), Tavit (Mikayelian), Garabed (Mkhalian) and Hovhannes (Mgerian). Boghos Vartabed Natanian, *Arachin deghegakroutiun vidjagis Nicomedio* [First report on the diocese of Nicomedia], Djezvedjian Press, Constantinople 1871, p. 19.

† The author means the Armenian Apostolic Church.

‡ Rev. Arshavir Varterssian's baptismal name was Karnig Paboudjian. He was a teacher before he was ordained in Cairo, Egypt in 1921.

village and gone to Egypt, where he'd been able to secure a position as an officiating priest in the Sts Peter and Paul church in Alexandria. Krikor Kahana, after the crushing of the Arab revolt by the British, having grown old, tired and becoming frightened by the lack of safety engendered by political events, returned to his birthplace to retire and remained without a position until his death, as a guest priest. He only officiated at services in church and joined in the morning and evening prayers.

100 – Community authority

With the establishment of the National Constitution in 1862, community rule was, for some time, in the hands of parish councils elected by the people. These were the villages' only and complete administrative organisations. They had government and community sectors and the mandatory function of *ekhtiar medjlis* (council of elders). The latter were set up by law and were unified for years with the constitutional town councils, as I've previously written.[*]

The parish council[†] was always chaired by the prelate's local deputy, who was usually the local leading kahana (*avakerets*). This position was carried out with the greatest authority by Garabed Kahana Mkhalian for over 40 years after Hovhannes Kahana Mgerian's move to Pera in Constantinople; the latter's influence may be imagined in the later words of Dr. Djerahian as *baghchedjik zelzeles* (Bardizag earthquake). This dual community and government representation continued in Bardizag for many years, until the village became the administrative centre of a *nahie* (group of villages), headed by a Turkish *miudir*.

The parish council, before the later organisation came into being, was strengthend by its role as the government's representative and carried out, for Bardizag, effective community actions. It took every community enterprise or problem in hand, be it governmental or concerning the community. The parish councils of those days were powerful and influential administrations, commanding great respect and authority towards the government and the village population.

To achieve satisfaction for the many and various demands made of it under its wide powers, the parish council elected or appointed various bodies to assist it.

First, a superintending body for the school, just as there always had been, usually made up of seven members[‡] that ran it – it appointed or dismissed teachers; collected and managed its income; rented out property belonging to the school,

---

[*] See Section 92.

[†] Parish council is the literal translation of the term *taghagan khorhourt*. It had responsibilities in many fields, as we shall see. I have retained the original term deliberately, to maintain simplicity.

[‡] These are the people known as *hokepartsou*. I have used the term 'trustees'.

having any necessary repairs carried out; prepared the school accounts; and monitored its work.

Second, it appointed one or two church guardians with the responsibility of maintaining the church's income and expenditure. In my day, the following people held that position at various times: Ghazaros Nahabedian, Hadji Khacher Khacherian, Hadji Krikor Agha Der-Antreasian, Hadji Garabed Agha Der-Garabedian, Hovhannes Agha Kiutnerian, Hadji Hagop Agha Djergayian, Hovhannes Agha Arakelian, and Sarkis Agha Djergayian. There were others I unfortunately cannot recall.

Third, it appointed a treasurer with responsibility for the money allocated for the poor. I can recall one or two of these: Hovhannes Agha Ghazarosian, Khacheres Bilidjian, and another, Mgerdich Nahabedian, given the nickname *Park Hor* [Glory to the Father] by the villagers, who was a son-in-law of the Kiutnerians.

These three, the school superintendents, church guardians and treasurer for the poor had, apart from their usual sources of income, their own special collection plates that used to be passed around the church congregation every Sunday.

Fourthly, the parish council appointed a secretary to the council, usually called the clerk, who recorded council decisions (the minutes), maintained the general public income and expenditure accounts as well as the records of the births, marriages and deaths from information provided by the priests.

It also had a *kehya* and a *jamgoch* [beadle]. The school superintendent body also had its male and female housekeepers. The appointment of the beadle was within the scope of the church guardians, but he, the *kehya* and housekeepers were employed under the authority of the parish council.

All these bodies and appointments were for the community sector. The parish council would appoint a *mukhtar* (headman - known in the old days as the agent or *chorbadji*) for the government sector as well as tax collectors who, in accordance with government orders and with the authority of the parish council, worked to satisfy government demands.

The parish council also had the responsibility for monitoring public safety and behaviour. It was assisted in this task by several Turkish policemen assigned to the village by the government, who operated according to the orders given by the council or its representative. They maintained their position thanks to the good will and good reports of the council, and tried to retain the sympathy of the local authorities with their discipline and loyalty. The parish council sometimes had the responsibility of catching and arresting evil-doers and criminals, calling for young men from the village that were used to handling guns, to join the police force assigned to the task.

Finally, the parish council had, within its wide and independent remit, the responsibility for monitoring public morals and punishing those who offended against them or created scandals.

In my youth I saw a person who was accused of animal-like behaviour. He was arraigned in the market, near the church wall, as a public spectacle, to be dirtied and spat upon by passers-by. The parish council also had the right of removal of criminals' personal civil rights until the convicted persons, through improvements in their lives, showed themselves worthy of being released from their punishment and having them restored.

The parish council in those days was a powerful ruling body that engendered respect, to which obedience was the law; but that power gradually passed to the government representatives and the authority of the parish council diminished accordingly.

At that time the parish council archive had a great number of files of papers concerning its activities as well as accounts and minute books, all of which were lost during the catastrophic year of the deportations. If those papers had been kept until today, the writing of Bardizag's history of those times would have been much easier and probably more accurate. In my present circumstances I can only rely on facts held in my fleeting and uncertain memory.

Apart from its usual day-to-day work, the parish council was also occupied with items of a public nature concerning community or governmental matters, such as:

The church
Construction or repair of the schools
Listing of the distribution of village government taxes
Election of candidates for the priesthood
Purchase or sale of community land
Public safety and health
Public works (roads, paving etc.)
Questions concerning inheritance and marriages
Care and protection of orphans
Relations with the prelacy, Armenian Patriarchate and government
Settlement of village disputes
Border questions
Protection of forests and agricultural land

and many other things which occupied a great deal of the council's time.

The parish council was elected for a period of four years, but it often continued beyond that term or resigned before it, depending on circumstances. Election processes were sometimes difficult and a temporary parish council would be appointed after consultations between the prelate, village priests and notables.

I add here, beginning with the first one of 1865, a list of all the lawful parish councils that worked in Bardizag until the beginning of the First World War.

The first council was elected in the year 1865. Its chairman was Sarkis Effendi Mgerian. During its period of office Mgerdich Mgerian was appointed head teacher as a sort of director of the community schools. He was ordained a kahana a year later.

The second council served under the chairmanship of Hadji Mardig Agha Der-Hagopian. (During the term of office of this council, Archbishop Nerses Varjabedian was elected Armenian Patriarch in Constantinople.)

The third was under the chairmanship of Hadji Mgrdich Agha Der-Hagopian.

The fourth, under the same chairman, during whose term of office the new school was built in 1881.

The fifth was under the chairmanship of Hadji Khacher Agha Khacherian.

The sixth under the chairmanship of Hadji Garabed Agha Der-Garabedian.

The seventh under the chairmanship of Nshan Agha Sinanian.

The eighth, under the same chairman, resigned before its term of office ended.

The ninth one too, under the chairmanship of Boghos Agha Kiutnerian, resigned early.

The tenth, under the chairmanship of Sarkis Agha Der-Sahagian.

The eleventh, under the chairmanship of Mgerdich Agha Alachayian. A very serious school question arose during the term of office of this council.*

The twelfth, under the chairmanship of Artin Agha Melkonian (Zobi).

The thirteenth, under the chairmanship of Aghasi Effendi Der-Mgerdichian.

The fourteenth, under the chairmanship of Hadji Hagop Agha Djergayian.

The fifteenth council, under the same chairman. The bath house was built at this time.†

The sixteenth council was elected in the days immediately following the re-establishment of the Ottoman Constitution in 1908, under the chairmanship of Minas Effendi Dzalian. The Provincial Deputies' Assembly was elected, after a long lapse, during this council's term of office. Elected lay members of the assembly from Bardizag were Aghasi Effendi Der-Mgerdichian, Hovhannes Agha Khacherian, Minas Effendi Dzalian and me.‡ The battle between the Armenian Revolutionary Federation's Bardizag committee and the town council over the school also took place at this time.**

The seventeenth, under the chairmanship of Hadji Mgerdich Agha Der-Garabedian. It was during this council's period of office that Seymen was extended into the Bay of Izmid, to enable ships carrying paper to approach it.

---

* See Section 132.

† See Section 139.

‡ This might be incorrect. Bardizag had to provide three lay and one ecclastical representatives to the assembly after the re-establishment of the constitituion in 1908. Minas Kasabian (Farhad), *Hayere Nikomedio Kavarin Mech*, p. 125.

** See Section 149.

The eighteenth and final council, under the chairmanship of Asadour Agha Der-Mgerdichian. Its term of office ended with the deportation of the villagers in 1915.

These were all the successively elected parish councils that held office until the catastrophic days of the deportations, according to an approximate historical check made.[*] The organisation of Bardizag as the centre of a *nahie* [group of villages] by the government coincided with the tenth parish council's term of office.[†]

101 – The foundation of an American girls' school

Mr Parsons, a man of very short stature who was all movement and life, gradually increased the extent of his missionary work in Bardizag. He planned to open a new girls' school for both day and boarding pupils, the importance of which wasn't appreciated in those days by us. Higher education for girls was considered to be superfluous and even detrimental to the strong family organisation, as well as being a scandal. He began to act on his decision when an American couple, the Baldwins, came to Bardizag to study the situation with the same aim in mind. We don't know why that couple rejected the idea after a time and went and settled in Boursa (Boursa) with the same idea, as a place with a more suitable environment for their plans.

Mr Parsons didn't give up hope and looked for people in the United States to assist him in his plans. The Baldwins were followed by an American lady especially for this work, but she didn't stay either. Finally Miss Farnham arrived in 1870 to assist Mr. Parsons. She was an unmarried lady who, within her frail body had a dedicated, spiritual and powerful soul. Thanks to her assistance, Mr. Parsons was to found the Bardizag American Girls' School in 1872, with the most humble beginnings in the silkworm house bought from the Gharevelegs. The work had found its real champion in that delicate, slim American lady.

It was obvious that Mr. Parsons and Miss Farnham had great belief in the education of girls; it would appear that they saw the community's salvation coming from homes, through spiritual and educated mothers.

The silkworm house had a number of repairs, additions and changes carried out to make it suitable to be a school, with classrooms, a hall, rooms for the teachers to live in and dormitories for boarding students. A kitchen, bathroom and washroom were built in the basement. Thus the building, now completed, opened its doors as the Bardizag American Girls' School.

The school curriculum was very modest at the beginning. The subjects being taught were Armenian and English language, and the elements of mathematics,

---

[*] The words used here are *modavorabes badmagan sdoukoutiamp*.
[†] The author is referring to the *Taghabedagan Khorhourt* (Village Council) that ran the affairs of the several villages around Bardizag which made up the *nahie*, of which Bardizag was the centre.

geography, basic algebra and geometry,* general history, Bible study, singing and physical education. The conditions for entry were easy for even the most modest purses. Miss Farnham became the headmistress of the school, the busiest person there: she ran it, gave most of the lessons, looked after discipline, kept the accounts and looked after the students' health and welfare. Lessons were given, in the early days, by Mr. Parsons, the head priest of the day† and, shortly after, by Armenag Der-Hagopian, who was Prof. Der-Hagopian's brother, and who had completed the Robert College syllabus.

The school developed over the years and became a necessity for the province and Constantinople, with many generations of girls applying to receive an almost free higher education. After the Protestants, Armenian Apostolic families gradually began to trust the school to give their daughters a good education too.

The American Girls' School remained in Bardizag until Mr. Parsons' tragic death‡ and for the next few years. It was during the time of the next missionary, Mr. Pierce, and almost immediately after the foundation of the American Boys' School, that it was moved to Adabazar, where living was much cheaper, the population larger, and there were greater opportunities to make use of other educational activists...

In Adabazar the school received a new – and more Armenian – name: *Adabzari Haiouhiats Varjaran* [Adabazar Armenian Girls' School], the principal being Miss Farnham, who had made it her life's work. The school moved to the Uskudar quarter of Constantinople after the First World War, being located in the old Constantinople College building, where it still exists.** Miss Farnham spent her life in the work she founded, then retired to America, from where she always maintained her interest in the school until her death. She was succeeded as principal of the Adabazar Girls' School by Miss Kinney, her long-time assistant, who was an unmarried American lady just as dedicated as she was, and who, with the same great merit, ran the school that was Miss Farnham's wonderful legacy. The vacancy left in Adabazar by Armenag Effendi Der-Hagopian was filled by Mr. Hovhannes Aliksanian, himself a graduate of Robert College, who taught in the school until his death in Constantinople in 1936. Classes were also given in Adabazar by Drs. Kavaldjian and Y. Djedjizian, *Verabadveli* [senior pastor] H. Djedjizian and several Armenian young ladies, all graduates of the Constantinople Girls' College. Miss Kinney died a few years ago, while still serving in the school.

The Bardizag Girls' School and the Adabazar Armenian Girls' School prepared generations of mothers in Bardizag, Adabazar, Izmid and other distant places, as

---

* The word used here is *yergrachapoutiun*. It could also mean trigonometry.
† The term used here is *joghovourti orvan yeretse*.
‡ See Section 102.
** This was in about 1937.

well as a significant number of dedicated teachers, although with modest training but with the greatest dedication and merit. In one of the final sections of this work I will have the opportunity to recall the names of about 20 of the final graduate students from Bardizag.*

102 – Mr. Parsons' martyrdom

Before closing the story of Mr. and Mrs. Parsons' missionary activity, I must record his death at the hands of criminals, which happened on what proved to be his final missionary journey.†

Mr Parsons set out on a missionary journey to the Armenian villages in the region around Lake Nicaea probably in about 1875. He took one of the Protestant Diudiuk Keiyian brothers from Bardizag as his guide. Having completed their missionary visit, they began the return journey. Night fell as they were in our mountains, near Manoushag, and they decided to stay there for the night. They expected to continue their journey at daylight the following morning. There was a Muslim Yoriuks' shepherds' resting place nearby, giving them confidence that they would be safe if they stayed where they were. They had a light evening meal with tea, having lit a fire to prepare it. The smoke and glow from the fire in the forest, at that time of night, attracted the attention of two of the young Yoriuk men, who stealthily approached and saw two unarmed infidels with their two horses and several full, good quality leather bags. Seeing this‡ they planned to kill the two foreigners who seemed to be so rich.

An hour or two later they returned to the same place, while the two travellers were sound asleep, dreaming with the satisfaction of having completed their spiritual obligations. The two miscreants killed both by using their guns, and then returned to their camp, having been disappointed at the contents of the bags, which contained nothing but books and printed papers of no value to them.

Travellers going to Bardizag saw the two bodies at the side of the road with the horses left to their fate on the following morning and reported it to authorities in the village. The authorities immediately raised a force of young men and sent them to the scene, to bring the bodies to the village. The two dead men were given a suitably solemn funeral the following day.

The Armenian Apostolic community, led by the priests and notables, took part in the funeral and mourning of the Americans by the local Protestants. Hovhannes Kahana Mgerian, who was in the village for a holiday, joined the other priests and

---

* See Section 154, sub-section 8.
† A bland version of the story of his death, edited to suppress every detail, was printed in *The Missionary Herald*, Journal of the American Board of Commissioners for Foreign Missions, Vol 76, No. 10, October 1880.
‡ The actual words used here are: 'The devil entered their stomachs and...'

gave a short address in the name of the Armenians, describing the age-old history of Armenian martyrdom at the hands of the Turks and fanatical and barbarian Islamic tribes, and added, 'Let the Europeans see, with their own eyes, and themselves feel with their own flesh what bitter and unbearable lives Christians live in this unfortunate land.' He then wished for peace for the souls of the dead and for our people's genuine feelings of sympathy on that sad occasion.

The Turkish government, alarmed, not because of the killing of Christians (something that was quite usual), but concerned in case political pressure was put on it, immediately arrested the two criminals, who were given sentences of 15 years imprisonment. One of them died in prison, and the other, having completed his sentence, was released.

After Mr. Parsons' death, Mrs. Parsons, respecting her husband's memory and work, didn't want to leave Bardizag. This was despite being a widow and alone (her children had gone to America to complete their education) but where her husband's last remains were buried. She selflessly continued her motherly work and service in the village. She only left it when she had grown old and, unable to work any longer, went to America to her family. This was after a new missionary, Mr. Pierce, had been working in the village and the Girls' School had long been moved to Adabazar.

103 – The immigration of the mountaineer Cherkez [Circassians] into Turkey

The Caucasian Cherkez [Circassian] mountain people in the Russian Caucasus expressed the wish to move to the other side of the border, to Turkey, in the years following the Crimean War.* This was because they weren't able to renounce their traditional, patriarchal customs and felt that they couldn't live under Christian law. They would, in Turkey, be free to live according to their traditions, settling in a Muslim state that would protect them and close its eyes to their frequent, lawless exploits.

The Turkish government, concerned to increase Muslim population numbers, agreed to their request and extended every care and accepted every sacrifice to assist them, even allocating a sum of money to aid their move into its territory.

These new Circassian immigrants mostly settled in areas where the majority of the population was either Arab or Christian. They were to act as a balance against the local population, towards which the government no longer had its former, ancient confidence. A great number of them were brought to the province of Izmid under this plan, where there were significant numbers of Armenians. They were made to settle in the Sakarya region, and in uninhabited areas between the roads to Izmid and Armash.

---

* The Crimean War ended in 1855, with the Treaty of Paris being signed in 1856.

The Circassian people were a handsome, sympathetic and noble tribe, with clean customs, and almost completely free of Islamic *namerham*[*] habits, but they weren't used to a sedentary life and especially in earning money and living honestly. They loved, above all else, stealing horses, domestic animals and capturing booty. These were regarded as bold, noble exploits, hence the reason for our people calling them 'horse thieves'. They were also known as 'woollen hats' because of the fur hats they wore.

They were hospitable, and graced with nobility, and their homes and surroundings were very clean. They were healthy and moved lightly, and suited their Caucasian dress. Their women were very beautiful, graceful and approachable. The Circassian people lived as a feudal society. They had beys, feudal princes whom they obeyed and respected like gods. But for all these good attributes, they had one failing – their inability to settle to a law-abiding life. Apart from this they were armed, with every house having its armoury.

The Turkish government gave them good, fertile land without charge, and assisted them in their difficulties during their first years until they became self-sufficient.[†] They became used, with great difficulty, to the circumstances of their new lives and wanted to unite them with their old, marauding ways, robbing ordinary travellers on the roads and stealing their horses, entering villages at night and stealing domestic animals, taking them to unknown places. They of course didn't deride money when they met travellers with full pockets in their forays. Under these circumstances their migration was a new form of evil in addition to those that had, for centuries, existed in the country; there were stories about them from the first days of their migration until our final deportation.

104 – Educational work in Bardizag during Sarkis Effendi Mgerian's time. Kevork Effendi Shirinian as inspector of the community schools and director of the *ousoumnaran* [senior school]

With Sarkis Pandigian's and Hagop Bodourian's ordinations as kahanas during Garabed Agha Mgerian's time, the only people available for the community schools were *Diratsou* Kapriel Semerdjian, *Diratsou* Taniel Hadjibakeyian[‡] and a few assistants, calld *khalfas*. The school continued like this for some time during which new people were found to supplement the existing ones, such as *Diratsou*

---

[*] This word is not known to me.
[†] Their robberies extended far beyond stealing horses and money; they arbitrarily took over land belonging to the settled population, without recompense. In the case of Bardizag, a great deal of land that was part of the village (apportioned by firman from the earliest days) was appropriated by them – as well as by later Muslim arrivals. Minas Kasabian (Farhad), *Hayere Nikomedio Kavarin Mech*, pp. 156-159 and 168-172.
[‡] This surname is written in this way in the original.

Hovhannes Mkhalian (later Garabed Kahana Mkhalian), his cousin* *Diratsou* Krikor Mkhalian, *Diratsou* Garabed Dolegian, Apraham Takvorian (nicknamed *engiuz peskiul* - walnut tassel), his brother Takvor Takvorian, Badveli Hagop Hovsepian and the *Chopdji* (named Atanasian), the last as a music teacher.

The schools in Bardizag continued their work for a time with these local people when, as a result of a re-organisation, Hovhannes Mgerian, Sarkis Effendi's brother, was appointed head teacher. This didn't last long because of the ordinations previously mentioned, as well as the retirement of teachers of advanced years and others resigning or dying. Under these circumstances, if not before, the parish council, under Sarkis Effendi Mgerian's chairmanship, saw the need to endow the community schools with a new organisation.

It managed to secure an able and skilled teacher from Constantinople who, with his ability and proficiency in teaching the Armenian language, also had a wealth of knowledge of French and natural sciences, things that were now looked for in Europe with the advancement of science. This new asset was Kevork Effendi Shirinian, the son of a provincial,† who had studied agriculture in Europe and had published a book about the subject. Shirinian was appointed inspector of the community schools, having as his colleagues the Takvorian brothers, Badveli Hagop Hovsepian and a few others in secondary positions.‡

The school curriculum was divided into two parts: the ordinary school and the senior one. In the first, the students learnt reading, writing, geography, mathematics, had Christian education lessons and learnt basic Turkish. The senior school added a higher education based on the first school's, adding classical Armenian, grammar, composition, oratory and science and other things. Shirinian's task was to be to manage Bardizag's educational efforts and, at the same

---

* Father's brother's son.

† Natanian tells us he was from Karahisar and was a *badveli* (Protestant pastor). Boghos Vartabed Natanian, *Arachin deghegakroutiun vidjagis Nicomedio* [First report on the diocese of Nicomedia], Djezvedjian Press, Constantinople 1871, p. 19.

‡ On his visitation in 1870, Boghos Vartabed Natanian quotes the schools as having 400 male pupils, of whom about 40 were studying the senior course. He adds that the schools owned property worth about 30,000 *kurush*, the income from which, he says, was used for the *boys'* school. He also states that the girls' school was in a sorry state, considered to be on the point of closing due to the local population's indifference, despite Shirinian's many protests to the notables. He adds that Shirinian wasn't properly renumerated for his work and occasionally had to work on a farm to feed his family! Boghos Vartabed Natanian, *Arachin deghegakroutiun vidjagis Nicomedio* [First report on the diocese of Nicomedia], Djezvedjian Press, Constantinople 1871, pp. 19-20. Kasabian states that there were two schools in the village in 1860: the boys' school had 450 pupils, the girls' 220. There were 7 teachers. The yearly budget was 32,000 *kurush*. Minas Kasabian (Farhad), *Hayere Nikomedio Kavarin Mech*, p. 260.

time, to give special attention and care to the senior school, teaching the most important subjects in its curriculum himself.

The students of this senior school at the time were some of the children of notables at the head of community affairs, such as Sarkis Effendi's son Ardashes Mgerian, Mgerdich Effendi Der-Hagopian's son Armenag Der-Hagopian, Minas Dzalian of that family and others like them. This situation could not escape public attention and especially that of those belonging to the old Khacherian party and their sympathisers, led by Hadji Khacher Khacherian, who looked, within the village, for opportunities to further weaken the Mgerians, who were already in decline due to their final bankruptcy.

Shirinian had hardly organised the educational work with his collaborators when a very serious problem arose about the school that, as time went on, would inflame passions between the opposing parties. People opposed to the village authority of the day began to stir up public opinion, presenting this school organisation as an arrangement designed to gain personal profit. Everyone began to protest: 'Brother, they've opened a school for their sons with the community's money. If they need teachers for their boys, they should pay for them themselves.'

A new, interesting and powerful weapon was used by the opposition in Bardizag for the first time. It was a new version of the protest letters that used to be sent to the Patriarchate. This new weapon was the publication of vitriolic, wounding, critical articles with false signatures in the Armenian newspapers that had been established in Constantinople for some time and were printed in that city.[*] These articles excited the people's interest and provided the opposition with new strength and enthusiasm.

In those days perhaps only one or two copies of any newspaper came to Bardizag. They had either been used as packaging material or brought in by travellers. When these copies appeared in public, be it in the market or the coffee houses, interested crowds would gather round the readers to listen to these critical articles that had been sent from Bardizag. These newspapers would pass from hand to hand, providing new and sought-after opportunities for people to talk, debate and joke with each other. Thus the entire village would live for a moment with the echoes of Bardizag that appeared in those newspapers, and the heads of the authors of the articles would, in the eyes of the villagers, be crowned with glory and would have the strength of gods.

The parish council, however, powerful in its authority, took no notice and derided the efforts of the opposition to promote scandal in the village and the floods of words that were spoken in the houses, coffee houses and written in the pages of the press, and calmly continued its work.

---

[*] Der-Hagopian has examples of these articles. See Hagop Der-Hagopian, *Bardizage khadoudig*, pp. 88-92.

Shirinian, a skilled and able man who was dedicated to his responsibilities, also calmly continued to do his educational mission in Bardizag. He was useful to the students, whose affection and respect towards him increased on a daily basis. It was obvious that the most reliable proof of the competence of the teacher was the student who best knew how to use him.

The opposition saw that it was powerless to change what had been built up in the school, despite all its efforts and with public opinion being apparently entirely on its side, prepared to deal a *governmental blow** and create a public scandal.

The days of the school public examinations arrived. The priests, notables and many idle, interested people were also present. The opposition prepared, in advance, the most suitable people from their number to administer the governmental blow – Tsadgan Boghos, Zobi Artin† and people like them – who, to give themselves Dutch courage, had already drunk several glasses of oghi or wine and who duly appeared at the place where the examinations were being held, apparently to praise the work carried out in the school.

At this fateful moment the examination concerned classical Armenian taught in the senior school. The students read, in turn, excerpts from their text books, translated what they had read into modern (western) Armenian, analysed sentences and gave answers to questions put to them about style and grammar. It happened that one of the teachers asked a student, 'What is that punctuation mark?'

The student replied, 'It is a *pout*.‡

At this, Tsadgan Boghos and his cohorts, greatly astonished, as they hadn't expected to see a *pout* in a book – as the villager, in colloquial language, called the main part of anything a *pout* – seeing an opportunity at their fingertips, began to chant, '*Pout, pout...!* What has a pout got to do with all this?'

A public argument began over this simple and innocent remark between the two sides - the authorities and the opposition - who shouted curses and unsuitable epithets at each other. Before the argument and battle had reached serious proportions, however, the members of the opposition who had created the argument were removed, and the examinations continued.

With both sides having these weapons in their hands, it was difficult to govern the school and Shirinian's short but fruitful period of office ended. He was forced to leave and seek his fate elsewhere. He settled in Adabazar after being in Bardizag, determined to work on the land instead of in schools as his work with basic elements – earth, water and air - would not be harmed by rebellion and indiscipline.

---

* Author's italics.
† Melkonian
‡ A punctuation mark (`) that is used for one of three purposes: (a) to replace omitted words; (b) to separate words drawn together because of missing words; (c) to separate a word from its appositive.

Shirinian, during his short term in office in Bardizag, had succeeded in producing a notable generation of students, many of whom, later, continued their education in the newly-established Robert College. Others with experience and education became well-known public activists, teachers, officials and merchants in Bardizag and elsewhere.

After Shirinian's departure, the school was left in a disorganised, neglected state for some time, in the hands of local people who maintained its existence, until passions had cooled.

I'll return to this subject in future pages.[*]

105 – A bandit group that robbed a government courier in Bardizag

A group of bandits succeeded in robbing a government courier from Anatolia at this time on the borders of Izmid one night, in the darkness before dawn. They rendered his accompanying officials and policemen helpless, and took a significant amount of rich booty. They then made their escape by skirting the upper areas of Bardizag, in other words the edge of the Upper Close Fields parish. They then saw a flickering light in one of the houses as they passed that way. Tired from their journey and the weight of the booty they were carrying, they decided to lighten their load and, before the sun rose, to escape swiftly to their hideout in the mountains. Using the light like a beacon in a storm at sea when their boat was in difficulties, they approached the house and knocked on the door.

It was Gabak Garabed's house. He was a poor man who worked in the horseshoe factory and who could hardly earn enough to feed the numerous members of his family every day, as he was forced to work for a pittance. The horseshoe makers of Bardizag were used to rising well before dawn, at about 2 to 3 am, seeking the warmth of the ever-glowing furnace fire against the cold nights, and working there until about 8 or 9 in the morning, when they would go home to rest for the remainder of the day.

Gabak Garabed never expected calls from his friends at that time of the night. He opened the window and saw a group of armed men clustered around his front door, accompanied by a string of laden mules. He came to the door, scared but intrigued, opened it and found himself faced by a powerful robber band. The leader entered and, pulling Gabak to one side, whispered something to him, from which he understood that they had come to leave their loads with him for a week. They would then return to retrieve them, when they would reward him generously for his services. Gabak naturally didn't refuse and accepted the robbers' delightful and promising suggestion. He immediately put the loads temporarily entrusted to him in a dark area of his house and, after providing the robbers with hospitality, sent them on their way.

---

[*] See Section 109.

Gabak closed the door and, forgetting his daily work for a time, went back to the room where his wife and children were still sleeping. He began to think about this event that appeared to be like something from the tale of Ali Baba and the forty thieves. Heaven had sent him an unexpected piece of good luck, to commiserate with the poorness of his house and his poverty. The bags were swollen with great riches; he was frightened of losing his wits from his small head. He had never seen so much money in one place, not even in his employer's possession.

He didn't go to work that day. He would say that he was unwell, and would lose a day's pay, but could he really leave his house unprotected when it had such a fortune in it, filling its normal emptiness? He thought and thought for a long time: what could he do? It was not difficult to finally reach the easy conclusion that the robbers had stolen that fortune. He therefore had the right to steal it too. There was, after all, the saying: 'The thief stole from the robber, God saw it and was amazed.' Gabak therefore decided, for once in his life, to amaze his God.

The robbers had told him that they would return in a week's time. 'Never mind,' he thought, 'lots of things could happen in a week. Maybe they would reclaim their loot, or perhaps encounter difficulties during their return. If they return at all, what of his would they take? I will tell them that I don't know anything about it and send them on their way. They are robbers, after all, and I can't be bold and demanding.'

So Gabak mused, and pictured his poor self as the richest man in the village, a man of unending luxuries and pleasure, a man who didn't need to work and sweat. The sweat that had poured off him until that day was enough for him to be able to live a harsh life up to that point.

These crazy thoughts and the need for air, it seemed, made him hurry out of his house after midday and wander about the Upper Fields for a time. Frightened of his shadow, and full of suspicion, he occasionally looked to the horizon with his dull eyes, while seeking a safe place to bury his treasure. He felt that its presence in his tumbledown house was dangerous. He eventually found what he was looking for.

That night, when everyone was asleep and all the lights in the village had been extinguished, he buried the contents of the bags deeply in various places where the soil hadn't been cultivated. He then filled the holes he'd dug, tamped down the earth and covered the signs of his excavations with stones, as if he wanted to deposit his riches in several safe banks.

Now he found peace of mind. His house was empty and his fortune was in safe hands, and was available whenever he wanted it.

He left his work, wandered here and there, claiming that he had some weakness which threatened to become permanent. Days passed, and the robbers didn't appear; the first crisis and fright passed and in that sense Gabak recovered himself and his spiritual peace. He ate and slept with relish, and forgot that the robbers could suddenly reappear.

This is exactly what happened ten days later.

The robbers knocked at his door one night. Gabak began to tremble, but what could he do? If he didn't open the door, a good shove with a shoulder would be enough to smash it down. So he went down and opened it. He showed the guests he had previously met into his house. They had come to demand the loot they had left. Loot..?

'What loot?' Gabak Aghpar didn't know anything about things like that.

The robbers thought that Gabak's denial was a joke, but a little later they became convinced that it wasn't. They did everything to make him see sense and persuade him not to cheat them. Gabak, however, didn't recognise them; he had no knowledge about anything like that. They'd come to the wrong door, they were deluding themselves etc. He was only a poor man – who could have trusted him with treasure like that?

The robbers, knowing that it was possible to get blood out of a stone but getting nothing from him, began to beat him severely, thinking the beating would weaken him and they could extract a confession. Gabak, however, had strong nerves and the spirit of a cat, and years of poverty had dulled his feelings. He screamed and cried during the long beating, and the only thing he said was 'I don't know anything'. The robbers, enraged, wanted to finish him off, not wanting him to live and enjoy their treasure. They beat him and beat him, breaking bones and bruising him very badly. Gabak became unconscious, stopped breathing and said no more. He had become like a hank of hemp thread; every part of him was damaged. The robbers saw Gabak's sons and wife were crying and wailing and that lights were beginning to be lit in the scattered nearby houses. Footsteps could be heard, and the whole parish was beginning to become agitated. The robbers decided to escape so as not to endanger themselves. They left the half-dead Gabak, convinced that he wouldn't survive.

The neighbours soon rushed in and calmed the family. Gabak was laid out in the room like a corpse where they stripped him. His whole body was bruised. They suddenly realised that his chest was rising and falling with shallow breathing and he still lived. They rubbed his body with oghi and vinegar to raise his temperature to normal. They bled him and finally, after he had suffered hours of crisis, saw his eyes open. He groaned continually; he had been reduced to the state of a piece of old rag, but he lived.

Gabak remained ill in bed for days; everyone in the village heard of the incident and it reached the government's ears. The robbers had beaten Gabak, apparently because he had kept their loot, while he knew nothing about it.

Government officials hurried to Bardizag to conduct a formal examination as they suspected that Gabak was holding the proceeds of the robbery of the government courier. The officials questioned the sick man who had nothing to say other than what he'd already said. They demolished Gabak's house: the walls, floors, wooden fittings, looked into any recesses – and everything - but found no trace of the loot. Gabak always denied everything.

The government officials, rendered hopeless by their abortive search and their failure to get a confession out of Gabak, arrested him when he was able to walk and imprisoned him in the Izmid government building.

Gabak saw that the situation had become grave. Under the circumstances it would be difficult to get rid of the accusations laid against him. He could foresee that he would be subject to new tortures and beatings in prison. All this forced him to seek Sarkis Effendi Mgerian's intervention who, thanks to the authority conferred by his membership of the provincial *irade* assembly, had great influence in government circles. Mgerian's defence proved valuable to him – he had been arrested on mere suspicion. There was no basis or proof to convict him. The government was just and the law didn't allow an innocent man to be jailed for a long time without being charged. This could only happen if there were reliable witnesses and correct facts – which they didn't have in Gabak's case. The government was forced to free him.

Gabak, however, from that day on, had no need to work to live. He became a personality surrounded by secrets. He was a very wealthy man, who was able to live to the end of his life with his family, without working and able to keep others too. Many shared in that treasure, either by defending him or by profiting from it. Others began to secretly follow him everywhere and people said that they found one or two places where he had buried these riches, dug it up and appropriated it for themselves.

Thus over the years he was surrounded and courted by many people, but always despaired of them. Everyone who approached him stole from him. These disappointments awoke very strong selfish feelings in him; he gave himself to eating and drinking, living his life as he understood it, having had a great longing for doing so for years. He married off his daughters and repaired and put his house in order. He provided new wardrobes for his wife and sons to make them look presentable. He saw that his wealth was slipping away with the years, and that his former poor life was likely to be visited upon his family for a second time. He had the wisdom to buy a plot of land in the market area of the village through friends. He built a house on the site at considerable expense with two sources of income on the ground floor – a coffee house and a shop – the rents from which cushioned his old age. They kept the threat of hunger away so that he was able to finally close his eyes without any misfortune befalling him. Of his wealth only that house remained as his legacy. He, the person who had been born as poor Gabak had become, through that sudden piece of good fortune, honoured by being called Garabed Agha or Garabed Effendi. But at the end of his days, true to his origins, he was buried as Gabak and joined his ancestors.

106 – Clashes between the young men of Bardizag and the Circassians[*]

In 1872–1873, a serious clash took place between several young travelling Armenian merchants from Bardizag and Circassian robbers in the forest called Sare Meshelig. The young men from the village were Tabakh Krikor, Baghdasar Ago, Gozgoz Serkis and one or two others who were returning to the village from Armash with their horses loaded with sacks of barley. Each had a six-gun[†] - for self-defence of course. They found that their way through a narrow defile was closed by three armed Circassians, who demanded their immediate surrender.

Tabakh Krikor, who was meeting the Circassians face-to-face for the first time, was mounted on his loaded horse. At the Circassians' sudden demand, he swiftly dismounted and, using it as his protection, took to his weapon, determined to protect his honour and goods. The Circassians, who hadn't expected the *giavours* [infidels] to defend themselves, became confused and, hiding behind tree trunks, prepared to open fire. The incident began with Tabakh Krikor and the Circassians firing at each other. Taking advantage of their confusion and acting quickly, Tabakh Krikor fatally wounded two of them before his fellow-travellers had even arrived on the scene. He fell, however, seriously wounded in the stomach. Krikor's companions arrived at this point and saw the bloody drama. The remaining Circassian, not being able to continue the battle against superior forces, left his wounded companions and escaped. The young travellers picked up their wounded friend, who was still alive but losing blood, put him on a horse and swiftly left the scene, frightened in case the remaining robber renewed the fight. The wounded Circassian robbers had already died. On their way to Bardizag, they thought of going to Izmid, which was much closer, to get their comrade first aid and also to inform the government of the incident. They had hardly got to the town, however, when Tabakh Krikor died from his wound and loss of blood. They informed the government of the incident; the officials came and examined the dead man's body and recorded the travellers' explanations and, putting them under protection, released them to return to Bardizag. They reached the village that night with their comrade's body. The whole village was agitated by this bloody incident. Tabakh Krikor's funeral took place the following day, in the late afternoon, with great solemnity and amid universal expressions of sorrow.

Archpriest Mgerian Kahana, who happened to be in the village, officiated at the burial of the brave man, and gave a powerful funeral oration full of sorrow and anger over his coffin in which, describing his heroic death, he lauded his marvellous

---

[*] Muslim mountaineers from the Caucasus who were brought to the province by the government and settled in the region. See Section 103.

[†] The text doesn't make it clear if these firearms were revolvers, just calling them *vetsharvadzian*.

act of self-defence and honourable death against superior forces, and strongly emphasising his words, ended with:

> Serf-like acquiescence has got to end; all of you who surround this coffin and are brave inside are citizens of this country, with equal rights for all without qualification of race or creed. It is the inalienable right of citizens to defend their honour, goods and lives against all villainous attacks with all the means at their disposal. Don't spare them: learn how to reply with weapons to all those who use arms against you, and let the malefactors know that they cannot be left unpunished for their illegal acts.

Sarkis Effendi Mgerian, the provincial *irade* assembly's Armenian member defended, with all the means in his power, the deceased Krikor's companions from government legal pursuit and anti-Armenian racial views. He proved that they had no part in the killing of the two Circassians, whose deaths had been caused by the dead Armenian, as a result of legal self-defence.

A similar incident took place several years later in the same place. It occurred between a horseman from Bardizag (nicknamed Yeldez because he was always alone) and two armed Circassians, for the same reason. Yeldez didn't have any companions with him; he usually travelled alone. He was returning alone from Armash with a loaded horse, which the robbers wanted to steal. Yeldez, despite his innocent look, with his head down and being taciturn and a poor looking person in general, was not someone who accepted things easily under those circumstances. So he took his single-barrelled pistol from his sash – the only companion he had and which he kept loaded – and suddenly fired at the Circassians. The bullet went through the first and wounded the second as he was behind him. Both fell to the ground like two birds killed by one stone. Yeldez looked around: there was no one there and the road was open before him. He mounted his horse and swiftly and safely reached Bardizag with only God and himself as witnesses to his heroic act.

Yeldez was an expert marksman well known in the village and the surrounding area for his prowess.

107 – The immigration of the *Giurdjis* [Muslim Georgians] to Turkey and the settlement of a group of them on the heights around Bardizag

It was the turn of the *Giurdjis* [Muslim Georgians], after the Circassians, to move into Turkey from the Caucasus after the end of the Russo-Turkish war of 1877.

A group of them was brought to be settled on the heights surrounding our completely Armenian area that consisted of four Armenian villages, containing approximately 20,000 inhabitants.

These new immigrants arrived in the last days of autumn and, so as to be protected from the winter, were temporarily billeted on us as guests. They were allocated houses on the edges of the villages without charge, the owners having been turned out. The government assigned several hills on the edge of our region for their permanent settlement: Sakar Bechke, Deosheme, Aghel Yeri and those behind our villages, where they gradually organised themselves, forming 15-20 Muslim villages. These Georgians were a peaceable and ingratiating tribe or race, the men, comparatively speaking, being reasonably clean and more presentable, while the women were poorly dressed and dirty. All of them were, however, fanatical Muslims, very demanding towards the women's modesty, but healthy and robust mountaineers.

Their main source of nourishment was made up of maize flour, of which a portion was mixed with water in earthenware pots every day and covered with the hot coals of their cooking fires. The result was a yellowish and easily broken up kind of bread which they used while still hot. This bread was prepared like a meal by the women, two or three times a day.

Both men and women utilised the time they were staying with us to the full by weaving fishing nets from hemp thread which they had brought with them in considerable quantities.

Thus they passed the winter as our neighbours, and when the first balmy spring days started, the snows melted and the cold abated, they left and went to the hills assigned to them. There they selected the places for their villages and, working together, cut down the centuries-old trees and determined a rational plot for each family on which they constructed their small underground houses or huts, using timber from the forest as building material. They constructed the walls with added timbers, and carefully covered the roofs with bark to prevent rain entering. An oven was put in one corner of each house, its smoke emerging through a hole in the roof and occasionally from the door when it was opened. Each house had an earthen floor on which mats and carpets were spread, thus making a more or less habitable dwelling in which they lived. They constructed gardens around the houses. Then they created fields by cutting down the trees and burning the timber, and maize seeds were sown, given to them by a solicitious government. They were also given domestic animals – horses, cows, goats and chickens, and reaped their first harvest of maize in that very year from the virgin land, securing their winter stores. The government looked after these immigrants very carefully until they were self-sufficient and even became rich. They lived tax-free for years, with the government waiting for them to be self-sufficient.

Before long they were able to sell what they didn't need in our village markets: the excess from their harvest and chickens, eggs, butter, animals for butchery, fruit, wheat, barley, wood, and much more besides. In this way agriculture, animal husbandry, the village economy and the utilisation of the rich forest all became their main activities, to which sericulture would be added, learnt from their neighbours. Thanks to all this they were able to secure everything required for a good life for themselves. Due to their commercial relations with Bardizag and the nearby villages, they eventually assisted their economic and material development to a significant extent.

It was Bardizag especially that, with their presence and activities, greatly developed and became like a small town. The shops multiplied, trade increased and some trades that had been cast aside were revitalised; for example horseshoe making, saddle making, blacksmithing and string making from hair,* that were dying trades among us.

Following the immigration of the Giurdjis and Laz,† Laz Armenian refugees also arrived in our region from Trabzon. They too formed a significant number of villages on the edges of those set up by the Giurdjis [Georgians].‡ Thus three Laz Armenian villages were founded in our area: Zakar Kiugh or Sakar Bechke [Zakar Village],** Manoushag and Jamavair, the latter on the heights behind neighbouring Ovadjek in a place called Kilisa Yeri (Church Place).

A number of other Laz Armenian villages were also founded near Adabazar, called Aram Village, Kegham Village and other small ones like them, whose inhabitants began to make lives for themselves like the Muslim Georgians and Laz on this new soil.†† They were, however, considered to be 'non-legitimate' and were denied the assistance given by the government to their new Muslim neighbours. In fact they never reached the economic prosperity that the Muslims immigrants did, especially as the land they held was limited and the soil poor.

On the occasions when the Armenian prelate of Izmid, Bishop Stepannos Hovagimi made his diocesan rounds, he would visit these newly-established Laz Armenian villages too, many of the names of which he had chosen for them, wanting to give them a genuine Armenian stamp. But the poor villagers often forgot those new names which they were not used to and which they pronounced

---

* Animal hair was used to make string and thin rope. This was called *mazmanoutiun*.
† This is the first time the author mentions the Muslim Laz immigration; it would seem that they arrived with the Georgians (Giurdjis), and are not to be confused with the Laz Armenians.
‡ The Laz Armenian people were Christian Armenians who had, from living among the Laz tribes, lost their Armenian speech and dressed and lived like Laz people. They had, however, retained their faith and were the kind of Armenians who were also known as *Hamshen*. For a detailed description See Minas Kasabian (Farhad), *Hayere Nikomedio Kavarin Mech*, pp. 81-89.
** Kasabian says that these Laz Armenian settlers came from Ordu, and the village itself was adjacent to the village of Deosheme. It had 65 houses and was founded in 1878 by about 7 families growing, with the influx of other refugees, to 287 individuals by 1892. Their first Kahana was ordained in 1892. The Minasian family (which included Khachig, Mgerdich, Haroutiun, Stepan, Avak Hadji, and Ohan) originated in this village. Minas Kasabian (Farhad), *Hayere Nikomedio Kavarin Mech*, p. 96.
†† See Minas Kasabian (Farhad), *Hayere Nikomedio Kavarin Mech*, pp. 81-89.

incorrectly. So every time the bishop would visit them, he would be surrounded by all the inhabitants - men, women and children - in a field, on their knees on the stony, dry ground, showing him the greatest respect and honour. He would begin a small question and answer session, to see if they had learnt the new names. When he saw that their recollection was growing weak, he would begin his lesson. Let us assume, for example, that he was in Kegham Kiugh [Village]. He would say the village name, repeating it several times: 'Kegham Kiugh! Kegham Kiugh...!' The population would repeat after him 'Kegham Kiugh! Kegham Kiugh...!' Then he would stop the lesson and would ask one or another of the villagers what the village name was and, if the answer didn't seem good enough, would repeat 'Kegham Kiugh! Kegham Kiugh...!' once more...

108 – Thieves made a forced entry into Hagop Agha Djergants'* house one night and burgled it

The many-branched Djergayian patriarchal clan was a notable house in Bardizag from the early days that was peaceable, diligent and thrifty in character and successful in business. The family always produced community activists who were decent and good-charactered people, although they weren't very bold or had great influence, but they always gave right-minded service. One or two branches of the family had chosen, from early times, to channel their activities into horseshoe making, encouraged by Garabed Agha Mgerian's example and had achieved wealth and social position in Bardizag.

A branch of the family was that of horseshoe maker Hagop Agha Djergayian, whose father was known as Kel Ekse because, through working in the open air in the sun, the nape of his neck had a burnt appearance. Hagop Agha had a younger brother, Hovhannes Djergayian, who had been taken with the new Protestant movement and had left the traditional Armenian Apostolic Church, being given, as a result, the nickname Djergayents Porod.† Years later he left Bardizag, having sold everything, and settled in Adabazar as being a more profitable and safer place, where he was followed by one of his father's brothers, Djerga Hadji Artin. The latter, however, always remained fathful to the Armenian Apostolic Church.

The Djergas were regarded as a wealthy family in Bardizag, something that was dangerous in those dark days.

One night, a gang of unknown thieves went to Hagop Agha's isolated house, which was located at the edge of the village. They made a hole in one of the walls and entered it, terrifying the family members inside who had suddenly woken up as a result of this unexpected visit by strangers. The thieves immediately demanded that Hadji Hagop Agha give them the money he had and the jewellery owned by the

---

* The author later calls him Hadji Hagop Agha Djergayian.

† *Porod* is a derogatory word used for 'Protestant'.

household, the kind and nature of which, amazingly, they knew very well as belonging to the family.

Hadji Hagop Agha was forced to submit to these demands and gave them all the money and jewels the family had. He parted with whatever he found in closed containers, at hand, or around the necks and in the ears of family members without discussion or bargaining, so as to preserve his and his family's lives. The thieves, pleased at what they had got and with Hagop Agha's quiet acceptance of the situation, left his house, not forgetting to apologise and asking him to wish them the enjoyment of his wealth. Hardly had the thieves left the confines of the village when all Bardizag knew of the raid and surrounded the family with general compassion.

Sarkis Effendi Mgerian attended a meeting with the priests and notables early the next morning, with some basic suspicions as to the identities of the thieves, and decided to raid the Albanian shepherds' camp located near Hormin Yasakh, as Albanian accents had been heard in the thieves' speech.

The notables called a young man known as Doner Nshan to see them. He had justly established a reputation as a swift-acting, brave and fearless person in the village. He was advised to gather several of his comrades and immediately go to the Albanian shepherds' camp, to search it and to detain the thieves at any cost.

Doner Nshan, who was already proud of the trust placed in him by the notables, went down into the marketplace, sat in front of a coffee house, called someone he knew and whispered some names into his ear, saying, 'Bring them to me here.' He sat there, with his legs crossed, smoking a hookah, while waiting for the people he had sent for. They weren't late in arriving at their chief's call. A small group gathered in front of the coffee house, and Doner Nshan explained his mission; he was going to leave the village shortly with the wish to reclaim its honour, and invited them to join him in that honourable task. He told them to arm themselves and wait in the nearby cemetery until everyone was present. Kaloust Artin, a neighbour of Hadji Hagop Agha and known to Doner Nshan and who always joined in things like this was among them. Unusually, however, he didn't seem ready to accept the invitation, saying he wasn't well. Doner Nshan's order was law and, even if it meant death, had to be obeyed. Artin, without wanting to, was forced to accept and, getting his weapons, joined the others.

The armed group set out immediately along the Chakhchi Valley road, went directly to the Albanians' camp and entered it. They reached it at about midday; it was empty of its inhabitants, as they were grazing their flocks in the nearby meadows, leaving one of their number as a guard.

Nshan's comrades searched every part of the camp – sacks, beds, property and other things, and found part of the stolen items. The Albanian guard was tied up at Doner Nshan's orders after seeing the evidence of the night raid they had made. The Albanian then pointed to Kaloust Artin, saying, 'Tie him up first, he led us.' Artin grew pale: he really did become sick. Nshan's men tied him up too.

Several of Nshan's men then went to the nearby area and found the Albanian shepherds with their animals. They searched them then and there, finding more of the stolen property in their belts and clothing. They tied them up too. Leaving a member of the group to guard the camp and animals, they returned to Bardizag with the thieves and looted items, where they handed them over to the notables in the church room.

The thieves confessed everything, in detail. They said that Artin had convinced them and led them to that house at night. He was the really guilty person; they had only followed what he'd said. Artin's house was also searched, where they found his share of the loot.

The thieves remained in Bardizag that night under guard; they were given bread and cheese as a meal, but refused the cheese as it was a fast day,[*] as they were Greek Orthodox Christians. Respecting their religious sentiments, they were given olives and halva.

On the following day the thieves were taken to Izmid and handed over to the government, with the necessary details of the incident. The government was, of course, very surprised that justice had been carried out so swiftly and sharply by the notables of the village. The thieves were tried, judged to be guilty and imprisoned for various terms. Artin, the leader, was found guilty, and was sentenced to be confined in prison for 15 years.

Artin survived his imprisonment and returned to Bardizag to live a quiet and modest life when his daughters and sons, grown up, were already working.

109 – Educational work in Bardizag after Shirinian's departure

After Shirinian's departure the village notables, seemingly at odds with each other, left the school to its fate and, with a view to saving appearances, entrusted it for a time to local people – the two Takvorian brothers. Hadji Apraham Agha Takvorian acted as a sort of overseer and Takvor Takvorian taught mathematics, geography and national history.[†] *Badveli* Hagop Hovsepian (a Protestant pastor) taught Armenian and composition, Mgerdich Effendi Geolliuian taught Turkish and Hagop Pirenian taught religious knowledge and church history. Sarkis Djergayian was also a teacher.[‡] These people divided the boys' and girls' senior school curriculums between them. Diratsou Garabed Shekhian, as overseer and teacher and Diratsou Garabed Deyirmendjian both taught in the first school. They were former students of the musician Cheopdji Kel, who had died at an early age. The

---

[*] Both Greek Orthodox and Armenian Apostolic Churches proscribe meat and dairy products on fast days such as Lent.

[†] It is not clear from the text whether 'national history' *azkayin badmoutiun* refers to Armenian or Ottoman history, but is probably the former.

[‡] The subject(s) he taught are not stated.

senior school was closed, being considered an unnecessary embellishment to the school with its noble traditions. Thus 'democracy' became triumphant in educational work in Bardizag.

There was no director, in the sense that we understand it, and lessons were divided between the teachers, who did the best they could.

The most notable of the teachers was Hadji Apraham Agha Takvorian. He represented the school trustees in the school itself and had to look after discipline in the school as well as the pupils' behaviour, in other words the formation of their characters. This held a more important place in the minds of the time than education itself did. He was an iron man in the school: cane in hand, he spent the whole day among the pupils. He would maintain discipline with great severity during study periods and when they entered and left classes.

Hadji Apraham Agha was known, by the villagers will, as Engiouz Pskiul [Walnut Tassel]. He considered it part of his duty not only to maintain discipline in the school, but also his permanent supervision outside it, in the market, at home or where the children played. He also paid attention that the education given in the school influenced their work and lives. He tried to develop politeness, cleanliness, neatness, love of the church and prayer, respect and obedience for their elders both within the home and outside, using his own methods. He tried to instill patriotic feelings and even a pure form of Armenian language in them, insisting on removing from their speech every word of Turkish origin, replacing them with real Armenian words and explanations. For example, he wanted *para* (money) to be replaced with the Armenian word *pogh*, *helva* by *hroushag*, *zeitin* (olive) by *tsitabdough*, *gaz* (oil) by *kariugh* and *khaife* (coffee) by *sourdj*, and for the children to use these words – and many others in the same way - always and everywhere.

He also organised a Sunday school with the object of making pupils used to Sunday being a holy day. The children in each quarter of the village would assemble in a particular outdoor place under the supervision of their appointed monitor after the end of the morning church service, after the family meal had been eaten. The children's mothers, sisters, infants and sometimes the men, as well as the neighbours, would all be there. The assembled children would sing *sharagans* [canticles] and patriotic songs for up to an hour. These awoke great enthusiasm in those listening and engendered warm feelings towards the school.

Hadji Apraham Agha's organisation and methods had, of course, their usefulness with their newness. Sometimes, however, they lacked soundness and respect for established customs, often resulting in all these good things being made laughable. The children loathed and hated these spurious obligations which seemed to be just for show. Their childish souls rebelled, especially when there was no love shown and the impositions made were not general customs. The threat of punishment was always present, with inexorable and merciless beatings being meted out. The latter inflamed the children against the good and constructive aspects of the efforts made, and the errors in the basic method demolished the whole work. The children wanted to grow up quickly so as to be free, like their elder brothers, from this tyrannical regime.

The other teachers tried to be useful, each in his lessons, within their capabilities without, however, much scruple and adding jokes, play times and mixing things into lessons from outside. In this educational situation the children were denied, from their earliest years, the demands of even the most enjoyable and innocent play. They were forced to learn things contained in books and couldn't appreciate their value in life. With a kind of necessity of relaxing the regime, the children would make the teachers, who didn't have the ability to impose their authority using Hadji Apraham Agha's methods, the butt of their naughtiness and persecution.

The pupils, tortured by them, waited for a certain age when they could leave the school like their seniors, to begin to work and earn a living – and what joy they would experience when that day came!

The most noticeable thing that was missing in the school was the following. The pupils didn't like the school and the teachers and looked for ways to escape from it. They would wander, with the greatest delight, through the fields and forests in freedom. It was where they could learn more concerning the world around them - and joyfully at that – than within the dour walls of the school. Absconding from school by pupils was usual in those days, despite the threat of the heavy punishment that their parents or teachers might inflict on them if they were caught. They preferred to be beaten than stay idle and oppressed in school all day, especially in good weather when the blue sky, the sun's smile, the green of the trees, birdsong, and colourful flowers and their scents were so beguiling for them.

Many left school after completing *dzaghgots* [first school]; most of these quickly forgot how to read and write. The number of pupils in each class in the upper classes lessened from one year to the next and hardly took reading and writing with them, after years of oppression and torture. This was the educational work carried out in the Bardizag community school - and everywhere else.

After Hadji Apraham, the most important person in the school was Badveli Hovsepian, teacher of Armenian language* and who taught classical Armenian, composition, as well as preparing events and training the participants for them. Apart from this, he also edited the many petitions that were addressed to the parish council prepared by certain people. These often took up most of his time. This teacher was, in the first instance, regarded as the most loyal servant of the community and its secretary, as he received his monthly salary from the public purse, irrespective of the fact that it was given to him for the work of teaching their

---

* The word used here is *haigapanoutiun*. This usually means classical Armenian, but I have taken it in a wider sense.

children. Many approached other teachers to write petitions for them, but the *haigapan* teacher was considered the person who could prepare strong and unbeatable documents.

The *badveli* was a man of delicate health, who was tired and worn out. He was easily aroused, nervous and absent-minded. The school was not the place for him of course; he should have been in a hospital, where his shattered health could have been restored, but the need to live had tied him to the school desk. During lessons his mind was often elsewhere; he had so many worries occupying it that he would walk from one wall of the classroom to the other, without being able to concentrate on the pupils' lesson. They would read and translate the set lesson as they saw fit, with the most amusing and outrageous mistakes, often knowingly wishing to amuse the class, which often erupted into laughter. These explosions of laughter would awaken him from his deep thoughts and, annoyed that bad behaviour had upset the peace of the class, he would run from one pupil to another. But he, surprised and confused, often wanted to calm his jangling nerves, not by dealing with the guilty boys, but by punishing the innocent. This led to even more laughter and indiscipline, caused by the natural rebellion against injustice by the innocent boys.

The *badveli's* state in the classroom was simply pitiful, where every ploy was used against this defenceless being, who was living in his subconscious dreams.

The third important teaching personality was Mr. Takvor, Hadji Apraham Agha's younger brother, who did not have his fervent religious severity and facial expressions. The pupils didn't dare play with him because they loved his humorous ways. He loved jokes and funny things; he was quick to understand humour, being a natural comedian. He too, however, was tired and satiated with the sameness of the work, into which he tried to make enjoyable changes by constantly joking with the pupils, sometimes parodying passers-by. In this way he succeeded in keeping his classroom a happy place that often resembled a theatre stage. Although the pupils didn't benefit from his mathematics lessons very much, at least they enjoyed themselves and his classroom was the most sought-after corner of the school.

The teacher of Turkish, Mgerdich Effendi Geolliuian who, years later, died at the hands of the enraged Turkish mob during the Ottoman Bank incident,[*] was a young man of sphinx-like mysteriousness. It was difficult to penetrate the depths of his soul because his eyes were in constant movement, giving him a sombre appearance, closing his inner self to the person opposite him. He looked after conduct in the court and tried to teach the Turkish language in its workaday and diplomatic forms, but to reduce the stress on the brains of the pupils he would often change the lesson to a form of lecture about divinity or deeply academic, lofty subjects.

---

[*] The capture of the Ottoman Bank in Constantinople by Armenian revolutionaries in 1896.

I could never forgive myself if I forgot another person on this list: a young and fresh person – Mr. Sarkis Djergayian - in whom the ideals of teaching were evident to a certain extent, and who didn't tire of the work or years of difficulties as much as the others. He did, however, have one natural fault, which was diametrically opposed to the skills of teaching. He stammered dreadfully, and even the most ordinary word required great effort and many attempts to articulate it. Then it would explode from the tip of his tongue, through his open lips. It was for this teacher that years later Rev. Tourian's father, Hadji Apraham Agha Tourian, would make this solemn and decisive announcement: 'Mr Sarkis is the most productive teacher in the school because he says one word each time in several syllables and with emphasis, and almost hammers it by force into the boys' brains like a nail...'

The children enjoyed a good time in the first school under *Diratsou* Garabed Shekhian and *Diratsou* Garabed Deyirmendjian. They utilised the parents' artlessness, giving their children the opportunity to demonstrate one or more of their talents and skills. These were responsive reading, the great and deep *art* of reading the *Djashou Book* [missal]. At solemn times they demonstrated their wonderful ability to sing *solos* in the presence of the entire congregation in church. These teachers naturally sought their just rewards in the morning or at midday, looking to the door of the school for gift parcels – a cooked chicken, a tasty morsel, a rare pastry; these had a greater value in their eyes than their salaries cashed by the treasurer which they received every month.

It was under these teachers that we, to enjoy the benefits of this educational system, began work, as students, in Bardizag's community school.

110 – Mr. and Mrs. Armen Lousinian in Bardizag's community schools

The school organisation that I presented in the last section couldn't last long after the experience of Shirinian's work, especially when the system used in the American Girls' School brought great changes in people's thinking concerning education in Bardizag.

It wasn't possible to operate the school using the old staff; a new man or men were required to satisfy the demands of the time. To satisfy this need, Mr. and Mrs. Lousinian were brought from Constantinople as the school directors at the beginning of the 1877 school year.

Armen Lousinian, like Meghbourian, was from Chengiler and had settled and married in Constantinople. He attended the Noubar-Shahnazarian School that was, in those days, the Armenian school that provided the best higher education in the capital. He was a notable student there. After completing his studies, he became part of intellectual life in Constantinople and made a name for himself as a capable teacher, publicist and poet. His wife too was a quite well educated woman and had some experience as a teacher. The leading priest, Rev. Hovhannes Mgerian, having been approached by the notables of Bardizag, recommended the couple as the most suitable candidates for running the village's education work.

They were to come to Bardizag to reform the school's educational programme and organise it in line with the new requirements, which would be continued, under their supervision, by known local people. They arrived in the village and were given the old prelacy, in the market area next to the church, as their home.

The Lousinians, however, didn't make major changes in the school programme. They added lessons in public speaking, outside of the boys' syllabus, which took place just before midday on Saturday in the presence of the students and teachers in the boys' upper hall. Some of the pupils recited chosen pieces by heart. They learnt these in advance and the performances they gave were a form of public speaking competition. They added dancing and needlework to the girls' syllabus, as well as French for the three highest classes. It was obvious that life's new demands spoke in the Lousinians – public speaking, dance, the teaching of a special international language used in high society – especially for the girls. Armen Lousinian and his wife took the teaching of the upper classes, as well as French, Armenian, composition, training in public speaking, needlework etc, upon themselves.

Another new thing was close supervision of work in the classroom and the attention paid to strict discipline in the school. They had small windows fitted into the classroom doors to make classroom supervision easier. They could thus monitor the work carried out and the pupils' conduct at any time of the day.

Lousinian was a short, nervous, light-spirited person who often appeared in front of classes by looking through the windows set in the doors, listening to the lesson being taught. He would sometimes burst into the classroom, interrupting the lesson, temporarily taking the teacher's place and making corrections and giving leadership. He looked at the pupils' work and attempted to liven up and instill movement in the teachers who, at the beginning, were very frightened of being found to be lacking and retaining the old indifferent way of doing things.

The Lousinians definitely created new life in the dead school generally and put the work of education in its proper groove with, as far as possible, the removal of the teachers' old habits and out-of-school activities.

Outside classes, they took special care of the pupils' behaviour, care, and especially of the cleanliness of their clothes and bodies and their neatness. The care that Hadji Apraham Agha took concerning cleanliness was stressed even more by them. Although the majority of the villagers of Bardizag loved cleanliness in the home and of the person, there were parents who were indifferent and behind the times. We know that boys especially tend to be lazy and indifferent to the rules of cleanliness, despite their parents' will and efforts. During the Lousinian era it was the rule that every boy and girl pupil came to school in clean and tidy clothes, washed face and hands and combed and arranged hair. The pupils were already used to these habits from Hadji Apraham Agha's time with his unforgiving strictness. Hadji Apraham mostly lost his all-powerful position during the time the Lousinians were in charge and had transferred to the girls' department with the same position. This was generally regarded as of a lower order, his place being been taken by a young local man, Haroutiun Daiyan, who had a civilised appearance with his European clothes and newly-grown beard. He was, at least outwardly, a new man, while Hadji Agha, in his long and wide trousers, had the appearance of an old woman, which was more suited to female society.

Lousinian unfortunately didn't want to just keep to surface cleanliness, he wanted to go deeper. External cleanliness didn't seem enough for him, and he furiously looked for inner cleanliness too, as if he could force the custom and love of it into their flesh. He often subjected untrustworthy pupils to the examination of their undergarments - their shirts and drawers – looking to find mites and other creatures unknown to civilised people. If the examination found evidence of them, such pupils were sent home to be cleaned and then returned to school. Fortunately there were very few such 'live' pupils.

A time came when the enthusiasm of the examiner of new worlds, exceeding rational limits, became an object of mirth. He became childish and excited people's displeasure through sheer tactlessness. The boys rebelled against his kind of *belief*, determined to stay less than clean. Lousinian was as stubborn as a boy and, determined to teach their parents a lesson, wanting to bathe the boys in the school itself, without thinking that there might have been reasons for their lack of cleanliness that were against their will. For example, lack of underclothes because of their poverty was a situation that could have been improved by simpler means, without resorting to the strict discipline that fomented rebellion. We knew that there were boys who only had one set of outer and under garments, whose mothers waited until the Saturday holiday to wash their children's bodies and their clothes. They had to wait for them to dry to be able to dress again, the children staying naked for a time until they did. Yes, there were these unforeseen circumstances, a situation that Lousinian could have sorted out by talking to the boys themselves.

The greatest danger or difficulty for a community leader, from the point of view of retaining his authority, is being a laughing stock. The Lousinians' lack of tact, the *dance* classes in the girls' school and their ridiculous and scandalous family life, more than laughable things, endangered their position even from the first year. However Sarkis Effendi Mgerian's protection, which was incontestable in Bardizag, kept the oncoming danger away for a time.

The second school year began, but the Lousinians lost something – not to say all – of their popularity with the people. Husband and wife weren't patient and circumspect. They were often seen drunk and arguing with each other. Their voices filled the lower marketplace and the shopkeepers, to prevent any danger, would rush, in their work clothes and bare arms, to re-impose peace in that stormy family home. Thus they died in public estimation, demeaning the post of teacher too.

They only just managed to complete the second year. Their only protector, Sarkis Effendi, who perhaps wanted to give them an opportunity to reflect on their actions, died in the winter of that year. This resulted in a gloomy and cold emptiness being built around them. The Lousinian sun was setting in Bardizag; their last act in the twilight of their tenure was the funeral oration given over Sarkis Effendi's coffin. It seemed as if that year was reserved solely for that event. It would be more accurate to call the oration a complete book with endless pages, all to laud the deceased great man's noteworthy public services and his powerful and unique leadership and position. Mixed in with laudatory comments to his memory, it had a resume of all his intellectual and oratorical gifts. But this good and praiseworthy oration was spoiled by Lousinian's usual total lack of tact. He was not able to grasp the occasion's solemn and awesome mystery, spouting an endless flood of words which he poured on the heads of the mourners from the height of the podium. It became insufferable. His oration was cut short so as to find time for the remains of the great son of Bardizag to be laid to rest.

The departed had known the Lousinians with all their faults and, as a man of noble character and generosity, had wanted to give them time to make a success of their efforts. His disappointment at the end of his life was that there was nothing to find in the Lousinians, and their lives would gradually disintegrate completely.

The Lousinians finally left Bardizag after only having the opportunity to serve for just two years.

It is worth saying a few words about Sarkis Effendi Mgerian before ending this section. He lived, throughout his life, his father's great traditions and virtues and became a notable person for a whole generation and a province, creating honour for his birthplace. This was because it is a truism that it is great men who value their birthplaces and make them worthy of it.

Sarkis Effendi's greatness gains greater value in my eyes than that of his father. His father, Garabed Agha, was a personality endowed with great talents who, in life, with his adroitness, skill, and tactful ways, rose from an insignificant birth to an enviable position. This raised him above ordinary people, and crowned him with glory and honour. It was a rise that was continuous and, like a shaft of light emanating from a tiny point, gradually grew wider, spread and enveloped its surroundings.

Sarkis Effendi, however, born and raised in this glory and honour, was suddenly struck by a catastrophe which laid him in the dust and mud and from which he couldn't recover. He was great enough, however, not to accept defeat, straightened his back, stood up and, although he had lost the greatnesses and values of the world, showed his real greatness through his inner strength and values. They were those of his heart and soul, which neither thieves could enter nor poisons pollute. The father was worthy of his son and the son was able to glorify his origins.

111 – A new and final census in Bardizag

I cannot determine the year that the final new census took place in the Ottoman Empire, but it was sometime between 1870 and 1880. Those conducted until then were not complete, as they only took account of the male population. The demands of administrative reforms and political events made it imperative that a complete census of the Ottoman Empire be carried out to establish its actual population. This would provide the comparative list of the constituent tribes and various elements of the population in this or that area, etc.

Officials were despatched to Bardizag for this purpose. Compiling the census took many days; the officials established their office in the *ghonakh* [government building]. The head of each household (or his or her representative) presented themselves to the census office and was obliged to have the members of the household recorded. This was done parish by parish. The record compiled consisted of:

> The name of the father of the family – his name, surname, date of birth, religion and nationality.*

> The name of the mother of the family – her name, surname, date of birth, religion and nationality.

> The sons and daughters of the family were recorded in the same way.

Every person was later issued with an identity document called a *Hamidiye*, based on these records.

The officials laid down, after the records had been compiled, that the notables were responsible for presenting the government at set times during the year with a list of all the births and deaths that occurred in the village during that time. The *Hamidiyes* of the dead had to be returned and new ones were issued in the names of the new-born. In this way the government always had an exact picture of at least the settled population of its subjects as a whole by area: of each vilayet, miutesarifate, kaza, miudiuriet, village, etc.†

Each of Bardizag's parish councils‡ kept a copy of this census, from which they deleted those who had died and to which they added the details of those born.

As far as I can rely on my memory, Bardizag, according to that census, had over 7,000 inhabitants, without taking into account those who had left the village and

---

* This means ethnicity.
† These are all Ottoman administrative regions from the largest (vilayet) to the village level.
‡ The words used here are *taghayin khorhourtner*.

settled elsewhere. I think the total number (including these) must have been approximately 10,000.*

112 – Records of ownership and government taxation

The government also had a record of land and property that, by occasional new checks being made, had been mostly completed. If someone built a new building or began cultivating a new area of unclaimed government land, that new building or cultivation, after the completion of certain formalities, was recorded against the owner's name. He would then receive an ownership *kocha*, giving the ownership number, type, place, area and borders and the value placed on it. It was on the basis of this last item that the government tax on it was determined. In the case of sale or purchase by one person to another, the transfer of ownership was made by the correct and lawful writing of a special document *(takrir)* before the appropriate officials, and would be registered in government records against the name of the new owner as part of his property.†

I should add, however, that there were property owners who often concealed their ownership of new property and didn't have it recorded either through indifference or negligence, despite these rules. Sometimes agreement was reached between the seller and buyer, both signing a document in front of witnesses, stating that the seller was giving it to the buyer. The property would thus remain in the seller's name. He would receive the tax demand, the new owner would pay him, and then he would give it to the government tax collector. This kind of transaction was illegal and created great difficulties in the future. It led to losses for the owners, as the *legal* owners never appeared before the government.

There was another even more illegal situation regarding property. When a person died, his estate was divided, according to law, between his lawful heirs. This took place in the presence of witnesses or before the representatives of the parish councils. The government often remained ignorant for years of this division, as the heirs didn't want to carry out their legal responsibilities and thus pay the requisite taxes. They were concerned that they would be cheated by unscrupulous officials (something that was usual in Turkey). As a result, although they got their portions

---

* A census carried out by the prelacy of Izmid in 1885 gives the following figures: Bardizag 6,297 individuals, 353 Protestants, 36 Catholics, absent from the village 600. See Hagop Der-Hagopian, *Bardizage khadoudig*, p. 238. Kasabian gives the following figures for 1886, collated by the Nicomedia prelacy as: 667 houses, 1900 males, 1874 females, giving a total of 3774 people. There were also 36 Catholics, 353 Protestants and 600 people absent from the village. The final total is, therefore, 4763 individuals. Minas Kasabian (Farhad), *Hayere Nikomedio Kavarin Mech*, p. 241.

† An example of such a sale document is shown in Appendix, Document. 6, Land sale document No. 1 (below).

of the estate, they couldn't obtain a lawful ownership document, as the government was dilatory in its application of the law. In this situation many, especially in matters regarding land ownership, would escape paying ownership tax or would club together to pay the dead person's tax, as well as the 10% tax. It was impossible to escape the latter as the 10% tax or excise officials would visit each village's cultivated land in turn and determine the crop yield in advance, to calculate the tax to be paid.

Despite all this, the government levied many taxes on its citizens, usually undervaluing the vast holdings of all kinds owned by the rich and overvaluing the receipts of the poor and incapable, who formed the majority of the population. The result was the overburdening of the poor with taxes and their suffering at the hands of the tax collectors. They often had to sell their land to pay back taxes which they couldn't otherwise pay. The government taxes were:

Emlak (ownership tax)

Arazi (land tax)

Aghnam (animal tax)

Bedeli askerie (military service exemption tax - for Christians only)

Temmetie (profits or income tax)

Ashar (10% tax)

Tarik (roads tax)

Mearif (education tax)

Miuriurie (travel tax)

Hunting permit tax

Service taxes – posts and telegrams, stamps

Law court taxes

Civilian taxes – Cleaning *(tanzifat)*; building tax; guards' tax; import and export taxes *(maks)* that was finally paid by the recipient on the goods he received.*

The military service exemption tax, like some others, was a certain annual charge. The amount paid was calculated on the number of a community's male inhabitants and was a large sum. At one time the cost was approximately a quarter of a lira per male inhabitant. It rose with time, on a yearly basis, and in my day was almost one lira per head. To ensure the collection of such a large sum, the government would present the total amount to the community's leadership, ordering that it should be levied as far as possible on able-bodied males only, leaving out the immature, the old, crippled and poor. Under these circumstances the

---

* Kasabian quotes the following taxes being paid in about 1910: military exemption tax (252,000 *kurush*); Land taxes etc. (118,118 *kurush*); roads tax (41,860 *kurush*). The total is 411,978 *kurush*. This sum was levelled on a population of about 8,000 people, or about 51.49 *kurush*/person/year! See Minas Kasabian (Farhad), *Hayere Nikomedio Kavarin Mech*, p. 208.

amount levied on all those subject to the tax was 100-300 *kurush* a year each; they actually had to pay more than this, to take into account those who had been left out.

The Patriarchate of Constantinople petitioned the Ottoman government at one time requesting that an extra 3 *kurush* be added to the military service exemption tax on all Armenian males. This was with the aim of repaying the debt, on a whole Armenian community basis,* that the Armenian Apostolic Monastery of the Two Jameses in Jerusalem had incurred. The sum thus collected by the government would be handed over to the Patriarchate for this purpose. The government permitted this request, but didn't hand over the extra money collected to the Patriarchate for many years. It was only when the Patriarch of the day, Archbishop Haroutiun Vehabedian, repeatedly petitioned the government, that he was able to recover a proportion of the amount collected and use it for the intended purpose. Not only this, but the government, seeing that the Armenian community was ready to make sacrifices for community needs and was able to pay, didn't reduce the military service exemption tax. On the contrary, it continued to collect it with a perfectly equable conscience and even subsequently gradually increased it. The monastery, as a result of these arrangements, didn't gain very much.

The benevolent Turkish government, seeing that the Christians were traders and artisans and, through their industry, had achieved a certain enviable position, had only one preoccupation. This was to always increase the taxes paid by them and never to allocate any of the amount collected to the people paying it. For example, Christians paid education tax but, from the time they opened them, had to finance their own schools, without receiving any benefit from the tax at all. The Armenians paid road tax, but there were no roads. The Armenians constructed and maintained their own roads. The 10% tax was paid, but agriculture and the village economy never profited from it. The entry of Christians into the highest governmental establishments too, especially in the higher centres of learning of law, agriculture and fine arts was in actual fact always refused due to certain plans. Only a few people, thanks to powerful patronage, were lucky to enter them.

If the government had only wanted taxes, we Armenians would regard ourselves as fortunate. We were also, apart from taxes, forced to pay enormous sums to government officials in the form of *bribes* so that, through them, an enterprise would be successful or some matter arranged.

Apart from these, we paid community taxes, the equivalent of 15% of those levied by the government, which paid for internal (village) expenses – schools, public building works or repairs and the prelacy's and patriarchate's *moukata*. Apart from community tax, there were church collections, the fees paid to the

---

* The word used here is *azkovin,* which I have translated as *community* rather than *national.*

priests for baptisms, marriages, deaths, for the church itself* and home blessings, as well as public collections when the harvest was in or for perceived needs.

The community taxes, when collected by community officials with those of the government, always provided a satisfactory result. Towards the end, however, the government separated community taxes from those of the government. This resulted in the community taxes, after that, being collected subject to the people's goodwill and community awareness. These things, no matter how noble, weren't powerful enough to produce good results, and the community treasury suffered from lack of funds. The Armenian community leadership added permanent properties to the Ottoman Armenian community's holdings, bought with the sums provided by the sacrifices of all Armenians, so as to provide for the public needs of the community itself.

113 – Horse thieves and Bodour Gabe

We met horse thieves during this story† who, years later, had settled down with permanent houses. They became owners of substantial land holdings which provided rich harvests, even becoming rich and having notable positions. Despite all this, they still hadn't stopped their horse stealing activities, as if they were driven by some inner urge. Horses were, for many of Bardizag's villagers, the only means of making a living, being used for transportation and buying and selling from village to village. Often the villager wasn't able to retain his ownership of it. He would suddenly be met in the forests or on the roads by a group of Circassians who would take the poor individual's horse, which he had often bought by going into debt, stealing his means of making his living. Protests to the government never met with any response. The poor man, without work and hungry, would weep at his misfortune. This was an impossible situation for any villager.‡ There was a need for a fundamental solution to this frequent criminal activity. God provided an avenging angel from the village that would put an end to this situation - alone. That angel was Bodour Gabe.

Before telling this story, let me tell you of two small incidents, separate from those I have related, concerning the Circassians' crimes.

A hearty young man named Ganno Hadji Garabed had a horse and earned his living by collecting wood. He was only able to bring two loads a day from the mountains to the village, eating a dry crust of bread on his way to assuage his

---

* The word used here is *jamouts*.
† See Section 103.
‡ Der-Hagopian quotes the 4th/16th July 1879 edition (No 2367) of the newspaper *Masis* of Constantinople, which states that in a two year period, the Circassians had stolen 180 horses from Bardizag. Hagop Der-Hagopian, *Bardizage khadoudig*, p. 191.

hunger. At that time a load of wood was worth 10-12 paras;[*] thus he made about 24 paras a day, of which the horse ate a little more than 5 paras worth, leaving the remainder to be used to feed his large family.

One day, this man was occupied in the forest preparing his first load of wood, leaving his horse to its fate to graze. Having completed arranging the load so he could tie it on his horse's back, he went to find it, but it had disappeared. The saddle had been left on the ground for its owner. Our man, losing his head, picked up his axe and ran as fast as he could, following the horse's tracks, in the hope of finding it. On the way he came face to face with the thief who, seated bareback on it, was swiftly disappearing. He grabbed the thief's leg and invited him to return his horse. The horse's new owner took no notice. He then swung the thief's leg to bring him down. The thief resisted with all his strength and grabbed his gun to kill Garabed. The latter, furiously angry, his eyes completely darkened with rage, took his axe and, in one motion, struck the thief's leg with its sharp edge, severing it. It fell at his feet. The thief fell off the horse, and our Hadji Garabed, springing on to the horse's back, galloped back to the village without stopping, leaving his load of wood in the forest. This young man was lucky, as he had to deal with only one thief.

Many years before this a charcoal burner disappeared in the mountains. Searches didn't locate him. The poor man was found, several days later, tied securely to a tree. He had died dreadfully from hunger and thirst. His body had already rotted and fallen apart. His remains were collected in a sack, brought to the village and buried. This man's name was Baghchi Baba. He was a good man and a diligent worker, who had become a victim of an unusual crime that, more than theft, was the result of fanaticism. He left a wife and two young sons who were able to improve their father's state.[†] But only God knows how they managed it through sacrifices and pain.[‡]

These kinds of incidents were usual, both far away and nearby, when Bodour Gabe began his *mission* that could be regarded as being godly as much as governmental.

Bodour Gabe was only as tall as a young boy, hence his nickname, Bodour, meaning 'short of stature'. He was an orphan, his father having died when he was young. He had two sisters and a brother at home, all of them younger than he was, being looked after by their widowed mother through public assistance. Already grown up, he determined to earn his own living and help his family as much as he could. Under these circumstances, he went, like a kitten, to all the khans and all the fields, providing his labour to anyone who needed it, to earn his daily bread. This is how this orphan grew up, in the bosom of free nature, used to hardships and with bravery and boldness. He was later appointed as the guard over the Mgerians' farm in Sarkis

---

[*] The word used here is *tahegan*, which is usually used to denote coins of the lowest value.

[†] The phrase used here is '...were able to improve his hearth.'

[‡] Kasabian tells us that there were 136 such killings known in the province in the 1895-1908 period. Minas Kasabian (Farhad), *Hayere Nikomedio Kavarin Mech*, p. 154.

Effendi Mgerian's time. In that position he often had dealings with horse thieves. He would suddenly open fire on them in the dead of night along the farm borders scaring the uninvited guests, who would hastily depart from those dangerous places.

He retained his position after the Mgerians' bankruptcy at the villagers' expense. With his guardian angel-like alertness, he protected the area around the Khans and to the borders of Hrom Kiugh (Yenikeoy) driving away the horse thieves.[*] They became used to passing through respectfully, during daylight, as travellers, unarmed, like all honourable men who had business in the vicinity.

Safety and peace were built up through Bodour Gabe's activities within the borders and areas belonging to Bardizag and Hrom Kiugh. That little man became loved by all, being able, alone, to establish peace in those places, to the point of exciting government envy.

Despite this, however, horse stealing continued in the mountains and on distant roads. Their victims were the charcoal burners from Bardizag who brought prepared charcoal down from the mountains. The amazing thing was that the charcoal burners, working for wealthy owners who had Circassian guards, always remained untouched. Those who plied the same roads but didn't have these guards, however, often lost their horses to the activities of the Circassian horse thieves, without regard to the protection money they were paid.

Bodour Gabe saw the hand of the Circassian guards in these thefts, because the Circassian, with his nobility, would want to respect the honour of his compatriots – so he met the two guards whom he frequently saw, accusing them of complicity in the horse stealing. His remarks went unheeded and the stealing continued on the same roads. A terrible battle took place between the Circassians and Bodour Gabe's comrades[†] during one of their night-time forays. The unfortunate result of this was the killing of the two Circassian thieves, one of whom died from his wounds where he was, while the other, badly wounded, would live for a few more hours, escaping and finding refuge in the Seymen customs house, among the Turkish officials there. The following morning the Turkish government received news of the incident with the wounded Circassian's testimony. The government, which hadn't any real acumen in catching thieves, decided to arrest Bodour Gabe and try him in accordance with law as an ordinary criminal. Bodour Gabe hid, determined not be handed over to the government.

The government resorted to spies to find his hiding place at any price with a view to arresting him. Days later a large contingent of police surprised him in his hiding

---

* For Bodour Gabe's exploits, see also H. Boghosian, *Anzoukagan Bardizag (housher)* [*Incomparable Bardizag (memoirs)*], Elegian Press, Paris, 1967, pp. 69-70 and Hagop Der-Hagopian, *Bardizage khadoudig*, pp. 191-194.

† His comrades are quoted as being his brother Kel Gabe and Goudjoug Olan (Bedig Asadour). Hagop Der-Hagopian, *Bardizage khadoudig*, p. 191.

place in the Ganno's silkworm house on the Ayazma road. The silkworm house was closely surrounded by the police, and when a detachment, led by an officer, tried to enter the building to arrest him, Bodour Gabe suddenly began firing at them from a lower window looking out onto the mulberry orchard. The policemen ran away, thus providing our hero with the opportunity to escape by jumping down from the building onto a newly-dug patch of soft earth, weapon in hand. He quickly got to his feet, using the gloomy, shadowy orchard to make his escape, leaving his pursuers looking foolish and disappointed.

So Bodour Gabe escaped the misfortune of arrest. No one knew his hiding place. He remained hidden for many days under the care and protection of those who loved him. They not only protected his person like a sacred relic, but also assisted his escape beyond Turkey's borders, to save their hero's honour and appreciating his manly, brave dedication to public safety.

A Greek sailing ship accepted him on board, dressed like a sailor, several months later, and he left safely through the port of Izmid, through the Dardanelles and finally landed at the Bulgarian port of Varna, where his younger brother had been working for some time. He spent his last days peacefully there and was buried in that free soil. His clean and noble heart had always beaten enthusiastically for justice and freedom during his brave and intrepid life.

114 – Mr. Pierce succeeds Mr. Parsons as a missionary, and the foundation of the American Boys' School

One or two years after Mr. Parsons' tragic death,[*] the American Missionary Board appointed a new missionary to the Nicomedia region – Mr. Pierce – who came to Bardizag to assume his new position.

Mr Pierce found that the soil he was to work was quite well prepared.

Miss Farnham still ran the American Girls' School, to which the villagers had given the nickname 'Marsovan',[†] with great results. Mrs. Parsons worked in the 'sisters meetings', with families, children and the sick. The Protestant community had its own meeting hall, pastor, services, first school and governing organisation. At the same time the passions on both sides concerning the Protestant movement had abated considerably. Mr. Pierce was a tall, active, happy, robust and practical American with a nature that was perhaps a little too familiar and which lacked the ability to inspire respect. He, of course, could not be satisfied by just walking along the road opened before him, but would like to stamp his own character on the missionary work entrusted to him.

---

[*] See Section 102.
[†] Referring to the very famous American school located there.

The Americans, in their newly established quarter of Bardizag located at the eastern edge of the village, didn't find anywhere to live for Mr. Pierce, as the one house they had was occupied by Mrs. Parsons and Miss Farnham. He therefore first secured a house near the entry to the village, close to the old cemetery, for himself and his family. He then rented, for a ten-year term, the silkworm house belonging to a branch of the Kiutnerian family, loaning the owners a large sum of money, the interest on which would be the rent of the building. He would be free to make alterations inside it and to add extensions to it at his expense. When the tenancy expired and the owners returned the loan, the building, in its new state, would be returned to them. The side of the silkworm house that faced the street was refurbished and was made suitable to be a family residence. The rear was rebuilt after some time with all the amenities required for a school, where the basis of the American Boys' School was put in place.

Mr Pierce had heard of the work carried out in the girls' school, in terms of a Christian education, with great satisfaction. Encouraged by this, he wanted to found an American boys' school – a high school. He found it impossible to understand the lack of a school for boys, alongside one that educated girls, leaving an uneducated and illiterate generation of boys. He planned to educate them in the same spirit and according to the educational requirements of the times, with the object of promoting mutual understanding and harmony between the sexes.

He set about this plan with a skilled man's understanding and experience, in modest and simple circumstances, within his house. Making all the necessary sacrifices to make this new work attractive and worthy of approval, he left the worry of perfecting it to the future. This school, like the other, had two departments – boarding and day school, to allow the admittance of students from other places and distant parts of the province.[*]

He was not, at first, too demanding concerning the level of fees or the conditions of their receipt: he had to get the parents used to the idea. Life was very cheap in Bardizag at that time. What he required were students, not profit. He thought that when parents became used to the American education system and methods, they would gradually begin to pay enough to cover the costs of their children's education.

He therefore closed his eyes to this and accepted all the students of any age that presented themselves, even young men with moustaches and of marriageable age who hadn't had the opportunity to receive an education. A very few of these paid a modest and reasonable fee, most, however, attending free. At the beginning the majority of the students were the sons of Protestant families. They were soon to be joined by those of the Armenian Apostolic faith. Years later they would form the overwhelming mass of students during the time of his successor, Mr. Chambers,

---

[*] According to Kasabian, the school started in 1876 with 18 pupils. Minas Kasabian (Farhad), *Hayere Nikomedio Kavarin Mech*, p. 251.

when his pure and liberal American mentality would draw great numbers of students from all parts to him who were thirsty for education and needed it.

The American Boys' School seemed to be the expression of a need in Bardizag. It developed swiftly, the number of students increased and the one building wasn't large enough to accept the flood. Mr. Pierce then rented Hadji Srab Kiutner's silkworm house, a few paces from the other one, so that he could recover at least a part of the ever-increasing educational costs of the rapidly escalating number of students. The new building was also used to provide a living for the poor or destitute students through teaching them a trade. Its basement was made into a trades' school, where non-fee paying students, at certain times of the day, learnt how to make furniture and shoes under the guidance of paid craftsmen, these being the two trades taught in the school.

The original (first) building was turned into a dormitory, dining hall, kitchen and laundry, while the upper floor of the second was devoted to school activities.

The Americans' view concerning the question of girls' and boys' education was very simple. It was to give them, in broad terms, the basic elements of intellectual education so that they could express themselves. It gave them the opportunity to read useful books – especially the Bible - and to arm them with the basics of mathematics for future work and life. This would encourage them to learn about the world and human reasoning in general terms but, more than anything else, get them used to thinking independently. This, in turn, would allow them, in any circumstance of work or life, to build healthy and skilled lives for themselves. It would develop their characters - right-minded and just – so they might live in accordance with Jesus' example, using all this as the basis for belief in God and, if possible, to ensure a modest livelihood for themselves.

This was the ideal pursued within the American Girls' and Boys' Schools: to prepare a community that was healthy in every way. Justice lays a responsibility on us to declare that they mostly succeeded in realising this ideal. They managed to prepare healthy, bold, rationally educated and especially decent and honourable generations. These produced individuals that saw reality and were distant from extreme and distorted ideals. These people were calm and dedicated to their work and its results, groomed with a degree of virtue, and with the strength to control themselves.

The Boys' School curriculum was very much like that of the Girls'. There was tuition in three languages, as well as mathematics, basic algebra and geometry, and natural sciences – anatomy, hygiene, basic physics and chemistry. The students had daily lessons in the Bible, as well as history and preparation for life beyond school in accordance with American traditions.

These two schools lived and worked side by side for some time, both having general and collaborating teachers – both male and female. However, as a result of certain circumstances, it was felt that the American Girls' School should be moved to Adabazar, I think in 1884/1885, where life was cheaper and fees were within the reach of a greater number of girls.*

These American schools combined learning the practical with study and education especially in the early days. The students had to do housework – making beds, waiting at tables in the dining hall, helping with kitchen chores and washing dishes, with the girls learning sewing etc. and the boys learning a trade.†

The Bardizag Protestant community purchased the abandoned silk spinning factory belonging to the Mgerians sometime after the 1890s. The other school buildings were emptied when their leases expired and the boys moved to this new building. Mr. Pierce then established his living quarters in the Parsons' house when Mrs. Parsons and Miss Farnham left Bardizag.

In the first years of the establishment of the American Boys' School, the following people worked as teachers there: Armenag Der-Hagopian, Badveli Samuel, Apraham Effendi Madteosian, Dr. Garabed Atanasian the doctor and teacher, Badveli Hovsep Djedjizian and other people who acted as assistants. Mr. Minas Selihian, who was well known in the Protestant community acted, for a time, as the school's administrator.

After a time it became the custom, in these schools, to choose teachers from the graduates of the Constantinople Girls' and Boys' colleges, usually Protestants and, later, with them, trustworthy people with different training, without considering that the religious denomination they belonged to was a problem.

While fanaticism still existed in the mind, generations of Bardizag Armenian Apostolic people remained distant from these schools, but in total contrast, all the children of the Protestant community of both sexes, after completing primary school, mostly followed the completing, or final, courses the schools provided.

Before closing this chapter, I would like to recall a sad incident concerning Mr. Pierce that was like that of Mr. Parsons, without having the same catastrophic end. Mr. Pierce decided to go on a journey to the Armenian villages around Geyve, with the aim of preaching and spreading the new beliefs. He went to Arslanbeg with the Protestant pastor of that village, Badveli Garabed Baroutdjian, who was originally from Bardizag They took two horses loaded with books and notebooks with them. From there the two men and their horses continued their journey through the mountains, as it was a shorter route, to complete their mission. They were held up

---

* See Section 101.

† We know that the Bardizag High School had, in September 1895, 127 students, of whom 102 were boarders. 60 of them came from Constantinople, 22 from Bardizag and the remainder from 25 other towns and villages in the Ottoman Empire. There were 8 graduates that year, with 3 becoming teachers, 1 going to Robert College, 1 to New York to study dentistry and the other 4 into business. See *New York Times* article, September 8, 1895.

by robbers in the mountains, robbed, beaten and left tied to trees. They spent hours in torment, shouting to attract any traveller's attention so they could be freed from their hopeless situation. Hours passed and they reached a crisis, when they had the good fortune to be seen by some travellers who hurried to free them from the threat of dying, and took them back to Arslanbeg. There Badveli Garabed Baroutdjian (my wife's father) fell into bed ill and died after some time as a result of the spiritual shock he had suffered. He left a widow and seven orphans (four boys and three girls). Mr. Pierce also became ill in Bardizag, but fortunately soon recovered.

Chapter 7

Present Times – The Tourian Era 1880 - 1914

115 – Government representation

As we've seen, Bardizag was governed by Turkish aghas for a long time during its history. Each of these aghas held, in his person, all the government departmental posts – public safety, tax collector, overseer of economic affairs, administration of inheritance and legacies, judicial authority and punishment and its implementation.

After the agha's authority had been abolished during the Mgerian era's last years (1850), the governance of the village had been handed over to a locally elected elders meeting *(ekhtiar medjlis)*, endorsed by the central government. Its chairman and executive authority was represented by the village headman or *mukhtar*. This assembly was elected by all the citizens who paid more than 50 *kurush* in ownership and land taxes *(emlak* and *arazi)*. The people who could be elected were those who paid more than 100 *kurush* of these same taxes. The headman had, under his jurisdiction, a police corporal *(chavoush)* and a few policemen.

Bardizag became the centre of a *nahie* or group of villages after 1880. It was governed by a headman or *mukhtar,* whose authority extended over the elders meeting and, before it was established, all the governmental departments that existed in the village at various times. The first of these government departments were, in time order, the six taxes *(rousoume sitti)*. These were later united and called the Public Debt Administration *(Douyoune Oumoumieh)*.

The Turkish government was under pressure from foreign powers to satisfy its European creditors who had no confidence in its financial administration. They had chosen, from its revenue, six taxes – the 10% tax on silkworm cocoons, salt, fish, hunting and hunting permits, postage stamps[*] and spirits (liquor), whose receipts would be administered by a representative body of foreigners set up by the creditors.

This administrative body, as a separate department of the government, collected all these taxes from all over the Ottoman Empire through its offices and representatives, the majority of whom were local officials. It paid, using the proceeds, the administrative costs of the new offices and the amount required as the creditors' yearly interest, and used the remainder to extinguish, year by year, parts of the national debt until it completely cleared it. The government had its representative in this body governed by foreigners, with the right to check its accounts in the name of the Turkish government.

The National Debt Administration in Bardizag was located in a rented building belonging to the community, next to the *ghonakh* [government building], known

---

[*] The word used here is *troshmatought*.

locally by the name of *mizan*. This office had its *miudir,* usually a Turk, a secretary, a *ghantardji* [weights and measures' inspector] and a *gholdji* [guard], both appointed from among local Armenians.

The National Debt Administration, although a foreign intervention in government affairs and, as such, not in the best odour, was something new. It was ordered and its accounts were accurate and mostly free from fraud and profiteering. It operated using European ways and methods. It paid its officials rational and satisfying salaries and, what is more, tried to increase the revenue obtained from the taxes under its control. It made these activities the subject of regular attention and care as was expected of them. They took special care of the development of the silkworm breeding houses and vineyards with the aim of increasing their yield, so that both the cultivator and Administration profited. Meanwhile the other taxes, collected directly by the government, continued to be dealt with in the usual Turkish way. The people were squeezed of the results of their hard-earned work, leaving the government coffers with only the remains of the amounts remitted, the majority entering the pockets of the intermediary tax farmers *(eshrafs)*, important and lesser officials.

The second branch of the government administration was, firstly, the official post office. This dealt with postal, then telegraphic, communications. This was, once more, a rented building, whose official was always appointed from the local population. This office, as I've said, was only concerned with postal matters for the first few years. Letters and packets of papers were handed over each day to a despatch rider on horseback, who would take them to Izmid and hand them over to the central postal depot there. He then received items for Bardizag and brought them to the village each evening.

After a time, telegraphic communications were added to the post office's responsibilities. To achieve this, a telegraph cable carried on poles was built from Bardizag to Izmid, the poles themselves being provided by the local inhabitants. Its use was also in the hands of the local people. A telegraph office containing the necessary machinery was set up in the post office building, thus linking Bardizag to the outside world for the first time.

The third part of government administration was the creation of a *taghabedoutiun* – or, in Turkish, *belediye* [municipality] in Bardizag,* with a salaried mayor, assisted by a villages' council made up of local people appointed by the government. This council also had its salaried secretary, architect and *spasavor* – or, in Turkish *chavoush* [steward]. The council had the authority to control the following:

> Market activities and the contents of shops
> Public and individual building permits – ensuring that buildings were constructed in accordance with the law

---

* I have used the term 'villages council' for this body.

Roads, pavements, public fountains

Managing road building according to the law.

The villages' council had its own sources of revenue – a tax for guards, a *ghantar* [cart] tax, a tax on permits etc.

Bardizag's mayors were always Armenians, initially sent in from outside, then appointed from local individuals, right up until the end. The mayors from outside the community were: Garabed Effendi Nersesian (from Izmid) and someone named Mgerdich Effendi (surname unknown - from Constantinople). Local people who became mayors of Bardizag were Hovhannes Arakelian, Hadji Artin Kiutnerian, Sarkis Djergayian and others.

These offices operated independently of each other until just after 1880, linked to the central government. This was until Bardizag finally became the centre of a group of villages *(nahie)* that included the neighbouring villages:

Dongel Armenian village

Ovadjek Armenian village

The Greek village of Yenikeoy

Three newly-established villages of Laz Armenians – Jamavayr (Kilise Yeri), Zakar Village and Manoushag[*]

10-12 Giurdji and Laz Muslim villages.

The central government always appointed the headman *(miudir)* and secretary *(kiatab)*, both Turks. The headman had a small police force under his jurisdiction, commanded by a corporal *(chavoush)* or sergeant major. The headman had an administrative council *(irade mejlis)* of the group of villages to advise him according to the law. Four of its members were appointed from Bardizag and one Muslim came from the neighbouring Giurdji village of Deosheme.

Each village had its elders meeting *(ekhtiar medjlis)* and headman. These constituted the links between the villages' government *(nahie)* and the communities that belonged to it.

Originally Bardizag was regarded as being made up of three separate parishes: the Armenians, Catholics and Protestants,[†] each of which had its elders meeting and headman.

---

[*] The foundation dates of these villages are quoted as being as follows: Bardizag, 1590; Dongel not known; Ovadjek 1605; Jamavayr 1894; Zakar Village 1878; and Manoushag 1884. Minas Kasabian (Farhad), *Hayere Nikomedio Kavarin Mech*, pp. 102-103.

[†] The division here is on purely religious grounds. By 'Armenian' the author is referring to the adherents of the Armenian Apostolic Church; 'Catholics' and 'Protestants' were Armenians from the village who had adopted one or other of those two faiths.

In the final days, the government altered the single 'Armenian' parish, dividing it into six, each having its own elders meeting and headman, thus putting the representation of the Bardizag Armenian Apostolic population into a strange situation.* In community terms it was one whole group, with one church, one school and one council, but in terms of its relationship with the government it was divided into six separate communities.

At one time, when Bardizag was regarded as one village community linked directly to the centre, it had its community authority, which at the same time was the elders meeting with its responsibilities. The government's aim was to split the two roles, as happened after the organisation of villages' group *(nahie)* but an old custom meant that Bardizag's elders meeting and *mukhtar*, to a certain extent, accepted the community authority's authority over them and conformed to its orders and suggestions in its activities. The government, this time, to sever this link too, divided the village into six parishes, with six independent elders meetings, making it impossible for them all to make the community authority understand anything in terms of defending community interests.† The government had a special aim in these arrangements: to weaken the community authority and reduce its appeal. It succeeded.

The members of the administrative council in Bardizag were often made up of the following people: Aghasi Effendi Papazian, Hadji Mgerdich Agha Der-Garabedian, Hovhannes Agha Arakelian, Sarkis Agha Djergayian, Khachig Agha Avedian etc., at different times and often more than once.

I can recall the following individuals among the Bardizag *nahie* headmen: first, an educated and refined Turk, Ali Fehmi Bey; the second was someone called Kurd Ali Bey, who was evil and accepted bribes during the dangerous days of the Armenian Question;‡ the third was Sefer Bey, a polite, noble Circassian, just before the days of freedom;** the fourth was Hagop Der-Hagopian, a noted journalist from Constantinople,†† during the first years of freedom; the fifth was the young Ittihadist‡‡ Ali Shu'uri Effendi, a two-faced person of dubious character, during whose term of office the deportation of the village population took place. There was

---

* This happened on 1 March 1895. See Hagop Der-Hagopian, *Bardizage khadoudig*, p. 250.

† The wording used here is: 'from the point of view of defending national interests' *(azkayin shaherou bashdbanoutian desagedov)*.

‡ During the reign of Abdul Hamid II.

** The author is talking about the period just before 1908, when the restoration of the Ottoman Constitution was proclaimed.

†† He was miudir from 1908 to 1914, and was the author of *Bardizage khadoudig*.

‡‡ The Ittihad party was also known as the 'Young Turks' and it ruled the Ottoman Empire from 1908 until the Armistice in November 1918. It was totally responsible for the Armenian genocide that began in 1915.

also a sixth whose name I've not been able to determine, during the years of the deportations, whose term of office lasted until the days of the Armistice.

I have to say that even taking the characters of these appointed headmen into account, their official capacities, relations with and attitudes towards us Armenians were governed to a very great extent by the central government's policies. This meant that even the good ones, to maintain their positions, were forced to adapt to situations and circumstances as they occurred, despite their feelings, in accordance with instructions from above. If not, being forced to live in a totally Armenian society throughout their tenure of office, they were inclined to fall into line with the local people's just demands and to win them over by using every possible means. The ones who left the people of Bardizag most satisfied were Ali Fehmi Bey and Cherkez Sefer Bey, who knew how to reconcile the demands of their positions with their personal feelings.

116 – The building of the road from Bardizag to Seymen

Bardizag and its port of Seymen were finally linked by road between 1880 and 1885.

The Turkish government had instituted a road tax *(tarik)* during those years, in accordance with which each able working adult male had to work for the government for four days a year or give its equivalent in cash, calculated at 4 *kurush* a day, a total of 16 *kurush*.

The government, with the profits from this newly established tax, planned to cover the entire country with a network of roads. This was to ease troop and commercial movement and to establish public safety from one end of the country to the other. There were no proper roads in the empire commensurate with its needs until then. The only roads that existed were those that were from the Roman and Byzantine eras and which were in a very poor state of repair. There were no railways at that time – just a few short lines – from Haidar Pasha to Izmid, Moudania to Boursa, Mersin to Adana, and from Jaffa to Jerusalem. Izmir's railway could also be added, being the only province where lengths of track had been built at various times, paid for with European capital.

The government, to satisfy this important need, sent skilled, bold overseers to every provincial centre to build roads, with the emphasis on collecting the tax and building the roads at the same time.

It was during this time that a new *miutasarif* was sent to Izmid by the name of Selim Serri. The government had found their man of action, who gave great impetus to the collection of the tax and, with an iron fist, raised the province's entire workforce and put it to work building roads throughout the province. The main road from Izmid, which was to link up with the one started in the province of Boursa, was begun; the network thus created was to extend, through Asia Minor, as far as Adana and Aleppo.

The Izmid main road began to advance through the province, towards Anatolia, passing through Devrend, Sabandja, Adabazar and Geyve, until it reached Biledjik, on the border of the province of Boursa.

The Bardizag notables took advantage of this building frenzy to persuade the pasha of Izmid to permit the people of the village to use the tax they had to collect, and their labour, to build a road from Seymen to the village, a distance of 5 kilometres (about 3.5 miles). Selim Serri, who had absolute powers in this regard, was good enough to give the villagers the required permission.

The government, through its expert officials, prepared the plan of the road to be built. This was to follow the old paved road apart from a small stretch, from above the Khans as far as Lemberloz. There a belt of vineyards in that area and the new road would therefore be diverted to the north. It then cut through cultivated gardens and vineyards, to reduce its steepness somewhat, forming a long curve. It would then continue, following the old roadway.

Construction began at the port, where the first turns of the spade furrowed the ground to a width of 8 metres (about 28 feet). The entire village joined in to pay for and build its own road.* This road, however, belonged for some distance to the Greek inhabitants of Yenikeoy, which was a part of our group of villages or *nahie*. They were supposed to assign some of the tax they collected, as well as their efforts, to this construction. With Greek stubbornness and unexplainable feelings of envy, however, that village's population was against joining the efforts until the very end. They undertook to work on other roads, rather than the one that belonged to the people of Bardizag, apparently because they had no need of it.

The people of Bardizag, inflamed by this opposition managed, alone, to complete the road as far as the entry to the village in 2 or 3 years. This gave Bardizag a link to the outside world and a main road that was safe to use in every season. Not only this: it was now possible to use horses and carts for transportation, while before the road was built all movement of goods was carried out with difficulty using horseback.

With the easing of transportation, transport costs were reduced and imports from outside increased. This was especially true of wagons of timber and flour from the Bolu area that, before then, used the old road with the greatest difficulty. The new road was also a clean and pleasant place to walk for the villagers and, in fine weather, every kind of group of people would meet on it, surrounded by greenery. Many, including the quiet ones, would, at about 4 o'clock in the afternoons, go down the road, laughing and joking, as far as Seymen, to have a coffee and a short rest there, enjoying the breeze off the water and then return in the same way; they

---

* It should be said, however, that building the road was not a simple exercise; there was much opposition in the village to its construction. See Hagop Der-Hagopian, *Bardizage khadoudig*, p. 214.

would reach their houses before it got dark, having enjoyed a long and healthy period of exercise.

117 – Tset Khacher's son Levon's unexpected act of bravery

Levon was the youngest son of the famous weather predictor Khachadour Chilingirian (Tset Khacher), from our parish. He was a twenty year-old who worked for a Turkish agha with his brothers burning charcoal in the mountains around Karamoursal. He was a simple and uneducated young man, still a bachelor, who had learned how to use weapons in Bodour Gabe's *school** for his own protection.

A Circassian robber band was active in those days in Izmid province, made up of three men who knew no limit to their marauding. They robbed travellers, entered houses at night to rob them by making holes in the walls and kidnapped rich people, taking them into the mountains and, using death threats, extorting great sums of money as ransom for them. They didn't even have the conscience to leave holy objects alone, even making places of prayer the scenes of their robberies and exploits, but who hadn't, until that time, been apprehended, despite bold government attempts.

One day, having been almost trapped by their pursuers, the robber band decided to move its area of operations, and journeyed from the Khodjeli region to go to the area around Karamoursal. On their way, the group was surrounded by government forces in the port of Khazekhli, but managed to escape through the line of troops and go into the mountains. There, during one of their forays, they found the Bardizag family's charcoal-burning camp.

There wasn't much to steal – just a few horses that they would take before retreating into the mountains to cover their tracks. Nevertheless the horses were loot. So they rounded up the brothers who had dispersed in the forest cutting wood for charcoal burning and brought them to where the stove was, in the camp. The brothers' hut was also located there. The robbers began to tie all the brothers up, but when the youngest brother's, Levon's, turn came, he resisted with a typical young man's anger. At this, one of the robbers hit him hard on the arm with the butt of his rifle, angering him to the point of rebellion. Levon, at this critical moment, turned to his brother and asked, 'Where is the iron with the hole in it?'† 'In the hut' was the reply. With one bound Levon rushed into the hut, picked up the gun and, suddenly emerging from the doorway, fired at one of the robbers who, trembling, fell to the ground lifeless. Levon fired a second round at another, who fell wounded to the

---

* Author's italics. Bodour Gabe was the most famous of the brave men in Bardizag. He protected the village against Circassian horse thieves and their assaults. See Section 113.

† A euphemism for a double-barrelled gun, probably a shotgun.

ground next to the first. The third, alarmed by all this, escaped into the depths of the forest.

Levon, seeing that the wounded man was still moving, but could no longer use his weapon, grabbed an axe and attacked him, but his brothers, who had been hiding behind trees during these events, shouted and warned him, seeing the robber extend his hand to his gun to protect himself. Levon, coming to himself, walked away with the axe in his hand and joined his brothers, who left the scene of the incident, looking for a safe place to hide, not knowing what to do.

After a time, when things had calmed down around them and their spirits had settled, they quietly approached their hut, checking to see what the situation was. They saw that the dead robber's body was still on the ground, while the wounded one had disappeared. They collected their horses and saw that one was missing. They understood that the robber who had escaped, taking advantage of the charcoal burners' flight, had returned to the scene and, putting his wounded comrade's body on the horse, had finally left that dangerous area.

Levon and his brothers collected their belongings, left their work, mounted their horses and went to Karamoursal. The described the incident to their agha, who informed the government. The government questioned Levon and his brothers and prepared a written report concerning the incident and the death on the basis of the charcoal burners' testimony. The brothers were released upon their agha's guarantee.

The government once more, led by one of the charcoal burners and with a squad of policemen, was sent into the mountains to visit the scene, retrieve the body and prepare a final report. A proper, legal examination of the body was conducted in Karamoursal: a man had been killed with Levon's double-barrelled gun. Finally Levon, with the completed report, was sent to the government centre of Izmid, where the responsibility for the death would be established.

Even before Levon and the officials accompanying him had arrived, the tale of the incident, couched in general terms and going from mouth to mouth, had reached the entire population of Izmid. Turks, Greeks, Armenians and Jews had all heard that a boy from Bardizag – who hadn't even grown a moustache – had had the bravery to defend himself against the robbers, kill two of them and forced the other to flee. It was this heroic boy that they were bringing to Izmid by mail steamship.

Everyone, big or small, rushed to the port when the ship's smoke could be seen on the horizon. Turkish and Christian women and girls filled the seashore roads and hung out of the windows. This brave boy was the talking point of the day and everybody wanted to see him for themselves. He had become the stuff of legend in their imagination.

The ship approached the port and the crowd became mobile. It squeezed up, climbed piles of goods, with people even getting on each other's shoulders to see the hero. Finally Levon appeared, surrounded by policemen, and passed, with his head down, red-faced with shame, through a passage between walls of people. This imaginary being received his natural comparison in the eyes of those present: a small boy, without hair on his face who, however, walked straight and upright on his feet. Then the clapping began, with calls of 'Yashasen,' 'Bravo' and 'Aferim, well done!'

Public opinion had judged the young hero: he was innocent of those two killings, having only defended himself – which was his right – and at the same time had helped the government destroy a robber band that had been a permanent problem for years in the province.

Levon was declared innocent and freed and, that same evening, returned to Bardizag with the praise and appreciation of high government officials for his unexpected bravery. His father, Tset Khacher Baba, who was justly known in and around Bardizag for his amazingly accurate weather forecasts, was delighted, but until then had not been able to predict the virtues of boldness and bravery in his son.

118 – The rebirth of silkworm breeding and the silk trade in Bardizag: the Pasteur method

We have seen the decline and fall of silkworm breeding and the silk industry in Bardizag* through the various sicknesses suffered by the silkworms themselves. This led to the abandonment of the silk spinning factories and silkworm breeding houses with the population of the village, considering the trade hopeless, turning away from the work that had brought its biggest income.

The great French scientist Louis Pasteur, however, was asked by the French government in the 1870s to examine the sicknesses suffered by silkworms and find a cure for them, so that the important and profitable silk trade in France could be rebuilt. After a few years of research and dedicated scientific study, he was able to find the absolute cure for the sicknesses by creating a method of producing healthy silkworms. That method has been known as *Pasteur's System* from that time until the present. It is based on the detailed examination of the silk moth that lays the eggs, as the only certain method of separating the sick worms from the healthy ones.

Pasteur's discovery was a turning point in sericulture and the silk trade that would, very swiftly, result in unprecedentedly brilliant results. Every country in the world involved in sericulture adopted Pasteur's discovery. Turkey utilised it too and, to teach Pasteur's system, the Public Debt Administration opened the Bursa Sericulture School, whose director was Kevork Effendi Torkomian, a rural economy graduate from a European university.

Greatly encouraged by Pasteur's discovery, people in Bardizag began, once more, to turn to their abandoned silk spinning factories. Silkworm houses were reopened, and ordinary people began to pay attention to the groves of mulberry

---

*   See Section 97.

trees. The old ones were pruned and returned to health and became the subject of care and attention. New mulberry orchards were planted on cultivable soil and, although there were initial squabbles, boldness and trust were created that led to new silkworm houses being built. All the villagers took to the resumption of the old trade with great enthusiasm.

At the beginning, when the breeders using the Pasteur system in Turkey were still not ready, merchants imported great quantities of silkworms into Turkey. The silkworn eggs were prepared using the Pasteur system, being obtained mainly from dealers in France and Italy. They supplied good quality materials and didn't disappoint those who worked hard to achieve a good harvest almost every time, thus making the work profitable. The cocoon harvest grew throughout Turkey, as it did in Bardizag and the surrounding area.

A wealthy man from Izmid, Hovhannes Agha Helvadjian, rented the Saroukhanian silk spinning facvtory from its European owners, wanting to replace his foodstuffs business with this new one, which promised to make bigger profits than his original business did and represented great hope for the future.

The machinery, lying rusted and unused for so long, began to turn, and the old life began in the village once more, in more promising circumstances.

The young people who graduated from school in Bardizag followed, in great numbers, the courses given in the Boursa Sericulture School. These courses lasted for two years, with teaching lasting for three months of each year. The graduates of these courses received certificates to show that they were able to use the Pasteur system.[*] Some took up the trade on their own account as a business, and several of them obtained posts as government sericulture inspectors.

The Pasteur system returned Bardizag to its old ways of living, the village gradually growing in size, occupying many of the villagers and great numbers of the women and girls as workers in the Helvadjian silk spinning factory.

These silk-working skills and the rebuilding of the trade in silkworms considerably improved the village economy and increased the buying power of the villagers themselves, resulting in an increase in the mercantile life of the village, especially in the import of European flour and woven goods.[†] This boom in the village economy was used by the Helvadjian house which, like the Mgerians, for a time, alongside the silk business, began to import great quantities of flour from Constantinople to satisfy public demand in Bardizag. Helvadjian was soon to be followed by a local merchant, Mr. Khachig Avedian who, thanks to his great success in the mercantile field, would become, in a very short time, a wealthy factory owner.

---

[*] We know that the author himself followed these courses and his certificate survives in his grandson's possession (see Appendix, Document 4).

[†] The word used here is *hiusvadzeghenner* which could mean either knitted or woven goods.

119 – An ordinary bandit called Nouri Bey achieves a very wealthy and influential position among the notables of the province of Izmid

Nouri was an ordinary bandit, a member of a robber band that was well known in the province. The government pursued the band wanting to destroy it. Various government officials had profited from it for years. They spoiled it for so many years that it had become totally outrageous and impossible with its boldness. When government efforts to arrest the band failed, it bribed one of its members to assist in the work of laying hands on it. This was the robber Nouri who agreed to betray his comrades on the condition that he should be declared innocent of his past acts. This was agreed.

Nouri, knowing he had saved his own skin, betrayed the robbers' hiding place in the mountains which was near Bardizag's borders. He advised the government forces to advance, on a certain night, without arousing suspicion, to the place he described and surround the hideout with strong forces so that the band couldn't escape. At this point Nouri would quietly abandon his comrades and go over to the government side, and the battle would begin between the two sides.

The government assigned this difficult and dangerous task to an experienced police squad, which it strengthened by getting volunteers from the neighbouring Armenian and Turkish villages. Bardizag also provided volunteers, one of whom was a well-known young man called Goudjoug Olan (from the Bodosian family), a married man with a wife and children, who was one of Bodour Gabe's old comrades.

The government forces silently advanced on the given night to the robbers' hiding place. It was like a tower, located on the top of a hill that was in the middle of a flat, open area. Everything went as planned and it was only at dawn that the robbers realised they were trapped, and prepared to defend themselves. Nouri, at this point, silently went over to the police lines and disappeared among their ranks.

The assault began on the robbers' position, which was brought under heavy fire. The robbers defended themselves with great energy, but circumstances were against them: they were closely surrounded and the government forces had greater numbers. During the battle, which lasted for some hours, some of the robbers were killed, some fell wounded and the remainder were arrested. The government forces too had its losses, one of whom, unfortunately, was our compatriot Goudjoug Olan, who was killed through his bravery and boldness. Through his thirst for battle he had moved so far forward towards the robbers' position that he was wounded and died shortly afterwards.

The dead young man left a wife and orphan children, who grew up without their father but who were able, later, to enrich their family home. This was without any substantial assistance from the government, for whose honour he had died. Their childhood years were spent mostly in poverty and they suffered a difficult period of abject misery.

Elsewhere, the robber Nouri gradually became the government's spoiled child, accumulating great riches and position and becoming a very wealthy man. He joined the officials in their profiteering and, working with them, became a tax gatherer, mortgaging whole groups of villages and wide expanses of land at the same time. These he then sold, piece by small piece, to less wealthy people, thereby assuring himself of great profits, some portions of which, of course, went to the greatest officials of the province.

Nouri, having become the well-known Nouri Bey, now robbed people to a greater extent than he did when he was part of the robber band, in totally safe circumstances. Nouri Bey, the man of the moment, poked his nose into everything to obtain the best and most succulent pieces from the public table, when people, rich or poor, needed government offices to assist them in making a *profitable* business successful.

120 – Yeghishe Vartabed Tourian in Bardizag as preacher and community schools' inspector (1880)

It is a well known historical fact that the economic development of a people often coincides with the advance of civilisation; so it happened with Bardizag. In the period after the village came out of recession, thanks to a fortunate election, Yeghishe Vartabed Tourian was invited to Bardizag as church preacher[*] and community schools' inspector, which he carried out for 10 years without a break. He tranformed the circumstances of the village's spiritual, intellectual and artistic development, and made sure Bardizag achieved an enviable name in the entire province. Tourian's ten years of work was a new era in Bardizag's history, unprecedented in its content and results, which I consider suitable to be called the *Tourian era*, as I previously separated the previous ones, calling them the *Agha Krikor Great Hadji Khacher Bab*, *Apraham Kahana* and *Garabed Agha Mgerian* eras.

I am going to divide this famous period in Bardizag's history into six parts:[†]

1. The construction of the new school building
2. The basic organisation of educational work
3. A new generation of teachers
4. Cultivation of spiritual life. Tourian the preacher
5. Lecture hall and theatre
6. Tourian's family, social and personal life.

---

[*] It is entirely possible that one of the reasons for his invitation to the village – not mentioned here in the text – was to counter the Protestant and Catholic missionaries' influence.

[†] I have amended the text here to reflect the actual titles used in this section.

1. The construction of the new school building

20 year-old Yeghishe Vartabed Tourian was a fresh, delicate-framed young man when he arrived in Bardizag. Despite his age, he made a great impression on the upper class of people in the village from the very first day. It was one that engendered confidence in him. He had limitless confidence, born of careful education, natural skills and talents, selfless and enthusiastic love of work and the inborn virtues of a noble person that endowed his whole being with charm and beauty. At the same time this confidence opened doors for every kind of sacrifice before him, and the things he started always became successful.

Tourian, in terms of the school, found himself in front of two ruins. The first was the school building that had suffered over the years, making it unfit for basic and new work within its walls and rendered it insufficient for the needs of the growing number of students. The second was the sheer exhaustion of the teachers and their incompetence in carrying out work already started.

Hardly had the school year ended when the decrepit state of the school building became the object of attention by Tourian and the people who admired his work. There was no room for hesitation. It was decided to demolish the building and construct a large and well-made new one. People found that an extra 1000 square arshins[*] had to be added to its existing area. So the street between it and the church wall was closed off and the neighbouring dwellings for the poor were demolished. The street was re-routed to go under the new building, from the north, where there was a narrow lane and the school playground already existed.

The work was given to a trained Greek architect (Mimiko Effendi) to complete. The building was to be in two halves – one for boys, the other for girls.

The architect drew up the plans for a large, three storey building (starting with the basement[†]), with two identical wings. Each wing would have, from south to north, a hall from one wall to the other for study and, next to it, a small hall, with a classroom on each of its three sides. The eastern wing would be for girls and the western one for boys, both of equal size and content, as if to confirm the equality of the two sexes.

Three storeys, with two wings, each with a hall and three classrooms, all in one school building: these totalled 6 halls and 14 classrooms, with the halls next to one another in the centre on each floor, and the classrooms at both ends. To ensure that light entered the new building from every direction, the old high wall was reduced from the southern end to the level of the second floor.

The foundations, below ground level, were to be of stone, with the whole of the building above ground level to be constructed of timber. The work began and the old building was demolished in a few days. The foundation trenches were excavated

---

[*] About 5445 square feet or 610 square metres.
[†] The floor (storey) below ground level.

according to the plans and filled with well-built stone walls. Gradually the great walls of the new school building began to rise above ground level on the north side of St. James church. They were unequalled in the province or even in many districts of Constantinople. Construction took two years. It was a period of enthusiasm and festival-like atmosphere for the whole people who, with unusual animation, built their children's house with love and sacrifice.

Prelate, vartabed, kahana, notable, men and women carried the building materials on their own shoulders. Many, both old and young, of both sexes, laboured for days alongside the paid builders as if it were their ordinary work. This huge three-storey building, on a foundation of a 1,000 square arshins, only cost 1,000 Ottoman liras, or one lira per square arshin, a sum that was negligible for such a building. This miracle was due to the villagers' mass free collaboration. The sum of 1,000 liras was accrued through donations made by the well-to-do, savings accumulated by the church treasury and large and small donations given by everyone during the silkworm season, resulting in a tidy total sum.

The opening of the new school was conducted in the presence of the prelate Bishop Stepannos Hovagimian, Tourian Vartabed, the village clergy and the entire population. The boys department was called the Nersesian School, in honour of the great Armenian Patriarch of Constantinople, and the girls department was named Shoushanian School, in honour of Shoushan, the daughter of the great national hero Vartan Mamigonian.[*] It seemed as if it was an attempt to tie both ends of our history together.

Tourian, after these two years, victoriously entered the new school with joy and spiritual satisfaction. He was accompanied by a crowd of his spiritual children, who filled the two upper storeys. The students numbered between 800 and 1,000 individuals.

The basement was excluded from educational work but would have its role to play, as we shall see later. During the two-year construction period, village education was continued in buildings and houses here and there. The elder boys were temporarily taught in the prelacy building behind the church on its western side that overlooked the market during the first year. The young boys and the girls had their lessons in both apses of the church itself during the same period. The ramshackle prelacy building suffered under the blows of the constantly-moving boys' feet and seemed liable to collapse, so it was left to its fate. The boys' school was moved to the Ghazarosian's silkworm house in the second year, which was then given the historic name 'Lazarian Djemaran' reminding us of the famous Armenian school in Moscow.[†]

---

[*] Commander-in-chief of the Armenian army at the battle of Avarair in 451 AD, where he was martyred.

[†] The author has added a personal note here. It would seem that he was one of these older students.

The construction of this school was under the patronage of the diocesan bishop through the parish council chaired by Mgerdich Effendi Der-Hagopian (father of Professor Apraham Der-Hagopian), and presided over by the leading cleric[*] Garabed Kahana Mkhalian.

2. The basic organisation of educational work

The Bardizag community school sometimes had brilliant times. These were during the tenures of the teachers Mourad of Peria, Monsieur Pascal, Shirinian, Sahag Kahana Pandig and the Lousinians. At no time, however, has it produced graduates completing a particular syllabus each year. In the old days the students would continue to attend school until they were satiated or grown up, leaving others to devote themselves to work and profit. The boy or girl would be a graduate only of their own will, when they were considered to be too old to continue school life.

Tourian cured that problem. He created a paced, established and regular syllabus spread over five years for the senior students, almost identical in content for both boys and girls.[†]

In the *nakhagrtaran* [middle school] the boys learnt a certain amount of Armenian (both classical and modern), Turkish and French, a whole mathematics programme, later adding the preliminary elements of algebra and geometry, and objective examination,[‡] as an introduction to the natural sciences. He later added the basics of anatomy of the human body, botany, zoology, physics and chemistry to the upper class syllabus. Religious studies comprised Bible study, as well as brief courses in Christian and national history, geography, handwriting etc.

The girls' courses did not include Turkish or, in the higher classes, natural sciences or mathematics. They learnt sewing, embroidery and home economics instead.

As for the precursors of first schools (there were none then, and the equivalent classes were called *dzaghgots*), the children remained in them for about four years, where they learnt to read and write, and to begin basic mathematics, Bible study and objective examination as preparation for the next level. Children were usually accepted into school at the age of five years old, and left at the age of 14 or 15.

Tourian was the life and soul of this work and its most important asset. Although he set the tired and worn-out teachers to work under his spirit and direction, it was he alone who taught the important lessons in the upper classes, being able to make the students enjoy the lessons and the school, which is a teacher's greatest value. He created enthusiasm for his work. He was assisted in his teaching by Karnig Effendi

---

[*] The title used here is *Avakerets*.
[†] In those days children's education was divided into three parts: *dzaghgots* [first school] lasting for four to five years; *nakhagrtaran* [middle school] lasting for 5 years; and *partsrakouin varjaran* [senior or high school] lasting between three and five years.
[‡] The word used here is *irakidoutiun*.

Giureghian, a young man from Uskudar, hired by the community council to teach Turkish and French.

After some time – about 3-4 years – Karnig Effendi became slipshod in his work, which he didn't like, wanting to be a medical practitioner in his circle of friends and acquaintances. He resigned from teaching after he was able to establish his reputation as a *healer* and gain a clientele. He then set himself to the work of healing, as it was permitted in those days to use practitioners without any qualifications, bearing in mind that there were not enough qualified doctors in the country, especially not in the villages.

Karnig Effendi was replaced by Apraham Effendi Madteosian (from Izmid), with the position of visiting teacher. He didn't have a real, in-depth knowledge of the subjects he taught, but had learnt much through self-study, and was able to deal with each subject as a middle school teacher, as he had enthusiasm and a good character.

It must be admitted that, under the circumstances of the time, Tourian's work, despite his efforts and dedication, didn't become regular and general because of his collaborators' lack of ability. But he tried to concentrate his efforts on one or two classes and, after five years of work, to present the first graduates.

This graduate class comprised seven students: K. Goudjoukian (later Archbishop Mgrdich Aghavnouni), H. Sekgiulian, M. Semerdjian, H. Djergayian, A Hapelian (Anania Kahana Hapelian, later a vartabed), H. Kiutnerian and me. Of the penultimate class which, over those five years had been completely dispersed, only Y. Der-Antreasian[*] remained, linked to the school as an assistant teacher for one or two years, and to whom Tourian gave private lessons outside school hours, to bolster his preparation.

From that day on, the Bardizag community school retained Tourian's syllabus and organisation and, on that basis, produced graduates year after year, whose numbers would be in the hundreds. During Tourian's ten years of office, the generation he produced became an active and noble group of young people that, years later, would take the leadership and development of community life on its shoulders.

3. A new generation of teachers

Tourian, when he found himself in front of these graduates that were the first results of his educational work, decided that the time had come to clear the ruins of the teaching staff. He had worked with them for better or worse for five years, but was now convinced that they were of no use, the fire for life and idealism having died in them. So he kept the most promising of the graduates, K. Goudjoukian, H. Sekgiulian, M. Semerdjian, A Hapelian and me in the school as assistant teachers alongside Y. Der-Antreasian, giving us all modest salaries. We were six fresh assets

---

[*] The author has written his name here as Y. D. Antreasian.

that he had inspired with his enthusiasm and fire for the education of the new generation. Of the old teachers, Hadji Apraham, Badveli Hovsepian and Mr. Takvor, as well as Apraham Effendi Madteosian – this last only appointed to fill a temporary need – gave up their positions in favour of the new ones.

Tourian, with this new teaching organisation, had a group of young collaborators around him whose preparation, although insufficient, had certain advantages over the old ones. We understood him, loved the work, were in the fullness of our youth and were ready to follow in his footsteps and were able to develop and gain experience. He divided the work of the school between us, taking care to prepare each of us for a specialist subject. He gave Y. Der-Antreasian Armenian, French and general history to teach; to H. Sekgiulian natural sciences and mathematics; K. Goudjoukian and M. Semerdjian the teaching of Turkish, national history and religion; likewise he gave the remaining pair of us the same subjects for the lower classes.

We, the new generation of teachers, under Tourian's direction, would gain in strength through years of collaboration and association with him and by adding experience in our new work. This was because our work as new assistant teachers would be an education of the highest order for us and, at the same time, an opportunity to learn pedagogy while we were working, under Tourian's authority and leadership.

These were days of joy, enthusiasm and idealism for us as a group in that part of our lives. All of us developed a necessary appetite for reading. We had placed our feet in – for us - an unknown world, with wide and enticing horizons and content, and vied with one another to devour the books that fell into our hands. Tourian's full library felt like a place of pilgrimage for us: we read great French classics – Chateaubriand, Voltaire, Rousseau, Corneille, Racine, Moliere, Lafontaine, Fenelon, Bossuet, Lamenet, Labruyere, Pascale and others. We read novels – by Lamartine, Victor Hugo, Miusset and De Vini, and the theory we learnt grew and deepened. We felt that we were becoming new men with new concerns and new visions. Each of us, with the excuse and charm of finding new things, would tell the others, in our social get-togethers, of our reading and that there was a lot more beyond the responsibilities of our lessons. We were driven to translate parts of the books and authors we loved, and Tourian joined in with witty observations from his joyful mind, opening our eyes to our mistakes and faults. The teachers' room gave the impression of being a classroom, thanks to this collaboration and these gatherings.

The school took on a new look as a result of these strenuous efforts. All of us teachers were dedicated, first to learning, then teaching, thus giving Bardizag's educational work order and producing results. The school reached enviable standards, putting the American High School into second place, with its healthy Armenian education and its superiority in many other branches. This reduced the

American High School to only having the responsibility of giving its students an American education and preparing them for entry to Robert College.

Bardizag's school, with its carefully prepared organisation and intensive work, became the whole province's educational establishment, with students being sent to it from Dongel, Ovadjek, Arslanbeg and even from distant Adabazar, Geyve's Ortakiugh, Merangeoz, Soleoz and many other Armenian-populated villages in the region.

One of the notable teachers in our group was H. Sekgiulian, who resigned and went and settled in Massua a year or two later, as the secretary of a merchant house. His place was filled by me, although before then, still being a youth, I was shy and indecisive. I hadn't been inspired with the idea of being fit to teach in the upper classes, many of whose students were taller than I was.

The school, after this, began to produce graduates with good preparation and sound middle school education year after year. Those among them that stood out were retained by the school as reserve teachers. They took over when fully trained teachers left Bardizag for other places with positions giving a better salary. Of these reserve teachers I must recall A Bodosian, Aram Mazlemian (later Archbishop Garabed Mazlemian), H. Garakian, K. Saraidarian, G. Nahabedian, A Arakelian, K. Bodourian, O. Ghazarian, H. Alodjian, M. Hovsepian and others, successively, all of whom dedicated themselves to teaching, firstly in their own school, and then in other Armenian schools.

4. Cultivation of spiritual life: Tourian the preacher

As a scientific man, Tourian's preferred subjects were classical Armenian, classical Armenian literature, church history and biblical studies. Over a period of time he amassed great expertise and authority in these subjects, especially aspiring to study them in the latest European philological light. He soon became known among us as an authority in those subjects.

This great man, despite all the pressing work that surrounded him, never failed however, to preach regularly in the church in Bardizag every Sunday. He was listened to by the congregation with the greatest animation. A new thing was that many Protestants loved to hear his sermons, which they found full of flavour. If all his sermons were recorded on paper, we would have volumes filled with them today, full of deep belief and couched in language and style of unmatched beauty and grace.

In those days, when religious propaganda was so emphatic, there was panic that the days of the Armenian Apostolic Church were numbered. Tourian's presence, arguments and his understanding of the Holy Bible in the light of the newest discoveries meant that the Armenian Apostolic Church found its greatest defender and the man of the hour. He silenced every attack and criticism levelled against the church, which had been the ark of salvation for the Armenian people through the centuries with the power of his arguments and even with wisdom culled from the Bible.

Thus Tourian was able in that way to stop the separatist movement in Bardizag that had appeared around the church, obliging people to treat it with love and respect.

The Protestants and Catholics did not, of course, return to the mother church, but those movements became meaningless things for many, reducing the fervency of the propaganda spread among them. The thought began to take hold in people's minds - and they began to be convinced - that these new Armenian churches didn't bring anything new. It seemed that the Protestant church, with its increasing number of variations, only arrived to give a spurious and illegitimate immunisation to Armenian spirits. It didn't seem to represent a safe and everlasting base for the construction of the people's spiritual and moral edifice. People also thought that a church's value consisted in the lives and works of the leadership that was faithful and prepared and that the reforms expected could not come from outside, but from within. They thought that it was not the form that would provide salvation, but the spirit, and that spirit existed within the Armenian Apostolic Church, although it had been buried by the centuries of dirt of tyranny and darkness. It was sufficient to have clergymen as prepared as Tourian to bring out that spirit in its most ancient and complete, shimmering brilliance.

As I've already said, Protestant propaganda stopped completely in Tourian's day and a new way of thinking took root among right-minded missionaries. This was to stop religious propaganda and dedicate themselves to the work of educating the Armenians spiritually and intellectually. They would also help, if necessary, the Armenian Apostolic Church to prepare the able and trustworthy clerics that it lacked, with whom the Armenian people would create its salvation with its own hands.

The people of Bardizag found its safety and spiritual peace under Tourian's spiritual supervision. It saw its God in itself and in its church once more, through Tourian's eyes.

After that, propaganda took on a laughable appearance. Bewildered, innocent-minded people, clinging to a saying or explanation from the Bible, thought that they would save their souls by moving from one Protestant church to another. Meanwhile, Tourian continued to preach his beautiful sermons that were full of content. He would turn to the people from the chancel with a prophet's voice and a disciple's conviction, occasionally wiping the sweat from his forehead with the corner of a handkerchief, as if he had made a special effort. He shouted God's eternal message of love, brotherhood, mercy, humility, justice, sin, the good and finally all that made up the core of religion into the people's ears. When he had put these spiritual things into their souls, he would turn his face to the altar, finding the senior kahana, Garabed Kahana Mkhalian, who only had a boy's stature close to him. The kahana, rubbing his hands and with feelings of immeasurable pleasure and satisfaction, would say, 'Well done, vartabed, you spoke very sweetly.' Tourian would then take a deep breath with a smile on his lips.

It would also happen that Tourian, animated by godly fire would roar, spilling from his lips Moses' and the other prophets' anger and passion, against aberrations contrary to spiritual life at a congregation that was frozen with fear and terror. Sometimes, with his crozier-staff in his hand, he would walk through the halls of God's house against sinners. At this point Hadji Krikor Agha (father of Y. Der-Antreasian), would shake his head as if encouraging him and murmur, 'Tell them, vartabed, tell them!' from his seated position below the chancel.

5. Lecture hall and theatre

Tourian, collaborating with us, his students-teachers, organised Sunday lectures in the school's upper halls in the years following 1885. These aimed at assisting in the development of adult minds and at the same time allowed us to gain experience in public speaking. He united the boys' and girls' halls, as a lecture hall, by opening the folding doors that formed the central dividing wall between them. Thus an enormous auditorium was created and, by pushing together two small bow-shaped platforms at one end, created a comfortably large stage.

Tourian would give us plans for lectures on scientific, moral and historical subjects that we would enlarge and develop as lectures, preparing ourselves to deliver them to the public without any notes in our hands.

Lectures took place on Sundays, after the church service and after everyone had eaten their main meal of the day. Adult men and women, girls and young men would all follow the lectures with great enthusiasm and pleasure. The women and girls would assemble in the girls' hall and the men and boys in the boys' hall, all seated at the desks there.

The speaker of the day would step onto the stage, from where his voice could be heard by the listeners in both halls. This allowed him and them to mostly see each other through the opened dividing doors. The village clergy, councillors, trustees, community organisation officials and the mixed crowd of people would always fill the halls and listen with the greatest interest to their sons' attempts at speaking. The latter, as if through the Miracle of the Upper Room, discovered their tongues and spoke about various subjects. Of course we inexperienced and new orators often displayed faults, hesitation and failings, but despite these, we talked about things that were new for the people.

It was here that the people heard new scientific things in the light of new investigations. They listened to something of the history of discoveries, descriptions of engineering and mechanical inventions, biographies of great men – both national* and foreign - moral reflections and incidents from national history. Both speakers and people gained equally from these lectures: the former gained in

---

* The word used here is *azkayin*; it is not clear from the text whether the author means Armenian or Ottoman. I am inclined to think the former.

developing a subject and presenting it in a cogent manner, and the latter, for its part, learnt new things and became linked to the development of the scientific and civilised world.

Tourian never missed any of the speakers' weaknesses or failings and, in the days following the lectures, would point out, in his witty and funny way, where they had gone wrong and making them familiar with public speaking using this practical method.

Apart from the lectures' immediate practical good, the lectures were a sort of attempt at examination for the people concerning work carried on in the school. The satisfaction generated by these attempts increased the love and spirit of sacrifice the villagers had towards its children's school.

Alongside these special assemblies of both sexes for lectures, Tourian also organised lectures specifically for women. Forming a sort of collaboration, they would get together on certain days, either in the halls or in various houses, when they would sing *sharagans* [canticles] or patriotic songs and where those who had the ability spoke in turn. The speakers presented incidents from the Gospels and Bible to those present and extracted moral and spiritual lessons from them. These women's gatherings were arranged like those of the Protestant Sisters – they were a form of mutual educational help. Usually Mrs. Srpouhi Mardigian, Mrs. Yeghisapet S. Sinanian, Mrs. Shoushan Drezian (mother of Diyonis Kahana Drezian) and several others spoke at them.

After Tourian departed, we - his students - continued to organise lectures. These were held even in coffee houses, bringing the word closer to the people. It was similar in my day, when lectures were organised in Der-Garabedian's coffee house. This was located in the middle of the market area of the village, run by Delo Krikor, and was quite spacious.

Tourian had a special love of the theatre; his brother's – Bedros Tourian's[*] - spirit lived in him to a great extent. Even before Tourian's time the people of Bardizag had the taste for theatrical performances, especially at the feast of Sts Vartanants. The tragedy of St. Vartan was staged on that feast day, having become a community tradition. The generation produced by Shirinian had been encouraged by performances put on by the theatre in Constantinople in those days of Armenian national revival. They collaborated in bringing to the stage important incidents and people from Armenian history – King Ardashes the Conqueror, King Arshag II, General Vartan - and other dramas by Terzian, Beshigtashlian and Tourian's tragedies. These they staged before a virgin audience, impressing it and gaining much applause.

I can recall, among these young men, Garabed Mgerian, Mihran Khacherian, Haroutiun Der-Antreasian, Mr. Takvor, Krikor Kiutian and others who, as art-

---

[*] The famous Armenian poet.

loving actors, would organise performances of plays in Bardizag, in earlier days, using Mgerian's *tolalekh* as a theatre.

Tourian utilised the upper boys' hall as a theatre, putting together the small platforms from both halls as a stage. By doing this, the girls' hall became the backstage area, where the actors got ready and dressed in their costumes to go on stage. We, his students, were the actors, who took both male and female roles, as the strict customs of the time forbade girls or women from taking part. The plays, apart from national tragedies, were also taken from incidents in the Bible and from works written by the Italian playwrights Metastos and Alfieri. Thus the stage would be filled with Adam and Eve, the first family; Joseph and his brothers; Saul and David, etc.

In those early days the stage was very poorly set up with virtually no decor. There was only a curtain to close the stage on one side and another one, on the other side, to screen off what was the backstage area. The actors almost always appeared on stage costumed in clothes worn at the New Year celebrations according to their taste and obtained from various houses. They generally had no reference to the period of the play being performed. The actors would say their lines, which they had learned by heart standing opposite one another. They did so with the simplicity of children in the kindergarten, without any passion, emotion, movement or expression relating to the characters they played. But this was the beginning of this art, a sort of experiment that, over a period of time, could bring forth artistic values and merits.

Encouraged by the response to these performances, Tourian later had one of the school's basement halls made into a theatre, furnished with simple wooden benches set out in rows on the earth floor. He also took advantage of a photographer's visit to the village, having him photograph one or two stage backdrops, doors and half-curtains. He had a quite a wide and deep stage built, with its various divisions and furnishings and, to one side, a room for the actors. The costs for all this work was paid for by Tourian out of his own modest pocket (he received five Ottoman liras a month which, added to his portion of the collections accrued for five summer Masses, meant that he had an income of 15-20 Ottoman liras a year), payable from the profits made from the performances.

Thus Bardizag had, for the first time, a hall set up with all the necessary fittings as a theatre. Performances were staged under the direction of Karnig Effendi Giureghian, who was the producer. He had considerable skills and expertise in this work, having worked with the Uskudar theatre troupe in his youth.

New plays were translated from foreign languages, and produced with better staging and picturing real life, although to do so was more demanding and difficult. They were mostly old patriotic dialogues, but we students gradually improved our acting skills, and were able to put some life and feeling in our expressions and movements. Mr. Takvor and Mr. Krikor Kiutian both showed great talent in these performances, the latter having been brought in from working in the market. Hagop Sekgiulian, Y. Der-Antreasian, Krikor Goudjoukian, me and others did so later.

Apart from this, Mr. Takvor, K. Kiutian and one of our friends H. Sekgiulian created comedies taken from Bardizag life. These were staged after the main performances, and were, if not the most artistic, certainly the most enjoyable and hilarious part, putting everyday life before the audience, in its own language, costumes and faces.

Years after Tourian had left Bardizag we, the generation he prepared, created a Graduates Union under my leadership. We had, as our aim, the construction of a large hall with all its fittings and conveniences, to honour and glorify the work of our much-loved vartabed.

The union was able to collect 150 Ottoman liras from its members, which it spent on the preparation and furnishing of the theatre. It joined the hall next to the Tourian theatre, which had the same area and dimensions to it, without compromising the structure of the school. It did this by removing the wall dividing them and replacing it with pillars to take the weight of the structure of the building. The stage was enlarged, taking up most of one end, with a room on either side of it. The floor of the auditorium was raised by an arshin (28 inches or 70cm) and a wooden floor installed, protecting the audience from the cold. Finally this large auditorium was fitted with comfortable wooden seats in long rows for 1,000 people. Apart from the exits, two new doors were opened up in the lower part of the theatre as fire exits, allowing the audience to leave quickly if there was danger. The four large windows in the theatre, which overlooked the school playground, also acted as emergency exits, as their sills were close to the ground.

The theatre ceilings were also panelled with wood; all this resulted in us having a large hall with every convenience specifically for an audience to attend lectures, events, theatrical productions and gatherings. This auditorium was presented by the Graduates Union to its school on the 20th anniversary of the beginning of Tourian's work.[*]

Plans were made, on the occasion of this presentation by the Graduates Union, to celebrate the 25th anniversary of the Bardizag community schools. Tourian had already left Armash by then, to take up the prelacy of Izmir, and was replaced by Torkom Vartabed Koushagian, who had come for a holiday to Bardizag.

A special delegation went to Karts village near Yalova to invite Bishop Stepannos Hovagimian, the prelate of Izmid (Nicomedia), to preside over the planned celebration. The prelate, occupied with the construction of public fountains, was unable to leave his work and the people of Bardizag who, left to themselves, arranged a brilliant event, at which the senior priest, Garabed Kahana Mkhalian spoke, presenting Bardizag's educational work until Tourian's arrival. Professor Apraham Der-Hagopian also spoke on behalf of the old graduates, telling stories

---

[*] This was in 1900.

from his student life. One of Tourian's students, Y. Der-Antreasian, spoke in the name of the new graduates, and I also spoke in the name of the Graduates Union, detailing the refurbishment of the theatre. Finally Torkom Vartabed Koushagian, as chairman of this event, lauded Tourian's educational work in Bardizag and the sacrifices made by the people for the sake of education, through which the community schools in Bardizag had achieved notable positions in the province with their order and progress.

We were able to enjoy the short-lived days of freedom in 1908 in this theatre, with performances by the famous Russian Armenian Armenian-Apelian artistic group. The villagers saw plays, brilliantly performed at the greatest artistic level, written by O. Telliot and Corrado, as well as Shakespeare's 'Hamlet', Shirvanzade's 'For honour' and others like Aharonian's 'Vale of Tears' that had become classics, all performed by this company.

It was this auditorium that, once again, saved us from the 'open and closed' crisis* during those stormy days of freedom, giving us the opportunity, within its walls, to convene frequent political and social gatherings.

6. Tourian's family, social and personal life

To really get to know the man, it is necessary to see and study him in his personal and social life. It is there that he betrays his spirit, freed

of the outward mannerisms of work and officialdom.

In previous pages I said that Tourian was a lightly-built, slim, 20 year-old young man above middle height with premature hair on his face when he first came to Bardizag. His thick moustache and beard gave him additional manly grace. He was a young man who gave the impression of being a mature one. In the early days he was given an apartment overlooking the street near the Torosians' newly-built house. This was in the lower part of the village, in a valley which, due to the winter rain and the overflow from the fountains, flooded with water, the sound of which was heard in the whole street. That part of the village was comparatively damper than the rest during the rainy and cold season. Tourian was thus, from the first days, badly affected by the damp and fell into bed ill, creating a crisis about his health among the notables. He was prone to colds, and Bardizag's climate, especially during that season, encouraged them.

When his chest was affected, Tourian's usually cheerful face was clouded, which killed his disposition to laugh and speak and painful thoughts upset his bright and happy spirit.

The villagers, with the greatest sympathy for their much-loved 'son', whom they seemed to have adopted, moved his home to the upper part of the village to a place

---

* The author does not elaborate on this statement anywhere.

near St. Minas. Khalfa Bedros Azarian's house (his brother was Mgerdich Kahana Azarian), which was built on a dry area on the edge of a steep slope, was given to him. This house was usually known as 'Great Bedros tower' as it was taller than the ones surrounding it and was buried in the surrounding greenery.

The change of house and place were beneficial for his health and he recovered and set to work. The winter months, after that, didn't affect him. The dry cold of the snowy season invigorated him and he came safely through them to the bright and joyful days of spring. These latter days were the preparation for Bardizag's incomparable summer with its greenness, flower scents, birdsong, and wonderful panoramas that filled his soul with cheerfulness and delight and strengthened his physical being.

Tourian had come to Bardizag alone. His father, mother and brother (Akribas Effendi) remained in Constantinople, in Uskudar, in their fathers' quarter of the city. His poor experience of the first year, despite the family-like careful attention he received, made it imperative that he had selfless motherly attention to protect him in his home. As a result, because it wasn't considered reasonable for the family to move, his aunt,[*] Hadji Hanem, came and occupied the place in Tourian's house that we couldn't fill.

Hadji Hanem, deprived of the opportunity of having a family of her own, was a substitute mother to her elder sister's son in his migration; she cheered him and his modest home with swift and complete motherly care, having the role of his guardian angel.

Hadji was a small, strong, energetic woman who didn't know fatigue, and whose movements spoke more than her lips did. She was quite taciturn, moving about instead of speaking. She cooked and cleaned and brightened that house and Tourian, with his lessons, devoted himself to his books, students and school with his heart and soul.

He was a good eater, like everyone from Constantinople, with particular tastes in food. He loved tasty aroma-rich Constantinople dishes, always accompanied by a sweet and Izmid's famous white *salamoura* cheese. She was the best at choosing the right items and the school's housekeeper, known by everyone by the nickname Tsvazegh Yeres (Fried Egg Face) for the dry, red skin on his face, who bought foodstuffs for the school, would bring them to her. She would choose the best and then make various good things with her small, delicate fingers. She prepared beans cooked with vegetables in olive oil, for example, that Tourian loved, as well as small stuffed vine leaf parcels *(dolma)* and other wonderful dishes made with aubergines etc., all of which enriched Tourian's modest meals.

In those days, life was very cheap in Bardizag, with good foodstuffs and good quality meat plentiful. Eggs, many kinds of fruit and chickens were all produced in the village, and fish was brought from the sea every morning.

---

[*] Mother's sister.

Tourian ate with great appetite and after his meal his face, showing that his stomach was satisfied, expressed his happy disposition, giving birth to sweet conversation and humorous anecdotes. At home Tourian would make innocent witticisms with Hadji, making the name sweeter and more decorative, calling her *Yerousaghemabadiv Hadji* (Jerusalem-honoured Hadji). Little Hadji would gently smile at her spoiled child's jokes, especially when she saw that, thanks to her care, his face filled out and took on a healthy colouring, that he grew in height and his body achieved maturity.

We've seen, in previous pages, that Tourian gave much to Bardizag and the villagers; Bardizag, in its turn, made him healthy, curing the delicateness of his constitution, making him able to withstand the pressures of his exhausting work.

Tourian's house was quite a distance from the school, so he took his midday meal there, saving his strength and energy. The school housekeeper would bring Tourian his lunch from his own house, giving him, at the same time, a piece of paper which only he could read, with the account of the day's purchases written on it, which Tourian always paid without demur. For Tourian, every activity, no matter how insignificant, had its humorous side, which he liked to stir up. For example, when the housekeeper presented the daily accounts, in which the main items of expenditure were written and priced, the final item was always 'sundries', written as *mainri-miunri* [this and that], which Tourian was used to looking for as the inevitable part of it. Looking at us, and saying the words the housekeeper had written down, he would laugh while he was still eating.

Tourian, if he had his Hadji in the house that nourished his gaiety over meals, he had us - his students, colleagues and friends - in the school and almost everywhere - on his walks, whom he liked to joke with. He would take an incident from the life and experiences of one of us and make a comic and witty verbal picture of it. Our literary, acting and oratorical attempts provided him with unending subjects for his wit, and happy laughter would completely overwhelm us and our surroundings. None of us could assume that we would remain free of those sudden and sweet witticisms. We felt our weaknesses at the time and tried to inject lively knowledge and judgement into our various attempts.

For example, one of us, in the steps of Milton and Pakradouni, wanted to write the legend of Adam and Eve, and the following words had flowed from his pen, in classical modern Armenian, in the description of paradise:

> You could see the haughty, brave imperious lion's mane there,
> And Adam measured, oh, a hundred loads.

Tourian read this for the fist time, in its innocent simplicity, and shouted, 'It's wonderful...!' through a suppressed gale of laughter, and added, 'These lines would have been even better with a small amendment.' Then he read the same lines again, with his change:

> 'You could see the haughty, brave imperious lion's mane there,

And Adam measured, uh uh, a hundred loads.'

He then added, 'Changing "oh" to "uh, uh", the words become even more expressive, showing the effort he is making to count the loads.'

It wasn't possible to remain unfeeling towards Tourian's observation, and spirited laughter erupted in the room.

The same author wrote, in another place: 'A star twinkled on the mist-bound horizon...'

The author's contradiction was plain to see, and Tourian, amid an explosion of laughter, shouted at the author, 'I must congratulate you on your eyesight, being able to see a twinkling star in the mist...'

None of us could assume that we would be free of his sudden and wonderful witticisms that were full of insight, and we were all aware of our failings. We therefore tried to use alert intelligence and criticism towards our own attempts.

The summer was the time we friends looked for. Tourian and we students loved, in the evening after school had ended, to go to a hill at the western end of the village called the Near Upper Fields, where one's gaze rested on a marvellous panorama containing the entire village, the gardens and vineyards, lower fields and the sea, all cradled by the hills enclosing the horizon.

There were several acacia and willow trees there, under whose delicate shade we would sit on stools and rest, next to a simple village coffee house. Apart from us there were very few people there on weekdays, with everyone busy with his work. We had the opportunity to spend happy hours there in a family atmosphere, talking, laughing and joking, sometimes playing a backgammon match or sometimes reading aloud – Tourian couldn't go anywhere without a book – and holding academic arguments. When the huge and cooled sun disappeared beyond the sea, the shadows gathered around us and it grew dark, we would begin the journey back to our homes, along the village's winding upper path. Our group would consist of fewer people when one or the other of us would leave and go down, through the mulberry groves, to our homes.

In the summer the annual holiday period gave us greater opportunities to enjoy ourselves. Tourian and we students utilised the time to go on pilgrimages, outside the village or in the area. We would go to places close by or further away such as to Manoushag or St. Minas. We would also visit sheepfolds and farms, mills and vegetable fields and vineyards. Sometimes we went to the banks of the Ovadjekh River - to the edge of the wonderful river or into deep shadows - still wet from the morning dew, to spend the complete day, sometimes the evening and all night too, enjoying Bardizag's cool, dry night air.

Our days slipped away in these beautiful places, with the simplicity of patriarchal custom. We became one with nature, squeezing life's essence and blazing spiritual enthusiasm from it. So it continued, for ten long years that are impossible to forget, and that he never forgot in the whole of his life.

After leaving Bardizag he found himself more greatly esteemed, more famous and in even higher positions. He longed for the life he led in Bardizag, which was never to be repeated. He always spoke about them, wanting to relive them with his feelings and in his dreams.

Hadji left Bardizag a few years later, giving her place to Tourian's mother and father - who was called *Zemba* [chisel] Hadji Apraham - when his brother, Akribas Effendi, having married, had moved into his own house. The notable traits in Tourian's character were made clear to us with these new acquaintances: he got his noble, scientific and self-contained seriousness from his mother and his subtle, witty happiness from his father.

His parents, from the beginning to the end, shared their son's company. When, several years later, his father Hadji Apraham died, he was buried in Bardizag's soil, which his son loved so much. Very soon afterwards his mother returned to Constantinople, to Akribas Effendi's house in Uskudar. This was when Tourian went to the Seminary of Armash to fulfil a national need and for work to be done there. This was near Bardizag, and he was able to relax occasionally by visiting the village.

Bardizag's winter, however, provided trouble for Tourian and his friends, while he was still with them. At that time the descent to the school or church in the early mornings was difficult for Tourian, at least in the vicinity of his home, as it was impossible for him, with his height, to retain his balance. He slipped, fell and was slightly injured several times on that frozen slope, although with no lasting effects.

The worst of these falls, however, was in his home, with the sudden collapse, under his weight, of a rotted timber balcony. He fell to the ground breaking his leg, making it impossible for him to stand. He was rescued by being carried on the strong back of one of our colleagues who composed the 'Adam and Eve' legend, and remained bedridden for many long days.

How sad those days were! The sudden cessation of the long years of games, dances and gaiety wiped the smiles from our faces and ended, at least temporarily, the revivifying effects of laughter in our souls. Dr. Garabed Atanasian, the American High School's physician, cared for him and bound up his leg until the bone had knitted completely. Despite this, his leg always remained frail, and he would occasionally have it treated by visiting the hot springs in Boursa, staying in his brother's daughter-in-law (Mrs Foulig's) parents' house in the Set Bashi quarter of the town.

Thus Tourian lived and laboured in Bardizag. He was a man of ideals, industry and great results. He had a happy, witty and noble character, which never allowed him to hurt anyone, big or small. He loved everyone and was loved by all in return. Those ten years became the most beautiful pages written in the history of Bardizag with the expressions of his life there.

121 – New ordination of kahanas in Bardizag

In Bardizag the need was seen, in 1884-1885,[*] for the ordination of priests for the church. The number of priests was very low, with some leaving and others dying, while those remaining were old and very tired. Of the old ones only Garabed Kahana Mkhalian, as the leading priest, Mgerdich Kahana Azarian,[†] Simon Kahana Tavitian and Krikor Kahana Paboudjian remained. The latter, however, had been ordained in the village of Nor Kiugh (New Village) near Iznik and later went to Alexandria, Egypt, working as a priest there, returning to his home village of Bardizag, where he was only a guest.

So the priests and the parish council, in a joint meeting, decided on three new candidates for the priesthood. These were: *Diratsou* Hovhannes Aprahamian (the parish council secretary), *Diratsou* Garabed Deyirmendjian (teacher of singing) and *Diratsou* Garabed Ghazarosian (an honourable merchant and fervent believer).

The result of the election was communicated to the prelate, Bishop Stepannos Hovagimian, who endorsed it. Bishop Madteos Izmirlian, who was Tourian's spiritual parent,[‡] was invited to Bardizag to conduct the ordination.

When Bishop Madteos arrived in Bardizag, the representatives of a number of villagers who were opposed to the election results presented themselves and, citing the insufficiency of the candidates' calling and their lack of value, introduced three others. These were better educated men from families well known in the village. They were Mihran Khacherian (painter), Boghos Nazigian (teacher) and Nigoghos Kechedjian (son-in-law of the Mgerians). They were of the Shirinian generation.

Bishop Madteos told them to present their protest and their list to the council, suggesting a final list of candidates from both sides for ordination be decided upon by all. He then withdrew to a separate room, awaiting the meeting's decision.

After days of negotiation, agreement was finally reached that the original list of candidates would stand. Acknowledgment was made as to the worthiness of those presented by the protestors. It was also agreed to delay the ordination of the latter, so that the village wouldn't have more priests than it needed. This situation would last until such time as gaps in the ranks of the priests appeared and the opportunity for new ordinations arose, with these men being ready candidates.

Upon this agreement, the bishop carried out the ordinations of Hovhannes Aprahamian, Garabed Deyirmendjian and Garabed Ghazarosian, calling them, in accordance with church rules, Sahag Kahana Aprahamian, Mesrob Kahana

---

[*] It would seem that the date should be 1882-1883, as an article of that year (*Hairenik*, March 22, 1883) comments on the split in the community of Bardizag over the candidates. See Hagop Der-Hagopian, *Bardizage khadoudig*, Paris, 1960, pp.182-183.

[†] This priest is accorded the title *avantabah*, possibly meaning sacristan or sexton.

[‡] This means that he carried out Tourian's ordination as a celibate monk giving him the rank of *apegha*.

Deyirmendjian and Nerses Kahana Ghazarosian. The three priests withdrew for their 40 day seclusion and preparation period, and then began working as priests with the old ones.

Through these ordinations the council lost its secretary and the church and school its singing teacher. On this occasion one of Tourian's first graduate students, Hovhannes Djergayian, who had not shown a preference for teaching, and was out of work, was appointed parish council secretary, and *Diratsou* Roupen Aprahamian, who was one of the new people, as singing teacher. Belonging to the Tourian generation, although he hadn't properly graduated, he had a certain skill and ability in church singing and served in the church as assistant musician.

122 – Stepannos Vartabed Hovgimian, prelate of the Izmid diocese: biographical outline, work and character

Stepannos Vartabed Hovagimian, whose baptismal name was Souren Hovagimian, was born in 1846 in Izmid, the son of a modest family. From his youth he showed the wish to study, and was accepted into the Armash theological seminary. Not being able to stay there long, he went from Armash to Izmir for the same reason. There he met the vartabed Shahnazarian, whose sympathy he was able to capture. He later went to the Noubar-Shahnazarian school in Khaskiugh, where he was a student for some years. He was then appointed an assistant teacher in the same school, during Bishop Nerses Varjabedian's term as inspector. He was ordained as a deacon by the bishop.

When Bishop Nerses Varjabedian was elected prelate of Izmir in 1871, Deacon Souren accompanied him and worked in the Izmid diocese under his authority. The bishop ordained him a celibate monk in 1873, renaming him Stepannos, in memory of the late famous prelate of the same diocese Bishop Stepannos Aghavni. Bishop Nerses was elected Patriarch of Constantinople in 1876 and took up his new position, retaining his post of diocesan prelate of Izmid and appointing Stepannos Vartabed as his locum tenens there. Stepannos Vartabed held the position until 1880, when the provincial assembly elected him prelate of the diocese, a position that he fulfilled with vigour, personal ability and good results until 1915, the year of the deportations and genocide.

The provincial assembly voted, in 1886, to send him to Echmiadzin to be consecrated bishop of Izmid. He received his consecration at the hand of the newly-elected Catholicos of All Armenians, Magar, and returned to his diocese.

Bishop Hovagimian was closely involved with public events in Bardizag during his long prelacy. He visited the village at least once a year, on the feast day of St. James of Nisibis,[*] in December, where he remained and preached until the start of

---

[*] The main Armenian Apostolic churches in Bardizag, all standing on the same site, were dedicated to this saint – *Mtspina Sourp Hagop*.

the Christmas period.* He would then leave and return to his prelacy in Izmid, to chair the Christmas festivities in the town.

A number of public works and historic events took place during his prelacy. Among these we can recall Hovsep Vartabed Ayvazian's return to the mother church;† the Shirinian (See Section 104), Lousinian (See Section 110) and Tourian educational regimes (See Section 120); the construction of the new school (See Section 120); the refurbishment of the church and the building of the *Sourp Takavor* [Holy King] church (See Section 124); the new *ghonakh*; the community bath house (See Section 139) and the new road (See Section 116); two ordinations of priests (See Section 121 and 141); the building of the Helvadjian silk spinning factory and the knotty problem connected with the water it required (See Section 126); the purchase of the building for the kindergarten (See Section 148) and the walling of the old cemetery (See Section 127); the preparations connected with the Tourian theatre and its furnishing (See Section 120 and 147); the immigration of the Laz Armenians into the Bardizag area and their settlement as well as many others which formed part and parcel of that era of Bardizag's history, and in which he had his prelate's, organiser's and supervisory role.

Bishop Stepannos Hovagimian was an irreproachable, spiritual, zealous, conservative, industrious, constructive churchman who lived very simply. He had great managerial ability and was boldly presumptive. His large prelacy, made up of more than 40 towns and villages, with an Armenian population of about 150,000 people, stretched over the governorships of Izmid, Bolu and part of the province of Boursa, which he ran, until the end, with the greatest vigour, authority and personality.

He knew how to communicate with, and was respected by, the government in his relations with it and was loved and respected by the overwhelming majority of the people in his prelacy. He was also able to capture sympathy on every side – among the province's non-Armenian tribes, the Muslims and Christians - showing great care for, and defending, their public and individual works and woes.

When he had occasion to make ordinary pastoral visits, without favouring great or small, large or small communities, he always took his large prelacy files with him. These he edited himself, without the aid of a secretary or assistant, as well as all the letters and official correspondence, which numbered in the thousands. He was never the delicate, severe individual who enjoyed rest and enjoyment. He would stay in one of the local church's rooms, no matter how unprepossessing, poor or unready it was, enjoying meals provided by one house or another in turn wherever he went. He was always, without fail, present at the morning and evening services wherever he was. He kept, with the greatest faithfulness, all the canonical fasts, even when he was unwell or sick.

---

* The Armenian Apostolic church celebrates Christmas (Theophany) on January 6.
† A well-known Catholic churchman who returned to the Armenian Apostolic Church. See Section 95.

As a churchman of high rank, he had a certain amount of education and speaking ability. He had a good, strong voice, and knew church music, which he often sang. He knew Turkish and French well. He often preached, even occasionally during the weekday evening services, in the simple, understandable language used by the people, sometimes reducing what he said to vulgar and basic terms, using sayings from the Gospels and holy works as his texts.

He almost always travelled on horseback, winter or summer, sometimes in the rain or snow, by the most dangerous and unsafe roads, visiting various corners of his vast diocese, without staying just in its centre.

This great churchman, despite these praiseworthy personal abilities and customs, had his human weaknesses and faults that occasionally made thinking and educated minds rebel against him.

He was extremely stubborn and egotistical, and was inclined to close his ears to advice given him. This was especially true of those who, as educated people, gave themselves the right to enlighten him and suggest caution with regard to the results of whatever work he was engaged in. He would not give way, sticking to what he knew, even though it was only the public good those people thought of. For him, those people simply spoke nonsense and were filled with the wish to make much of themselves. He felt that they were trying to smother and complicate the work being done under a deluge of empty words and explanations. He dealt with this sort of people everywhere, without mercy, and would always approach simple souls, who could be easily managed, to complete his plans. These people, with him at their head, would be enough to do what was right and reasonable in terms of decisions and actions. Thus he was the great friend of spiritually poor people, who understood him and whom he led wherever he wanted.

He was a man of biting, wounding sarcasm towards those he didn't like, even when they were present, as if to annoy and drive them from his presence. These excesses of his often resulted in loss of patience and gave rise to arguments and scandal, causing damage to his authority and esteem. To counter this he was always surrounded by the 'hadji aghas'* whose company he preferred. He was the central and domineering personality among them, who hung on his every word with the greatest respect and humility. Each had become worthy of his trust either by a real or feigned charitable and community spirit. They knew how to take advantage of his sympathy towards them, wishing to centralise community works and affairs in their hands.

He could not accept meetings and constitutional organisation, in other words democratic principles, being born with a dictatorial character. He only recognised one kind of meeting: that of village parish councils or notables. These were always made up of his men who, in concert with the priests, could realise his plans and will everywhere. It was said that he hated the constitution, something that had

---

* A derogatory term meaning conservative people of position and wealth.

considerable truth in it. For him, a church council was indeed sufficient, made up of the notables and priests he liked. This weakness of his sometimes made him a party to, and defender of, fraudsters and profiteers, with his unwitting trust in them being the reason for their fall into temptation by profiteering.

His hatred and opposition for his enemies reached unusual and extreme lengths. It sometimes reached the level of the persecution of the best people who, concerned for the public good, were tempted to criticise the people he trusted and make their activities seem suspicious. Completely filled with jealousy of his authority, he would arm himself and consider those criticisms and interventions as dangers to it. What was worse, he would try, with all his strength, to destroy the best and most beneficial public works created by his enemies, considering them to be unjustified obstacles in what he considered to be his monopoly.

In other words, he had friends that always remained so until the end of his life, and enemies whom he could never forgive until his death. He was a man of strange contradictions – of both positive and negative virtues. He was a good, able and active churchman, but didn't want to see any other greatness, value and individuality around him, only slaves and yes-men. One master was enough: as if 'a man cannot serve two masters' was the tenet that formed the basis of his administrative rule.

We should be just, however, and say that his dedication to his people was without limit. He was a great churchman, despite all his faults, and brave and intrepid in defending the people's interests and existence.

He travelled, often on foot, on the long roads of deportation, with his people, comforting them. He was their unquenchable symbol of hope. He led his people in the deserts as Moses did and suffered with them. Dispensing solicitude and care around him and later, when he began the return journey to his prelacy, Izmid, his grateful people gave him a wonderful demonstration of love and esteem. They unhitched the horses from his carriage and pulling it themselves, to the sound of clapping and good wishes, in an atmosphere of incredible enthusiasm.

With the arrival of the Kemalist forces he left with his flock once more, to Bulgaria. He settled in Sofia and, in his final years, was prelate of the Armenians of that country. He was always loved and respected and died on hospitable Bulgarian soil at a great patriarchal age and was given a magnificent funeral.

123 – The ordination of a young man from Bardizag as a celibate monk

The prelate of the diocese, Stepannos Vartabed Hovagimian, had returned from Echmiadzin in 1886 having been consecrated a bishop. He was petitioned by Mr. Hagop Pirenian, of the martyr's family[*] who requested ordination as a celibate monk.

---

*   See Section 64.

Hagop Pirenian, faithful to the traditions of his father's house, was an honourable, spiritual and religious young man. Giving his spare time to reading church books and writings, he faithfully followed church services both morning and evening, living an almost hermit-like life.

He was one of the students of the Shirinian period and had been able to acquire considerable education and improve himself. He acted as an assistant teacher in Bardizag's community schools, usually taking religious studies and church history lessons. He continued teaching during the first years of the Tourian era, when the life and work of the vartabed from Constantinople emphasised the long-held wish within him.

The prelate always needed assistant clerics to collaborate with him and help in the work of his extensive diocese. He therefore ordained the young man, based on the certificate of good conduct issued by the Bardizag parish council. This was his first religious ordination and took place in 1886.

The ceremony took place in the church in Izmid, and Hagop Pirenian was renamed Hovhannes Apegha,[*] it being the name of the martyr. On this occasion Tourian, who was present as his spiritual guarantor, preached one of his superb sermons. He presented the lives and works of great Armenian Apostolic churchmen of the past, putting lessons and examples before the newly ordained apegha. This was to create the spirit of those great men and the grace of their virtues in him.

Hovhannes Apegha Pirenian was a good, honourable and zealous cleric, acting for a time as the deputy prelate in various parts of the diocese, making pastoral visits. Then, right up until his death, he became the permanent preacher in the church of the densely-populated Armenian quarter of St. Garabed in Adabazar, making his home there. Unfortunately his life was short; he wasted away under the pressure of work and pious denial, dying there after only a few years of office, and where he was esteemed and loved.

The people of Adabazar had taken to this promising, old-fashioned churchman and made his illness the subject of their care and compassion. They felt that he deserved their approbation for his dedication to his church and the improvement of the people's religious and spiritual life.

124 – The repair of St. James church and the building of the church of the Holy King

People saw the need, a few years after the community schools were constructed, to carry out important repairs to St. James church. After a life of over 40 years,[†] although it was strongly built and would last, the plaster on the walls, the eaves and

---

[*] Apegha is the lowest ordained monastic rank.
[†] It was built in 1830-1831, so this must have been in about 1870-1871.

wooden roof had all suffered as a result of rain and the passage of time. A full, basic repair of the building was therefore begun to prevent the damage from increasing and to save large-scale, expensive repairs in the future. The opportunity was taken to re-gild all three altars. Thus the church building regained its integrity and beauty, the work costing approximately 200 Ottoman liras, paid for by the people.

I have not been able to determine if it was several years earlier or later than this that the building of a new, second church in Bardizag was started. This was despite the one church being sufficient for the population of the village until then. The village was, however, swiftly increasing in both population and size, especially towards the high Near Upper Fields. This was a parish that was some distance from the church. It meant that devout people had a difficult trek in winter to attend services morning and evening. There was also a group of people still living an almost hermit-like existence nearby, who venerated the pilgrimage site, its traditions and memory.

The plan was to build a chapel-church of modest proportions to retain the memory of the old days. At the same time it would serve to keep the feelings for church-going and devoutness alive in the people who lived in the Near Upper Fields parish. They would have somewhere for them nearby. They could go there, morning and evening, to pray or make a vow, to make the sign of the cross or light a candle and have a separate evening service on Saturday night and a Mass on Sunday morning.

A neat little church was therefore built with funds donated by the people, named the Holy King, whose care was entrusted to the relatives and descendants of the hermit group, the Jamgochian family.

No decision was made for a priest to be based there permanently, to prevent any separatist feelings between the two churches. Instead, an arrangement was made for one or two of the priests from the lower (St James) church to go to this new church in turn on a Saturday evening and Sunday morning to conduct services.

This arrangement continued for some time, but was discontinued later as the original aim was never justified and the people preferred to attend St. James church.

The church of the Holy King, however, always remained open in its unfinished state, with naked walls and without furnishings, where old people went to pray and receive spiritual comfort.

125 – Khachig Agha Avedian becomes a silk spinning factory owner

Khachig Agha Avedian was the son of a modest Protestant family. He was orphaned early. His widowed mother, to keep and bring up her children, had gone as a servant to Constantinople for many long years. She died and left her young son, Khachig, in whom she saw enterprise and ability, a modest sum of money.

Khachig Avedian started a bakery with that money, in the days when such a commercial enterprise was profitable in Bardizag. He became successful in a short time. An alert person and gifted with commercial instincts, he gradually enlarged his business and succeeded in adding the sale of European flour to it. He grew wealthy in this latter business and built an enviable position for himself in the Bardizag marketplace.

After a time his mercantile competence and the experience he had gained led him to try to make a profit from Bardizag's main crop – silkworm cocoons. During the fresh cocoon season, when they were plentiful, the villager, short of ready cash, wasn't too demanding in terms of prices for them. He was forced, not having patience and to gain time, to sell the crop as soon as he could in the Public Debt Administration's public auction. Avedian took part in it, becoming Hovhannes Effendi Helvadjian's powerful competitor who, for many years, had operated the Saroukhanians' abandoned silk spinning factory, which belonged to European owners, on a rental basis.

Avedian would dry and stockpile the cocoons he purchased, financiers in Constantinople advancing him credit. Then, taking advantage of the rise in price and the lack of cocoons on the market in winter, he would sell his stock in either Constantinople or Boursa. He thus secured great profits and, through his trading enterprises, made a secure and trustworthy position for himself and became a well-known name in those markets.

The European owners of the Saroukhanians' silk spinning factory had been forced, until that time, to retain their ownership due to the fall in prices of everything to do with silk-making skills. I referred to this in previous pages.* They now saw the resurgence of the trade after Pasteur's discovery and decided that the time had come to sell their silk spinning factory, which had never brought them much of a profit through rental. So they suggested to Helvadjian that he bought it for a modest sum. Helvadjian tortured them with suggestions for huge discounts on the price, convinced that they wouldn't find another buyer. He was mistaken. His commercial juggling and wish to profit by his position made the owners turn their attention to other potential customers.

Avedian heard, through his contacts, about the owners' intentions and their irritation in the face of Helvadjian's games. They only wanted to transfer ownership to a buyer for the paltry sum of 1,000 Ottoman liras. Avedian approached the owners skilfully and, without making it public, offered to buy the silk spinning factory for the asking price. The owners agreed and, without a word of the transaction reaching Helvadjian's ears, the deal was completed. Helvadjian was faced with a fait accompli.

Helvadjian was annoyed, having lost the opportunity, but what could he do? The prize had slipped through his fingers. He was forced to empty the factory and end the work of years. He had to give way to Avedian, who was now the owner of a large silk spinning factory, much land and a cocoon warehouse – all for the small sum of 1,000 Ottoman liras.

---

* See Section 97.

Thus Avedian became a silk spinning factory owner, having his own works in Bardizag, just as the Mgerians had in the past, and began to operate it, while continuing his trade in flour.*

126 – Helvadjian builds his own silk spinning factory in Bardizag. Helvadjian's water problem

Having been balked, Helvadjian took in hand the building of his own new silk spinning factory. He chose a piece of land at the western end of the village near the old cemetery as the site for it. The Mgerians' abandoned factory was nearby, also owned by European financiers; Helvadjian didn't want to purchase it, considering its price to be greater than the cost of building a new one.

His years of brilliant trading activity began to deteriorate with the building of this silk spinning factory. Its completion would bring about his final bankruptcy, resulting in the well-known house of Helvadjian passing into history like others before it.

Helvadjian purchased a number of groves of mulberry trees in the area through intermediaries for his new silk spinning factory. He then secured the piece of land he'd selected for the factory, which cost him a considerable sum of money. He then began the construction of the factory with a capacity of over 100 *mandjelekhs* [spindles]. He also had a small but neat house built next to it for his family to live in. This was separate from a large cocoon storehouse of several storeys that he had built with individual, separate floors.†

He ordered a huge steam cauldron *(shokegatsa)*, as well as mechanical assemblies, spindles and much else from Europe. The transfer of the cauldron from the port to the factory took many days and much effort, providing an interesting spectacle for days for the villagers. It took 12 pairs of oxen days on end, with the slowness of a tortoise, to pull it up to the village.‡ He finally completed the building,

---

* Kasabian gives details of the Avedian factory workforce etc. for the years 1910-1912 as:

    Capacity - 98 spindles; Number of Armenian women workers – 75; Number of Armenian Greek-Orthodox (called *hai hrom*) – 42; Number of Foremen -7; Armenian Greek-Orthodox foremen (called *hai hrom*) –1; Ages of female workers 13 to 60; Number of workers aged 13 to 16 – 35; Actual number of hours worked – 10.5;

    13 to 16 year-olds' daily wage – 2 to 3 *kurush*; Older workers' daily wage – 3 to 6 *kurush*. Minas Kasabian (Farhad), *Hayere Nikomedio Kavarin Mech*, pp. 210-211.

† The wording here is *irarme anchad barab kedinnerov gghziatsadz*.

‡ Der-Hagopian, quoting the Istanbul newspaper *Sourhantag* dated 3th May 1899, tells us that this cauldron weighed 12,000 kg (12 tonnes) and 26 pairs of buffaloes were unable to get it into place after they got it to the village. The entire male population of the village was needed to finally move it to the site allocated for it in the silk spinning factory. Hagop Der-Hagopian, *Bardizage khadoudig*, p. 233.

equipped according to the newest European system, having spent tens of thousands of liras. Helvadjian, in all his life, had never opened his pockets so wide.

The factory had to have its own source of water to work. His friends and collaborators had assured him that Bardizag's subsoil, due to the richness of its outflows of water, would present no problem in providing enough water for the factory.

He hired skilled men and labourers to find water; preliminary surveys brought Helvadjian to the conclusion that it could, without great expenditure, be brought to the factory from the floor of the valley near the Near Upper Fields. He began excavations which lasted for days. The soil began to show signs of wetness and he had hopes that the water would finally appear. In reality water did burst out of the ground. Helvadjian was delighted, although he restrained his pleasure, frightened that he would make people envious. For a moment he forgot all the great sacrifices he had made, which now appeared to him to have ended.

The excavations were deepened to make the water more plentiful so that there was enough for the factory. He was delighted that the amount of water from the source gradually increased and appeared to be very rich. But catastrophe was not long in coming. The more Helvadjian's water source grew, the less the Near Upper Fields public fountain flowed; it finally ceased. This was followed by the drying up, one after another, of the other fountains in the Holy King and Palaghents quarters of the village, and threatened the flow of others. The inhabitants of the quarter and all the other villagers became alarmed. It seemed as if Helvadjian was collecting all the villagers' water to run his factory. A serious situation developed between them. The village council took over the matter so as to prevent clashes between Helvadjian and the village populace.

To examine the problem legally, the excavations officially ceased and negotiations began between Helvadjian and the villagers, represented by the council, which the diocesan prelate, Bishop Stepannos, joined.

The villagers said that the water was for their fountains; they would not give Helvadjian even one drop. He replied that he had extracted water at his own expense, and it was his. But Helvadjian himself realised the weakness of his words and, finding himself in a strange moral dilemma, looked in vain for a solution.

The solution to the problem remained with the authorities. Inspectors came to examine the site and prepare written reports to be sent to the government. They were detrimental to Helvadjian: the water belonged to the public fountains. The new source had tapped the sub-surface water basin that fed the fountains and, being deepened, had made it run towards the new cut, drying up the already-existing fountains.

At this, Helvadjian blanched, and began pleading with the diocesan bishop and the council, among whom he of course had friends.

There was an attempt to bring reality to the situation, keeping the interests of both sides in mind. There was no doubt that the water belonged to the village fountains, but Helvadjian, with his excavations, had increased its flow at great expense. It wasn't fair that he should be totally deprived of it, especially as he was going to use the water to operate his factory. This was considered to be an enterprise that was the source of many kinds of profit for the village, with workers, officials, woodsmen and transporters, all of them villagers, benefiting. So Helvadjian's business had to be encouraged. It was with these thoughts in mind that intermediaries suggested that the fountains should be given their share of the water, in the old quantities, allowing the remainder to flow to Helvadjian's factory as his property, obtained by his sacrifices and at his expense.

Helvadjian, although he gave the appearance of disliking the solution, must of course have been inwardly delighted that the problem had been solved in accordance with his friends' realism.

The councillors, however, were adamant; all the water was theirs, and they wouldn't spare even one drop for Helvadjian. If he had incurred expense, he still had no right to disturb the water basin and, at the most, could demand the payment of the amount he had spent, assuming that the law allowed him to do so, as he hadn't asked for permission to extract water in the first place.

In the end, after many days and weeks of negotiations, it became possible to reach a lawful and just solution on the following basis.

> All the water belonged to the Near Upper Fields' and Holy King quarter's fountains and they would receive it in the same quantities as before.
>
> The remainder belonged to the community, as a source of profit for the schools.
>
> The community undertook to have this water flow to Helvadjian's factory, at an annual cost of 10 Ottoman liras, for as long as the Helvadjians remained the factory owners.
>
> Helvadjian would withdraw his demands for compensation.

Several people had a great part in this arrangement in the community's interests: Aghasi Effendi Papazian, Hovhannes Agha Arakelian, Hadji Artin Agha Kiutnerian and other community representatives, as well as – especially – the Palaz family's son-in-law Garabed Khalfa Andonian, on behalf of the councillors.

127 – The enclosing of the old cemetery with a wall

The old (upper) cemetery, located in front of the Mgrians' silk spinning factory, had ceased being used for many years. It had been been filled with graves from the time of the foundation of the village, as it was the community's only cemetery. It was, at the same time, in the centre of the village, as the various blocks of houses had been built outwards from it. The community authorities, because of this, had reserved a piece of land as the new (lower) cemetery, further away, at Dantsin Broun, bordered on two sides by the junction of the road to Hrom Kiugh (Yenikeoy) and that going to the port. That was a beautiful place, small, attractive and slightly higher than its surroundings and with slopes on three sides. It was a place that had lain deserted among the vineyards and roads, as it wasn't suitable for cultivation and was protected by wild trees. It probably originally belonged to Great Hadji Zakar's heirs.

For this reason the old cemetery had remained undefended and ownerless like an orphan, becoming a walkway and grazing place for animals. It was in a poor condition that wounded many devout people's feelings. They could see the lack of respect for their ancestors' memory.

To rectify this poor situation, the young men who had grown up under Tourian's tutelage* formed a 'Cemetery Association' having as its aim the collection of enough money to pay for a wall to be built around it, and giving that holy place care and attention. The association, to obtain the necessary funds, was given permission by the village authorities to make collections among the people each Sunday. This was apart from its members' monthly subscriptions. A few years later, a total of 150-200 Ottoman liras were collected by this means, giving the association's operations committee the courage to begin the construction of the wall around the cemetery.

Craftsmen and labourers were hired, as were packhorse owners to transport stone, cement and sand. Construction began opposite the Mgerians' factory, beginning at the point where the corner of the street to the port began. The wall gradually began to appear above ground level, about half an arshin (14 inches or 35cm) thick and two arshins (4 feet 9 inches or 1.5m) in height. To conserve their capital, the Association had the good idea of using free collective labour each Sunday to supplement the paid work done during the week.

One Sunday the wall had reached a point just opposite the Mgerians' factory where the edge of the cemetery bent sharply to accommodate the entrance and the area leading to the Mgerians' nail workshops and forges. This area formed part of the old cemetery at one time. The people, fired with the older people's descriptions and wanting to right an old injustice, built the wall, with great enthusiasm, high and straight, re-attaching that area to the cemetery.

Now the Bardizag Protestant community had purchased that factory from the Mgerians either that year or one or two previously. The Apostolic community had remained indifferent to the sale. The Protestant *mukhtar* [mayor], Artin Agha Kourouian, now intervened in the name of his community, wanting to prevent the seizure of that part of their property. The people, however, reinforced in their feelings by the skulls and bones they revealed during their work, continued construction without regard for the mayor's intervention and protest and, as if by a miracle, finished erecting the wall on that area in a few hours.

---

* The author infers that he was also a member.

The Protestant community, in the knowledge of its just rights, took the problem to the Protestant National Office* in Constantinople, which had the wisdom and greatness to ignore that trifling question, not wishing to tarnish relations between sister communities. Thus the former boundary of the old cemetery was restored.†

It took more than a year to complete the whole wall, and thus protect the cemetery's sanctity and respect. It guaranteed the villager a place to rest in the summer months on its lush green grass and in the shade of its big trees that, although fewer with the ravages of time, represented the remains of a glade in the once-present forests. Its position was higher than the surrounding streets and, being an open space, encompassed a beautiful panorama towards the sea and the surrounding heights. Passing time there became a pleasure, and the people were near the remains of our ancestors.

The village authority of the day wanted to preserve the newly built wall against damage and bring the schools a small income. It therefore handed the area's protection and maintenance to someone who rented it for a small sum, permitting him to keep a small buffet in the upper part of the cemetery where there were no burials. He dispensed coffee, fruit juices and sweets there, providing the place with chairs and a good place to play backgammon for visitors who wanted to enjoy those amenities. This buffet was a method of putting a permanent guard over the cemetery, where women and boys, the old and young, would come to cool down among the greenery with complete freedom, especially on Sunday evenings, without having to pay anything if they didn't want to use the buffet.‡

128 – The first revolutionary act in Bardizag

The Russo-Turkish war ended in 1877 with Turkey's complete defeat. The Treaty of San Stefano was then signed. 'Armenian Reforms' were seen officially for the first time as the Turkish government had, by the treaty, to institute reforms in all the Armenian-inhabited parts of the empire. This was to protect the Armenians' lives, honour and assets against all barbarian races and tribes. In the next year (1878), the Berlin Congress, editing that treaty, accepted the 'Armenian Reforms' question and made it an international one, placing their realisation under the superintendance of the six participating powers.

---

* The words used here are *Poghokagan Azkabedaran*.
† Kasabian gives the date of reconstruction as 1893. Minas Kasabian (Farhad), *Hayere Nikomedio Kavarin Mech*, p. 277.
‡ Writing in 1912, Kasabian states that it was only a partial building (*gisagadar*). He adds that the organisation was then dissolved, and the wall left to deteriorate. He says that the wall now presented a poor appearance. Minas Kasabian (Farhad), *Hayere Nikomedio Kavarin Mech*, p. 277.

The Armenian people, armed with this international written agreement, gradually became more demanding, but subsequent events in Turkey showed that Turkey was not sincere in its undertakings. In fact the situation the Armenians were in deteriorated in the interior provinces. As a result of this, Armenian revolutionary organisations were born that, through newspapers printed in Europe, preached and stressed the necessity of the Armenian reforms, hoping to force European diplomacy to act and provide a basic solution under public pressure. Within the country, Armenian revolutionary activity was limited, in those days, to the preparation of minds and the organisation of demonstrations.

An Armenian from Amasia appeared in Bardizag in about 1890. He was known as Amasiali. He ran a coffee house in Izmid called the Amasiali Khahven. This unknown individual approached us schoolboys, as to a generation that was idealistic and ready to make sacrifices. He especially got to know me and my friend the secretary to the council, Hovhannes Azkabedian (Djergayian). He spoke familiarly to us about the Armenian Question and the necessity for every knowledgeable Armenian to make sacrifices. He called upon our patriotic feelings and urged us to begin work, collaborating in the efforts and dedication to improve the political situation of the Armenian people. At the end he brought out one or two copies of Portougalian's paper *Armenia*, published in Marseilles. We thumbed through them with a sense of horror and admiration, and saw articles written in a bold and inflammatory style, like a boy's thoughtless and bold attempts at writing. Their purpose was to place before European public opinion a picture of the moral decline of the Ottoman authorities and the deterioration of its character. They further wrote about the deliberate and culpable plot against their most solemn promises and undertakings. The writers pointed out its new injustices and the persecution of the Armenians that had been taking place for some time and which were getting worse day by day. These persecutions had the object of emptying the provinces of their Armenian populations, or to make them slaves where they lived and to eliminate them according to a pre-determined plan.

The spirit of idealism was still fresh and powerful in us, and like all boys, we were ready to go down the road of idealism. We became enthusiastic. These newspapers brought a new message to our virgin souls; it was imperative that we determine our position and share in this planned work.

Our revolutionary activity was to be in accordance with the newspapers' spirit, which we would receive secretly and regularly. We would begin a mission to prepare the people of Bardizag and collect funds for the holy work (*sourp kordz*) which we would send to the editors of *Arevelk* in Constantinople, receiving receipts for our remittances.

Amasiali, having made these arrangements with us, left and returned to Izmid, to his work. He promised us that he would occasionally visit us and bring us new orders and suggestions. We made several dependable friends our comrades and organised the first revolutionary committee in Bardizag, made up of seven people.

We usually got together in the *Tolalikhi Baghchali* coffee house, which had a separate room for those who wanted to be alone. This room became our meeting place, where we read the newspapers that arrived. We wanted to keep our enthusiasm bright and to determine the direction of our activities.

Our committee made appeals every evening to various sectors of Bardizag society. Having read the papers in the coffee house, we destroyed them; then, as a group, in the dark, we'd knock at doors that were ready to open before us. We'd go in and, standing, say a few words about the salvation of Armenia. Wallets would be opened and our pockets would be filled with the greatest confidence and belief in the cause.

We succeeded in collecting 60 Ottoman liras through our approaches after a month or two. We sent half, 30 liras, to *Arevelk,* receiving a receipt in return. It had been collected from only about 100 to 150 houses; we still had a lot of work to do. We were waiting for another opportunity to send some more money when we suddenly found ourselves in danger. The Baab Ali demonstration had taken place in Constantinople. A crowd of Armenian protesters, led by revolutionary leaders, went to Baab Ali to present a written demand concerning the Armenian Reforms. The government used force to disperse the demonstrators. Some of the leaders were immediately arrested and thrown into prison. In the chaos that followed injured people fell to the ground while others ran away to hide themselves.[*]

One of the injured people had escaped and arrived in Bardizag. We looked after him for days and helped him recover and, when the atmosphere had become calm, he quietly returned to Constantinople.

The Turkish government, using their usual methods, had extracted confessions from those arrested, revealing that a revolutionary organisation and a network of secret activity existed from one end of the country to the other. The Turkish government, faced with this, found it necessary to implement a policy of repression. It stirred up Armenian hearts and, after the resulting arrests had taken place, began to arrest and detain Armenian revolutionaries throughout the country.

The man known as Amasiali was arrested in Izmid and taken to Constantinople's central prison. The turn of the revolutionaries in Bardizag would not be long. A policeman arrived in the village from Izmid one day with a name written on a piece of paper which read Yeghsapetian Ohannes. He went to the mayor demanding that the man be handed over to the government. There was no one of that name in Bardizag. Everyone, however, understood that the name Yeghsapetian Ohannes should read Azkabedian Hovhannes, and was the false name

---

[*] It took place on 18 September 1895, and was immediately followed by a massacre of over 2,000 Armenians in Constantinople.

of one of our comrades. That mistake of penmanship was an opportunity for us to gain time. The village authorities sent the policeman away, saying that there was no one of that name in Bardizag. But there was no doubt that the mistake would be corrected very soon and our comrade hunted. Friends suggested that Azkabedian escape abroad, but difficulties were seen in carrying that out. We therefore contented ourselves with destroying papers and newspapers in our houses that could be compromising and anxiously awaited developments.

The same policeman returned to Bardizag a few days later, this time demanding the handing over of someone named Hovhannes Azkabedian. He was handed over and was taken to Constantinople. Marknag Mgrdich, our coffee house leaseholder was also arrested and taken to Constantinople a few days later.

The Turkish government had achieved its aim: its policy of terror. What had happened was a childish thing, without being a serious danger to the country. Elsewhere, in Europe, the voice of the Armenian revolutionaries was joined by those of pro-Armenian publicists on the occasion of the event and the subsequent arrests. Sultan Hamid II's wary and suspicious government was frightened to enlarge what in itself was an insignificant thing and stir European public opinion against it. European opinion still had great weight and significance for the Turkish government, until it became used to its uselessness and derided it. The government therefore decided to pardon those arrested and set them free, first making them swear to remain faithful to the country's laws.

After an absence lasting approximately two months, all those in prison were released. Our comrade, Hovhannes Azkabedian, and our host the coffee house owner Marknag Mgrdich were both released. They both gave their stipulated oath in the church in Izmid, then returned to Bardizag.

Feelings calmed down; the immediate danger had passed from over our heads. We divided the remaining 30 liras between the two men who had been imprisoned as compensation. We ended our dangerous revolutionary activities, not seeing any use for those disorganised, youthful attempts that were without consistent, long term plans. We felt that the Armenian people were still not ready for supreme sacrifices and armed mass rebellion. We felt that, if it really was necessary, armed rebellion was the only method of imposing our will on the government and forcing it to abide by the terms of the treaty and carry out the reforms.

Our movement, in Bardizag, passed into history as an abortive act, and we became wiser, devoting ourselves to our own work.

A few years after us, a new revolutionary committee was formed in Bardizag, with the name of *Hnchagian*,[*] the members of which were people from the generation after ours. We never knew the name of our political party; it would appear that we were *Armenagans*, members of the first Armenian revolutionary party.

---

[*] The Social-Democratic Hnchagian party, founded in 1882.

The Hnchags wanted to continue the work we had started, under almost the same circumstances. Having learned from us, they didn't find the villagers agreeable to financial sacrifices. The new members wanted to add threats or terror to their requests for aid. The Armenian revolution accepted terrorism among its methods, because the revolutionaries were more vulnerable in the country than the people who didn't want to contribute.

The Turkish government, restless before this new movement, emphasised its toughness against the revolutionaries. They were gradually driven to work secretly, meaning total inactivity: they were heard, but weren't present.

The Dashnaks* appeared much later, especially among the youth, but they were a name rather than real revolutionary activists in Bardizag. This lasted until the days of freedom exploded in 1908† and there was freedom of speech. This resulted in 'revolutionism' becoming the fashion of the day. We older ones remained aloof, seeing danger in those thoughtless and ignorant attempts.

129 – Mr. Chambers, the third American missionary‡ in Bardizag

I have not been able to determine how long Mr. Pierce stayed in Bardizag, but he worked as a missionary in the Bithynian plain for more than 15 long years. His permanent residence was in Bardizag. He displayed both dedication and merit, especially by founding the American Boys' High School. He was followed by Mr. Chambers, who came from the plains of Erzerum and was a noble, sympathetic missionary.**

Mr Chambers arrived in Bardizag speaking excellent Erzerum Armenian. He had learned it as well as any Armenian and it sounded very harmonious and sweet when he spoke. He not only spoke Armenian without difficulty, but preached in it smoothly and clearly. He even wrote in Armenian, although with some hesitation, concerned about spelling mistakes, as he was used to completing any task without making any errors.

He was a tall man who was slightly built and always had a smile on his face. He was able to create a family atmosphere around him. He was accompanied by his wife, Mrs. Bessie Chambers, and their two adolescent sons, Robert and Lawson

---

* The Armenian Revolutionary Federation, founded in 1890.
† The year in which the Ottoman constitution was restored and Sultan Abdul Hamid II was dethroned.
‡ He and his wife were actually Canadians, but worked for the American Missionary organisation.
** See H. F. B. Lynch, in his *Armenia: travels and studies*, London, 1901, Vol II: The Turkish provinces, p. 217, where he describes how he met him in Erzerum and was very impressed.

Chambers, who had opened their eyes to the world in Armenia, if I am not mistaken.

Mr Chambers was over 40 years old when they moved to Bardizag. He had matured with great and measured experience while still retaining his youthful vigour. His physical weakness was his chest, which had become weak due to Erzerum's severe and cold climate, and which would be affected by Bardizag's cold and damp winter.

He found an important Protestant community and the American Boys' High School in Bardizag. It had been transferred to the Mgerians' silk spinning factory, which belonged to the community and which had had some alterations to make it suitable to be a school. This school became the object of Mr. Chambers' greatest care and attention. He believed that it, with the church, was the best means of building good and noble characters in the young generation. He was a much-sought after person in that regard.

Mr Chambers was the most educated and refined of all the missionaries called to serve in Bardizag. He was a gentleman* in the real and full sense of the word. Naturally clever and thoughtful, he had received a notable education that he had deepened with years of continual reading. This had placed him on a par with any intellectual. It was for this reason that the American university he had studied in later gave him a doctorate, in recognition of his meritorious services.

He had gained a notable position in American Missionary Board circles and was both loved and esteemed. The well-known Mr. Peet called him 'a very fine man'† after his death, when I had a meeting with him. His thoughts and suggestions were listened to with pleasure and satisfaction by Missionary Board people.

He was a fervent, good and honourable Christian, who never just looked at the exterior, the outer shell, but at the depths of souls and life. For him religion wasn't an important habit, custom or robe, but a living force and a tangible reality. These virtues of his had made him a supremely wide-thinking personality. For him, the Christian hadn't sought to be Protestant, Apostolic or Catholic, but tried to live the life of Christ and be fruitful in His kingdom, whatever sect he belonged to.

He knew the Armenian people. He came from Armenia, a place he had lived and worked in for years, and had used his eyes to see the truth. He was interested in the Armenian's past and present life, which had been a singular and wonderful Christian martyrdom. He had seen, with his own eyes, the fruits of irrepressible Armenian faith. These were embodied in the monuments that he saw around him. They were Armenian monasteries and churches, a rich religious literature, art that appeared in all its forms. Finally, he appreciated the Armenian people's durability, intelligence, purity of family and social life, thriftiness and diligence.

---

* The author has used the transliteration of this word here for emphasis.
† Written in English in the Armenian original.

For Dr. Chambers, this truth had the force of a proven conviction: the sum total of Armenian virtues was far greater than its faults. He felt the latter had been given to it by the environment and difficult political circumstances it lived in. He loved our people with conviction and without reservation. Our nation wasn't foreign to him. He knew it was made up of his unfortunate brothers and sisters who had been condemned to live in darkness and shadow for centuries. The nation had been demeaned and persecuted although, on the surface, it had seemingly freed itself to a certain extent and still retained its clean and noble core.

His conviction and experiences had been the reasons why he asked himself: 'What have I come to do among this people?' The answer was: 'to teach and educate it and clean it of its grime.' He felt, in the clean depths of his consciousness, that the life of this people had taught him a great deal – the depth of its faith and unending passion to suffer for its God. He had therefore come to the conviction that it was not the church or Christianity that was lacking in it, but education and cleansing of its filth.

He thus came, with the greatest open-mindedness, to dedicate himself to the task of raising the nation up and ennobling it. It was with these thoughts that he felt the attempt to erect a new church alongside the Armenian Apostolic Church was wrong. He accepted the fact that it was a mistake and that he must not appropriate it for himself, so he abandoned the idea of propaganda to which his two predecessors had surrendered themselves. He saw, with distress, that he could not, from one day to the next, make the Armenian Protestant a livelier and more real Christian than a member of the Armenian Apostolic Church. He therefore extended his hand to the weak side, the development of Christian culture - to the difficult, arduous work of preparing real Christians - rather than just Protestants.

His predecessor, Mr. Pierce, had left him a school. He decided to build this educational establishment into a Christian cultural furnace according to his own sincere convictions and experience. This was so that the generation educated there could take that Christian culture with it in its lfe and spread it among its people.

Two important questions captured his attention concerning his plans for this educational mission. The first was to secure a good, Christian model of teaching staff deserving of confidence, making his pure, religious and noble person a centre of inspiration among them. Secondly it was to secure a clean environment for the school with a range of suitable buildings, where it would be possible for the work to be accomplished. He only kept Professor Apraham Effendi Der-Hagopian out of the old schoolteachers. The latter was one of the students of the Shirinian era who had, later, received an inspiring and rational education in Robert College, Constantinople. Over a period of time he added the following teachers:

Minas Dzalian from Bardizag

S. Magarian, a graduate of Robert College

Hovsep Djedjizian from Adabazar, a graduate of Robert College

Yervant Djedjizian from Adabazar, a graduate of Robert College

H. Domboulian from Adabazar, a graduate of the Bardizag American Boys' High School

Dr. H. Der-Stepanian, a graduate of both Robert College and London Medical University[*]

A. Yakoubian (from Kayseri) a graduate of the Djenanian School, Konya

S. Kasabian from Agn

H. Touradian from Amasia, a graduate of Marsovan College

Me (I was one of Tourian's students).

There were others who taught at different times and for various lengths of time, many for a decade or double that and for even more years without a break.

When choosing teachers, Dr. Chambers looked at the *man* and his character before and above anything else. He then came to his education and how ready or prepared he was. He was deeply convinced that it was the teacher's personality and life that built the student. As a Christian, he didn't seek, in the teacher, denominational doctrine, rather a person who didn't discriminate between Protestant and Armenian Apostolic students. The teacher was called to work among students that were mostly from Armenian Apostolic families, encouraged by Dr. Chambers' broadminded and liberal spirit. The students would be certain to retain the faith of their fathers in his hands. I do not know of a single student who, during Dr. Chambers' tenure, forsook the Armenian Apostolic Church and joined the Evangelical Protestant Church.

The Bardizag American Boys' School was a high school in the American sense. It had a curriculum designed to giving the student an intellectually rational education. This was linked to the work of preparing good and useful men in the practical American spirit. The man of work had to be physically healthy and vigorous. His development was to be aided by open-air games and exercise, turning the atmosphere of the school into a pleasant one for all the students without exception. Secondly, the spiritual and moral man's preparation would be assisted by daily lessons from the Holy Bible in a thoughtful, very carefully prepared way, with Sunday worship specifically designed for the school.

Despite this, Dr. Chambers did not believe in just the power of the spoken word and lectures to prepare the man required. This was especially so if the life the student lived and his daily work didn't join together to form good habits in him. Efforts were therefore made to form associations among the students, membership of which was left to the individual. In them work and speech joined together, putting miniature pictures of future life before the students.

---

[*] It is not clear which medical establishment this was. There does not seem to have been a 'medical university' in London, United Kingdom, with this name. It might have been University College Medical School, part of the University of London.

Thus within the school there was the 'Patience Association', 'Christian Effort Association', 'Christian Youth Association' and so on, which the student joined of his own free will and swore to maintain its moral and spiritual principles in life.[*] These were, for example, to resign from vices, to live the life of Christ[†] as portrayed in the New Testament: of love, brotherhood, service, mutual help and sacrifice. These associations had their separate meetings on Sunday afternoons, each inviting a teacher as chairman, elected by the votes of the members, who ran the meeting.

Members or invited guests spoke on appropriate subjects at these meetings, as opportunities for inspiration for the members. The students thus lived in a healthy, serious and spiritual atmosphere, at the same time assimilating autonomy and harmonious collaboration.

The senior management of the school was very demanding in terms of the students' and teachers' personal lives. It was the life lived every day that would build the man's value, and even a small error or scandalous act by a student was subject to very strict censure, so as to zealously maintain the school's high moral integrity.

The students had group trips under the leadership of the unmarried resident teachers on Sunday evenings during good weather. These excursions took them to the tops of the local hills, to the bosom of nature, the shadows of the forests and into the midst of greenness. They visited to the flanks of massive outcrops of stone and the depths of the valleys. These trips eased the pressure of school life and self-contained fatigue, providing the pleasure of clean air and beautiful scenery. The teachers gave the students opportunities for experience, personal observations and studies, presented to them as things, appearances and scenic views that cultivated their imagination and taste.

The syllabus included the teaching of four languages: Armenian (both classical and modern), English, Turkish and French. The ruling language in the school was, of course, Armenian. The students were also taught mathematics (arithmetic, basic algebra and geometry); natural sciences (geography, basic physics and chemistry, anatomy and botany), history (general and national history[‡]), basic psychology and lessons in the Holy Scriptures. It had, apart from these subjects, a weekly assembly for recitations.

The school also organised a series of lectures every winter. These were seriously and carefully prepared and given by teachers and specially invited speakers. The choice of subject was left, in the widest sense about the world and life, to the speaker.

---

* Garo Kevorkian, who has written extensive articles about his life as a student in the school, was a member of the *Chanasirats* [Diligence] Association. See Garo Kevorkian, *Everybody's Yearbook, 3rd year*, Beirut, 1956, pp. 183-243 (see picture on p. 196).
† The words used here are *medz vartabed* or great doctor or master.
‡ The author does not make clear what *national history* was. It might have been Ottoman history.

There were, among these lectures, some about scientific, historical and topographical subjects using magic lantern slides.

The school continued its life within the Mgerians' silk spinning factory building for some time, with dormitories in nearby houses specially rented for the purpose by the school authorities. Dr. Chambers had established his home from the first day in Mr. Parsons' house at the western edge of the village, from where, each morning, he would walk to the school. He ate his midday meal there with the teachers and returned home in the evening, always on foot.

Gradually the number of students increased to overflowing, reaching over 300. Most of them were boarders. Their families could afford the annual fees, which were only from 15 to 20 Ottoman liras per student, gradually rising with the cost of living to the latter figure, which was still a small amount for an organised school like this.

Dr Chambers, seeing this increase in the size of the school, had been planning for a building – or buildings – for some time to be owned by the school and began looking for donors to obtain the funds for this project. The first school building, constructed on ground purchased during Mr. Parsons' time, was the magnificent four storey building later named Pierce Hall, in memory of the original founder.

The student body was moved into this building, which had been planned with all that was necessary on each floor: school, dormitories, canteen, kitchen, baths, wood store etc.

After a time, that huge building wasn't sufficient to include the student body in comfortable circumstances. It was thanks to a gift by Miss Newnham, the daughter of a noble British family and the director of the newly established Favre Boys Home, that the school's second building, Newnham Hall, was constructed in a mulberry orchard next to the school grounds. This was a separate building where all the lessons were taught. After that Pierce Hall acted as the students' house.

After these two buildings, a third one, a house for Dr. Chambers and his family, was built behind the other two. It was located on a prominent piece of land that had been newly purchased, the cost of which was defrayed by the Missionary Board, and where Dr. Chambers lived until he retired.

The fourth school building located opposite Dr. Chambers' house was Chambers Hall, paid for by funds collected by the Bardizag High School Alumni Association and presented to their Alma Mater in appreciation of their much-loved principal and teacher. It had a large, well-lit hall in the upper storey used for various functions; the lower floor was divided into two, one part being the library and the other being used as a sports hall, fitted with all the necessary equipment, during the winter.

The Favre Boys Home was also a new building, built with funds provided by British and Swiss pro-Armenian donors. It was separate from the other buildings, and held a number of orphans from the Armenian massacres of 1895. These boys were looked after, brought up, taught and prepared for a self-sufficient life[*] through donations made by foreign friends. They enjoyed a family atmosphere and parent-like care under Miss Newnham's robust and intelligent direction. This establishment was totally separate in its organisation and finances from the American High School, which was under Dr. Chambers' fatherly direction. One or two American and Swiss ladies worked there under Miss Newnham, and when a teacher or organiser was required for a time, Mr. S. Magarian and other assistant Armenian teachers took over.

All of these buildings were constructed according to the plans created by Hovhannes Leylozian of Bardizag, who was a member of the Khalfa Leylozian family that was famous in the building trade.

Dr Chambers, appreciating the many years of good and faithful service provided by Armenag Der-Hagopian in the American School from the very beginning, and regarding him as one of the pillars of the teaching family, gave permission for him to have his own house in the school grounds, with the proviso that if it had to be sold, the American Missionary Board would buy it.

Having had all these school buildings completed, Dr. Chambers then had a large area levelled and fenced in as a playground and for open-air exercises. It was located below and in front of the buildings, and extended as far as the public road going to Kirazlekh. This whole complex formed a large and attractive American parish in the village, costing a great deal of money.

In his mind, Dr. Chambers had planned to gradually raise the educational standard of the school until it reached that of a college. This plan was thwarted by the Armenian catastrophe of 1915, when the Armenian population of Turkey was sent on the road to slaughter and destruction.

I have given considerable space to Dr. Chambers' work and that of the American High School in Bardizag's contemporary history. This is because they formed part of that history and especially as Dr. Chambers has his unique place in it, as a man with noble character and as a public activist. His greatness consisted of taking Mr. Pierce's Protestant establishment and transforming it into an Armenian-national educational one. It was imbued with the spirit of open mindedness – or more correctly with a total lack of discrimination – where many generations of Bardizag students were inspired and taught. The shocks and decline suffered by the community schools after Tourian's departure meant that boys, after completing the courses in that school, went to the American High School to finish their education. The latter provided many of them with their final lessons through Armenian national spirit and traditions.

The High School was also, for the Armenian young generation, a source of Christian propaganda and spiritual life where it learnt to treat religion and spiritual life with the greatest seriousness. The community schools were always slack in that

---

* Each boy was taught a trade, so that he could make a living when he finally left home.

regard and failed in their duty to give their students proper religious and moral teaching.

Apart from - and more than - this, Dr. Chambers has been a patriotic Armenian among us, inside an American skin, and had often expressed himself thus: 'I would have been very happy to have been born an Armenian.' He appreciated our nation with its moral and spiritual history very much. In his social dealings with the people of Bardizag, Dr. Chambers was a selfless friend, ready to serve them in their times of need without suspicious thoughts or intentions.

One of us, one day, talking about him said, 'It seems to me, looking at the Gospels, that Christ was someone like him.'

In the days after the Bank incident,[*] when there was an attempt to massacre Armenians who had gone to the market in Geyve (a town under the jurisdiction of Izmid) by Turkish and Islamic mobs, Dr. Chambers spontaneously hurried to the scene with the prelate Bishop Stepannos Hovagimian to look after and comfort those who had suffered, at the same time informing Bible House and the American embassy in Constantinople, in writing, of the details of the massacre.[†]

Dr Chambers, after so many years of exhausting work, received the right to enjoy two years of leave, so went to America with his wife. His position was filled by Mr. Allen, a young American who had been born and brought up in Armenia and who spoke, read and wrote Armenian just as well as any of us and loved our nation very much.

The Chambers' returned to Bardizag two years later, where they had important work that was in their hearts and souls. Many of their friends and acquaintances went to Constantinople, Izmid and Seymen to meet them. When the carriage bringing them to the village reached the lower cemetery, almost the whole population – in all its classes – of Bardizag welcomed them with the young men, with indescribable enthusiasm and love, uncoupling the horses from the carriage and drawing it themselves for a considerable distance to welcome their friend, the sincere Armenophile, as a gesture of thankfulness and respect. Dr. and Mrs. Chambers were extremely affected by this great demonstration. Their lips trembled, finding it impossible to articulate their thanks. They had tears in their eyes, which only those who loved them could understand.

They finally parted from Bardizag and the work they loved in 1910-1911, having earned the right to retire. But they stayed in Constantinople in Uskudar, in the old

---

[*] This was the capture of the Ottoman Bank in Constantinople on 26 August, 1896 by revolutionaries belonging to the Armenian Revolutionary Federation. It was followed by a massacre in the city, with between 5,000 and 6,000 Armenians killed.

[†] Kasabian makes no reference to this particular event, but describes, in some detail, the massacre that took place in Ak-Hisar on Wednesday, 27 September 1895. Minas Kasabian (Farhad), *Hayere Nikomedio Kavarin Mech*, pp. 149-153.

American Girls' College building for two years before they left. It was as if longing for the Armenian people and their love was an impediment to their departure. They wanted to get used to the pain of leaving. They finally went to America, where their two sons, Robert and Lawson, were already settled.

It was there that they heard of the catastrophe that engulfed the Armenian people: their final and complete martyrdom. Neither he nor his wife was able to bear the blow; their Christian conscience could not grasp the nature of the crime visited on an entire people before the eyes of Christian humanity. It was impossible for them to live in this world and breathe its air that was so stifling and deadly. They died within a few years of each other – he in 1917, she in 1923 – as if not to see the unending cemetery of the people they loved.*

Those of his students who lived in America collaborated in a beautiful thought to show their gratitude and respect, putting up a memorial to him in one of the halls in the university where he had studied.

The strong Armenophile traditions live on in the family and the sons, who are professors and work in the USA, retain them, and the younger, Lawson Chambers, never forgets his old friends, maintaining correspondence with many of them in clear and almost faultless Armenian.†

Mr McNaughton, one of the Smyrna (Izmir) missionaries, replaced Dr. Chambers. He was only able to run the school for two years before the Turkish government, after joining the war, exiled him to the country's interior as the subject of an enemy country (Mr McNaughton was a British subject). It was only through the intervention of the United States embassy that he was brought back, on the condition that he left the country.

He was replaced for the 1914-1915 scholastic year by a young American missionary, Mr. Reid. He then saw complete desolation all around him, with the entire population of Bardizag deported and the populations of the other towns and villages scattered, like fallen leaves, by the dreadful storm of exile. History had ended for the Armenian people and put an end to his work.

130 – Garabed Effendi Helvadjian, the son of the family, is abducted by bandits and taken to the mountains. The fate of the Helvadjians' silk spinning factory

Garabed Helvadjian was the silk spinning factory's manager. The Helvadjians, as we have seen, were from Izmid, and had their main residence there, where they were occupied with their commercial enterprises. As the factory manager, Garabed Effendi lived with his family in Bardizag during the week, in the house they built for

---

* They are buried in the cemetery in Woodstock, Ontario, Canada.
† This was written in the 1930s.

themselves,* but in the summer he and his family went to Izmid every Saturday evening, as a change, returning on Sunday night when the air had cooled.

When he was returning with his wife to Bardizag one Sunday evening - the roads were deserted on a Sunday as people didn't work on that day - and was near the edge of a *tavouk* called Ouzoun Chayir, about one kilometre above Seymen, a robber band that was lying in wait ambushed them, demanding their surrender. Seeing that self-defence was impossible, they did so. The robbers released Garabed Effendi's wife, assuring her amid her tears that her husband would come to no harm. Taking Garabed Effendi with them they went, in broad daylight, through the gardens and vineyards to the rear of a height to the south and above Bardizag. They met a villager on their way there, to whom they gave a written demand, signed by Garabed Effendi Helvadjian and addressed to his father. This was for a ransom of 1,000 Ottoman liras, and said they would kill him if it was not satisfied immediately.

Garabed Effendi's wife, upon her release, hurried back to Seymen from where she took a boat home and told her father-in-law Hovhannes Helvadjian of the incident. The elder Helvadjian went to Bardizag that same evening, where he got hold of the paper his son had signed. He couldn't believe his eyes, and said to those around him, 'This isn't the work of robbers, it's a game set up by *efes* from Bardizag† so they can extort some money.' They tried, in vain, to persuade him that this couldn't be considered to be a joke, and that not even the stupidest villager would try such a thing. Finally Helvadjian, sticking to his guns, decided on a stratagem: he handed the messenger 500 liras for the robbers. This sum was taken to the place the robbers had stipulated. They accepted the money and had Garabed Effendi write a note saying that they demanded the remainder and not a penny less. The note was written in a trembling hand, with a terrified Garabed imploring his father to hurry payment and save his life.

Having this new demand, Hovhannes Helvadjian realized that, in his stupidity, the robbers now had two hostages - his son and the 500 liras. Frightened of losing both, he sent the robbers a second sum of 500 liras. They, thanking Garabed Effendi for accepting their hospitality, released him with a friendly handshake.

Helvadjian, seeing his son alive before his eyes, forgot his great and sudden sacrifice and regained his peace of heart and mind, leaving the defence of justice and law to the government.

The government, having heard of this incident at the time, had hurried, based on the intelligence it had received, to surround the robbers' lair with a large force, awaiting the freeing of the Helvadjian son after the ransom had been paid. The robbers pocketed the ransom and, with the greatest aplomb, passed through the encircling police lines that same night and escaped without the slightest danger or

---

* See Section 126.
† Bold young men who operated the tobacco smuggling trade.

difficulty. They probably made their way to some inlet on the coast and took a waiting boat that carried them to some peaceful port like Constantinople or abroad.

The Turkish government hadn't been able to apprehend the criminals; especially not a band that had become so rich suddenly. This presented a real difficulty for it.

The factory owner Hovhannes Effendi Helvadjian wasn't able to stand the strain of all this in his dotage, especially as he had never in his life handed out such a *royal* gift. He died soon afterwards, leaving his factory and various commercial enterprises to the care of his sons. But the Helvadjians' bad luck didn't end there. About a year later the price of silk rose suddenly - beyond all expectations – to three times that of the normal rate. The Helvadjians were delighted as they had a vast quantity of cocoons in stock that they had bought at very low prices. Their wealth had trebled through one piece of good luck. They would be able to pay off all their debts and still have a fortune left.

They speculated on the basis of their vast stock of cocoons, while the prices kept rising. They held on to their stock, so as to sell it at the highest possible price. In these circumstances they took on large loans to pay for the purchase of future stock. The interest rates were low and their credit rating was good. The prices rose and rose to incredible heights, then suddenly fell dramatically. The Helvadjians said that it was a stock market (bourse) tactic to force the factory owners to sell their stock. 'We won't sell, we'll hold on' they said to each other. The price of silk continued to fall, initially quietly. The Helvadjians continued to hold on; then the prices began to fall very swiftly. The Helvadjians were concerned and began to panic, but they bravely held on until the end. Unfortunately prices fell below its usual level, and refused to rise again. The family found their economic strength faced with an irrecoverable disaster but didn't give up hope; it still endured in the hope of an assured rise in silk prices. But the creditors didn't have the same patience, calling in their loans, the total interest on which was a significant sum.

Prices by now had sunk to such low levels that even selling the stock the family held would not recoup its value. It would still leave them with such a huge debt that the only recourse was to sell their fixed assets to pay it off. To pay off their creditors and to try their luck once more required money, but every door was shut to them now. The impending disaster grew with each passing day. Bankruptcy became inevitable and they had not only to sell their vast stock of cocoons, but also the factory itself with all its buildings, equipment and land. The Helvadjians, having lost everything, sat on barren soil and passed into history.

The Helvadjian silk spinning factory was bought, sometime later, by an important person from Bardizag, namely Ardashes Effendi - the son of Sarkis Effendi Mgerian, whom we have met before[*] - who, having held important positions in the commercial and money changing world in Constantinople, had amassed

---

* See Section 92.

great experience and a significant amount of capital. Thus Ardashes Mgerian took into his hands, years later, the work his forefathers did, and ran it very skillfully and successfully until the general war destroyed that very promising commercial and engineering enterprise.[*]

131 – Ordination of Mgerdich Vartabed Aghavnouni

Before Tourian left Bardizag, one of the members of the graduate class, Krikor Goudjoukian, who had worked as a teacher of Turkish for a number of years in Bardizag's community schools, had felt the calling to become a celibate cleric and to serve in the Izmid diocese as an assistant to the prelate Bishop Stepannos Hovagimian.

Goudjoukian's educational development, meek nature, sincere faith and honourable way of living made him absolutely right for that holy calling, so his wish received Bishop Hovagimian's approval, especially as the large Izmid (Nicomedia) diocese needed more than one assistant working under his direction.

With all this in mind, Krikor Goudjoukian was ordained as an archdeacon in Bardizag by the Bishop in 1888. Two years later (in 1890) at the Feast of Pentecost, the 27 year-old was ordained as a vartabed[†] in the church in Izmid, being renamed Mgerdich Vartabed Aghavnouni, a change of surname that justified his father's nickname *Eghmnag* (*aghavni* – dove) and retained the memory of the one-time prelate Bishop Stepannos Aghavni.

Many people from Bardizag, with the priests, attended this ordination, as did Yeghishe Vartabed Tourian and Hovhannes Kahana Mgerian. The latter had come to his birthplace, Bardizag, for a holiday at that time, and had made the wonderful suggestion concerning the new cleric's surname to the ordaining bishop.

Mgerdich Vartabed worked for many years in the Izmid diocese as locum tenens and chairman of the Provincial Ecclesiastical Assembly. He was appointed locum tenens of the prelacy of Goudina (Keotahia-Afion Karahisar) in 1895/1896 by the Constantinople Patriarchate during Ormanian's patriarchate and, years later, was

---

[*] Kasabian tells us that the Mgerian silk spinning factory was operating in Bardizag in 1910-1912, and gives details of its workforce etc. as:

> Capacity - 90 spindles ; Number of Armenian women workers – 140; Foremen -7; Ages of female workers – from 13 to 60; Number of workers aged 13 to 16 – 35; Actual number of hours worked – 10; 13 to 16 year-olds' daily wage – 2 to 3 *kurush*; Older workers' daily wage – 3 to 6 *kurush*.
> Minas Kasabian (Farhad), *Hayere Nikomedio Kavarin Mech*, pp. 210-211.

[†] Normally a celibate monk would be ordained as an *apegha* (the lowest of the celibate monk grades). I am not sure from the text whether this was the case in this instance.

sent to Egypt with the same position, being ordained bishop by the Catholicos of All Armenians Kevork V in Echmiadzin in 1910.

He served as prelate in Egypt for nine long years, working quietly and peacefully. His prelacy coincided with one of the most brilliant periods of Armenian community life in Egypt. He resigned just before the First World War and returned to Constantinople, where he was appointed preacher in Uskudar's St. Garabed church for a time. He was exiled, during the dark days of the deportations, by the Turkish government to the Armenian Apostolic monastery of the Two Jameses in Jerusalem, where he remains to this day,* having been accepted into the brotherhood of monks there. He became a member of the monastery synod during the reign of Catholicos-Patriarch Sahag. After the Armistice, he was appointed locum tenens to the Jerusalem patriarchate during the reign of Patriarch Yeghishe Tourian, a position he still holds to this day, as well as during the reign of Patriarch Torkom Koushagian, being a member of the governing council of the monastery at the same time. He is also a teacher in the newly-established seminary, while conducting research into the existence of the ancient Armenian monasteries in the Holy Land, the results of which have appeared as a three-volume book published by the Jerusalem patriarchate's publishing house.

---

* Mkhalian means 1937. The archbishop died on 24 August 1941, in Jerusalem, and is buried there.

Chapter 8

Present Times – The Next Phase

132 – Educational work in Bardizag after Tourian's departure

In 1890 Tourian was invited to be the main teacher in the newly-established seminary in Armash monastery, to collaborate with Archbishop Ormanian, to whom its directorship had been entrusted. He was given the title of deputy abbot (the Armenian Patriarch in Constantinople retaining the title of abbot for himself, as was the custom). Tourian, regarding his work in Bardizag as completed, with the students he had taught being able to continue the work, accepted the invitation.

Before he left, Tourian, in concert with the village authorities, wished to divide his legacy among his students. So he advised that the schools' directorship be divided between three people from among the best of his student-collaborators: Y. Der-Antreasian, M. Semerdjian and me, as we had already taken on the responsibility for the most important parts of the curriculum in those days. The basic Armenian language, Turkish, French, natural sciences and mathematical subjects were all being taught by a graduate of the initial class, A Hapelian (later Anania Kahana then Vartabed Hapelian), and two others from the second class, A Bodosian and Aram Mazlemian (now Archbishop Garabed Mazlemian). They were assisted by several deputy teachers of both sexes.

Unfortunately this arrangement didn't work once he had left, Y. Der-Antreasian resigning in the first year. He went to Izmid as director of the community school there.

At this, the schools' trustees of the day cast aside the idea of a triumvirate running the schools and took on their senior direction itself, dividing the work between teachers. The schools re-opened with this organisation and continued its work. After a time, however, the trustees saw the need to have a representative in the schools and, informally, entrusted that position to me, without any kind of title, so as not to excite envy and suspicion within the teachers' circle.

This school year passed peacefully, without any difficulties, apart from a small problem that would have remained completely unnoticed if those who 'wanted to catch fish in troubled waters' during events in the future hadn't taken advantage of it. It was the following. A union had come into existence among the students whose organisers were individuals in the fourth class and their chairman one of the teachers. The object and plan of this union was unknown to me, but they had set themselves the task of providing poor students with writing materials. The trustees had given their permission for this and for which the union had a collecting box located in the corner of the main boys' hall, under the responsibility of one of its members. They sold, to anyone who approached them, whatever writing materials were necessary, during breaks and self-study times.

This commerce, in the school and at those times, attracted the trustees' representative's (my) attention, as something inimical to school discipline and detrimental to the students' regular education, being a permanent opportunity for their distraction. So I presented the problem to the trustees, advising them that it be halted during school hours and only be allowed during the lunch break or in the evenings after school had ended for the day. The trustees found this reasonable, and told the union's chairman that from then on the sale of writing materials could only continue during lunch and after school. Unfortunately neither the chairman-teacher nor some of the members liked this arrangement that had been made for their benefit, ascribing an anti-union stance to me, which was untrue.

The school re-opened and continued its work the following year in peaceful and quiet circumstances. During the year, however, one or two incidents happened that poisoned the peaceful relations between the trustees and their representative (me).

The first of these was this. Lent had begun. It had been the custom for many years, during Lent, to take all the students, as a group, to church immediately after school finished in the evening, to be present at the evening services. Despite this custom and without getting the trustees' approval, the teachers decided among themselves that the students could be given the opportunity to have a break, letting them go, with the strict instruction that they must all attend the evening services without fail. This arrangement was reached in this way: the days had grown longer with the season and the weather was improving significantly, therefore school could start earlier, resulting in work ending sooner, well before the church bell rang.

Because of this, they didn't consider it reasonable to hold the students in the school hall without anything to do while waiting for the church bell to ring. It would have been against the students' well-being and an opportunity for a lack of discipline to keep them in the school. The halls would become playgrounds, with the students talking, arguing and chasing each other. All this was also detrimental to the importance and special status of the study areas. At the same time the students, kept in the school against their will, only to be then taken to the church, would develop feelings of antipathy which, in terms of religious teaching, was not to be recommended. On the other hand, if they were given a break, they would rest and renew their energies and, without difficulty, perform their religious duty in good spirits and without any bad feeling.

One of the trustees noticed this change to the established custom. He too had children in the school, as well as having a paying student from Arslanbeg in his home, who was attending Bardizag's school. So to understand the situation and somewhat annoyed, he came to the school with some of his friends one morning and invited their representative (me) to join them to provide an explanation.

I quietly explained the reasons behind the change, while admitting that a mistake had been made in implementing it before getting the trustees' approval.

The protesting trustee, seeing that my sincere words were having an effect on his friends and would lead to the change being approved, and with the object of creating a problem, dared to insult me in my position as their representative, attempting to dismiss me, saying I had no right to speak in a trustees' meeting.

Seeing that I had already won the case before the majority of those present at the meeting, and allowing somewhat for the fact that the trustee was angry, I considered it sufficient to point out that the insult was unnecessary and that I had spoken, not as a member of the trusteeship, but to give the trustees an explanation in answer to the trustee's question.

A second problem was soon raised, thanks to the nature of the same trustee.

This man was a travelling cloth merchant. He looked for customers for his wares, with his package of materials on his shoulder, by walking the streets. The trustees, wishing their assembly room in the school - which had served from Tourian's time as a classroom and meeting room - to have the old curtains replaced and couches and cushions re-covered, had asked this man to bring several appropriate swatches of cloth at some reasonable time for them to make a choice and to place an order.

One day several trustees and this cloth-merchant trusteeship member came to the school with the required swatches and entered the room where I was sitting, awaiting the bell for the next lesson - I taught in that room.

The trustees looked at and examined the spread-out swatches of cloth and began joking about quality and price with their friend. Wanting to join this jovial company, having completely forgotten about the previous incident, I made a mistake and jokingly said something about not liking the materials. Our cloth-merchant trustee, who hadn't forgotten the incident and who hadn't learnt how to forgive if necessary, angrily began: 'Is that you talking?' He then added inflammatory things and curses to words and descriptions that could not have been accepted without difficulty by anyone with any self-respect. I, becoming very angry indeed, this time had the boldness to give a full and appropriate lesson to this man who, under the veneer of being a trustee, had given himself airs. The poor man had not expected such a justified reposte by someone who was just a teacher, as he was a person who had the ingenuousness of seeing everyone around him as slaves. He dried up, taking on a confused and beaten air. I could see that doing a worthwhile, long-term job with these people was impossible. It was obvious to me that this man would continue his destructive activities by secretly using underhanded methods to destroy his enemy (me), as it was very easy for a trustee to remove a teacher from the school and get someone else – even a piece of wood – to take his place. I turned to the trustees and said that I had lost confidence in this man's honesty as a trustee and as a man and, to maintain educational work before the storm broke – which it soon would – I considered it best to resign immediately and give my place to someone else. I also said that I knew that it wouldn't be difficult for the trustees, and would free me from this – now dangerous – position of being a teacher and trustee representative. I then left the room and went home.

At the unexpected result of the incident, the trustees held a full meeting, which divided into two equal and opposing camps, with three members on each side, the seventh member having resigned long before this incident.

One of the opposing camps of trustees defended their friend, who was one of them. The other three, who were completely neutral, despite the fact that one of them was the chairman and the man's brother-in-law, defended my position and called for the trusteeship meeting to exercise wisdom and care over the permanent solution to the basic problem. The chairman called for the resignation of the whole trusteeship to give the opportunity for me to return to my post. This was on the basis that I was one of the best assets the school had, if not the best, and to approach the parish council* to elect a new trusteeship for the school made up of neutral people. This wise suggestion was totally opposed by the three stubborn trustees.

The three trustees who backed me in retaining my position as a teacher took the initiative of presenting the problem, in all its details, to the parish council and also to present their collective resignations there. With their resignations, the trusteeship no longer had a quorum and, according to the rules, had to be considered as dissolved.

The opposing camp, wishing to continue in their position and to succeed in their destructive activity, thought of using the rules to bolster their position. So they persuaded the former trustee who had resigned to return to his position, which he accepted, making the number of trustees four out of a total of seven. They then approached the parish council and, basing their case on the swiftly and artificially manufactured majority being maintained, suggested that the number of trustees be brought up to the right level. The parish council, a slack and weak body in those days, under external pressure, buckled, and appointed three new trustees in place of those who had resigned. It was therefore reconstituted and remained in place, as it had not finished what it was to do in the school.

During this flurry of activity, I remained away from my former post. New incidents, of course, happened which strengthened the points I had made and which had made me withdraw. The meeting's chairman, however, saw me one day and invited me to resume my position. I refused. I couldn't be certain of the trustees' neutrality, especially with its new membership. The chairman then put a legal problem before me: that I had no right to resign during the school year and that the problem with the trusteeship was a personal one for the meeting itself, which it couldn't deal with.

---

* The word used here is *taghaganoutiun*.

Despite the fact that all these words were a means to gain time and avoid a probable scandal, I decided to comply with the rules, returning to my post, at least until the end of the school year, on the newly-elected chairman's assurances that *the problem was simply a personal one with the trustee, and that the trusteeship itself could not be involved.**

I returned to my post, without any position in the school and, like any and all teachers, concerned myself with the lessons I taught. This time, however, another teacher who was assisted by the trusteeship, without any official position, collaborated with the said trustee in his treachery and underhanded games. I heard about the fact that I was hated and that there were secret activities being carried on by the student members of the writing materials sales union and their chairman-teacher and the trustee against me. Notes were entered into the school's ledgers, apparently inserted by that teacher: 'he was early'; 'he was late'; 'he gave low marks'; 'he gave high marks', all to justify my forced resignation at the end of the school year.

The examination days arrived; the students of the 3rd class created a problem with me, clearly encouraged by my enemies, because they would not abide by the arrangements I made. I took the problem to the trustees who, without any legal basis, sided with the students, destroying my prestige and spreading indiscipline among the rest of them. To preserve my prestige, I refused to accept the trustees' illegal and dangerous ruling, the result of which was that I refused to accept responsibility for that class's examinations. The class therefore did not have any examinations for the subjects I taught. The students wanted to take part in the public examination of only one of the four subjects I taught, while I, whose sole right it was, in accordance with the rules and traditions of the school, demanded that they were examined in two subjects. The trustees however, took the students' part against me.

So what had been prepared happened. At the end of the school year I was dismissed by the trustees with the official announcement: 'We thank you for your service, but have no use for you next year'. The trustees had achieved their aim.

My unjustified dismissal, due to the circumstances outlined above, became a very serious matter in Bardizag. I was loved and considered to be of value, and regarded as the victim of enmity. The whole population of the village split in two: on the one side the trustees' backers - their relatives and relations, the locum tenens priest† and the slack parish council; on my side were the majority of the villagers, who refused to be involved with my dismissal. The people's approach to the community authorities, with threats being made, battles and severe clashes taking place, had no result. My unjustified dismissal stood, with passions running high, but

---

* Author's italics.
† This refers to the kahana who acted as the local deputy for the prelate.

not in the interests of the school or public. I therefore accepted an invitation to take up a post as teacher and director in a nearby Armenian-populated village school,* with a satisfactory salary and conditions, and swiftly decamped† and left the place I loved, to which I would not have the opportunity of returning.

The trustees, now masters of the situation, organized the teaching in the school for the next school year, keeping the teachers in their positions and, to replace me, invited Y. Der-Antreasian to come from Izmid where he lived, and teach. He accepted the position offered, and returned to Bardizag to collaborate with the trustees to distribute the teaching of various subjects. Of the teachers, Mr. Asadour Hapelian was dissatisfied with this distribution and left, taking up Der Andreasian's former position in the school in Izmid. However, at this same time, the latter was invited to take up a teaching post in the Armash seminary. He accepted, despite already accepting the position in Bardizag, as he couldn't be sure of the Bardizag public's troubled state as he would have belonged to a grouping, against his will, in the hands of the trustees.

The trustees became totally confused at this unexpected situation, seeing its position eroded in the eyes of the public. This all happened precisely at that time that I had gone, for a few days, to the village where I had accepted the new post, to clarify my position and to reach agreement with the local community authorities, which was completed between us.

I could see, with my own eyes, the disorganized and hopeless state the Bardizag community school and its trustees were in. In these circumstances and under public pressure, with the agreement of the trustees, the parish council took the initiative of approaching me, *the bad person*, as the good people had left. I was invited to the parish council offices and asked to return to my post at the school. I replied to the meeting that I had been dismissed against my will and had now accepted a new job, in a nearby village, and it was a matter of honour for me not to renege on my acceptance, so I regretted that I would not be able to accept their suggestion.

The parish council suggested that they get me released from my new job with an official approach to the village concerned, and insisted on doing so. As a final and irrevocable condition, I demanded the election of a new trusteeship, as I found it impossible to depend on the present one, so as to be able to work and produce good results. The actioning of this second demand was beyond the capability of the council, so it suggested peace negotiations between me and the trustees. I refused this suggestion, as I couldn't work with the present trusteeship with a calm state of mind. The negotiations then ended.

It is a common Armenian national (or community) custom to satisfy personal passions to the detriment of the community purse. The trustees sent a delegation to

---

* This must have been the school in Chengiler.

† His actual words are: 'I shook the dust from my feet...'

Constantinople to look for a teacher so that the schools in Bardizag could be reopened. Two teachers were hired: someone named Mr. Simonig Semerdjian and an expert in Turkish language, Boghos Effendi Kalebdjian, who received a salary of five Turkish liras a month each, an amount that was equal to, if not more than, the total monthly salaries of all the other teachers put together. The schools reopened.

The year ended but, despite the great sacrifices made, the schools couldn't achieve the same results as had previously been reached, and public feeling in Bardizag was very much against the trusteeship. Mr. Simonig Semerdjian was dismissed the following year and Minas Effendi Dzallian was invited to be the schools' inspector and teacher of Armenian. During that year Minas Dzallian became convinced that he couldn't do a worthwhile job under the trustees' auspices, and resigned at the end of the school year. To bring the schools to a reasonable state was extremely difficult for the trusteeship that, however, didn't want to give way. It was scared that it would look small and lose its standing, especially now that the country's political circumstances, especially towards the Armenians, were in a very delicate state.* Passions were so emphasised that the trusteeship didn't hesitate to utilise them against its opponents, as we shall see, in its stubborn determination to stay in power. So it continued to work, if not for the benefit of education, which no longer had a place in their minds, but simpy to maintain their wrongly understood prestige. After Dzallian, the inspectorate was given to the teacher Mr. Aram Mazlemian,† who was now the trustees' man. Mr. Mazlemian, surrounded by his student friends, ran the schools, with only the shadow of the old ones remaining.

The fall of Tourian's schools and their decline continued like this until the days of freedom,‡ with a falling number of students and a gradual reduction of moral and mental development, and a significant number of Bardizag students leaving and attending the American Boys' High School instead.

During the days of freedom the clique of trustees and its friends and advisors was cleaned out and swept away; those wretched individuals, tied to the pillar of disgrace, hardly had the courage to appear in public.

---

* The author is referring here to the state of the Ottoman Empire in about 1894-1895, when there were serious moves against the Armenians by Sultan Abdul Hamid II, culminating in the mass killings of 1895, when between 200,000 and 300,000 Armenians were massacred.

† Mkhalian doesn't give his first name, but it is recorded by Teotig in his *Golgotha of the Armenian clergy and its flock in the calamitous yoar of 1915*, edited by Ara Kalaydjian, New York, 1985, p. 402.

‡ Mkhalian is referring to 1908, the time of the restoration of the Ottoman constitution. Kasabian states that in 1909-1910 the community boys' school had 330 pupils with 10 male and 15 female teachers and that its budget was 53,000 *kurush*, while the girls' school had 290 pupils, 6 female teachers and a budget of 9,000 *kurush*. Minas Kasabian (Farhad), *Hayere Nikomedio Kavarin Mech*, p. 261.

It remains for me to continue the history of the schools in Bardizag from the days of freedom through the following years, but I will leave that until later,* presenting other events that are connected to this time of unbridled passions.

133 – The ordination of a vartabed: Mr. A Mazlemian dedicates himself to celibate priesthood

Aram Mazlemian, after several years of teaching, following Mgerdich Vartabed Aghavnouni's example,† had the wish to become a celibate monk. He therefore approached the deputy abbot of the Armash seminary, but found himself in difficulties realising his wish there, and returned to Bardizag to his post as a teacher.

Then his friends, the trusteeship quoted in the previous section, came to his aid, presenting his wish to the diocesan prelate Bishop Stepannos Hovagimian. This churchman, in accordance with his *good* custom, loved and defended the trusteeship that had taken on the mission of destroying the Bardizag schools, as if to erase Tourian's work. So he was pleased to approve the request put before him. He was spurred on by the candidate's rejection by the deputy abbot of Armash whom he didn't like from his early days, and ordained Mazlemian a vartabed (archimandrite) in Bardizag in 1894, giving him the ordination name of Garabed.

This ordination took place at the time of Minas Dzallian's resignation as schools inspector. The trustees, having reached their goal, formally handed the school inspectorate over to the newly ordained monk, who at the same time was appointed the Bardizag church's preacher. His position as inspector didn't last long; he left his work to take up spiritual work in the diocese under the Bishop. He became diocesan locum tenens and participated in the provincial assemblies.

He was later elected to the prelacy of the diocese of Banderma-Balekeser. He and the people of his diocese were deported from there in 1915, and he had a very bad time, often in danger of his life. He finally was able to stop within the Aleppo vilayet borders, in a Turkish village near Radjo station from where, at the order and with the permission of the Ittihad Turkish government, he was able to escape to the Armenian Apostolic monastery in Jerusalem towards the end of the war. He became part of the Catholicosal-Patriarchal brotherhood there and was a member of the Synod for a time. After the Armistice‡ he returned to Banderma to resume his diocesan position until the Kemalist Turkish forces advanced, when he and his people left the region, escaping to Athens, Greece.** There he was appointed to the

---

* See Chapter 11, Section 154, item 8.
† See Section 131.
‡ November 1918.
** This was in 1923.

prelacy of Old Greece, which he holds to this day,* showing great robustness and individuality despite the difficulties and political problems that surround him. He received his consecration as archbishop from the late Catholicos of All Armenians Kevork V in Echmiadzin.

In his life he has been a robust, battling person, but often hasn't been able to choose good and reliable friends, being cheated by them.

134 – Days of terror in Bardizag

At the time when the peaceful running of the schools was interrupted and passions were running high, four people who opposed the trustees were arrested, charged with revolutionary activity. They were H. Khacherian, Vahan Djelgouni (now Hovhannes Kahana Djelgouni), Boghos Kourouyian and Hagop Kondaiyan. They were incarcerated in Constantinople's central prison. In a previous section† I told the story of the first arrests of people accused of revolutionary activity in Bardizag. As a result of new Armenian demonstrations in Constantinople, the Turkish government renewed its policy of terror and began to pursue every form of revolutionary activity throughout the country.‡ Spies and informers proliferated and there was no limit to the severe persecution that took place, resulting in an atmosphere in the country in which only informers and spies could draw breath freely. Evil people everywhere utilised the opportunity presented by the government's dreadful policy to gain position and wealth for themselves. One of these was the chairman of the trustees who, in his stupid passion, found great approbation in government circles. He became, for a time, a member of the Preliminary Court** in Izmid, and the chairman of the village council in Bardizag.††

Everybody in Bardizag found the arrests unjustified, because if three of those arrested had been known as Hnchags by many, H. Khacherian was simply an opponent in principle of the trustees, and at no time had any dealings with or joined in any revolutionary activity, being the son of an old, well-to-do family and an old man himself. He had never felt drawn to those suspicious, dangerous movements. Everyone knew this in Bardizag, and his being accused of being a revolutionary and incarcerated

---

* Mkhalian was writing this in about 1937.
† See Section 128.
‡ It would appear that the author is writing about the Sultan Abdul-Hamid II anti-Armenian policy of repression and massacre that took place in 1895-1896. Minas Kasabian (Farhad), *Hayere Nikomedio Kavarin Mech*, pp. 148-149.
** The words used here are *nakhatad tadastan*.
†† The author does not provide this individual's name. He does, however, detail the village councils in order in Section 100; it would appear that this person was one of the following individuals who were chairmen during this era: Mgerdich Agha Alachayian, Artin Agha Melkonian (Zobi) or Aghasi Effendi Der-Mgerdichian.

was simply a way of silencing a confirmed opponent and subjecting him to terror. The others, although they were known Hnchags, had never partaken in any work or activity that justified their arrests, but were part of the group opposed to the trustees.

These innocent men were held in cells in prison for several months under severe questioning, suffering great expense. The treatment they received disturbed their mental tranquillity. Finally archpriest Hovhannes Kahana Mgerian, who was the arrested Vahan Djelgouni's grandfather, and Hovhannes Kondaiyan, a bookseller in the Bible House and father of Hagop Kondaiyan, collaborated and, through the intervention of the Armenian Patriarchate, the Armenian Protestant National Authority and well-known Armenian government people, succeeded in obtaining freedom for the four imprisoned men who, very depressed, returned to Bardizag. Although the plot hatched by evil people had eventually been thwarted, fear had entered all hearts and the trustees' opponents were forced into silence.

135 – The Yildiz bomb: new and terrible fear in Bardizag

In 1905, a few years after the events described above, a bomb exploded at the Friday Selamlik on Sultan Abdul Hamid II's route. The Sultan, having been delayed, escaped the attempt on his life, but the entire country, from one end to the other, was plunged into crisis and horror. The criminal or criminals had to be found.*

Spies and informers were put into action and evil people found a new opportunity to satisfy their passions. Many, on mere suspicion, were put in prison, for days or months, and subjected to terrible torture to force confessions from them. The plotters who tried to kill the sultan were searched for, with the greatest rigour, everywhere, even in the depths of the provinces. Several days after the attempt on the sultan's life, a special ship arrived in Seymen from Constantinople and anchored there. A large elite group, with secret orders, disembarked and made its way up to Bardizag.

Aghasi Effendi Der-Mgeridchian and his brother, the pharmacist and community activist Garabed Der-Mgerdichian were both arrested, as was one of the people who had been arrested previously – Boghos Kourouyian who bred silkworms – and also Ghazaros Kanchilian, a grocer and a good, quiet man, the latter two being Protestants. The shops belonging to the arrested men were meticulously searched, as were their goods, houses and papers, which were collected into packets for examination. Not satisfied with all this, they demolished the walls of the arrestees' houses, blocked up places were opened up in the search for suspicious items and, finally, the Der-Mgerdichian-owned mulberry orchard, located next to their house,

---

* This is the famous 'Yildiz bomb' incident that took place on July 21, 1905, organised by the Armenian Revolutionary Federation. The sultan escaped because he was delayed by the Sheikh-ul-Islam, who wanted to speak to him, just before the sultan was due to enter his carriage to return to his palace.

was completely dug up to the depth of at least half an arshin (about 15 inches or 38cm) using hired labour and under strict supervision. In other words the most rigorous search was made in all the places that were expected to achieve results, as well as those that weren't, as the accusations against them were so great and serious.

Fortunately they couldn't find even one shred of evidence to prove the arrested men's guilt, and the group, in Bardizag itself, became convinced of their absolute innocence. But in accordance with their instructions, they took the arrested men and their papers with them the next day to Yildiz palace, where the questioning of suspects was taking place.

The whole village, faced with such a serious and worrying situation, was terrified, as it could endanger its very safety.

The arrested men didn't stay in Constantinople very long. They were questioned and their papers examined, and their total innocence proved. They were released, and returned to Bardizag, spending several days in a fearful state that was almost as bad as death for them. The questioning they had suffered revealed the nature of the accusations levelled against them. These had been laid before the authorities by an evil and rascally woman who was the first wife of the Der-Mgerdichians' third brother, who had been convicted of immorality and had her marriage to him annulled in accordance with canon law. No one else had any part in the accusations that time.

136 – Fire calamities

Fire was the greatest calamity for Constantinople and the surrounding area, where the majority of buildings were of wooden construction, apart from the old ones, and there was still no fire protection insurance in the country.

Outbreaks of fire had hit Bardizag as both major and minor incidents more than once, suddenly leaving part of the population with nothing but ashes. We've seen, in the earliest part of this work,* the burning down of the first church. After that, however, the walls of the houses were built of clay bricks for a time, removing most of the risk of fire. But the villagers returned to constructing their houses of timber in the old way. This was perhaps because lumber, prepared timber and building materials were plentiful in our area. The houses took comparatively less time to build, as well as being light in construction, standing up to earthquakes better and having the advantages of being free from damp and being well ventilated.

Fires usually broke out in Bardizag in autumn and winter. They happened in autumn because branches of trees and flax plant stems would be piled around the houses. These, dried by the wind, were readily combustible materials if a spark should accidentally fall among them, such as, for example, a lit cigarette butt thrown out of a window. Again, in winter, when it was cold the brazier or oven was kept constantly lit.

---

* See Section 9.

If the fire had not been damped down at night, a sudden explosion in the fire itself could send showers of sparks onto these dry, combustible materials while everyone was in a deep sleep, suddenly waking them up due to the smell of burning and the heat of the flames.

In Bardizag, after the first church burnt down, one major outbreak of fire is recalled (called the Great Fire), which happened probably during the 1840s or a little later, before I was born. A complete, newly-built group of houses on the eastern side of the village was destroyed by fire in a few hours. Traces of it could still be seen in my day, with many plots of land still empty where burnt houses had stood. This fire, which started in a pile of flax plants, was a noted event in Bardizag. People in the village were used to calculating the time of an event, like prehistoric man, as being either before or after 'the year of the fire' *(yangheni darien)*.

Several fires, both large and small, broke out in my day too, the worst of which happened in the market area, in a narrow and crowded street right next to the Golimanents fountains, in the house of someone nicknamed 'Chorab Fez', and which was only put out thanks to superhuman efforts and keeping the fire within the confines of that house alone.

The people of Bardizag displayed the greatest boldness and an estimable spirit of collaboration when fire broke out. Everyone without exception would rush to the scene of the fire with the determination to prevent a catastrophe. Carpenters would, with the greatest daring and skill, climb to the points on the surrounding houses which were the most endangered, covering them with wetted carpets or pouring buckets of water onto the flames to quench them. Armed with axes, they would demolish parts of the building on fire, to isolate the flames and the fire itself. The women and girls would bring water from the nearest fountains or houses in various containers and the fire, before long, would be quenched, thanks to that brave and irresistible public collaboration.

The villagers in my youth bought, through public collaboration and assistance, two portable pumps and all their necessary equipment as community assets, which were kept in the church's narthex. An elite group of young men was trained as firefighters under the leadership of Baghdasar Ago (Daiyi), one of the heroes of the Armash road incident.[*] The *fortoumdji* was Ghaladji Karekin, from the famous clan of Ghaladjis, a lively and high-spirited young man. During the construction of the new schools, the opportunity was taken to build two wide and deep cisterns in the church courtyard to act as water reservoirs in case of fire, filled by the rainwater flowing from the school roof into guttering and through down pipes. These reservoirs were always kept full in case of emergencies and especially for the sake of the school building.

---

* See Section 106.

No other fire worthy of recollection occurred in Bardizag apart from these events I have recorded. The neighbouring Armenian village of Arslanbeg was much less fortunate and suffered a dreadful fire that reduced it completely to ashes in one day. It was reconstructed with government and community assistance[*] and the local people's enthusiastic work, on a new and regular plan, with wide, straight streets crossing one another at right angles aligned to the cardinal points of the compass. Two years later, however, the whole village was destroyed by fire again, leaving it a heap of ashes. But the villagers, left to themselves this time, rebuilt the village with unmatched enthusiasm and effort on the same plan and under the same circumstances.

137 – Nshan Agha Sinanian and his farm

The Sinanians were a quiet and likeable family in Bardizag. They were able, but had the harmless weakness of wanting to show off. At the same time they were experts in understanding the Turks' psychology and successful in their efforts to cultivate them as friends.

Nshan Agha Sinanian was the son of one of the branches of the Sinanian family, and his father was Sinan Khachadour.[†] Nshan had four brothers: he and Sinan, the oldest, resided in Bardizag; the other three, Stepan, Mgerdich and Mihran, were established in Constantinople, where for a time they were clerks in a fruit business *(Meyve Hosh)*, later becoming owners of their own business and offices.

The eldest, Sinan, was the son-in-law to one of the Der-Sahagian brothers of that famous family, and lived at the eastern end of the village, occupying himself with the manufacture of wooden cereal containers of specific sizes.[‡] This was like a hobby to him. At the same time he was mostly a man of taste and pleasure, regarding life as an opportunity for recreation. He had created a beautiful garden next to his house, a sought-after meeting place during summer evenings for Bardizag's Turkish officials and their friends, who were either from the village or from outside, who liked to gather there and enjoy themselves, surrounded by flowers and fresh green plants. In this way Sinan had managed to cultivate influential and useful friends through whom he was able to arrange his and other people's business with ease.

Nshan Agha, on the other hand, was the son-in-law of the notable farming and landowning Bedigian family. He lived with them in his own part of their house, thanks to his wife's inheritance, and succeeded in establishing a position for himself

---

[*] The word used here is *azkayin,* which can be translated as 'national'. The author uses it here to indicate that the help received was from Armenian sources, rather than those of the government.

[†] The author has used this name. I have refrained, in this instance, from making it Khachadour Sinan.

[‡] The author quotes the sizes as *demirli, yolcheg* and *ghouti*.

in Bardizag in a short time. He rose from being a travelling merchant to the notable state of farm owner.

The Bedigians, within the Khans area, had large and good quality land holdings where Nshan Sinanian began to concern himself with the cultivation of mulberry trees, tobacco and cheese making on a large scale – he had flocks of sheep on his land. These rural activities were successful and made him rich. Early each morning he would go the market area of the village, leading his saddled horse, which he tied up at the corner of a shop. He would drink a coffee in front of the Der-Garabedians' coffee house or another similar establishment, then talk to various people to arrange matters about his business. Having completed this, he would spring lightly into the saddle, gather the skirts of his light fabric coat under him and, giving himself the air of a nobleman, would gallop his horse the length of Bardizag's main street, attracting the gaze of many, and go to his farm.

He spent his days there, occupied with the farm and the supervision of the labourers, directing their efforts. Sometimes he would mount his horse again and would walk it gently through the fields to briefly visit his flocks that were grazing in the meadows. He would give orders to the shepherds and then turn his horse's head to go down to Seymen, taking one of the farm boys with him. There he would leave the horse with the farm boy to take it back to the farm and take a boat to Izmid to see his acquaintances, merchants and customers. At a particular time in the evening the farm boy would bring the horse to Seymen once more. The Agha would mount it and, having briefly visiting his farm and animals again, return home, soothed by its regular pace.

Nshan Agha Sinanian's presentable appearance and his financial means allowed him to entertain great friends especially during the summer, during the day in the charming shady copse on his farm and at night. Whole lambs were spit-roasted, often basted with wine or oghi, which was always accompanied by his famous fresh cheese sweet dish *(yoshmir)*. All this was the means to gain influential friendships in Izmid government circles beginning with the mutesarif and including all the notables who had position and authority. Thus he became a known and respected man in Bardizag and Izmid. He began to be approached by many with their worries and troubles, and became an invulnerable personality with his personal businesses. His only misfortune was his lack of education, which was a serious impediment to giving his position great weight.

It was at this time that an abduction took place at the site of the warm springs at Yalova. It could well have resulted in complications for the Turkish government. A lady, belonging to the French aristocracy, accompanied by a Miss Paraghamian,[*] had gone to the famous Sultan Hamid warm springs for a cure. A robber band had heard of their visit and, wanting to capitalise on the wonderful opportunity that

---

[*] A girl from Bardizag who must have been her maid.

presented itself, abducted the two ladies and took them to the mountains, demanding a 10,000 liras ransom for their release. Nshan Agha Sinanian was to have an important role in the arrest of this bold robber band and, for his selfless government service, would receive a notable reward.

Let me tell the story of the incident with its main details. Sultan Abdul Hamid II grasped the seriousness of the problem. This was at the time when European public opinion was so involved with the question of administrative reforms that were felt to be so necessary in Turkey. He tried, with all the means at his disposal, to free the women from the robbers, to prove the robustness and authority of the Turkish government.

The government itself paid the ransom and freed the abducted women without injury, but in accordance with the sultan's order, boldly pursued the robber band that, having pocketed the ransom, had disappeared from the area. To prevent them escaping by sea, the whole length of the Marmara coastline was put under strict surveillance. The only route left for the robbers was overland, so they decided to return via the area around the Bay of Izmid and travel through the mountains to Uskudar, in other words to Constantinople. Following this plan, the band travelled at night, resting in various hiding places, and moving towards the edge of the sea in the Bardizag area. It made its way through it one night, as far as the forest near the government factory, where it was confronted by government forces.

The robbers defended themselves there, and a fierce battle developed between them and the government forces, without either side winning. The way ahead was closed to the robbers, who swiftly retreated and made their way to Nshan Agha Sinanian's farm, where they sought protection, leaving the worry of saving them to him, so that he could show them the way to go to Constantinople safely.

Sinanian found himself confronted with a serious dilemma. If he tried to help them escape, it would seriously endanger his person and position if they were caught, which was highly likely. To betray them, however, to the government would also be dangerous, as the robbers were determined not to surrender, and would fight to their last breath. If they escaped under such circumstances, it would be impossible for him to keep his work on his farm in the deserted Bardizag countryside and he would never be safe, as his life would constantly be under threat.

So he came to a firm decision: to get the robbers to Constantinople, disarm them there and hand them over to the government safely. I don't know if the government knew of this plan, but in any event caution determined that the government's approval was secured. The reality was that through Nshan Agha Sinanian, the robbers went to Constantinople without incident, by sea, disguised as sailors in a sailing ship. The robbers settled in a hotel there, waiting for a safe way of going abroad to be found.

Now that the robbers were no longer a threat and were defenceless, Nshan Agha handed them over to the government, earning a certificate of commendation from it saying that he had carried out an important service. His collaborator in this episode in Constantinople was his brother, Stepan Effendi Sinanian. The government rewarded him for his selfless and consummate assistance, presenting him with the Medal of Medidjie, fourth class.

This government reward raised Nshan Agha's position and value before the local government, as someone who had been commended and decorated by high government circles. Now he had free access to every government office. He participated in government celebrations, such as the sultan's birthday or the anniversary of his enthronement, dressed in his uniform with his medals on his chest and a sword by his side. He would be received in Izmid on these occasions with full official honours.

In his greatness and influence, Nshan Agha did not have a detrimental effect on Bardizag public interests and helped the community to the best of his ability. He was chairman of the village council twice, trying to provide good service through good stewardship.[*]

The only thing that somewhat badly affected the villagers was his reluctance to pay the rent for grazing his sheep on the community-owned meadows, claiming that he used his own land for that purpose. This was simply an excuse, to show that he was following the rules. It would appear that he wanted the villagers to respect his position and withdraw the demand, which he felt was not appropriate either to his greatness or magnanimity. The rents from the meadows were income used for the community schools. After a time, however, he conformed to public demand and paid, like everyone else.

Nshan Agha knew how to utilise his position and his only son, Hagop Effendi Sinanian, one of the final graduates of the Tourian era of the community school, succeeded in being accepted into the newly-established government agricultural school in Halkale. Hagop Effendi Sinanian successfully graduated from that school and was appointed a government agricultural inspector. He served in that capacity in the province of Izmid, and when the deportations took place, remained free when, in those days, his father, Nshan Agha, was already dead.

Unfortunately this pleasant, noble and worthwhile young man didn't live for very long. After the Armistice he married into the Kiutnerian family, becoming Hadji Artin's son-in-law, but a sudden grave illness carried him off while he was still full of energy.

138 – Laz Armenian bandits

We have read, in previous pages, of the formation of Laz Armenian villages, alongside those of *Giurdjis* [Muslim Georgians], in our mountains.[†] Two of them,

---

[*] He was the chairman of the 7th and 8th village councils. See Section 100.
[†] See Section 115.

Zakar village and Manoushag, were located within the local area and were in everyday trading contact with Bardizag.

Zakar village was about one and a half hours distant form Bardizag in Sakar Bchki, which was turned into the name Zakar. The other, Manoushag, was at two hours distance from Bardizag, and was located around the well-known pilgrimage site known as Menemeshe.

Both villages had their kahanas and simple places of prayer. The priest in Zakar village was Margos Kahana, a peasant but a fervant believer and a dedicated churchman; Manoushag's was Hagop Kahana, a slightly better educated, honourable and good priest, who was more refined in the values of the spirit and heart. Those villages had their elders, representatives of the great houses who, in concert with the priests, governed their communities. They were a tribe of intrepid mountain people, who lived in concord with the neighbouring Islamic immigrants.

At the beginning they mainly gained their livelihood from growing *lazoud* [maize] on their land, from which they prepared, like their Muslim neighbours, their daily *djat* [bread] and sold small boxes of various sizes and cups etc. carved from solid blocks of wood, in Bardizag. Later they had their own domestic animals: horses used for transporting wood and lumber, cows and goats, from the milk of which they produced clarified butter, a much sought-after item. They also supplied animals for food and occasionally grew wheat and barley for sale, and spent the winter hunting in the forests.

There were no wealthy people among them; they lived simple lives in patriarchal families, self-sufficient and satisfied with their state, and had a courteous relationship with us and their Muslim neighbours.

A catastrophic incident occurred, however, which poisoned the good relations with their neighbouring Muslims for a time, creating an atmosphere of suspicion and distrust between them.

One day, I think it was in about 1900, two Laz Armenian young men, Avedis and Sarkis, both honourable villagers who earned their own wages, armed with Mausers[*] as a precaution against any evil surprise, were driving their horses, loaded with wood, down from the forest towards their village. On their way down, the met two Muslim brothers called Loghman oghlou Mehmed and Ahmed oghlou Mehmed of Deoshme village, both of whom had suspicious pasts. These two demanded that Avedis and Sarkis hand over their weapons, which the two Laz Armenians refused to do. At this unexpected refusal and defence by the 'infidels', the two criminals became angry, and tried to disarm them by force. The two Laz Armenians, defending themselves, fired at the criminals, killing one of them; the other saved his life by escaping.

The Laz Armenian youths had no confidence in government justice and were fearful of the revenge that would be exacted by members of the dead man's

---

[*] It is not stated whether these weapons were pistols or rifles.

community after this incident. They therefore went into the mountains, leaving their homes, and decided to preserve their honour and lives against any attack with their weapons. Fear made them into bandits with the result that from that day on they adopted hiding places in the mountains as their places to live.

After a time young men from Bardizag collaborated with them, taking them food and defending them. One of these young men was a person called Parnag, who had, at some time, been a Regie* overseer and was now a tobacco smuggler,† an occupation in which the two Laz Armenian young men could provide assistance.

The two now slept during the day, so as to be active on the deserted roads at night. They adopted tobacco smuggling as their occupation which, although dangerous, was profitable for bold and brave men. They occasionally went to the Adabazar and Khandedig areas at night, making friends and creating their hideouts on that long road. They bought their stock of tobacco there and returned to the Bardizag region where they sold it all and made a living for themselves.

The smuggling of tobacco, fraught with danger, was not very different from banditry – the latter was also considered to be a profitable business in Turkey, although linked to danger, but available to bold and brave men such as our young Laz Armenians.

Avedis and Sarkis, apart from smuggling, also took up banditry, robbing travellers or surprising rich Turkish or Greek villagers by night in their gardens or fields, obtaining ransoms for their release. The saying is 'One's appetite grows with eating'. The Laz Armenians continued their trade, despite their real wishes, on the roads and in the way they had to. They were often pursued by government forces but were impossible to find and became invulnerable, something that increased their boldness and bravery. Public perception was that the suspect bandits were just two Lazes, their other collaborators being simply friends of the night or of dark corners of their hideouts and their advisors. All the latter were reliable citizens like everyone else, moving about and travelling like ordinary people, and following their own ordinary work in the village or in their homes when they were not involved in any night time activity with the real bandits. Everyone in Bardizag, however, knew the whole truth about those secret activities, but was careful about talking about it. The villagers were frightened of thieves, but these two didn't do them any harm, especially as their existence in the mountains and on deserted roads forced the Muslims to respect Armenian Christians.

They were cautious, for a time, in their exploits vis-a-vis their compatriots, but eventually came to the conclusion that every rich man was a thief. This applied to any Armenian or Turk, with his fraudulent activities that crushed the poor and

---

* The government tobacco organisation.
† Tobacco smuggling in Bardizag was known as *ayinga*, and the smugglers as *ayingadji*. See 'Rural economy' in Section 156.

weak in their penury. The latter were not able to defend their interests, which mostly went into rich men's pockets. In those days socialism was the doctrine that was preached among us, with its attractive and just outer appearances. It was mostly the poor who were very interested in it, as were the bandits, who could turn its principles into an occupation.

With these thoughts in their minds, they heard that the newly-established silk spinning factory owner Avedian of Bardizag had the habit of bringing the sums of money made in his trading activities from Constantinople to the village on a Sunday. This was a day which was not suspicious in terms of profit and earnings. Bardizag's port and the road to the village were usually deserted on Sunday as it was a day of rest. So one Sunday the thieves waited on his route as he was due to return then. They hid in a copse about a quarter of an hour below the village, within the area of vineyards, in daylight. The road was empty as usual with no one moving one way or the other. Suddenly Avedian appeared on the road in his carriage pulled by horses. The disguised thieves stopped the carriage and robbed him, with death threats, of everything in his pockets, about 500 Austrian Kremnitz.[*]

The thieves then, before Avedian's confused and frightened eyes, went through the vineyards and mulberry orchards and disappeared into the distance towards Hromin Yasakh. Avedian and his friends settled their suspicions on the Laz Armenian bandits, as it would be unbelievable for foreigners to have the audacity, in broad daylight and so near the village, to carry out such an exploit. They reported their suspicions to the government, accusing the Laz Armenian bandits of the crime, with Parnag being presented as their collaborator and leader.

The government arrested Parnag, imprisoned and questioned him, and threatened to keep him under permanent surveillance, to force him to tell the truth. Parnag resisted; money was plentiful, and his comrades would look after his home and children. They would look after him, at the same time, while he was in prison.[†] Under these circumstances, not being able to find a legal basis for the accusation against him, the government released him. As a suspicious person, however, he was kept under surveillance and every time something happened and the Laz Armenians were suspected, the first person looked for and arrested was Parnag.

One day the government heard that the two bandits were in their home village, Zakar, in Sarkis' brother's house. It immediately mobilised a large force of police and sent it to the village. This was done secretly at night and the force was joined, on the way there, by a large contingent of armed Muslim volunteers. The government force captured the village by surprise, closed all the ways out of it and surrounded Sarkis' house. The thieves were in the house but, without any fuss,

---

[*] An Austrian Kremnitz was equal to 4 Austrian Gulden or 10 Latin Monetary Union Francs, and was in use from 1848 until 1916.

[†] If a prisoner in a Turkish jail had money, he would usually buy his meals, bedding, tobacco etc. from outside.

suddenly emerged, weapons in hand. Several volleys were enough to frighten the surrounding police force and the volunteers into panicking and, cutting through their lines, the two escaped into the mountains without injury.

The police, disillusioned and embarrassed, wanted to vent their spleen on the people in the house. They searched every part of it as well as Sarkis' brother, his wife and children, shouting obscenities and beating them. They found a considerable sum in Sarkis' wife's belt, all of it Austrian Kremitzes. They arrested her and Parnag from Bardizag, throwing them both into the Izmid government building's prison.

The government was determined to use this proof of the robbery to destroy the Laz Armenian bandit band. This was at a time when the Armenian revolution had already started in Turkey's interior and had created concern in government circles. Noting that the bandits were ready *fedayees* (freedom fighters)* for the Armenian Case,† the government increased the pressure on the detainees, especially on Parnag. Parnag gradually became convinced that he was going to be the scapegoat in this vexed question of the Laz Armenian bandits. He weakened under the pressure put on him, a weakness that would result in an unjustifiable crime committed by him, which was to betray his comrades so as to save his own skin. He came to an agreement with the government to hand them over, on the condition that he remained immune from prosecution, under the following circumstances.

Parnag, released from prison, found his comrades and persuaded them that to continue what they were doing within the area was now dangerous for them. He suggested that they descend to Bardizag at night and continue on, using deserted roads, to the Black Sea coast. Then, travelling like ordinary people from village to village, they could reach the borders of their original homeland, near Ordu, shake off any pursuit and end their lives as bandits.

What happened was that he brought his comrades down at dead of night and entertained them in his brother-in-law's house in Bardizag's Lower Fields parish. According to the arrangements made between Parnag and the government, a detachment of police, under the command of an officer, came and hid behind the trunks of the ancient mulberry trees opposite the front door at about midnight. The idea was that the two men would be killed as they opened the door and emerged. Parnag and his comrades ate and drank, then came into the yard to start the planned journey to the Black Sea coast. When they opened the door and came into the street, the police opened continuous fire from their hiding places and killed both men, as it would have been impossible to arrest them without suffering losses. This is the gist of the *official* report of the incident of the slaughter of the two robbers or bandits, with the police officer and the police receiving various medals for their *intrepid bravery*.

---

* Armenian revolutionaries were known as *fedayees*. This is a Turkish term meaning 'self-sacrifice' and was given to them by the Armenian population throughout Turkey as a sign of respect and affection.

† It was otherwise known as the 'Armenian Question' in diplomatic circles.

But the real truth was completely different. Not being able to be sure that they could kill the two men under the circumstances presented without suffering losses, the men's own friends killed them in the yard while they were putting on their sandals. The bodies were thrown out onto the street, at which point the brave policemen fired their rifles into the air, concealing the horrible killings in a haze of smoke, flames and noise.

The evil men were tried and convicted by public opinion and were discredited until the curtain of deportation finally covered every foul deed.

139 – The construction of the community bath house

Bardizag didn't have a public bath house, despite having plentiful supplies of water. It was a completely Armenian village that hadn't felt the need for one. It was the same for all the surrounding Armenian villages. For Muslims, however, a bath house was a necessity, as an establishment linked to religion. We Armenians took care of our baths and washing within the family home, in wooden bathrooms.[*] This meant that our people didn't enjoy the benefits of washing and bodily cleanliness with its health requirements, often doing without bathing, especially in cold weather, as there was none of the current kind of regular and protected bathrooms in the houses at that time.

When Bardizag became the centre of a group of villages *(nahie)*, there were always a number of Turkish officials in the village accompanied by their families. With this and the above-mentioned situation in mind, it became necessary to have a bath house in the village. The community authorities, under the chairmanship of Aghasi Effendi Papazian, took the decision to build one. This was considered to be a community necessity and at the same time a source of revenue for the community schools. The diocesan prelate, Bishop Stepannos Hovagimian, approved of and endorsed the council's decision and dedicated his efforts to its construction.

A plot of land at the lower part of the village, on the edge of the road leading to the Upper Cemetery, was bought as the site for the bath house. Experts in bath house construction were brought in, and local wall builders and labourers worked alongside them. Building materials had been previously stockpiled for its construction and building began. The administration and superintendence of the construction was handed over to Hadji Artin Kiutnerian and, very soon, the community had its own bath house.[†]

---

[*] The word *lokaran* could either mean bathroom, bath house or bath tub. I have used the first.
[†] This is the basic chronicle of the building of the bath house. There are many anecdotes about its construction. I personally have heard many (often scurrilous) stories about it from elderly people. Der-Hagopian recounts a more colourful version the story. Hagop Der-Hagopian, *Bardizage khadoudig*, Paris, 1960, pp. 215-217.

The bath house was a neat building. It was eminently fit for its purpose, with two baths, each of which had two basins, with hot and cold water taps. There was a breathing room* in the area where the two baths met, with only one basin. In the bath house courtyard there was a large two storey hall, furnished with rows of couches. There was a small buffet in the corner of this hall which served coffee and soft drinks for customers.† A sufficient flow of water was secured for it, and it began operating.‡

The bath house was rented out to a tenant who bid for it at auction, in return for a specific sum of money, and men, women and children bathed there at prices set by the village authorities.

140 – The Ottoman Bank incident in Constantinople and its repercussions on life in Bardizag

On August 15th, 1896, Armenian revolutionaries, armed with bombs, captured the Ottoman Bank building in Constantinople. They threatened to destroy that internationally important currency exchange establishment if the great European powers didn't fulfil their commitments as defined by the Treaty of Berlin by putting pressure on the Turkish government to stop the massacre of Armenians and realise the promised reforms.**

That protest by the revolutionaries was a bankrupt exercise. The European powers' ambassadors negotiated with the revolutionaries and persuaded them, with false promises and arranging official permission for them to go abroad, to end the protest, thus saving the Ottoman Bank.

Unfortunately for our people, hardly had the revolutionaries left the bank and embarked on a ship to go to Europe, when a terrible massacre began in the streets and quarters of Constantinople, and thousands of Armenians were killed by the Turkish mob and much Armenian wealth was looted. All this happened under the ambassadors' indifferent and unsympathetic gaze. It was organised, aided and abetted by the guilty Turkish government, with the whole of the Armenian

---

* The author uses the word *shncharan* here.
† The construction of the bath house was completed on 1 January 1903.
‡ Even after the bath house construction had been finished, the supply of water was a problem. The higher parishes wouldn't allow water to flow to it, so eventually the Izmid government got involved, and the higher parishes hired a lawyer: mediation was used and the problem was settled. Eventually water flowed to the bath house and it was used until 1915.
** The Ottoman Bank incident was organised by the Armenian Revolutionary Federation (Dashnaktsutiun) and commanded by a young man known as Papken Siuni, leading Dashnak fedayees. It took place on August 14th, 1896. See Christopher J. Walker, *Armenia: the Survival of a Nation*, Croom Helm, London 1980, pp. 164-166.

population of Constantinople living days of terror. There were, of course, many Armenians in the city from the provinces who had settled there for years because of their businesses or who had arrived for a few days for personal reasons.

There were people from Bardizag among those killed; one of them was Mgerdich Effendi Geolliuian, a former teacher in the community schools who, now established in Constantinople, had been working as a lawyer there for years. Another was a young man named Hovnatan who was a basketmaker. I don't recall any other villagers among the slain.

The prelate of Izmid, Bishop Stepannos Hovagimian was also in the city at this time, staying in the Izmid Hotel in Galata Yuksek Kalderem, who certainly would have been killed if he hadn't escaped from the hotel via the roof, going from one roof to another with great difficulty and finally gaining refuge in a Greek chicken seller's shop, until the city returned to normal. Hadji Artin Kiutnerian was also there and, in his haste to escape from the murderers, jumped down from the top of a wall and was left hanging, dangling by his leg, which had caught on a spike hammered into the wall itself and was badly injured as a result. His recovery took a long time, but at least his life was saved. Maybe it was then that he understood the importance of his former *government service* and had a pang of conscience.[*]

Along with many others, I too was in the city at the time, but had the good fortune to escape the hell in Constantinople on an Izmid mail ship the day after it all began.

It was a few days later that the Armenian patriarchal elections took place and Archbishop Maghakia Ormanian was enthroned as patriarch. The Turkish government, immediately after those horrific days, sent the provincial people back to their birthplaces and closed the ways into the city to Armenians, so to make the city safe against Armenian revolutionary activity. But the real reason it did all this was to destroy the Armenian community economically, to keep the provinces under the threat of massacre, and to wipe the word 'reform' from the lips of the Armenians, who were now hungry and without employment. Despite this, an exception was made for the Armenian Catholics and Protestants, as it was in the government's interests due to the approaches made about them by the European powers.

The restriction imposed, especially for Bardizag, was a great blow, because many villagers were in constant contact with Constantinople due to their work or trade.

Then there was a new evil: to help people who wanted to go to Constantinople to do so, the Armenian Catholic authorities began to take advantage of the situation, making it a propaganda tool. Many Armenian Apostolic Church adherents, so as to

---

[*] Author's italics. It would appear by Mkhalian's innate sarcasm that in his opinion Kiutnerian must have done something on behalf of the government that was perhaps not in the best interests of the Bardizag community.

enter Constantinople and continue their work, forsook their church and registered as Catholics. Thus many people appeared among us who, for reasons of work and profit, turned Catholic. The Protestant public, however, broadmindedly remained morally superior, not wanting to take advantage of the Armenian nation's great calamity trying, however, to facilitate the movement of large numbers into and out of the city.

141 – The final ordinations in Bardizag

The need was seen in Bardizag, in about 1907, for new kahana ordinations. Of the two previous generations of priests, only five individuals remained: Garabed Kahana Mkhalian, Mgerdich Kahana Azarian (both old), Sahag Kahana Aprahamian, Mesrob Kahana Deyirmendjian (both ill and incapable of continuing their ministry and who would soon pass away) and Nerses Kahana Ghazarosian, meaning that only three were able to minister to the needs of the population of the village.

The village council of the day, wishing to find a solution to this problem, convened a general assembly that included the priests, during which they elected four candidates for ordination as kahanas. These were: Asadour Hapelian, a teacher; Roupen Aprahamian, the choirmaster; Nighoghos Parounian, a tailor; and Hagop Der-Garabedian, a craftsman. The last two were good and devout young men, and quite well educated.

This election was presented to the prelacy for ratification. The prelate came to Bardizag, examined each of the new candidates in accordance with canon law and, having established their worthiness, approved their selection and prepared to ordain them.

As usual, certain elements of the population rebelled at these proposed ordinations, protesting that some of the candidates weren't worthy, and presenting more worthy candidates of their own. The people who lived in the Lower Fields parish presented, as their candidate, Hagop Drezian, a graduate of the community school and, for some time, the secretary in the government military cloth factory. Those of the Upper Fields parish presented Levon Gondiurian, a graduate of the community school and a teacher. The Baghdasarents parish presented Mikayel Baghdasarian, a graduate and teacher. The council had no problem with the worthiness of these new, people's, candidates but thought that there were too many in total and the necessity was for fewer. If the people's demands were met, the total number of kahanas, including the candidates officially chosen and those chosen by the people would be ten. This was considered to be excessive for the needs of the Bardizag church. It was also greater than the people of the village could properly support. On that basis the council rejected the new candidates, considering that it had the power to have its candidates ordained.

The ordination ceremony began, but on the Calling evening,* a great number of protesters had the temerity to upset it. The disorder and shouting grew to such an extent that the bishop stopped the ordination. He left the village the next day, to give time for passions to cool.

The four official candidates for the priesthood were in a very difficult position. They could neither return to their work nor accept the sacrament of ordination. This unresolved situation lasted for months.† Eventually the village authorities and the protesters finally agreed to have all seven candidates ordained together, leaving to God and the individual candidate his way of supporting himself.

On the basis of this agreement, the prelate was invited to the village for the second time. He performed the ordination of all seven candidates, calling them Anania Kahana Hapelian, Parnapas Kahana Parounian, Pilibbos Kahana Aprahamian, Partoghomeos Kahana Mkhalian,‡ Tioniseos Kahana Drezian, Madatia Kahana Gondiurian and Dimoteos Kahana Baghdasarian.**

The newly ordained priests had hardly completed their 40-day seclusion and begun their ministry when they found they had great difficulties in making a living for themselves, so they looked for positions outside Bardizag. In a very short time Tioniseos Kahana went to the Dardanelles†† as a priest, and Rev. Dimoteos went to Bolu, where he had relations already established there.

A few years later Rev. Anania Hapelian had the misfortune to lose his wife and wore a cowl‡‡ to act as preacher in the church and director of the community schools. With these movements, the number of working priests reverted to the numbers previously determined – three old and four new now ones - a total of seven, who could secure a modest living for themselves in their birthplace as community elders.

Mgerdich Kahana Azarian didn't live for very long after his ordination and died several years before the First World War. He left a memory of an honourable,

---

* In the Armenian Apostolic Church the candidate, on the evening before his ordination, goes through the ceremony of 'Calling'; he is ordained the following day, then goes into 40 days of seclusion, after which he begins his ministry.

† This is an excellent example of the differences that usually occurred between the village authorities and the villagers themselves concerning any community undertaking!

‡ Hagop Der-Garabedian reverted to the ancestral family name of Mkhalian at ordination.

** Their fates are recorded in Teotig, *Koghkota hai hokevoraganoutian yev ir hodin aghedali 1915 dariin*, edited by Ara Kalaydjian, New York, 1985, pp. 347-352.

†† This appears to have been a bishopric based on the area.

‡‡ He first became a *gousagron kahana* [celibate kahana] then was consecrated as a vartabed.

dutiful and zealous priest. With his death, at the time of the deportation (1915) there were six priests and a preaching vartabed who all shared the deportation of their people with all its difficulties.

Garabed Kahana Mkhalian, the senior member of the group of priests was, by 1915, 90 years old. Although the miudir permitted him to remain in the village and not join the deportation, he didn't want to be parted from his large family. He reached Meskene, on the eastern borders of the vilayet of Aleppo with them, where he died under the weight of his years, suffering and exhaustion. He retained, to the end, his positive attitude despite the endless movement of our people and gradual reduction in their numbers. He thought that he would finally settle in this Arabic-speaking region, allowing our children, according to him, the opportunity of learning Arabic, a rich and beautiful language.

Anania Vartabed Hapelian, as the representative of a military family, tried to return from Izmid to Bardizag with the other families in the same category. He was sent to a nearby Turkish village, Hasar Keoy, where he lived until the Armistice.[*]

Anania Vartabed went to Izmid after the Armistice and re-opened the local church. Some time later he returned to Bardizag to preside over the re-opening of the church in the village. But when the Kemalist movement began and the Greeks began to retreat from our region, he too left and went to his relations on the island of Midili in the archipelago, and then went to Lyon in France, where he died after suffering a stroke and becoming paralysed.

Of the remaining five priests, only Nerses Kahana Ghazarosian survived the deportation. All the others died on the road. Nerses Kahana worked for a time as a priest the church in Bardizag after the Armistice. He too, with the advance of the Kemalist forces was forced seek refuge in Constantinople, where he served as a priest in various parishes for a number of years before dying at an advanced age a few years ago.[†] He was a very good man and a dedicated and selfless priest, wherever he served.

Apart from these priests who were ordained in the church in Bardizag, there were other priests outside the village who were born there. In the years before the First World War, the Armenian Apostolic church in the Rumanian town of Fokshan[‡] had a kahana who had been ordained there named Hagop Kahana Tadavorian. He died in Constantinople after moving there. Mesrob Kahana Andonian, ordained in the church in Adrianople, who went to Bulgaria after the

---

[*] A considerable number of people from the village were members of military families. Rev. Anania collected them together in Izmid and obtained permission for them to return to Bardizag, but the miuder of the village refused to allow them back, hence their distribution around Muslim villages in the area. Der-Hagopian, Hagop, *Bardizage khadoudig*, pp. 37-39.

[†] Some years before 1937.

[‡] This is the transliteration from Armenian.

Armistice, served for a time in the Armenian Apostolic church in Sofia and died there. After the Armistice Housig Kahana Ghazarian, a graduate of the Bardizag community school and a teacher was ordained as a kahana in the church in the Rumeli Hisar quarter of Constantinople. He continues to serve there to this day with great worthiness. Tovma Kahana Shigaher (Shigoyian), a graduate of the community school and at one time secretary to the Associations[*] in Bardizag, was ordained after the Armistice by Bishop Stepannos Hovagimian in the church in Izmid. He then went to Constantinople and served in various quarters of the city. At present he is serving in the Holy Trinity Church in Pera. He is much appreciated and is an alert priest.

Another, Arshavir Kahana Varteressian, was ordained in the church in Cairo by the prelate Archbishop Torkom Koushagian.[†] He was a graduate of the Bardizag community school, followed courses in Armash seminary and was, for many years, a teacher in the provinces of Turkey and in Constantinople.[‡]

Two others were ordained by Archbishop Garabed Mazlemian in Greece. One was Hovhannes Kahana Djelgouni, a graduate of the community school, and grandson of the archpriest Hovhannes Kahana Mgerian and serves in Dede Aghadji. The second, Bsag Kahana Hampartsoumian, who went to school in Izmid, served for a time in Greece and has recently moved to the Armenian church in Cairo as a permanent priest there.

Thus at the time I'm writing this (August 25th, 1936) priests born in Bardizag serve:

> In Constantinople – Dadjad Kahana Pashayian (ordained early in the Holy Cross church in Uskudar and rich in years and service), Tovma Kahana Shigaher and Housig Kahana Ghazarian.
>
> In Greece – Hovhannes Kahana Djlgouni.
>
> In Cairo, Egypt – Arshavir Kahana Varteressian and Bsag Kahana Hampartsoumian, in the St. Gregory the Illuminator church.

142 – Antranig Garabedian becomes director of the Community schools

Antranig Garabedian had studied to become a teacher in America and was a serious and educated person. Garabed Vartabed Mazlemian relinquished the directorship and teaching positions in Bardizag, to serve as locum tenens in the diocese. A few years later Asadour Hapelian, one of Tourian's first graduates, entered the

---

[*] The author doesn't make clear what these associations were.
[†] Rev. Arshavir was, until his ordination, Karnig Paboudjian, although it seems that he was using Varteressian as his surname before then.
[‡] His biography appears in Garo Kevorkian, *Amenoun darekirke (Everybody's yearbook)*, 6th year, 1959, Beirut, 1959, p. 598.

priesthood as a kahana. The parish council, under the chairmanship of Asadour Agha Der-Mgerdichian, then invited Mr. Antranig Garabedian, with his wife, to become the school's director. This was in 1912.

This gentleman ran the Bardizag community schools for two years with great success, especially as by that time the passions concerning the school had died down. He had a fruitful and useful time among us, not just because of his training, but also because of his good character and calm life. When the First World War broke out and Turkey also took up arms, he left his work in Bardizag and went to Izmir, where he continued his work as a teacher, from then until the days of the Kemalist movement, when he was a victim of the ferocity of Turkish bandits and the work he was so much admired for came to a premature end.

143 – The links between the Armash seminary and Bardizag

The monastery of Armash had, from the early days, been an important centre of learning for the diocese of Izmid, many people gaining a measure of education there which they couldn't have obtained in their places of birth, as there were no regular schools even in the most important places with large Armenian populations.

These students from Armash were, at the time, mainly from the great and honourable houses or the sons of priests. This was especially true when the Armash abbacy was part of the prelate's responsibilities. In those dark old days, anybody with some education owed it to the monastery of Armash and became priests, teachers and community activists in their birthplaces.

People in Bardizag with this educational background were Hovhannes Kahana of the Great Derder family, Garabed Kahana Der-Krikorian, Sahag Kahana Pandigian, Krikor Kahana Somoundjian and others who, before they became priests, served as teachers for years.

The monastery of Armash provided, in the same way, teachers and instructors for many provincial centres, who in great part assisted in the organisation of the educational effort of those places, serving in them for long periods of time.

The educational work carried on in this fashion in Armash lasted until 1880. The last abbot, Archbishop Khoren Ashekian, ascended the Patriarchal throne in Constantinople in 1888 and the abbacy of Armash became, from then on, part of the patriarch of the day's duties.

Taking advantage of this administrative change, the educational system was altered so that the monastery of Armash became the Armash Seminary. It thus became an establishment that was restricted to producing celibate monks and priests under the patronage of the Armenian Patriarch in Constantinople. Its administration was placed into the hands of Bishop Maghakia Ormanian, who was given the title of deputy abbot, who was concerned with its finances and overall supervision.

The seminary's aim was to produce educated celibate churchmen who would be able to become church leaders* in provincial dioceses. This was in accordance with the new requirements of the time, realising the people's spiritual and mental development and protecting its existence according to the laws of the land.

The trustees of the seminary, under Apig Effendi Oundjian's chairmanship, were able to raise the seminary's educational and organisational levels to a notable level, and endow it with new, good and sound buildings. The new school building was constructed using the donation made by Goudigian. A number of buildings inside and outside the seminary walls for pilgrims, which were used for silkworm production during the season and were an important source of revenue for the seminary at one time, were refurbished by the trustees. Its watermill was also brought up to modern standards by being mechanised. The trustees also paid attention to the seminary's farm. The seminary's administration also cared for the Karageomriug (Little Armash) church in Constantinople, the income from which was assigned to it and, joined to the income from the farm and the annual income from pilgrims, brought in a total annual income of between 1,000-1,500 Ottoman gold liras, which was enough to satisfy the needs of the seminary and the monks.

Bishop Maghakia Ormanian was its main driving force during the first two years of the establishment of the seminary, with some of the older monks assisting him – Hovhannes Vartabed Mavian, the school's director, Arsen Vartabed, spiritual overseer of Khasgal, Mampre Vartabed, the teacher of Armenian, as well as three secular teachers of Turkish, French, the sciences and mathematics. Baba Hampartsoum, who had found refuge in the monastery in his old age, taught musical notation and was the church's choirmaster.

Two years later, Yeghishe Vartabed Tourian was invited to the seminary as Ormanian's chief assistant for the 1891 school year, and who, after a time, took over the directorship of the seminary itself. Tourian's move from Bardizag to Armash was the first and main link between the two and he, as one who had served for ten long years in the village's community schools, had earned the right to be a citizen among us.

After another two years, Yervant Der-Antreasian was likewise invited to join the seminary's teaching staff as the teacher of French to Armenian translation and general history. He served there for two years and then went to Constantinople, where he remained until the Armistice.

After Der-Antreasian, I was invited to serve in the seminary as teacher of natural and mathematical sciences.† I too stayed there for two years when, because of the events of 1896, the seminary students dispersed and it temporarily closed its doors.

---

* The words used here are '...who could carry out shepherding functions...'
† The latter in Armenian is described as *chapagan kidoutiun*.

Many young men from Bardizag and graduates from the Bardizag community school were students in Armash seminary. Of the latter I can recall Moushegh Seroyian, from the seminary's first grade, and Tatoul V. Tourian, of the second grade. The students from Bardizag were the following: Mgerdich Koushagian (Torkom Vartabed) in the second grade in 1893; in the higher grades were Yeghishe Vartabed Khacherian, a promising young churchman who unfortunately died young; Karnig Bodourian, who didn't finish the course, but was a respected teacher; Karnig Paboudjian (Arshavir Kahana Varteressian), who had previously served as a teacher for many years; Kevork Mesrob (ordained as a deacon who later forswore his oath), who was a well-known teacher and author of text books and Vartan Choullerian.

The Armash community school, administered and run by the abbacy of Armash, had employed Siragan Boyadjian and Minas Semerdjian, both from Bardizag, as teachers, the latter one of the first graduates of the community school during Tourian's tenure as director.

The most brilliant student from Bardizag in the seminary was Torkom Vartabed Koushagian, later bishop and Armenian Patriarch of Jerusalem. Torkom Vartabed, before finally leaving the Armash seminary, had been the monastery's deputy abbot for a time, then had gone to Sepastia (Sivas) as prelate of that diocese, where he was consecrated bishop (1910). Leaving Sepastia, he went to Egypt for a holiday, where the diocesan assembly unanimously elected him prelate of the united Alexandria and Cairo dioceses. He served there for many years with great ability and skill. He still held that position when, in 1931, he was elected Patriarch by the order of Armenian Apostolic Church monks in Jerusalem, which was officially endorsed by the British government. Patriarch Torkom Koushagian, with his great intellectual ability and energetic activity, added lustre and value to that high office and, to the same extent, secured a special place in the ranks of worthy people from Bardizag.

Chapter 9

The Constitutional Revolution and Bardizag 1908 - 1915

144 – The re-establishment of the Turkish constitution (July 1908): days of freedom

Sultan Hamid's tyrannical and bloodthirsty government ignored the necessity of basic reforms in the country to ensure its peaceful development. Instead it worked, in terms of the fate of the Ottoman Empire, to forge dissention between the great powers. This was to gain time using its rotten diplomacy and to see its fate linked especially to friendship with the German Kaiser and the Triple Alliance he presided over, in return for certain monopolies such as the German project to build the Baghdad railway.

British diplomacy, in regard to Sultan Abdul Hamid's position, seeing danger for peace in Europe – and for inter-governmental stability – signed, upon the initiative of King Edward VII, an accord with France called the *Entente Cordiale* and an agreement with the Tsar of Russia in Riga, to either anticipate or face any danger to the peace of Europe.

The Young Turk party seeing, in the jealous and competitive diplomatic negotiations and agreements made between the powers, danger to the existence of Turkey, redoubled its efforts. It succeeded in winning over the officer corps of the Turkish Army of Macedonia, the most modern and well armed part of the Ottoman armed forces, to its side.

In these critical circumstances the Young Turks, having secured this army's aid, entered into negotiations directly with the sultan with the view to preventing danger to the country. It suggested that the constitution, which he, during his first years on the throne had prorogued, be proclaimed once more. If he refused, they threatened to mobilise the Macedonian Army and have it march on Constantinople to establish constitutional rule and dethrone him.

The sultan was powerless and alone before this threat, in the atmosphere of mistrust that had been created around him, with the government being completely made up of an association of spies and criminals only concerned with personal gain. To save their skins and to gain time under the new circumstances, the members of the government, in the age-old diplomatic way, gave way to the demand. It re-introduced the constitution, against its wishes, as well as a parliament and ministries responsible to it, and handed over the country's administration. With this peaceful revolution, events in Turkey began to take place in swift succession. The Macedonian Army, under the command of Shevket Pasha, marched to

Constantinople to preserve order and ease the imposition of the constitution. The Young Turks returned in droves to Constantinople from abroad. The atmosphere in the country became electric and packs of spies and informants drew breath outside the country while others concealed themselves. Others fell under the ferocious anger of the people.

A temporary government was formed from the most trustworthy elements of the old regime, awaiting parliamentary elections and a government made up of people trusted by the parliament. Newspapers felt free and tongues loosened. New, self-assured and bold language began to flood public places; more than anything else, instead of servile, flattering explanations, the boldest, most extravagant reasoning became the rule in the newly established liberal order. Every citizen began to adjust his position in relation to this new state: the Turks, the greatest majority, from one day to the next, became revolutionaries of the most liberal, unbridled mentality. The Young Turk party grew in leaps and bounds, encompassing almost all officialdom and the students. It was a torrent that drove people, without realising it, into a storm of liberalism.

The Armenians, who had suffered most under the old regime, had every reason to explode to the point of madness. The Armenian revolutionaries appeared behind the Young Turks in the newly-established liberal circus, and the Armenian people marched on the liberal road and became politicised in the widest and deepest sense. Young people, both girls and boys, entered the ranks of the Armenian Revolutionary Federation *(Dashnaktsutiun)* and mature people into those of the Social Democrats *(Hnchags)*; the world now belonged to the revolution and the political parties. They had brought freedom: the Red Sultan had been restrained and the vision of wonderful days ahead could be seen in their eyes.

The Armenians had their Yildiz too: the Constantinople Patriarchate and the enthroned tyrant there, Patriarch Ormanian. So began the work of reform; the patriarchate was cleansed of its old-fashioned representatives and the patriarch dethroned. Then, with every form of ignominy, under curses and spittle, he was dragged through the streets. This was despite the fact that the Turks had the wisdom to keep their sultan, although the blood of innocents had not yet dried on his hands.

The churches and parish councils were emptied of their old and suspect people. Many of them were only guilty of having the courage to retain the Armenian nation's administration in their hands in the most dangerous of times, sometimes against their will, during Patriarch Ormanian's day.

These passions and this madness swiftly spread like a plague to the provinces and, in the first instance to us – to Izmid, to Bardizag, that was so close to the capital – the forge of liberalism. Within the village nearly everybody became a revolutionary, from schoolboys and schoolgirls to mature people, men and women, who began to swear by the sun of Freedom.

The unreliable elements in the den of the parish council seemed confused by the warm shafts of the light of freedom. They hid like owls and bats, taking refuge in ruins and dark places, keeping quiet while being annoyed at the turn of events. It was in those days that a handsome idiot, a young Dashnak lad,* had the boldness to demand the government seal from the *miudir* of the day, the noble Circassian Sefer Bey. The boy was swiftly brought to his senses by a number of older and far-sighted people. They had suffered during the old regime and wanted to see the rule of law respected and for people to be careful of extreme boyish escapades.

Many, in those irresponsible days, grabbed the collar of the chairman of the trustees whom we know already† who had, in the days when his authority was supreme, dared to accept money from various people in his positions as trusteeship chairman and head of the council. They now, with bloodshot eyes, demanded its return. He was forced to satisfy many, so that he would not be faced with an unpalatable situation. This continued until he had the sense to leave Bardizag for a time, going to Izmid, far from meetings that upset him.

After that, a veritable flood of orators and speakers began to disturb the atmosphere in Bardizag, despite it having been peaceful and dormant for many years. Revolutionaries such as the Young Turks; Dashnaks (Khajag, Shahrigian‡ and others, including one of the founders of the party Simon Zavarian**); and Hnchags (Sabahgiulian): all visited Bardizag. The church and the High School lecture hall were used for their speeches. The large audiences listened to the paeans of praise for freedom and constitutional order and the heaping of derision on the old regime's tyranny, obstructionism and crimes. It heard the blackening of Sultan Hamid's government's name and its creatures with soot and spittle and words and sentences like roars of thunder, with threatening fists and powerful stamping of feet. In this way the speakers tried to make the new mentality the people's patrimony, to mobilise it against any future contingency.

There were, among the revolutionaries, people who had lived in the country for years, courting and making up to the government, cursing the revolutionaries and their evil work. Now, however, from one day to the next, they had gone to the other extreme, heaping fire and brimstone on Sultan Hamid's collaborators. Among these was a young Protestant pastor whose spoken Turkish was very rich and who very early had, with skipping, harmonious and sonorous words, prayed for the long life of the sultan. He now heaped curses – almost swear words – at him, becoming a brother of the revolutionaries, knowing of course that the beast was tied up in his cage.

There were, of course, boyish games, the result of a certain psychological state and approached, in their entirety, tragic-comic theatrical productions.

---

*   The words used here are ...*siroun khent me, tashnagtsagan dgheg me*...
†   See Section 132.
‡   See Garo Kevorkian, *Everybody's Yearbook*, 3rd year, 1956, Beirut, 1956, pp. 211-212.
** See Garo Kevorkian, *Everybody's Yearbook*, 11th year, 1964, Beirut 1964, pp. 262-266.

When this liberal current, after a time, lost its agitation and became smoother and cleaner, the revolutionaries began to teach liberalism, each party to the people in its own ranks.

A new village council was elected in Bardizag under the pressure of the current of liberalism, with voting going to completely new, fresh forces and, to some extent, those opposing the old authorities. The new council was organised under the chairmanship of Minas Effendi Dzalian, with Hovhannes Koushagian, Karnig Varteressian[*] (later Arshavir Kahana Varteressian), me, and others of like mind being members. The council, wishing to remain faithful to the ruling mentality, elected one of the newly-ordained kahanas, Madatia Kahana Gondiurian to be locum tenens. It also formed a trusteeship for the community schools from new people, some of them being members of the council. The schools' teachers were reorganised, using experienced local people from those prepared during the Tourian era and mostly from the subsequent generations of students. The oversight and directorship of the schools were in the hands of the trustees.

The prelate, Bishop Stepannos Hovagimian was never a friend of constitutional order during the whole of his tenure and hadn't convened a provincial deputies' assembly for years. He had never convened regular religious or political assemblies and their assisting bodies. He was now carried along by the new powerful winds of change and prepared to form a central provincial authority with all its lawful departments. Bardizag was called upon to provide four lay delegates, once more from the ranks of the opposition. These were Hovhannes Khacherian,[†] Aghasi Papazian, Minas Dzalian and me, apart from those of the church.

The ship of freedom began to sail with these constitutional organisations, on both governmental and Armenian national stormy seas with wild and great hesitation.

When the storm created by the Turkish constitution had eased somewhat, three revolutionary committees were formed in Bardizag: Young Turk, which didn't last long, Hnchag[‡] and Dashnak,[**] the last two filled with hatred and envy and violently against each other. As we've seen, the local authority was headed by Minas Dzalian, with the government's senior authority being represented by an Armenian *miudir*,

---

[*] He seems to have begun to use this surname instead of his family name of Paboudjian at this time.

[†] Also known by the nickname *Pondodig*.

[‡] One of the main Hnchagian members was Yervant Topouzian, who was one of the 20 Hnchag activits hanged by the Turkish government in June 1915. H. Boghosian, *Anzoukagan Bardizag*, Paris, 1967, pp. 34-35, Christopher J. Walker, *Armenia: The Survival of a Nation*, Croom Helm, London 1980, p. 198.

[**] A leading light in the Bardizag Dashnak organisation was Hovhannes Khacherian, who survived the deportation and returned to the village in 1918. Unfortunately he died soon afterwards of illness. Haroutiun Boghosian, *Anzoukagan Bardizag*, pp. 34-35.

Hagop Effendi Der-Hagopian,* a young journalist, well known by the Constantinople public.

The major portion of the youth of the village was carried away with political activity at this time. The only avenue open to neutral young people was public works, an otherwise useful activity, dedicated to the development of the village economy. It used all the free effort and vigour available during these liberal days, creating, on a neutral basis, more than one organisation dedicated to the public good.

145 – Various organisations in Bardizag

I will present these village organisations† in order:
1. Protection of Village Cultivable Land
2. The organising of the Armenian General Benevolent Union (AGBU) Bardizag branch
3. The establishment of the People's Bank
4. The Steamship Company
5. The Builders' *(diurger)* Association
6. The *Dashnaktsagan* (ARF) retail co-operative
7. The Public Garden Association

1. Protection of Village Cultivable Land

This organisation existed for a few years before 1908, but I thought it was worth recording it among the others.

It was not a collaborative association. Forming an association before 1908 was a dangerous task for the organisers, even more so for groups acting under the auspices of the community council.

---

* He was the author of *Bardizage khadoudig*, published in Paris in 1960 by his own printing house, which owes much to *this* work.

† There is a strange omission from this list. The Bardizag Basketmakers Union, founded in 1910, was established to promote the basketmakers' interests and had links with people in the same trade in Constantinople and other places. Minas Kasabian (Farhad), *Hayere Nikomedio Kavarin Mech*, p. 207. Der-Hagopian tells us, quoting Vahram Mouradian, a basketmaker from the village who published a note in the newspaper *Manzoume* edition 1175, 27/10 May 1905, that the basketmaking trade was started in Bardizag in 1835 by someone from the village named Mardigian, who had learnt it from Turks in Saraylou. In his turn he taught the Baghdasarians and Yakoyians. At the time Mouradian wrote in 1905, great quantities of baskets were being ordered by merchants in Constantinople, and there were 120 Bardizag basketmakers who worked for 13 hours a day all year round. A master of the craft could produce 6 grape or 4 vegetable baskets a day. Hagop Der-Hagopian, *Bardizage khadoudig*, p. 231.

Village cultivable lands had been left without any protection for many years, leaving their upkeep to the will of each landowner. Bardizag had great areas devoted to viticulture, orchards and fruit trees, with cultivation of vegetables and legumes taking place in the spring and summer. Apart from these, maize, tobacco and grain were grown, which were mainly left to God's care and protection. Neither the government nor the village authorities felt the need for guards. It was only during the grape season, when the grapes showed signs of ripening* and provided temptation for passers-by and small children, that the vineyard owners would come together and each appoint a paid guard for their own vineyards, until the grapes had been harvested. The vineyards were guarded for no more than two months, but this was a special and permanent arrangement which wasn't used for any other purpose. Many villagers complained that thieves and animals damaged their crops, preventing them from enjoying the fruits of their labours. This led to a certain degree of disappointment and the weakening of the will to cultivate the land.

A solution was needed for this problem, so that the working villager remained tied to the cultivation of his land and the village economy benefited and profited from it.

I had the boldness,† in view of this situation, to gather a few friends together, wanting to organise the regular and organised protection of village agriculture throughout the year. For the success of this work, it was necessary to find sources of revenue, so it was decided to impose a tax with comparative rates on the villagers, based on the quality of each landowner's cultivation. The collection of this tax would be entrusted to a collector, who would be paid a percentage of the sum he collected. To this sum would be added the annual amount accrued from the rent of pastureland each year. The total value of these two important sources of revenue would be about 60,000 *kurush*, which would be sufficient to ensure our scheme's success.

We also decided that the protection of agricultural land would be given to a trusted creditor on a reducing basis, on the condition that he would be liable for any losses or destroyed crops, whose assessed value would be debited from the sum to be paid. The creditor would also, according to season and need, have foot and horse guards, the number to be agreed in the contract. Their number in spring and summer would rise to 20, and in winter would be reduced to a minimum after harvesting had been completed and only ploughed fields and trees in gardens left. All the villagers' cultivation would be under protection: sown fields, vineyards, mulberry plantations, smallholdings and forests.

---

* The author has used the dialect term *khar ihnal* – the correct term to describe the stage the grapes had reached in their growth.
† Very modestly, the author has described his initiative in the third person singular, beginning this paragraph with the words 'The author of these lines...' *(Ays dogherou heghinage...)*

After the group had fixed these basic terms of the plan, it compiled a complete list of land ownership, showing their extent and kind, utilising government records for this purpose.* The amount to be paid by each landowner for the protection of the land was determined on the basis of this listing.†

After completing this preliminary work, the plan was presented to the village authority of the day for examination and approval. The council approved it and put it under its aegis. The local government, seeing its usefulness, ensured the necessary aid for the tax to be collected.

The Defence of Village Cultivable Land organisation had been born in these circumstances under the patronage of the village and government authorities, so the group began its work, appointing a tax collector. It came to an agreement with an agricultural creditor and rented the village meadows by auction to an agent; so it took the organised work under its conscientious and serious control.

This organistion was a blessing for the whole village: no land remained uncultivated and the theft of harvests or their destruction ceased. Everyone became the master, without loss, from then on, of the whole result of his labours. No animal was able to approach the crops and damage them. The forests grew and increased in extent becoming, for their owners, a notable source of income, whereas for years past no profit had been made from them at all, and they had been the cause of extra expenditure. Even the fruit that dropped from the trees remained where it fell, waiting for its owners.

All the villagers prayed for and felt gratitude to the organisers of this successful effort. They saw, with amazement, that the amount of tax paid just on the harvested grape crop, which in the past had been quite small, was now large. It was enough to cover the cost of protection of all the village's cultivation for a complete year. The freedom of Bardizag's agriculture had arrived – well before its time.‡

---

* The first list compiled by the government was that of 1838-1839. See Section 68.

† Kasabian tells us that the land held by the villagers was actually significantly less than 1838/1839 formal documents showed. This was because of the appropriations made by the new Muslim immigrants, despite protests by the villagers and government surveys. Part of the land was handed over to the Laz and Giurdji incomers by officials and the local mufti in 1898. The Laz Armenians, however, received no benefit from these arrangements as they were Christians. Minas Kasabian (Farhad), *Hayere Nikomedio Kavarin Mech*, pp. 168-170.

‡ Kasabian describes this organisation, founded in 1909, (which he calls the 'Bardizag Agricultural Union') in a different light, stating that its original object was to promote and develop all the branches of agriculture practised in the village. It had over 1,000 members of both sexes in 1909-1910, but the ideas they had were never realised due to internal wrangling and lack of cohesion, but defending their land, as described, was possibly the best outcome. Minas Kasabian (Farhad), *Hayere Nikomedio Kavarin Mech*, p. 202.

2. The organisation of the Armenian General Benevolent Union (AGBU) Bardizag branch

The AGBU, organised in Egypt during the time of the Armenian massacres,[*] taking advantage of the freedom of 1908, took the decision to extend its farsighted work dedicated to the Armenian nation among all the Armenians. To achieve this it sent a delegation from Egypt to Constantinople made up of M. Antranigian and Dr. Daghavarian.

This delegation, during its mission, also called at Bardizag, approaching notable local people and explaining the AGBU's plans and aims and appealing to their patriotic spirit to found a local branch of the AGBU in the village.

The villagers accepted the invitation to bring their participation and assistance to the work this union, devoted to the nation, was conducting, resulting in the organisation of the first branch of the AGBU in Bardizag, with a few but honourable members, who paid, according to their ability, the entry sum and determined their membership dues.

The Bardizag branch of the AGBU elected its local committee under the chairmanship of Dr. H. Der-Stepanian and me (acting as secretary), which worked with the greatest enthusiasm and maintained its existence until the date of Turkey's involvement in the First World War.

The AGBU Bardizag branch, limited in numbers because in those days many people's attention and vigour had been captured by the revolutionary organisations, kept its philanthropic work alive in the area and, after the ending of most of the useless enthusiasm and work around us, continuing its dedicated and useful efforts.

3. The establishment of Bardizag's People's Bank

The lack of financial resources among the poor villagers and the loss of a significant part of their earnings, which went to fatten the pockets of usurers who, charging exorbitant rates of interest (40%-50%), lent money to the working and poor people, was very noticeable. Instead of improving their lot by these loans, these people gradually fell further into debt, eventually being forced to sell what they had in the most unfavourable circumstances to free themselves from its ever-increasing burden.

Seeing this, I[†] came to the conclusion that something should be done among and for the people to secure their earnings by using reasonable and lawful interest rates. I created a plan for the foundation of a People's Bank, the capital of which would

---

[*] It was founded in 1906. See Haroutiun Kevorkian and Vahe Tachjian (organisers), *A century of history of the Armenian General Benevolent Union*, Cairo-Paris-New York 2006, Vol 1, 1906-1940 pp. 17-26.

[†] The author uses the third person singular here once more.

accrue from shares worth 20 *tahegans* each,* until such time as capital to the value of 1,000 liras had been accumulated. This would be used to lend small amounts (at an interest rate of 12%) to needy villagers to facilitate the completion of their efforts.

This idea was embraced by all sections of the village population, and almost 5,000 shares, each worth 20 *tahegans* that had been put on the market were sold, creating the capital required – 1,000 liras. Many – boys, girls, women and adults - bought more than one share, often registering 5-10 shares each. These were days of enthusiasm, and public-spiritedness and patriotism was expressed by people of all classes; it was sufficient for a person, who had the necessary ability, to inspire them.

This modest banking organisation began work is short order (within three months), lending small amounts (one to three liras) to those who applied, accepting as collateral the shares the individual had in the bank and, if they weren't sufficient, or if they had none at all, to have a guarantee in which there was confidence.

The People's Bank had its executive administration, a paid secretary and an office. The loans, receipts and loan extensions, when necessary, were made under the responsibility of the administration and accounts, receipts and official papers were maintained.

This establishment worked for the people in a regular and successful manner until the dreadful date of the deportation, keeping its capital circulating among the people, dealing a mortal blow to the work of usurers, or at least moderating their conditions to make them more accessible. The wish of the founders of the bank, like all banks, was not to secure its shareholders shares, but to work for the people's good, on the condition that the capital created remained available and any profits made paid the costs of the secretary and office as well as a modest dividend to the bank's administration and shareholders, as a mark of the value placed on their responsibility and sacrifice and thus to preserve the usefulness of the work.†

4. The Steamship Company

Spurred on by the results of the foundation of the People's Bank, I then turned my attention to another important public need. This was to replace the ferry boats‡

---

* This word is usually used for the smallest value coins in circulation at the time. Its actual value is not stated here, but I assume that 1 *tahegan* = 1 *para*.

† Kasabian states that there were *two* 'banks' in Bardizag, which he calls *sendoug* [cash boxes]. The first (the one described here) he calls the 'Agricultural and merchant bank' (founded in August 1911). In 1911-1912 its remitted capital was 12,660 *kurush*, profit 5,667 *kurush* (each shareholder receiving a 2.40 *kurush* dividend), loans totalled 126,460 *kurush*. He quotes the calotype newspaper *Meghou* [Bee], No 21, Bardizag 1912. The other was the 'Bardizag savings bank', founded in 1910. It was guaranteed by the Builders' *(diurger)* Association. Kasabian states that it never received much encouragement. Minas Kasabian (Farhad), *Hayere Nikomedio Kavarin Mech,* p. 205.

‡ He uses the colloquialism *bazar khayekhner* here.

service with a steam-driven one, without damaging community revenues and, at the same time, securing travellers' safety and comfort.

The reader will recall that the Bardizag community authorities, to secure important revenues for the community schools, and to provide the people with a service had, for many years, established a community-owned ferry boat service between Seymen and Izmid for travellers, the majority of whom were people from the village.*

The fare per person per journey in my day was two *kurush*, of which only a quarter went to the community, and from which the expenses incurred by the boat and its equipment (and its replacement) were paid. The remaining three quarters of the fare was given to the hired boatmen, of whom there were three in each boat. The community owned three boats that had been bought and equipped. It was responsible for their upkeep, maintaining them in a serviceable condition. Under these circumstances the community's quarter share was much reduced and was of very little value, but provided, once a year, a significant sum to the community's finances, which was the most important of the revenues assigned to the schools.

A plan was therefore drawn up to run that service from then on using a small steamship carrying 100 passengers at a time safely, allowing improvements to be made to the old system. The first thing was to secure, for the community, 20 *paras* (a quarter of the 2 *kurush* fare) per passenger, as pure revenue without cost, which would double the schools' revenue from this enterprise. The second was the lessening in journey time. The third was to make the passage comfortable and safe and pleasing for the customers.

A Steamship Company was created using this plan with 1,000 liras capital, each share costing 10 Ottoman liras, through 30-40 wealthy members. The Company came to an understanding with the community authority, under the abovementioned conditions, keeping the fares the same, of which a whole half a *kurush* would be paid to the community treasury according to the number of tickets controlled by the authority itself.

The authority was pleased to agree to this suggestion, as its former revenue was now secured in this way for each passenger, without any cost or concern, and at the same time it would be able to sell the boats it owned and collect the prices paid for them.

Having come to an agreement with the authority, the Company began looking for a suitable vessel to buy. It was successful in purchasing the Catholic Azarian family's† steamship the *Ararad* [Ararat] in Constantinople for approximately 700 liras, and had certain repairs carried out on it. The Company also bought a stock of coal, hired a captain and an engineer and a ticket seller as its representative who would, at the same time, serve on board as a seaman.

---

* See Section 82.

† The author does not make it clear whether this family was from Bardizag, there being a family of that name in the village.

The Constitutional Revolution and Bardizag 1908 - 1915

This steamship service began running between Izmid and Seymen in wonderful and successful circumstances, drawing everyone's attention to it and exciting admiration for the Bardizag community's initiative and taste and its concern for the development of its schools.

Unfortunately this laudable enterprise, as a result of a bankrupt Freedom, didn't last long, existing for only three years.[*] During the whole of that time the Company wasn't able to make a profit for itself, but closed its accounts every year without loss and paid the village authority its revenue regularly. Despite not making a profit, all of us were sure that with the experience we had gained and with rational economies, a profit for the Company shareholders would have been made.

This enterprise, too, was destroyed in the general catastrophe, just like the bank. When the deportation days arrived, the bank's capital was left to the people in the form of loans, whose final reckoning was impossible to make. In the case of the Company, it too remained with the people, but had paid for itself and wasn't a burden for us.

When, however, we were blown like chaff by a fierce barbarian wind under distant stars, the Turkish captain and engineer commandeered the ship and took it to Constantinople in the wholesale looting of Armenian wealth, considering it their property. Later we learnt that Ardashes Effendi Mgerian had managed to re-assert ownership of the vessel and sell it, as he had been designated as the owner of the Company's assets, as owner of four shares in it, when the final reckoning was made by the members.

Ardashes Effendi paid some of the members their shares after the Armistice, when they were able to see him in his office in Constantinople. Like many others, I was unable to collect mine, despite the fact that the idea was mine, and I had taken on most of the preliminary work and sacrifices, personally buying the ship and supervising its refurbishment, having to remain in Constantinople for many long days because of the work.

5. The Builders' *(Diurger)* Association

Other idealistic young people were imbued with this spirit of community collaboration. One of them was K. Bodourian,[†] a student at the seminary and a teacher, who planned and organised a new association under the name of Builders *(Diurger)* Association.

This association's basic aim was to establish collaboration between the builders of Bardizag, of whom there was a considerable number, to secure sources of work and earnings. They would use the capital that the Association accrued to purchase

---

[*] It would seem from internal evidence that this was from 1912 until 1915.
[†] Probably Krikor Bodourian.

building materials and use them to build new houses on suitable ground, which they would then sell to new buyers, providing the members with permanent work.

The Association was formed and went to work,* buying timber, wood, lime, tiles etc on the open market when the prices were favourable and storing them in rented warehouses. Experience and opportunity, however, showed that it would be more useful and simpler for the Association if, instead of building houses with these materials in the future, which might not sell and suffer falls in prices, they sold the stockpiled materials themselves. There was a greater demand for them than for building houses. The Association eventually came to the conclusion that its capital should be used for trading in building materials for profit. This proved to be more profitable and simpler, resulting in the Builders' *(Diurger)* Association becoming a trading company.

In the beginning it concerned itself solely with building materials. It then branched out and dealt in other things such as European flour and imports like sugar, rice, soap and so on. The Association, however, retained its name, but opened its doors to all classes of people, mostly shopkeepers, grocers and bakers who, despite being members of the Association, were also its customers. The Association became, in Bardizag, a significant trading house, with great prospects for future profits, binding local shopkeepers to it as their wholesaler. These then severed their trading links with Izmid wholesalers and other local individual traders, becoming customers of the mercantile Association they had founded and partners in the profits made by it. Under these circumstances the Builders' *(Diurger)* Association became an important trading and labour establishment in Bardizag. It made its purchases mainly in the larger market of Constantinople, especially for flour and groceries, and expanded its trading activities, securing for itself a good reputation and great trading markets and profits.

K Bodourian remained the life and soul of this important enterprise until the spring of 1915, when he was suddenly arrested, with several others and exiled to the interior before the deportation, from where he would never return. He remained alive during the war and went to Jerusalem after its capture by the British. He then went to Egypt, where he caught typhus and died within a few days.

His friends continued to operate the establishment until the time of the deportation† when community needs, with the end of Bardizag's existence, ended this successful enterprise too.

---

* It was founded in 1908. Minas Kasabian (Farhad), *Hayere Nikomedio Kavarin Mech,* p. 203.
† August 1915.

6. The *Dashnaktsagan* (ARF) retail co-operative

The revolutionary (political) parties had not displayed any initiative during all this activity, although party members had joined this or that organisation.

The Bardizag ARF (Dashnaktsutiun) committee, however, did not want to be left behind the others in this period of enthusiastic community activity and, desiring to increase its attraction among its members and sympathisers, planned to open, with their assistance, a retail co-operative shop, perhaps to demonstrate, in a tangible way, its socialist doctrines. Because it didn't have anyone skilled enough in its ranks to run such an establishment, it placed its organisation, administrative responsibility and financial affairs in the hands of the manager of the Builders' Association, K. Bodourian.*

The *Dashnaktsagan* (ARF) retail co-operative was not a usual grocery shop; the committee wanted to provide its members and sympathisers with the best quality products at reasonable prices, and at the same time to ensure profits for its members and customers, according to their purchases or orders.†

7. The Public Garden Association

Bardizag's summers and autumns were wonderful and everyone really felt the need to enjoy them. Bardizag's pure, cold water, the unique views of the fields and countryside, clear blue sky and sea, velvety, gentle breeze from the sea and the delicacy of the scents of the fields, vineyards and mulberry copses brought with them dry and cool nights under a dome of marvellous stars. All this had an irresistible sweetness, the enjoyment of which was to live in immortality.

Ancient open areas existed around the village: the Upper Threshing Floors, Lower Threshing Floors, the nearby Upper Fields, Avazoud and the Upper Cemetery where the villagers were used to going and spending many hours, lying full length under the trees. These places, however, mostly remained in their virgin state, uncultivated and uncared-for and had not had man's skills devoted to them. The development of new tastes now demanded something more than them just being beautiful places.

---

* It was founded in May 1911, and the cost of membership was 20 paras. The members had to pay a subscription of one para a week, for five years. There were 100 founder-members and others joined during its life. Kasabian states that the grocers in the village were much against this enterprise. It also opened a bakery. Minas Kasabian (Farhad), *Hayere Nikomedio Kavarin Mech*, p. 206.

† There is no mention here of how long the co-operative shop lasted; it might have continued until Bodourian's arrest in 1915.

It was this demand that gave birth to outside coffee houses, places of amusement established in unpopulated areas, where someone could find a cup of cold water, a cooling drink or a measure of oghi, a table and chair and where he could occasionally reserve a game of backgammon or cards. Such venues appeared in the summer in those places; for example on the eastern side of the village was Sinanian's garden, Ghaladji's coffee house and, later, Doudou's coffee house. At the other end of the village was the Upper Cemetery buffet and the coffee house in the Upper Fields, where the locals would go to get a breath of air after the work of the day.

There was nowhere, however, among these places where someone could enjoy themselves with his entire family for a few hours. To satisfy this need and to give satisfaction to the new tastes created during the time, a 'Public Garden Association' was created among the young people.

To achieve its aim, the Association chose one of the best places at the edge of the village, with singularly beautiful views and within reach of people of any age. This was one of the Lower Threshing Floors' small promontories at the edge of the village that looked north, and was a continuation of the area of the village itself, but which, however, was only just the size of a large threshing floor, and whose three sides descended steeply, giving it the character of a promontory in empty space. The views from here encompassed the village's mulberry plantations, vineyards and widespread green fields, village road, surrounding range of hills and, in the centre, far away, the Bay of Izmid, with that town itself clinging to the shore, the hills that were behind it, as well as Seymen, Bash Iskele, Deniz Bashi, Kileze and the valley that was Asia Minor's gateway, through which the white cloud of steam of the railway to Baghdad snaked.

The Association created the Public Garden in this area, planting trees and flowerbeds, placing fountains among them, creating gravel paths and an open space in the centre where chairs, benches and tables covered with clean white cloths were set up, with temporary parasols over them until such time as the trees grew tall enough to create shade in the garden.

A clean, neat buffet had been set up in a corner of the garden, where it was possible to buy coffee, tea, chocolate, pastries, cool drinks and alcoholic beverages, with good and attentive service.

The Association had also brought flowing drinking water from a nearby source for the use of customers and for the garden itself. Thus, that isolated place that baked under the summer sun and was subject to snowstorms in winter despite its marvellous beauty and being deserted by everyone, was now changed into a small heaven by a fairy's hand, like a large, green and scented flower vase hanging from the heavens.

It was to this garden that, during the short years of freedom,[*] the houses in the village would empty and all their occupants – old and young, men and women -

---

[*] 1908-1914.

would come in friendly groups, to spend a few enjoyable hours there, under the eyes of the stars, caressed by the breeze, in a clean and amiable fellowship until late at night, mostly devoid of the old rough customs and rigidity. Visitors and guests who came to Bardizag from Constantinople and other places to enjoy cheap – almost free – summer holidays, would be transported by the beauty of that place and would think themselves in an imaginary village, full of life and song.

The Garden Association, as the tenants of a community-owned plot of land, paid a yearly rent to the community treasury like those of the Upper Fields and the Old Cemetery.

146 - New plans being considered

In all this activity, the idealistic, enterprising young people of Bardizag didn't think its work was complete in terms of the development of the village's social life and the strengthening of its economy. Other plans were being considered which time and opportunity would have allowed to be developed if only fate had not treated us so mercilessly stopping, before its time, life in all its many facets.

One of the plans that was being considered was the saving of the useless flow of water from the fountains and having it flow into the houses. This would have ended the heavy and dangerous task of carrying water by our mothers and sisters, and the chore of having to wait in lines on the stone pavement for hours in the sun or rain, for their turn at the fountain itself.

Another being considered was the construction of large water reservoirs in several high places above the village and connecting the water flowing from the various sources to them. Each fountain in the village would remain where it was, and the flow of water to them would be stopped at night by using taps. When the taps were turned off, stopping the flow through the fountains, the water would fill the reservoirs, and then, using underground pipes, be led into the houses, for a fee.

Many houses would, under this scheme, have clean flowing water, and the women and girls of the family would not have the chore of going to the fountain for water for washing clothes and other necessary things. Drinking water, if they wanted it, would be supplied directly from the fountains, being clean, flowing spring water. This plan was an eminently practical one and would have provided a new source of revenue for the public economy and jobs for certain people as employees of a water company.

A second plan was the provision of an autobus service from the village to Seymen, which would be used for the transportation of passengers and goods, speeding up the journey, making it cheaper, more comfortable and safer.[*]

---

[*] The distance from Bardizag to Seymen was about 3 miles (5 km).

The implementation of these schemes would have been the inspiration for new plans for the benefit of the community. Bardizag had people with the necessary skills who could have translated the plans into reality. Unfortunately we lived in a country and under a government where it was much more difficult to do good than evil.

147 - Theatrical and artistic life in Bardizag

During the days of freedom and enthusiasm, not only were we lucky to see tourists, revolutionary activists and visitors during the good weather, but also to have Armenian artists among us who had gained international reputations, and who came to improve and inspire our theatre with artistic expressions we were not used to seeing before that time[*]. Our earlier theatrical productions had mostly been amateur attempts, as we have seen before,[†] lacking in artistic understanding and implementation. The villager was able, for the first time, to experience the arts of the theatre and of actors, when the eastern Armenian Armenian-Apelian theatre group[‡] was among us, presenting rich programmes.

This group remained in Bardizag for about two to three months, and presented, with the greatest success, performances of Shakespeare's Hamlet and Othello; Korradon, Avedis Aharonian's 'Vale of tears', Shirvanzade's 'For honour' and others.

The spacious theatre auditorium would fill to capacity with priests, teachers, notables, officials, tradesmen, shopkeepers and individuals of every class: in all about 1,000 people. They followed, with the greatest seriousness and restraint, these worthy artistic performances in which human emotions gushed forth and the actors, becoming one with the types and characters they played, transported us all to unknown, although human, new worlds. These were filled with the compulsive warmth of love, violent, jealous passions, confused, erroneous social superstitions and flowing, unbridled vanities, to which we, the audience, would respond to in the depths of our souls. We would display storms of emotion at social injustice, the complete trampling of rights, crimes and the horrors of carnage, from one moment to the next.

Each of these performances would only secure a sum between 20 and 25 Ottoman liras, a very small amount for the theatre troupe; when I tried, using the ploy of justifying it, one day saying to Mr. Apelian that our people loved to appreciate the group's art, but unfortunately were too poor to reward it to the extent it deserved, he replied, 'We're not looking for money, but a people that follows our

---

[*] 1908-1914.
[†] See Section 120.
[‡] Hovahnnes Haroutiun Apelian was a noted actor in the eastern Armenian theatre. He and A Armenian founded the Apelian-Armenian theatre group in 1908. They came to Bardizag shortly after this.

artistry and knowledgeably applauds us. This spiritual pleasure is worth more than money to us.'

They were wonderful days for our people, whose spirit rejoiced with the breath of the new times and the shivers produced by a new art.

Gomidas Vartabed, the tragic, unique and singular artist also visited us. He spoke to us about the human instinct to create songs, taking their expression and style from surrounding circumstances and spiritual factors. He spoke especially about village songs, when the peasant, like learning a new language, copied the proud and noble sounds of the mountains, the rustling of the leaves of the trees, the echoes that could be heard in caves, the roar of thunder and lightning and, setting all this to music, produced a natural and wild song on his lips, like that of nature.[*]

Gomidas Vartabed also pictured the expression of the manifold feelings of the virgin soul of the villager through song, during his daily labours, in his life, be it happy or sad, joyful or tragic, and which had given birth on his lips to songs of the field, weddings, dance, sorrow or praise and lullabies, providing a new language for his many feelings.[†]

Many of Gomidas' students later followed him to Bardizag and organised concerts of popular songs using and training local people to form a choir, and Armenian song, based on minstrels' works, was heard from its lips. These were later replaced by the patriotic songs that were written in a European form and style, and which we had heard since our childhood and youth.

It is not superfluous to mention the new, bold oratory used by the political activists. They spoke using simple language, short and sharp sentences, utilising a flow of special and powerful words and all the variations of tone and movement that gushed from their souls. They electrified their audiences, creating in it the stirrings of new ways of thinking and turmoil in their souls and feelings.

One of the spiritual pleasures that were enjoyed in Bardizag in those days of freedom was the celebration of the 1,500th anniversary of the translation of the Bible into Armenian and the 400th anniversary of Armenian printing.[‡] These two things were commemorated on a nationwide scale, and were very great celebrations. A choir was

---

[*] Aghavni Mesrobian provides us with recollections of Gomidas' visit to Bardizag in the summer of 1913. Her description of Gomidas' day, when he would go to the *Tsadgan Chour* [Leaping Water] waterfall arm-in-arm with Ghazigian Vartabed (with whom he stayed in the village and who was an old friend) on one side and Roupen Zartarian on the other, surrounded by members of the Kousan choir and their families, friends and pupils, is both compelling and tender. Kourken Kasbarian, *Gomidas in his contemporaries' recollections and testimonies*, Yerevan 2009, pp. 350-353.

[†] Panos Terlemezian's famous painting of Gomidas sitting under an awning amid the trees was painted at this idyllic time, probably in Bardizag.

[‡] This was officially proclaimed by the Catholicos of All Armenians in 1913 and was celebrated in October of that year.

formed in Bardizag made up of students from the community school and the American high school, under the direction of our compatriot, the high school student Vahram Kondaiyan. They sang songs collected by Gomidas with the greatest success.[*]

148 - The founding of a kindergarten and the purchase of its own building

The Bardizag community school still didn't have a kindergarten as that important branch of teaching children in those days had not, in many places, been given any real importance, except in certain European countries.

The child, in those days, spent the first three or four years of its life at home. It was left to its own devices, falling down and getting up again, breaking things, resulting in being often smacked by its mother, elder brother or sister. They would, however, occasionally smile at it, cuddle it and show it affection. The child of course didn't understand these conflicting things that affected its small person, and because it didn't understand, liked to surrender to its usual and natural games and naughtiness. It would then perhaps be astonished at being scolded and smacked for things which seemed so natural to it.

The child was sent, after a time, to an experienced *doudou*[†] each day where it continued to behave in the same way, often suffering smacking or receiving smiles, to which was added dancing, singing, the first attempts at reading and enjoying a nap on the floor.

The child, at the age of five or six would finally enter school, where it didn't find anything very different from what it already preferred.

With, however, the Russian Armenian female kindergarten teacher[‡] Mrs. Madagian's mission and dedication, the necessity and skills used in this important part of education were spread far and wide in Turkey. They started to be used in Constantinople – where the first Armenian kindergartens were established – and kindergarten teachers[**] were trained, not just in Madagian's school but also in American missionary establishments. In the provinces, Bardizag was the first place to want its own kindergarten where the little ones could be taught using the latest methods and means.

While people thought like this the village council, so as not to lose time, rented Gabak's newly-built house[††] in the market area, which then had a number of alterations made to it, making it into a temporary kindergarten where children, both

---

[*] The pictures that exist of the Bardizag American Boys' High School buildings decorated with branches etc. around their windows were taken during this celebration.
[†] This dialect word can mean older woman, elderly lady, aunt, child minder or something similar, depending on context.
[‡] The word used here is *mangabardizbanouhi*.
[**] The Armenian text uses the feminine gender here, just as in Footnote 4 above.
[††] See Section 105.

boys and girls from the age of four years old were brought. This formed the Bardizag kindergarten establishment, with a group of women trustees, under the supervision of the village council.

The first directress of this new establishment was a young lady from Bardizag named Varsenig Hetebian, who had some knowledge and experience and who had a female assistant and a woman housekeeper.

Our children who, until then filled the *doudous'* courtyards in unsuitable and unhealthy conditions, now had the best and purpose-built building where they would enjoy the benefits of the new kind of education. Those children, with bright and smiling faces, wearing red coveralls with the Armenian initials A M. (meaning *Azkayin Mangabardez* – Community Kindergarten) in white on their collars went there now. They carried their small lunchboxes, laughing and skipping through the streets, to spend their day in play, singing and dancing, forming a large happy family of children, where the talents of their little souls would reveal themselves, within a loving and motherly atmosphere.

That part of the market area became a much-improved place after that, as if the villagers had, in that tall building, caged its chicks in the sun under a blue sky, where they chirped all day, taking a snatch of happy song back to their homes, providing encouragement to the people who were working.

A year or two later the Bardizag kindergarten had its own building in the centre of the village, near the community school.

The leading priest Hovhannes Kahana Mgerian, concerned to spend his old age in his birthplace, had a proper and stylish house built on land belonging to his family, with all the requisites for easy living. After he passed away, his heirs decided to sell it. The Bardizag village authorities, taking advantage of the opportunity, wanted to buy the new building and use it for the kindergarten's needs. They bought it for about 200 Ottoman liras, and the children went there, into their own home.[*]

This all happened in the years just before the beginning of Turkish Freedom.[†]

149 - The conflict between the community authorities and the local ARF[‡] committee

The community authority of the day was chaired by Minas Effendi Dzalian, whose election was assisted and secured by the Bardizag ARF committee's sympathy and vote.

---

[*] A Womens' Charity-Kindergarten Association had been set up in the village in 1904 with the aim of collecting enough money to build a kindergarten. By 1910 it had handed over 100 Ottoman liras to the village authorities for this purpose. The organisation disintegrated after that through bitter wrangling. Minas Kasabian (Farhad), *Hayere Nikomedio Kavarin Mech*, pp. 207-208.

[†] In other words just before 1908.

[‡] ARF – Armenian Revolutionary Federation (Dashnaktsoutiun).

This *loving agreement** didn't last long due to a minor school problem.

A young teacher, who was a member of the ARF, had an argument with a colleague, just like anyone else, and dared to insult him. The insulted teacher formally protested to the school trustees, seeking justice. The trustees examined the incident seriously, listened to both sides, and determined that the complaint was real and justified. There was an offence which the accused didn't deny. The insulted teacher wanted to defend his honour in front of the relevant authority, which was coming to the conviction that an offence had been committed by the accused teacher.

It never entered the heads of the trustees to give this childish spat any real importance. This sort of thing was not unusual between two citizens and the teachers were citizens. But there was the question of the insulted teacher's demand and his moral position, so the trustees decided to suggest to the accused's side that he should see his colleague and, justifying what he said, to close the matter.

The teacher concerned didn't agree to this innocent and tactful decision. He was given time to think about it and give satisfaction to the insulted teacher. The accused refused; we† had not known that a member of the ARF could not be guilty, and even if he was, that to say he was sorry would be an inadmissible disgrace. This position maintained by the Dashnak teacher made us understand much about future public incidents, so the trustees, having consulted with the village council, suspended him as a rebel against lawful authority: so the parcel of incidents began to disintegrate.

The Dashnak committee, determined to defend its comrade with all its strength and means, ignoring the fact that he was guilty, adopted the tactics detailed below against the community authority that became, after this, the usual ones employed against those it considered to be the ARF's enemies.

The first was the unofficial and oblique approaches made to the authority or their representatives, trying to persuade them to rescind their decision and allow the teacher to return to his various duties, using persuasive language and threats. Naturally, the community authority didn't want to kill off its prestige and would not give way. It was left to the Dashnaks to make good its threats.

Next, it organised a strike by the school students that were under its influence, to try to stir up public opinion. The authorities stood firm and insisted on its point of view.

The third tactic was the organisation of public demonstrations and approaches to the authority, and clamorous, demeaning and incorrect articles in the newspapers. The authority once more stood firm and the teacher remained suspended.

---

*   Author's own italics.

†   The author, it seems, was a community school trustee – yet another of the positions he held along with his teaching between 1908 and 1915.

The fourth was verbal and physical attacks on the authority members, especially on the chairman,* even in the council chamber. The authorities stood firm once more, and invited the protesters to stop their wrongful activities and use lawful means.

The ARF committee still had actions to take using the methods it knew, and its fifth tactic was the demand for a general public assembly to examine the problem. The authority agreed to this, although the demand was illegal and inopportune. The majority of those present at the meeting agreed with the authority's stance and the examination of the problem was aborted.

The committee hadn't succeeded in this new game and, in despair that all their tactics had failed, finally took the problem to the (Armenian) provincial education authority court.† There, thanks to party and friendship ties, and the fact that some of the court assessors were Dashnaks, and without any prior examination or seeing the need for the Bardizag authority's information, it came to the strange conclusion which it communicated to the Bardizag authority, that: 'Seeing that it is not legal to suspend a teacher during the school year, and considering the punishment meted out to the teacher is sufficient, he should resume his duties.'

This decision made by the education authority was very strange. If the suspension of a teacher during the school year wasn't lawful, naturally the question then had to be asked as to when it was. At the same time the education authority accepted the suspended teacher's guilt, for which an illegal (sic) suspension was considered to be sufficient punishment, and it ordered him to be reinstated. But it forgot that with this patchwork decision it wielded an axe, striking at the foundation on which the community authority's rule was based, as there had been a very serious rebellion that had lasted for several days.

The Bardizag community authority then presented the problem to the education authority with all the details of its successive stages, and pointed out that their decision could destroy the community authority's prestige and created a dangerous precedent in Bardizag, in terms of the good administration of community works.

The ARF committee, the suspended teacher and the whole population of the village were now spectators. The struggle was now between the representatives of two national‡ bodies. The education authority, finding itself in a difficult position, and in its turn regarding its prestige damaged either outside or separate from it, took

---

* In all probability Minas Dzalian.
† Kavaragan Ousoumnagan Khorhourti Tadasdan.
‡ I use this term here because the local (provincial) education authority was an arm of the main education authority under the control of the Armenian Patriarchate in Constantinople.

the problem to the provincial political assembly,* asking that it make the Bardizag authority see sense.

The political assembly, jealous to maintain the education authority's prestige, adopted its thesis, and ordered Bardizag's authority to adopt the latter's decision, without even examining the explanatory document submitted by the village authority.

Bardizag's authorities held out, sticking firmly to its point of view, which was shared by two deputies† of the provincial deputies' assembly.‡ The other Bardizag deputies also shared the same view, an important point not noticed by the provincial political assembly.

The Bardizag community authority submitted a lengthy document containing the facts and relevant arguments to justify its position.

The political assembly didn't want to listen and repeated its order to bow to the education authority's decision, and threatened to punish the rebellious Bardizag community authority that that had not been able, in the midst of everything that had happened, to bring a recalcitrant teacher to heel and dismiss him.

The community authority repeated and stressed its point of view and held firm. Then the provincial political assembly, losing its head, dared to declare the Bardizag community authority dissolved and wrote to the locum tenens of the diocese to retrieve its official seal.

The Bardizag community authority, bereft of any hope of making the simplest thing understood, firstly by the teacher, then the Bardizag ARF committee and, step by step, the provincial education authority and the political assembly, and at the same time certain of the lawfulness of its position, approached the Armenian Patriarchate in Constantinople. The result of this approach was the Patriarchate's intervention in this minor matter and its irrefutable statement that the political assembly's decision to declare the dissolution of the Bardizag community authority was not legally justifiable. Thus the Bardizag authority remained the master of the situation and continued its work in the village undisturbed.

This problem lasted for a whole year, involving the school trustees, the student body, community authority, ARF committee, the population of the village, provincial education authority, political assembly and, finally the Patriarchate in Constantinople - and for what? - so a Dashnak teacher was spared the task of justifying himself to his colleague, whom he had dared to insult, as that would *apparently* have been demeaning. He could, for example, have said, 'Friend, as I was annoyed, I couldn't remain cool, and am upset that, despite not wanting to, I was tactless enough to insult you. I hope you will forgive me.'

---

* Kavaragan Kaghakagan Joghov.
† It should not be forgotten that the author himself was one of these deputies.
‡ Kavaragan Yerespokhanagan Catholicosate Joghov.

If the ARF had been able to have the greatness and nobility to make their member-teacher understand this and have him do so, he would not have suffered. There would not have been so many meetings at intervals, with the situation lasting a whole year, forcing everybody to understand what the ARF wanted – to apparently spare one of its member's feelings of dignity.

In all this, however, if there was something regrettable, it was the lightminded, demeaning and inappropriate way that the provincial education authority and the provincial political assembly that stood behind it both acted towards a lawful community authority. This was despite the fact that it had two individuals in it who were members of the highest provincial authority to whom they owed their existence and authority. These were individuals who, by experience, skill and understanding of the law remained far above them. On the other hand the national authority they belonged to had the confidence of the majority of the local people.

This was a reprehensible, lightminded and tactless error made by the provincial political assembly, and when it had completed its two-year term of office and gave its report to the national deputies' assembly, that and other similar acts were severely criticised and it was reduced to appearing like a 'poor, wet chicken'[*] as a result of voting by the deputies' assembly.

The Bardizag community authority, after having steadfastly defended its position and maintaining the prestige of the national authority at all costs, spontaneously resigned, being replaced with a temporary authority which remained at the head of Bardizag village affairs until the catastrophic year of 1915.

---

* The author's exact words.

Chapter 10

Deportation and Short-Lived Post-War Life

150 – Incidents that were precedents in Armeno-Turkish relations

The enthusiasm, solidarity and collaboration between Ittihad and the Armenian political parties in the first days of freedom didn't last long. The Hnchag party, even from the first days, was suspicious of the liberal Turks and didn't believe in the sincerity of their loud pronouncements that all Ottoman citizens were equal. But the Armenian Revolutionary Federation (ARF), which had worked with Ittihad to re-establish the liberal regime in the Ottoman Empire, retained for a long time, in its innocence, its faith in it. The ARF showed more eagerness than the Turks in giving the Turkish constitutional (sic) state its complete and unreserved independence, erasing the old ways of governing that existed from the old days and giving weight to Ittihad policies with all its spirit.

The foreign nations' Capitulations and the Christian patriarchates' rights remained the same. It became, however, almost scandalous when it was seen that among the native Christian races, the Armenians, that had suffered so much and been the most persecuted of all under the old regime, through the pressure exerted by the ARF, the dominant political force in the Armenian public arena, now subscribed to that Ittihad policy. It tried to destroy the final and only weapon in the nation's hands – through its naive, sincere dedication to the freedom of all the people. If it wasn't for the robust opposition to that Turkish effort by the other patriarchs, especially by the Greek Orthodox Ecumenical Patriarch, we Armenians would have, with our own hands, engineered our own destruction. The Turks knew that it wasn't possible for them, from one day to the next, to escape from their governmental shackles. They demanded that the foreign powers relinquish their Capitulations. Unsuccessful in this, they therefore decided to remove the internal freedoms enjoyed by the Christian communities. The Turks did not succeed in this aim either, and naturally would not because, although there was talk of a liberal regime, it was only talk and there was no real attempt to persuade jurists.

The first misunderstandings between Ittihad and the ARF became apparent, although without causing a final split, when the question of the election of the deputies to the Ottoman parliament became the subject of negotiation between them. The Turks wanted, with the apparently greatest broadmindedness, not to take the racial question into account in it. After all, wasn't everyone now a free and equal Ottoman citizen in the country? The parliamentary elections, therefore, should be conducted, not according to racial lines, but on the principle of the merit of citizenship. This was a beautiful and laudable principle, but never practical with the country's current mentality, where races living next to each other hated and were suspicious of one another. It was also a country where merit had no place, other than in terms of belonging to the same race or religion.

The Turks, therefore, against their will, retreated from that principle for a time, agreeing to the election of deputies to the new parliament from the subject races on a proportional basis, but the number of seats assigned to the Armenians didn't satisfy the ARF. But it accepted, for the sake of solidarity, still trailing behind Ittihad.

Thus only a small number of seats was assigned to the Armenians in the Ottoman parliament, disproportionate to their total number in the country, but at least it was a beginning.[*] The Armenian people had a voice within the highest lawmaking authority. The questions raised and articulated in parliament concerning seizures of Armenian-owned land, the Armenians' losses and the necessity of redressing their deprivation, however, were received, just as under the slackness of old regime, by the total deafness of the Ittihad government. That was a delicate question for it, fanning racial hatreds. The righting of every mistake was impossible, and the Armenians had to be satisfied with their present position. It was thought that those injustices and sacrifices had now been consigned to history, and they had become the owners of equality of citizenship before the law. This was something which, after all, was an assurance for the future.

During this period, however, the new Turkey was passing through various political crises which angered Ittihad, despite the re-establishment of constitutional order that was regarded as a universal panacea. The dismemberment of the Empire by the European Great Powers continued.

Austria finally annexed Bosnia and Herzegovina,[†] which had, under the terms of the Treaty of Berlin, been placed under its temporary jurisdiction. The Turko-Italian war broke out a little later on and African Tripoli (Tripolitania) was captured by the Italians.[‡] The Turkish government had neither the time nor the disposition to impose justice for its Christian citizens in the circumstances the country was in.[**]

Apart from all these external difficulties, an anti-constitutional, reactionary movement had begun in the interior of the country, through Sultan Abdul Hamid II's

---

[*] The 'reformed' Ottoman parliament opened on 14th December 1908.
[†] The annexation was declared on 5th October 1908, and Turkey accepted an Austrian offer of £2,500,000 for the territory on 12 January 1909. On 5th October 1908 Prince Ferdinand of Bulgaria declared his country independent of the Ottoman Empire. The Ottoman Empire recognised its independence on 19th April 1909.
[‡] The war for African Tripoli (Tripolitania, now Libya) lasted from Sep. 29th 1911 until 18th October 1912 and ended with the Italians' victory.
[**] The author has condensed all the international events of the time between 1909 and 1912 – because they had no real bearing on Bardizag or the Armenians directly – into this one paragraph.

duplicity and agents bribed by him, which threatened to strangle the constitutional order in its embryonic state. The Ittihad government, rendered confused for a time, with the ship of state striking obstacle after obstacle decided, forgetting everything else, to at least save constitutional freedoms. It escaped the danger, convening parliament in St. Stefano. Meanwhile it invited Shevket Pasha, with his army, to advance to Constantinople and preserve constitutional order. Shevket Pasha's army had clashes with the Sultan's armed forces on the streets of Constantinople, but within a few days succeeded in crushing this attempted military counter-revolution and captured the sultan himself, who was declared to be deposed, and exiled to Salonica (Thessalonniki).

The reactionary movement fomented by Sultan Abdul Hamind II brought to light the old anti-liberal mentality that existed from one end of the country to the other. Adana was engulfed in the blood of the Armenians of the city and the looting and destruction of their assets.[*] This time too the Armenian people drank from the cup of bitterness, and found themselves faced with puppet and sham liberalism. The ARF, however, as a revolutionary party, tied its fate to that of Ittihad. It regarded this movement to be a threat against the ideals of the revolution itself, being convinced that, after this danger was past, the Armenian people would see justice done by Ittihad, at least on this occasion.

The shaken liberal order was re-established. Constantinople was captured and parliament returned to the capital. A new Sultan, a person who was debauched and devoid of individuality and boldness, ascended the throne.[†] He was simply a puppet in the hands of all-powerful Ittihad.

The danger which re-appeared in the country was counter-revolutionary, and especially against the Armenian people. It was like a symbol to the vast majority of the Turkish people – the re-establishing of the liberal order - brought the ranks of the Ittihad and ARF closer together. Precautionary measures were taken to deal with the potential threat, by arming the people that were in favour of the liberal order, in other words the small Ittihad party group and the ranks of the Armenian political parties as a political army to protect, if necessary, the endangered constitution. Thus Ittihad, driven by the need to save itself, gave the Armenians weapons to be held until such time as the threat to constitutional order receded.

Two questions arose in these days to endanger this closeness and solidarity of Ittihad and the Armenian people and especially the ARF that spoke for it.

The first was the examination of the Adana catastrophe and the demand for justice. Despite the ARF's optimism and hopes, this simply degenerated into

---

* The Adana massacre of 1909 cost 30,000 Armenian lives. See Hagop H. Terzian, *Cilicia 1909: the Massacre of Armenians*, translated by Ara Stepan Melkonian and edited by Ara Sarafian, Gomidas Institute, London, 2009.
† This was Mehmed V, who reigned from 1909 until 1918.

buffoonery and bankruptcy. Along with the real criminals, a number of Armenians, whose only guilt was self-defence, were hanged. This showed that under the disguise of Ittihad liberalism, the same Turk still existed, with all his barbarism and blows against real justice. Although the ARF was in despair, it curbed its emotions concerning the massacre of innocent people in Adana to maintain its revolutionary organisation.

The second question was that of army service for Christians as a condition of their equality of citizenship. Ittihad was very hesitant over this. The military service exemption tax was an important source of revenue for the government, which had great need of funds. At the same time the government didn't want to provide Christians, whom it didn't trust, with weapons. On the other hand, apart from the Armenians, none of the other races had any faith in the liberal order and didn't display any interest in the work of saving the country. They had no faith in its existence either, and were drawn towards the governments of the countries around Turkey that were their racial brothers wanting, as if by centrifugal force, to link their communities' fate to them. It was only the Armenians that had honestly placed their faith in the liberal order and the reforming changes needed by the demands of the country. The Turks therefore couldn't see the use of the conscription of the Greeks and Bulgarians, whom they didn't trust, into the Turkish armed forces. Meanwhile the Armenians considered it a necessity as a means of self-defence, although they[*] didn't share this thought with the great majority of their fellow Armenians.

The ARF, despite Ittihad's hesitation and the other Christian races' antipathy, wanted the endorsement of the law for Christians to serve in the armed forces, as a basic condition that emerged from the principles of the liberal order. The Armenian revolutionaries and the ARF therefore arranged great demonstrations across the country to defend their point of view, strengthened by the people's demands. One of these demonstrations took place in Bardizag, and the people were dragged towards the ARF's wishes.

Ittihad shelved the question for a time, with the liquidation of the defeat in the First Balkan War and the territory under its control reduced. It later saw the need for a large army to maintain its existence in which it could usefully and profitably use all the local races they trusted with weapons. Those they didn't trust would be used as labourers and technicians in its support. It therefore accepted Christian enlistment. This was on the condition that anyone who didn't want to serve in the armed forces would not be forced to do so, paying the military service exemption tax instead.

The Turks knew that the Armenians and other foreign races, in whose hands the richest enterprises in the country were, would not want to force their sons to serve

---

[*] The text here is not clear; one can make an assumption that the author is talking about the ARF.

in the armed forces. They would therefore have to pay the tax which would bring in, during wartime, significant revenue. Only the sons of those who were unable to pay would be conscripted. This meant two kinds of profit – who could ask for more?

Ittihad, which believed in constitutional liberal order in the first days, wanted to prevent the planned dismemberment of the country and preserve the government's independence. It saw that it had not succeeded in its attempt at providing a universal panacea. The events of the six years after the promulgation of the constitution, both internal and external, had made it desperate. All of European Turkey and Tripolitania in Africa had passed into foreign hands, and no end could be seen to this continued dismemberment. There was new agitation on the horizon, foreign powers retaining all their privileges and the Christian communities their juridical independence. Nothing had changed in the country. Although a constitutional parliament and ministries devolved from it were the authorities, the constitutional order had not succeeded in uniting the country's citizens and the distrust between them was gradually increasing. Even the Armenians, despite their total dedication to the Turkish constitution, although seeing no profit or assistance from it for their continued existence, had finally succeeded, through the demand and the help of foreign powers, of imposing foreign checks and a unique regime in the Armenian-populated areas of the country.[*] Thus the country, instead of uniting, was faced with the danger of further divisions. Ittihad, in its rage at these events, lost all hope and, losing it head, reached a dreadful way of thinking. This was to make a final basic attempt to succeed, or to destroy and bury its fury and every movement that impeded its aims under the ruins.

It was while Ittihad was in this mood that the First World War broke out.[†] The opportunity was made for Ittihad: it was the time for a decisive decision to be made. Europe had divided into two camps opposed to each other for a terrible struggle. Should – or must - Turkey remain neutral in this war of nations? Ittihad, in its current hopeless and angry state, couldn't make up its mind. In a general war – that of the Balkans – Turkey had been defeated, a wound that still had not healed. The Allies (Great Britain, France and Russia) had prepared that war and Turkey's defeat. The new administration of the Armenian-inhabited provinces was also their work. The Arab world in its turn was also in ferment, wanting to find its independence. It

---

[*] The author is referring to the administrative changes made to the government of the six Armenian provinces: their re-organisation into two administrative districts, each under a European Inspector-General appointed by the Turks but approved by the great powers. They were appointed in April 1914 – Westenek, from Holland, a colonial administrator, and Major Hoff, of the Norwegan army, the first based in Van, the second in Erzerum. The onset of the First World War forced this scheme to be abandoned. See Christopher T. Walker, *Armenia: The Survival of a Nation*, Croom Helm, London 1980, pp. 194-195.

[†] War was declared in Europe on 3rd August 1914.

seemed as if the suffering races in Turkey wanted to make the Allied powers their allies for the sake of justice. Turkey and Ittihad could see the death of their independence in an Allied victory. Ittihad didn't have the foresight and wisdom at that critical time to make friends with those it considered enemies, by moving forward with reforms and the autonomy of the races under Turkey's patronage. The Allies' enemy, Germany, and its allies looked to be all-powerful to the Turkish leaders. They therefore tied their fate to a German victory, determining to fight a final life-or-death battle by fighting alongside Germany and its allies. The natural result of this decision by the Turks was the destruction of the Armenian people and, immediately after the declaration of war, they began to strengthen their feelings against their consciences and justice – feelings that were never very strong in their centuries-old bloody history.

151 – Collection of weapons and deportation

Turkey entered the war in November 1914 joining the Central powers and allying itself with Germany. The Turkish government declared mobilisation and called all citizens of military age, be they Christian or Muslim, to the colours.[*]

Bardizag, upon mobilisation, sent almost all its young men, approximately 1,000 individuals,[†] to serve as unarmed soldiers, building roads and repairing means of communication under the harshest conditions and with great sacrifices.[‡] Those who didn't want to serve in the army paid enormous sums of money as military exemption tax, and that several times. Apart from this, the people were forced, under the greatest threats, to contribute to the military aid organisations named *Tekalife Harbiye* and *Hilale Adjmer*.[**]

---

* Walker tells us that mobilisation was actually ordered on 28 October 1914. Christopher J. Walker, *Armenia: the Survival of a Nation*, Croom Helm, London, 1980, p. 198.

† According to Der-Hagopian, mobilisation was actually declared in Bardizag on 9th August 1914. During the next three days about 1,500 men registered for service. Some of these, by paying military service exemption tax, stayed in the village. The first 500 to be drafted marched, to the accompaniment of the village ARF trumpet band, to Karamoursal. Hagop Der-Hagopian, *Bardizage khadoudig*, p. 35.

‡ The 19 year-olds of Bardizag were also called up and sent to Constantinople, as the Turks had no confidence in the Christians. They were assigned, as auxiliary soldiers, to the labour battalions. Boghosian and his friend Vahram Manougian became clerks and had to keep track of arriving and departing soldiers, sending them to the Dardanelles front. Haroutiun Boghosian, *Anzoukagan Bardizag*, Elegian Press, Paris, 1967, p. 56.

** This appears to be the occasion recorded by Hapelian when, to demonstrate their fidelity to the Ottoman constitution, the village collected 400 liras for the Red Crescent and handed it over to the miudir, who informed the appropriate authorities and spoke of his satisfaction towards the village's population. Hagop Der-Hagopian, *Bardizage khadoudig*, p. 38.

Despite this complete acceptance of their civilian responsibilities by the people of Bardizag and the whole of the Turkish Armenian community, more than 20 people from the village - doctors, teachers, government officials, artisans and ordinary people - without any specific accusation or trial, were suddenly arrested in Bardizag and exiled to the country's interior in the spring of 1915.[*]

Later, in the weeks before *Vartavar* [the feast of the Transfiguration of Jesus],[†] the government officially informed the people and all the inhabitants of the *nahie* [village group], both Christian and Muslim, that all weapons should be handed in within ten days, retaining the right to return them to whomever it pleased.

The people of Bardizag handed over, in the main, hunting rifles and self-defence weapons. The government, however, before everyone's gaze, returned all the weapons handed in by the Muslim population, confiscating all those belonging to Christians.

On the *Vartavar* Saturday (the day before the feast itself) more than 40 *bashe bozouks* [irregular Turkish soldiers] in civilian clothing and wearing white armbands laid siege to Bardizag, preventing the movement of the people to and from the village. The government, on the same day, invited between 50 and 60 notables[‡] – vartabeds, kahanas, local members of the *Irade* and *Belediye* assemblies, parish councillors, trustees, teachers, all the *mukhtars* and several young men[**] to the government building.

A special official sent by the government in Constantinople to search for weapons, Ibrahim Bey,[††] an individual with an untrustworthy past demanded, in the presence of the local miudir and the commandant of the Izmid gendarmerie that all the weapons, bomb-making materials and other military stores that were apparently kept in the village be surrendered immediately without argument. He gave the individuals summoned two hours to think about and say their final words

---

[*] Der-Hagopian quotes the date as April 1915, and provides the following names: Dr. H. Der-Stepanian, the teacher Karnig Bodourian, Boghos Kourouyian, Siragan Tsintsinian, Mihran Der-Garabedian, brave men like Baghdasar Ago, Parnag, Gabak Ago, Mihran Bodourian (Gabedj), Biber Ardash and others. Hagop Der-Hagopian, *Bardizage khadoudig*, p. 35.

[†] This is celebrated in July.

[‡] Anania Vartabed Hapelian, whose diary is quoted in Der-Hagopian, gives the date of this event as 27 June, and further states that he was one of those called in, with Aghasi Effendi Der-Mgrdichian, Sahag Der-Sahagian, Mgrdich Der-Garabedian and Minas Avedian. He gives the name of the Turkish miudir of the village as Ali Shu'uri. Hagop Der-Hagopian, *Bardizage khadoudig*, p. 37.

[**] The author himself was one of these people, as will be seen.

[††] Anania Vartabed Hapelian provides the following detail about this individual: 'Ibrahim Bey is the general director of prisons'. Hagop Der-Hagopian, *Bardizage khadoudig*, p. 37.

about it.* If not, he threatened, he would massacre everyone in the village down to the youngest infant in accordance with the permission he had been given. He then invited them to go to the community school building to think about it and come to a decision.

The school building was surrounded by a cordon of soldiers shortly afterwards. When the invited individuals, who had assembled in one room, were trying to find some sort of escape from this dangerous and deadly situation, a policeman brought a bundle of wet canes and a bucket of water and put them in a corner outside the room.

We, within reason, and trying to maintain our coolness, came to the conclusion that we should reply by saying that there were no weapons or bomb-making materials in Bardizag, but that it was probable that there might be a few weapons still held by individuals who had been frightened of handing them in before.

After the period of grace had expired, Ibrahim Bey, the *miudir* and the commandant of the gendarmes, accompanied by a number of gendarmes, came into the school building, bringing with them a *falakha*† and took over the boys' upper hall. The *miudir* then came to us and invited us to present ourselves and inform them of our answer.

The kahana who was the locum tenens of the diocese in Bardizag, Madatia Kahana Gondiurian, who later died on the road to exile, went, with two local silk merchants, to see the government representatives with the task of giving them our collective answer.

Talk, justification or truth didn't have any value; we were now a people deemed to be outside the law, and every injustice and illegality was forgiven, even praised.

The only answer our representatives received was to be laid full length on the floor and the soles of their feet beaten without mercy with the wet canes, as if they were masterless dogs. 20 or even more than 30 strong blows were delivered, first to one foot, then the other. The sound of cries and unspeakable screams created a storm in the quiet atmosphere of the school, and the rest of us, deathly pale, shook with terror where we were. They were beating our representatives to death... On that day, until noon, all of us shared the horrible beatings in groups of three. Only the *mukhtars* and one or two delicate people were spared.‡

---

* Ibrahim and his group arrived in Bardizag in May, settling themselves in the government building *(ghonakh)* and demanded the surrender of all weapons. Here, as everywhere else, the people brought what poor weapons they had. Hagop Der-Hagopian, *Bardizage khadoudig*, p. 36.

† A kind of whip.

‡ Hapelian states that he was spared being beaten twice 'thanks to the noble personality of the commandant of the gendarmes and the village's *miudir*'. Hagop Der-Hagopian, *Bardizage khadoudig*, pp. 37-38.

After the beatings, several of us who were considered to be trustworthy were cross-examined separately, and were given the task of talking to various classes of people and turning over any weapons found to the government. This delegation managed to retrieve some weapons, among which were 15-20 Mauser rifles.[*]

That night several of us were released with the duty of collecting all the remaining weapons in the village and handing them over. By the following morning the number of Mauser rifles collected had risen to about 50.

On the following morning Ibrahim Bey and his men beat those of us that were regarded as political figures for the second time with wet canes and with increased severity. They also beat several others who were innocent of the charge, but had respected the political parties, according to the advice given by the Ittihad government. There were no new revelations, nor could there be, as all the barbarities carried out were only based on suspicion.

Various parts of the church were searched during the morning, with large and deep areas of that innocent building being demolished. Nothing was found apart from an old picture depicting an Armenian king, probably used in a theatrical performance.

During the day and in the evening, these honourable and faithful citizens of a constitutional government, who had been dreadfully treated, were released in two separate groups, as it had become certain that there were no arms and bomb depots in Bardizag. They had to sign a document promising to hand in all weapons that might still be in the village to the government, with the threat of death if, upon a second inspection, any arms were found there.

The 'officials' then visited every home, both in the village and outside it and every silk-spinning factory and khan, and collected everything they found – knives, saws, sickles etc - in other words anything that could potentially cause an injury. These totalled several hundred items, among which there were only 50-60 weapons.

There was nothing more to be done by Bardizag; the village that had been an obstacle to the Turkish government's aims was already denuded of its fighting youth, which had been conscripted months before, and now that the 'weapons' had been collected, it was ready to subject itself to the government's most rebel-rousing and illegal orders like sheep.

A few days later the order for the deportation of the village was published:

> The Armenian people are untrustworthy, the country is at war and the enemy is shelling the gates of Constantinople so, on the basis of military precautions, it has been found necessary to remove it far from the coastlines, to the interior, to Biledjik, Eski-Shehir and Konya.

---

[*] Hapelian states in his diary that he was one of these people and made an announcement about handing over weapons in the Holy King church. Hagop Der-Hagopian, *Bardizage khadoudig*, p. 38.

The government was reticent with the whole truth, in fact they hid it, apparently being frightened of unarmed children, women and the hopeless rebellion of an army of old people. There was a final weapon in the people's hands: its wealth and portable assets which it could use to protect its existence for a time. This too was to be purloined and the people sent, naked and hungry, on their unending journey, so as to ensure the total extermination of the community.

The *muidir*, the man called Shu'uri Bey, an evil man with no character, worked with Ittihad with all his energy while pretending to be sympathetic to us and being our friend.

The people of Bardizag, the majority of whom lived from day to day, had no money or savings, and therefore had to sell what they had to acquire funds for the journey, leaving everything else to God.

The whole village took on the appearance of a market: every family bringing onto the street its furniture and whatever it had to sell to those who appeared. Only the grape harvest had been brought in, the majority of which still hadn't been sold and turned into cash. The village filled with a great crowd of Muslims from the neighbouring villages – Laz, Georgians Tatars, Circassians and Turks – who had come to enrich themselves for next to nothing. This community sale was a dreadful financial catastrophe for the Armenian villagers, with items worth 5-10 liras being sold for 5-10 *kurush*, with everything selling at this sort of price. Houses that were filled from top to bottom were emptied in a few days. Most of the owners only made 3, 5 or 10 liras to put in their pockets. There were some who didn't want to sell their possessions under those conditions and decided to make the journey without doing so, preferring death to this forced robbery. The *miudir*, for his part, found ways to lessen what entered their pockets.

He told the village notables that if the people of the village would collect 100 liras for each of the two military organisations named *Tekalife Harbiye* and *Hilale Adjmer* and the community undertook the purchase of a 100-bed military hospital and defray all its costs until the end of the war, he would telegraph the Minister of the Interior, Talaat Pasha, requesting that the people of the village remained where they were. He expressed hopes that his request would be granted. He knew the whole truth, of course, concerning the fate of the Armenians, but he tried to expedite their destruction by leaving the majority of the people without money. Hoping for the best, however, has always made people credulous. We were convinced of the *miudir's* sincerity, collected the 200 liras and handed it over to him, as well as giving him an assurance that the hospital would be set up, paid for and maintained, so that he would make his promised approach to Constantinople, to the Minister of the Interior.

Days passed without any answer. The *miudir* was engaged in his destructive work, while we approached him for an answer to his petition on our behalf. He expressed sorrow that he hadn't received a reply. It may be that he never telegraphed Constantinople, and pocketed the money collected as his portion of the robbery of the community. He also had the callousness to say that perhaps the amount was regarded as being too small for such a large village, and advised us to collect another 100-150 liras for the same organisations, repeating our petition, hoping it would be successful. The villagers' answer to this new suggestion was unequivocal: it was no longer in a position to make such a sacrifice, but there were people from Bardizag in Constantinople who would want to assist their birthplace for the salvation of their compatriots, if we had the opportunity to apply to them. The *miudir* told the notables to select two people and he would send them to Constantinople to perform that duty for the village.

It was forbidden, in those days, to enter Constantinople, but the *miudir* issued passports for a delegation of two people to go there to make the proposed collection. I was one of the two people selected.[*]

We departed for Constantinople using the passports provided. But we had hardly begun our mission to collect the amount now required from our compatriots when I received a letter from my wife, who wrote to me saying, 'What are you waiting in Constantinople for? Everyone here has put his affairs in order and is preparing to leave, while we are totally unready.'

We had already collected 30 liras, and many of our compatriots had expressed willingness to make a contribution, whenever we needed it, which we had deferred until nearer the date of our return.

I approached the various official Armenian circles, Archbishops Zaven and Tourian, Professor Der-Hagopian[†] and Americans whom I knew, who said to me, 'The Armenian deportations are inevitable, and the interior provinces have already been emptied of their Armenian populations.' I asked where they had been sent to; the answer was, 'We don't know. They are all moving in the direction of the Mesopotamian deserts.' I then asked if they had news of the deportees. The answer was negative. There was a dark and frightening uncertainty. I began to guess the terrible, catastrophic truth. All the *miudir's* words were lies and his advice was treachery. We were forced to leave our homes, land, harvests in our fields, gardens and vineyards and to take to the road in complete uncertainty.

I hurried to return to Bardizag to protect my family and share in its fate, with all the other Armenians. The *miudir* wasn't there when I reached the village. Members of my family, waiting for me, hadn't sold anything. The general 'market' continued, with lower and lower prices being paid for purchases – almost to the point of

---

[*] Mkhalian does not reveal who the other person was.
[†] Not to be confused with Hagop Der-Hagopian, the journalist and former *muidir* of Bardizag.

begging – when everyone, seeing potential customers, begged them to buy what they had to sell. This wasn't an ordinary market - it was more like giving things away just to obtain a few coins.

I was able to sell a few things. My family consisted of 10 people: eight members of my immediate family, my mother-in-law and my sister-in-law. We had no money. The temporary director of the American High School, who had succeeded the previous one who was a British subject from Canada,[*] hearing of my state, sent me two months' salary, a sum of 18 liras, as a gift or loan which, added to what we had, totalled the small sum of 50 Ottoman liras, or five liras per person.

The *miudir*, having emptied the nearby Armenian-inhabited villages of Dongel and Ovadjek of their populations, returned to Bardizag. I was forced to appear before him and give him the report on the mission. I wasn't of course forced to see him, but I was frightened that after we left the village he would remember me and have me brought back, forcing me to leave my family unprotected on its journey on unknown roads. I went to the government building, presented myself and told him that there were hopes of a successful collection, but when we received the news that the population of the village was to be deported, we considered that our efforts were useless and our potential donors didn't want to pay. We had collected 30 liras, of which we had spent five, leaving the small sum of 25 liras from the donations we had received. I asked him to allow me to distribute it among the priests who were almost destitute. His reply: 'I cannot permit you to give the money collected in the name of the *Tekalife Harbiye* and *Hilale Adjmer* to the priests. But if you want to, you may.'

This reply had the strength of a threat for me, so I gave it to him, adding, 'I won't take the responsibility and give it to you; you can give it to whomever you like.' He pocketed the money as he had, without doubt, done with the previous sums, saying, with the greatest effrontery and impertinence, 'Give it to me so I can "eat" it.' And he did.

The whole village, with a population of 2,000 families,[†] was 'invited'[‡] to leave it in three days' time,[**] going down to Seymen, then by boat to Izmid station, from

---

[*] This director (Mr McNaughton), in the days following the declaration of war, was deported to Yozghad near Ankara as a suspicious person, where he was due to remain for the duration of the war, but the American embassy in Constantinople intervened on his behalf and he was permitted to return to the capital, on the condition that he and his family left the country. (Author's note)

[†] The number of individuals has been estimated as 8,000 although Hapelian quotes the number of families as 1,500 and the total number of people being deported as 10,000. Hagop Der-Hagopian, *Bardizage khadoudig*, p. 38.

[‡] This is the author's word.

[**] Hapelian gives the date as August 4th, 1915. Hagop Der-Hagopian, *Bardizage khadoudig*, p. 38.

where we would move onward by train.*

We had nothing more to sell, only having items and clothing for the journey. We were forced to pay to have them transported, as well as paying our fares. The means of transport were lacking and it wasn't possible to carry what we had on our backs. The Turkish carters demanded 40-50 *kurush* for an hour's journey. What could we do? We had to pay and wait. We paid – everyone paid – robbery had taken on the force of law. The *miudir,* at the last minute, appropriated a house as a place of refuge where each of us could leave old people who couldn't walk, and where they could wait for death, for the sum of two liras each. About 20 old men and women were left there; the muidir pocketed the payments made for their keep.†

Before leaving,‡ we were invited to take the possessions we were leaving behind to the church or the Protestant meeting house, handing the keys over to the government, with the assurance that when we returned, each household could recover its possessions. Many innocently believed this and took their things to the appointed places, with some considering the American High School or the houses of Turks they were acquainted with outside the village to be the safest places.

The muidir and the government knew that the people would not have the opportunity to return, but wanted us, who had been robbed, to assist them in their looting. The *miudir*, to complete this work, also captured an Armenian girl, forcibly bringing her back from Seymen to Bardizag, with the object of marrying her.**

We found ourselves, in Seymen, faced with another form of robbery. Several Turks from Izmid, who were apparently government-appointed officials, had arrived to collect train fares to three specific stations – Biledjik, Eski-Shehir and Konya, leaving the choice to the people. They didn't issue any tickets, only writing

---

*   Mkhalian makes no mention of the 250 people who took to the hills under the leadership of Zalem Garabed, who was accompanied by his two brothers, Minas and Boghos, rather than face deportation. Hagop Der-Hagopian, *Bardizage khadoudig*, pp. 53-54.

†   This house – actually a silk spinning factory - belonged to Nigoghos Giuleser, and was located near Goudjoug Forest. Hagop Der-Hagopian, *Bardizage khadoudig*, p. 37.

‡   Several families weren't deported at this time because they had converted to Islam: they were those of Hovhannes Derderig and Onnig Hagopi Chakher. They were later exiled to Bozanti. Apart from them some other families were allowed to remain. These were the families of Dr. G. Khacherian, Garabed Aliksanian (of the Izmid *Sandek Emin*), Hagop Sinanian (the agricultural inspector) and the accountant of the government factory. Hagop Der-Hagopian, *Bardizage khadoudig*, p. 37.

** The girl involved was Takouhi Seferian, who was in love with Ali Shu'uri the *miudir*. She was frightened of revenge by her compatriots, so went, on each day of the deportation, down to Seymen with the people, secretly returning to her lover each evening. Hagop Der-Hagopian, *Bardizage khadoudig*, p. 37.

down the names of those who paid on pieces of paper that, probably, were blown into the water by the wind. Many paid the fare to Konya as our deportation's final destination, to save them being shunted from one place to another.

We crossed the bay in boats, it costing 5 *kurush* per person for a 45 minute journey. We then had to wait in Izmid station, in the open, for days, as only one train a day was reserved for us deportees and it was difficult to move such a large crowd with just one train. It took two weeks to clear all the people from the station, sending them to the interior, under unclear circumstances.[*]

Here, in the station, there was a new and unexpected robbery. The government, on the basis that many of the deportees had not paid their fares before boarding the trains, forced those still waiting to buy tickets for a second time, saying that it was to compensate for those who had departed on previous trains without paying. They said that if we didn't, we would be sent to the pre-arranged destinations on foot. Was it possible not to accede? We weren't going from the market to our homes, but to Biledjik, Eski-Shehir and Konya. It was sufficient to look at a map of Asia Minor to make one's blood run cold. So we paid. Thus even before leaving Izmid, many people had spent the little money they had in their pockets.

In all this there was only one piece of good news for the people of Bardizag: after about half of them had taken the road to exile, the rest were told that permission had been given by the government in Constantinople for the families of soldiers to remain in their villages. Which family from Bardizag hadn't got a son in military service or hadn't paid military service exemption tax? This too was a new, roguish, impudent swindle, a means of salvation for many. Soldiers' families were separated and a number of them were permitted to return to the village.[†] Some were sent by boat back to Seymen, with others going to villages around the station on the way to Adabazar called Devrend. We later heard that these families had been distributed in

---

[*] Boghosian tells us that the station was patrolled by Turkish guards, who treated the people waiting to be deported with a total disregard for humanity. H. Boghosian, *Anzoukagan Bardizag*, p. 63.

[†] Boghosian tells us that

... [the officer in the station] began to advise me to calm down, without realising that I had already been able to save my family, saying that orders had come giving permission for soldiers' parents to stay in their homes, and it was possible that it would be put into practice the following day. He added that the provincial governor agreed with it. As soon as I heard this, I began to advise the soldiers' families to delay their departure.

H. Boghosian, *Anzoukagan Bardizag*, pp. 67-68.

small groups among the Muslim villages, being used as slaves and workers without wages.*

The American High School directors tried to get its teachers freed. An appeal to the local government had no result, so it asked for permission to go to Constantinople. The answer was that the presence of the American director of the establishment was necessary, as the government could not accept responsibility for American property. At this, the American consul in Izmid was contacted and asked to go to Constantinople on the school's behalf. The consul asked for permission; the reply was that under the present circumstances his remaining at his post was a necessity. Finally the government officials in Izmid raised every obstacle against the school's wish to have their teachers exempted from exile. When the director met his American fellow-directors who were returning to Constantinople from the interior provinces, he sent word through them to the Missionary Board. The Board wrote to the director saying that the Ministry of the Interior had agreed to the High School teachers being spared deportation. When he presented the letter to the *miutesarif* of Izmid, that official replied that there had been no such written communication, so the American High School teachers had to share the fate of the rest of the people.

152 – Bardizag during the years when it was empty of its population

After the deportation of the entire village community, the only people remaining in Bardizag, apart from Turkish officials, were several old men and women, one or two unreliable families, the *miudir's* female housekeeper and her only son, a woman called Gadar who was originally from Arslanbeg and who, having become widowed, had married a man from Bardizag who had a son. It was this woman who had facilitated the relationship between the *miudir* and Takouhi Seferian (or Sefer-Andonian), months before the deportation. Two more families remained, having

---

* Anania Vartabed Hapelian's diary entries:
August 10, Tuesday ...The young man in Izmid named Ibrahim Bey who was the *sevk memorou* [deportation official] had delayed the departure into exile of a number of families (having been bribed heavily by me) as being permitted to return to the village, as the Ottoman government had allowed the families of military doctors, officers and soldiers to stay in their villages. Today, in accordance with that order, about 200 families returned by sailing boat to Seymen, to return to their own houses in Bardizag, but due to a misunderstanding (in actual fact the *miudir's* intransigence) part of this poor remnant of the population remained in Seymen, and the remainder in the houses near the cemetery.
August 17, Tuesday: On the order of the *miutesarif* of Izmid, Mazhar Bey, and organised by the *miudir* of Bardizag, the people (in Seymen and the houses near the cemetery) were sent, in groups of five families, to the neighbouring Turkish, Georgian, Circassian and Tatar villages. I and my group were assigned to the Turkish village of Hasar Keoy (about one hour from the Greek village of Yenikeoy) comprising about 80 houses. The people were unwelcoming, rough and hated us. We were forced to stay in a ruined, dirty, smelly coffee house with no roof for 8-10 days.

promised to turn Muslim.*

Among the families remaining were those that had permits because one or another of their family members was in an important government position. These were the Khacherians – because of Captain Dr. Garabed Khacherian; the Aliksanian family, for Garabed Effendi Aliksanian of the Izmid *Sandek Emin;* and the Sinanian family, as Hagop Effendi Sinanian was the provincial agricultural inspector. Another family was also given a permit – that of Yermia Effendi Seferian – who was formerly an official in the government factory and who, before the deportation, had been exiled as a suspicious person. He and his family were allowed to return as the family of a soldier, as his son was an officer in the army. The B. G. Nahabedian family also returned, as they were related by marriage to the Seferians.†

Some time later Yeremia Effendi died,‡ but his family lived safely in Bardizag. The families that had converted to Islam weren't so lucky. The female members and childen were allowed to stay in the village, while the males were rounded up and exiled to the interior of the country.

These were examples of Bardizag's old community who were allowed to stay in their homes. Bardizag, under these circumstances, seemed to have become the home of owls and, without its population, presented an empty and sad picture: looted houses mostly with open doors, with dogs and cats wandering about and entering and leaving them at will, looking for food and familiar faces and, disappointed in their expectations, howling and miaowing piteously.

Movement and life had completely stopped and the totally empty village was deserted, resembling a huge, empty, abandoned coffin.** It was a dreadful scene where horror and terror reigned and people flitted about like ghosts, often frightened by the sound of their own footsteps. It wasn't possible to go out at night and enter even the best known wide streets as it seemed as if spirits wandered in them in the dark, ready to pounce on even the boldest people and kill them by squeezing them in their dreadful claws.

---

* According to Arthur C. Ryan's statement of 28 March 1918, he went to Bardizag in October 1915, where he found 60 people, of whom about 30 were incapacitated. They were located in houses near the American High School, and provided with funds by the school to keep them alive. He adds that at least 12 of these people died before 20 Nov 1915. Arthur C. Ryan, *Statement on the misrule of Turkey and her cruel treatment of non-Muslim subjects,* 28 March 1918, Chicago, USA.
† Anania Vartabed Hapelian also tells us that he met Garabed Effendi Melkonian in Bardizag on Monday, 16 Nov. 1915. Hagop Der-Hagopian, *Bardizage khadoudig,* p. 42.
‡ Anania Vartabed Hapelian gives the date as Sunday, 4 October 1915. Hagop Der-Hagopian, *Bardizage khadoudig,* p. 40.
** It should be borne in mind that there were between 1,200 and 2,000 houses in the village in 1915.

The small group of Bardizag's non-Armenian and discordant inhabitants, as if persecuted by the village's emptiness and loneliness, with the expressions of normal life in that dismal environment having become unnatural and dissonant, had moved closer to each other to protect themselves in that kingdom of corpses and ghosts. They too would have liked to escape these living conditions that had become a source of terrible suffering for them and to join the departing caravans of people. They doubtlessly envied their compatriots going into exile, who at least had the comfort of each others' company.

The *miudir*, to escape this nightmare, permitted Muslim refugees to come down from their villages to fill Bardizag. There were many houses and shops, and these newcomers swiftly appropriated the best and most comfortable houses, opened shops and several coffee houses, as well as grocery and butchers shops in the market area around the *ghonakh* [government building].

To bring life to the empty village, the government also brought about 100 families from the Macedonia region and settled them in the village.

The Muslim Laz people descended from their mountains as far as Seymen. Coffee houses and shops opened there too, in the attempt to get life re-started. The newcomers occupied themselves with fishing and operating the boats and, in this way, created a caricature of life as it was in Bardizag and its seaport.

A part of the rich harvests of the innumerable fruit trees, vineyards and fields around the village rotted where they were, the remainder becoming the property of the people who passed by. Everyone, be it from the village or outside, gathered as much as he could as if it were the result of uncultivated growth. All the gardens, orchards, vineyards and fields were completely stripped of their produce, and no one even tried to continue to grow them for future crops. The country gradually returned to its former uncultivated state before people had come to settle there.

When Bardizag began to come to life with the Muslim refugees and life became a little more bearable, the wholesale looting and destruction of the empty houses began in earnest during both night and day, both openly and secretly, and in which the *miudir* and his assistants took part.[*]

The Protestant meeting hall and the Armenian church were first despoiled of their contents – the things that had been stored in them by the people being deported. These things – beds, clothes, carpets, home furnishings, etc. were all sold

---

* Arthur C. Ryan was a witness to the looting:

> I spent much of the time between October 6 and November 20 1915 in Bardizag. While there I saw Turkish officials collecting the moveable property of the deported Armenians. After gathering this property into the Armenian Gregorian church, it was transported to the seashore and placed on steamers. I suppose it was sent to Constantinople.

and the proceeds went into the officials' pockets, leaving only odds and ends to the new administration.

After these available items had disappeared, the houses became the targets for any Muslim who wanted to enter and search them. First, all the things that could be moved were removed from the houses and courtyards and sold – tools used in agriculture and the timber trades, fuel, firewood, timber for building, planks of wood, lumber, straw, grass, etc. After clearing out the houses, the time had come for the buildings themselves to be demolished, but carefully, without making the extent of the horror of the demolition obvious. Window shutters and frames, doors, cupboard drawers, cooking utensils, tables, chairs etc. were all removed. The turn then came for the ripping out of floors, ceilings and roofs, with the rain, snow and wind providing assistance. The buildings then began to sag inwards onto their foundations. Beams and timber would then be extracted, if not as lumber for building, then as firewood, to be sold as such.

This demolition increased with time and necessity. Houses on the outskirts of the village became fewer, and the silk spinning factories in the mulberry orchards began to be demolished or appropriated by the Muslim refugees. These appropriations became, unwittingly, the buildings' salvation, because they were retained and protected, and we would find them when we returned after the Armistice.

This destruction widened the streets, and light entered the narrow streets that were previously always dark. This left the prominent houses and those that were being lived in standing within the area of destruction and emptiness.

There was an unlimited mania for destroying edifices erected by Christian effort over the centuries, without even the smallest sense of responsibility. When firewood ran short in the village, the necessity to obtain it meant that marauders would cut down venerable walnut, peach, pear, apple, cherry, quince and mulberry trees that were in the orchards. Fires were used to burn vineyards and fields; if it was possible they would have burnt the land too.

> 'One day these officials came to our compound [The American High School] and broke into one of the houses in which Professor Hagopian had lived and carried away all the goods that remained in the house. I watched them break open the door and carry them away. My protest was laughed at by the officials and I was told that these articles belonged to an Armenian before he had been deported and that the government would take care of them in his absence.
>
> Arthur C. Ryan, *Statement on the Misrule of Turkey and Her Cruel Treatment of non-Muslim Subjects,* 28 March 1918, Chicago, USA.

Community establishments, like the other buildings, were subjected to destruction or desecration.* The altars and cross-holders in the marvellous St. Hagop church were totally demolished and used to build fireplaces in the coffee houses. The *khachkars* [cross stones] set into the walls were smashed and their carvings obliterated. The chancel's marble floor panels were removed and taken to the community school building. The latter was made into an orphanage by the Turks for Turkish orphans.† Its basement floor was covered with the marble panels from the church. At the same time the floors and ceilings of the Chelengs' house were repaired with wood and the building had extensions built on to it, using materials taken from the church. This house was then allocated to the Turkish orphanage's teachers.

They removed the church bell with the greatest effort and difficulty from its place‡ and demolished the bell tower, leaving the church, damaged and denuded of

---

* Anania Vartabed Hapelian, in his diary entry for Monday 16 November 1915, tells us:

> *Miudir* Ali Shu'uri, the Commission chairman Ihsan Bey and I had the good fortune (sic) to enter the church of St. Hagop, which hadn't heard prayers or blessings for about four months. Its holiness and dedication desecrated, it had been deprived of its function as a place of prayer and was filled with confiscated items: furniture, beds, baskets, pictures, chandeliers, bottles etc., with everything displayed in a mess. They remain there, all piled up, a den of thieves and thievery. Oh, Lord my Christ... In concert with the two officials I examined all the [sacred] objects and ornaments which were kept in the chapel of St. Stepannos and in the vestry. I was reduced to tears, bowed before the altar and carefully collected all the church vessels and ornaments that had been dishonoured. The chapel on the right, which had remained closed until this time, was forcibly opened by the *miudir*. The wealth of the church, consisting of holy vessels, chalices, copes and other things were all examined and the valuable items put into an iron chest which was then locked. The key was kept by the *miudir*. Very much affected, I left the Lord's House, perhaps for the last time.

Hagop Der-Hagopian, *Bardizage khadoudig*, pp. 41-42.

† Der-Hagopian, quoting Mgerdich Hairabedian, tells us that the Turkish orphanage in Bardizag was set up in early 1916 to take care of Armenian orphans sent back from Aleppo to Constantinople by order of Djemal Pasha. He further states that there were a few (number not quoted) Turkish orphans there as well. There were other such institutions in Adabazar, for example. He says that when the USA declared war, the orphanage in the village was transferred to Bardizag's American High School. These Turkish and Armenian orphans stayed there until the Armistice, when they were separated. (The Armenian orphans were then taken care of by the Armenian relief organisation in Constantinople.) Hagop Der-Hagopian, *Bardizage khadoudig*, pp. 272-276.

‡ Hapelian gives the date of its removal as 20 November 1915. Hagop Der-Hagopian, *Bardizage khadoudig*, p. 40.

its ornaments and richness, to become a storehouse, with the sole purpose of insulting Christians. Tombstones were removed and broken up, simply for the love of destruction, fuelled by a fanatic barbarian urge.* The Protestant Meeting Hall was turned into a mosque, with a minaret-like tower being built at its southern edge.

The only buildings to escape this universal destruction were more than one of the American High School buildings and their contents,† guarded by a Turkish official, thanks to the American Embassy's efforts.

Thus, during the four short years of the war, the efforts of Turkish barbarity and nature were employed in turning vibrant, lovely Bardizag, the queen of Bithynia's villages, into ruins and desolation, with homes, shops, silkworm houses and khans demolished. They left what remained, like the living dead, in a decrepit state. The cultivated areas were rendered unrecognisable by being trodden down and made into gravelly wastelands. The much-used roads, streets and squares became sites where thorny bushes grew, whose dark green leaves covered the cobbles laid by the hand of man, and which were now the haunt of hedgehogs, lizards and snakes.

153 – After the Armistice

Those deported from Bardizag who returned immediately after the Armistice found their birthplace in this sad state. They could hardly recognise it as it had changed so much, its beauty and grace destroyed and desecrated.‡

Some became very angry and swore to take revenge. They understood that the Turks had only one concern towards them: *to kill them and destroy the results of their centuries-old efforts.*** The war had nothing to do with this at all.

The returnees, making supreme efforts, began the work of restoring the old, good living.

---

* Many of the pieces, which still existed in the early 1960s, were used as hardcore in the construction of the town hall that was built in that decade. I have personally seen others, wiped clean of their inscriptions, used as floor slabs, with one being used as a door step and another (Rev. Sarkis' tombstone dated 1832) as a paving stone in front of a public fountain.

† These two buildings were Chambers Hall (later totally emptied), and the director's home. Both are still standing, with the house being lived in to this day.

‡ Der-Hagopian tells us:

> ...The port (Seymen) had been wrecked. The silkworm houses and vineyards on the way up to the village had been destroyed. All the stones in the [new] cemetery had been taken away. Less than half of the houses were still standing. Of the population of 10,000 only about 2,000 returned to their ruined birthplace.

Hagop Der-Hagopian, *Bardizage khadoudig*, p. 51.

** Author's italics.

A certain number of deported people from Bardizag who, because they were members of soldiers' families, had been allowed to stay in small groups from one end of Asia Minor to the other, hurried to return to their birthplace. They came from Eski-Shehir, Chai-Stasion, Afion Karahisar, Konya, Ereili, Cilicia and the far corners of Mesopotamia, Rus-ul-Ayn and even from the deathly plains of Der Zor itself. They were the remnants of humanity, who had only survived through a miracle after suffering untold privations. Oh to see their village once more, to drink its cold, pure waters - these things would make them forget everything! This longing drew them back to Bardizag, where soldiers' families that had been living among the Muslims around the village and Devrend had already arrived. Some had also returned from Constantinople, to see, with their own eyes how unconscious, illiterate and fanatical barbarity could wreck the expressions of life and human endeavour.

This current of returning villagers, which gradually increased, forced the Muslim refugees, who had taken over the village and its surroundings, away from the houses and shops they were living in or opened. They retreated to the mountains and their villages. Only the Turkish officials, the police and the Armenian and Turkish orphans and their teachers remained in Bardizag during those first days.

The returnees were not, of course, all of the people from the village who survived the catastrophe, only a proportion of them. Many had begun to make new lives for themselves where they were and didn't want to return, in those days of uncertainty and confusion, to their birthplace. Others, not knowing if they would have anywhere to stay in their ruined village, went to Izmid* and Constantinople, where life continued almost as it did in the past. Despite all this, Bardizag was fortunate in finding a proportion of its inhabitants among the survivors – almost 40% - resulting from the following.

> 1. As, among the Armenian population of Izmid province, the people of Bardizag were the last to be deported, they were, in part, able to take advantage of the rule about soldiers' families being allowed to remain. Between 300 and 400 families were distributed among the Muslim villages around Bardizag and the interior as a result.
>
> 2. The Bardizag Protestants and Catholics were able to take advantage, in the early days of the deportations, of a published order, under which they were considered to be free to remain where they were on the date of the order.
>
> 3. As the majority of Bardizag's population were artisans, a class that were found to be necessary in military service, many succeeded in remaining free

---

* Boghosian's book is mainly about the people of Bardizag who lived in the town. He quotes the following families from the village as being merchants in Izmid after the war: Teoleolian, Khashmanian, Aliksanian, Semerdjian, Sinanian, the Kembelian brothers, his two uncles Boghos and Garabed Boghosian, as well as the Patougian family. See Haroutiun Boghosian, *Anzoukagan Bardizag*, p. 102.

and provided their skills as tradespeople, working for government building projects and in factories.

Apart from these, there were many people from the village who, seeing their lives in jeopardy in the deportations and not being able to take advantage of the situations detailed above, used all their acumen, ingenuity and boldness, despite every difficulty, to escape from the caravans of deportees and stay somewhere. They were like flotsam carried along by the current, where they were able to live, finding a common language between them and the local influential Turks, who protected them.

As a result of all these favourable circumstances, more than 3,000 people from the village were able to survive – both old and young – while the number deported was more than 8,000. As a clarification of this statement, I can recall our family, consisting of five houses, totalling 31 people. After the catastrophes of the war, the number who survived was 21; in other words we lost ten individuals, but this comparison was only matched by a few families. The family of one of my brothers, which had been established in Constantinople years before, had not been deported; the families of my other two brothers grouped together and, as a soldier's family, stayed in Bardizag, living in the Muslim villages, and survived. It was only my own family that suffered deportation; we all survived by a miracle. Unfortunately my sister's family was wiped out on the road to Der Zor.*

The first priority of the people who returned was to find somewhere to live, then something to eat. Many of them found that their houses had been wrecked or demolished so moved into another house or building that was available. They had, of course, brought what few belongings they had retained from the journey. Their clothing was, naturally, reduced to rags, but even in that condition they could be used for something. The families that had remained in Bardizag during the war helped the newly-arrived people as best they could, even giving them some of their possessions.

Before long the Allied powers' military authorities, as well as European and American philanthropic organisations and the AGBU began the task of collecting Armenian deportees and orphans, getting them ready and finding places for them to stay and be looked after. Money, clothing, shoes, underclothes, medicines and other such necessities were distributed among the deportees before winter arrived, so as to protect them from sickness and death.

Miss Newnham, the daughter of a well-to-do English family, who before the war was the directress of the Favre Boys Home that was located within the confines of the American High School, arrived in Bardizag at this time. She became the Bardizag representative of the European organisations providing assistance† and it

---

* In this one instance, the author has written these lines in first person singular.
† Der-Hagopian states that she was also the local representative of the British 'Lord Mayor's Fund' and distributed clothing and foodstuffs on its behalf. He also states that she set up a health clinic. Hagop Der-Hagopian, *Bardizage khadoudig*, p. 52.

was she who distributed the items held in the American High School and money and other aid sent from Constantinople.

Miss Newnham, apart from this, was able to take possession of the some of the buildings that belonged to the American High School that had been requisitioned by the Turkish authorities. They had taken them to house the Turkish boys' orphanage after they emptied the community school building. These were the Favre Boys Home building and Newnham Hall, built with funds provided by her family. She used the latter as her newly-established orphanage, collecting local and other Armenian orphans and putting them under her motherly care.[*] The other buildings belonging to the American High School remained in Turkish hands for some time.

A small Armenian community was created under these circumstances in Bardizag and a poor picture of the old life began to emerge. Returning villagers lived there from day to day, largely through aid arriving from outside and small profits made from some commercial activity in the form of mutual assistance – someone doing something for another person, and that person repaying the service with one of their own – without being able to do anything basic in the task of rebuilding the old life in its entirety. First, the means to do this were absent; secondly, the victorious Allies had a plan to create an independent Armenia where all the Armenians would finally go and settle, therefore their state everywhere was one of waiting and trying to live from day to day.

While waiting for the fate of the Armenians to be determined in their minds and in practice by the Allied diplomats, the Bardizag survivors decide to use their time to repair the damage done to the village and build an illusion of their former brilliant lives. The catastrophe and suffering they had experienced had made them into brothers. The divisions between people of the Armenian Apostolic, Protestant and Catholic faiths had lost their significance; they had all suffered simply because they were Armenian Christians, without regard to sect. So they joined together and created a single community authority[†] in the village. 72 electors voted and, in accordance with the votes cast, created a sort of parish council, with Armenian Apostolic, Protestant and Catholic members. The initiators were H. Kondaiyan, H. Koushagian, G. Nahabedian, M. Avedian and B. Kourouyian. Gradually they were joined by Nshan Kourouyian, Khachig Teoleolian, Onnig Der-Krikorian, Siragan Boyadjian, Krikor Saraydarian, Hagop Alodjian, Nshan Khacherian, Hagop Ghazigian and others.

This newly created community authority became the owner of all the public buildings and property. Things left here and there, mainly building materials, were found and appropriated in the name of the community. It made small repairs to

---

[*] Der-Hagopian quotes a figure of 500 orphans, with Hagop Alodjian as the orphanage's director. Hagop Der-Hagopian, *Bardizage khadoudig*, p. 52.

[†] The words used here are *hamazkayin ishkhanoutiun*.

community property to bring them into a usable condition, such as coffee houses, shops, bakeries, storehouses etc., both in the village and in the port, and rented them out through an auction. It was thus possible for community revenue to be accrued, allowing the church and school to be opened.

The community authority, having taken up collections from its members, the people and funds from the various aid organisations, had enough money to repair and rebuild the church and its demolished parts – the chancel, cross holders, belltower, windows and doors and brought it to a usable state. It appealed to the Armenian Patriarchate in Constantinople for a kahana, and one named Drtad Kahana was sent to the village from outside to cater for the community's spiritual needs. Anania Vartabed Hapelian, who was born in Bardizag, and was acting as locum tenens of Izmid at that time, was invited to conduct the church's official opening and re-consecration services. Services were held in it from then on.

The opportunity was taken to collect the church's books and vessels and robes from various places, thanks to which it was possible to conduct daily services and Mass on Sundays, which the community longed for, having been denied them for the whole of the war period and not receiving any spiritual comfort at all for those long years. St. James also acted as a prayer meeting hall for the Protestants, as their own meeting hall was still configured as a mosque.

The Apostolic community conducted morning service and Mass early each Sunday morning, and then the church was turned over to the Protestants for their Sunday service, being led in turn by local teachers of the Apostolic and Protestant faiths.

It was at this point that Bishop Garabed Mazlemian arrived in Bardizag, and conducted an Armenian Apostolic Bishop's Mass. He also preached a sermon in the Protestant service. His presence generated great enthusiasm in the village.

Nerses Kahana Ghazarosian and his family arrived in the village after a time – he was the only priest from Bardizag still living[*] after the deportations. Drtad Kahana departed and Nerses Kahana became the village's priest once more.

After divine worship was resumed, the community authority began work to re-open the community school, and succeeded in this worthwhile and good plan. In those days the village had a population of about 800 people, providing the school with 263 students of both sexes, with survivors Ghazaros Nahabedian, Siragan Boyadjian

---

[*] Seven kahanas had been ordained in 1908. See Section 141. Rev. Anania Hapelian tells us, in his diary entry for Friday 4 May 1916:

> I received a letter from Shamen written in Armenian by Nerses Kahana Ghazarosian and dated 7 April, telling me of the deaths of four priests, his son Onnig, his son's wife Hamasig and his grandson Nerses. Only he and his wife and two grandchildren are left.

Hagop Der-Hagopian, *Bardizage khadoudig*, p. 49.

and the elder Krikor Saraydarian being appointed teachers. The younger Krikor Saraydarian was appointed assistant teacher and chief chorister of the church.

It was amazing that the parents paid school fees for their children's education, just as they did before, although not enough at the time of course. It was notable that people that had returned from the vale of tears and death were able, along with their daily bread, to provide something for their children's education. The deficit in the school's budget was closed by part of the rents received for community property that had been let. The Public Debt Administration that used one of the community's buildings not only began to pay rent regularly, but also paid a certain amount for the war years during which it had paid nothing.

Although the community authority re-opened the church and school and set up their funding, it also dealt with arguments arising in the community, solving them by arbitration. It also concerned itself with the defence of the community against the neighbouring Muslims, relations with which were becoming strained and therefore threatening, as a result of unfortunate incidents, clashes and hatred. At one stage this danger became serious, as the Muslims were armed. As the Armenians didn't have means of self-defence, the community authority petitioned the Armenian Patriarchate in Constantinople and the Allied military authorities, presenting them with the seriousness of the situation and succeeded in defending the local community by means of the provision of military guard units, assisted by local forces.*

The antipathy between the two elements gradually increased, with friendly, neighbourly and trade links ceasing. With the withdrawal of British units from the Nicomedia region and its capture by Greek forces, the Muslims' boldness increased. The attitude of the Muslim and Turkish population that existed immediately after the Armistice, when it was cowed and servile, had changed and was succeeded by a sort of pride and arrogance which was not reassuring in any way. This mentality was encouraged by development of a Turkish nationalistic movement in the country's interior.

Miss Newnham, in these uncertain circumstances, transferred her orphanage for a time to a place on the coast towards Constantinople named Derindje,† where allied governments had storehouses and the area was still under military control.

---

* It was inevitable that, having suffered so much, some Armenians wanted to exact vengeance from the local Muslim inhabitants, especially as they had been responsible for the partial destruction of the village and cemetery. They formed themselves into armed bands and had skirmishes with the local Muslim forces. Hagop Der-Hagopian, *Bardizage khadoudig*, pp. 54-57.

† This was the place where the Armenian Assistance Organisation, organised just after the Armistice to care for all the Armenian orphans still living, had its holiday camp for them. See Eblighatian, Madteos M, *National Assistance Organisation, general report for the first six months, 1 May 1919 – 31 October 1919*, 2nd edition, Antelias, Lebanon, 1985, p. 366.

Later, when Derindje was emptied and the allied forces departed to Constantinople with the plan of finally leaving Turkey and the western part of Asia Minor entrusted to the care of the Greek army, many people left Bardizag and, like a retreating army, gradually moved, with Miss Newnham's orphanage, first to Derindje then, finally, to Constantinople.

The life that had only just begun in Bardizag stopped, where a state of war became apparent, with daily clashes between untrustworthy and thoughtless Armenians and Muslim elements. Crimes were committed and mutual attacks, looting and killing took place.

Under these circumstances disaster could not be long in coming. After some time, the Greek army was not able to defend its positions against the forces led by Mustafa Kemal, who represented the strength of Turkish nationalist sentiment. It retreated, losing all discipline, becoming a mob, and was pushed into the Ionian Sea.

The Turks advanced victoriously, the Greek defeat and retreat putting an end to Bardizag's existence, resulting in the remaining Armenian population finally deserting its village and going to Constantinople, while the Greeks were fighting against the pursuing local Muslims.

When Mustafa Kemal succeeded in capturing Smyrna (Izmir) and put an end to Greek rule in Asia Minor the Allies, amid the greatest scandal (it was of almost criminal dimensions) found it impossible to understand each other and to work together. They left Constantinople and Turkey, with the Greek army following them and hurrying to cross into Thrace ahead of Mustafa Kemal's forces. After Izmir, the Turkish army captured the sultans' capital.

As a result of these precipitate actions, many of the people of Bardizag, like the rest of the Armenians and Greeks of Asia Minor, drew breath in Constantinople and, no longer having any confidence in their existence and lives in Turkey, hurried to seek refuge in the Greek islands, Bulgaria and the Ionian coast of Greece, dispersing to the four corners of the world like chaff, like poor refugees and, as such, becoming an undesirable people, without a homeland or possessions.*

---

* After the final evacuation of the village, a group of young men from the village hid in the hills and continued fighting. Der-Hagopian recalls several of them: Djidjig Hovhannes, Chavoush Ohannes Djoboyian, Tsemeroug Ago Shekhian, Terzi Garabed, Vidin Gabe, Chilingir Hovhannes, Melkon, son of Baghdasar Ago, Haroutiun Gannoyian, Keghetsig Apelian (Kiutiukdji), and Haroutiun Odadjian. There were others. Very few survived. Hagop Der-Hagopian, *Bardizage khadoudig*, pp. 56-57.

Chapter 11

A Composite Picture of Bardizag Public Life

154 – Explanation

We have, up to this point, taken into account the public and individual lives of the people of Bardizag in all their facets, as far as is possible in chronological order. I should like to attempt to create, in this new chapter, a synthesis of the whole picture of the village as it would appear at the point of the destruction of its centuries-old existence.

The reader will have put before him sections which will encompass public life in all its aspects:

1. Bardizag's position, geography and topographical description
2. Climate and health
3. Economic life
    A. Rural economy
    B. Labour
    C. Trades
    D. Shopkeeping
    E. Peddling and administration
    F. Womens' and girls' labour, both in the house and elesewhere
4. Family life
    A. Birth
    B. Marriage
    C. Death
5. Social life - leisure
6. Public life
7. Religious and spiritual life
8. Educational work
9. Popular superstitions and beliefs

1. Bardizag's position, geography and topographical description

Bardizag, near the edge of the Bay of Izmid (Nicomedia), one hour south of its southern shore, was a small town* located on the side of a hill approximately 29 degrees east of Greenwich (longitude) and 41 degrees north (latitude). It was at an altitude of about 250-300m (820-1025 feet) above sea level, and spread along the side of the hill on an east-west axis. Each end spread up the hillside (southwards) like

---

*   The author used the term *kiughakaghak*.

a horn, from the Serops' and Deledjegs' houses in the east, and the Near Upper Fields in the west. In the opposite direction, northwards, the central part of the axis formed a small hill,* with the Protestant Meeting House built at one edge with, on the two arms of the north-western end, the village's two new built up areas, located on the roads leading to the lower (new) cemetery and the Chaghchi Valley. From one end of the village to the other (east to west), in other words from the American High School compound to the new Armenian Catholic monastery located near Ghoumloukh, it was about a quarter of an hour's distance, measured at ordinary walking pace. The market area was located in the centre of the road stretching from one end of the village to the other, with the village's sidestreets going north and south off it. These were narrow and steep; carts and carriages were unable to enter them, the main road being the only one they could use. The Armenian Apostolic cathedral† of *Mtspina Sourp Hagop* [St James of Nisibis] was located on the north side of the main street opposite the market area, as was the large, magnificent community schools' building, the prelacy and the community-owned *ghonakh* [government building].

The upper stories of houses on both sides of the sidestreets often overhung them, bringing the top floors so close together that only a narrow strip of sky could be seen between them. They were sometimes even joined together as if to form bridges over the street, therefore only leaving passageways for people at ground level.

The houses and blocks‡ of buildings created dense masses, close together, and there was no room for squares and gardens. In fact no open spaces or important squares existed within the village at all. In some places a sort of square was created at the point where several streets formed an intersection, where a greater expanse of sky could be seen above people's heads. The one or two small open areas in the village were the remnants of old threshing floors, such as Khachman Gal, the Bordjoghlou's Gal and others.

It was only at the edges of the village that newly built houses or new blocks were to be seen with gardens around them containing mulberry and fruit trees, as well as open areas such as the Upper Threshing Floors, Lower Threshing Floors, Boyakhane, Baghcha, Ghoumloukh, and the Upper Cemetery.

The houses were usually built of wood on square stone foundations set into the ground, with the wooden construction beginning above ground level. The walls, both inside and out, were plastered with mud. In more recent times lime plaster was generally used. The roofs were always tiled and pierced with chimneys taking away the smoke from the ovens. There were no houses with flat roofs as the local climate

---

* The author has used the word *por* (belly) here.
† The author uses the term *mayr yegeghetsi* here.
‡ The word used here is *tagh*. This could mean village ward, parish, block or area. I have chosen to use block in this context.

wouldn't permit it. There were still houses left from the old days whose walls were thick and built of mud bricks, but they were nearly all gone. The houses weren't very tall, mostly two stories high with low ceilings; the rooms were usually small and lit by small windows, so that they remained warm in winter and reduced running costs.

As a result of the village's position, the lines of houses ascended the hill and higher ones looked over those below in northerly and southerly directions, towards the fields, sea and the range of hills. The eastern and southern sides of the village were closed off by the heights in those directions. The prevailing winds that blew through the village came from the north and west; in summer they were wonderfully cooling, while in winter they were damp, cold and mixed with snow. The southern warm winds only lasted for a short time, at the beginning of autumn, and didn't cause any discomfort.

There were no constantly flowing streams of water in the village apart from the fountains which dried up immediately outside it. It was only in the winter and spring, the rainy seasons, when several torrents of water were created which cleaned the village, taking with them months of accumulated village excrement. The most important of these currents was the one called *Kak Tsor* [Excrement Valley]* that flowed from the slopes of the Upper fields, entered the village and, from the market's lower (western) end, ran to one of the edges of the Upper Cemetery. It then flowed through the gardens, occasionally through deep hollows, northwards. Secondary ones, called *Jamoun Tsor* [Church Valley] and *Tbrotsin Tsor* [School Valley] flowed from above the village and, passing through the central part, emerged below its lower area, near the bath house, where it joined Excrement Valley. Finally the fourth important stream of water was the one called *Veri Galeri Tsor* [Upper Threshing Floors Valley] flowing from the heights on the eastern side of the village, which joined the Kirazlekh Valley, outside the village. It was therefore Excrement Valley and the flows that joined it that seemed to have the duty of flooding the village in winter and cleaning it. All these currents dried up in summer, only flowing for the occasional day when there was a sudden storm. There were small bridges or culverts in the market area and various streets for the convenience of passers-by when the streams of water were running. The largest of these bridges was called *Charsoui Keopriu* [Charsou's Bridge].

If we were to leave the village for a moment and look around us, we would see that the view to the south of the village was closed off by the side of a hill, St. Minas, which forms the main pivot of the range of hills stretching from east to west and parallel to the sides of the hills along the opposite edge of the Bay of Izmid. The lower slopes of this mountainous point, from north to south, formed depressions in which water collected, making floods or valleys. A quarter of an hour's very difficult

---

* It is a peculiarity of the dialect spoken by the villagers that streams and flows of water that were generated during the rainy season were called valleys *(tsor)*, possibly a local version of the word *dzor* meaning stream. I have used the former.

walk above the village (southwards) was sufficient to reach the summit, which swept downwards on the other side. A further half an hour's walk south from there brought the traveller to the bank of the Ovadjekh River which, where our village was, formed the biggest watercourse. On the other side of the river was another mountain pivot, parallel to St. Minas. The land belonging to Bardizag extended to the edge of the river.

Immediately to the east of the village was one of the slopes of St. Minas Hill, which extended as far as the open fields. The upper part of this slope was known as Kirazlekh, from whose sides streams of water flowed to the village. The first of these was named *Kirazlekh Tsor* [Kirazlekh Valley]. Then, above this was the *Deven Ingadz Tsor* [Valley Fallen from Deve]. In the middle was *Vari Galeri* or *Hadji Bakeyents Tsor* [Lower Threshing Floors or Hadji Bakeyents Valley]. These all ran (part of the last being used to irrigate the cultivated fields) eventually into the Excrement Valley flow at the base of the Zepperi Chayiri.

The Kirazlekh Valley didn't dry up in summer and almost always flowed in winter. A part of the Kirazlekh lower slope had been given the name *Goudjoug Orman* or *Tezoug Andar* [Dwarf Forest]. It was a wonderful place, although it obscured the village view from the east. If someone took the trouble to climb to the summit of its lower slope he would be rewarded with a marvellous panorama of the area. The young people from the village made a habit of going there in the evenings, especially during the days of freedom.*

Kirazlekh's higher slope gradually rose eastwards then suddenly ended in an escarpment, the bottom of which was filled with a constantly-flowing stream called *Khoroung Tsor* [Deep Valley] squeezed between the sides of two mountains and where the flow of water had created a number of very small lakes in the cool shadows. This was where the younger boys from the Upper and Lower Threshing Floors parts of the village would go to bathe in the cold water in summer and eat the wild fruit in the surrounding forest to their heart's content. The new lower slope of the Upper and Lower Ayazma was to its east and which, falling gradually, became part of the plain.

The border between the lands belonging to Dongel and Bardizag was delineated by the stream called *Kor Tsor* [Kor Valley] that flowed a little further on. The road to the Armenian villages began at the eastern end of Bardizag, following a natural trackway for most of the way to Dongel, Ovadjek and, in the far distance, Arslanbeg, which was located three hours distance east from the village.

The western side of Bardizag opened and spread out, forming a complex web of mountainous heights. The bottom of the village stretched from the middle of Excrement Valley in that direction, through Ghoumloukh and, half an hour's distance away, gradually descended, forming a new depression called *Chiftligi Tsor*

---

* From 1908 to 1915.

[Farm Valley] which, like Deep Valley, had a stream that flowed continuously in summer and winter, although not so abundantly. This too, like Deep Valley, had formed small lakes, among which the one called Eyreg, whose cold water, used as a swimming pool by the local boys in the summer, was famous. The *Teghentan Aghpiur* [Yellow Fountain], a mecca for sick people, was near this stream.*

The slope opposite Farm Valley rose steeply and formed Yasakh Mountain, whose summit, opening out, became a promontory called Bazigian's Chairi. The fountain called *Chourin Ken Eradz* [Ignored Water Fountain] was located at its south-western corner near the stream. The southern side of Yasakh Mountain sloped down, finally forming a dry flat area called Douzloukh. This was to the west of Farm Valley, and ended with another gentle downward slope to a depression called *Douzloukhi Tsor* [Douzloukh Valley] or the continuation of *Tsadkan Chour* [Leaping Water]. This new valley, running parallel to Farm Valley for some distance joined, at a slightly lower level, the road to the distant Upper fields, to form the larger *Chagharchi Tsor* [Chagharchi Valley]. The continuation of the Yasakh heights, in other words the lower slopes of Douzloukh, suddenly separated from it, forming a line at one point, where the previously-mentiond Leaping Water, a small but beautiful waterfall about 15m (48 feet) high, sprang forth.

Westwards, beyond Douzloukh, the ground rose once more and reached the high, distant Upper Fields, but a depression was formed at the point where the Yasakh joined it, and from where *Vartabedin Tsor* or *Keshish Souyou* [Priest's Valley] flowed. This valley too, without forming a large distinct bed, joined the above-mentioned Chaghchi Valley. This flow of water coursed through the middle of Chiftlig Farm's cultivated fields to the western boundary of the village at the corner of the Upper Cemetery, and was called *Chakhchi djampan* [Chakhchi Road]. Made up of the union of three water courses, it formed the most important constantly-flowing river at a point near the western side of Bardizag. It was sometimes impossible to cross in winter, due to the strength of the current, taking people and horses with it, as has often happened. Unfortunately there wasn't a bridge there, as the cost of building one spanning a 30-50m (100-165 feet) width would have been prohibitive.

Chakhchi Valley had been named because of the several *chaghats* [mills]† built on its banks. The first one was built on it with, lower down, those of Diannos, Chora Fez, the Djezels or Khacherians and, lowest of all, the *Hrom Kiughi* [Roman Village's]‡ or Ghazig Mger's, being constructed. The ground suddenly rose above

---

* It was a mineral water fountain locally and considered to be medicinal.
† The author, using the word *chaghats*, implies that the mills were wind driven, as the meaning of the word is simply 'mill' and used in that way. I think he means *chraghats* - the first syllable meaning water - water mill, as the ones he refers to were located on the banks of the rivers or flows of water.
‡ This alludes to the Greek village of Yenikeoy.

and on the opposite side of the Chaghchi Valley, creating the *Otsig Otsig Djampoun* [Snake-Snake's Road] or Bayiri, which became part of the surrounding heights and formed the rather large area named the Distant Upper Fields. This had the *Vartabedin Aghpiure* [Priest's Fountain] with the St. Sarkis pilgrimage site at its summit, as far as *Sakar Bchke*, Bardizag's western boundary. It was there that the Laz-Armenians and the Muslim Laz people built their adjoining villages named Deosheme. The Laz-Armenians called theirs *Zakar Kiugh* [Zakar Village] in Armenian, which sounded similar to the name *Sakar*.

An extensive mountain range began beyond this border, through which, using a natural defile, the road know as *Antreresi Djampan* [Reverse Face Road], led to the Turkish villages located on the northern side of Lake Nicaea. Bardizag's Manoushag pilgrimage site, on the top of a mountain, was located on that road near the source of the Ovadjekh River, and was where the Laz-Armenians had built a second village named Manoushag. This was three hours distance from Bardizag itself in a south-westerly direction.

A new depression begins at the edge of Sakar Bchke where a valley with a winter flow of water ran north-east, alongside Bardizag's land boundary and having the height named *Hormin Yasakh* [Romans' Yasakh] opposite it at the lower end, which closed the view of Bardizag in a south-westerly direction. This new valley, after a number of twists and turns, joined Chaghchi Valley at a point below an area of land called Kestanelig that was adjacent to the Distant Upper Fields, near the Khacherians' mill. Chaghchi Valley, by its length and volume of water, was the largest within Bardizag's boundaries.

The Chaghchi Valley below the Hormin or Azarians' depression took the name *Hormin Tsor* [Roman Valley] and formed the boundary between the land belonging to Bardizag and *Hormin Kiugh* [Yenikeoy Greek village] where the lower fields were. Finally this valley, the extreme end of which was given the name *Engezli Boghaz* [Walnut Pass], flowed into the Bay of Izmid, close to the western side of Seymen, at the place known as *Khntsorasdan* [Apple Land in Armenian] and *Kechedji Elmalek* in Turkish.

Only the northern side of the village now needs to be described. There was a triangular area of cultivated land below the village, one edge of which was secured by the village's west to east line, and the other two by Excrement Valley and Hadji Bakeyents Valley (the continuation of Kirazlekh Valley), which met to complete the triangle lower down. The whole of this area was covered by mulberry trees and, interspersed among them, a great number of fruit trees – mainly pear, apple and quince. There were two further large promontories of cultivable land bounded on one side by Excrement Valley and Chaghchi Valley and, on the other, by Kirazlekh Valley and Deep Valley, which gradually descended and formed their edges, becoming part of the Khans' farmland to the north. All this land, close to the village, was covered with mulberry trees and, lower down, by vineyards as far as the edge of the farmland about half way between Bardizag and the sea.

The road from Bardizag to Seymen was built on the slope on the western edge of Excrement Valley, and began near the Upper Cemetery, at the entrance to the village and ended at the edge of the sea. Plantations of mulberry trees, vineyards and fields had been planted on all the cultivable land in every direction. The road to the port, at a point about a quarter of an hour's distance from the village, passed the New Upper Cemetery. The road forked at its entrance, with a path running northwest off it which went through the lines of vineyards and gardens down to Roman Valley. It continued from there to the Greek Yenikeoy village, a distance of about three quarters of an hour. The road itself continued from the cemetery in a northeasterly direction and reached the agricultural station called Khaner at the edge of the fields. Farmers' summer living quarters, sheepfolds, barns, stables and silkworm houses could be seen there. A new, unpaved road split off here, heading east, through the Khans, over the Alaman heights, descending gradually to the sea. It followed the coastline from this point, passing near Ovadjek's port called Bash Iskele, then continued to Deniz Bashi and the Ovadjek River, passing over it via the Kilez Bridge. It joined the main road from Izmid to Anatolia a short distance further on. This was the land route to Izmid, reasonable in dry weather, but very difficult in winter. The road, near the Khans, turned north and continued in parallel with the now united Excrement and Deep Valleys, following a route through the farmland, reaching Seymen after about half an hour. This cultivable land had farmed areas within it, as well as areas of stunted forest and meadows, becoming marshy near the sea and was a breeding ground for malaria.

Seyman was an industrial area, without a settled population, with only warehouses, shops and bakeries located there. It had a long wooden jetty extending into the sea, used for loading and unloading cargo from ships and boats.

2. Climate and health

Bardizag had a good, mixed, healthy climate. The seasons followed one another in a regular manner. Summers were warm and dry, with occasional short, heavy storms, when lightning struck the cliffs and hailstones the size of walnuts covered the ground. It would become quite cold in autumn, with the mornings and evenings having the lowest temperatures. The saying 'Khash, icheri kash'* had become a saying among us. Autumn would arrive with its inevitable fogs, dew, dripping dampness and mould. The hot, fierce wind from the south, called *gheblan*, blew during autumn, clearing the deciduous trees of their leaves. Winter, with its cold winds, snow and blizzards, often covered the ground with a thick layer of snow and

---

* Khash is a heavy, hot boiled meat stew utilising the fat of the meat as well, and eaten in autumn and winter.

ice. Spring, with its frequent rain and occasional snow would turn the month of March into an uncertain time, the villagers having used up all the firewood that had been stored, forcing them to burn wooden implements when they ran out of it.

In summer the temperature would occasionally reach 40 degrees C in the shade, dropping to freezing in winter. Extremely low temperatures sometimes occurred, freezing the sea in rare cases. Bardizag's autumn, usually very pleasant, was sometimes cold and damp, while the temperatures in the village in spring were often low, preventing it drying out. The summer and winter were comparatively drier seasons, especially the former, which was Bardizag's best and most attractive one. Its temperature and dryness were reasonable and a gentle breeze blew off the sea after midday which, mixed with the rays of the sun until sunset, dying down then, gave way to a sweet and warm stillness in the evening and night, turning them into the most beautiful times of the summer season, when people and their animals slept on the dry ground outdoors in that wonderful climate.

As Bardizag was located on a slope, it had no fear of water accumulating or floods of flowing water or rain inundating the village. Because, however, of its clay subsoil which sucked in every bit of moisture, it could remain wet or damp for days. This made the ground very muddy, with the narrow streets, most of which rarely saw the sun, only drying out with difficulty. Light and air never penetrated them, leading to people getting coughs and colds that could become dangerous illnesses. This climatic circumstance was emphasised by the short winter days and the late rising of the sun from behind the mountains when, hardly freed from that obstacle, it set behind the western peaks.

Bardizag's climatic conditions and position encouraged chronic local illnesses, as I said: colds with all their complications, bronchitis, pneumonia and pleurisy, all of which, lasting a long time without any attention, led to tuberculosis of the lungs. This disease always killed one or two people each year. The fens and puddles collecting in low places along the seashore were malaria breeding grounds, which affected the people working in the fields and the port. Alongside these local sicknesses, there were occasional epidemics brought in from outside which affected the children most of all, especially smallpox, measles, German measles (rubella),[*] scarlet fever[†] and whooping cough, all of which took many children's lives at the time when there were no vaccinations or regular medical care among us.[‡] There were a considerable number of individuals in the village with *grdod* [pock-marked] faces, distended bellies due to *dalakh* [malaria], or who were sick.

---

[*] The word used here is *chrdzaghig*.
[†] The author has used the word *garmroug* here.
[‡] It should also be borne in mind that sanitation was very primitive.

Bardizag was visited, from time to time, by cholera and plague*, which took many lives in the years when the people were ignorant and superstitious. Typhus and meningitis occurred in the village, as did other other ordinary illnesses.

The care of sick people was incredibly bad, especially in the old days. If someone was ill in a house, local and related women, driven by mistaken pity and compassion, would fill the sick person's room day and night, turning the air unbreathable. The windows were only opened occasionally, so the sick person wouldn't get cold, and a brazier or fire would be lit in the room in cold weather. The people visiting the sick person would gather and hold conversations in his room. Each of them, certain she was a doctor, would suggest trying this or that medicine, based on the sick person's external symptoms, without thinking that different sicknesses could have the same ones. In other words they would kill the sick person with love and kindness.

The village 'doctors', in the main, were women who tried to cure the patient with poultices of vinegar, plain water or some kind of mixture. They also used leeches, cupping glasses, incisions, hot creams, *krekh* [syringing] and cauterisation. They fed the patient *ardale* [gruel], bitter flour, hot bread, hot excrement, fresh meat, grasses, aniseed, garlic, onion, soaked linden tree leaves, boiled quince seeds, aphids, puppy dog meat, mice, and all sorts of other things to try to cure the patient! All this was done without any systematic or scientific basis, the 'doctor' simply saying 'We did this, and it very useful.'

The treatment and care given by the women was supplemented by that of the barbers, occasionally by shepherds or farriers, the last two on the basis of their experience of treating animals. To all these must be added the priest who, in his duty of bringing God's aid to the sick, tried to be helpful, using the knowledge he had gained at other sickbeds.

Approaches were made to *bakhedji* or, in Armenian, *koushag* [fortune tellers] apart from the utilisation of all these ready medicines and experience. They, in their diagnosis of the sickness, determined the fear and dread that existed in the patient and recommended mystical cures: no sick person was ever free of fear.

This was how it was, and continued even in my day, and was considered to be the unfailing way of curing the sick, especially among the lower classes who found it difficult to break away from their old customs and ways.

In my youth Berber Minas and Chakhr Hagop were experts in cupping and pulling rotted teeth with horrible pincers which were inserted into the mouth with difficulty. The *adzerou choban* [goatherd] often intervened with mothers giving birth when the birth itself was difficult.

---

* The word used here is *jandakhd*.

A Composite Picture of Bardizag Public Life

Beordjen, a local medical assistant[*] ruled, with Hypocratic authority, over every ill person when I was a boy, through the power of his unfailing cures. There were similar medical assistants from about 1850 who, although they had not received any special education or preparation in medicine, formed the class called *hekim* (literally doctor in Turkish) and added their knowledge of medieval medicine to their experience in curing people.

Beordjen means, in the Bardizag lexicon, a sort of bean, a nickname that had been given to our *hekim* [doctor], who had only one arm as the result of a machine accident. Because he had been in a government hospital for a long time recovering, he had gained significant experience in diagnosis and the methods of effecting a cure from the 'doctors' there and, having returned to his birthplace, spent his time as a *hekim*. The only laxative he had available was *sinemek* [senna] leaves which were boiled in water and the infusion given to the patient, thus beginning the cure for every sick person. He also had various tablets or pills, the content of which only he knew and kept in a cupboard in his house, and which he gave with infusions of various grasses to sick people who came to see him. He also recommended various ointments, as palliatives for inflammation. He was a sort of doctor who treated people for modest fees.

He wore a teacher's trousers and an *aba* [long coat], one sleeve of which hung loose and waved gently as he walked. He worked in Bardizag for a very long time as the village's only *hekim*, taking his comfort to the sick who felt the need for his intervention.

It was in Beordjen's final days that a new doctor appeared in Bardizag from Constantinople. He was an Armenian Catholic known as Dr. Alanian, who with his title brought new methods to the art of medicine. He looked well, wearing European clothes, and was serious and quite well trained in his profession. He was much esteemed and loved by the people of Bardizag until his death that occurred among us. He really comforted the sick and inspired confidence in his new ways of healing them.

There was also a Greek doctor who either arrived after Dr. Alanian's death or worked with him named Dr. Atanas. He too was a practitioner like Dr. Alanian, without qualifications, probably a medical student from Athens medical college who hadn't completed the course and who, having worked alongside doctors, had gained some experience in the art of healing.

Dr Atanas was loved by the people of the village, and loved, in his turn, the environment he was in. He made a good living in the village and the need for doctors had become general. He was a small, bent man, easily aroused and nervous by nature, whose zeal and feelings would become evident when a patient often didn't agree or carry out his instructions to the letter, seemingly expecting a miracle.

---

[*] The word used here is *poujag*.

On one occasion, when my father was on his deathbed, having caught a virulent and dangerous form of pneumonia, worrying all of us, we approached Dr. Atanas who, after examining him, gave him several pills. My father instinctively had no faith in his treatment, so didn't want to take them. The doctor, on his second visit, wanted to see the beneficial results of the medicine he had prescribed, and was greatly surprised that the pills hadn't been taken. He became very angry, and began to have an impassioned argument with my father from where he sat, unfortunately not having the strength to prevail, and eventually got up and left. My father died one or two days later.

Dr Atanas worked in Bardizag for many long years, married a local girl and became almost a native of the village.

Later, to legalise his medical art, he took an examination in the medical faculty in Constantinople, where he succeeded in obtaining a certificate in pharmacology. It was illegal to practice medicine without completing the necessary courses and taking the relevant examinations but in those days, as there weren't enough doctors to satisfy the country's needs, pharmacists had the right to give basic treatment where doctors were absent. This was the case in Bardizag.

In those days a young man from the village, Aghasi Effendi Der-Mgerdichian, as a regular student of the medical school in Constantinople, received a pharmacology certificate and, returning to Bardizag, opened the first pharmacy in the village. In the old days pharmacies were shops belonging to *akhtars* [herbalists]. Before that, every doctor or hekim prepared his own medicines. Now each (doctor/hekim and pharmacist) had his own trade, so to complete the medical service in the village a certified doctor was necessary. That role was filled by a person named Dr. Djerahian.

Dr Atanas, seeing that there was nothing more he could do in Bardizag, went to Armash, having been invited there to be the newly-established seminary's permanent doctor.

Dr Djerahian was quite a skilful and experienced doctor. At the same time he was a happy, witty and friendly person, advantages that were sought after in a doctor. He created great sympathy around himself, adding jokes, witticisms and laughter to his treatments, which occasionally helped the patient more than the prescribed medicine.

It was at this time that Karnig Effendi Giureghian, a teacher who had been invited to Bardizag with Yeghishe Vartabed Tourian, wanting to withdraw from the sterile world of teaching, began a practical course of medicine through visiting his sick friends, using what he saw in medical textbooks to experiment on sick people, until they said, 'Karnig Effendi knows local illnesses and how to treat them very well.' His medical certification was public sentiment.

Dr Djerahian scorned him, but didn't want to openly oppose him, not considering him to be a great obstacle, especially as he saw that he had a large, sympathetic circle of people.

One day he was invited to visit a sick person in a notable's family home in the village. There he understood that Karnig Effendi had been called before him but, after long days of treatment without result, they had been forced to call him in. Dr. Djerahian did his utmost and succeeded in making the sick man well. Days later the notable house owner met him in a convivial situation and, taking advantage of the situation, wanting to praise him, expressed his appreciation of his treatment, saying a few words of thanks in public. Dr. Djerahian used a short story to reply: 'A camel driver,' he said, 'had a much-loved camel that he prized above all the others. Unfortunately it fell ill and all the treatments he gave it failed and it was in its death agony. The camel driver, greatly affected, said, "Dear camel, if I've wronged you in any way during my lifetime, please forgive me."

The camel, in its death agony, replied, "I forgive you for everything except one thing."

"What is that?" the camel driver asked, annoyed.

The sick camel, referring to the donkey that led the caravan of camels continued, "I cannot forgive the insult of having a base animal walk at the head of our caravan."'

Dr Jerahian fell silent. The assembled company burst out laughing, causing the notable home owner much confusion, as he had asked Karnig Effendi to treat the sick person before calling the doctor in.

One day, however, Dr. Djerahian suddenly disappeared. He went to Constantinople and didn't return. His departure, like his arrival, was like the disappearance of a comet.

The field of work remained in Karnig Effendi Giureghian's hands after Dr. Djerahian's departure and who now counted, among the ranks of his friends and admirers, the in-laws and relatives of the well-known Hairabedian family of Bardizag, whose son-in-law he had become. He too, like Dr. Atanas, went to the medical faculty in Constantinople a year or two later and obtained, after taking an examination, a pharmacist's certificate. Then, like Aghasi Effendi Der-Mgerdichian, he opened his own pharmacy, giving him ample opportunity to continue his harmless medical treatments.

Karnig Effendi, armed with his new diploma, began work with greater boldness and success. He never accepted fees from his patients for visiting them, being satisfied with the prices paid for his medicines. But his success would suffer stormy crises when the missionary Mr. Pearce would invite a doctor, Dr. Garabed Atanasian from Ghourtbelen, who had qualified in America, to come and lecture and provide a medical service in the American Boys' High School. Dr. Atanasian was to be the second qualified doctor in Bardizag.

Dr Atanasian was a stern and severe man, supremely jealous of his art and, at the same time, of his interests. He joined* Aghasi Effendi's pharmacy as a doctor, during the hours when he was free. Despite this, he persecuted *Doctor* Karnig Effendi with every means at his disposal for as long as he remained in the village, to prevent him from practicing medicine and be satisfied with being a pharmacist.

It often happend that, unknown to one another, both men would meet at the bedside of a patient. Karnig Effendi's appearance there was enough to anger Dr. Atanasian, who would attack him with his cane, driving him out of the sick person's house, frightening and terrifying him. His attacks on Karning Effendi went to such an extreme that he made him lose heart. Karnig Effendi chose to follow a safer and more peaceful trade, regarding being a doctor as an amateur occupation. At last, therefore, Karnig Effend resigned from that – for him – dangerous, incident-filled trade and took up that of an exciseman, which was far more profitable for him and without any danger. The imposition of medical rules in Bardizag had its satisfactory result, removing unqualified people from practicing it.

Dr Atanasian brought something new to his art. He added surgery and obstetrics, establishing, in the minds of women who were going to give birth, the necessity of a doctor's presence, especially in delicate situations, and stopping, to a great extent, the intervention of shepherds or women known as nurses at births, thus preventing frequently occurring problems.

He had the word *dznoutsich* [midwife], rather than *mangaparts* (a synonym for midwife) inscribed on his sign, perhaps regarding the latter as not being impressive enough. He found the first to be more forceful, as if to prevent any opposition to the expected operation.

He was never discouraged by lack of success in using new methods, stubbornly continuing his treatments even if the results were not what he expected. He had great faith in science and tried to follow new scientific things.

One day, when replacing the loosened sutures on an infected wound, he wanted to use the skin of a live frog to immunise it, once the wound had been cleaned and washed out, but the frog wouldn't obey his wish, and hadn't previously mixed with human flesh... His lack of success in using new scientific methods didn't discourage him however. He was stubborn in his experiments no matter how diametrically opposed the results they produced were to his expectations. He had great faith in science and attempted to follow new scientific things.

After a time, finding the work in the village too mundane, he wanted to use the Pasteur system to raise silkworms, without realising that he was going against his principles by doing so. Several years later he moved to the provincial capital, Izmid, where he hoped to find more and better paying patients.

---

* The word used here is *gabvetsav*.

Dr Atanasian's place was taken by the new doctor, Dr. Hovsep Der-Stepanian, a graduate of the medical university of London,* who had been invited to the American high school as its physician during Dr. Chambers' term of office as director.

The new doctor was a sympathetic, sociable, lively and witty young man. As a sociable person and able doctor, he gained great esteem among all classes of people in Bardizag without exception and took his art to all the sick. His success was so great that he made Bardizag his new homeland (he was from Rodosto) and established his whole family in the village – his mother and sisters – and later built his own house on a very nice plot near the public park. If he was to have severed his official link with the American high school, he would have been able to continue his work in Bardizag itself, loved and esteemed by everyone. Unfortunately he was one of the people in Bardizag who was regarded as suspicious by the Ittihad government in 1915, and was deported with a number of other people to the district of Soultanie near Konya. He was able to remain safely there, having been joined by his family during the catastrophic years of the genocide. After the Armistice he went abroad, to the city of Tehran, where he continues his work as a much-loved doctor.†

During the years that Dr. Der-Stepanian spent in Bardizag, two dreadful epidemics affected the village: smallpox and scarlet fever, causing great losses among the old and especially the young. In each instance between 100 and 200 people died from them in the village. In the case of smallpox, there were many who died despite being vaccinated against it, as we didn't know that the vaccination had to be renewed every 5-6 years. There was also a small cholera epidemic but, thanks to the scientific study of its causes, it was possible to implement several precautions, sterilising all food and drink, thus preventing a catastrophe.

During Dr. Der-Stepanian's time another doctor practiced in Bardizag. This was Dr. Khosrov Hairabedian, a native of Bardizag who, after some years, moved to Izmid and settled there. He is living, at present, on the Greek island of Corfu.‡

At the same time, and for 3-4 years before the 1915 deportations, another doctor arrived in Bardizag and practiced there. This was Dr. Garabed Khacherian, of the well-known village family, who also taught hygiene and citizenship in the village's community schools. He was, at one time, elected chairman of the village council** and was a member of the governing bodies of some of the well-known community intitatives.†† He served as a military doctor during the First World War and, at the Armistice, after settling in Smyrna (Izmir), he was forced to find refuge in Midili, then Thessaloniki, after the Greek army was defeated. He continues his medical

---

* Possibly University College Hospital, part of London University.
† This was written during the 1930s.
‡ This too was in the 1930s.
** Taghabedagan Khorhourt.
†† See Section 145.

practice in the latter city, while giving his great experience to the public life of the local Armenian community.*

This brief history of medical services in Bardizag demonstrates several basic improvements in the treatment of the sick and in the prevention of disease. Some of these were, for example, the more regular care of the sick, the necessity for air, light and cleanliness for them, respect for, and confidence in, scientific medicine, the importance given to the quality and quantity of food provided to older people and especially to the children, the swift adoption of precautions against disease and many others.

Bardizag had a population of between 7,000 and 8,000 people. This increase stemmed from the immigration to this new village of the original 20 or so families in only three centuries.† Before closing this section I should like to add some figures to the comparison of the increase made in my day that I have gleaned from Minas Kasabian's (Farhad) important, locally prepared volume *The Armenians of the province of Nicomedia.*‡

According to one statistical table in this volume, in the eleven years from 1899 to 1909 there were 2,077 births, and 1,347 deaths, a difference in favour of births of 750. These figures relating to Bardizag's population give a general average figure of 25.1% births and 16.3% deaths, giving a difference of 8.80% as the percentage increase during those eleven years, which is a good figure for such a people living in such dense and primitive circumstances.

3. Economic life

To give an overall picture of Bardizag's economic life I shall be taking the following factors into account:

A. Rural economy (cultivation and animal husbandry)

B. Labour

C. Trades

D. Shopkeeping**

E. Peddling†† and administration

F. Womens' and girls' labour, both in the house and elsewhere

---

* This was in the 1930s. For the second edition of his diary of the Smyrna (Izmir) events of 1922, see Dora Sakayan, *Garabed Hacherian: An Armenian Doctor in Turkey. My Smyrna Ordeal in 1922* (Yerevan State University, 2011).

† This might be a simplification. According to some sources there have been influxes of people from Agn etc., which would have increased the population over and above its birthrate. See Hagop Der-Hagopian, *Bardizage khadoudig*, p. 21.

‡ Minas Kasabian (Farhad), *Hayere Nikomedio Kavarin Mech*, Azadamard Press, Bardizag 1913. He is quoting figures extracted from pp. 226-235.

** I have made the following sub-section separate from this one.

†† The words used here are *shrchig vadjaraganoutiun*.

A. Rural Economy

Bardizag was regarded as being poor economically, limited to living within itself, without important external trade links despite a constantly increasing population and being restricted by limited cultivable land. As a result of these work and profit circumstances, there were no really rich people in Bardizag. The local person's main assets consisted of his land – mulberry orchards or vineyards, forest, fruit trees and a limited number of domestic animals. As I said, the lack of capital there was noticeable. A capital sum of 100-200 Ottoman gold liras was considered to be considerable wealth in the village.

The limited area of cultivable land in the area was the reason that the villager, utilising experienced gained, had been driven to using it for only those crops that would secure the greatest profit within the smallest area. For this reason Bardizag's agriculture consisted, in the main, of vineyards, fruit orchards and especially mulberry orchards to feed silkworms, as well as tobacco, alongside minor crops like wheat, barley, maize, beans, chick-peas and other things like them.

Viticulture – which at one time held an important place in the village's economy – was, in my day, suffering a decline, especially when phylloxera[*] had already begun to threaten the health of the vines. Despite this, every family, with a few exceptions, had its small vineyard, located in the immediate vicinity of the village, just beyond the mulberry orchards. These areas were in Upper and Lower Ayazma, the slopes of both sides of Deep and Excrement Valleys, Dandzin Broung, Lemberloz, along the sides of the road to the Greek village (Yenikeoy), in Douzloukh and the sunny parts of Chakhchi Valley. The main kinds of grapes were *Misket, Tergeomleg, White and Black Tokhat, Gradana, Ghara Geote, Kechi Memisi, Skh Bdough, Tourshoutsou Khaghogh, Salar Khaghogh,*[†] a small number of *Amasia* vines and various others.

Bardizag's grapes weren't for export or for the market; buying grapes for money was considered to be shameful. When the grapes were ready for eating, the vineyards owners' daughters, wives and young sons would, once or twice a week, go and pick those that had ripened, bringing them back in various sized baskets for their own use, always leaving some for those who didn't have a vineyard.

Grape harvesting took place in September, when the entire village population would go in crowds to the vineyards, in a festival-like atmosphere.[‡] They would return home with their horses heavily laden with the crop, giving some to anyone they met on the road. The grapes would be put into large *laza* [barrels] to be

---

[*] A kind of plant lice that is very destructive to grapevines.
[†] Some of these varieties are recognisable: *Misket* (Muscat), *White and Black Tokhat* (Tokay), *Skh Bdough* (Tight Fruit), and *Tourshoutsou Khaghogh* (Pickling Grapes).
[‡] The grape harvest took about two weeks. It should be noted, however, that the custom in many families was that grapes weren't to be eaten until after the feast of the Assumption of the Virgin Mary in August. Apig Der-Minasian says the harvest took place in October. See Hagop Der-Hagopian, *Bardizage khadoudig*, p 205.

trodden. Every house, during the grape harvest, would choose for itself the kinds of grapes that were considered to be of the highest quality and with long-lasting qualities to create a reserve, either trodden or spread out on mats, with the remainder being stored in barrels.

Clean, small feet would tread the grapes in the barrel to extract the juice. At the same time the children treading them would sing to make their work pleasureable. At one time a certain amount of this juice was used to make a stock of sweetmeats for the house, various kinds of *rechel, basdegh* [grape sheets], strings of sugared fruit etc., but in my day, with sugar being cheap, they were not needed. It was used instead to make high quality village wine which would make a person's blood course through his veins, enlarging them and giving his face a ruddy colour, a good appetite and making his lips and tongue even more supple and talkative. It created a happy atmosphere in company and on special occasions made the home a party venue. All the grape harvest in Bardizag was turned into wine and oghi, the latter being *distilled twice* making it very strong: a small glass would make ones eyes stand out from their sockets.

Unfortunately, in the state I find myself in while preparing this work, I am not able to provide figures showing the amount of grapes harvested and turned into wine and oghi. Grapes, wine and oghi were for local consumption only, although there were people who exported a proportion of the wine they prepared to Constantinople, where it was sold by well-known establishments.

Certain families in Bardizag were renowned for the quality of the wine and oghi they produced and which formed a significant source of income for them. Usually, however, the produce of the vineyard was mostly a pleasure and a necessity for weddings, baptisms, engagements etc.* Fruit growing was usually an extension of viticulture as the fruit trees, in places, shaded the vineyards, mulberry plantations and the gardens next to the houses.

Bardizag didn't have specific orchards. In the old days there had been oak coppices and stands of cherry and apple trees, but experience had shown that there was no profit to be made from them, and they were abandoned.

We had many kinds of fruit trees in the village: sweet or oily plum, pear, apple, cherry, morello cherry, mulberry, fig, quince, peach, chestnut, oak and walnut. The last stood on the banks of the streams and rivers with their great height. I can recall, of course, the name of the valley and the end of Chaghci Valley known as *Engezle Boghaz* where walnut trees grew.

All these fruits, in their many varieties, were the product of Bardizag's soil and climate. Every house had some of them in their gardens, in greater or smaller numbers. The usual trees were: pear, apple, cherry, plum, mulberry, fig, quince and walnut. The fruit was for local use, apart from one or two kinds of cherries – *gardje*

---

* All of these occasions were known under the general term *hargink*.

got [short stemmed] and *Dalbasi* with full, firm and juicy flesh - which were much favoured in the markets of Constantinople. *Manavs* [fruit merchants] from Constantinople would come to Bardizag at cherry harvesting time and would rent these much-prized trees in the gardens, which were put under guard, the crop harvested and then sold in Constantinople. Fruit was usually eaten fresh in Bardizag, with a proportion dried in the sun or in the ovens and, when boiled up with sugar water, produced wonderful *khoshab* [sweets].

The fruit that usually lasted the longest before softening were pears, apples and quinces which were kept like holy relics in winter and often served as *hivanti gamag* [special treats for the sick] when a sick person, in his agony, longed for this or that ripe fruit that was difficult to find in the market during that season.

For the villager, sources of income were the raising of silkworms, using the leaves of the mulberry trees around the village itself and growing tobacco. The silkworm and tobacco leaf were profitable exportable crops, almost the pillars of the villager's tottering economic edifice.

There was almost no house that didn't raise silkworms; from the most affluent to the poorest, all took part, to a greater or lesser extent, in that trade using their mulberry trees.

The silkworm season usually began in mid-April and ended at about the end of May, a period of between 40 and 50 days of very hard work, involving all the members of the family without exception, turning the house or specially a constructed shed in the garden into a silkworm shed.

The silk moth caterpillars hatched from eggs (called *hound*) in spring either due to the ambient temperature being high enough or in heated hatcheries, and were about the size of an ant. The small black caterpillars, which were fed on chopped mulberry leaves from their first days, then on leafy branches, grew very quickly to about the length and thickness of a little finger, when they would begin to spin their *khozag* [cocoon] around themselves.

These caterpillars, in their lifetimes, went through four phases called *koun* [sleep or rest]: the first lasted 5-6 days; the second 4-5 days; the third, 8-10 days; and the fourth lasted for 10-12 days. The last two stages were also called small *alad* and great *alad* respectively. When the caterpillars were small they were placed on mats or special trays that were lined with cloth that made *angoghin* or *salk* [beds] over a period of days and which were stacked into tiers, one on top of the other, each with its branches of leaves.

Every time a stage was completed and the caterpillars stopped eating for a day or two and shed their skins, the old beds would be cleaned and moved to new places. At the final stage *(koun)*, the great *alad*, each bed would be raised by about half an *arshin* (about 14 inches or 330 mm); the caterpillars would stop eating, each would clean out its bowel and look for a place to spin its cocoon. It was then that leafy thin oak branches would be put (vertically) in the beds, in lines a little apart from each other, forming a sort of copse on the beds. The caterpillars would then ascend these branches, choosing a place among the leaves to spin their cocoons, tying strands of silk to the leaves as they did so. The cocoons looked a little like hens' eggs, completely covering the caterpillar.

The branches would look like Christmas trees at this point, covered with a veil of white and yellow cocoons, pleasing the whole family that had been looking after them, that could now see the results of their labours, satisfying them. The whole house would now be filled from top to bottom with cocoons, the family now being relegated to the garden.

Harvesting the cocoons would begin a week later, being gathered from the branches and laid on mats in thin layers. These were *fresh* cocoons. The caterpillars were still alive in them, having pupated *(harsniag)* and, if they were left, would become moths, puncturing the cocoons and emerging to lay their eggs. But the cocoons would lose much of their value in that state, so they were put into a steam oven while still fresh to kill the enclosed pupas and prevent them being punctured, if the owner didn't want to sell them immediately in their fresh state.

The Bardizag cocoon harvest weighed about 60,000 to 100,000 kg (132,000 to 220,000 lb or nearly *60 to 100 tons*), worth between 12,000 to 20,000 Ottoman liras, and was the village economy's greatest source of income.

The cultivation of tobacco was a long drawn-out activity, lasting almost a whole year, which became very important when the Turkish government, on behalf of a European company, made it into a monopoly named the Ottoman Tobacco Regie. The company was able, through this monopoly, to take control of all tobacco grown in Turkey and was the only organisation in the country allowed to sell it. This monopoly, like all the others, resulted in smuggling in which, as we shall soon see, the Bardizag villager participated to a notable extent.

Tobacco cultivation went through the following stages: seed planting in containers[*] and their care; the preparation of the fields – ploughing and manuring; planting out; weeding around the plants' roots several times; collecting the leaves and making strings of them (all this took between one and two months); drying them in the sun and turning them a golden colour by leaving the strings hanging in the damp autumn air; when the leaves softened they were removed from the strings and made into small bundles according to quality and, finally, the bundles made into bales.

The tobacco was ready to be sold in this state. The sale took place by auction in the Regie's depots in the main towns with, apart from the Regie, certain dealers allowed to bid, on the condition that what they purchased would be exported. This sale by public auction was enshrined in the Regie's charter, with the object of

---

* This is inferred from the text.

protecting the grower's profits, so that the Regie, as a monopoly, would not assess the tobacco harvest as it would prefer to.

The Regie, however, had received the right, on the basis of the same charter, to limit tobacco cultivation to certain areas, the products of which were regarded as the most prized. The main areas in which tobacco was allowed to be cultivated were the province of Bithynia, the Asian shores of the Black Sea (Samsun and Bafra), the European shores of the Aegean Sea (Drama and Seregh) and so on, making it easy for the Regie to keep production under its control without great expendture or problems.

To restrict smuggling, the crop, still in the fields, was assessed twice, the size of the harvest being agreed with the cultivator. The cultivator had to provide the amount of tobacco, in accordance with the second assessment made, to the Regie's depots. The cultivator, however, to maximise his profits and to save the amount to be used as contraband and which could be sold at a higher price, would find a way to come to an understanding with the Regie's assessor, and reduce the harvest assessment. He had a second method of doing this: replacing good quality crops with those of lower or useless quality, which he handed over to the Regie to fulfil his agreement, while keeping the best quality crop for smuggling.

The Regie had also had the right under its charter to maintain its own *gholdjis* [guards]. These pursued the smugglers, night and day, on land and sea, trying to seize the contraband tobacco they were carrying or hanging in the houses in the villages where it was being cultivated. The government also assumed the responsibility of defending the Regie's guards' efforts to catch the smugglers, if officially called upon to do so.

Bardizag was inside the permitted tobacco cultivation zone, but didn't have large areas of land or farms to devote to it, only small ones, each belonging to one or two people. The Regie had to deal with them individually, giving each of them the necessary permits, so it only gave permission to a few who, with the advantage of having somewhat larger pieces of land, were also regarded as being trustworthy. This meant that the ordinary villager was denied access to that profitable trade. At the same time the young men of Bardizag, as brave and bold *ayingadjis* [smugglers] made a name for themselves throughout this tobacco growing region.[*] The Regie therefore hesitated in granting permits in Bardizag to all who wanted them. Under these circumstances the annual crop of tobacco produced by Bardizag was about 40,000 kg (88,000 lb or 40 tons), bringing an income to village of about 4,000-5,000

---

[*] Some of the men from Bardizag who were famous *ayingadjis* were Biber Ardash, Biber Hovhannes, Bolig Hagop, Parnag, Agosto Artin, Chatal, Antranig and Aksham Nigo. The last generation of these men were represented by Chavoush Hovhannes, Ataments Krikor, Perkhadzin Vanes, Chinig Minas, Bolig Barkev and Godjag Sde. There were, of course, many others whose names have not come down to us. See Hagop Der-Hagopian, *Bardizage khadoudig*, pp. 200-203, quoting Apig Der-Minasian.

Ottoman liras. Good quality tobacco would reach a price of 10-12 *kurush* per kg (2.2 lb) in public auction.

This lack of confidence in the Bardizag villager demonstrated by the Regie and the limiting of tobacco production on village land were the reasons for the villager to find a way of reducing his losses, with the village becoming an invincible and famous centre of smuggling. The village's bold and manly young men obtained contraband tobacco from various places and, armed to the teeth, transported it by boat or on horseback either to Constantinople or to the inner provinces of Asia Minor and as far afield as Konya, selling it very profitably in those places, where it was greatly sought after. They were often accompanied in their forays by Muslim Turks from Anatolia, to prevent racial problems disrupting their activities.

This practical alliance between the Turks and the young men from Bardizag became almost like an army ranged against the Regie, with deadly clashes occurring between them and the guards employed by it on their journeys. They smugglers almost always emerged victorious from such clashes, as the guards, only earning one or two liras a month, really didn't want to put their lives in danger.

The government, that had taken on the responsibility of protecting the Regie's interests in the country, was often slack in its efforts against those heroic men and often impressed by the sheer elegance of their methods.

I previously mentioned the exploits of the Laz-Armenian bandits, who operated in concert with young men from Bardizag.[*] At this point I would like to recall Biber Ardash and his comrades, whose fame extended from Izmid as far as the gates to Cilicia. Biber Ardash, their leader, was like a figure from old legends, manly and intrepid and with, at the same time, a humble and noble character. Two others, Kurd Sarkis and his comrade Little Sarkis, both died one day on one of those brave forays, leaving the fear they generated and the charm of their names to those who came after them.

One night Kurd Sarkis, on his way to Constantinople in his boat filled with contraband tobacco, was surprised by a Regie steamboat with inspectors on board. Losing his coolness and becoming extremely angry, he attacked the steamboat, incapacitated the captain and engineer, and weapon in hand, pursued the inspectors all over the vessel. Being alone against many, however, he finally succumbed during this unique and heroic combat.

It was not only on deserted and distant roads that clashes took place; they often happened in the village itself between visiting inspectors and the smugglers, when through the Regie's spies – a profitable and safe occupation for those of bad character – it heard of the existence of a stock of contraband tobacco stored in one of the houses. In this instance the Regie's inspectors took the local *mukhtar* with them and surrounded the house under suspicion. Suddenly, however, there was a

---

[*] See Section 138.

flurry of activity, with all the girls and women of the local area – and all the young people – armed with sticks and staves, sprang into action and attacked the inspectors, totally confusing them and driving them away. Meanwhile other women and girls secretly moved the contraband from the house to safe places some distance away and, when the inspectors, as a result of this unexpected attack returned and, protected by government forces, entered the house they regarded as suspicious, apart from turning it upside down, they found nothing and retreated empty-handed, bewildered and ashamed.

In this work of smuggling, no danger or victim was enough to stop the young Bardizag *ayingadjis* continuing their daily struggle against the Regie until, finally, as a result of the Armenian question, the government's attitude changed, and it saw a danger to itself in those armed clashes with Armenian smugglers inside villages and on deserted roads, and so began to persecute them. It was only then that smugglers stopped their activities, laid down their arms and took to safer occupations.

It only remains for me to write here about another farming activity, that of animal husbandry.

The Bardizag villager didn't keep great flocks of sheep, goats or herds of cows, as the land available wasn't enough to profitably take advantage of that important branch of farming. Only Nshan Agha Sinanian had flocks of sheep on the Bedigs' land. Enor Keyian and Tavlou Artin had their flocks of goats on the heights above the village as well as having a modest cheese-making concern.

Generally speaking, individual villagers had their horse or horses, maybe a cow or two, or one or two oxen, or perhaps one or two mules. Specific people, however, utilised them as a result of the trade they followed. There were about 200-300 horses in the village which were used for riding and as pack animals. Some of them were used to transport wood, charcoal or timber from the high forests to Seymen. Horses were also used to move the harvest home from the fields or gardens, or to take manure to them. They were also used by pedlars[*] to transport goods to and from Turkish villages.

There were about five to ten pairs of oxen too, which were harnessed to ploughs or carts for agricultural work. There were about 100 cows, used by their owners to provide milk and yogurt, which they sold locally. The cow owners, as a group, hired a herdsman who would collect the animals in the early morning to take them to graze below the village in summer and to the heights above it in winter, returning them each evening to their owners.

Certain families also had, especially at the edges of the village, communal grassy areas where they would keep poultry – several hundred hens, ducks and geese – kept for their meat, eggs and feathers.

---

* *Sherchig vadjaraganner* [travelling merchants].

This was the extent of animal husbandry in the village, which didn't satisfy its needs.

With the need for cheese and meat increasing every year, there were wealthy people who, at the beginning of spring, would buy flocks of lactating sheep from the Rumeli region and bring them to the borders of the village, taking their milk during the summer to make cheese. When the sheeps' milk dried up, they would fatten them to sell either locally or in Constantinople as meat animals, as mutton was considered to be the best meat to eat. Apart from these, Bardizag butchers would secure, as a group, flocks of a kind of sheep called *gharaman* from the interior of Anatolia, which would be grazed by a shepherd on land belonging to the village, then used in accordance with market needs, flocks of them being slaughtered as required.

The perusal of this section devoted to rural economy leads us to the conclusion that Bardizag could not provide enough bread, meat or milk for itself, in other words its food, using its land. It therefore brought those necessities from outside. This is why, when the surrounding agricultural provinces had poor harvests, the village was often short of food and once or twice even suffered famine. It was then that the Armenian authorities in Constantinople provided aid.

Milk, yogurt and poultry products were occasional luxuries, given only to the sick, or when needed for special occasions. Then the villager was forced, for a time, to open his purse wide, which was usually firmly closed on ordinary days because of his thrift and economic situation.

B. Labour

The lack of agricultural work in the Bardizag rural economy meant that new means of employment had to be found for the villagers. One of these was working in mechanised factories. As we've seen in previous pages,* the Imperial Cloth Factory had been built about one and a half hour's distance from Bardizag, employing several hundred workers, mainly Armenians from the three local Armenian-populated villages – Bardizag, Ovadjekh and Arslanbeg. There were about 50 workers from Bardizag there, mostly weavers who were well paid, as well as important officials. The latter were Hampartsoum Ghazarosian, the *ousda bashi* [manager], who had been rewarded for his services with a medal; Yeremia Effendi Seferian, who was first the secretary and accountant and who succeeded Ghazarosian as manager; Hagop Effendi Drezian (later Diyonisius Kahana), an office official; Mihran Effendi Ghazarosian, the bakery overseer; Garabed Agha Drezian, the master of the dyeing house; and Haroutiun Seferian, the master weaver. These workers would depart together on a Monday morning for the factory, then work and stay there until midday on Saturday, returning to their homes

---

* See sections 75 and 89 above.

together, where they would stay with their families. These workers from Bardizag were generally esteemed and sought-after people and were, comparatively speaking, well-off by village standards.

Apart from these there were about 200-300 people, mostly women and girls, who worked in the two silk spinning factories belonging to the Helvadjians and Avedians that had been established in the village. These women had to work for more than ten hours a day for very low wages; the average daily wage was, at the most, 4-5 *kurush*, and the lowest was 1 to 1½ *kurush*. But it was permanent work for the women and girls who had no opportunity or means to find work outside their homes and who assisted their family's domestic economy with the little they earned.

In my day the Der-Sahagian family had their own silk spinning factory, first of all in the village, then lower down, in the Greek village of Yenikeoy, as they needed cheap labour, and where the women and girls working in it were mainly Greeks, under expert supervisors from Bardizag. These factories also provided work and profit to the officials, the cocoon buyers and horse keepers who transported firewood and goods.

Bardizag had a class of male worker called *chapadji* or *renchber* [labourer] that was employed at certain times of the year in and around the village and for the care and maintenance of its extensive vineyards and mulberry plantations. The vineyards and mulberry plantations would be dug over at least once a year with a spade (this tool was called *bed* by the villagers). There were conscientious landowners who had their lands dug over twice a year, the first time with a spade, and the second, after harvesting had been completed, with a hoe. There was therefore always the need for men to do this work as the landowner or wealthy person couldn't personally do so. The digging-over of the land began in March, after the rains had ended and the land had dried out. The second, for the mulberry plantations, started after the harvest, at the beginning of summer,[*] and for the vineyards, in September or, more usually, in October.

The labourers *(chapadji* or *renchber)* usually earned 7-8 *kurush* a day, and used their own tools. They rested about 4-5 times a day and stopped work when the evening bell sounded; they only worked for 6-7 hours a day when the landowner supervised them.[†] Apart from their daily wage, they were also given a breakfast of hot soup or *ghatekh* and bread by the landowner.

It sometimes happened that the time allotted to this village-wide activity was less than usual, because of occasional rainstorms. Then the limited number of these diggers would become demanding, wanting 10-12 *kurush* a day for their work. It

---

* The cocoon harvest was in May. See above.

† It is to be noted that even skilled women working in silk spinning mills for many more hours a day received only 3-6 kurush at the most (see above), while these labourers earned almost twice as much.

was at that point that other unemployed men would, for a few days, be paid to become labourers, taking advantage of the situation.

The *renchber* labourers also found building work, as assistants working under the supervision of master builders, but there weren't many opportunities for this, as the number of new buildings being constructed in the village was very few due to its economic situation.

C. Trades

In the village's final period, the most notable tradespeople or artisans in Bardizag were the carpenters,* furniture makers, basket weavers, ironsmiths, light leather shoe makers *(yemenidji)*; on the second or third levels were the farriers, horseshoe makers, tailors, coat makers [abadji], coopers, ropers or string makers [mazman], saddlers, painters, cobblers, feltmakers, millers, coppersmiths and various other small trades. Carpentry was a popular trade, with about 100 families involved in it. There were several families that passed down the trade from father to son – the *paraghams* – the Andonians, Bodosians, Zakarians, Jamgochians, Azarians, etc. But because there wasn't enough work for all of them in the village, some had stopped plying their trade, while the majority worked outside, especially in the provincial capital Izmid, where the scope for work and profit was the reason that so many of them settled there and become part of the town's Armenian community. It was the same for some other artisans too. There were ironsmiths, coopers, farriers, inkeepers, saddlers, feltmakers, coat makers, etc., who had moved from Bardizag and settled there. Some artisans had gone and settled in Constantinople. These were basket weavers, coppersmiths, coffee mill makers *(djezvedjis)*, cobblers and tailors. There were farriers and horseshoe makers and others from Bardizag in Adabazar, who went there to take advantage of the great opportunites presented by the work available.

The carpenters in the village earned about 20-25 *kurush* a day, a good wage in a village environment, but the lack of a steady flow of work actually meant that they had a somewhat precarious living.

After the carpenters, the ironsmiths had plenty of work in the village, almost constantly repairing metal tools, especially after Muslims and Armenians settled in villages in the area, and who would come to Bardizag for all kinds of things or to have their tools repaired. The basket weavers too worked the year round; there were a number of wealthy people in that trade who would have children and workers brought in from outside to work for them. Basket weaving, the newest trade in Bardizag, was a very prosperous one. Among the basket weavers one can recall the Ghodjakhavoukhs, Yakos, Rayises, Topouzes, Ghourous, Sepetdji Minas, the

---

* Carpenter is possibly a misnomer for *hiusn*. It should perhaps be cabinet maker, a more highly skilled form of carpentry.

Basmadjis etc., who worked for the Constantinople fruit merchants *(maive hosh)* on behalf of the *manavs* [merchants], and who also employed woodcutters and transporters, the latter taking finished goods down to the port. Boats loaded with these baskets would distribute them to the fruit and vegetable centres around the Bay of Izmid.

Making *yemenidji* light leather shoes was, in my day, also a busy trade. They were worn by villagers everywhere, both indoors and outside. Their manufacture was notably in the hands of the Berberians, Kondas and several others who, after satisfying the needs of the villagers, had a very comprehensive trade in the surrounding Turkish, Laz and Giurdji villages. The trade also had a repair sector, with worn out yemenidjis and shoes being refurbished. Some people carried out this repair work as their means of livelihood in the village; others would go from one village to the next and, despite the modest content of the work, made good money and maintained their families.

Tailoring in the European style was a new trade, whose practitioners gradually increased with the general use of those styles. They were the Alemshahs and Khosrov Der-Nersesian at first, followed in my day by Nighoghos Parounian (later Parnapas Kahana), Garabed Gabeyian, Onnig Tavitian and another person. It was a trade that promised much.

The charcoal, lumber and ordinary carpentry trades were important from the old days. Bardizag was on the edge of the rich forest belt on the Black Sea coast and very near to the Constantinople marketplace. In those areas, in ancient historic times, centres producing firewood and lumber were famous and a part of that historic trade was continued by the people of Bardizag, thanks to its location.

We had a considerable number of charcoal burners who had become masters of that trade; there were also wealthy people linked to it for profit. There were two of these in my time – the Kiutnerians, a family in that trade from the old days, and a new person, Asadour Kondaiyan - who both filled the gap left by families who had disappeared. Apart from them there were minor families that sold all they produced locally – the Edjems, Toumayians and one or two others.

The great wealthy families used to rent the distant, high forests and reach agreements with the charcoal burners and would send them into the mountains. The charcoal produced would be brought down by them using their own caravans of 10-12 horses each to Seymen and stored in their own warehouses, to be sold to the shipowners who presented themselves to buy cargo from the port. They also carried out, especially in summer, lumber preparation work *(varol, samanli)* and the masters of that trade *(barmakhdji)* took the lumber too to Seymen and held it in warehouses there. Bardizag's charcoal, mainly prepared from oak, was sold on the Constantinople market, while the lumber went to the Greek islands to make casks for wines and spirits, olive oil and olives.

Both charcoal burning and lumber production were profitable businesses. The carpentry associated with the preparation of baulks of timber was a specialist trade, carried out according to the needs of the village. Horses were used to transport them to the village from the mountains. Each horse transported two lengths of timber, one on either side of its body, one end of each secured to the saddle, the longer part trailing behind the horse on the ground. The horse, loaded like this, would then be led down difficult and narrow paths, dragging them along.

The wealthy people involved in these trades had their own caravan leaders *(ghatardjis)* who almost always was mounted on the lead horse *(bineg)* and would slowly lead the caravan along unsafe roads, being burnt by the sun in summer and battered and soaked by the rain and snow in winter – which was worse that the work itself – work which they carried on for years. These men usually died early. Each caravan was accompanied by a *wool head* (a Circassian)[*] guard, mounted and armed, with the task of protecting the caravan from attacks by his compatriots.

We will see other new trades that operated in Bardizag, especially bakeries and the raising of silkworm eggs, which I will talk about in the sub-section devoted to shopkeeping and commerce, regarding them as commercial enterprises.

D. Shopkeeping

This sub-section may be regarded as part of 'Trades' (above), as hand-made goods formed the major part of the artisans' work, mixed in with, to a certain extent, work with charcoal.

Baking was not only a trade, but a commercial business. At one time every house used to prepare its own dough and bake bread in the neighbourhood's ovens. This continued in Bardizag but to a much lesser extent as, although home-baked bread was tastier and cheaper, with changes in taste and the new activities that the women and girls were engaged in outside their homes, it was not a viable task for many. This was because they would have to bake a huge quantity at a time, sometimes wasting all of it if something went wrong.

For these and other reasons baking became very important and many people were involved in this trade in the market, providing the villager with his daily nourishment – bread.

The commercial baking of bread was the reason that the village watermills had less and less work to do and went through a period of decline, not just because of the work the bakeries were doing in Bardizag, but also because of the plentiful supply of flour on the market from Europe and neighbouring countries.

Apart from bakeries, there were also grocery and fishmongers, butchers, drapers and barbers' shops. The latter, apart from cutting and dressing hair and shaving faces, also had a sideline of providing hot drinks (coffee and tea) and spirits (wine,

---

[*] They were called this because of the lambswool *papakhs* (hats) they wore.

oghi and cognac) for their customers who, to deal with personal matters or to see friends for one reason or another, would spend some time in them. There were about 20 grocery shops, perhaps 10 butchers, 4-5 fishmongers, 10-12 drapery shops and 10-15 coffee houses and barbers' shops in Bardizag's market area.[*] There were more than 100 people in these shops who were involved in their own businesses and made up the village's bourgeois class.

We may add the completely new trade of silkworm caterpillar *(hound)* production to this list; the people producing them didn't have shops, but worked scientifically in their homes, employing girls at the cocoon stage. They also had a certain amount of capital which they used. There were 5-10 of these people, who had studied sericulture in the Brousa (Boursa) Sericulture School.[†]

The grocers sold dry legumes, cereals and vegetables, regional crops,[‡] stores of foodstuffs[**] and paper products. Customers would also find beans, chick peas, lentils, flour, rice, kerosene, olive oil, soap, candles, matches, salted fish, salted olives, salted cheese, as well as items specifically for schoolchildren. These things were brought from Izmid market or from ships' captains who called in at Seymen, bringing certain imported items from the Greek islands as well as others produced locally. These shops were usually busiest in the mornings and evenings, after people made the journey to work and later returned to the village.

Fishmongers supplied fresh fish to the villagers every day. They also had stores of salted fish. They had arrangements with fishermen settled in places on the seashore and would go down before dawn with their horses, load them up with the night's catch and return to the village. The fish was weighed and recorded in the Public Debt Administration's building *(mizan)* and then brought to the shops for the customers. Fresh fish, fried or baked, was the villagers' preferred meal. Everyone, as soon as fresh fish appeared in the shops in the morning, would buy a few coins-worth of fish, which the fishmongers were used to stringing on a kind of grass *(sez)* brought from the seashore, and the buyer, with the strung fish dangling from his fingers, would take them home.

There were various kinds of fresh fish caught according to season, all of which were tasty and fine, as that caught in the bay always was.

Fresh fish was almost always the villagers' main midday meal, with some people having the habit of sprinkling it with a cup of wine.

---

[*] The market area was located on both sides of the main street running through the village.
[†] See the author's certificate in the Appendix.
[‡] The words used here are *kaghtayin perker*.
[**] *Snntagan bahesdner.*

At grape harvest time (September or October) fish called *palamoud* and *torig (lekerde)* arrived from the Black Sea, and were regarded as providing the finest meals when accompanied by newly fermented wine.

In spring fish caught in the fresh-water lakes around the Izmid and Sabandja areas appeared, which was transported at night, to retain its freshness, from distances of between 8-10 hours distant from the village.

Butchers provided fresh mutton, goat, lamb, kid and beef, which were slaughtered in the marketplace, in front of each butcher's shop for interested people and packs of dogs to see. There was no abattoir; cleaning up was left to the dogs' appetites. After fish, meat was the main element of the villagers' diet, which was comparatively cheap in the village market.

Game was also available, especially wild boar, which was hunted in the high mountains in winter.

Shops selling cloth and haberdashery were quite busy, with mainly women and girls as their customers - especially those who worked - who continually approached them for home and clothing necessities, as well as those preparing for weddings and to complete their sons' or daughters' wedding clothing chest (dowry). These shops were at their busiest during the fresh cocoon season when most people had some money, especially in my day, when the number of seamstresses had diminished and tastes become more refined, with much more presentable clothes being required.

I have already talked about barbers, who had more than one occupation – both as barbers and haircutters and club owners – where they ran buffets. Over a period of time there was a move to separate the barbers' shops from the coffee buffets. Thus one or two new-style barbers' shops appeared where only haircutting and shaving was carried out.

E. Peddling[*] and administration

There was also a fairly large class of travelling salesmen (pedlars) in Bardizag. Each of these had his own horse which he would load up with what he could sell – vinegar, salted olives, soap, cloth, various kinds of seeds as well as other things of this nature – then taking them to all the nearby Turkish villages. They would travel to Anteres and Khodjeli, and to the various newly-established Muslim settlements, where they would barter their goods for local ones, sometimes paying in coin for what they bought. They would collect wool, goat hair, wheat, barley, oats, cheese, yogurt, chickens, eggs and occasionally animals for slaughter, and would return loaded with what they had bought, selling them off a little at a time.

There were pedlars who actually plied their trades in the places they visited, or who sold things made in Bardizag such as rugs, dyed cloth and items woven from string. They would also stay for a time in the centres they visited, working as

---

* The term used here is *shrchig vadjaraganoutiun*.

painters, repairers or pewterers and carry on other minor trades, being paid for their work in local produce of one kind or other.

After a significant number of new immigrant villages had been established in the heights around Bardizag, the village's commerce, restricted for many years to just the village and the locality, gained new impetus and the number of shops and their size and range of goods increased. Increased amounts of money circulated in the village, and Bardizag became a minor centre of trade, greatly changing and reforming the village economy.

The shopkeepers and merchants becoming wealthy, started to generalise and extend their credit arrangements for customers for longer periods - even up to a year - in anticipation of the main harvest, when they would be paid and accounts would be closed.

This bourgeois class, with its many branches of work and earnings, to which government and other officials, teachers, silk spinning factory owners, the wealthy and one or two property owners must be added, formed the village's ruling class and the element that represented public opinion, and from which community public administations were elected - *taghagan khorhourt* [parish councils], *hokapartsoutiun* [trustees], *yegeghetsbanner* [churchwardens], the village and *nahie* [group of villages] *taghabedagan khorhourt, kiughakhoumpi khorhourt* [villages' assemblies], *mukhtar* [headman] and *ekhtiar medjlis* [council of elders] as well as imperial tax collectors.

F. Womens' and girls' labour, both in the house and elsewhere

I should like to close this section on Bardizag's economy by presenting a few lines about the work carried out by the women and girls, which had its particular and important influence on the village economy.

We have seen, in previous pages, the work carried out by women and girls of the village as workers in the silk spinning factories, as well as their participation, with the men, in the silkworm production business. By women doing so, the men had the opportunity, to a significant extent, of continuing their separate occupations. It is therefore possible to say that the village's greatest source of income, the cocoon crop, was the result of the intensive work carried out by the women and girls. The women, again, were used to working either in the fields during harvest time as daily wage earners, or providing services in wealthy houses such as laundry and other household activities, bringing significant income to the family's domestic economy.

The women also had to continue their ordinary daily work in their own homes – looking after and feeding their children, doing the home laundry, preparing and cooking meals, serving at table, washing dishes and *boulashekh* [utensils], sewing and repairing garments – as well as the preparation of cloth and stores for the winter. In my day, however, the last two were much reduced in many homes, while for others, who regarded them as one of their sources of income, they were very tiring and needed great stamina and strength to do them successfully.

For example, the preparation of cloth by the women consisted of many different activities – the harvesting of the flax, separating out the seeds, softening the flax in running water, drying it, bringing it home from the fields on their backs, the beating of the woody parts with *mengene* [sticks], carding and spinning into thread, making it into hanks, weaving the cloth itself – when the cloth was finally finished it would have taken a whole year of complicated and diverse activities to produce.*

Similar complex work was that of preparing foodstuffs for the home. One of these was the boiling of wheat, milling it using manual milling methods, splitting it into different parts, winnowing it and so on. Another was the preparation of many different kinds of sweets made from fresh or dried fruit cooked with *roub* [syrup] or sugar water. Still others were the melting of lambs' tails and pressing fat produced into storage vessels and the baking of various pastries etc.

Women also had to carry out many other tasks, such as harvesting wild salad items, fruit, as well as various kinds of mushrooms available according to season, which they would use immediately or dry for use in winter. Pickles – using cucumber, cabbage, peppers, tomatoes and grapes – were also prepared and stored. Wine was also fermented and oghi distilled. Water had to be brought in from fountains on women's backs or shoulders in pitchers. They took care of and fed the livestock owned by the family: horses, cows and chickens. They also had to bathe the children and, occasionally, the elderly, before the bath house in the village was built. It is not easy to complete the list of work and things the women of the village did.

It is said that the European woman works much harder than her eastern counterpart; that could be true for some, but I am sure that the European woman would buckle under the weight of these many and disparate tasks, no matter what race she belonged to. I can say, without doubt, that the Armenian woman especially – and she alone – had the work of ten to carry out, which she did victoriously and with great energy.

It was unfortunate that a significant number of women and girls had to work as maids and *snndou* [wet-nurses] in wealthy homes in Constantinople. This unfortunate reality had its particular reasons. Firstly, there was not enough work available in the village for all the women who were forced to work to make ends meet. Secondly, the woman from Bardizag had the advantages of being well brought-up, preferring cleanliness, was capable of learning and refinement, and was presentable and healthy – more so than others from other places. The result of this was that the needs of Constantinople gave preference to the women or girls from Bardizag, when there was a requirement for a maid or hired wet-nurse to look after a child. These

---

* The author has not mentioned the washing and drying of bales of newly produced cloth and the activities connected with whitening it, all of which were labour intensive.

advantages the women or girls from Bardizag possessed were, in a way, their misfortune, as it forced them, because of the lack of available work and poverty, to leave their own homes for an indeterminate time and work in houses in Constantinople.

The Bardizag woman or girl didn't leave her home easily because those who did were needy and subject to unexpected problems, forcing them to leave their hearths and loved ones to help provide for them. For me, who has known the woman from Bardizag closely, it was a dreadful and incomprehensible sacrifice. It was always found that when a woman was faced, for the first time, with the necessity of having to make such a sacrifice, it wasn't easy for her to accept such a bitter fate. She would object to the idea for days, with tears in her eyes, until even the strongest will was crushed under the tyranny of necessity. I have seen so many women who didn't want to leave their children and give their motherly care to those of another family, in a strange house: for days they'd say, 'I'll stay hungry, I'll die, but I won't go...' but in the end misfortune always spoke louder.

This was the secret of those poor, unfortunate Bardizag women's submission in the real pain of their leaving their hearths.

As a result of these circumstances, there have always been between 50 and 100 women working in houses in Constantinople, a kind of sacrifice to motherly dedication and love. For some of these Bardizag women, this necessary employment outside their own houses assisted them to see new visions for their children. These received a certain amount of education thanks to their mothers' and sisters' sacrifices This resulted in them having the opportunity to obtain important positions in Bardizag or even in Constantinople as master craftsmen, merchants and people who had mastered liberal trades.

4. Family life

The family, in Bardizag, was organised in an Armenian patriarchal way. The father was the master of the family who had to be obeyed by all the family members, beginning with the mother, completely and without reservation. He was the hearth owner and received every honour and respect. The care and protection of the family was his responsibility and every family member looked to him for sustenance.

The mother was responsible for the running of the house and all the work required within it. She had to cook the meals, wash the dishes and utensils, do the weekly washing and baths, lay and clear the table, look after the little ones, feeding them milk and putting them to sleep to the sound of lullabies. She mended all the clothes that needed sewing, looked after the sick, helped her husband in the cultivation of his fields and milked, fed and cared for the domestic animals. She wove cloth if necessary, brought kindling and firewood on her back from the forest to the yard in the autumn. She carried the baby outside the home, brought water from the fountains... She was, in a sense, the only servant in the house. If she however had a grown daughter or daughter-in-law, they had to help her in the work done in the house and in looking after the children. As much as this was an obligation for daughters, it was also an apprenticeship for their future responsibilities.

The boys had a more privileged position in the home. It was considered to be almost shameful for a boy to help in the house. At the most he could help his father in his work, for example, cleaning and grooming their horses and taking them to pasture, and other such things.

This picture of family life in Bardizag, to a certain extent, belonged to the old days. From my days the curtailment of the fathers' and sons' privileges could be seen but, in principle and to a great extent, the situation remained the same. Thus the father could have his own ideas and point of view in matters pertaining to the family, but couldn't impose them against his wife's will.

The family was an indissoluble union, with strict morals. Throughout the village, over the years, I can only recall one or two dissolutions of marriage that had been regarded as illegal,* with the ties of marriage retaining their existence, even if the husband or wife lived away from the family.

The daughters and sons too, up until a certain age, had no say or opinion concerning family matters, especially in the father's presence. Corporal punishment (slaps and beatings) were accepted as the means of educating the little ones, and utilised as a rule, with both sons and daughters sharing punishment if the father was easily aroused. In reality these customs had eased, and slaps and beatings had begun to be regarded as coarse and brutal, especially towards the older ones.

When the patriarchal way of living had begun to change for the better, the work carried out by the girls and women was restricted to that which took place in the home, and thus lost much of the hardship and effort of the old days. When the sons grew up and reached employment age, some of the father's work would be shared between them, but every son brought his wages to his father who would give him what he needed. The sons, for as long as they remained under their father's authority and leadership, couldn't amass their own wealth; their wages belonged to the family group, to be used as the father saw fit.

The boys were considered to reach maturity at 18-20 – in my day it was a little later, 22-25 – and the father and mother would select a prospective bride for their mature son and introduce her to him.† It was seldom that a son would refuse the choice made for him by his parents and if that happened, it would be regarded as

---

* The words used here are *amousnatoghoutiunner voronk aborini ngadvadz ein*.

† The words used here are *yev anor ge nergayatsnein zain*. This must be taken in the sense that she would be pointed out to him at a distance at first, before formal negotiations took place.

almost scandalous. Even although it created bad feeling between son and parents, the son's will was respected.

Married sons and their wives would remain in the family house, until such time as the number of people living in it forced the father to build another or make extensions to the existing one, settling the son's family in a separate part or in the new house.

As for the daughters, at maturity (15-16 years old), later a little older, it would happen that they would be considered as prospective wives for the son of another family. Then, in accordance with the decision made by her parents that she would hear from her mother, she would be officially affianced *(khoskgab)* or engaged *(nshandouk)*. A daughter's refusal would be considered to be very grave, even scandalous, as bad as impertinence and impudence, and she would be forced to accept. But over time this tyrannical strictness lost its authority, and girls achieved a measure of independence concerning their future in such a delicate matter. There were girls who fought their parents so as to achieve their emancipation, and customs were considerably relaxed for both girls and boys, in terms of giving their feelings more freedom in the choice of a partner in life.

When the son's (future bridegroom's) father gave the decision for the marriage to take place, the girl's (bride's) family would agree and it would take place. The girl would take the dowry prepared for her (under and outer clothes, items for the home and jewellery) and go to her husband's home, to spend her married and motherly life there, with complete loyalty and obedience.

When the father of the family died, the first-born son in reality inherited his father's authority in the home. Although he was the head of the house, he would consult his brothers and take account of their suggestions and advice concerning the governance of the home. This stopped when the patriarchal way of living ceased, and the various sons had moved to separate establishments. Each would have his own work in accordance with the opportunities that presented themselves. They would stop working together and each had his own house and work, becoming completely independent.

A. Birth

The appearance of a new-born child in a newly-established household was considered to be the greatest blessing, a gift from God, a condition of the continuation of the house's patrimony and future generations. On such an occasion everyone would have smiles on their faces, and the mother and child would be given the best possible love and care. The whole house would seem like that of a wedding.

The birth of a boy would provide great joy in the house, but the birth of a girl, especially if it was the second or subsequent one, would be met with frowns and it would be felt that the mother was responsible for not producing a boy.

As soon as the child entered the world, a neighbouring woman or girl would run to tell the good news to the members of the household, relatives, in-laws, neighbours, the godparents, saying, 'Congratulations, we have a boy (or girl).' It was the custom to reward the messenger with a small coin, on behalf of the household and relatives, with a slightly larger one if the newborn was a boy.

The child's umbilical cord would be tied at its belly and then cut. The baby would then be washed and swaddled tightly like a little mummy and put on its mother's breast. They would have the mother rest on a richly decorated and comfortable high bed. She, in her great joy and making sure other people didn't see, would look at her infant occasionally, inwardly delighted at the birth of this God-given child.

When the father, older brothers and sisters returned to the house after the birth, the midwife would, swiftly and swollen with a sort of pride, present the child to them, and would place it on all the arms extended from every direction to receive it. She would say, 'It's a chubby, large baby.'* In their joy, they would try to work out who it looked like saying, with affectionate explanation: 'It has dropped from the father's (or mother's or brother's) nose, may I die for God's eyes.'† Of course, the belief that the child had 'fallen from its father's nose' was a great joy for everyone – it was the true descendant of the house.

Congratulatory visits from female relatives and neighbours lasted for days, with the visitors each bringing a dish of sweet soup. They would have the new mother sit down and put a spoonful of the soup from each dish to her lips as a sign of pride and to honour the donor.

If the child was born weak, and didn't seem as if it would survive, it would be rushed to the church to be baptised, so that it wouldn't die without receiving that sacrament, which would have been a great sorrow for the family. But when the child had entered the world in the usual way, the baptism usually took place on the first Sunday after it was born, to give it, during the service, its first Communion.‡

The infant, wrapped in clean whites, baptised and blessed, would be brought home from the church. Everyone would then, with the greatest reverence, approach and kiss God's newly anointed one, upon whose face the Holy Chrism had not yet dried.

The household, godfather and relatives would, on this occasion, give the child gifts – gold coins, tiny rings and earrings, all tied to the baby's cap, hands and its beautiful new clothes, to dress and decorate it.

The baby's mother got up after a week and would begin her usual work in the house and breastfeed her baby. When the baby was 40 days old, the mother and

---

* *Tomboulig khoshor bebek men e.*
† *Hore (more gam yeghpore) kiten ingadz e, asdoudzo achkin mernim.*
‡ Kasabian provides the number of children born, both male and female, during the period 1899-1909 – See Appendix, Table 1 below.

child would be taken to the church on the first Sunday after that day to receive Communion and be blessed.

The child would then grow up under the care of its mother and elder sisters. It would occasionally be taken down to the street, where it would roll about and slide on the stones and in the grass, putting whatever it found in its mouth to gain its first experiences of the world around it. But this important work had its negative side: its face and its clean clothes would get dirty. It would then be picked up and receive gentle slaps on its hands and bottom, making it scream and cry with great tears falling from its lovely eyes. Then loving arms would cuddle it and kisses would dry its hot tears, resulting in smiles like rainbows. So it grew up, until its legs grew strong, it stood up and tottered about *(kal yeller)*, and was ready to go to a practiced child-minder *(varbed doudou)* or the kindergarten.

B. Marriage[*]

The wedding of a mature boy or girl was an important event in a family's life. In the old days, the villagers would marry them off at an early age, 'before they had opened their eyes' as they said, to preserve their moral standards. In the final days the age for marriage was considerably greater.[†]

The settling, making a home, etc. for a boy or girl was quite a difficult thing for a family. It was necessary to prepare for years beforehand to cope with the needs of someone getting married. This was especially true for a girl, for whom the preparation of her *djeyiz* [dowry chest] was quite expensive. Undergarments and outer clothes, in either half-dozens or dozens, parcels of various kinds of cloth, lace, towels and ribbons – all this and more – had to be prepared for each girl to be married *(hars yellogh)*. This was the work and sacrifice of years. It was a mother's pride, otherwise she would be considered to be useless – and a village woman never liked to be that.

The good reputation of the family of a prospective bride or groom was most important, as was their character and way of living, social status, means and diligence, as well as the health and attractiveness or grace of the candidate. Another important factor considered was the candidate's training for the responsibility of running the house and, for boys, having the means to support a family.

First the *khoskgab* [promise] or *nshandouk* [engagement] would take place between the two families, in the presence of the priest and or those invited. Each

---

[*] Although the author uses a single family to describe the events connected with marriage, the reader must keep in mind that *at least 40 separate pairs of families* would be involved, each with a bride and groom during the same days.

[†] There were set rules governing engagements and marriages promulgated in 1864 by the village council and endorsed by the diocesan bishop of the time. See Appendix, Document 2 below.

would give a token to the other with the bride-to-be receiving a piece of jewellery and the husband-to-be usually receiving a silk handkerchief.

From the days of my youth, it was considered reprehensible and scandalous for an engaged couple to have friendly relations or see each other, be it in the house or outside. Usually the engaged girl would run away and hide herself if she was to see her fiancée. They had to look at one another secretly from a distance, otherwise they would be discredited, especially in the case of the girl and, if it should happen that the engagement was broken off, no one else would ask for her hand, saying she was 'open'.*

Despite this, the engaged young people would seek each other out, far from envious eyes, during excursions outside the home on feast days. At Christmas this would happen in Avazoud; at Easter in the Lower Threshing Floors; at Assumption in the Upper Fields; at Holy Cross near the Upper Cemetery, on the roads to Chahgchi Valley or to the port, where they, dressed in their new-fashioned clothes in striking loud colours, would go to enjoy those festival pastimes.

These places, on festival days, would be like markets, where pedlars of cold drinks, sweets, pastries, nuts and raisins would rend the air with their cries, moving among the youthful crowds while carrying tables loaded with their wares on their heads. The engaged young man would approach one of them, fill a large handkerchief with whatever it was that was sold and, giving it to a small boy, would have him take it to his fiancée where she was resting in the shade under the trees with her female friends. This was often the opportunity for the engaged boy and girl to approach each other under the same tree, in a warm, friendly and happy atmosphere, to enjoy a sweet and loving conversation, relieving their longing.

In these circumstances it seemed as if boldness was the rule, with repressed feelings being expressed, when eyes and hands spoke more than words. The young man would use an enjoyable mixture of jokes and bright conversation. But these social meetings were innocent and remained so, simply being the necessary expression of spiritual pleasure between the two young people.

It was also usual, on these festival days, to send parcels to the husband-to be from his future mother-in-law so that he could invite his friends to a modest party. The husband-to-be would, on these occasions, have the boldness – a sought-after boldness much encouraged – to send word to his future mother-in-law to prepare such a parcel. At this, the lady would get busy, and prepare one containing many different things: fruit, cheese, roast chicken or other roasted meat, accompanied by a bottle of wine, and would send it to him. He and his friends would be honoured by this and eat and drink together. In my day this sending of parcels to the husband-to- be was considered to be somewhat odd and coarse. The young man, with the easing of customs, got used to visiting his future mother-in-law's house, where the

---

* The wording used here is *pats aghchig men e*.

engaged couple had the opportunity and pleasure of seeing and talking to each other in a warm, family atmosphere. There was another custom that applied during the period of engagement. The boy's family, neighbours and relatives would arrange, days in advance, a visit to see the girl *(aghchigdes)*, sending word of their intended visit to her family. The object was to introduce the girl - their son's intended bride - to everyone *(poloraganneroun)* and to form a friendly link between them. This was a very good and worthwhile custom, as both sides wanted to get to know each other.

On the evening agreed, after every invited person had finished their meal, they would assemble in the young man's house and, when the company was complete it would, led by the boy's father and mother, go in a body to his fiancee's parents' home where, likewise, all the family, their neighbours and relatives were waiting. It was not the done thing for the husband-to-be to be present at this event. A warm welcome awaited the visitors, who would be led to the most favoured seats in the best room of the house. After mutual compliments and respectful conversation, a rich buffet table, loaded with delicacies, would be prepared in the prospective in-laws' honour. Apart from dry and fresh fruit, there would be preserves and sausage, different kinds of cheese, various dishes and, in the centre, a traditional roast or boiled chicken, dressed to suit every taste and age and accompanied by pure, refreshing village wine. Toasts – both blessings and good wishes - were pronounced and drunk, with expressions of mutual friendship – even affection – between the two houses.

During this party, the bride-to be, who, until this time, had not made an appearance, would enter the room where it was being held, dressed beautifully and with good taste, being led in by a woman who had already married. Every eye would be on her, carefully measuring and assessing her with great interest: her height, the grace of her movements, her face, expressions and dress. She folllowed the woman leading her and approached each of her future in-laws in turn and kissed their hands; in their turn they would slide a gift of money into her beautiful hands.

When this solemn ceremony was completed, the bride-to-be, modestly, and with her eyes downcast and pale-faced (which made her even more attractive), would stand in a corner in an attitude of respect and gravity, with everyone's eyes riveted on her, until her mother told her to fill a glass of wine for each of the guests. The girl would then bring a tray, loaded with glasses of wine, offering one to each person in turn who, with delighted compliments and blessings, would almost suck its contents as if he or she tasted something new and different, and which they couldn't take from their lips.

They would spend many hours enjoying themselves, becoming merry with drink, when talk would be wittier and then, sometime after midnight, they would part company with some reluctance.

It was very rare and almost scandalous for an engagement to be broken and the engaged couple almost always set up house with the endorsement and seal of holy matrimony.

The time for weddings in Bardizag was at the end of autumn, when everyone had finished the year's work and the filling of the house's stores had been completed. That time was one of relaxation and enjoyment for the villager, who had emptied the fields, vineyards and gardens of their crops, got what he could from the mountains and brought all of it to his house in the village. It was at this point that wedding dances began in the houses and mature girls and boys would become engrossed *(vodk ou kloukh g'ellayin)* in making preparations for their future family life. Thus there would be many weddings on the feasts of St. James[*] and St. Sarkis,[†] with the marrying couples forming a long line across the church from one wall to the other.[‡]

There were only a few weddings in the *Paregentan* week before Lent, as weddings were forbidden by church law during the whole of Lent.

The wedding, for the entire family, was a great and symbolic event, taking many days to come to fruition and creating a generally festive atmosphere. A people who remained bereft of artistic pleasures – having almost no theatre, music, dances and lectures (which had only just started among us in their simple, primitive forms) - used these important family events, which took place under the patronage of the church and were blessed by it, as village life's spiritual pleasures.[**]

Preparations for the wedding began from the Friday before the ceremony. With the aid of relatives and neighbours, the majority of the dishes for the wedding feast would be prepared: the traditional stuffed vine leaves *(dolma)*, meat with onions and meat with cabbage and leeks. From that day on snacks would be prepared too.

From then on, the girl to be married would invite her friends to visit her, sending, as an invitation, apples with cloves pressed into them and, from that first evening, they would dance and sing in her house.

---

* The feast of St. James is celebrated, in the Armenian Apostolic church, in the second half of December.

† The feast of St. Sarkis is celebrated, in the Armenian Apostolic church, in the first half of February. Boghosian tells us that most of the weddings took place on that feast day. Haroutiun Boghosian, *Anzoukagan Bardizag*, Elegian Press, Paris, 1967, p. 11.

‡ It was a tradition in Bardizag that marriages took place only on these two feast days, and just a few later. The village, therefore, would have wedding parties taking place in many houses – all at the same time! We know that there were more than 50 weddings in Bardizag in 1897/1898. See *Pounch*, 14 Feb 1898, No 2589, quoted in Hagop Der-Hagopian, *Bardizage khadoudig*, Paris, 1960, p. 244. Kasabian provides the number of marriages each year from 1899 to 1909 – See Appendix, Table 1 below.

** The author is referring to the Tourian years here, when Yeghishe Vartabed Tourian had begun to reform the village's community school. See Section 120.

The festivities in the groom's house started on the next day (the Saturday evening), when he would gather his friends in a coffee house in the market to prepare them for the wedding, inviting them to the gathering by means of paying for them to have their hair cut and beards trimmed. He gathered them around a party table and, after they had enjoyed themselves, would lead them to his home as a group, singing and dancing through the streets.

They would partake of the evening meal in the house, after which a table full of small dishes would be set before them, accompanied by wine. The groom, thus having secured the opportunity to provide his friends with comfort and pleasure would, with a friend, leave the house with a basket full of lemons with a few oranges mixed in with them. These were distributed to important friends, the notables of the village and the priests. He would enter each house and say, 'You are invited to the wedding,' (*harsnik hrammetsek*) giving the household a lemon as an invitation.

When the visits to the list of guests was completed he and his friend would, finally, go to his future mother-in-law's house, kiss the bride's father's and mother's hands, and give them the same invitation, as well as an orange and a lemon.

The bride's mother would then invite the two young men into a special room, complimenting them and laying out snacks, chicken and wine for them. The would drink several glasses of wine and, when it was time to leave, would often join the bride and her friends' dances, distributing sweets to all of them, creating great excitement in the house, with the dances gradually becoming more lively and vigorous, and the songs more harmonious and sonorous. The bridegroom and his friend would spend a short time enjoying themselves like this with the girls then, saying goodbye, swiftly leave to go home to rejoin the groom's friends there with the desire to stress their enjoyment and animation and to keep the wedding house prosperous *(shen bahel)*.

Saturday night ended with the commencement of these wedding festivities, when the groom's friends, well after midnight, gradually departed and returned to their homes to rest.

At dawn on Sunday everyone, as usual, would go to church. When Mass ended, the groom would once more assemble his friends in a coffee house and, starting from there, they would go to the godfather's house, to officially have him join their group. The groom and his group of friends would be complimented and entertained outside the godfather's house, usually with oghi and wine accompanied by small dishes, served by one of the family's boys. The godfather would then join them, taking his place with the groom. The group would then go the bride's house, to officially invite the bride's brother. There too they would be entertained in the same way. The bride's brother would then join the group which would, its mission accomplished, return to the groom's house. There they would eat a meal and prepare for the blessing of both the dowry and the groom's clothing *(halav)* that would take place that afternoon in the house.

Well-known village people of some status would be specially invited on this occasion to be present at the blessing, and who would gradually arrive. A procession would be formed outside the bride's house made up of women and girls, who would bring the bride's dowry to the groom's house; the priests, accompanied by the church choir and musicians-teachers would arrive too, with a package of religious vestments and crosses.

When everything was ready, the priests and choristers would robe themselves and both *halavs* would be brought and put on a table in front of the priests. After they were blessed, the leading priest would suggest that a collection should be made among the groom's friends (called *yughakin* – oil price) for the church, which would be handed to the priests.

The blessing of the dowry and clothes would take place with the greatest solemnity. The bride's dowry would be returned to the women, who would take it back, in the same procession, to the bride's home, while the groom's friends would take his, except for his hat, which would remain on the table, and lead him to a separate room, to dress him in the clothing that had been blessed. They would then lead him back to the priests and guests. There the groom's father would receive, from the priest, his son's blessed and sanctified hat, approach his son and put it on his head, kissing him on the forehead. The son would kiss his father's hand. Then congratulations would begin to be expressed. The groom would then kiss the hands of all those present and receive their heartfelt congratulations.

After the ceremonies and congratulations ended, a rich table would be laid for the priests and guests with hospitality being provided by the groom and his friends. As it grew dark in the evening, the guests would gradually leave, and the house would be left to those of the family who had been invited.

No one slept on the Sunday night. It is a night of vigil. The evening meal would be eaten and then everyone gathered, separated according to age, around the tables filled with snacks – the young people, the older generation and women all separate - with dancing and singing continuing until dawn.

At this point – very early on Monday morning - the festivities would cease and everyone would begin preparations for 'getting the bride' from her family home. A huge procession would be formed led by little boys and girls carrying lighted candles, followed by the groom and his friends, then the mature men and women, all of them holding lighted candles. The bridegroom's house would empty, with only a few women left behind to look after and clean it, ready for officially welcoming the bride and groom.

The procession would walk slowly, the streets filling with the sounds of songs and lit by the candle flames. The shutters of the neighbouring houses would be noisily thrown open and people, awakened by the noise and only just out of bed, sleep-tousled, would look out of the windows to watch the procession going by. It would finally arrive at the bride's home and break up inside its walls, filling the entire house. The people crammed inside would stir and draw breath and the house would be transformed from an insignificant building into a village palace filled with the light of the candles, with the sunrise gradually lighting up the house, street and the nearby buildings. The bride's friends, meanwhile, would dance with greater verve and enthusiasm. The crowd, now increased by the new arrivals, would be even happier.

The house would finally calm down and become peaceful. The in-laws would be busy veiling the bride, accompanied by songs and sad farewells. The beadle *(jamgoch)*, at this moment, would shout his cries in the gloom, seemingly making them even louder, with his staff striking the ground and making the stones lament. He would approach the bride's house, before the door of which his deep, loud cries would fly through the air in waves once more, upwards, with the strength of a link binding the heavens and the earth together. Shortly after this the tolling of the church bell would be heard over the village houses, like a song from heaven reaching the earth.

Everyone then readied to go to the church. The procession would re-form, its ranks now swollen by the coming together of the members of the two families along the street, accompanied by lights and songs. It would then move forward, with slow, measured tread, with the bride and groom in the centre, with the 'bride's sisters' *(harsin kourere)* leading her to the ceremony of Holy Matrimony.[*] The bride-to-be and her future husband would have already, in the previous week, taken Holy Communion.

The procession would disperse in the large church. The bride and groom, with the godfather, would be led to the nave, and the families would take their places in the apses.

Mass would have already begun; the bride and groom would be led to the chancel, in front of the raised altar, and the nuptial crowns placed on their heads, with the offering of prayers, readings, hymns and rites. The church had joined them together, and nothing could separate them.[†]

---

[*] It should be borne in mind that there might be up to fifty couples in the church who were to be married at the same time during the service, thus there would be a similar scene at the same number of houses!

[†] The godfather held a cross over the couple's heads during the wedding ceremony. When the number of couples being married was more than the number of crosses available, the prayerbook called *Mashdots* would be held instead, provided it had a cross on its cover.

At the end of the Mass, the newly-married couple led by the priests and accompanied by the choir and the families, singing *sharagans* [canticles], would go in procession to the groom's house.* On their way they would be bombarded by handfuls of wheat thrown from the windows – the blessing of bread – on their heads, and, from the windows of the groom's house, a shower of small coins – the blessing of an honourable living – thus creating much excitement among the young boys in the procession, who would scrabble about to collect them.

A sacrificial animal would often be slaughtered on the doorstep, under the feet of the bride and groom, to protect the newly-married couple from the troubles of the world. The bride would be escorted to the bridal chamber, under the protection of the girl called the 'bride's sister'† who was her family's representative, and who would hand her over to her new home.

Congratulatory visits by friends and acquaintances would begin, being received by the new husband's parents. An hour or two later the ceremony of removing the crowns would be carried out by the priests. They would bless the wine as the symbol of Christ's blood, and the newly-married couple, the godfather and everyone in the house would put it to their lips. Their gifts for the priest performing the blessing, as was his right, were put on a plate. The house would regain its tranquillity after a

---

* Boghosian tells us that the sharagan that was sung was *Aravod louso* [The morning light]. Haroutiun Boghosian, *Anzoukagan Bardizag,* Elegian Press, Paris, 1967, p. 12.

Boghosian has an anecdote about one such wedding procession he was in before 1908 that showed the people's spirit...
> 'I was in the wedding procession and, when we reached the *ghonakh* (the government building), the older men stopped the band from playing. They then began to sing, at the tops of their voices, in chorus, "*Azadn Asdvadz ayn orits yerp hadjetsav shounch pchel...*" [From the day free God was pleased to blow life...] and the entire procession joined in.
> Naturally there were severe punishments imposed by the Abdul Hamid government for any demonstrations of Armenian patriotism at that time. Knowing this the men, who were generally armed with pistols on such an occasion as this, were ready to defend themselves if the police intervened. Instead of intervening, however, the government officials who were in the building extinguished the few lights they had lit, deciding that it was more sensible to keep a low profile.

This is, of course, a famous early Armenian patriotic song titled 'Song of Freedom' written by Mikayel Nalbandian (1829-1866)! Haroutiun Boghosian, *ibid*, 1967, pp. 13-14.

Finally, with a number of couples being married at the same time, each would have to wait their turn. It is said that in years when there were a great many marriages, these processions took from early morning until midday to be completed.

† Today she would be called the 'maid of honour'.

time, with everyone leaving to get some rest; only the family, the newly-married couple and the 'bride's sister' remained in the house.*

On the Monday evening the celebrations would be continued by the groom and his friends and near relations, although in a less boisterous way because of everyone's tiredness. The party would end early so people could get some rest.

The house would be quiet on the Tuesday. The groom and his close friends, whose numbers would have lessened considerably, would go for a stroll to the village's parks and places of amusement to pass the time but, after the evening church service, the original large group would make its way to the bride's mother's house, to cheer it up as it was now lonely without its daughter. The groom's group would eat there that evening and, after the meal, gather around a table laden with small dishes, holding a party for a few hours. At about 8 or 9 in the evening the group, carrying lights and singing, would leads the in-laws and their close relations in procession to the groom's house for an exchange visit to their daughter's (the bride's) new home.

That evening would cement the new relationship between the two families, the groom's friends having provided that opportunity and then departed. First the two sets of in-laws would eat together and then gather around a table of snacks, spending some of the sweetest hours of the entire wedding together, when it seemed that the little ones would be grown up, the old got younger, and all the mature people celebrated the joining of the two houses. The in-laws – mothers and fathers, with their newly-married children – would dance sweet dances, holding hands, singing simple village songs, making the entire house shake with their jumping, measured dance steps.

They would only separate in the early hours of the morning, recording sweet memories in the book of their poor lives.

On the Wednesday evening, after sunset, the 'bride's sister' would finally hand the bride, her family's daughter, over to her new masters, the groom's family, as an important and sweet new member of it. Up until this point the bride was still part of her own family, receiving her daily meals, which she shared with her 'sister', from her parents' home. The 'bride's sister' would finally depart, as her delicate and responsible task had been completed.

Meanwhile, the groom and his friends would be entertained in the godfather's house, where they would eat and enjoy themselves for a long time, joking, singing and dancing until, very late, they escorted the groom back to his home.

---

* The 'bride's sister' not only had to look after her and hand her over to her new home, but acted as her chaperone until the wedding night, which was on the Wednesday after the wedding ceremony.

The Wednesday night was the wedding night, when as the Bible says, 'they would know each other' and become husband and wife, by the will of God.

On Thursday morning family members, neighbours and in-laws would congratulate one another, with everyone having smiles on their faces. That was the day when *khash** was prepared, to be eaten with great appetite and enjoyed by all.

The new husband's friends would visit him at his home on the Sunday, where they would have the opportunity to see the newly-married couple, with the honour of spending a few hours enjoying themselves with them and giving the couple gifts of sums of money for their new home. In addition, friends of the husband's family, neighbours and relatives would also arrive in the evening to congratulate them, bringing gifts too.

This long wedding celebration would finally officially end with the bride's dowry chest being opened in the presence of the two sets of in-laws and their female friends and the contents displayed. It would be sent from the bride's mother's house to that of the groom during the week following the wedding and placed in the bride's room. Several weeks later her mother, with her relatives, would visit their new in-laws in the girl's new home and both sets of women, other newly married women and mature girls would open it, show off its contents and officially hand it over.

Certain customs often appeared during these celebrations that were comic or laughable, leftovers from the customs of the old days.

There was, for example, the custom of stealing the bride from the groom's house. The 'bride's sister' would be kept occupied or diverted to relax her guard on the bride, and as soon as the opportunity presented itself the bride would be gently removed from her presence and hidden in an obscure corner of the house. The 'bride's sister' would be surprised when she found the bride missing, while the 'thieves' would then jeer at her for not carrying out her responsibilities properly. In her confusion she would 'break into forty pieces', begging and pleading for them to restore the bride, promising to give them any gift they wanted for her. Sometimes they replaced the bride with someone else (often a young man) who had previously dressed like one. Those present, who knew what was going on, would laugh loudly among themselves at the bride and her 'sister', who would be surprised at this display of hilarity, while the bride herself was nearby and safe. After some time, during which they would confuse and annoy the 'bride's sister', someone would approach the fake bride and lift the veil covering his face showing the person's beard and moustache. The 'sister', faced with reality, often could not restrain her laughter until such time as, under strict circumstances, she was able to find the real bride.

Another custom was the game of examining the bride. They would give the groom's little brother a slipper, seat the bride next to him and the examination

---

* *Khash* is made from sheep's stomachs, which are cleaned, boiled and dressed with spices and garlic. (Author's note)

would commence. The little boy, under orders, would ask her, 'If my feet are dirty, will you wash them? If I have a hole in my sock, will you darn it? If my trousers tear, will you repair them?' and other such questions, striking her back gently with the slipper after each one and awaiting an answer. The bride of course had no option other than to agree, so she would lower her head at each question, replying, 'Yes'.

The bride had no right to speak or make a noise for a long time, and would even have to cover her face, as the rules of modesty so demanded. She would have to speak through an interpreter during the first days, normally the little children of the house playing that role. In my day this rule had lost its strictness, and the bride would begin to speak to her mother-in-law, sisters-in-law, and little brothers-in-law within a week, when she had become part of the household by kissing their hands. She would, however, retain her silence for a time in front of her father-in-law and elder brothers-in-law until such time as she produced one or more children and had been given permission to speak. Many of these customs had ended in my day, but in general the picture was the same.

The number of marriages in Bardizag during the 11 years from 1899 to 1909, according to Minas Kasabian's (also known as Farhad) statistics, was 570 which, based on the population of the village, gave a 6.9% rate. That of the Armenian villages in the province was less than this, while that of Arslanbeg was 10.13%.[*]

This low marriage rate in Bardizag may be explained by the poverty of the community and its difficult economic circumstances. This was especially true for the young people of the village who, needing to form families, were deterred by the 'ennoblement' of taste and exacting demands when, as a result of this mentality, the costs of getting married had greatly increased. It was a known social fact that the number of marriages declined in proportion to the development of civilisation and its demands.

C. Death[†]

In the section devoted to health[‡] I showed how, due to an erroneous understanding of the feelings of love and care, a sick person's room was usually filled with women who had come to see him or her. When the sick person, having exhausted every medicine and remedy became dangerously ill, and the final death agony began, the crowd of women grew, with the room filling up completely, the crowd even extending outside it.

The priest would give the dying person Holy Communion, so he or she would not die without the final sacrament, something that would create a crisis of conscience for everyone.

---

[*] See Appendix, Table 1 below.
[†] The original title of this sub-section was 'Customs to do with death' *(Merelagan sovoroutiunner)*.
[‡] See Section 154, sub-section 2 (above).

Those present would want to hear the dying person's last words and will, as a sacred legacy at that dreadful time, if he or she could only speak in the throes of death. When the dying person relapsed into unconsciousness, his or her loved ones surrounding the bed would begin to express sorrow, shaking their heads, with confused and pale looks and tears, sighs and sobs, silently saying *akh, vakh* [oh dear, alas], until he or she gave their final breath. Then all their repressed sorrow would burst forth...

The women of the neighbourhood would hasten to close the deceased's eyes, mouth and lips, to give it grace and final respect before the body was cold. The keening women* would begin the sorrowing and praise for the departed, with all those present accompanying them with streaming eyes and expressions of deep emotion. All the neighbours, wearing black cloths on their heads - and even passers-by - would go into the room where the body lay, with their own words of sympathy and sorrow. Every time a new face appeared at the door, a cry of sorrow would be heard. There would be new paroxysms of grief by members of the family. They displayed great sorrow near the body of the dear departed, as if they had lost their minds, tearing their hair out, having seizures of grief, beating their knees and making the worst stupid movements and expressions: shouting, calling, shrieking and crying.

The body would be washed and prepared for burial shortly afterwards. A fresh, clean bed would be prepared and the body dressed in clean underclothes and his or her best clothes. The body would then be surrounded with flowers. The sorrowing and crying would continue, ceasing occasionally to calm people's raw nerves.

Women and girls - and men too - formed into groups in the street outside the house as if bereft of the will to live, saddened and emotional. They would talk about the person who died, recalling events from his or her life.

The body would be kept in the house for at least one night, or at least for 24 hours in accordance with custom.

The priest and choir would finally arrive, the family bier would be prepared, the body would be placed in the coffin, and young men would come to carry it down. The sorrowing women's emotions would reach extreme proportions at this moment of final parting, with them not wanting to part with the body. They would cling to the coffin to prevent its departure, and it would only be possible to lift it and take it down to the door of the house with great difficulty. It would be followed by the deceased person's nearest and dearest as far as the street, with them in their dishevelled state crying and shrieking, making all those present very emotional.

Women, in Bardizag, never took part in funeral processions, although apparently they did in the old days. The coffin would move off to the

---

* These were women who were brought in for the purpose – professional mourners. They were called *yegheramayr*.

accompaniment of the singing of requiem *sharagans* mixing with the sounds of sorrowing women at the door and hanging out of the upper windows looking on to the street.

After the procession had gone, songs of praise for the departed continued for a time in the house, followed by numbness and fatigue, creating calm in everyone, with sad expressions on everyone's faces and their heads bowed.

After the burial service in the church, the procession would go to the cemetery, led by a cross and candles, and accompanied by *sharagans*. There would be a short requiem service near the old cemetery and some of the mourners would leave the procession, with the satisfaction of knowing that they had paid their last respects to the dead person. The majority, with the priest, continued their procession as far as the New Cemetery. The singing stopped on the way, but when the procession reached the cemetery gates, they started once more. There, in the entrance, the main part of the interment service would take place, under an awning. The coffin would then be lowered into the grave and it would be filled in. The priest would pray over the new grave and a stone would be placed at its head. With all the ceremonies now over, the priest and his entourage would approach the group of mourners who would kiss the holy missal in his hand. Every mourner would kiss it in turn and, passing in front of the others, would say, 'May you be comforted by the Holy Spirit.'

Slices of bread, cheese, some olives and sweetmeats would be placed near the cemetery entrance and, nearby, there would be a young boy carrying a bottle of oghi. This was the *hokehats* [bread of the spirit]. All those present would drink a glass of oghi and eat a piece of bread etc. and then return to the village.

The New Cemetery was some distance – more than a quarter of an hour's walk - from the village. A hearse was never used and it was regarded as a sacred and inevitable duty for each mourner accompanying the coffin to take his turn to help to carry it, with each vying with the others for the privilege of doing so.

Finally, as all the mourners left, taking the road to the village, they would be led by the priest, who would be the first to enter the deceased's house. The priest would perform another small act of worship and give words of comfort and sympathy to the crowd of women assembled there. A table would then be laid, served by the neighbourhood women, and everyone would eat something to renew their energy.

The bereaved would receive visits of condolence and sympathy throughout each day, for a week or two after this. The visitors would be concerned not to leave them alone in their grief. Neighbours, acquaintances, relatives and mourners would surround them with friendly feelings of heartfelt sympathy. These visits brought out very tactful attitudes towards the bereaved family. The visitors were careful not to speak of the deceased person in the family's presence. If it really was necessary to do so, it would be done very gently, so as not to reopen their wounds and sorrow. In fact many other subjects were talked about – work, the season, human experiences

– as if to help to heal their shattered nerves and lift their spirits, and to help in the knowledge of their inevitable retun to life.

The departed were never, of course, forgotten, but their memory, cleaned of the hurt of their tragic death, remained in the depths of their spirits. The women, after that, on the 40th day after the death and requiem days, used to visit the departed's grave, planting a bush or tree to cast shade on it. Wealthy people, apart from that, would decorate the grave with a tombstone, as a permanent protection against the ravages of time. From time to time prayers would be said, with a requiem service conducted in the deceased's memory.*

5. Social life - leisure

The expressions of social life in Bardizag were gatherings of friends or relations in houses during the long winter nights. In the clement seasons, picnics were held by families and friends at cold springs or under the trees in the gardens or vineyards. Apart from these, there were gatherings, in the coffee houses that were within or outside the village, of mature and young men who were artisans or were earning good wages, both in the morning or the evening and especially on Sundays.

Gatherings in houses were reserved for the pleasures of talking and joking; these occasions were usually accompanied by meals and glasses of wine and oghi. The get-togethers usually began in a serious manner with conversation about this and that - about work, earnings, incidents from past and present life, and political and national events – with the addition of witticisms and jokes about this or that person. When stomachs had been satisfied and the assembled male members had become tipsy, singing and dancing would often begin inside the house or in the open. This happened especially when fresh young people gathered together, with jokes, wit and racy stories encouraging the onset of great hilarity among them.

Some individuals, who were naturally able to add spice to these gatherings, were sought everywhere, and who knew how to, had those surrounding them hang onto their every word. On many occasions, however, gatherings would be very restrained and serious in the houses, where the grace and allure of the novel, fairy tale or real stories would be sought, told or read by a talented or able local person.

Apart from these impromptu gatherings, there were also congratulatory visits on name and feast days, especially at New Year, Christmas and Easter in every house, when ordinary life would change and be replaced by celebrations. These congratulatory visits were opportunities for social conversation about everything and anything, accompanied by hospitality. They were the popular training schools where people listened and learnt to increase their stock of experiences.

---

* Kasabian provides the number of deaths, both male and female, each year from 1899 to 1909 – See Appendix, Table 1 below.

50 to 100 years ago* there were no coffee houses in the village, only one or two barbers' shops where mature men would go, once a week, to be shaved as well as having their hair, faces and necks washed with warm water. The men of the neighbourhood would gather at the edges of their blocks of houses, streets or in open spaces, often with elderly women joining them in those olden days. These social gatherings would take place in the sun in winter, so that the people could warm themselves, while in summer it would be in the shade to cool down. In any event the people would talk about their daily work and natural and climatic conditions.

In my day, when only traces of this primitive life remained, the number of coffee houses had increased enormously, as had the popularity of Turkish-style *odas* [rooms] where customers were not only shaved but could also enjoy a cup of coffee or oghi, creating opportunities for social gatherings.† Individual coffee houses were patronised by customers of particular ages, with some catering for young and others for mature men. Even in my day the generations didn't really mix.

There were one or two coffee houses in Bardizag that reminded one of the old barber shops - those of Berber Minas and Chakhr Hagop. Apart from these one may recollect those of the Kondaiyan, Djezels, Der-Garabedians, Khacherians, Kechedjis, Dzallans, Djouloum Artin, Taniel Agha Der-Sahagian, Gozgoz Garabed, Keghi, Tolalekh, Gabak and Boghos Kiutnerian. Some of these were in the names of those who rented them, who divided the mature clientele among themselves. There were other coffee houses that were more active in the summer months, when families would patronise them in the cool of the evening. These were Doudou Ghodjakhavouents, Upper fields, Upper Cemetery, Markenag Mgerdich's, and the 'Gardens', all of which were situated in areas around the village.

The Bardizag villager was used to going to bed early, especially during the winter when the family had no visitors, to economise on fuel for heating and candles for light. But the household elders – the mature men, mother, daughter and daughter-in-law - would get up early, before dawn, before the church bell pealed. The men would hurry to the market, while the women would be occupied with the thousand and one things they found had to be done in the house: bringing water from the fountains, baking bread or other household tasks, such as weaving darning, knitting etc.

The coffee houses would already be open in those early hours, when it wasn't possible to see one another in the dark and passers-by had to rely on their memories to find their way around the village. They were warmed by heaters or braziers, with customers arriving one after the other to take their places on the benches around the walls. Those who particularly felt the cold would sit on chairs nearer the heat source in the coffee house's warm, smoke-filled atmosphere. This was the ordinary man's time; the *aghas* and notables would arrive later, when some of the old customers had

---

* 1835-1885.
† See Section 154, (3), (D) above.

already left. A general conversation would begin while waiting for the dawn, dreams would be described, as would be any new thing that had happened in the village. Those skilled in the art of conversation would keep the company interested, broaching the oddest subjects, both old and new, until such time as everyone had his cigar in his mouth or was drawing on the mouthpiece of a hookah, drinking his hot coffee or tea at the same time.

Some coffee house keepers were famous as conversationalists and wits, and would charm their customers, pricking this or that person in the village with his smart jokes. The famous names from the days of my youth onwards were: Lop, Delo Krikor, Setrag, Shelem Serkis and Dzallan Hadji Mgerdich, who often turned their coffee houses into theatre auditoriums, where farce, satire, ridicule and jokes were all mixed together.

The customers, when the church bell finally pealed, would suddenly realise that God existed and detach themselves one by one from the crowd, to go and pray in church.[*] After church, be it in winter or summer, all the coffee houses would empty, with everyone going about their business: to their place of work, shop, garden or vineyard.

The coffee houses were never busy during the day, with only the idle rich, shopkeepers and *tadargabord* [literally empty-bellies, meaning rogues] as customers. These last would be busy morning and evening, those times being the best for their trade. When it grew light, the time was up and the shops would open from one end of the market area to the other, with people taking a short walk to see what baskets of fresh fish Blosh Bedo or others had in stock, what slaughtered goat's meat Dedo Khacher had, or what meat Kel Nigo had, to come to a decision as to what to buy for the day's meals.

The coffee houses served those without work, and shopkeepers, as places of relaxation where they could play cards, backgammon dominoes and dama during the day. They pulled others in who would watch the games with the greatest attention and partisanship for one or other of the players, giving them encouragement etc.

Love of reading didn't exist at first, but when I was a boy many had Protestant Armenian bibles[†] which they loved to read in their free time. Others glanced at newspapers or had them to read. The American missionaries, to provide a helpful, clean and pleasant pastime for the people, opened a reading-room–shop, at one time, using the Bedigs' premises in the market area of the main street, where those who wanted to read could find the Bible or sections of it, moral and religious *dedrags* [tracts], good, improving short stories and, finally, the Bible House journal *Avedaper*.

---

[*] Or, as is said in Bardizag dialect: *dzoung me* or *peran me aghotk me enel*: literally 'to make a knee or mouth of prayer.'

[†] These were published in modern (western Armenian) by the Protestant missionary organisations.

The coffee houses also fulfilled the role of writing rooms for their customers, where arrangements were made concerning work, earnings and trading. Haggling took place over hiring labour as well as negotiations and agreements between landowners and farmworkers, wealthy people and those from the mountains and various business partners. The amortisation of loans between creditors and those who owed them money also took place.

Some of the coffee houses, later on, became taverns where customers, group by group, would assemble around tables and would drink alcohol accompanied by pickles. This was the natural result of the gradual demise of viticulture, with many houses no longer being able to produce their own oghi or store of wine. This lack was filled by the coffee houses turned taverns.

There were certain classes of people whose social position didn't allow them to mix with the customers of the coffee houses. These were the priests, teachers, notables and aghas and the representatives of the great houses. However, the need for them to talk to one another brought them together in certain shops or outside them, seated on stools. This was especially true of Aghasi Effendi Papazian's pharmacy, which was the meeting place for the doctors, teachers and those who were considered to be educated, and who were involved in more serious conversations.

The women too had their social meeting places. In summer, when their housework had been completed, they would come into the street in front of their houses in neighbourhood groups, needing to talk. In winter they would take whatever they were making in the form of socks, sewing or a lace border and get together in someone's house. Another opportunity to talk presented itself at the fountains when they waited their turn, each holding their clay pitcher. They would squat next to their friends giving themselves up to *sweet (anoush)* conversations, often forgetting and losing their turn to get water.

These womens' meetings in the streets were quite usual, especially on a Sunday, when working with one's hands was forbidden, as there was concern that Sunday should be kept holy. After the main meal had been eaten in the morning and the men and children left the house and dispersed, the women of the house, each taking a hassock or cushion, would approach the group of women that was forming, put what she was going to sit on on the ground and take her place in the group, which gradually grew larger. Anyone who took a walk through the village on a Sunday at that particular time of the afternoon would have the opportunity to see groups of women ranged along the sides of the streets, deep in enjoyable conversation with each other.

There was no lack of subjects for the women to talk about: anything and everything, as well as every meeting of one with another, all of which provided ample subjects in their social circle. Cloth made in the home, their stores for the winter, materials for clothing, each other's dresses, the children of the household, the sick, health, the dead, engagements, weddings, baptisms, silkworms, cocoons, and everything else one could think of could be mentioned or discussed in detail as if to make the effort to see and make them the subjects for discussion or conversation.

There were often disagreements, arguments and fights between neighbouring women for even the most trivial reasons which, with their expressions, would be scandalous and improper and which would be followed by the protagonists mutually ignoring one another for long periods, until time brought them together again – with everything forgotten - and all wounds healed.

I previously mentioned the lack of reading among the villagers, but there were people who did read. Such people were the priests, who utilised the contents of the church library (or repository),* mainly reading religious or historic works. They would find old books or tracts† in the houses they visited, which they would borrow and read. Towards the end, bibles in modern (western) Armenian could be found in houses, often accompanied by a Nareg,‡ the Book of Psalms, *Bghntse Kaghak* [Copper City] and *Yerazahan* [Interpretation of dreams], translations taken from classical authors, all read by chosen readers and listened to with great interest.

Later still, newspapers from Constantinople began to appear in the village: Utudjian's *Masis,* Aladjadjian's *Pounch,* Panosian's *Manzoume* and Djivelegian's *Djeriden,* which would be brought by chance, as containing interesting news, by people returning to Bardizag.** Newspapers excited great interest in the village, especially among the great number of illiterate people. They would gather round the newspaper reader to hear of the events in Constantinople, be they political or national, with great interest. Smiles would appear on their faces listening to the pictures of ordinary life described in their pages.

The re-establishment of the Ottoman Constitution in 1908 brought both *Azadamard*†† and *Piuzantion*‡‡ to Bardizag, newspapers that were opposed to each other. The number of people reading them had now increased as the generation that had gone to school had greatly increased in numbers. Thus quite a few copies of each were sold by individuals in the village. Subscribing to newspapers had not yet become a

---

* The word used here is *madenataran.*

† The word used here, *dedrag,* could mean notebook, tract, paper-bound book, pamphlet, copybook, tablet or stitched book.

‡ The book of religious poetry (considered to be a prayer book with healing prayers in it) written by St. Gregory of Nareg, and which is a masterpiece of Armenian religious and spiritual writing.

** Der-Hagopian gives examples of articles referring to Bardizag taken from Constantinople newspapers, quoting *Hairenik,* (1892-1895), *Manzoume* (1902), *Piuzantion* (1906) and *Masis* (1854-1856). He quotes many others throughout his book. See Hagop Der-Hagopian, *Bardizage khadoudig,* Paris 1960. Pp. 64-74 etc.

†† The Armenian Revolutionary Federation (ARF) newspaper.

‡‡ A moderate Armenian newspaper. See Main Editorial Board, Armenian Encyclopaedia, *Encyclopaedia of the Armenian Question,* Yerevan, 1996, p. 86.

habit in Bardizag and people objected to paying in advance for them. The newspaper could suddenly be closed down, and their editors didn't have the habit of returning the subscriptions they had received. There were a large number of people who read them without buying them too. A newspaper was a commodity that the consumer could utilise and enjoy in one fell swoop, but it was never used up; another person could do the same. Thus a newspaper would pass from hand to hand for days on end, gradually deteriorating on its long journey, eventually displaying the total exhaustion of the paper it was made from and looking like strips or rags. It then needed each piece to be laid next to the other to be read. These attempts, however, encouraged reading among the many becoming, inevitably, a necessity in many hands, eventually resulting in people having to pay for what they needed.

It would, of course, be interesting to have an idea of what the children's, girls' and older boys' social life and play was like, as they didn't go into coffee houses or become part of street gatherings. Their social life was in the games they played and their wanderings in the streets and open spaces in good weather. When I was young, adolescent boys, who didn't enter coffee houses, and adolescent girls, who hadn't the courage or the effrontery to mix with the groups of mothers and younger married women, spent their time in the open areas around the village on Sundays, such as the threshing floors, Upper Fields, Avazoud and the cemeteries, devoting their free time to invigorating games and morally innocent pastimes. The boys would play *chelig chboukh, esir, binder bire, yergan esh,* have running and jumping competitions, the string game,* *vras ar giuleshe,* and so on, creating enthusiasm around them and drawing great crowds of onlookers. The girls would play *gap* [jacks or five-stones] sitting down, and *madzoun madzoun* [yogurt, yogurt], *dzar dzar* [tree, tree] *achkgabouk* [blind-man's-bluff], dance and play ball games on their feet and so on. The boys and girls always played separately and at a distance from each other. Kites would be flown when the winds blew in autumn, and when the snow fell, they would enjoy themselves by making snowballs, sledging and making snowmen. These games, in the end, became the preserve of the little boys and girls. The older ones considered them to be beneath them, only fit for small children. Schoolboys, after the day's schooling had ended, would throw their books and school things into a corner of the house and rush out to play, with their faces reddening and sweat covering their entire bodies through their enthusiasm. They argued, shouted, rushed and jumped about, living the best time of their lives.†

---

* Possibly skipping.
† Der Hagopian has an article in three parts in his book which was written by Bared Elegian, titled *Bardizagi ladjere* [The young boys of Bardizag], which gives a marvellous description of the things the young boys got up to in the village and the raids they made on Yenikeoy village. See Hagop Der-Hagopian, *Bardizage khadoudig*, pp. 260-272.

The boys, once again, would boldly and fearlessly wander about in the surrounding unpopulated areas and woods, busy with gathering wild fruit, stripping blackberry bushes that were loaded with berries, collecting medlars from wild trees, grapes from wild vines *(djiveg)*, apples, pears, quinces, strawberries *(chileg)*, wild plums *(mamoukh)* and *glglag*, the reddish fruit of a climbing plant that was made into necklaces and crowns by stringing them onto various kinds of grass stalks.

They would, occasionally, in their youthful innocence climb over the walls of someone's garden and steal the unripe fruit from the trees in it, while the flowers were still attached.

During the winter the little ones would organise games in the house, such as *gap, balek kachdi, ktana* and others like them, which they could play without causing problems in the home. The girls too had their own games played in the house, such as *khnam khnam*, as well as dramas taken from family life and acted out in their innocent way.

I can recall other good pastimes, such as bird and rabbit hunting (although this was done by a minority) and fishing in the rivers and the sea.

Flocks of birds would fly to Bardizag in summer, whose meat was good to eat such as partidge, quail, cuckoo etc.. In winter wild duck was hunted on the sea or at the edges of the rivers, as well as wild geese occasionally. Crustaceans such as crabs, crayfish, *shifata, chakhle gotig,* mussels, *darakh* etc. would be caught under water. Again, in the cool of our forests, trout would be fished for along the edge of the Ovadjek River, and crayfish would be sought by turning stones over on the bottom of the river. In autumn snails would be sought in the clumps of grass or bushes which, skewered and prepared in various ways, would provide delicious meals.

The hunting of large animals had ceased when I was a boy, as the Muslim and Laz Armenian refugees that had settled around us had cleared the forests of any game. Famous hunters were still remembered in my day that, in the idle days of winter, would ascend the mountains to hunt for bear, wolf, fox, wild boar, deer, mountain goat etc. Some I can recall from my youth were Gregh, Seghpos and Palabeyekh. There were others. In my day the famous bird and rabbit hunter was Gel Gel Nshan, who could bring down a bird in flight. Both Sinan and Zakar Kevork were famous fisherman.

6. Public life

I have had the opportunity in the course of this work to mention the notable personalities of the village authority [*Azkayin ishkhanoutiun*] and in the village itself. My task, in this sub-section, is to provide a picture of Bardizag's public life.

Community rule everywhere among us, in the beginning, was of a feudal nature. Among Armenians, public affairs were organised and run by the priests and patriarchs of the great houses. Later, and in my day, that work was carried out by the elected parish council having, as its chairman, the highest-ranking kahana *(avakerets),* with the title of Locum Tenens.* The rights of this community authority included:

> Church and educational work
>
> The election or appointment of kahanas, teachers, school trustees, seat holders or mukhtars, church or poor treasurer and leader [reyis]
>
> Public building construction or repair of the church, schools, poor house, roads, fountains and bath house
>
> Collection of government taxes and their remittance
>
> Land border problems (both public and private)
>
> Protection of public property
>
> Forestry
>
> Aid to the poor and orphans
>
> Marriage disputes and court cases
>
> Settlement of matters concerning inheritance.

It was a kind of internal government conducted, in the old days, with great independence. In my day Bardizag became the centre of a group of villages *(nahie)* and government intervention became noticeable in public matters, thanks to which a number of matters that were, in the past, dealt with by the village authority were now dealt with by the government itself.

In the beginning the community authority didn't keep any written records. The notables would come together and form a consensus about any particular question and that decision would be acted upon. There are no papers existing from those days, but there were some in the church's office. Various other papers (promissory notes, memoranda, contracts, accounts and diaries detailing various events) were held by individuals in their houses. Apart from these, notes would often be found in the margins of books and manuscripts, which were utilised by Garabed Kahana Mkhalian when he wrote his history.

History, however, was mainly transmitted by word of mouth from father to son that, over time, erased or altered many memories, which became legends or stories.

After the establishment of the National Constitution† in 1862, however, along with other written records that were begun slightly earlier, statements of income and expenditure, accounts for public works, copies of government statistics, records of decisions made in meetings, regular records of births, marriages and deaths, government and community tax returns, official papers and letters and statements

---

* The term in Armenian is *arachnortagan pokhanort* meaning diocesan bishop's (local) representative.

† The author is referring to the constitution approved by the sultan for the internal governance of the Armenian community (it was not yet considered to be a nation) by the Armenian Patriarchate.

of arrangements made concerning inheritance existed and were kept. They were all destroyed in the storm of deportation in 1915.

It would have been possible, if those files of documents existed today,[*] to recreate the history of Bardizag, and especially of the final period in a much more detailed and lively way, while I have been forced to use facts presented by general eyewitness recollections that aren't necessarily reliable.

At the beginning of the division of the village into parishes[†] as a result of the implementation of the National Constitution, the official written records were mainly created by the priests, leaving the recording and accounts of public works to the officials appointed to oversee them, the government tax collectors, *mukhtars*, church officials and the school and poor relief treasurers. In my day the parish council had its own paid secretary who created and looked after the records and account books. Of those secretaries I can recall Diratsou Hovhannes Aprahamian (later Sahag Kahana Aprahamian) and Hovhannes Djergayian (Azkabedian), the latter being one of my school friends. He was succeeded by an assistant secretary who worked with the council secretary.

The parish council and the school trustees met once a week, on the Sunday when they had their regular meetings. They also occasionally convened extraordinary meetings if there was an important matter that required an immediate decision. The parish council's meeting venue was a room in the church[‡] while the school trustees held their meetings in the director's offices in the school itself.

The parish council, as the highest competent authority, was very busy and its meetings often lasted the whole of Sunday afternoon, until it got dark, as there were so many different questions put to it in a village with such a large population. I have to say that the council worked very diligently and with great patience and with justice. There were, of course, members of the council who abused their position, but the majority of the abuses were the work of officials, collectors, construction and repair overseers, mukhtars and treasurers who were little different from similar government officials.

Among the things that most occupied the parish council, even more than community questions, were complicated family and personal matters they tackled with the aim of securing peace, justice and right in the arguments between the citizens of the village. There was also the care of orphans; solving problems concerning

---

[*] The author wrote this prior to 1937.
[†] I believe the author is talking about the *original* division, i.e. the village being divided by religion, with a Protestant, Catholic and Armenian parish. Much later the government divided the village into 6 parishes: Church Parish *(kilise mahlesi)*, Valley Parish *(dere mahlesi)*, Avazoud Parish *(kumluk mahlesi)*, New-Upper Fields Parish *(yeni mhalesi)*, Protestant Parish and Catholic Parish. See Hagop Der-Hagopian, *Bardizage khadoudig*, p. 32.
[‡] Known as *jamoun odan*.

inheritance on the basis of government law; peacefully solving marital problems; protection of community morals or ethics and of the weak; and the levying of military service exemption tax on each household, with the rich giving the most and the poor either being freed from paying it or paying only a proportion of it.

There were times when the parish council found it necessary to occupy itself with general economic questions. Thus, when the shortage of small denomination currency was creating problems for the church and the market, it decided that it would create low value paper money tokens, guaranteed by the community treasury and under its authority, for circulation and use in the church. So it had small paper tokens printed, each worth 10, 20 or 40 *paras*, and authorised with the parish council's seal stamped on them, and put into circulation. They were also used in the market for ordinary purchases and transactions.

These paper tokens were sold to particular people under the community treasury guarantee, and distributed among the people. They were used for a long time, not only in the village, but in Seymen and neighbouring villages. The government had no objection to the use of such tokens, as there was so much freedom in those days. This was before Bardizag had been re-organised as the head of a group of villages *(nahie)* and the Armenian Question didn't exist. After some time forgeries began to appear, so they were withdrawn by the parish council, ending their use.

The revenue shown in the income and expenditure accounts consisted of:

The weekly church offertory
The voluntary tax on the price of oil at Christmas and Easter
The collection made at cocoon harvest
Rents from community-owned property
Fees paid by school students
Profits made from community-owned boats
The community tax that was 15% of that paid to the government
Occasional community collections
Various other minor sources of revenue.

All of these added up to a significant sum, used to defray the costs of running the church and community school, repair or construction of community-owned property, expenses incurred by the parish council, school trustees and bodies that assisted them, the prelacy and partriarchate's *moukata* tax and sundry other expenses. This was a heavy and complex financial account that was balanced without much difficulty.

Community property was obtained by purchase and far-sighted initiatives made by the community authorities, gifts made by individuals, bequests or by the efforts of various associations.

The Bardizag community was thus the owner of many properties – houses, shops, coffee houses, bakeries, storehouses, official government buildings, fields and boats -

in the village, Seymen and Izmid. I have been unable to determine the revenue from the latter. The community owned the *ghonakh* [government building], *belediye* [town hall] and the *mizan* [Public Debt Administration office] in the village. Likewise it owned Seymen's *geomriuk* [customs house] and the harbour. The properties would be rented out by auction on a yearly basis to those who applied.

These explanations leave no doubts concerning community activities. The great interest taken and sacrifices made by the villager resulted in the *azkin doune* [community's house] with its properties, its own public buildings – church, schools etc. – being the most envied and well-to-do, especially with its solid, beautiful St. James cathedral, its enormous three-storey school and its separate kindergarten, all of which formed the most eye-catching and massive structures in the village.

The Bardizag villager, alert and sensible, extended his interest beyond his individual work to vigilance over the community authority's good and regular activities. The groupings in the coffee houses and groups of workers working together presented them with the opportunity to form public opinion which was respected by official authority – the priesthood, community authorities, school trustees, teachers etc. – who were always forced to take the people's thoughts and opinions, formed around their work, into account, the profitable flow of which was important in making their work easier and more helpful.*

The villager was used to paying his community taxes with good grace, most of which were voluntary, but he was equally demanding of the community authorities or of officialdom.

7. Religious and spiritual life

The people of Bardizag have always been deeply devout but not to the extent of being like Pharisees, who made hypocritical demonstrations of their faith. This devoutness showed itself in the critical zealousness they displayed towards church officials. For that reason it was the rule that the spiritual life and moral cleanliness of a kahana [married priest] or vartabed [celibate monk] had to be impeccable. Education and - more than this – his devoutness and honourable life and customs were sought after in a kahana. The history of the village shows that people were very strict with their priests, not hesitating to punish those who failed to do their duty or were unreliable.

---

* These opinions were often of a violent nature. Most of the community projects, be they the rebuilding of the church, the road to Seymen or the bathouse (to take three examples) or the ordination of priests, appointment or dismissal of teachers, were accompanied by vociferous opposition, even physical violence, with final decisions sometimes taking months to come to fruition. There are many examples quoted throughout this work.

It was natural that the Bardizag kahanas, as a result of the people's way of thinking, had to be exemplary in every way. The priest, in Bardizag, could not have anything to do with scandal or scandalous society. He had to be a patient, sober, abstemious person who always used good language. He could not enter coffee houses, and ordinary pastimes and places of recreation weren't for him. Temporal occupations and covetousness in him led to scandal. The priest was the dedicated official of the church and God and he had always to remain as such. His house had to be holy in its contents and his wife and children exemplary. The priests whose sons were of a prodigal nature or daughters that were less than modest would be vilified: 'he (or she) doesn't seem like a priest's child' sounded very bad in a Christian villager's ear.

People who had this mentality towards their priests, as faithful Christians, were also strict with themselves and never tolerated any form of scandal that could reflect on their personal honour or religious convictions.

The Bardizag villager was generally peaceable, clean living and church loving. Before Protestantism began among us, everyone rushed to church in the early morning and in the evening, to play his part in public worship.

It was usual, at home, to pray before going to bed and in the early morning as soon as one got up. People would often continue their prayers on the way to church, without taking any notice of other people going there too. People would be seated at the table and pray before the meal, and, when it had ended, would pray again. This was a habit bequeathed by our forefathers and was imperative and all-important. It must also be said, however, that secular education, after a time, greatly reduced this fervent and devout habit.

Again, not to go to church on a Sunday was considered to be a sin. The market was completely closed on that day and commerce stopped completely. Much later, when coffee house life began, although coffee houses were closed during the time of the Mass, they opened immediately after it as meeting places and for various pastimes.

People's conduct in church was very circumspect. Both men and women entered it barefoot, with clean feet, crossing themselves and praying as they did so. Talking to anyone in church was considered to be wrong and, if it really was necessary to address someone, they had to whisper in the person's ear, because every believer considered himself to be in the invisible presence of God, who was looking down at them – his children - from the altar and listening to their innocent and good prayers.

The faithful obeyed the church's commands with the greatest willingness. On festival days, especially at Christmas and Easter, great crowds of men, women and children would take Communion; doing anything else would have given the individual a crisis of conscience and he or she would be in receipt of public opprobrium, being considered as unreliable.

They remained faithful to holy matrimony: the wife obeyed her husband as her lord and respected him, while the husband loved and protected his wife. Divorce and dishonourable promiscuity were very rare occurrences, and would be subject to severe persecution. Arguments and misunderstandings between husband and wife did of course occur. There were some men who had the audacity to raise their hands and beat their wives while they were angry, but this sort of incident was rare, and the man who did so suffered public criticism and disgrace.

Fasting was obligatory; fast days during the week were faithfully observed,[*] as it was during Lent. At the beginning of Lent the *khoukhoulidj* or *khoukhoulin*[†] – an onion with seven feathers pushed into it – would be hung by a string from the ceiling above head height with everyone watching it, like the sword of Damocles, as if it was ready to release its feathers and put out the eyes of anyone who broke their fast.[‡]

On Paregentan Monday, food utensils would be covered in ashes and then washed, removing any oil or clarified butter from them. Animals were only slaughtered for their meat on a Saturday during the year, for the Sunday meal. It was often difficult to find meat on other days of the week in the market. It was the same during Lent and on fast days during any week. It was considered to be absolutely scandalous to see meat for sale on those days. This strict regime was somewhat relaxed some years after Protestantism took root among us, in parallel with the development of education, especially when Turkish government officials started living in Bardizag.

Preaching in church was not usual or necessary. The congregation only heard sermons when the diocesan bishop made a formal visit to the village once a year, or when a vartabed or a high ranking churchman happened to visit it. The longing for a sermon then ensured that the church would be absolutely full. Much later, however, in an attempt to offset Protestant influence, the priests, after the reading of the missal, would stand in the chancel, in front of the Mass book, and give carefully prepared admonitions and interpretations of the daily readings from the Bible to the people.

During Tourian's days, the sermon became obligatory and a fixed item in the Mass on Sundays and festival days, and the practice was continued after his departure by local preaching vartabeds. I can recall Anania Vartabed Hapelian and Garabed Vartabed Mazlemian among those that did so.

Regular visits were made by each parish priest to his parishoners' homes. They visited them not only on feast days to bless the homes or on the occasions of marriages, baptisms or deaths, but also at various other times out of interest for their well-being, concerns and pain, economic and family problems, as well as their neglect of their religious duties, and would comfort, advise and make suggestions.

---

[*] Usually Wednesday and Friday.
[†] The actual word used is unclear here.
[‡] It should be explained that this custom was universal among Armenians. Small children would be frightened into behaving themselves with the threat that it was watching them. But during each week of Lent a feather would be pulled out, and at the end of the fast period, the onion itself would be removed, much to everyone's relief.

The priest, again, as a referee, would intervene in domestic disputes, those between friends and neighbours and to provide spiritual help. They took the comfort of readings from the Gospels and other holy books to the sick and for the ears of the bereaved.

The devout feelings of the faithful were reflected in the sacrifices they made for the church and its spiritual officials. There were separate collection plates for the poor and for the church itself on either side of the entrance to the narthex. On silent days[*] the believer would throw his 10-note[†] into them on his way into church, and on Sundays the plates would be circulated among the congregation in the church, the majority paying their dues both to the church and for the poor. Later two more plates were added: one for the school and one for the Holy Redeemer Hospital.[‡] On two occasions in the year – Christmas and Easter – an 'oil-cost' collection would be made among the faithful, with everyone or a representative of every family participating, giving a sum of 2, 3, 4, 5, or 10 *paras*.[**] The sale of candles on one occasion during the year, and collections for 'oil costs' for weddings and blessing of the dowry *(halav)*, were important sources of revenue set aside to cover church needs.

The people paid the priests' fees on various occasions to provide them with an income. Offertories, weddings, baptisms, funerals, house blessings and requiems all had their costs. The priests in Bardizag lived honourably. Their status was slightly above middle class, without any real difficulties. The priesthood was considered to be an honourable profession among us, both in terms of position and income. This meant that when candidates for the priesthood were elected there was great competition and arguments within the community.[††]

It was an important obligation for the faithful to visit the Holy Places, especially those of Jerusalem[‡‡] and occasionally of Holy Echmiadzin.[***] From very early on in the village's history representatives of the great houses were *hadjis*,[†††] in other words had visited the Holy Places associated with Christ. When the father of a family raised his children and had settled them, then he and his wife, and

---

[*] Weekdays, when Mass wasn't said and there was only a morning and evening act of worship.

[†] The word used here is *dasnots*, which was probably 10 *paras*, but the currency denomination is not stated.

[‡] *Sourp Prgich Hivantanots* – the Armenian-owned hospital in Constantinople.

[**] I have used the word *paras* here as the author uses *tahegan* i.e. the smallest denomination coins.

[††] See Section 141 for example.

[‡‡] The Armenian Patriarchate of the Two Jameses.

[***] The seat of the Supreme Patriarch and Catholicos of All Armenians in what was then Russian Armenia.

[†††] Those who went to Jerusalem adopted the title 'hadji', thus becoming, for example, Hadji Hovhannes (followed by his surname). If the entire family went together, then the title would be attached to their surname and used thereafter.

occasionally his children too, would go on a pilgrimage to Jerusalem. He had carried out his worldly responsibilities; now it was time to think of God and go on a pilgrimage to those sites that gave birth to the truth of his spiritual beliefs, wishing that as a true believer he should be prepared for heavenly life. This devout custom was much relaxed in my day both by the diminution of faith and the pressing economic situation.

A pilgrimage to Jerusalem was a religious act, and thus the object of certain religious ceremonies. Before they set out, the pilgrims would go to the church, pray, confess and take Holy Communion, and occasionally make gifts or wills to the church or community establishments. Then, following the priest and choir, they would visit the cemetery and have their dead blessed, then bid farewell to the village and their relatives.

The pilgrims, on their return, would be met at the entrance to the village by the priest and choir, who would lead them in procession to the church, then to their homes.

Apart from this great and worthwhile pilgrimage, the Bardizag villager was used to going on a pilgrimage every year to the Holy Mother of God church in Armash and to that of Manoushag in significant numbers, whose history we have read in previous pages.[*]

A beautiful custom among us was that the working day ended for those outside the village with the pealing of the church bell in the evening, as if that moment was reserved for the praise and worship of God.[†]

The gift of *madagh* [a sacrificial animal] was pleasing and regarded as a duty when an unexpected success occurred or a real difficulty was overcome, and was an expression of thanks to God by the believer. It also provided him with the satisfaction of knowing that he had provided bread and a meal for the poor. This provision of sacrifices was made by individuals and, occasionally, during feast days, as a community act in places of pilgrimage, when many animals were slaughtered and a great deal of food – cracked wheat *pilav* and boiled meat - having been blessed, was prepared and distributed to every poor person and to everyone else.

---

* See Section 40.

† There was another side to this. In the village itself, as Patriarch of Jerusalem Archbishop Torkom Koushagian, himself a native of the village tells us:
> ...But the most notable thing about this village was the liveliness of its life which filled me with spiritual satisfaction. After the pealing of the evening bell, when the men, women and children returned home from the vineyards, workshops and schools, the whole village would resound from one end to the other with the noise of the singing and shouting of the children and adults. Visitors in a glade in the Tzoug Forest or on St. Minas Hill, listening to it, were never able to understand what an expression of gaiety or joy this loud noise was.

Quoted by Hagop Der-Hagopian, *Bardizage khadoudig*, pp. 67-68.

Just as for Christians everywhere, the memory of those who had departed from this life was sacred, so for every family it was a pleasing duty, at times of great solemnity, such as a new birth, wedding or when a death occurred, to have a requiem or office said in church, during Mass, for the repose of their souls. On the Requiem Monday after a feast day, families would visit the graves of those who had died, having them blessed, wanting to perpetuate their link forever.

Graves, as roofless churches, were holy. It was a scandal for parties to be held among them or to allow animals to tread on them. They were therefore maintained properly by everyone.*

Thus religious life was expressed in all its ways – in the home, church and cemetery – on solemn occasions and in the people's ordinary lives and in their social relations.

Men would stand in church without any head-covering, although this wasn't general, and women with their heads covered. Men and women stood separately, with the young women and girls usually going up the stairs into the gallery, while old women, who weren't strong enough to join them, stood behind the ranks of the men, in the right-hand side apse.

8. Educational work

The people of Bardizag, being intelligent and far-sighted had, from the early days, given great value and importance to the education of their children, as a lasting value in the life of a society. Bardizag was among the first – if not the first - village in the province to have its school teach its children how to read, write and learn *hisab* [a form of accounting] and to give them a sort of religious and temporal education. They were also concerned, when the opportunity arose, to take advantage of high quality outside establishments such as, in the old days, the seminary of the Evil-Slaying† Monastery of Armash, for the education of its children. In those old days there were people from Armash who worked in Bardizag either as kahanas or schoolteachers. I can recall the names Garabed Kahana Der-Krikorian, Krikor Kahana Somoundjian and Sahag Kahana Pandigian who, before they became kahanas, had been teachers in Bardizag's community schools. There were also boys from great Bardizag families who, wishing to acquire higher education, had the opportunity to attend the Scutari (Uskudar) Armenian Gymnasium during its finest era. Hadji Garabed Agha Mgerian sent one or two of his sons to that school during the days when amiras were its trustees.

In my youth, Bardizag's most productive and finest educational era was when Shirinian and Yeghishe Vartabed Tourian were community school teachers. Some people of the Shrinian era later followed courses in the newly-established American

---

* This was not necessarily true. The old cemetery in the village itself became a public park, as described above. See Section 145 (7).
† The word used here is *Charkhapan*.

Robert College in Constantinople, and became notable and well-known individuals in Bardizag. Some of these were: Professor Apraham Effendi Der-Hagopian, his brother Armenag Effendi Der-Hagopian (a teacher in the American High School in Bardizag for many years), Minas Effendi Dzalian (a teacher and author of schoolbooks), Nshan Effendi Kondayan (secretary and interpreter in the Bible House), Ardashes Effendi Mgerian (an official of the currency exchange establishments in Constantinople and later the owner of a silk spinning factory), and Aghasi Effendi Der-Mgerdichian (a graduate in pharmacology of the government Medical University) who opened the first pharmacy in Bardizag, at the same time giving long and important service in Bardizag's public life.

Those of the Shirinan generation who went into business in Bardizag or Constantinople formed a mostly educated and practical class. Of these last I can recall Hadji Artin Kiutnerian and Artin Srab Kiutnerian, Hovhaness Khashmanian, Mgerdich Sinanian, Mihran Sinanian, Kelesh Hagop's two sons (whose names I can't establish), Haroutiun Der-Antreasian, Hadji Mgerdich Der-Garabedian, Garabed Der-Garabed Mkhalian, Haroutiun Djergayian, J. Khacherian and many others who worked as clerks in offices in Constantinople and/or in Bardizag as shopkeepers and merchants. It was at this time that remarkable women also appeared: Mrs. Shoushanig G. Drezian, Mrs. Yeghisapet Sinanian, Mrs. Srpouhi Mardigian, Mrs. Mariam Kasabian, Mrs. Makrouhi H. Arakelian, Mrs. Mariam Koushagian, Mrs. Ovsanna Yakoyian, Mrs. Varteni Hairabedian, Mrs. Zarouhi A Der-Mgerdichian, Mrs. Aghavni Kondayan, Mrs. Dirouhi Kiutnerian and others who later worked as leaders in the women's religious assemblies and lecture halls.

It would be unforgivable if, in this story of the educational work carried out in Bardizag, I forgot to mention the generation before that of Shirinian that emerged during Sahag Kahana Pandigian's teaching era. These were, in the main, children of the great houses who, having gained considerable education, had important roles in Bardizag's public life when I was a boy. Among these I can recall Mihran Khacherian and Hovhannes Khacherian, Hagopig Der-Hovhannes Mgerian and Garabed Der-Hovhannes Mgerian, Mihran Der-Antreasian, Hadji Haroutiun Der-Garabedian, Nigoghos Dzalian, Hadji Haroutiun Hairabedian, Zenop Der-Sahagian, Mgerdich Der-Garabed Mkhalian, the two Sarkis Djergayians, Hovhannes Arakelian, Hadji Hagop Djergayian, Badveli (Protestant Pastor) Hovsepian, Mr. Takvor Takvorian (these last two were, for many years, teachers in the community school), Mgerdich Geolliuian (a teacher, later a lawyer), Hovhannes Aprahamian (secretary to the parish council and later a kahana), Garabed and Nshan Ghazarosian (the first became Nerses Kahana), and many more like them who worked in Bardizag as trustees and members of the parish council for many a long year. Professor Apraham Der-Hagopian actually belonged to that generation.

The students who graduated from the regular courses in the community school were those taught by Yeghishe Vartabed Tourian and his students, whose numbers reached the hundreds. An important number of them from this generation dedicated themselves to teaching, several entered the church as either celibate monks or kahanas, and many became merchants and artisans, with a very few becoming clerks or officials.

Let me recall some of the teachers: Y. Der-Antreasian, A Hapelian, M. Semerdjian, A Mazlemian, A Bodosian, H. Sekgiulian, K. Saraydarian, K. Goudjoukian, H. Garakian, G. Nahabedian, A Arakelian (having graduated from Bardizag's community school, he then graduated from the Berberian school in Constantinople), K. Bodourian, M. Mardigian, M. Derderian, L. Geondiurian, O. Srab Kiutnerian, O. Ghazarian (later Housig Kahana), me and many others.

A significant number went from the Bardizag community school to the American Boys' High School, graduating from there, then dedicated themselves to teaching and providing profitable and appreciated service as teachers, both within the village and elsewhere.*

Many who entered the church, both celibate monks and kahanas, began their careers as teachers and then were ordained. Among these I can recollect, before all the others, the celibate monks Vahan Vartabed *Bardizagtsi* [of Bardizag]†, who obtained his education outside the village, Hovhannes Vartabed Pirenian (of the Shirinian generation) and, from the Tourian generation, Archbishop Torkom Koushagian, Armenian Patriarch of Jerusalem, Archbishop Mgerdich Aghavnouni,‡ Archbishop Garabed Mazlemian,** Yeghishe Vartabed Khacherian (of these monks Archbishop Torkom Koushagian and Yeghishe Vartabed Khacherian also graduated from the Armash theological seminary), Rev. Anania Hapelian†† and Arsen Vartabed Ghazigian (of the Armenian Catholic Mkhitarist order).

---

* There was also a YMCA branch in Bardizag, founded in about 1890. It had a reading room and library. It was this organisation that published the monthly journal *Paros*. It was influenced very much by Dr. R. Chambers, the director of the American Boys' High School. It closed in about 1912. There was also a Young Ladies' Diligence Union in Bardizag, also founded in about 1890. Minas Kasabian (Farhad), *Hayere Nikomedio Kavarin Mech*, pp. 269-270.

† Rev. Vahan of Bardizag's surname was Der-Minasian. He was a writer and satirist who was not afraid of laughing at himself, as well as being a representative of the Constantinople Patriarchate to various places. The renowned satirist Hagop Baronian has penned a marvellous piece about him in his series *Azkayin Chocher* [National leaders]. See Hagop Baronian, *Collected works,* Academy of Sciences of the Armenian SSR, Yerevan, Volume 2, 1964, pp.149-158, and Hagop Der-Hagopian, *Bardizage khadoudig*, pp. 126-135.

‡ See Section 131.

** See Section 133.

†† Rev. Anania was ordained a kahana but was later consecrated a celibate kahana *(shoushdag)* when his wife died. He was later promoted to the rank of Archimandrite as a celibate monk, eventually reaching the rank of archpriest *(dzairakuin vartabed)*.

I should like to recall the kahanas who served in Bardizag: Tionisios Kahana Drezian, Pilibbos Kahana Aprahamian, Partogh Der-Garabed Kahana Mkhalian, Madatia Kahana Geondiurian, Dimoteos Kahana Baghdasarian, Mesrob Kahana Andonian and Parnapas Kahana Parounian. Those serving outside the village were: Housig Kahana Ghazarian, Toma Kahana Shigaher (Constantinople), Arshavir Kahana Varteressian (Cairo), Bsag Kahana Hampartsoumian (Cairo) and Hovhannes Kahana Djelgouni (Dede Aghadj). There may be others that I have forgotten.

Government officials were: Garabed Aliksanian (first a teacher, then *sandek emini* in the provincial centre, Izmid), Hagop Sinanian (a graduate of the Halkele agricultural school and agricultural inspector), Hairabed Hairabedian and Z. Hairabedian (clerk in the Public Debt Administration), two others who held the same position but whose names escape me now, and Hovhannes Djergayian, the secretary to the parish council.

The following went into trade: Ardashes Kiutnerian, Hagop Kiutnerian, M. Kiutnerian, Garabed Mardigian, Aghasi Ellezian, Khachig and Hagop Teoleolian, Ardashes Berberian, Hagop Ghazigian, Hrant Gevregian, Mgerdich Shlemian, Onnig Ashdjian, Mikayel Bedigian, Garabed Gerevamian, Aghasi and Onnig Paraghamian and Hagop Khashmanian.

A significant number of the Tourian generation were certified silkworm breeders, having completed special courses in the Broussa (Boursa) Sericulture School. Among these I can recall: Haroutiun Djergayian (from the Shirinian era), Yervant Der-Mgerdichian, Mgerdich Drezian, Aghasi Paraghamian, Vahan Djelgouni, Haroutiun Arakelian and me. Hagop Kondayan and Boghos Kourouyian, who received their primary education in Protestant schools, should be added to this list.

There are quite a number of doctors and pharmacists who attended the government medical faculty. I can recall from among them: Dr. Aivazian (from the oldest generation who practiced in Constantinople), Dr. Garabed Mazlemian (a military doctor), Dr. Khosrov Hairabedian, Dr. Garabed Khacherian, Dr. A Kiudian (a dentist), Dr. Shahen Diuzian, the two Teoleolian brothers, Dr. Vahakn Mkhalian, Dr. Hairabed Hairabedian, Dr. S. A Kiutnerian, Dr. Albert Giureghian and Dr. Mampre Djangalozian. Pharmacists were: Kevork, Anoushavan and Nerses Kiutnerian, Aram Diuzian, Vahram Papazian, Asadour Margarian and Mgerdich Mardigian (who had studied engineering chemistry[*] in the United States of America).

Bedros Kiutian was a graduate of the government law school who, as an intellectual, was arrested and killed before he even reached his place of exile in 1915.

---

[*] The words used here are *djardarakidagan kimiapanoutiun*. This might also be translated as chemical engineering.

Some of the female students of this generation dedicated themselves to teaching in Bardizag's community schools, the kindergarten and elsewhere, in Armenian villages. Unfortunately I don't have their names so I cannot record them here.

The American boys' and girls' schools played an important part in educational work, the latter first in Bardizag then, later, in Adabazar while it continued its existence. There were a significant number of graduates or those who had partly completed the courses of study in the community schools and then gone to the American schools.

I have a partial list of the girls from Bardizag who either attended or graduated from the *Haiouhiats Varjaran* [Armenian Girls' School], willingly prepared for this work by Hovhannes Effendi Aliksanian, who was, for many years, a very successful teacher there. It consists of the following names: Soultanig Kourouyian (1895), M. Daiyan (1896), H. Kemeloyian (1896), O. Tertsagian (1900), A Boghosian (1901), Z. Boligian (1905), V. N. Azarian (1905), P. N. Dzalian (1906), T. H. Berberian (1907), H. M. Atanasian (1907), A K. Kembelian (1908), A M. Avedian (1908), Y. L. Pashayian (1908), D. B. Azinian (1909), V. M. Hetebian (1910), Y. S. Gevregian (1911), N. M. Atanasian (1911), A G. Der-Garabedian (1913), P. S. Magarian (1913), K. M. Dzalian (1913), H. K. Mkhalian (1913), N. S. Paravazian (1913), L. D. Toumayian (1914), N. H. Kiurkdjian (1914), S. K. Giureghian (1914), S. D. Der-Sahagian (1914) and A E. Papazian (1915).

Unfortunately it has proved impossible to obtain the list of female students of the American Girls' School who were from Bardizag while it was still in the village, but there were probably about 20 of them. Some of these young ladies, before they married and created their own homes – and even when they were married, with all that entailed – worked for many years as teachers in the Bardizag community schools or elsewhere.

The American Boys' School maintained its existence in Bardizag until the disaster of the First World War,[*] from about 1876, a few years before Tourian came to the village, with the majority of its first students being from the village. The number of graduates from Bardizag was about 50, some of whom, as we've seen, dedicated themselves to teaching using a harmonious synthesis of Armenian and American methods. Here are their names: Haroutiun Kiurkdjian, Azarig Azarian (a teacher in the same school for a time), Hagop Kondayan, Hovap Arabian (a teacher in the same school for a time), Mgerdich Kanchilian, Onnig Der-Nersesian, Mgerdich Djezelian, Kevork Leylozian, Mardiros Reyisian, Ghazaros Nahabedian (a teacher in the same school for a time), Garabed Berberian, Hagop Khashmanian, Mergeros Khashmanian, Zora Kasabian (a teacher in the same school for a time), Yervant Basmadjian (a teacher in the same school for a time), S. Kasabian, M. Gevregian, L. Kamian, Onnig Berberian, Dr. Vahakn M. Mkhalian, Hmayag

---

[*] 1915.

Ghazarosian, Minas Nahabedian, Hagop Daiyan, Asadour Magarian, Vahram Der-Mgerdichian, Sarkis Seferian, Mgerdich Der-Hagopian, Vahram Kondayan (a teacher in the same school for a time), Barkev Ghazarian, Garabed Sinanian, Sarkis Dongligian, Minas Basmadjian, Vahram Babokhian, Nigoghos Petoyian, Haroutiun Hairabedian, Hrant Der-Antreasian, Ardashes Tadavorian, Arshavir Hapelian, Hagop Saraydarian, Onnig Mkhalian, Zarmair Zakarian, Levon Saraydarian, Hagop Babokhian, Vahram Derderian, Haroutiun Kiutnerian, Nigoghos Vadjaraganian, Krikor Dzalian, Hovhannes Parounian, Krikor Vartabedian and many others who left before graduating. Many of the graduates of both the girls' and boys' schools went on to study in the Constantinople Girls' School and Robert College, later gaining important positions in their careers.

Apart from the graduates from Robert College I have mentioned (see above), there were others from Bardizag: Toros Torosian (1887), Stepan Magarian (1889), Mardiros Reyisian (1902), Hadji Mikayel Der-Garabedian,[*] Hovhannes Garakian (1909), Mgerdich Mgerian (1912), Sarkis Mgerian (1912), Bedros Srabian (1913), Vahram Kondaiyan (1913), Onnig Dzalian (1923), Aram Kondaiyan (1927), L. Azarian (1929), V. Azarian (1934), Apraham Bodourian (1935) and H. Shirinian (1936).

It is unfortunate that I wasn't able to obtain a list of the young ladies from Bardizag who went to college prior to 1914, but I can record those who graduated after that year: Arpine Der-Garabedian (1920), Baidzar Yesayian (1924), Rosa Vartanian (1926), Aghavni M. Mkhalian (1927), Mannig Arakelian (1928), Vartanoush Vartapourian (1929), Marie Boyadjian (1932), Arsine Konaiyan (1932), Srpouhi Mardigian (1933) and Markarid Melkonian (1936). I am grateful to Aram Konaiyan, himself a graduate from Robert College and at present a teacher there, for these lists of young men and women graduates.[†]

I have already written about the Armenian Catholic monastery and school in Bardizag in the section about its foundation and have nothing further to add here.[‡]

The people of Bardizag were naturally inclined towards education and development, a virtue that eased its narrow environment's economic difficulties and strengthened early links with Constantinople and other developed centres. Not having the opportunities within the village to settle its sons in trade and industry, the people of Bardizag gave impetus to their education and learning, extending the time spent in education in the establishments that were in its care.[**] It regarded education as the means to achieve a better working life and, thanks to these circumstances,

---

[*] No date quoted.
[†] This was written before 1937.
[‡] See Section 94.
[**] Mkhalian makes no mention of the Pro-education Union that was set up in Bardizag in 1910 with the aim of providing scholarships for deserving young people in the schools in the village. It had two such students in the American High School in 1913. Minas Kasabian (Farhad), *Hayere Nikomedio Kavarin Mech*, p. 267.

Bardizag was, in the Izmid province, considered to be a centre of learning with its several community and foreign educational establishments.[*] It produced generations of students that went into intellectual occupations, the church, teaching, journalism, official positions, liberal professions (the famous singer Mrs. Zabel Aram and her daughter, the well-known dancer Miss Adrine Aram Zabel, Miss Marie Bodourian the pianist and K. Alemshah the musician, were all from Bardizag), medicine, pharmacology, agriculture, sericulture (using the Pasteur system), all of which demanded a certain amount of education. They thus became leaders in public works compared to other places which had communities with larger populations[†] in the same province, driving it to aim for targets beyond material things in spite of natural misfortunes and sacrifices due to a very poor economic situation.

The boys and girls of Bardizag were ardent and clever students who, finding education opportunities in Robert College, Constantinople College, Adabazar Girls' School, the Berberian and Central schools, Armash Seminary, Mourad-Raphayelian School and the monastery of St. Lazzaro in Venice, became notable students and brought honour to their origins and the educational establishments that prepared them.

It is proper that I should, in this section devoted to education in Bardizag, devote space to certain annual community events.[‡]

The people of Bardizag were perhaps the only community in the whole of the province that had the habit, every year, of celebrating three Armenian national festivals – Sts Vartanants[**] (known popularly as Vartanants), Holy Translators[††] and the anniversary of the Armenian national constitution of 1862.[‡‡]

---

[*] Mkhalian is silent on the subject of the classes held by both the Hnchag and the ARF clubs in Bardizag from 1910 onwards. The one run by the Dashnaks trained people in handicrafts, virtually free of charge. The Hnchag class was held in the winter. Both classes were successful. Minas Kasabian (Farhad), *Hayere Nikomedio Kavarin Mech*, pp. 271-272.

[†] The author means Armenian communities.

[‡] The author uses the word *azkayin* here, which could be taken to mean national.

[**] This is an important Armenian Apostolic Church commemoration, relating to the 5th century. Sts Varanants celebrates the martyrdom of the Armenian army under the command of General Vartan Mamigonian in defence of 'faith and fatherland' against the invasion of Armenia by the Persians in 451AD.

[††] This feast commemorates the creation of the Armenian alphabet in about 405AD by St. Mersob (also called Mashdots) and the translation of the Bible very soon afterwards by St. Sahag and St. Mesrob.

[‡‡] The Armenian National Constitution was promulgated in 1862 for the internal government of the Armenian community *(millet)* in the Ottoman Empire, under the jurisdiction of the Armenian Patriarch of Constantinople, who was responsible for it to the Sultan.

Vartanants was usually celebrated by the staging of the story of the heroic resistance and martyrdom of Brave Vartan and his comrades-in-arms. It was regularly staged on the feast of Sts Vartanants, which occurs on the Thursday of the week before the beginning of Lent, when the government still allowed this expression of national sentiment. This happened regularly even before Tourian's days. The youth of the day would rehearse the play for days before the festival and stage it to a vast audience on the Wednesday evening in the school hall or, before that, in a suitable place, such as the Mgerians' *tolalikh*. The production of this historical play didn't, of course, represent any great value in a literary or artistic sense. For our people it fulfilled a need, in terms of educating their national feelings: to awaken love and enthusiasm in them towards this magnificent historic incident and to strengthen their national feelings and faith still further. The people of Bardizag came to this performance and, for a moment, lived in its past, witnesses to their forefathers' fierce struggle to preserve Armenian national identity and faith, thus stressing their national consciousness about these unforgettable Armenian values.

The young people who performed only did their duty. It was usual for the profit made from this performance to be given to the community schools.

The Holy Translators feast took place in summer.* In Bardizag, apart from celebrating it in church, it became a habit during the Tourian years to do so as a national event.

On that day, after the festival celebration in church, Mass would be said and, after it had ended, the officiating priest in his robes, led by the choir singing the appropriate sharagan [canticle] of the day, would go to the upper halls of the Nerses-Shoushanian community schools. This procession was followed by all the priests, the parish council, trustees, boys and girls attending the schools, and a great crowd of men and women.

The officiating priest would take his place on the stage with the Gospel in his hand with the priests, officials, everyone else below him, with the males of the population in the boys' hall and the women in that of the girls, the dividing partitions between the two having been opened. Recitations and speeches to mark the occasion would be made, emphasising the value and significance of the festival. Armenian patriotic songs would be sung by the students, the aim of which was to glorify the role the invention of the Armenian alphabet and the translation of the Bible played in Armenian national life and existence. This was a singular and marvellous episode in the Armenian renaissance which was the greatest Armenian value in all its history. It put into motion the whole store of that people's energy, through the centuries, giving it an honourable place in the history of nations as a civilised people, despite its weakness and small size. It was the celebration of Armenian education. Then the priest would bless the Armenian school, the students and teachers, and close this wonderful event with a benediction.

---

* The church calendar shows that the feast is celebrated in October.

The celebration of the anniversary of the promulgation of the Armenian national constitution of 1862, like Vartanants, began very early on in Bardizag. It was the celebration of freedom and autonomy, and would take place in the open, outside the village in the open space named Avazoud, which was shaded by ancient trees, in the bosom of nature and under a high and wide dome of blue sky, on the Sunday after Ascension,* just like it was celebrated in the open spaces around the Holy Redeemer Hospital in Constantinople, on the occasion of the implementation of the constitution and liberal rules covering our community's internal governance. A procession was formed outside the community schools made up of students, official bodies and, with the participation of the priests and, with waving flags, would move off, led by students singing patriotic songs and others dedicated to the constitution. It passed through the market area of the main street and continued along the road to Avazoud through the blocks of houses, with a great crowd of people following it, which grew as the procession continued on its way, like a flood that was forcing its way to the sea.

When it reached Avazoud, the whole crowd would be seated on previously arranged benches and chairs in the deep shade of the trees, in comfortable conditions in the free, open air. The whole of Avazoud would be filled with the celebrating crowd, with every hummock and stone becoming a seat as well. It was like in an ancient amphitheatre, with every eye fixed on a stage that was built on the stump of an enormous hornbeam tree and reached by ascending a small set of steps. Orators would go onto this stage one after another and express their praise for the liberal order and the people's autonomy. The speeches would be punctuated by patriotic songs sung by the students, which made a great impression on everyone with their harmony and immediacy. The speeches, in that free and large environment, fell upon the heads of those present like the sparks from rockets, with their deep meaning, and would make a great impression on everyone with their enthusiastic spirit, as the celebration of a great victory that had been achieved.

It is worthwhile recalling, among these celebrations, those of the end of the school year held by the community schools and attended by great crowds of people, where comprehensive reports would be given concerning the educational effort in the village and the very useful plans they envisaged for the future.

Finally, a few words about newspapers that appeared in the village: immediately after the days of freedom began several calotype newspapers were printed in the village by students or teachers, which gave local news and expressed their point of view concerning public questions.† They also printed *panahiusoutiun* [pieces of old oral poetry]. The titles of these papers were *Panper Bardizagian* [Bardizag Herald],

---

* Ascension Day was usually in May.
† The author is referring to the Armenian national constitution of 1862.

Tarman [Remedy], *Meghou* [Bee], *Baikar* [Debate or Struggle] and *Gshir* [Scales]. None of them lasted for very long.*

The Alumni Association of the American Boys' High School also had its journal *Bardizag*, with a new issue produced half-yearly, that lasted for some years† and was printed in Constantinople, concerned with the school and lives of the graduates. The editor was Dr. Hovsep Der-Stepanian, the school's doctor, a teacher, and an alumnus of the school.

9. Popular superstitions and beliefs

Belief in the evil eye *(nazar)* was usual for the Bardizag villager. Everyone was frightened of the *nazar* and its coming, and defence against it was of great concern in the people's customs. If someone had a child who was healthy, beautiful, with lovely pink cheeks, white skin and above natural height or development, it was usual to fix a talisman on its shoulders made of beads to prevent the evil eye affecting it.

People never had the boldness to show their babies to everyone they met, worried in case it was affected by the evil eye. It was the same with the animals they took special care of – a handsome horse, a cow that gave a lot of milk, a large sheep – each would have a bead talisman. Grown people would often have an amulet or talisman too under their clothing, against their bodies, as a form of armour against it. Again, when someone succeeded in building himself a house, having done everything in his power to do so, he would often nail an old horseshoe or a piece of hoof over the door to protect the house against the evil eye.

---

* *Panper Bardizagian* [Bardizag Herald], edited by the young Hovhannes Mgerian (later kahana) in 1867. Hagop Der-Hagopian, *Bardizage khadoudig*, p. 224; *Tarman* [Remedy], edited by the Bardizag Hnchag group. It appeared in 1895-1896, and was distributed secretly. *ibid.* p. 224; *Meghou* [Bee], an illustrated, satirical newspaper produced by Apig Der-Minasian. Another newspaper with the same title appeared later, in 1912, published weekly by the local Dashnak group. It was edited by Kegham Koushagian (the poet, who was Archbishop Torkom Koushagian's nephew). *ibid.* pp. 224-245; *Baikar* [Debate or Struggle], a Hnchag newspaper published every two weeks. *ibid.* p. 224.

Der Hagopian also gives the titles of other calotype newspapers – *Paros*, the YMCA journal, edited by Hagop Alodjian and Krikor Mkhalian, the author of this work. 17 monthly issues were printed in Constantinople from February 1910 until August 1911; *Bardez Azkayin dzaghgants* [Garden of national flowers] produced in about 1867; *Touafi* produced alternately in Armenian and Turkish using Armenian transliteration (also in 1867). Hagop Der-Hagopian, *Bardizage khadoudig*, p. 224.

† From October 1909 to at least October 1912. Der-Hagopian states that it lasted until 1914. Der-Hagopian also tells us that there was another journal with the same title that appeared in about 1880, edited by Armenag Der-Hagopian and Minas Dzalian. Hagop Der-Hagopian, *Bardizage khadoudig*, p. 224.

This fear of the evil eye made the villager cautious of ostentation. The wish to hide one's property under a cloak of modesty and mystery had the force of an obligatory tax for everyone. The purchase by anyone of a large piece of highest quality meat from the market, a large, choice fish or a basket filled to overflowing with goods could attract the evil eye, so they would be sent home almost secretly.

If someone met another person in the street and cordially exclaimed over how good he looked, there was the fear of the evil eye, of failure or sickness, so the person who received the compliment would pinch his own buttock as an antidote to it. The explanation 'They were eaten with the eye' *(achkov geran)* was used when someone suffered a misfortune or had an accident.

A curse was also something that was horrid to many. People were frightened of a curse, just as they were of the evil eye. Parents' curses were especially bad. The explanation 'He is holding his father's and mother's curse'[*] had the strength of truth. If someone, in a fight, finding himself in increasing difficulty, rained curses on his opponent, people often said, 'Fire is falling from his lips; I'm afraid of his curses, they'll stick.' It was very easy to get the better of a superstitious and credulous person: it was enough to say to him, 'Behave or I'll curse you...!'[†] A curse, in other words, was an anathema, also used occasionally by the church against stubborn and unfeeling, guilty people. Having tried every usual thing in vain to make them be good, the anathema was the way of handing them over to God's judgement, to put the fear of God into them, which had great force in the old, devout, happy days.

The belief in fear *(vakh)* had great power over ordinary people. It is well known that great fear, physiologically speaking, can have a devastating effect on a human body and nerves. It is for this reason that on many occasions illnesses that could not be adequately diagnosed were attributed to the effects of fear.[‡] 'He has been frightened' was the usual diagnosis in these circumstances, and the sick person would often say, 'I was frightened, count my forty days.' They were convinced that the terrible results of fear would appear within 40 days and, if the sick person died, they would say, 'The poor person was frightened, and was laid to rest in 40 days.'

If it was suspected that someone had been frightened and thus fallen ill, the *bakherdjis* and candle wax drippers would be approached, the sick person's relatives taking a piece of cloth belonging to him with them, wishing that the place where it happened and the relevant circumstances be established. The person they went to, by dripping oil or melted candle wax into cold water, and looking at the shape the wax made when it solidified, would think they understood that the sick person had been frightened in such-and-such a place and under these-or-those circumstances. These diagnoses would be followed by the remedies: to secretly take some sugar at night to the place where the sick person had been frightened and sprinkle it there,

---

[*] Hore-more anedzke ge prne.
[†] Khelok getsir, kez g'anidzem, a....!
[‡] It should be noted that the author is a layman, and was writing in the 1930s.

or make some dough which included some hair and other things taken from the sick person, and throw bits of it, after dark, in various places – into the valleys, the sea and into deserted places.

Another remedy for fear was also for a number of women to go, at night, without speaking to anyone, and get water from seven different fountains in a container and sprinkle it at crossroads then, silently, return home.

Again, the frightened person would be taken to see prayer-saying women who would seat the sick person opposite them and mutter unintelligible prayers over him, occasionally pretending to yawn and touching him, thus thinking that they had rid the sick person of the fright or banished the evil spirits from him.

Several other sicknesses may be linked to those brought on by fright connected to death-step *(merelgokh)*.* Apparently, if an ill person, in his scatter-brained, poor state of health showed a lack of proper respect for someone who had died and whose cortège had passed him and he hadn't risen to his feet, the result was that this illness would come upon him – a strange lack of strength to stand up, a lack of appetite, melancholy, a state of not being able to come forward – all these were the symptoms of a person with 'death-step'. For this too they would prepare a sort of remedy made of various mixtures of water and give it to someone to pour on the deceased's grave. Sometimes the sick person and his relatives would go to the grave, where they would pray, wash his head and face and pour the water on the grave. If the sick person wasn't able to go to the cemetery, another way of curing him of the 'death-step' sickness was for several women to go to the deceased's grave, get a little of the soil from it, mix it with water, leave it for three nights in the open air, then have the sick person drink it.

In my day, belief in evil spirits (djinns, *peris* and *kezmez aghegner*) had much diminished, being the remnants of beliefs that had reached us from the dim, distant past, only being held by illiterate peasants *(ramig)*. It was as a result of these beliefs that many couldn't sleep without fear at night in an isolated house, or would hesitate at passing a cemetery, lonely places or ruins in the dark, as they thought there were evil spirits there, where careless people, who had the boldness to pass those places that were regarded as being dangerous, could bump into them.

When I was a boy, stories were told that were considered to be true about visits to stables by evil spirits resulting in horses and other animals being strangely affected, with their manes and tails being spontaneously braided and tied into knots. They also told how they saw spirits, with heads like those of horses or goats, emerge from the spouts of fountains.

Spirits were also used to torturing poor mortals lying in their beds, sitting heavily on their chests (nightmares) about which people said that the spirits called *khebligs* were at work, preventing the person affected from standing up. There is no doubt

---

* I have coined the expression 'death-step' as it is the literal translation of the Armenian expression.

that this was the result of a certain physiological state suffered by a person when he had been lying on his back for a long time.

Certain odd and specific sounds made by various sinister animals or birds were linked to these beliefs. Thus the howl of a dog near a house at night was considered to be a bad omen by the people living in the neighbouring houses and who, terrified, would leave their beds, shout 'Hosht! Hosht!' and, throwing pieces of bread, try to make the dog leave the area. The same fear was felt when an owl, perched on a roof at night, would hoot in its usual way. The household would fearfully rise, disturbed by gloomy thoughts, and try to make it fly away from their house and, if they found the way to do so, would kill it with a rifle bullet. They believed that these animals and birds signalled disaster or death. One can imagine the dire concerns that households with sick people in them suffered when an owl screeched on their roof or a dog howled in the street near their door.

There was also the belief in what could be called a 'meeting' *(hantebk)*, which was considered to be an accident involving spirits. When a person unexpectedly suffered a stroke or wasn't able to move a limb without a specific reason, it was said the he had suffered 'a meeting'.*

I cannot, among all these things, ignore the general belief in dreams coming true, which were regarded as a kind of revelation of the future, for either good or ill. When someone got up in the morning, they would often say, 'I had a very bad dream last night, may God preserve us,' and a spiritual crisis would begin in the household, with the family awaiting some sort of misfortune. If a bad thing did happen the next evening, the person who had the original bad dream would say 'My dream happened.'

This belief in dreams was often buttressed by stories in the Bible, where this or that person's dreams were proved to be true by events that happened later. Dreams were therefore considered, on that basis, to be heavenly visions in people's lives. On those occasions those concerned would approach dream interpreters or peruse books of interpretations of dreams which usually contained explanatory formulas for ordinary dreams, providing pleasure or worry for days on end.

Dreams are, of course, spiritual visions and capable of explanation, being the subject of special scientific study. In this sense those interested may read psychological studies, based on the research done by competent scientists. Here I only have regard for popular thought and belief concerning them. But what I would like to say is this: dreams, as spiritual visions, have had a deep significance in the formation of certain human beliefs. Some elements of religion among people, such as the idea of the immortality of souls and the existence of spirits, owe a great deal to dreams and many other things, stretching from the beginning of man's existence and reaching us to form part of certain religious perceptions.

---

* *Hantebk ounetser e.*

I will end this section with a few words on popular faith in the curative powers of some local fountains. It is not the scientific study of their attributes that will concern me here, only the popular belief that those waters had properties that were supernatural, and had divine spiritual influence.

We have already seen that the famous Sokhmiar (St Minas) fountain was regarded as curing fevers.[*] Apart from this, at one end of the village, in Avazoud (Ghoumloukh) there was the one known as *Lius Aghpiur* [Fountain of Light], a trickle of flowing water that was considered to be the remedy for eye problems. If someone had bad eyes, he would go to this fountain early in the morning and bathe his eyes and face with its water, with the belief that he would be cured. Scientific analysis of this water was never carried out. I have no idea, on a scientific basis, what properties it had to have been given the attribute of curing eye problems.

Again, there was, further on from Avazoud, *Teghentan –Teghnoutian Aghpiur* [Yellow Fountain] near the edge of Yasakh Valley, which emerged drop by drop from the red soil there, forming a pool with bits of rust on its surface, in a small depression in a glade in the forest. It had an inky taste. Everyone who felt weak or who had jaundice would go there in the early morning, taking a bag containing their breakfast with them and, before eating, would drink a cup or two of its water, wash their hands and face in it and pray. They would then tie a piece of cloth taken from their clothing to the branch of a nearby tree[†] and, certain that they would be cured, sit down on the grass in the first rays of sunlight and eat their breakfast with a great appetite. After breakfast they would drink some more water from the fountain and return, seemingly eased, to their homes.

Many benefitted from their pilgrimage to this sacred fountain. But when a person who had jaundice couldn't go there, he would ask someone he knew to bring him some of that healing water in a container. The friend would take the container, go to the fountain, fill it and return to the village without putting the container on the ground or allowing it to touch it, in other words keeping it in the air, and give it to the sick person.

My father would tell the story of a Turk from Deyirmendere who asked him to bring some water from this fountain on his return home, with the deeply-held belief that he would be cured of a stubborn illness. My father forgot the request, and only recalled it half way back to Deyimendere. Not wanting to disappoint the sick man, he filled the container with water from nearby Hasar Dere and took it to the Turk, thinking that in this instance faith would be more influential than the water itself.

---

[*] See Section 18.

[†] This is a universal custom among Armenians that still exists, with people tying ribbons or pieces of cloth – and even plastic bags(!) to branches of trees or bushes outside monasteries and churches, holy places and near fountains, in the belief that their spiritual pleas would be granted.

The sick man drank it with the greatest longing and faith as water from Teghentan Fountain, and regained his health.

Chemical analysis of the water from this fountain was carried out by Ghougasian Effendi, the well-known lecturer in chemistry in the Constantinople medical university, who had come to Bardizag on a visit in my day. He found it contained traces of iron. It was this iron that, entering the bloodstream, helped in the recovery of the sick patient, with the assistance of his faith in the curative qualities of the water of course.

An oath was sacred and a matter of honour for the person who swore it. If however he was forced to betray it, then it was usual, so he would remain unpunished for going against it, to break a piece of newly-baked, hot bread in two over his head, an act, according to belief, that neutralised the oath itself.

APPENDIX

Main street - market scenes.

(Top) Bardizag street.
(Bottom) Upper cemetery.

(Top) Mgerian silk spinning factory.
(Bottom) Helvadjian silk spinning factory.

(Top) Lousaghpiur, Avazoud.
(Bottom) Upper Ayazma, Minas Agha's oak grove and silkworm house.

Appendix

(Top) Nshan Sinanian's farm. *(Bottom)* Chapel of St Minas.

(Top) Yeghishe Tourian's visit to Bardizag.
(Bottom) Manoushag on a pilgrimage day.

Appendix

(Top) Seymen.
(Bottom) Gdouts Monastery (Lake Van).

(Top) Armash Monastery.
(Bottom) Izmid railway station.

Appendix

(Top) Destruction of houses in the village during the war.
(Bottom) Girls' class, Community School.

(Top) Kindergarten class.
(Bottom) Boys' class, Community School.

Appendix

Community School graduates.

(Top) Kahanas in Bardizag before 1915. Left to right: Mesrob Kahana Andonian, Mgerdich Kahana Azarian, Garabed Kahana Mkhalian, Sahag Kahana Aprahamian, Nerses Kahana Ghazarosian.
(Lower left) Garabed Kahana Mkhalian.
(Lower right) Hovhannes Kahana Mgerian.

Appendix

(Upper left) Archbishop Boghos Karakoch, prelate of the united sees of Izmid and Armash.
(Upper right) Armenian Patriarch of Constantinople Nerses Varjabedian.
(Lower left) Archbishop Stepannos Maghakian.
(Lower right) Bishop Stepannos Aghavni.

(Upper left) Yeghishe Vartabed Tourian.
(Upper right) Archbishop Stepannos Hovagimian.
(Lower left) Archbishop Garabed Mazlemian.
(Lower right) Archbishop Mgerdich Aghavnouni.

Appendix

(Upper left) Armenian Patriarch of Jerusalem Archbishop Torkom Koushagian.
(Upper right) Yeghishe Vartabed Khacherian.
(Lower left) Vahan Vartabaed Bardizagtsi (Der-Minasian).
(Lower right) Armenag Der-Hagopian.

(Upper left) Artin Amira Kazaz.
(Upper right) Dr Hovsep Der-Stepanian.
(Lower left) Dr Garabed Khacherian.
(Lower right) Minas Dzalian.

Appendix

(Upper left) Yervant Der-Antreasian.
(Upper right) Prof. Apraham Der-Hagopian.
(Lower left) Aghasi Der-Mgerdichian.
(Lower right) V. Kondayian.

(Top) Armenian Catholic monastery.
(Lower left) Father V. Hatsouni.
(Lower right) Father H. Torosian.

Appendix

(Upper left) Father G. Daiyan.
(Upper right) Father Y. Daiyetsi.
(Lower left) Father Arsen Ghazigian.
(Lower right) Father M. Bodourian.

(Top) American Boys' High School after 1908. *(Bottom)* High School in winter.

(Top) Foundation ceremony, Newnham Hall.
(Bottom) Newnham Hall.

(Top) Pierce Hall, October 1913, decorated to commemorate of the 1,500th anniversary of the invention of the Armenian alphabet and the translation of the Bible into Armenian.
(Bottom) Chambers Hall.

Appendix

(Upper left) Mr Justin W. Parsons
(Upper right) Dr R. Chambers (1849 - 1917).
(Lower left) Mrs Elizabeth (Bessie) Chambers (1845 -1923).

(Top) Some of the members of the American High School Chanasirats [Diligence] club, 1907. Left to right, standing: Aram Shahbazian, Kegham Kerestedjian, Manoug Margosian, Hagop Kouyoumdjian, Vahram (surname unknown), Vramshabouh Papazian, Gobernig Giulmezian. Left to right, seated (teachers): Mgerdich Der-Hagopian, Lawson Chambers, Dr Robert Chambers, Mrs Bessie Chambers, Hrant Malkhasian. Left to right, seated cross-legged: Garo Kevorkian, Zakar (surname unknown), Giragos Giragosian, Hovhannes Semerdjibashian, Haigazoun (surname unknown).
(Bottom) High School, 1919. Near East Relief officials.

Appendix

Document 1 - Donations[*]

The following donations have been made for the publication of this book for the love of unforgettable Bardizag and as a sign of respect for its history's author.

An honourable compatriot	£30 *Sterling*
Rev. Arshavir Varteressian (Cairo)	220 Egyptian *kurush*
Rev. Antranig Bedigian (New York)	165 Palestinian *kurush*
Mr Ghazaros Nahabedian (Cairo)	300 Egyptian *kurush*
Haroutiun Selihian (Toronto)	$15 Canadian
Dr Garabed Khacherian (Salonika)	1120 *drakhmis*
Onnig Dzalian (Cairo)	200 Egyptian *kurush*
Onnig Mkhalian (Cairo)	200 Egyptian *kurush*
Levon Kamian (Cairo)	150 Egyptian *kurush*
Vahram Ziver Hagopian (Cairo)	100 Egyptian *kurush*
Bedros Bedrosian (Alexandria)	100 Egyptian *kurush*
Nerses Kiutnerian (Mehallah Kebir)	100 Egyptian *kurush*
Mrs Kayiane Margarian (Simbillavi)	100 Egyptian *kurush*
Dr Sahag Der-Garabedian (Alexandria)	100 Egyptian *kurush*
Dr Sahag Yeramian (Cairo)	100 Egyptian *kurush*
Mihrtad Boyadjian (Cairo)	100 Egyptian *kurush*
Vartan Bardzankian (Salonika)	500 *drakhmis*
Dr O. Somoundjian (Giumildjine)	400 *drakhmis*
S Tatarian (Canada)	$5 Canadian
M Garabedian (Geneva)	150 *francs*

Apart from the above, many people have paid for their copies prior to publication through Dr. G. Khacherian, Ardashes Khacherian, Hagop Khashmanian and Haroutiun Kiurkdjian. Sincere thanks to all.

I gratefully wish to acknowledge that the majority of the photographs printed in this book were prepared by the artist Mr. Artur Ashdjian, himself from Bardizag.

---

[*] This list appeared in the original Armenian edition.

Document 2 - Rules governing betrothals and marriages in Bardizag. Promulgated and approved by the village council and the diocesan prelate in 1864.*

Betrothals

1. Betrothals take place when the girl is 12 years of age and the young man is 18. If they are younger, the betrothal is invalid.

2. Legal betrothals take place at the church door with the agreement of both sides, in the presence of the kahanas and village council. There will be a detailed examination of family relationships and the heartfelt agreement between both sides.

3. Betrothals that take place separately in houses are illegal, whether the girl and young many are of the correct ages or not.

4. When a betrothal takers place, the young man's and girl's kahanas will testify that it is taking place with the good will of both sides. With the parents and guardians on both sides being present, one handkerchief (mahrama) and a 10 or 20 lira note will be presented by the young man's side to that of the girl. A handkerchief only will be given by the girl's side to that of the young man. These are the only signs of the girl and young man being betrothed.

5. After the betrothal being made in this manner, it will be recorded in a special register held by the village council and the betrothal tax of 12 kurush will be paid by the young man's family.

6. The young couple, from the day of their betrothal until their wedding day, may not take presents to one another. They may not congregate with relatives and be henna'd as bride and groom, or give or take gold, or send dishes of food or articles of clothing to each other. Expensive things or events that create disorders are completely forbidden.

7. If either the girl or young man take no notice of these rules and conduct themselves as they did before, apart from being considered to have disobeyed them, if one day the betrothal has to be annulled on reasonable grounds, there will not be any claims for the extra costs by either side, under any circumstances.

8. An annulment of a betrothal may be declared by the village council if there are seen to be reasonable grounds to do so.

---

* First published in the monthly journal *Huis – Troshag haireniats*, (Hope – flag of our native land) edition 5, 1864, published by Armash Monastery. It was later published as a separate booklet. See Der-Hagopian, Hagop, *Bardizage khadoudig* (Dappled Bardizag), pp.421-423, and Kasabian, Minas (Farhad), *Hayere Nikomedio Kavarin Mech*, p. 238.

Appendix

9. The girl's dowry will be considered to be made up of five sets* of plain clothes. They will be put into a chest and will be sent to the bridegroom's house on the Monday evening after the wedding.

10. By putting clothing into the girl's marriage chest or separated for the groom, nothing may be given to relatives apart from the following:

    1 shirt, 1 set of white drawers, 1 belt and 2 handkerchiefs for the bridegroom

    1 shirt, 1 pair of trousers *(shalvar)* for the mother-in-law

    1 shirt, 1 handkerchief for the godfather.

Nothing – not a single cloth or article of clothing - may be given to anyone else.

Weddings

1. When both sides decide to have the wedding, both sets of future in-laws and their kahanas and seatholder will present themselves to the village council a week before the date of the wedding. There they will complete their wedding negotiations *(kesemet)* only by word of mouth, without giving anything to each other and will pay the fees for the wedding and the right to the seat.

2. Taking the bride like a beggar from house to house with her head covered is forbidden.

3. It is forbidden for young men on the bridegroom's side to gather together and create a disturbance on the Saturday evening before the wedding.

4. The vulgar custom of a mixed crowed of men and women going from the bridegroom's house to that of the bride and back again on the Sunday of the wedding is abolished. Both *hinayma* and taking and getting cloth articles is forbidden. Only one woman may take the articles of clothing reserved for the bridegroom and wrapped in one parcel, as detailed in the 10th article concerning betrothals (above), from the bride's house to that of the groom.

5. The dowry is blessed on the Sunday of the wedding either during the day or in the evening in the presence of relatives, in-laws and godfathers and it is forbidden to sing vulgar songs on this occasion.

6. Gluttony, drinking and games played by a mixed crowd of men and women, as well as shouting, saying that the house is a wedding house, is forbidden from the evening of the Sunday until dawn of the following day.

7. The people who get the bride before the morning church bell sounds are to be ready to go to church at the time of morning worship *(jamerkoutiun)*. When they go to get the bride from her home and bring her to the church, celebrating or shouting or music being played in the streets is forbidden.† Only the bridegroom's parents and relative may go and get the bride and, without partaking of a meal,

---

*   The word used here is *tserk*.

†   However, see Chapter 11, (4)(b) Marriage, footnote 4.

bringing her to the church accompanied by the kahana. They will conduct themselves with decorum and the ceremony of Holy Matrimony will take place there before the altar of the Lord.

8. After bringing the bride and groom to the church, the groom's friends are forbidden to go to coffee houses, make music, get drunk or provide examples of bad conduct in the streets.

9. The wedding ceremony will be completed in church early on Monday morning and the kahana of the house, without a cope, and singing canticles (sharagans) will lead the married couple to their home and, having immediately completed the *takverats* [removal of the crowns] ceremony there, the wedding will be completed.

10. As with all laws, it is forbidden for the people, to prevent ruinous expenditure, to employ musicians and have music played, which is a primary reason for such expenditure. But if any one person wants to have music played only in his own home, he must first obtain a permit from the village council, promising that music will not be played in the streets.

These rules are established by the united will of the village council, kahanas and notables of this village.

Promulgated on 12 November 1864
In Bardizag

Seeing the importance and usefulness of these rules, I order that they be put into use and their terms be considered to be law from now on.

Archbishop Stepannos (Maghakiants)
(Prelate of) Nicomedia

Appendix

Krikor Mkhalian's Ottoman identity document, issued after April 27, 1909 during the reign of Sultan Mehmed V. Reshad.*

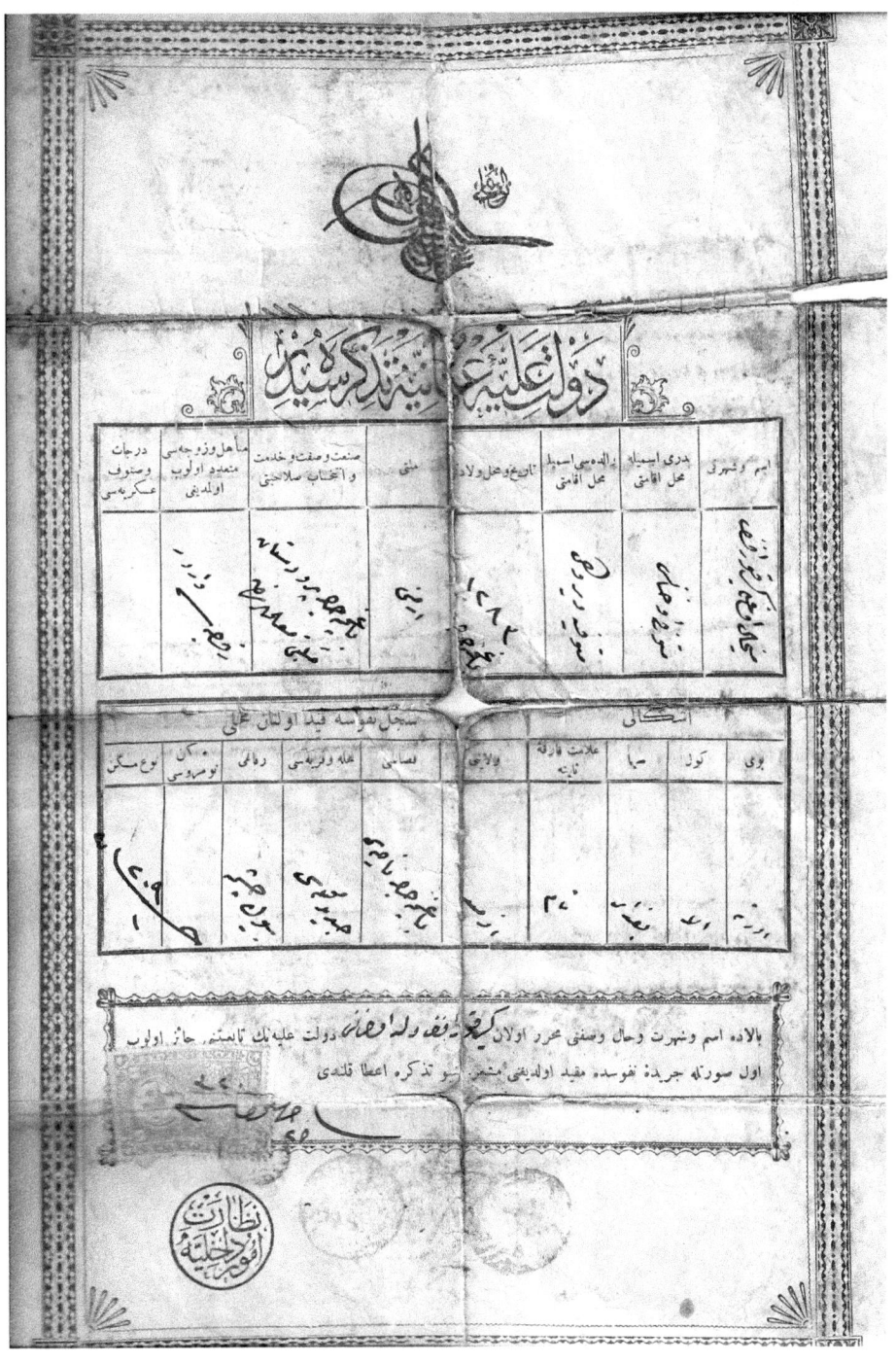

* Krikor Mkhalian archive.

Krikor Mkhalian's 1st class sericulture certificate from the Boursa (Bursa) Sericulture School dated February 27, 1889[*]

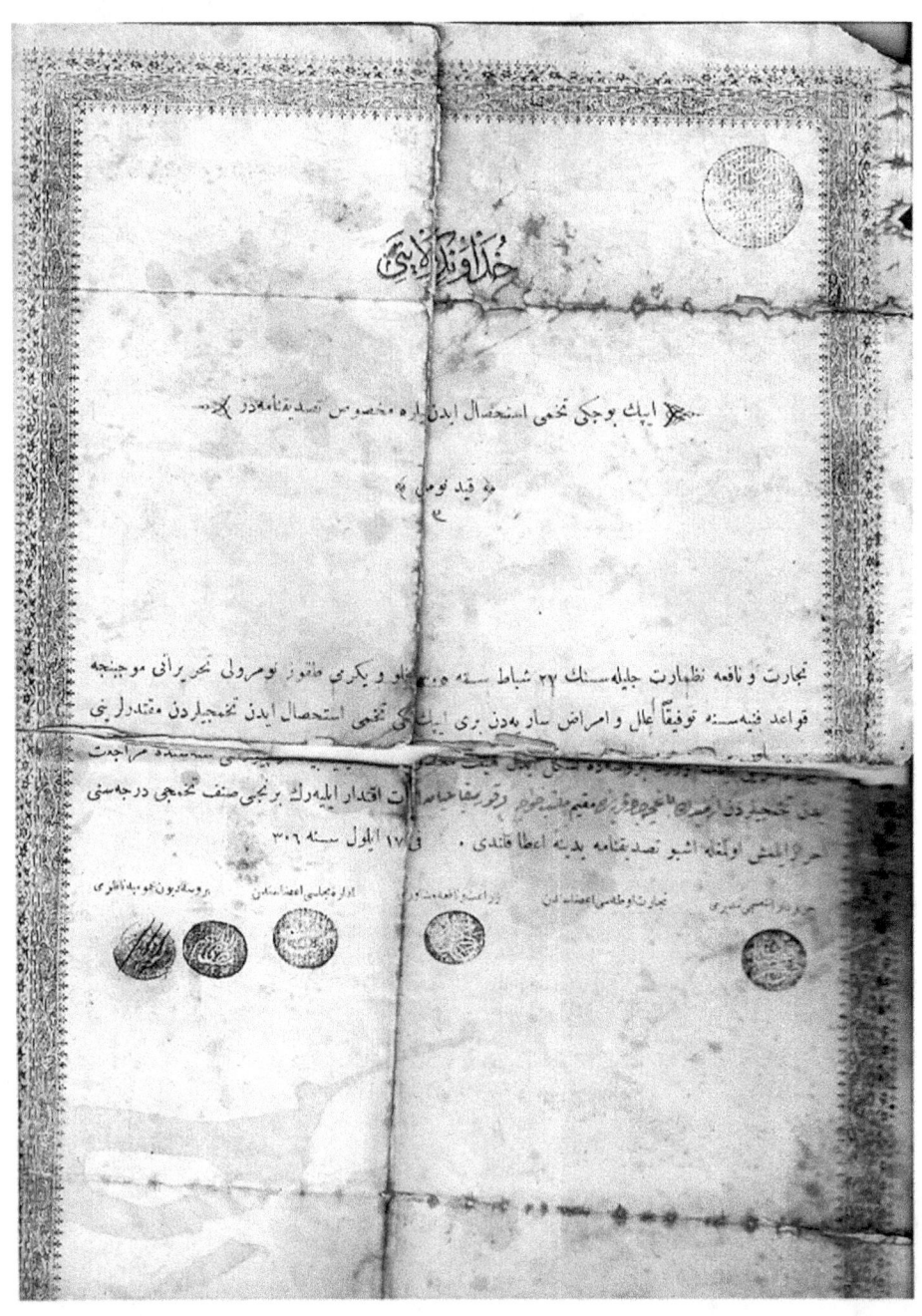

---
[*] Krikor Mkhalian archive.

Appendix

Krikor Mkhalian's educator/teacher certificate of competence issued by the Armenian Patriarchate, Constantinople, dated March 12, 1911[*]

---

[*] Krikor Mkhalian archive.

Bardizag land sale documents - 1[*]

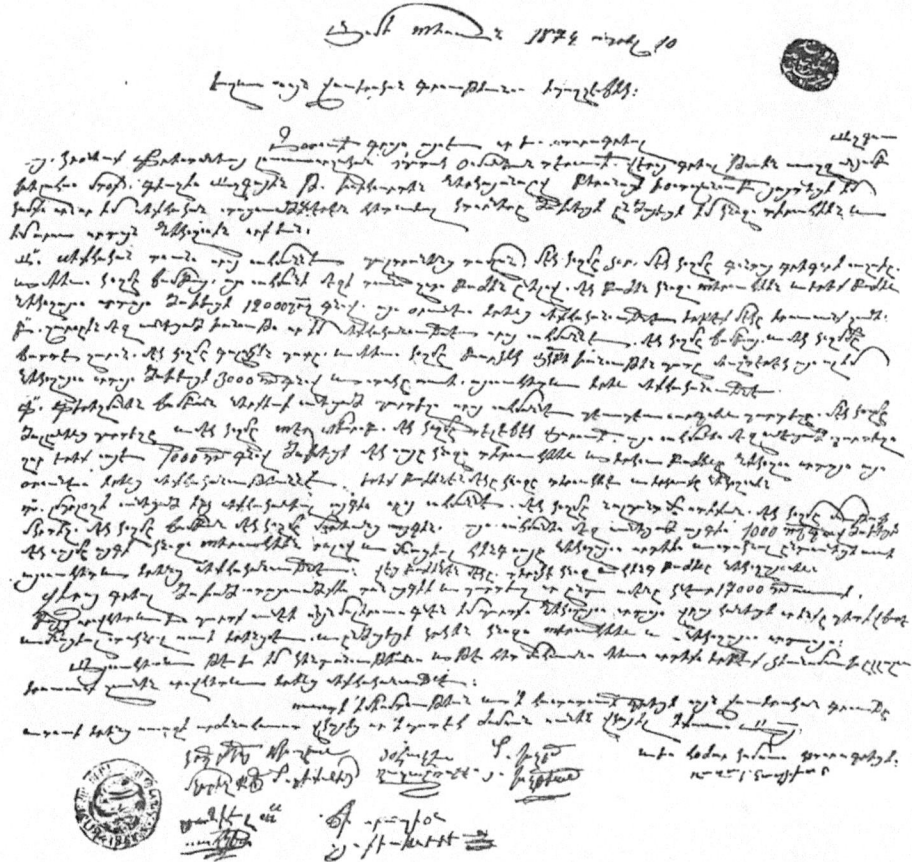

---

[*] This document appeared in Mkhalian's work on p. 974.

Appendix

Bardizag land sale documents - 2[*]

---

[*] This document appeared in Mkhalian's work on p. 975.

Table 1 – Births, marriages and deaths, Bardizag 1899 – 1909[*]

Year	BIRTHS Male	Female	Total	MARRIAGES Number	DEATHS Male	Female	Total
1899	117	95	212	68	70	65	135
1900	99	96	195	69	63	57	120
1901	102	102	204	47	58	58	116
1902	108	81	189	62	60	56	116
1903	96	85	181	50	99	70	169
1904	117	122	239	59	58	56	114
1905	107	90	197	46	49	56	105
1906	107	83	190	47	58	42	100
1907	75	83	158	40	53	64	117
1908	64	86	150	40	62	52	114
1908	80	82	162	42	81	60	141
	Final total: 2,077			Total: 570	Final total: 1,347		

[*] Kasabian, Minas (Farhad), *Hayere Nikomedio Kavarin Mech*, Azadamard Press, Bardizag 1913, section relating to Bardizag only, taken from the table inserted between pp. 230-231.

Appendix

Table 2 – Extract of census taken in 1909-1910 for the Nicomedia diocesan authorities, by religious affiliation[*]

Town/Village	Date founded	Origin of inhabitants	Figures for 1909-1910					
			Religion	Families	No of houses	Males	Females	No of people
Izmid	1580	Palu, Kemakh, Yerevan	Armenian Apostolic	900	812	2057	2232	4289
			Protestant or Evangelical	68	61	274	269	543
			Armenian Catholics	18	18	31	35	66
Bardizag	1590	Sepastia, Agn	Armenian Apostolic	1500	1460	4156	4100	8256
			Protestant or Evangelical	135	116	274	269	543
			Armenian Catholics	41	41	120	105	225
			Sabbatarians or Pentecostals	not stated	not stated	not stated	not stated	30
Ovadjek	1605	Agn, Erzerum	Armenian Apostolic	573	500	1730	1573	3303
			Sabbatarians or Pentecostals	not stated	not stated	not stated	not stated	30
Dongel	Not known	Not known	Armenian Apostolic	81	75	232	187	419
Dongel's Saint	1904	Not known	Armenian Apostolic	80	61	371	220	591
Manoushag	1884	Not known						
Jamavayr	1894	Trabzon, Ordu	Armenian Apostolic	51	41	143	121	264
Zakar kiugh	1878	Trabzon, Ordu	Armenian Apostolic	65	68	211	193	404
			TOTALS	3512	3253	9599	9304	18963

Note: The totals in these 4 columns do not include Sabbatarians or Pentecostals

---

[*] Extract from the tables in Kasabian, Minas (Farhad), *Hayere Nikomedio Kavarin Mech*, pp. 102, 103, 242-244.

Sources

The following books and publications have been used in the preparation of this annotated translation:

Aghavnouni, Bishop Mgerdich, *Miapank yev aitselouk hai Yerousaghemi [Members of the [Monastic] Brotherhood and Visitors to Armenian Jerusalem]*, Published by the St. James' Press, Jerusalem, 1929. (In Armenian)

Bardizag, Bardizag American High School Alumni Association's half-yearly journal, Bardizag, 1909-1912 (In Armenian)

Baronian, Hagop, *Yergeri joghovadzou [Collected works]*, Academy of Sciences of the Armenian SSR, Yerevan, Volume 2, 1964. (In Armenian)

Bedigian, A A, *Krchanegarner Bardizag kiughin [Sketches of the Village of Bardizag]*, Paris, 1950. (In Armenian)

Boghosian, Haroutiun, *Anzoukagan Bardizag (housher) [Incomparable Bardizag (Memoirs)]*, Elegian Press, Paris, 1967. (In Armenian)

Central Executive, AGBU, (edition directed by Kevorkian, Haroutiun and Tachjian, Vahe), *Tar me badmoutiun Hai Parekordzagan Enthanour Mioutian [A century of history of the Armenian General Benevolent Union]*, Cairo-Paris-New York, 2006, Vol 1, 1906-1940. (In Armenian)

Carmont, Pascal, *The Amiras, Lords of Ottoman Armenia*, Taderon Press, London, 2012.

Der-Hagopian, Hagop. *Bardizage khadoudig [Dappled Bardizag]*, Paris 1960. (In Armenian)

Eblighatian, Madteos M, *Azkayin khnamadaroutiun enthanour deghegakir arachin vetsamsia 1 Mayis 1919 – 31 Hogdemper 1919 [National Assistance Organisation, general report for the first six months, 1 May 1919 – 31 October 1919]*, 2nd edition, Antilias, Lebanon, 1985 (In Armenian)

Kasabian, Minas (Farhad), *Hayere Nikomedio Kavarin Mech [The Armenians in the Province of Nicomedia]*, Azadamard Press, Bardizag 1913 (In Armenian)

Gasparyan, Gourgen, *Komitase jamanakakitsneri housheroum yev vgayoutiunneroum [Gomidas in his contemporaries' recollections and testimonies]*, Yerevan, 2009. (In Armenian)

Kevorkian, Garo, *Amenoun darekirke [Everybody's yearbook]*, 3rd year, 1956, Beirut, 1956. (In Armenian)

Kevorkian, Garo, *Amenoun darekirke [Everybody's yearbook]*, 5th year, 1959, Beirut, 1959. (In Armenian)

Kevorkian, Garo, *Amenoun darekirke [Everybody's yearbook]*, 6th year, 1958, Beirut, 1958. (In Armenian)

Kevorkian, Garo, *Amenoun darekirke [Everybody's yearbook]*, 11th year, 1964, Beirut, 1964. (In Armenian)

Kevorkian, Garo, *Amenoun darekirke [Everybody's yearbook]*, 12th year, 1965, Beirut, 1965. (In Armenian)

Kevorkian, Garo, *Amenoun darekirke [Everybody's yearbook]*, 13th year, 1966, Beirut, 1966. (In Armenian)

Kevorkian, Raymond, *The Armenian Genocide, a Complete History*. I. B. Tauris, New York, 2011

Kuyumjian, Rita Soulahian, *Archeology of Madness. Komitas, portrait of an icon*, Gomidas Institute, Princeton, New Jersey, 2001.

Haikakan Hanragitarani Klkhavor Khmpagrutyun, *Haikakan Hardsi Hanragitaran* [Main Editorial Board of the Armenian Encyclopaedia, Encyclopaedia of the Armenian Question], Yerevan 1996. (In Armenian)

Boghos Vartabed Natanian, *Arachin deghegakroutiun vidjagis Nicomedio* [First report on the diocese of Nicomedia], Djezvedjian Press, Constantinople 1871.

Ryan, Arthur C, *Statement on the Misrule of Turkey and her Cruel Treatment of non-Muslim Subjects*. Chicago, USA, 28 March 1918.

Sakayan, Prof. Dora, *An Armenian Doctor in Turkey. Garabed Hacherian: my Smyrna Ordeal in 1922*, Yerevan State University, 2011.

Teotig, *Goghgota hai hokevoraganoutian yev ir hodin 1915 aghedali dariin [The Golgotha of the Armenian clergy and its flock in the calamatous year of 1915]*, edited by Ara Kalaydjian, St. Vartan Press, New York, 1985. (In Armenian)

Terzian, Hagop H, *Cilicia 1909, The Massacre of Armenians*, translated by Ara Stepan Melkonian and edited by Ara Sarafian, Gomidas Institute, London, 2009.

The Missionary Herald, journal of the American Board of Commissioners for Foreign Missions, Vol 76, No 10, October 1880.

Walker, Christopher J, *Armenia, the Survival of a Nation*, Croom Helm, London 1980.

Gomidas Institute
42 Blythe Rd.
London W14 0HA
United Kingdom

*For more information about Bardizag and Nicomedia
please visit our website at www.gomidas.org*

www.ingramcontent.com/pod-product-compliance
Lightning Source LLC
Chambersburg PA
CBHW081144290426

44108CB00018B/2432